Pāli Canon Teachings and Translations

THE COMPLETE WORKS OF SANGHARAKSHITA include all his previously published work, as well as talks, seminars, and writings published here for the first time. The collection represents the definitive edition of his life's work as Buddhist writer and teacher. For further details, including the contents of each volume, please turn to the 'Guide' on pp. 799–807.

FOUNDATION

1 A Survey of Buddhism / The Buddha's Noble Eightfold Path
2 The Three Jewels I
3 The Three Jewels II
4 The Bodhisattva Ideal
5 The Purpose and Practice of Buddhist Meditation
6 The Essential Sangharakshita

INDIA

7 Crossing the Stream: India Writings I
8 Beating the Dharma Drum: India Writings II
9 Dr Ambedkar and the Revival of Buddhism I
10 Dr Ambedkar and the Revival of Buddhism II

THE WEST

11 A New Buddhist Movement I
12 A New Buddhist Movement II
13 Eastern and Western Traditions

COMPLETE WORKS 15 **COMMENTARY**

Sangharakshita

# Pāli Canon Teachings and Translations

EDITED BY VIDYADEVI

Windhorse Publications
38 Newmarket Road
Cambridge CB5 8DT

info@windhorsepublications.com
www.windhorsepublications.com


First published in 2023.



Cover design by Dhammarati
Cover images: Front: Manuscript, detail, Thailand, 19th century
© British Library Board (Or 16009 f001r)
Back flap: Sangharakshita leading a women's study seminar at Padmaloka, June, 1980. Courtesy of Urgyen Sangharakshita Trust



Typesetting and layout by Tarajyoti
Printed by Bell & Bain Ltd, Glasgow

**British Library Cataloguing in Publication Data:**
A catalogue record for this book is available from the British Library.

ISBN 978-1-915342-06-5 (paperback)
ISBN 978-1-915342-05-8 (hardback)

# CONTENTS

# FOREWORD

I am writing this foreword in the Sangharakshita Library at Adhisthana in Herefordshire, UK. Here, in a quiet room that smells of book-dust and hums with silence, are the Dharma books that Sangharakshita collected over many years as the nucleus of a library for the Triratna Order and movement. In the archive section of the library are some shelves with the books that Sangharakshita brought back from India in 1967, when he returned to the UK after twenty years in the East and founded a new Buddhist movement. These battered old volumes look like they saw a lot of service, but they are nevertheless well-preserved, for Sangharakshita was someone who loved books and looked after them. And here is a small hardback, in the Oxford World's Classics series, covered in thick brown paper, and signed 'Sangharakshita' in blue ink that has faded to ancient grey. It is a well-read edition of *Some Sayings of the Buddha*, an anthology assembled and translated by Frank Lee Woodward, one of the Pali Text Society's pioneering English translators of the Pāli canon.

This copy of *Some Sayings* is a 1951 reprint, so it must be a replacement for a copy that Sangharakshita had owned before then, for in his first book of memoirs, *The Rainbow Road*, he describes carefully reading this book in 1949. At that time he was living in the town of Tansen, Nepal, with his friend Buddharakshita. They had both recently gone forth as *sāmaṇeras*, or novice Buddhist monks, and they had settled for a while at the Mahachaitya Vihara, where they were looked after by a local Newar Buddhist called Anagarika Sushila. Sangharakshita writes,

> When we had ceremonially given thanks to Sushila and her assistant for our meal, we returned to the vihara and after a brief rest settled down to our studies again. Since it was the hottest, the afternoon was also the quietest time of day, and we could usually count on not being disturbed for at least four or five hours. While Buddharakshita ploughed his way through Hindi translations of the Pāli canon, I renewed my acquaintance with *Some Sayings of the Buddha*. I also did a little writing, and besides maintaining the journal I had been keeping since our departure from Benares, worked on verse translations of the hymn, 'Salutation to the Three Jewels', and the five most popular *paritrāṇa sūtras*, or canonical texts recited as a means of blessing and protection. (*Complete Works*, vol. 20, p. 434)

A few months later, while living with Bhikkhu Jagdish Kashyap at the Benares Hindu University, studying Pāli, logic, and Abhidhamma with him, Sangharakshita returned to his work on these texts. Indeed, this work on these verse translations was of some symbolic significance within Sangharakshita's inner life. Under the conditions of months of settled peace which he called his 'academic interlude', Sangharakshita found that there were two Sangharakshitas:

> Sangharakshita I wanted to enjoy the beauty of nature, to read and write poetry, to listen to music, to look at paintings and sculpture, to experience emotion, to lie in bed and dream, to see places, to meet people. Sangharakshita II wanted to realize the truth, to read and write philosophy, to observe the precepts, to get up early and meditate, to mortify the flesh, to fast and pray. (Ibid. p. 451)

These two Sangharakshitas came into conflict, and Sangharakshita II burned all of Sangharakshita I's poems. In his memoirs, Sangharakshita writes:

> After this catastrophe, which shocked them both, they learned to respect each other's spheres of influence. Occasionally they even collaborated, as in the completion of the blank verse rendition of the five *paritrāṇa sūtra*s that had been started in Nepal. (Ibid. p. 452)

Working on blank verse renditions of some important early Buddhist translations was something that could satisfy both sides of Sangharakshita's character. These renditions are included in the first part of this volume: 'Translations'. They were published in a collection of poems entitled *The Enchanted Heart*, duplicated on recycled paper in 1978 under the Ola Leaves imprint, in which each of the six translations was marked '1949', suggesting that they were printed unchanged from that time. They were reprinted in *Complete Poems* (1995), but for the *Complete Works*, they have migrated from poetry (vol. 25) to Pāli canon (vol. 15) – a reminder, perhaps, of how they once bridged the two sides of Bhante's mind.

The translations consist of five discourses and what Sangharakshita calls a 'hymn' – more familiar to many Buddhists as a translation of the *Tiratana Vandanā* (often called the '*iti pi so*' in the Theravādin Buddhist world). The five discourses are taken from an ancient Pāli canonical collection called the *Khuddaka-pāṭha*, originally put together as a handbook for novices to memorize and reflect on, and which was later used as a collection of texts recited for protection (Pāli *paritta*, Sanskrit *paritrāṇa*). It makes sense that Sangharakshita, as a novice monk, should have spent time familiarizing himself with these old texts. He did so by taking the prose translations in Woodward's *Some Sayings of the Buddha*, and rewriting them in blank verse (lines of unrhymed iambic pentameter, which is to say, of non-rhyming verse which has ten syllables per line in a stress pattern that goes, 'di *dah* di *dah* di *dah* di *dah* di *dah*'). This was an appropriate thing to do, for the original Pāli poems were composed in strict metre, in patterns of long and short syllables. The *Maṅgala Sutta*, *Tirokuḍḍa Sutta*, and *Nidhikaṇḍa Sutta* are each in a metrical form called *anuṣṭubh*, consisting of patterns of eight syllable *pada*s or 'feet', while the *Ratana Sutta* is in a metre called *triṣṭubh*, with eleven syllables per *pada*. The *Karaṇīya Mettā Sutta* is in a complicated metre called 'Old Ārya'. There is no way to translate these metrical forms into English, which is why Pāli poetry is most often translated as prose. By putting Woodward's translations into blank verse, Sangharakshita was returning the text to poetry. Blank verse gives a steady rhythm and structure to the line, making reading a pleasure, especially reading aloud.

While these early translations appear to be something of a spiritual writing exercise, Sangharakshita's translation of the *Dhammapada*, also in the first part of this volume, is an altogether more serious and complex achievement. As his own Preface indicates, Sangharakshita managed to translate about one-third of the whole text by the 1980s, then completed the rest of the 423 verses in the year 2000, while on retreat at Guhyaloka in Spain. His translation of the *Dhammapada* thus belongs to the mature phase of his writing and teaching.

As Sangarakshita explains in his Preface, the *Dhammapada* is the Pāli version of an ancient collection of Buddhist verses, arranged in thematic chapters, such as 'The Elephant' or 'Flowers', in which most (though not all) of the verses mention the theme. It would appear that all the ancient Buddhist schools had their own version of the *Dhammapada* (which some of them called the *Udānavarga*), drawn from a floating collection of verses on ethics, wisdom, and liberation. These collections are valued for compressing the spirit of the Dharma into memorable words and vivid images. The value of the *Dhammapada* as a distillation of the Dharma was brought vividly to mind on a study retreat we held recently here at Adhisthana. We were studying another Pāli text, the *Udāna*, but conversation ranged widely over Buddhist teachings. One of the retreatants had successfully memorized the entire *Dhammapada* in Sangharakshita's translation, and we soon discovered that on almost any Dharma topic that we might discuss, there was some relevant *Dhammapada* verse that our friend could retrieve from his memory and bring into the conversation. It was a lesson not just in the value of memorizing the Dharma, but in the importance of the *Dhammapada* as a verse summary of many central Dharmic themes.

Whereas in 1949 Sangharakshita had put prose translations of Buddhist poems into blank verse, his translation of the *Dhammapada* is entirely in prose. The reason is no doubt connected with Sangharakshita's aim in making another translation of a text that had already been translated many times – to convey, as he says in his preface, 'a directness and sense of urgency' that he believed was missing from many existing translations. This directness would have been compromised by the compressed artificiality of verse. Indeed, a distinctive feature of Sangharakshita's translation is a concern for accuracy, to the extent of incorporating explanatory phrases which spell out what was merely implied. Take, for example, verse 146, from the *Jarāvagga*, or the chapter on Decay (usually translated as Old Age), the Pāli of which runs:

*ko nu hāso kim ānando niccaṃ pajjalite sati*
*andhakārena onaddhā padīpaṃ na gavessatha*

Sangharakshita renders this pithy challenge as follows:

> What mirth can there be, what pleasure, when all the time (everything) is blazing (with the threefold fire of suffering, impermanence, and insubstantiality)? Covered (though you are) in blind darkness, you do not seek a light!

The words and phrases in brackets are not, strictly speaking, there in the Pāli. This use of brackets is frowned upon by some translators as unnecessarily interfering with the reading experience. But Sangharakshita was concerned both to make clear what the Pāli actually says and also to spell out what it means such that the reader can feel the meaning. It is not just that the world is ablaze (*pajjalita*), but it is blazing *with the threefold fire of suffering, impermanence, and insubstantiality* – the three characteristics (*lakkhaṇa*) of conditioned existence – which are like flames that not only burn all the time (*niccaṃ*), but burn *everything*. Covered (*onaddhā*) *though you are* – in case you thought this verse did not apply to you – in blind darkness (*andhakārena*), you do not seek a light!

The effect of these explanatory additions is to give Sangharakshita's translation of the *Dhammapada* an unrushed and stately quality which nevertheless preserves the 'directness and urgency' that Sangharakshita sought to convey. This is also very evident in his regular translation of the word *bāla*, usually 'child' or 'fool', as 'spiritually immature person', and its contrary, *paṇḍita*, usually 'wise one', as 'spiritually mature person'. Let us take the example of verse 63, from the *Bālavagga*, or chapter on the Spiritually Immature:

*yo bālo maññati bālyaṃ paṇḍito vāpi tena so*
*bālo ca paṇḍitamānī sa ve bālo ti vuccati*

Valerie Roebuck, whose 2010 translation of the *Dhammapada* for Penguin is scholarly and reliable, translates this verse as follows:

> The fool who knows his folly
> Becomes wise by that fact.

But the fool who thinks he's wise –
He's called 'a fool' indeed!

It is easy to admire the concision and music of this translation, especially the use of alliteration, which livens the language considerably. Now here is Sangharakshita's version:

> The spiritually immature person who recognizes his immaturity is to that extent mature; the spiritually immature one who thinks of himself as mature is termed immature indeed.

Whereas it was easy to agree with Roebuck's translation, and to shake one's head at the foolish fool, reading Sangharakshita's version one feels oneself on much less certain ground. Am I, as a reader, sufficiently spiritually mature to recognize my foolishness? Perhaps not; perhaps I quite foolishly think myself mature. Suddenly the verse makes one reassess oneself. While Sangharakshita's translation may be less elegant than Roebuck's, it conveys more of an urgent challenge to the reader.

As well as these translations of Pāli verse, this volume of the *Complete Works* contains the transcripts and edited reimaginings of seminars that Sangharakshita conducted in the 1970s and 1980s, each connected one way or another with Pāli Buddhism. The period in which Sangharakshita held these and other study seminars was one of consolidation. Sangharakshita was creating deep connections between his teaching of the Dharma and the wider Buddhist tradition, and initiating his students and disciples into a method of study, a unique combination of Dharma enquiry, historical criticism, and creative exegesis for the contemporary world. These seminars helped form the intellectual and cultural ambience of the FWBO/Triratna. The discussions held during the seminars were transcribed, in some cases edited, and then printed out for study and discussion throughout the Movement. Some underwent a more radical form of editing through the work of the Spoken Word Project, and, with the removal of digressions and asides, and through much judicious shaping of the prose, were reimagined as books.

The first seminar included here is *Living With Awareness*, a book-length reimagining of a seminar on the *Satipaṭṭhāna Sutta* (the 'Discourse on the Establishment of Mindfulness'). This discourse is one of the most important of all early Buddhist discourses. The Buddha sets out the practice of mindfulness (*sati*) as the 'direct path' to the realization of Awakening, and does so both in depth (in the form of detailed instructions for practice) and breadth (in the form of teaching mindfulness of body, feelings, mind, and mental states or qualities). Because of its importance for the meditative life of the Buddhist tradition, the *Satipaṭṭhāna Sutta* has been the subject of many commentaries and studies. In recent years, Windhorse Publications (publisher of the *Complete Works*) has brought out three books on *satipaṭṭhāna* by Bhikkhu Anālayo, each of which combines remarkable scholarship regarding the different versions of the discourse with a deep commitment to practice and realization. One might wonder how Sangharakshita's work stands up in the light of Anālayo's contributions.

Here in the Sangharakshita Library at Adhisthana, I have pulled out a copy of *The Way of Mindfulness*, by Bhikkhu Soma of the Island Hermitage in Ceylon, inscribed by the author 'to Āyasmā [i.e. Venerable] Sangharakshita', and dated 15 August 1950. This is another of the books in the small library that Sangharakshita brought back from India in 1967, and no doubt he read it very carefully. It is a translation of the *Satipaṭṭhāna Sutta*, together with the traditional Pāli commentaries on the text relating to the practice of mindfulness as well as to the correct understanding of the ancient teaching. One might have expected that in his seminar Sangharakshita would draw on this authoritative commentarial tradition, but in fact he does not.

One does not have to read many pages of *Living With Awareness* to realize that Sangharakshita is doing something very different from either Anālayo or the commentarial tradition. Apart from a brief introduction to the traditional setting of the discourse and an account of its wider importance, Sangharakshita's approach diverges completely from any traditional Theravādin commentary. Commenting, for instance, on the connection between *sati* and memory, he recalls a story by Charles Dickens rather than anything from the Buddhist tradition. He is trying to bring mindfulness alive in a modern western context, to make mindfulness more *indigenous*.

To each stage of the practice of *satipaṭṭhāna*, Sangharakshita brings unexpected perspectives. The most striking may be his presentation, in Chapter 6, entitled 'Getting Down to Essentials', of how to practise mindfulness of the four material elements (*mahābhūta*s) which make up the physical body. Whereas the traditional account of the contemplation of the elements is analytic, a matter of considering how, upon analysis, this body is composed of earth, water, heat, and wind, none of which can be considered 'I' or 'mine', Sangharakshita draws out another theme, that of how these elements are alive, or can be experienced as living entities or forces. Indeed, the lack of awareness in the modern world of these elemental forces is part of the problem that a western Buddhist, educated to believe that the universe is a great machine, needs to address. Sangharakshita comments:

> I would go so far as to say that a universe conceived of as dead cannot be a universe in which one stands any chance of attaining Enlightenment. (Whether you stand any chance in a living universe is of course up to you.) It may be difficult for us to get back to the view of the world that came naturally to our ancestors, but poets have persisted in seeing the universe as alive: surely no poet could have a totally Newtonian outlook, the kind of attitude that Blake termed 'single vision' and 'Newton's sleep'. Milton, for example, traces the origin of mining to Hell itself: in *Paradise Lost* the devils start excavating minerals in order to manufacture artillery to use against heaven. One could even interpret the whole Romantic movement as expressing a great protest against the Newtonian picture of nature and a reassertion of essentially pagan values. (pp. 138–9)

This is classic Sangharakshita: first, an accurate, historically-grounded account of a Buddhist teaching – in this case, mindfulness of the material elements of the body – and then a leap into how one should relate to this teaching as a modern Western Buddhist, and how to practise the Dharma today. Sangharakshita's approach is almost the opposite of a secular approach to Buddhism: rather than making the Dharma accessible by translating it into secular terms, he questions the assumptions of the modern Western mind so that we can enter into the greater vision of the Dharma. The same approach informs the second edited seminar included in this volume. Entitled *Living With Kindness*, it is based on a seminar on the *Karaṇīya Mettā Sutta*, a verse discourse included in this volume in Sangharakshita's 1949 translation. But the version that Sangharakshita discusses here is by H. Saddhatissa, from the latter's translation of the *Sutta-Nipāta*. Saddhatissa's translation is distinctive in aiming to convey the spirit of the text in contemporary language. Sangharakshita's commentary likewise seeks to draw out the contemporary meaning of the rather archaic and sometimes difficult Pāli.

Again we see Sangharakshita applying his distinctive method to a text which, in this case, is part of the everyday liturgy of Theravāda Buddhists. First he discusses each Pāli word, going into any translation issues that might arise, then he places it into the context of the Dharma as a whole. Thirdly, he draws out the meaning of the teaching for the modern world. For instance, the *sutta* states that the one who seeks to practise the cultivation of *mettā* or loving-kindness should be *subharo*, which Saddhatissa translates as 'easily supported'. This refers to a monastic practitioner, and Sangharakshita goes on to place in historical context the renunciate lifestyle of traditional Buddhist monastics, who wandered for alms and were supported by lay people. One who is *subharo* will be easy for the laity to support, not fussy or demanding. But Sangharakshita then goes on to critically discuss the implied idea that productive economic work might be unsuitable for monks or for anyone seeking to practise the Dharma. He writes:

> Today we have the opportunity to reappraise the whole question of work and financial support. We do not necessarily have to accept the traditions as they have come down to us, especially when these are influenced by Indian social and cultural conditions of some 2,500 years ago. (pp. 281–2)

He goes on to update this whole economic model, based on the underlying principle that all of us in a complex society are supported by the work of others. He concludes:

> The principle behind this term *subharo* therefore comes down to taking from the world and from society no more than you need, and freely contributing whatever you can. (p. 283)

This principle allows him to draw out the best attitude for a Dharma practitioner in regard to our economic participation in the contemporary world, while providing a historical context for the tradition of Buddhist monastics not doing any work.

Following these two seminars repurposed as books, the current volume continues with a previously unpublished edited seminar (from 1983) on 'Evil', chapter 9 of the *Dhammapada*, newly prepared by Vidyadevi, the editor of this volume. In this seminar, Sangharakshita comments on his own translation, allowing us to appreciate his approach to these ancient verses. The next items are two more short seminars, on the *Maṅgala Sutta* (entitled *Auspicious Signs*) and on the *Tiratana Vandanā* (entitled *Salutation to the Three Jewels*). These were published in the 1980s in the 'Sangharakshita in Seminar' series, having been transcribed by volunteers and then carefully edited by Sangharakshita. Highlights include an extraordinary discussion, in *Auspicious Signs*, of the word *santuṭṭhi*, meaning 'contentment', in terms of working with its opposite, which is not being content, or rather, being bored. Sangharakshita explains how boredom is a mood one has to just be with, that in fact one has to feel through. The only satisfactory way out of it is to stay with one's experience until some genuine impulse to act arises.

Both *Auspicious Signs* and *Salutation to the Three Jewels* include extended discussions between Sangharakshita and the seminar participants, who in both cases are young men, about the disadvantages of the nuclear family and of the couple relationship, and even of the possibility of taking young boys aged 7 or 8 away from their mothers to live in men's communities. One may or may not agree with all that is said. One should bear in mind, however, that in Sangharakshita's new Buddhist movement, Order members are neither monastic nor lay. If they are going to avoid simply falling into the default social institution of the couple relationship, they surely need to have some critique of it. This is the context for what is said, which is no doubt the kind of thing idealistic young spiritual seekers, whether male or female, have discussed since Buddhism began.

The final item in this volume is another publication from the 'Sangharakshita in Seminar' series. *The Threefold Refuge* is a long discussion of an eponymous booklet by Nyanaponika Thera. Nyanaponika (1901–1994) was born in Germany but lived as a Theravādin monk in Sri Lanka, initially at the Island Hermitage, which was a base for generations of English-speaking *bhikkhu*s, such as Bhikkhu Soma, mentioned above. Nyanaponika was for many years the director of the Buddhist Publication Society, the publisher of *The Threefold Refuge*. Nyanaponika first translates a passage from the Theravādin commentator Buddhaghosa on the meaning and significance of Going for Refuge to the Buddha, Dhamma, and Sangha, then contributes his own commentary on the importance of Going for Refuge, as well as commenting on Buddhaghosa's commentary.

Anyone familiar with Sangharakshita's presentation of the Dharma will understand why he chose to hold a seminar on Nyanaponika's booklet, for the centrality of Going for Refuge is a fundamental and distinctive emphasis of his approach. The seminar discussion itself shows the evolution of Sangharakshita's thought concerning the exact nature of Going for Refuge, especially the role of intellect, emotion, and volition, as well as the levels of Going for Refuge and its connections with other formulations of the Buddhist path. So important is this discussion that Sangharakshita summarized it in chapter 19 of *The History of My Going Refuge* (now in *Complete Works*, vol. 2), a long talk from 1986 that became a book setting out the evolution of his understanding of Going for Refuge.

One might suspect that Sangharakshita brought to the discussion of Nyanaponika's booklet an already well-developed set of thoughts about the significance of Going for Refuge, which had not yet found their final form. I think this explains his sometimes apparently nit-picking criticism of Nyanaponika's formulations, which, after all, appear to have been closer to his own thoughts and feelings than those of anyone else in the Buddhist world. Nyanaponika emphasizes the importance of Going for Refuge as a heartfelt individual act, as against the mere recitation of the refuges and precepts to reaffirm one's belonging to a Buddhist group. But this very congruence of vision allowed Sangharakshita to go into details. Most importantly, the seminar shows him teasing out the importance for Going for Refuge of Perfect Vision as against what he considered to be Nyanaponika's slight over-emphasis on intellectual understanding. To read through *The Threefold Refuge* seminar is to retrace an important part of Sangharakshita's own journey to what he regarded as a satisfactory account of the nature and ramifications of Going for Refuge to the Three Jewels as the defining and central act of the Buddhist life.

Dhivan Thomas Jones
Adhisthana
October 2022

# A NOTE FROM THE EDITOR

In 2011 Windhorse Publications issued a revised edition of Sangharakshita's translation of the *Dhammapada*, incorporating several changes to the translation requested by Sangharakshita. He had asked Dhivan Thomas Jones to indicate any problems or mistakes in translation, and ten changes were made in accordance with Dhivan's suggestions. The alterations occur in verses 71, 82, 109, 151, 185, 248, 271–2, 276, 302, and 353.

Unfortunately, Dhivan's work was not acknowledged in the 2011 edition as it should have been. I want to take this opportunity to rectify that error, in accordance with Sangharakshita's wishes (expressed in an email to Dhivan in 2017) and to acknowledge Dhivan's valuable contributions to this translation. Sangharakshita himself clearly appreciated Dhivan's work on this text, which was so close to his heart, concluding his 2017 email with the words: 'So far as I am concerned, critical scholarship is definitely welcome within Triratna.'

I am very grateful to Dhivan also for writing the foreword to this volume and for casting his scholarly eye over the whole text, as a result of which we have made a few changes and added a few extra explanatory notes.

Vidyadevi
Herefordshire
October 2022

# PART I
# TRANSLATIONS

# DHAMMAPADA

The Way of Truth

# PREFACE

The Buddha was born towards the end of the fifth century BCE, renounced the world at the age of 29, attained Enlightenment six years later, and spent the remaining forty-five years of his life communicating the truth he had discovered to anyone who was willing to learn.

He communicated that truth orally, by means of the spoken word, though many people were also deeply moved by his mere presence. His words made a deep impression on his hearers, so that some of them remembered them all their lives and both before and after his death repeated them for the benefit of others. In this way there sprang up and developed an *oral tradition*, which not only preserved the Buddha's teaching but organized, edited, and amplified it in various ways. The process of oral transmission lasted for several hundred years and probably it was not until the first century BCE that the Buddha's discourses and sayings began to be committed to writing.

By this time that tradition had become very rich, the more especially as it now included exegetical and commentarial material by several successive generations of the Buddha's followers. By this time, too, those followers had become divided into a number of different schools, each of which transmitted, in its own language, its own particular version of orally transmitted material. When the oral tradition of the Buddha's teaching came finally to be written down, therefore, it was written down in at least four different languages or dialects, one of them being the language now known as Pāli.

This Pāli version of the oral tradition, which was committed to writing in Sri Lanka in the first century BCE by members of the Theravāda school, is the only version of that material to have survived complete in the original language, and as such it is of enormous historical and spiritual importance. It is divided into three *piṭakas* or 'baskets', a basket of monastic rules, a basket of discourses, and a basket of further teaching, the last being actually the work of latter-day followers. The basket of discourses or Sutta Piṭaka is divided into five collections, the fifth of which is the *Khuddaka Nikāya* or 'Little Collection'. The 'Little Collection' consists of fifteen separate works, some very long and some quite short. The *Dhammapada* is one of these.

Though none of the other literary versions of the oral tradition has survived complete in the original language, a handful of separate works, or portions of works, fortunately are still available to us. Thus in addition to the Pāli *Dhammapada* we have a Prakrit *Dhammapada* and a Sanskrit *Dharmapada* (also known as the *Udānavarga*). The Chinese Buddhist canon also contains four texts of this name, all translated from different Sanskrit originals. Such comparative studies as have so far been made reveal no basic discrepancies among the various recensions of the work, whether Pāli, Prakrit, or Sanskrit. As I have written elsewhere,

> All consist of the same type of material organized in the same way, that is to say, of verses embodying ethical and spiritual precepts grouped more or less according to subject under various sectional headings. Though the total number of verses is not the same, and though the selection of verses, as well as the number and nature of the sections into which they are classified, differ considerably from one text to another, all the *Dhammapadas* have certain blocks of verses in common. Some of these blocks are found elsewhere in the Sūtra Piṭaka; others appear to be peculiar to the *Dhammapada* literature. It would seem, therefore, that taking these blocks, which together constituted the basic text... each of the early schools composed a *Dhammapada* of its own.[1]

That the Pāli *Dhammapada* is at present the best known of this class of Buddhist canonical texts is largely the result of historical accident. Since its appearance in a Latin version in 1855 it has been repeatedly translated into the principal European and Asian languages,

> the depth and universality of its doctrine, the purity and earnestness of its moral teaching, and the sublimity of its spiritual ideal, combined with the refined simplicity and pellucid poetical beauty of its language, winning for it an honoured place in world literature.[2]

Small wonder, then, that the *Dhammapada* should now be one of the best known and best loved of all Buddhist scriptures, or that for many Western Buddhists, irrespective of school, it should be a perpetual source of inspiration.

For me it has been a source of inspiration, encouragement, and guidance for well over fifty years. Indeed, I sometimes think that the *Dhammapada* contains, at least in principle, as much of the Buddha's teaching as most of us really need to know in order to progress towards Enlightenment. As the Buddha himself tells us in verse 100,

> Better than a thousand meaningless words collected together (in the Vedic oral tradition) is a single meaningful word on hearing which one becomes tranquil.

There are many such meaningful words in the *Dhammapada* – words that are of infinitely greater value than the tens of thousands of meaningless words we hear every day of our lives.

Four episodes in the history of my relationship with the *Dhammapada* stand out with particular vividness. The first occurred in 1944. I had just arrived in Delhi, and being already a Buddhist went looking for a Buddhist temple. Eventually I found one, the first I had ever seen. Inside the entrance there was a bookstall, and among the books I bought that day was an English translation of the *Dhammapada* complete with the Pāli text in *devanāgarī* script. Thereafter the orange-covered pocket volume accompanied me to Sri Lanka, to Singapore, and then back to India, where it was the constant companion of my years as a freelance wandering ascetic.

It is to those years of wandering that the next episode belongs. I was staying at a Hindu ashram in North Malabar, and during my stay devoted the period of my morning walk to learning the *Dhammapada* by heart in the original Pāli, reciting the verses out loud as I strode along the road. As I knew no Pāli, though I had learned the *devanāgarī* script while in Sri Lanka, I had to recite the verses parrot-fashion with only a general idea of their meaning. At that time I was a great believer in the value of learning scriptures and poetry by heart, as I still am today.

The third episode in the history of my relationship with the *Dhammapada* finds me living in Benares with the venerable Jagdish Kashyap, my first teacher, with whom I studied Pāli, Abhidharma, and Logic. One of the texts I studied with him was the *Dhammapada*. Though I never became a Pāli scholar, as Kashyapji perhaps hoped I might, I at least managed to acquire from him a knowledge of the language sufficient to enable me, many years later, to attempt a *Dhammapada* translation of my own.

The last of these episodes took place in Poona, not long before my return to the West in 1964. In 1956 hundreds of thousands of Hindus, who had been treated as untouchables by members of the higher castes, converted to Buddhism, and since then I had spent much of my time travelling from place to place throughout central and western India teaching them the fundamentals of the Dharma. On one of my visits to Poona I conducted a four-week training course in Buddhism, in the context of which I gave a running commentary on all twenty-six chapters of the *Dhammapada*. Few, if any, of the participants had encountered the *Dhammapada* before, and I was deeply moved to see the effect the inspired words of the Buddha had on them all, including the uneducated and even illiterate. They could well have exclaimed, as did so many in the Buddha's own day, that it was as though what was overthrown was raised up, or what was hidden revealed, or the way pointed out to him that wandered astray, or a light held up in the darkness so that those that had eyes might see.

During the seventies and eighties, back in England, I led seminars on different chapters of the *Dhammapada*, though without ever covering the entire work as I had done in Poona. It was at this time, and in connection with those seminars, that I started translating the *Dhammapada* and got about a third of the way through the text. Circumstances then obliged me to put the work aside for a while, and as in the interval several new translations of the *Dhammapada* had appeared I eventually concluded there was no need for me to finish mine. Copies of the chapters I had translated did, however, circulate in duplicated form among friends and disciples, many of whom assured me that they found my version of these chapters more useful than any other. They also urged me to finish the work of translating the remaining chapters and in the end I promised to do so. This promise I redeemed last year, here in the peace and solitude of the green valley that is Guhyaloka, and in this way, totally immersed as I was in the inspired words of the Buddha, spent one of the happiest months of my life.[3]

There have been more than thirty English translations of the *Dhammapada* or the 'Way of Truth', or 'Footfalls of the Law', or 'Statement of Principles', as the work has been variously called, and it might have been thought that notwithstanding the urgings of friends and disciples another one was hardly necessary. But of a text like the *Dhammapada* there cannot be too many translations, not only because the more translations there are the more widely the work is likely to be known but because no single translation can fully exhaust the meaning of the original. In this present version I have striven not only to be accurate but, in particular, to reproduce the directness and sense of urgency I detect in many of the verses – a directness and sense of urgency that most other translations entirely fail to capture. At times, indeed, it is as though the Buddha is speaking personally to us across the centuries, reminding us of our faults, encouraging us to persevere, and pointing out the ultimate Goal. For this reason I have not burdened the translation with a commentary, so that to the extent that the exigencies of translation permit there should be nothing to stand between the reader and the Buddha.

A few words about the way in which I have translated certain key terms may not be out of place.

Originally I had rendered the word *arahant* as 'the New Man', but since then the expression has been so seriously devalued that I have had to drop it. Instead, I have translated *arahant*, more literally, as 'the (Supremely) Worthy One', the bracketed adverb and initial capitals indicating that inasmuch as an *arahant* is one who has attained Nirvāṇa or Enlightenment, he (or she) is 'worthy' in the highest possible sense. The term *bhikkhu* is often translated 'monk', but this rendering I have avoided, partly because the word 'monk' is so overlaid with Christian connotations as to be quite misleading when used in a Buddhist context and partly because of the confusion that has been created by the appearance, in recent years, of Zen 'married monks' of both sexes. The literal meaning of *bhikkhu* is one who lives on alms, and I have therefore translated it as 'almsman'. Though *brāhmaṇa* is a multivalent term, and as such difficult to translate by any one word, its meaning within the context of the *Dhammapada* is reasonably clear, and I have therefore left it untranslated, except that in the few instances where it refers to a member of the Vedic priestly caste I have given it in its anglicized form. The term *samaṇa*, literally 'one who strives (spiritually)', is quite accurately rendered by 'ascetic', which is the usual translation, but in order to emphasize the latter's ultimate derivation from the Greek *askeīn*, 'to exercise', and to dissociate it from any suggestion of self-mortification, I have spelt the word with a 'k' instead of with a 'c'.

The terms *bāla* and *paṇḍita* designate two contrasting types of persons – 'the fool' and 'the wise', as they are usually translated. *Bāla*, however, means not so much a fool as one who is childish, lacking in moral sense. I have therefore translated *bāla* as 'the (spiritually) immature person' and *paṇḍita*, accordingly, as 'the (spiritually) mature person'. *Dhammaṭṭha* has been rendered as 'the man of principle' rather than as 'the righteous' in order to avoid the latter word's rather biblical overtones.

Now that it is at last finished, this latest translation of the *Dhammapada* goes forth from the secluded, peaceful valley where most of the work on it has been done into a world which is far from peaceful. It goes forth, in particular, into a Western world increasingly dominated by the forces of greed, as represented by consumerism, hatred, as represented by ruthless economic competition, and delusion, as represented by a variety of ideologies from scientism to religious fundamentalism. Thus it goes forth into a world greatly in need of the qualities of simplicity, contentment, kindness, gentleness, serenity, and self-control inculcated by the Buddha in the *Dhammapada* – qualities that lead, in the long run, to the enjoyment of that vision of the Truth which alone can satisfy the deepest longings of the human heart. May this present translation play a part in making those qualities more widespread and more active among us.

Sangharakshita
Guhyaloka
Spain
31 July 2000

# DHAMMAPADA

## 1: PAIRS

1 Experiences are preceded by mind, led by mind, and produced by mind. If one speaks or acts with an impure mind, suffering follows even as the cart-wheel follows the hoof of the ox (drawing the cart).

2 Experiences are preceded by mind, led by mind, and produced by mind. If one speaks or acts with a pure mind, happiness follows like a shadow that never departs.

3 Those who entertain such thoughts as 'He abused me, he beat me, he conquered me, he robbed me,' will not still their hatred.

4 Those who do not entertain such thoughts as 'He abused me, he beat me, he conquered me, he robbed me,' will still their hatred.

5 Not by hatred are hatreds ever pacified here (in the world). They are pacified by love. This is the eternal law.

6 Others do not realize that we are all heading for death. Those who do realize it will compose their quarrels.

7 As the wind blows down a weak tree, so Māra[4] overthrows one who lives seeing the (unlovely as) lovely, whose senses are uncontrolled, who is immoderate in food, lazy, and of inferior vigour.

8 As the wind does not blow down the rocky mountain peak, so Māra does not overthrow one who lives seeing the (unlovely as) unlovely, whose senses are controlled, who is moderate in food, and whose faith and vigour are aroused.

9 He is not worthy of the yellow robe who takes it (while still) not free from impurity, and lacking in self-restraint and truth.

10 He is worthy of the yellow robe who has made an end to all impurity, who is well established in virtuous conduct (*sīla*), and who is endowed with self-restraint and truth.

11 Those who take the unreal for the real, and who in the real see the unreal, they, wandering in the sphere of wrong thought, will not attain the real.

12 Those who have known the real as the real, and the unreal as the unreal, they, moving in the sphere of right thought, will attain the real.

13 As the rain penetrates the badly thatched house, so lust enters the (spiritually) undeveloped mind.

14 As the rain does not penetrate into the well-thatched house, so lust does not enter the (spiritually) well-developed mind.

15 The evildoer grieves in both worlds; he grieves 'here' and he grieves 'there'.[5] He suffers and torments himself seeing his own foul deeds.

16 The doer of good rejoices in both (worlds); he rejoices 'here' and he rejoices 'there'. He rejoices and is glad seeing his own pure deeds.

17 The evildoer burns in both (worlds); he burns 'here' and he burns 'there'. He burns (with remorse) thinking he has done evil, and he burns (with suffering) having gone (after death) to an evil state.

18 The doer of good delights in both (worlds); he delights 'here' and he delights 'there'. He delights (in this life) thinking he has done good and he delights (after death) having gone to a state of happiness.

19 He who for his own benefit constantly recites the (canonical) literature[6] but does not act accordingly, that heedless man, like a cowherd that counts the cows of others, is not enriched by the asketic life.

20 He who for his own benefit recites even a little of the (canonical) literature but lives in accordance with its principles, abandoning craving, hatred, and delusion, possessed of right knowledge, with mind well freed, clinging to nothing in this or any other world, *he* is enriched by the asketic life.

## 2: MINDFULNESS

21 Mindfulness is the Way to the Immortal,[7] unmindfulness the way to death. Those who are mindful do not die, (whereas) the unmindful are like the dead.

22 Knowing the distinction of mindfulness the spiritually mature (*paṇḍitas*) rejoice in mindfulness and take delight in the sphere of the Noble Ones (*ariyas*).

23 Absorbed in superconscious states (*jhānas*), recollected, and ever exerting themselves, those wise ones (*dhīras*) realize Nirvāṇa, the unsurpassed security.

24 Whoever is energetic, recollected, pure in conduct, considerate, self-restrained, of righteous life, and mindful, the glory of such a one waxes exceedingly.

25 By means of energy, mindfulness, self-restraint, and control, let the man of understanding (*medhāvī*) make (for himself) an island that no flood can overwhelm.

26 Out of their evil understanding the spiritually immature (*bāla*) abandon themselves to unmindfulness. The man of understanding guards mindfulness as his chief treasure.

27 Do not abandon yourselves to unmindfulness; have no intimacy with sensuous delights. The mindful person, absorbed in superconscious states, gains ample bliss.

28 As a dweller in the mountains looks down on those who live in the valley, so the spiritually mature person, the hero free from sorrow, having driven out unmindfulness by means of mindfulness, ascends to the Palace of Wisdom and looks down at the sorrowful, spiritually immature multitude (below).

29 Mindful among the unmindful, wide awake among the sleeping, the man of good understanding forges ahead like a swift horse outdistancing a feeble hack.

30 By means of mindfulness, Maghavā (i.e., Indra) attained to the chieftaincy of the gods. Mindfulness is always praised, unmindfulness always despised.

31 The almsman (*bhikkhu*) who delights in mindfulness (and) who regards unmindfulness with fear advances like fire, burning up fetters gross and subtle.

32 The almsman who delights in mindfulness (and) who regards unmindfulness with fear is not liable to regression. He is in the presence of Nirvāṇa.

## 3: THE MIND

33 As a fletcher straightens the arrow, so the man of understanding makes straight the trembling unsteady mind, which is difficult to guard (and) difficult to restrain.

34 As a fish threshes from side to side when taken from one abode to another and cast on dry land, so the mind throbs and vibrates (with the strain) as it abandons the domain of Māra.

35 (The mind) is frivolous and difficult to control, alighting on whatever it pleases. It is good to tame the mind. A tamed mind brings happiness.

36 The mind is extremely subtle and difficult to grasp, alighting on whatever it pleases. Let the man of understanding keep watch over the mind. A guarded mind brings happiness.

37 Far-ranging and lone-faring is the mind, incorporeal and abiding in the cave (of the heart). Those who bring it under control are freed from the bonds of Māra.

38 His wisdom does not attain to perfection whose mind is unsettled, who is ignorant of the Real Truth (*saddhamma*), and whose faith wavers.

39 There is no fear for someone who is awake, whose mind is uncontaminated by craving, (and) unperplexed, (and) who has given up vice and virtue.

40 Perceiving the body to be (fragile) like a clay pot, (and) fortifying the mind as though it were a city, with the sword of wisdom make war on Māra. Free from attachment, keep watch over what has been won.

41 Before long, this body, devoid of consciousness, will lie rejected on the ground like a useless faggot.

42 Whatever foe may do to foe, or hater to hater, greater is the harm done (to oneself) by a wrongly directed mind.

43 Neither mother nor father, nor any other relative, can do one as much good as a perfectly directed mind.

## 4: FLOWERS

44 Who shall conquer the earth and the Realm of Death with its deities? Who shall make out the well-taught Verses of Truth as an expert picks flowers?

45 The Learner (of the Transcendental Path) shall conquer the Realm of Death with its deities. The Learner shall make out the well-taught Verses of Truth as an expert picks flowers.

46 Seeing the body as froth, (and) thoroughly comprehending its mirage-nature, let one proceed unseen by the King of Death, having broken the flower-tipped arrows of Māra.[8]

47 As a great flood carries away a sleeping village, so death bears off the man who, possessed of longing, plucks only the flowers (of existence).

48 The Destroyer brings under his sway the man who, possessed by longing, plucks only the flowers (of existence), (and) who is insatiable in sexual passions.

49 Let the silent sage move about in the village as the bee goes taking honey from the flower without harming colour or fragrance.

50 One should pay no heed to the faults of others, what they have done and not done. Rather should one consider the things that one has oneself done and not done.

51 Like a beautiful flower, brightly coloured but without scent, even so useless is the well-uttered speech of one who does not act accordingly.

52 Like a beautiful flower, brightly coloured and scented, even so useful is the well-uttered speech of one who acts accordingly.

53 As many garlands are made from a heap of flowers, so one who is a mortal born should perform many ethically skilful deeds.

54 The fragrance of flowers, of sandalwood, of aromatic resin or jasmine, does not go against the wind, (whereas) the fragrance of the good does go against the wind.

55 Sandalwood or aromatic resin, blue lotus, or wild jasmine, of all these kinds of fragrance, the odour of virtue is unsurpassed.

56 Insignificant in comparison is this fragrance of aromatic resin and sandalwood. The fragrance of virtue it is that blows among the gods as the highest.

57 Māra does not find the path of those who are virtuous, who live mindfully, and who are freed through Perfect Knowledge (*sammadaññā*).

58 As pink lotuses, sweet-scented and lovely, spring from a heap of rubbish thrown in the highway,

59 so among those who have become (as) rubbish, (among) ignorant, ordinary people, the Disciple of the Perfectly Enlightened One shines forth exceedingly in wisdom.

## 5: THE SPIRITUALLY IMMATURE

60 Long is the night to the wakeful, long the league to one who is exhausted (with travel). Long is the process of faring (through repeated existences) to those spiritually immature ones who do not know the real truth (*saddhamma*).

61 If he who goes about (in search of truth) does not find one better than or (at least) similar to himself, let him firmly lead a solitary life. There is no companionship (for him) with the spiritually immature.

62 The spiritually immature person vexes himself (thinking) 'Sons are mine, riches are mine'. He himself is not his own, even; how then sons? how then riches?

63 The spiritually immature person who recognizes his immaturity is to that extent mature; the spiritually immature one who thinks of himself as mature is termed immature indeed.

64 Though throughout his life a spiritually immature person attends upon (or: honours) one who is spiritually mature, he does not necessarily know the truth, any more than the spoon knows the taste of the soup.

65 If for a moment a wise man attends upon one who is spiritually mature, he quickly perceives the truth, as the tongue at once detects the taste of the soup.

66 Of evil understanding, the spiritually immature live as enemies to themselves, committing sinful deeds, the consequences of which are bitter.

67 That deed is not well done which, being done, one repents, (and) the result of which one suffers with tearful face and lamentations.

68 That deed is well done which, being done, one does not repent, (and) the result of which one receives gladly.

69 So long as it has not ripened, the spiritually immature one thinks sin as sweet as honey; (but) when sin does ripen, then the spiritually immature one suffers a downfall.

70 Month after month, a spiritually immature person may eat his food with the tip of a blade of (sacred) kusa-grass,[9] (yet) his worth is not a fraction (lit., not a sixteenth part) of those who have ascertained the truth.

71 Unlike milk, which curdles immediately, the sin that has been committed does not at once bear fruit. (Instead) it pursues the

spiritually immature person like a fire covered with ashes, burning him (only after a time).

72 The spiritually immature person wins (theoretical religious) knowledge only to his own disadvantage; it destroys his better nature while splitting his head.

73 One who is spiritually immature desires a false reputation, honour among fellow almsmen, authority over monastic settlements, and respect from the families (living) round about.

74 'Let both those householders and those who have gone forth (from the household life) approve what I have done; let them be subject to me in all undertakings, great and small.' Such is the wish of the spiritually immature, (as a result of which) his craving and conceit increase.

75 One thing is that which leads to (worldly) gain; quite another the way that leads to Nirvāṇa. Thus comprehending, let the almsman, the disciple of the Buddha, take no delight in respectful greetings, but devote himself to solitude.

## 6: THE SPIRITUALLY MATURE

76 Should one see a man of understanding who, as if indicating a (buried) treasure, points out faults and administers reproof, let one associate with such a spiritually mature person. To associate with one like this is good, not evil.

77 Let him instruct, let him advise, let him restrain (one) from uncivilized behaviour, (and the result will be that) he will be dear to the good and detestable to the bad.

78 Do not associate with evil friends; do not associate with low fellows. Associate with spiritual friends; associate with superior men (*purisuttamas*).

79 One who has imbibed the Truth lives happily with well-seeing mind. The spiritually mature person delights in the Truth made known by the Noble (*ariyas*).

80 Irrigators draw off waters; fletchers straighten arrows; carpenters shape wood; the spiritually mature discipline themselves.

81 As a solid rock cannot be shaken by the wind, so the spiritually mature person is unmoved by praise or blame.

82 Hearing the teachings (of the Buddha), the spiritually mature become clear (or calm) like a deep lake (suddenly) becoming clear and undisturbed.

83 True men give up everything; the righteous do not speak wishing for sensuous pleasures. Touched now by pleasure, now by pain, the spiritually mature show neither elation nor depression.

84 Not for one's own sake, nor for the sake of others, should one desire sons, wealth, or territory; one should not desire success for oneself by unrighteous means. He (who behaves in such a way) is virtuous, is wise, is righteous.

85 Few among men are those who go to the Further Shore. The other (ordinary) people chase up and down this shore.

86 Those people who conform themselves to the well-explained Truth of Things and who are desirous of (reaching) the Further Shore will pass over the Realm of Death, so difficult to transcend.

87 Forsaking dark ways, the spiritually mature person cultivates the bright. Coming from home to the homeless (life), he (abides) in solitude (which) is hard to enjoy.

88 Giving up delight in sensuous pleasures the spiritually mature person, the man-of-no-possessions, should purify himself from (all) mental defilements.

89 They whose minds have cultivated to perfection the Factors of Enlightenment[10] and who, free from clinging, delight in the giving up of attachment, those bias-free radiant ones become Cool (*nibbutā*) even in this world (i.e., in this life).

## 7: THE (SUPREMELY) WORTHY

90 The burning fever of passion does not exist for one who has finished his journey (i.e., completed his spiritual evolution), who is free from sorrow, wholly emancipated, and released from all the bonds (of conditionality).

91 The mindful who leave home do not delight in an abode; like wild geese quitting a lake, they abandon whatever security they have.

92 Those who do not accumulate (material or mental possessions), who thoroughly understand (the true nature of) the food they eat, and whose range of experience (lit., pasture) is liberation through (the realization of) the Empty (*suñña*) and Unconditioned (*animitta*), their path, like that of birds in the sky, is difficult to trace.

93 He whose impurities are extinct, who is not attached to food, and whose range of experience (lit., pasture) is liberation through (the realization of) the Empty (*suñña*) and Unconditioned (*animitta*), his path, like that of birds in the sky, is difficult to trace.

94 He whose senses are pacified like horses well controlled by the charioteer, who has eradicated conceit and who is free from impurities – the very gods love a man of such (good) qualities (as these).

95 Like the earth, he offers no opposition; like the main pillar (of the city gate), he stands firm. He is (pure) like a lake free from mud. For a man of such (good) qualities (as these) there are no more wanderings (from life to life).

96 Tranquil is the thought, tranquil the word and deed, of that supremely tranquil person who is emancipated through Perfect Knowledge.

97 He is a superior man (*uttamapuriso*) who does not (merely) believe (but) who knows the Unmade, who has severed all links (with conditioned existence), put an end to the occasions (of good and evil), and who has renounced (lit., vomited up) all worldly hopes.

98 Whether village or forest, plain or hill, delightful is that spot where the (Supremely) Worthy dwell.

99 Delightful are the forests where ordinary people find no pleasure. Those who are free from passion delight (in them), (for) they do not go in quest of sensuous enjoyment.

## 8: THE THOUSANDS

100 Better than a thousand meaningless words collected together (in the Vedic oral tradition) is a single meaningful word on hearing which one becomes tranquil.

101 Better than a thousand meaningless verses collected together (in the Vedic oral tradition) is one (meaningful) line of verse on hearing which one becomes tranquil.

102 Though one should recite a hundred (Vedic) verses, (verses) without meaning, better is one line (or: a single word) of Dhamma on hearing which one becomes tranquil.

103 Though one should conquer in battle thousands upon thousands of men, yet he who conquers himself is (truly) the greatest in battle.

104 It is indeed better to conquer oneself than to conquer other people. Of a man who has subdued himself, (and) who lives (self-) controlled,

105 neither a god nor a celestial musician (*gandhabba*), nor Māra together with Brahmā, can undo the victory – the victory of a person who is (subdued and controlled) like that.

106 If month after month for a hundred years one should offer sacrifices by the thousand, and if for a single moment one should venerate a (spiritually) developed person, better is that (act of) veneration than the hundred years (of sacrifices).

107 Though one should tend the sacred fire in the forest for a hundred years, yet if he venerates a (spiritually) developed person even for a moment, better is that (act of) veneration than the hundred years (spent tending the sacred fire).

108 Whatever oblations and sacrifices one might offer here on earth in the course of the whole (Vedic) religious year, seeking to gain merit thereby, all that is not a quarter (as meritorious) as paying respect to those who live uprightly, which is (indeed) excellent.

109 For him who is of a reverential disposition, constantly respecting his elders, four things constantly increase: life, beauty, happiness, and strength.

110 Though one should live a hundred years unethical and unintegrated (*asamāhita*), better is one single day lived ethically and absorbed (in higher meditative states).

111 Though one should live a hundred years of evil understanding and unintegrated, better is one single day lived possessed of wisdom and absorbed (in higher meditative states).

112 Better than a hundred years lived lazily and with inferior energy is one single day lived with energy aroused and fortified.

113 Better than a hundred years lived unaware of the rise and fall (of conditioned things) is one single day lived aware of the rise and fall (of conditioned things).

114 Better than a hundred years lived unaware of the Deathless State is one single day lived aware of the Deathless State.

115 Better than a hundred years lived unaware of the Supreme Truth (*dhammam uttamaṃ*) is one single day lived aware of the Supreme Truth.

## 9: EVIL

116 Be quick to do what is (morally) beautiful. Restrain the mind from evil. He who is sluggish in doing good, his mind delights in evil.

117 Should a man (once) do evil, let him not make a habit of it; let him not set his heart on it. Painful is the heaping up of evil.

118 Should a man (once) do good, let him make a habit of it; let him set his heart on it. Happy is the heaping up of good.

119 As long as it bears no fruit, so long the evildoer sees the evil (he has done) as good. When it bears fruit (in the form of suffering) he recognizes it as evil.

120 As long as it bears no fruit, so long the good man sees the good (he has done) as evil. When it bears fruit (in the form of happiness) he recognizes it as good.

121 Do not underestimate evil, (thinking) 'It will not approach me.' A water-pot becomes full by the (constant) falling of drops of water. (Similarly) the spiritually immature person little by little fills himself with evil.

122 Do not underestimate good, (thinking) 'It will not approach me.' A water-pot becomes full by the (constant) falling of drops of water. (Similarly) the wise man little by little fills himself with good.

123 As a merchant (travelling) with a small caravan and much wealth avoids a dangerous road, or as one desirous of life shuns poison, so should one keep clear of evil.

124 If one has no wound in one's hand one may (safely) handle poison. The unwounded hand is not affected by poison. (Similarly) no evil befalls him who does no wrong.

125 Whoever offends against an innocent man, one who is pure and faultless, to that spiritually immature person the evil (he has committed) comes back like fine dust thrown against the wind.

126 Some (beings) arise (by way of conception) in the womb. Evildoers are born in a state of woe. Those who do good go to heaven. Those who are free from defilements become utterly 'Cool'.

127 Not in the sky, nor in the midst of the sea, nor yet in the clefts of the mountains, nowhere in the world (in fact) is there any place to be found where, having entered, one can abide free from (the consequences of) one's evil deeds.

128 Not in the sky, nor in the midst of the sea, nor yet in the clefts of mountains, nowhere in the world (in fact) is there any place to be found where, having entered, one will not be overcome by death.

## 10: PUNISHMENT

129 All (living beings) are terrified of punishment (*daṇḍa*); all fear death. Making comparison (of others) with oneself, one should neither kill nor cause to kill.

130 All (living beings) are terrified of punishment (*daṇḍa*); to all, life is dear. Making comparison (of others) with oneself, one should neither kill nor cause to kill.

131 Whoever torments with the stick (*daṇḍa*) creatures desirous of happiness, he himself thereafter, seeking happiness, will not obtain happiness.

132 Whoever does not torment with the stick (*daṇḍa*) creatures desirous of happiness, he himself thereafter, seeking happiness, will obtain happiness.

133 Do not speak roughly to anyone: those thus spoken to will answer back. Painful indeed is angry talk, (as a result of which) one will experience retribution.

134 If you (can) silence yourself like a shattered metal plate you have already attained Nirvāṇa: no anger is found in you.

135 As a cowherd drives cows out to pasture with a stick, so do old age and death drive the life out of living beings.

136 A spiritually immature person performs evil deeds not realizing (their true nature). By his own actions is the man of evil understanding tormented (lit., burned) as though consumed by fire.

137 Whoever inflicts punishment on the innocent, (or) who offends against the unoffending, he speedily falls into one of the ten states:

138 He meets either with intense physical pain, or material loss, or bodily injury, or serious illness, or mental derangement;

139 Or (he meets with) trouble from the government or a serious accusation, or bereavement, or loss of wealth:

140 Or else his houses are consumed by fire, (while) on the dissolution of the body that man of evil understanding is reborn in a state of woe.

141 Not going about naked, not (the wearing of) matted locks, not abstention from food, not sleeping on the (bare) ground, not (smearing the body with) dust and ashes, nor yet (the practice of) squatting (on the balls of the feet), can purify a mortal who has not overcome his doubts.

142 If one who is richly adorned lives in tranquillity, is calm, controlled, assured (of eventual enlightenment), and devotes himself to the spiritual life, laying down the stick with regard to all living beings, then (despite his being richly adorned), he is a *brāhmaṇa*, he is an asketic, he is an almsman.

143 In the (whole) world is there a man to be found who, restrained by a sense of shame, avoids censure as a good horse avoids the whip?

144 Like a good horse touched by the whip, be zealous and stirred by profound religious emotion. By means of faith, upright conduct, energy, concentration (*samādhi*), and investigation of the Truth, (as well as by being) endowed with (spiritual) knowledge and (righteous) behaviour, and by being mindful, leave this great suffering behind.

145 Irrigators draw off the waters; fletchers straighten arrows; carpenters shape wood; righteous men discipline themselves.

## 11: DECAY

146 What mirth can there be, what pleasure, when all the time (everything) is blazing (with the threefold fire of suffering, impermanence, and insubstantiality)? Covered (though you are) in blind darkness, you do not seek a light!

147 Look at this painted doll (i.e., the body), this pretentious mass of sores, wretched and full of cravings (or: much hankered after), nothing of which is stable or lasting!

148 Wasted away is this body, a nest of disease, and perishable. The putrid mass breaks up: death is the end of life.

149 When like gourds in autumn these dove-grey bones lie here discarded, what pleasure (can one take) in looking at them?

150 (The body) is a city built of bones and plastered with flesh and blood, (a city) wherein lie concealed decay and death, pride and hypocrisy.

151 Even the richly decorated royal chariots (in time) wear out; likewise the body also perishes. (But) the Truth (*dhamma*) of the good does not perish, (for) those who are good indeed speak of it to the good.

152 The man of little learning lives like a stalled ox: his flesh increases but his wisdom does not.

153 Many a birth have I undergone in this (process of) faring on (in the round of conditioned existence), seeking the builder of the house and not finding him. Painful is (such) repeated birth.

154 House-builder, (now) you are seen! Never again shall you build (me) a house. Your rafters are all broken, your ridgepole shattered. The (conditioned) mind too has gone to destruction: one has attained to the cessation of craving.[11]

155 Those who have not led the spiritual life (*brahmacariya*), or obtained the wealth (of merit) in their youth, (such as these) brood over the past like aged herons in a pond without fish.

156 Those who have not led the spiritual life (*brahmacariya*), or obtained the wealth (of merit) in their youth, (such as these) lie like worn-out arrows, lamenting the things of old.

## 12: SELF

157 If a man (really) regards himself as dear, let him well and truly protect himself. During one or another of the three watches (of the night) the spiritually mature person should keep wide awake.

158 First establish yourself in what is suitable, then advise others. The spiritually mature person should not besmirch himself (by acting otherwise).

159 Should you act as you advise others to act, then it would be (a case of) one who was (self-) controlled exercising control (over others). The self is truly difficult to control.

160 One is indeed one's own saviour (or: protector). What other saviour should there be? With oneself well-controlled, one finds a saviour (who is) hard to find.

161 The evil done by oneself, born of oneself, produced by oneself, destroys the man of evil understanding as a diamond pulverizes a piece of rock crystal.

162 He whose unprincipled behaviour is without limit, like a māluvā creeper overspreading a sāl tree, does to his own self that which his enemy wishes (to do to him).

163 Easily done are things which are bad and not beneficial to oneself. What is (both) beneficial and good, that is exceedingly difficult to do.

164 The man of evil understanding who, on account of his (wrong) views, obstructs (or: rejects) the message of the (Supremely) Worthy, the Noble Ones, the men of authentic life, that wicked person, like a kaṭṭhaka(-reed), brings forth fruit (i.e., performs actions) to his own destruction.

165 A man besmirches himself by the evil he personally commits. (Similarly) he purifies himself by personally abstaining from evil. Purity and impurity are matters of personal experience: one man cannot purify another.

166 (Consequently) one should not neglect one's own (spiritual) welfare for the welfare of others, great as that may be. Clearly perceiving (what constitutes) one's personal welfare, one should devote oneself to one's own good.

## 13: THE WORLD

167 Don't follow inferior principles. Don't live heedlessly. Don't entertain false views. Don't be one who (by following inferior principles etc.) keeps the world going.

168 Get up! Don't be heedless! Live practising the Dhamma, (the Dhamma) which is good conduct. One who lives practising the Dhamma (*dhammacārī*) dwells happily (both) in this world and the other (world).

169 Live practising the Dhamma. Do not live behaving badly. One who lives practising the Dhamma (*dhammacārī*) dwells happily (both) in this world and the other (world).

170 Look upon (the world) as a bubble; look upon (it) as a mirage. The King of Death does not see one who looks upon the world in this way.

171 Come, (just) look at this world, which is like a decorated royal chariot in which the spiritually immature sink down (or: are dejected), but (with regard to which) there is no attachment on the part of those who really know.

172 One who having formerly been heedless later is not heedless, lights up the world like the moon (when) freed from clouds.

173 One who covers over the evil deeds he has done with (ethically) skilful actions, lights up this world like the moon (when) freed from clouds.

174 This world is (mentally) blinded; few see clearly. Few are those who, like birds freed from the net, go to heaven.

175 Swans fly on the path of the sun.[12] Those with supernormal powers travel through the air. The wise, having conquered Māra and his army, are led (away) from the world.

176 There is no wrong that cannot be committed by a lying person who has transgressed one (good) principle (i.e., that of truthfulness), and who has given up (all thought of) the other world.

177 Truly, misers do not get to the world of the gods. (Only) the spiritually immature do not praise giving. The wise man rejoices in giving, and therefore is happy in the hereafter.

178 The Fruit of Stream Entry is better than sole sovereignty over the earth, (better) than going to heaven, (better) than lordship over all the worlds.

179 That Enlightened One whose sphere is endless, whose victory is irreversible, and after whose victory no (defilements) remain (to be conquered), by what track will you lead him (astray), the Trackless One?

180 That Enlightened One in whom there is not that ensnaring, entangling craving to lead anywhere (in conditioned existence), and whose sphere is endless, by what track will you lead him (astray), the Trackless One?

181 Those wise ones who are intent on absorption (in higher meditative states) and who delight in the calm of renunciation, even the gods love them, those thoroughly enlightened and mindful ones.

182 Difficult is the attainment of the human state. Difficult is the life of mortals. Difficult is the hearing of the Real Truth (*saddhamma*). Difficult is the appearance of the Enlightened Ones.

183 The not doing of anything evil, undertaking to do what is (ethically) skilful (*kusala*), (and) complete purification of the mind – this is the ordinance (*sāsana*) of the Enlightened Ones.

184 Patient endurance is the best form of penance. 'Nirvāṇa is the Highest,' say the Enlightened Ones. No (true) goer forth (from the household life) is he who injures another, nor is he a true asketic who persecutes others.

185 Not to speak evil, not to injure, to exercise restraint through the observance of the (almsman's) code of conduct, to be moderate in diet, to live alone, and to occupy oneself with higher mental states – this is the ordinance (*sāsana*) of the Enlightened Ones.

186 Not (even) in a shower of money is satisfaction of desires to be found. 'Worldly pleasures are of little relish, (indeed) painful.' Thus understanding, the spiritually mature person

187 takes no delight even in heavenly pleasures. The disciple of the Fully, Perfectly Enlightened One takes delight (only) in the destruction of craving.

188 Many people, out of fear, flee for refuge to (sacred) hills, woods, groves, trees, and shrines.

189 In reality this is not a safe refuge. In reality this is not the best refuge. Fleeing to such a refuge one is not released from all suffering.

190 He who goes for refuge to the Enlightened One, to the Truth, and to the Spiritual Community, and who sees with perfect wisdom the Four Ariyan Truths –

191 namely, suffering, the origin of suffering, the passing beyond suffering, and the Ariyan Eightfold Way leading to the pacification of suffering –

192 (for him) this is a safe refuge, (for him) this is the best refuge. Having gone to such a refuge, one is released from all suffering.

193 Hard to come by is the Ideal Man (*purisājañña*). He is not born everywhere. Where such a wise one is born, that family grows happy.

194 Happy is the appearance of the Enlightened Ones. Happy is the teaching of the Real Truth (*saddhamma*). Happy is the unity of the Spiritual Community. Happy is the spiritual effort of the united.

195 He who reverences those worthy of reverence, whether Enlightened Ones or (their) disciples, (men) who have transcended illusion (*papañca*), and passed beyond grief and lamentation;

196 he who reverences those who are of such a nature, who (moreover) are at peace and without cause for fear, his merit is not to be reckoned as such and such.

197 Happy indeed we live, friendly amid the haters. Among men who hate we dwell free from hate.

198 Happy indeed we live, healthy amid the sick. Among men who are sick we dwell free from sickness.

199 Happy indeed we live, content amid the greedy. Among men who are greedy we dwell free from greed.

200 Happy indeed we live, we for whom there are no possessions (*kiñcanas*). Feeders on rapture shall we be, like the gods of Brilliant Light.[13]

201 Victory begets hatred, (for) the defeated one experiences suffering. The tranquil one experiences happiness, giving up (both) victory and defeat.

202 There is no fire like lust, no blemish like demerit (*kali*), no suffering like the taking up of the (five) constituents (of conditioned existence), no happiness like peace.

203 Hunger is the worst disease, conditioned existence the worst suffering. Knowing this as it really is (one realizes that) Nirvāṇa is the highest happiness.

204 Health is the highest gain, contentment the greatest riches. The trustworthy are the best kinsmen, Nirvāṇa is the supreme happiness.

205 Having enjoyed the flavour of solitude and tranquillity, free from sorrow and free from sin, one enjoys the rapturous flavour of the Truth (*dhamma*).

206 Good it is to see the spiritually developed (*ariyas*); to (actually) dwell with them is always happiness. By not seeing the spiritually immature, one indeed will be perpetually happy.

207 By living in company with the spiritually immature one grieves for a long time. Association with the spiritually immature is always painful, like association with an enemy. Association with the wise is pleasant, like the coming together of relatives.

208 (Therefore it is said: ) Follow one who is wise, understanding, and learned, who bears the yoke of virtue, is religious and spiritually developed (*ariya*). Follow one of such a nature, as the moon follows the path of the stars.

## 16: AFFECTIONS

209 Devoting himself to the unbefitting and not devoting himself to the fitting, he, rejecting the (truly) good and grasping the (merely) pleasant, envies those who are devoted to the (truly) good.

210 Don't associate with the dear, and never with the undear. Not seeing those who are dear is painful, (as is) seeing those who are not dear.

211 Therefore let nothing be dear to you, for separation from the dear is (experienced as an) evil. There exist no bonds for those for whom there is neither the dear nor the undear.

212 From the dear arises grief; from the dear arises fear. For the one who is wholly free from the dear there exists no grief. Whence (should) fear (come)?

213 From affection (*pema*) arises grief; from affection arises fear. For one who is wholly free from affection there exists no grief. Whence (should) fear (come)?

214 From (sensual) enjoyment (*rati*) arises grief; from (sensual) enjoyment arises fear. For one who is wholly free from (sensual) enjoyment there is no grief. Whence (should) fear (come)?

215 From (lustful) desire (*kāma*) arises grief; from (lustful) desire (*kāma*) arises fear. For one who is wholly free from (lustful) desire there is no grief. Whence (should) fear (come)?

216 From craving arises grief; from craving arises fear. For one who is wholly free from craving there is no grief. Whence (should) fear (come)?

217 People hold him dear who is perfect in right conduct (*sīla*) and vision (*dassana*), who is principled (*dhammaṭṭha*) and a speaker of the truth, and who carries out his own (spiritual) tasks.

218 He is called 'One whose stream goes upward'[14] in whom is born an ardent aspiration (*chanda*) after the Undefined, whose mind (*manas*) would be permeated (by the thrill of his progress so far), and whose heart (*citta*) is unattached to sensual pleasures.

219 When a man long absent (from home) returns safely from a distant place, his relatives, friends, and well-wishers rejoice exceedingly at his return.

220 Similarly, his own good deeds receive him when he goes from this world to the other (world) as relatives (receive) a dear one on his return (home).

## 17: ANGER

221 Let one give up anger, renounce conceit, (and) overcome all fetters. Suffering does not befall him who is unattached to name-and-form (*nāmarūpa*: i.e., psychophysical existence), (and) who is without (material or mental) possessions (*akiñcana*).

222 I call him a charioteer who holds back the arisen anger as though (holding back) a swerving chariot. Others are only holders of reins.

223 Overcome the angry by non-anger; overcome the wicked with good. Overcome the miserly by giving, the teller of lies with truth.

224 Speak the truth; do not get angry; give your mite to those who ask (for alms). On these three grounds one goes into the presence of the gods.

225 Those silent sages who are harmless (*ahiṃsakas*) and always (self-)controlled go to the Immovable Abode, whither having gone they do not grieve.

226 They come to the end of (their) defilements (*āsavas*), those who keep awake, who study day and night, (and) who are intent on Nirvāṇa.

227 This is an old story, Atula,[15] not just one of today. They blame him who is taciturn; they blame him who is talkative; they even blame him who speaks in moderation. There is no one in the world who is not blamed.

228 There has not been, nor will there be, nor is there anyone now, who is absolutely blamed or absolutely praised.

229–230 Who is entitled to blame that man who is like (a coin of) Jambunada gold,[16] a man who is praised by the wise, by those who have tested him day by day; one who is free from faults, a man of understanding, (and) whose wisdom and understanding are (well) integrated? Even the gods praise such a man. By Brahmā, too, is he praised.

231 Be on your guard against bodily agitation; be controlled in body. Giving up bodily misconduct, live well behaved as regards the body.

232 Be on your guard against verbal agitation; be controlled in speech. Giving up verbal misconduct, live well behaved as regards speech.

233 Be on your guard against mental agitation; be controlled in mind. Giving up mental misconduct, live well behaved as regards the mind.

234 They are the perfectly restrained ones, the wise who are controlled in body and speech, (together with) the wise who are controlled as regards the mind.

235 You are now like a withered leaf; Death's men have approached you. You stand at the door of departure, and you do not even have provisions for the road.

236 Make a lamp (or: island) for yourself; strive quickly, (and) become one who is spiritually mature. With stains removed, (and) free from blemish, you will reach the celestial plane (*bhūmi*) of the spiritually developed (*ariyas*).

237 You are now of advanced age; you have gone forth into the presence of Death. There is no (resting) place for you in between, (and) you do not even have provisions for the road.

238 Make a lamp (or: island) for yourself; strive quickly, (and) become one who is spiritually mature. With stains removed, (and) free from blemish, you will not undergo repeated birth and old age (any more).

239 The man of understanding removes his stains gradually, little by little, and from moment to moment, just as the silversmith (removes) the impurities of silver.

240 Just as rust springing from iron, (having) sprung from that eats it (away), even so his own actions lead the transgressor to an evil state (*duggati*).

241 Non-repetition is the stain of the (orally transmitted) sacred verses (*mantas*). Inactivity (in maintaining them) is the stain of houses. Sloth is the stain of beauty (of complexion). Heedlessness is the stain of one who guards.

242 Misconduct is the stain of a woman. Stinginess is the stain of one who gives. (Both) in this world and the other (world) stains are indeed evil things.

243 A greater stain than these is ignorance (*avijjā*), which is the supreme stain. Abandoning this stain, be stainless, almsmen.

244 He has an easy life who is shameless, impudent as a crow, disparaging (of others' merits), obtrusive, arrogant, (and) of a corrupt way of life.

245 Life is hard for one with a sense of shame, who always seeks purity, who is unattached (or: strenuous), who is humble (and) of a pure way of life, and discerning.

246 Whoever in (this) world (of ours) destroys life, tells lies, takes what is not given, resorts to the wives of others,

247 and is addicted to the drinking of intoxicants (*surāmeraya*), that man in this world himself digs up his own roots (of merit).

248 Know this, good man: Those having an evil nature are uncontrolled. Don't let greed and unrighteousness subject you to prolonged suffering.

249 People give (alms) according to their faith and at their good pleasure. One who is discontented about the food and drink of others does not attain concentration (*samādhi*), be it by day or by night.

250 One in whom this (kind of attitude) is extirpated, (it being) destroyed at its roots (and) abolished, he attains concentration (*samādhi*), be it by day or by night.

251 There is no fire like lust. There is no grip like anger. There is no net like delusion. There is no river like craving.

252 The faults of others are easily seen; one's own faults are seen with difficulty. One winnows the faults of others like chaff, but one covers up one's own as a dishonest gambler (covers up) a losing throw (of the dice).

253 He who pays attention to the faults of others (and) is always irritable, his defilements (*āsavas*) grow. He is far from the destruction of the defilements.

254 There is no track in the sky. There is no (true) asketic outside (this Teaching). The race of men delight in illusion (*papañca*). The Tathāgatas (i.e., the Buddhas or Enlightened Ones) are free from illusions.

255 There is no track in the sky. There is no (true) asketic outside (this Teaching). There are no conditioned things that are eternal. There is no vacillation in the Enlightened Ones.

## 19: THE MAN OF PRINCIPLE

256 He is not a 'man of principle' (*dhammaṭṭha*) who rashly judges what is advantageous (*attha*). The spiritually mature person who judges both what is advantageous and disadvantageous –

257 who judges others impartially, carefully, and in accordance with principle – that man of understanding, guarded of principle, is said to be 'a man of principle'.

258 A man is not spiritually mature (or: learned) merely because he talks a lot. He is said to be spiritually mature who is secure (in himself), friendly, and without fear.

259 He is not a vessel of the Teaching (*dhammadhara*) merely because he talks a lot. He who, having heard only a little, personally sees the Truth, he (truly) is a 'vessel of the Teaching', that man who is not neglectful of the Teaching.

260 A man is not an elder (among almsmen) because his head is grey. Though of mature age, he is called 'grown old in vain'.

261 He is (truly) called an elder (among almsmen) in whom are truth and principle, (together with) harmlessness (*ahiṃsā*), (self-)control (and) restraint, (and) who is without stain and wise.

262 One who is jealous, miserly, and dishonest is not accounted 'good' (*sādhurūpa*) merely by reason of his speechifying or beautiful complexion.

263 He is said to be 'good' (*sādhurūpa*), that fault-free man of understanding, in whom this (kind of behaviour) is extirpated, it being destroyed at its roots (and) abolished.

264 A man who is without (religious) observances (and) who speaks what is false is not an asketic (merely) by reason of his shaven head.

265 He who stills (*sameti*) all his evils, small and great, is said to be an asketic (*samaṇa*) because those evils have been stilled.

266 One is not an almsman (merely) because he begs (alms) from others. One is not an almsman (merely) because of having adopted a bad (teaching).

267 He is said to be an almsman who lives in the world with discrimination (*saṅkhā*), having by means of the spiritual life (*brahmacariya*) set aside merit and demerit.

268–269 One who is confused and ignorant does not become a silent sage (*muni*) merely by observing silence. But that spiritually mature person who, as if holding a pair of scales, accepts the best and rejects the evil, *he* is a silent sage. He is a silent sage for that (very) reason. He is (also) called a silent sage (*muni*) because he understands (*munāti*) both worlds.

270 A man who harms living beings is not one who is spiritually developed (*ariya*). He is said to be spiritually developed who is harmless towards all living beings.

271–272 Without having attained to the destruction of the defilements (*āsavas*), almsman, you should not rest content with rules of conduct and religious observances, or with much learning, or with the attainment of concentration (*samādhi*), or with living in seclusion, or with (thinking) 'I enjoy the bliss of emancipation (that is) unknown to ordinary people.'

## 20: THE WAY

273 Best of ways is the Eightfold (Way). Best of truths are the Four (Truths). Passionlessness is the best of (mental) states. The Man of Vision (*cakkhumā*) is the best of bipeds.

274 This indeed is the Way; there is no other that leads to purity of vision. Enter upon the Way; this Way is the bewilderment of Māra.

275 Following this Way you will make an end of suffering. This indeed is the Way proclaimed by me ever since I knew how to draw out the darts (of craving).

276 By you must the zealous effort be made. The Tathāgatas (i.e., the Buddhas or Enlightened Ones) are only proclaimers (of the Way). Those who are practitioners, absorbed (in higher meditative states) (eventually) win release from the bondage of Māra.

277 'All conditioned things are impermanent.' When one sees this with insight (*paññā*) one becomes weary of suffering. This is the Way to Purity.

278 'All conditioned things are painful.' When one sees this with insight (*paññā*) one becomes weary of suffering. This is the Way to Purity.

279 'All things (whatsoever) are devoid of unchanging selfhood.' When one sees this with insight (*pannā*) one becomes weary of suffering. This is the Way to Purity.

280 One who does not make use of his (spiritual) opportunities, who, though young and strong, is lazy, weak in aspiration, and inactive, such a lazy person does not find the way to insight (*paññā*).

281 Guarded in speech, as well as controlled in mind, let one do no (ethically) unskilful thing with the body. Purifying these three avenues of action, let him attain the Way made known by the sages.

282 From application (*yoga*) arises the (spiritually) great (*bhūri*). From lack of application the (spiritually) great wanes. Having known these two avenues of increase and decrease (of the great) let him so establish himself that the great may flourish.

283 Cut down the (whole) forest, not (just) one tree. From the forest arises fear. Cutting down both wood and brushwood, be 'out of the wood', almsman.

284 To the extent that one has not cut down the last little bit of this 'brushwood' of (the craving of) man for woman, to that extent his mind will be fettered, as the sucking calf to its mother.

285 Cut off your sticky affection, as one plucks with one's hand the white autumnal lotus. Develop the Way of Peace, the Nirvāṇa taught by the Happy One.

286 'Here shall I stay during the rains, here in the cold season and the hot.' Thus thinks the spiritually immature person. He does not understand the dangers (to life).

287 That infatuated man whose delight is in offspring and cattle, death goes and carries him off as a great flood (sweeps away) a sleeping village.

288 Sons are no protection, nor father, nor yet (other) relatives. For him who is seized by the End-maker (i.e., Death), there is no protection forthcoming from relatives.

289 Knowing the significance of this, let the spiritually mature person, the man restrained by good conduct, speedily cleanse the Way leading to Nirvāṇa.

290 If by renouncing a limited happiness one would see an abundant happiness, let the spiritually mature person, having regard to the abundant happiness, sacrifice the limited happiness.

291 He who, contaminated by (his) association with hatred, seeks happiness for himself by inflicting suffering on others, is not released from hatred.

292 What is to be done, that is neglected; what is not to be done, that is done. Of those who are arrogant and heedless the defilements increase.

293 Those who ever earnestly practise mindfulness with regard to the body, not following after what is not to be done (and) steadfastly pursuing what is to be done, of these mindful and fully attentive ones the defilements come to an end.

294 Having slain mother and father and two warrior kings, and having destroyed a kingdom together with the (king's) revenue collector, the brāhmaṇa goes free from sin.[17]

295 Having slain mother and father and two learned kings, and having killed a tiger as the fifth, the brāhmaṇa goes free from sin.[18]

296 Wide awake they always arise (in the morning), the disciples of Gotama, (those) who day and night are constantly mindful of the (virtues of the) Buddha.

297 Wide awake they always arise (in the morning), the disciples of Gotama, (those) who day and night are constantly mindful of the (qualities of the) Dhamma.

298 Wide awake they always arise (in the morning), the disciples of Gotama, (those) who day and night are constantly mindful of the (characteristics of the Ārya) Sangha.[19]

299 Wide awake they always arise (in the morning), the disciples of Gotama, (those) who day and night are constantly mindful of the (transitory nature of the) body.

300 Wide awake they always arise (in the morning), the disciples of Gotama, (those) who day and night delight in non-injury (*ahiṃsā*).

301 Wide awake they always arise (in the morning), the disciples of Gotama, (those) whose mind day and night delights in meditation (*bhāvanā*).

302 It is difficult to go forth (from home to the homeless life); and difficult to delight therein (once one has gone forth). (At the same time) household life is painful, (and) painful, likewise, is living together with those who are not (one's) peers. Travellers (on the road of birth, death, and rebirth) are oppressed by suffering, so do not be (such a) traveller oppressed by suffering.

303 He who is perfect in faith and good conduct, (and) possessed of fame and wealth, he is honoured everywhere, to whatever country he resorts.

304 Like the Snowy (Mountain Range), the good are visible even from afar. The wicked are not seen, like arrows shot in the night.

305 He who sits alone, lies down alone (and) walks alone, without weariness, (and) who strives, (all) alone, to subdue himself, (he) will take delight in the (solitude of the) forest.

## 22: THE WOEFUL STATE

306 One who tells lies arises (by way of rebirth) in a state of woe, as does one who, having done something, says 'I don't do (that sort of thing).' These two sons of Manu (the Primeval Progenitor),[20] men of base actions, on departing (this life) have the same (painful destiny) in the other world.

307 Many 'yellow-necks' (i.e., wearers of the yellow robe)[21] are of bad qualities (or: of an evil disposition) and uncontrolled. These bad people, on account of their bad deeds, arise (after death) in a state of woe.

308 Better to swallow a flaming, red hot ball of iron, than to be an immoral, uncontrolled man living on the almsfood of the land.

309 A heedless man who resorts to the wives of others comes by four (evil) states: acquisition of demerit; not sleeping (soundly) as desired; thirdly, blame; (and) fourthly, (rebirth in) a state of woe.

310 (The result is) acquisition of demerit and a wretched (future) course; the short-lived enjoyment of an apprehensive man with an apprehensive woman; also the king imposes a heavy penalty. Therefore let not a man resort to another's wife.

311 Just as (sharp-edged) kusa grass, wrongly taken hold of, cuts the hand, so the life of a religieux, wrongly grasped, drags down to a state of woe.

312 Any unprincipled act, and any sullied religious observance – a (slack) spiritual life (*brahmacariya*) filled with suspicion – this is of little benefit.

313 If you have something to do, attack it vigorously. One who lives the homeless life half-heartedly scatters much dust of passion around.

314 An ill deed is better left undone, (for) an ill deed torments one afterwards (with remorse). Better done is a good deed, having done which one is not (so) tormented.

315 Like a frontier city well-guarded within and without, so guard yourself. Let not the (fortunate) moment (of human birth etc.) pass you by. Those who allow the fortunate moment to pass by grieve when they go to the woeful state.

316 Those who are ashamed of what is not shameful, (and) not ashamed of what is shameful, such beings, taking upon themselves wrong views, go to an evil state.

317 Those who see what (morally) is not fearful as fearful, and who see what (morally) is fearful as not fearful, such beings, taking upon themselves wrong views, go to an evil state.

318 Those who think what (morally) is blameable not blameable, and who see what (morally) is not blameable as blameable, such beings, taking upon themselves wrong views, go to an evil state.

319 Knowing the (morally) blameable as blameable, and the (morally) free from blame as blameless, those beings, taking upon themselves right views, go to a happy state.

## 23: THE ELEPHANT

320 I shall patiently endure abuse, just as the (trained) elephant endures in battle the arrow (shot) from a bow. The many are indeed ill-natured (or: badly behaved).

321 The tamed (elephant) is led to the assembly; the king mounts the tamed (elephant). Among men, best is the (self-)controlled person who patiently endures abuse.

322 Trained mules are best, also (equine) thoroughbreds of Sindh, and the mighty (fighting) elephants. (But) best of all is the self-controlled man.

323 One does not go to the unfrequented realm by such vehicles as these, as does a controlled one go (to it) by means of a well-subdued, disciplined self.

324 The elephant called Dhanapāla is difficult to restrain when his temples are streaming with must (in the time of rut). Shackled, he refuses (his) food. The tusker remembers the (delightful) elephant forest.

325 When one is sluggish and gluttonous, given to sleep, (and) a roller-about like a great hog fed on grains, such a stupid person goes again and again to a womb (to be reborn).

326 Formerly this mind (of mine) went wandering about where it wished, as it liked, (and) according to its pleasure. Today I will control it radically, as the wielder of the (elephant driver's) hook restrains the (rutting) elephant.

327 Be delighters in non-heedlessness. Keep watch over your mind. Lift yourself clear of the difficult road (of the mental defilements), as an elephant sunk in a bog (hauls himself out).

328 Should you get a sensible companion, one who is fit company (for you), who behaves well, and is wise, (then) go about with him joyous and mindful, overcoming all (external and internal) dangers.

329 Should you not get a sensible companion, one who is fit company (for you), who behaves well, and is wise, (then) go about alone, like a king forsaking a conquered country, (or) like an elephant (living solitary) in the Mātaṅga forest.

330 It is better to go about alone; there is no companionship with the spiritually immature. Going about alone one commits no sins, like an elephant living unconcerned in the Mātaṅga forest.

331 Friends are good in time of need. Contentment is good in every way. At the end of life (a store of) merit is good (or: a meritorious action is good). Good is the leaving behind of all suffering.

332 Here reverence for mother is good; reverence for father is also good. Here reverence for asketicism is good; reverence for holiness is also good.

333 The lifelong practice of virtue (*sīla*) is good. A (firmly) established faith (in the Three Jewels) is good. Good is the getting of wisdom (*paññā*). The non-doing of evil is good.

334 The craving of the man who lives carelessly increases like the māluvā creeper. He runs from existence to existence, like a monkey in the jungle (leaping from tree to tree) in search of fruit.

335 Whoever in the world is overcome by this wretched, adhesive craving, his sorrows grow like the bīraṇa grass that is rained upon.

336 Whoever in the world overcomes this wretched, adhesive craving, so difficult to overcome, his sorrows fall from him like drops of water from the lotus leaf.

337 I tell you this: Be of good cheer, as many of you as are here assembled. Dig out the root of craving, as the seeker of the usīra (digs out) the bīraṇa grass. Don't let Māra (the Evil One) break you again and again as a river (in spate) breaks the reed.

338 Just as a felled tree shoots (up) again if the root is uninjured and stout, so this suffering (of ours) arises again and again if the propensity to craving is not destroyed.

339 The currents of his passion-based thoughts carry him away, that man of wrong views for whom the thirty-six streams (of craving)[22] flowing towards what is pleasurable are strong.

340 The streams (of craving) flow everywhere, (and) the creeper (of craving) having sprung up remains (clasping its objects). Seeing that creeper sprung up, sever its root with (the knife of) wisdom (*paññā*).

341 Delights arise for a being, (delights) that rush on and are saturated (with craving). Those seekers after pleasure who are attached to what is agreeable, those men are indeed bound for (re) birth and old age.

342 Attended upon by craving, the race of men run about in terror like a trapped hare. Fettered and bound (as they are), suffering befalls them again and again for a long time.

343 Attended upon by craving, the race of men run about in terror like a trapped hare. Therefore let him allay craving, the almsman who is desirous of his own freedom from passion.

344 Just look at him, the man who having been delivered from the jungle of craving (i.e., from the household life) and drawn to (the life of) the jungle, (nonetheless) having been thus delivered from the jungle (of craving) runs (from the jungle) to the jungle (of household life). Freed, he runs (back) to (his former) bondage.

345 That is not a strong bond, say the wise, which is made of iron, wood, or (plaited) grass. Passionate fondness for jewelled earrings, (and) longing with regard to sons and wives –

346 that is a strong bond, say the wise. It drags one down, is loose (fitting) yet difficult to be got rid of. This (bond) they too cut off, those longing-free ones who, giving up sensual pleasures, go forth (from the household life).

347 The passionately lustful man falls back into the torrent (of repeated existence), just as the spider returns to (the centre of) its web (after running out and feeding on a trapped fly). This too the wise man cuts off and renounces; free from longing, he leaves behind all suffering.

348 Give up what is 'before' (in time), give up what is 'after', give up what is 'in between'. Crossed to the Further Shore of existence, (and) with mind wholly released, you will undergo birth and decay no more.

349 For the person of disturbed thinking, whose passions are acute, and who looks (only) for what is 'lovely', craving grows apace.

350 He who delights in calming down (his) thinking, who meditates on the ('lovely' as being truly) unlovely, (and) who is always mindful, he will cut through the bond of Māra (the Evil One).

351 The one who has arrived at (spiritual) perfection, who is devoid of fear, free from craving, and without (moral) blemish, (that person)

has wrenched out the darts of (mundane) existence. This is the last body (he will wear).

352 One who is free from craving, not grasping, skilled in the explanation of (doctrinal) terms, and who would understand the words (of the Buddha's Teaching) in context, that person is truly called 'a wearer of his last body', 'very wise', (and) 'a great man'.

353 I am all-conquering, all-knowing, (and) unattached to all things. All-abandoning, freed through the destruction of craving, (and) having by myself thoroughly comprehended (the destruction of craving), whom should I point out (as my teacher)?[23]

354 The gift of the Dhamma surpasses all gifts. The taste of the Dhamma surpasses all tastes. Delight in the Dhamma surpasses all delights. The destruction of craving overcomes all suffering.

355 Possessions strike (down) the man of evil understanding, but not those who are seekers of the Beyond. Because of his craving for possessions, the man of evil understanding strikes himself (down) as if he were striking (down) others.

356 Weeds are the blemish of (cultivated) fields, lust of this (human) race. Hence what is given to those free from lust is productive of much fruit (in the shape of merit).

357 Weeds are the blemish of (cultivated) fields, hatred of this (human) race. Hence what is given to those free from hate is productive of much fruit (in the shape of merit).

358 Weeds are the blemish of (cultivated) fields, delusion of this (human) race. Hence what is given to those free from delusion is productive of much fruit (in the shape of merit).

359 Weeds are the blemish of (cultivated) fields, covetousness of this (human) race. Hence what is given to those free from covetousness is productive of much fruit (in the shape of merit).

## 25: THE ALMSMAN

360 Restraint with the eye is good; good is restraint by the ear; restraint by the nose is good; good is restraint with the tongue.

361 Bodily restraint is good; good is restraint in speech; restraint of the mind is good; good in all respects is restraint. The almsman who is in all respects restrained is freed from all suffering.

362 He is truly called an almsman whose hands are controlled, whose feet are controlled, whose speech is controlled, who is controlled in thought (or: supremely controlled), whose delight is within, (and) who is collected, solitary, content.

363 The utterance is sweet of that almsman who controls his mouth, who speaks in moderation, who is not puffed up (with his knowledge), (and) who explains the meaning (of the Buddha's words) and their practical application.

364 An almsman who abides in the Teaching, who delights in the Teaching, who reflects on the Teaching, and who bears the Teaching in mind, will not fall away from the True Teaching (*saddhamma*).

365 Let one not despise what he has gained (by way of alms); let him not live envying the gains of others. The almsman who envies the gains of others does not attain to (meditative) concentration.

366 Even if an almsman's gains (by way of alms) be very little, let him not despise what he has gained. The gods praise him who is of pure livelihood (and) unwearied.

367 He is indeed called an almsman for whom nowhere in the mind and body is there anything of which to say 'This is mine,' and who does not grieve for what does not (really) exist.

368 The almsman who dwells in loving-kindness, (and) who is happy in the mandate of the Buddha, would attain to the state that is peace (i.e., Nirvāṇa), to the quieting of conditioned existence (and) to bliss.

369 Almsman, empty this boat! Emptied, it will go more (quickly and) lightly for you. Having cut out lust and hatred, you will then go to Nirvāṇa.

370 Cut away five, abandon five, (and) in addition cultivate five. The almsman who has transcended the five attachments is called 'One who has crossed the flood'.[24]

371 Be absorbed (in higher meditative states), almsman! Don't be heedless. Don't allow your mind to whirl about among sensual pleasures. Don't through heedlessness swallow a (red hot) iron ball, (and then) when it scorches you cry out 'What torment!'

372 There is no absorption in higher meditative states (*jhāna*) for one who is without wisdom (*paññā*); there is no wisdom for one who is unabsorbed in higher meditative states. He in whom are found (both) absorption in higher mental states and wisdom is truly in the (very) presence of Nirvāṇa.

373 For the almsman who enters an empty cottage, who is of peaceful mind, and who perfectly comprehends the Dharma, there is a joy surpassing that of men.

374 Howsoever one grasps (the fact of) the rise and fall of the aggregates (of conditioned existence), he attains a joy and delight that, to the discerning person, is (as) nectar.

375 Here (in the world) the first thing for the wise almsman is this: control of the senses, contentment, restraint through observance of the (almsman's) code of conduct, and association with friends who are virtuous, of pure life, (and) energetic.

376 Let one be hospitable (and) well-mannered. Being on this account full of happiness one will make an end of suffering.

377 Just as the jasmine (creeper) sheds its withered flowers so, almsmen, should you totally get rid of lust and hatred.

378 He who is tranquil in body, tranquil in speech, (and) possessed of (mental) tranquillity, who is well integrated, (and) who has left behind worldly things – such an almsman is said to be at peace.

379 Yourself reprove yourself. Yourself examine yourself. Thus self-guarded (and) mindful the almsman will live happily.

380 One is one's own protector; what other protector should there be? Therefore control this self of yours as a trader (manages) a noble steed.

381 The almsman who is full of joy (and) happy in the instruction of the Buddha will attain to the State of Peace, to the blissful allaying of (mundane) conditions.

382 A youthful almsman, even, who commits himself to the Buddha's instruction, lights up the world like the moon (when) freed from cloud.

## 26: THE BRĀHMAṆA

383 Exert yourself and cut off the stream;[25] do away with sense-desires, brāhmaṇa. Having known the destruction of mundane conditionings, be a Knower of the Unmade, brāhmaṇa.

384 When the brāhmaṇa has 'crossed over' in respect of the two states (i.e., calm and insight), then all the fetters of that knowing one come to an end.

385 I call him a brāhmaṇa for whom there exists neither the Further Shore nor the hither shore, nor both, (and) who is without distress and free from (all) bonds.

386 I call him a brāhmaṇa who is absorbed (in higher meditative states), who is unstained (by passion), whose task is done, who is free from the defilements (or: unbiased), (and) who has reached the Ultimate Goal.

387 The sun shines bright by day; the moon shines at night; the armed warrior shines bright; the brāhmaṇa who is absorbed (in higher meditative states) shines bright. But the Buddha shines bright by day and by night, (shining) with splendour.

388 'Brāhmaṇa' means one who 'bars out' evil; he is said to be an asketic (*samaṇa*) who lives in quiet (*sama*); he is said to be a 'goer forth' (from the household life) who has 'sent forth into banishment' his own impurities.[26]

389 One should not strike a brāhmaṇa, nor should the brāhmaṇa (who is struck) give vent (to anger). Shame on (or: woe to) him who strikes a brāhmaṇa! More shame on (or: woe to) him who gives vent (to anger).

390 For a brāhmaṇa there is nothing better than a mind restrained from (its) likings. To the extent that the harming mind turns back (from harming), to that extent suffering is stopped.

391 I call him a brāhmaṇa by whom no evil is done by the body, by speech, (or) by the mind, and who with regard to these three is restrained.

392 As a brahmin worships the sacrificial fire, so let one pay homage to the person from whom one comes to know the Truth (*dhamma*) taught by the Perfectly Enlightened One.

393 One is not a brāhmaṇa on account of matted hair, or (one's) clan, or birth. He in whom there exists both truth and principle (*dhamma*), *he* is pure, *he* is a brāhmaṇa.

394 What use (your) matted hair, (you) man of evil understanding; what use your deerskin garment? Within, you are a dense jungle (of passions), (yet) you touch up the outside.

395 The man who wears rags from a dust heap, who is lean, whose veins stand out all over the body, (and) who, alone and in the forest, is absorbed (in higher meditative states), *him* I call a brāhmaṇa.

396 I do not call him a brāhmaṇa who is (merely) womb-born or sprung from a (brahmin) mother. If he is a man of possessions (*sakiñcana*) he is (simply) called 'one who addresses others familiarly'. I call him a brāhmaṇa who is free from attachment and without possessions (*akiñcana*).

397 I call him a brāhmaṇa who, having severed all bonds, does not tremble, and who has unburdened himself of all attachments.

398 I call him a brāhmaṇa who has severed the bond (of hatred), the thong (of craving), and the cord (of wrong views) together with its concomitants, who has lifted the crossbar (of ignorance), (and) who is Enlightened.

399 I call him a brāhmaṇa who, being good, patiently endures abuse, flogging, and imprisonment, and whose strong army is the strength of patience.

400 I call him a brāhmaṇa who is without anger, who (scrupulously) observes (religious) vows, who is ethical, free from lust, (and) controlled, (and) who wears his last body.

401 I call him a brāhmaṇa who, like (a drop of) water on a lotus leaf, or a mustard seed on the point of an awl, does not cling to (lit., is not smeared with) sensuous pleasures.

402 I call him a brāhmaṇa who in this very life has personally known the destruction of suffering, who has laid down the burden (of conditioned existence), (and) who is detached (from the world).

403 I call him a brāhmaṇa whose knowledge is deep, who is a man of understanding, who knows what is and what is not the Way, (and) who has reached the Supreme Goal.

404 I call him a brāhmaṇa who socializes with neither householders nor homeless ones (*anāgārikas*), who lives free from attachment (lit., lives houseless), (and) who desires little or nothing.

405 I call him a brāhmaṇa who has abandoned violence towards living beings, be they moving about or stationary (or: whether trembling and afraid or firm-minded), and who neither slays nor causes (others) to slay.

406 I call him a brāhmaṇa who is conciliatory among the antagonistic, peaceful among those who have recourse to violence (*daṇḍa*), (and) who is unattached among the attached.

407 I call him a brāhmaṇa from whom lust, hatred, pride, and hypocrisy have fallen away like a mustard seed from the point of an awl.

408 I call him a brāhmaṇa who would utter gentle, instructive, true speech by which one would give offence to no one.

409 I call him a brāhmaṇa who takes, in this world, nothing that is not given (to him), be it long or short, small or great, pleasant or unpleasant.

410 I call him a brāhmaṇa in whom are found no longings either for this world or the other (world), who is (utterly) free from longings (and) who is released from all defilements.

411 I call him a brāhmaṇa who, through perfect knowledge, is free from doubts, (and) who has achieved the plunge into the Deathless (*amata*).

412 I call him a brāhmaṇa who here (in this world) has transcended good and bad, together with attachment, and who is free from sorrow, without passion, (and) pure.

413 I call him a brāhmaṇa who is spotless and pure as the moon, clear(-minded) and undisturbed (by the defilements), and in whom delight (in conditioned existence) has been extinguished.

414 I call him a brāhmaṇa who has passed over this dangerous (or: muddy) track (of the passions), this fortress of delusion that

is repeated existence, who has crossed (the flood) and reached the Further Shore, who is absorbed (in higher meditative states), who is passionless and free from doubts, (and) who, being without (further) clinging, is at peace (in Nirvāṇa).

415 I call him a brāhmaṇa who, having here (in the world) given up the pleasures of sense, goes forth as a homeless one, and who has destroyed (craving for) sensuous existence.

416 I call him a brāhmaṇa who, having here (in the world) given up craving, goes forth as a homeless one, and who has destroyed craving for (conditioned) existence.

417 I call him a brāhmaṇa who, having discarded human bonds and transcended celestial bonds, is delivered from all bonds (whatsoever).[27]

418 I call him a brāhmaṇa who has given up attachment and aversion, become tranquil (lit., cool), (and) free from the substrates (of conditioned existence), (and who thus is) a hero victorious over the whole world.

419 I call him a brāhmaṇa who knows, in every way, the passing away and arising of living beings, who is unattached, living happily, and Enlightened.

420 I call him a brāhmaṇa whose track gods, celestial musicians,[28] and human beings do not know, that (supremely) worthy one who has destroyed the defilements.

421 I call him a brāhmaṇa for whom there is nothing before, or after, or in between, who is without (material or mental) possessions, (and) who is unattached.

422 I call him a brāhmaṇa who is foremost (among men), excellent, heroic, a great sage, the victorious one, the one who is passionless, washed (clean of the defilements), (and) Enlightened.

423 I call him a brāhmaṇa who knows his previous lives (lit., abodes), who sees heaven and the state of woe, who has reached the extinction of births, who is a silent sage, a master of the higher knowledge (*abhiññā*), (and) who has accomplished all that is to be accomplished.

# GLOSSARY

*Aggregate*: (Pāli *khandha*) All phenomena are 'compounded' or 'put together', and are therefore aggregates of other phenomena. Traditionally, these are divided into five types: form (*rūpa*), feeling (*vedanā*), perception (*saññā*), volition (*saṅkhāra*), and consciousness (*viññāna*).

*Brahmā*: The most powerful and longest lived of all the 'gods', q.v.

*Brāhmaṇa*: See note 17.

*Conditioned Existence*: (*paṭicca-samuppāda*) Everything arises in dependence upon conditions, thus the mundane world is spoken of as conditioned existence.

*Deathless*: (*amata*) a synonym for Nirvāṇa (q.v.).

*Defilements*: (*āsavas*) The biases toward sensuous experience (*kāma*), conditioned existence (*bhava*), speculative opinions (*diṭṭhi*), and ignorance (*avijjā*).

*Dhamma*: The Truth; the teaching of the Buddha.

*Eightfold Way*: One way of describing the path leading to Enlightenment, consisting of Perfect Vision, Perfect Emotion, Perfect Speech, Perfect Action, Perfect Livelihood, Perfect Effort, Perfect Awareness, and Perfect *Samādhi*.

*Empty*: (*suñña*) Absolute reality is not 'conditioned' or 'compounded' of anything, and is therefore described as Empty.

*Fetters*: See Note 24.

*Four (Ariyan) Truths*: These are the fundamental truths of Buddhism: the existence of unsatisfactoriness (*dukkha*), craving (*taṇhā*) as its cause, its cessation (*nibbāna*), and the way leading to its cessation (the Eightfold Way, q.v.)

*Further Shore*: (*pāra*) a synonym for Nirvāṇa (q.v.).

*Gods*: (*devas*) Beings that dwell on the higher, more blissful, planes of existence. See also Note 13.

*Immovable*: (*accuta*) a synonym for Nirvāṇa (q.v.).

*Nirvāṇa*: (Pāli *nibbāna*) lit., 'blowing out'; the extinguishing of all the fires of craving. Nirvāṇa or Enlightenment is the goal of all Buddhists.

*Noble Ones*: (*ariyas*) Those who have gained Enlightenment or are shortly to do so, consisting of Stream Entrants (q.v.) (*sotāpannas*), Once-Returners (*sakadāgāmins*), Non-Returners (*anāgāmins*), and Enlightened beings (*arahants*).

*Perfectly Enlightened One*: (*sammāsambuddha*) The Buddha.

*Stream Entry*: (*sotāpatti*) The point at which one has established transcendental insight such that one can no longer fall away from the path. Traditionally, Enlightenment will then be attained within a maximum of seven more lifetimes.

*Supernormal powers*: (*iddhi*) the powers and influence that emanate from a highly concentrated state of mental absorption.

*Unmade*: (*akaṭa*) That which is not compounded or conditioned, i.e., Nirvāṇa.

# FURTHER READING

John Brough (ed.), *The Gāndhārī Dharmapada*, Oxford University Press, London 1962 (includes introduction and commentary).

John Ross Carter and Mahinda Pālihawadāna (trans.), *Buddhism: The Dhammapada* (Sacred Writings vol. 6), Book-of-the-Month Club, New York 1992 (includes Pāli text).

Bhikkhu Kuala Lumpur Dhammajoti (trans.), *The Chinese Version of the Dharmapada*, University of Kelaniya, Sri Lanka 1995 (includes introduction and annotations).

K. R. Norman, *Pāli Literature*, Otto Harrassowitz, Wiesbaden 1983.

K. R. Norman, *The Word of the Doctrine (Dhammapada)*, Pali Text Society, Oxford 1997.

Sangharakshita, *The Eternal Legacy*, Windhorse Publications, Birmingham 2006 (*Complete Works*, vol. 14).

Gareth Sparham, *The Tibetan Dharmapada*, Wisdom Publications, London 1983 (a translation of the Tibetan version of the *Udānavarga*).

## AUSPICIOUS SIGNS (*MAṄGALA SUTTA*)

For welfare wishing, many gods and men
Have pondered on 'the most auspicious sign':
Tell us the most auspicious sign of all.

Not to serve fools but men of wisdom deep,
And to give worship to the worshipful –
This is the most auspicious sign of all.

Life in a suitable locality,
With deeds of merit done in former times,
And aspiration to the Perfect State –
This is the most auspicious sign of all.

Much knowledge, and much skill in arts and crafts,
A well-learnt discipline, and pleasant speech –
This is the most auspicious sign of all.

The maintenance of parents past their youth,
The loving nurture of one's child and wife,
And following a peaceful livelihood –
This is the most auspicious sign of all.

To give in charity, live righteously,
To help one's kindred in the time of need,
And to do spotless deeds that bring no blame –
This is the most auspicious sign of all.

To cease and utterly abstain from sin,
Shunning all wit-destroying drinks and drugs,
And to be vigilant in doing good –
This is the most auspicious sign of all.

Reverent demeanour, humbleheartedness,
Contentment sweet and lowly gratitude,
And hearkening to the Law at proper times –
This is the most auspicious sign of all.

Patience in provocation, pleasant speech,
The sight of those who lead the holy life,
And talk about the Truth in season meet –
This is the most auspicious sign of all.

Asceticism and the life sublime,
The vision splendid of the Noble Truths,
The seeing of Nibbāna face to face –
This is the most auspicious sign of all.

He whose firm mind, untroubled by the touch
Of all terrestrial happenings whatso'er,
Is void of sorrow, stainless, and secure –
This is the most auspicious sign of all.

Those who accomplish such good things as these
In every place unconquered do abide,
Moving in perfect safety where they will –
Theirs are the most auspicious signs of all.[29]

## JEWELS (*RATANA SUTTA*)

Whatever beings are assembled here,
Creatures of earth or spirits of the sky,
May they be happy-minded, every one,
And pay good heed to what is said to them.

Hence, all ye spirits, hear attentively.
Look lovingly upon the race of men,
And, since they bring thee offerings day and night,
Keep watch and ward about them heedfully.

The riches of this world and of the next,
And all the precious things the heav'ns may hold,
None can compare with the Tathāgata.
Yea, in the Buddha shines this glorious gem:
By virtue of this truth, may bliss abound!

The waning out of lust, that wondrous state
Of deathlessness the Śākyan Sage attained
Through calm and concentration of the mind –
Nothing at all with that state can compare.
Yea, in the Teaching shines this glorious gem:
By virtue of this truth, may bliss abound!

That flawless meditation praised by Him
Who is the Wisest of the wise, which brings
Instant reward to him who practises –
Naught with that meditation can compare.
Yea, in the Teaching shines this glorious gem:
By virtue of this truth, may bliss abound!

Those persons eight whom all the sages praise
Make up four pairs. Worthy of offerings
Are they, the followers of the Happy One,
And offerings made them bear abundant fruit.
Yea, in the Order shines this glorious gem:
By virtue of this truth, may bliss abound!

Whoso, desireless, have applied themselves
Firm-minded to the lore of Gautama,
They have won That which should indeed be won,
And having plunged into the Deathless State
Freely enjoy the Peace they have attained.
Yea, in the Order shines this glorious gem:
By virtue of this truth, may bliss abound!

Just as the firm post at the city gate
Doth stir not though the four winds on it blow,
So do I call him a good man and true
Who sees the Fourfold Āryan Truth of things.
Yea, in the Order shines this glorious gem:
By virtue of this truth, may bliss abound!

Who clearly comprehends these Noble Truths
Well taught by Him of wisdom fathomless,
However heedless be they afterwards,
Into an eighth birth are not doomed to fall.
Yea, in the Order shines this glorious gem:
By virtue of this truth, may bliss abound!

As soon as he with insight is endowed
Three things become discarded utterly:
The lie of a perduring self, and doubt,
And clinging to vain rites and empty vows.
Escaped is he from the four evil states,
And of the six great sins incapable.
Yea, in the Order shines this glorious gem:
By virtue of this truth, may bliss abound!

Whatever evil deed in act or word,
Or even in his private thought he does,
Incapable is he of hiding it.
For such a thing (so hath it been declared)
He who has glimpsed the highest cannot do.
Yea, in the Order shines this glorious gem:
By virtue of this truth, may bliss abound!

Just as a forest grove puts forth its flowers
When the first month of summer heat doth come,
So, for the highest good of all, He preached
The Truth Sublime which to Nirvāṇa leads.
Yea, in the Buddha shines this glorious gem:
By virtue of this truth, may bliss abound!

The Highest One, the Knower of the Highest,
The Giver and the Bringer of the Highest,
'Tis He Who taught the highest Truth of all.
Yea, in the Buddha shines this glorious gem:
By virtue of this truth, may bliss abound!

The old is withered out, the new becomes not;
Their minds desireth now no future birth.
Whoso have utterly destroyed the seeds
Of all existence, whose desires are quenched,
Extinguished are those wise ones as this lamp.
Yea, in the Order shines this glorious gem:
By virtue of this truth, may bliss abound!

Whatever beings are assembled here,
Creatures of earth or spirits of the sky,
To th' gods-and-men-adored Tathāgata,
To th' Buddha, let us bow: may bliss abound!

Whatever beings are assembled here,
Creatures of earth or spirits of the sky,
To th' gods-and-men-adored Tathāgata,
To th' Teaching, let us bow: may bliss abound!

Whatever beings are assembled here,
Creatures of earth or spirits of the sky,
To th' gods-and-men-adored Tathāgata,
To th' Order, let us bow: may bliss abound![30]

# OUTSIDE THE WALLS (*TIROKUḌḌA SUTTA*)

Outside the walls, at crossroads, do they stand,
And, to their homes returning, outside doors;
But when a meal of food and drink is spread,
A sumptuous meal, no man remembers them:
Such is the way of things. Wherefore it is
That in compassion for their kin deceased
Men make fit offerings at the proper time
Of food and drink, saying 'Be this a gift
Unto our kinsmen: may it gladden them.'
Then do those earth-bound kinsmen gather round
Where'er that feast of food and drink is spread,
Nor fail to render grateful thanks and say
'Long live our kinsman who hath made this gift!'
For there in ghostland is no herding seen,
Nor any ploughing of the fruitful fields;
There is no trading, as on earth there is,
Nor is there any trafficking with gold.
We, the departed spirits, there exist
On whatsoever things are offered here.
Even as water from the high ground flows
Down to the marshes lying at its foot,
So are the offerings that on earth are made
Of service to the spirits of the dead;

And as filled rivers flow to fill the sea,
So are the offerings that on earth are made
Of service to the spirits of the dead.
'Presents he made, did this and that for me;
They were my kinsmen, comrades, bosom-friends.'
Thus recollecting actions past, a man
Should give unto the ghosts in charity.
For of a truth, wailing and sorrowing
And many lamentations naught avail:
The ghosts are helped not when their kinsmen weep.
Besides, this alms unto the Order given
Will be of service for full many a day.
So is this duty to one's kinsmen told.
Unto the ghosts it is a gift of grace;
Unto the brethren of the Order, strength;
Unto yourselves, an ample merit won.[31]

## THE BURIED TREASURE
## (*NIDHIKAṆḌA SUTTA*)

In a deep hole beside some pond or stream
A man hides treasure, thinking in his heart,
'In time of need it will avail me much,
Or if perchance the king condemneth me,
If robber robs me, or to pay my debts,
Or else in time of famine, or when some
Mischance befalls me unexpectedly.'
Such in this world the weighty reasons are
For which a treasure is deposited.
But all this treasure cunningly concealed
In a deep hole beside some pond or stream,
It profiteth its owner not at all.
For either from its place it vanishes,
Or else his wits astray go wandering
And he remembers not its hiding-place,
Or else 'tis stolen by the serpent-gods,
Or goblins filch it from the secret place,
Or heirs unloved bear it by stealth away.
For when exhausted all one's merit is
That heap of treasure wholly perisheth.
But by much giving and by righteousness,
By self-control and taming of the self,
There is a precious treasure well concealed

For man or woman who will dig it up.
This is a treasure incommunicable,
Which thieves and robbers cannot steal away.
Let then the man of wisdom do good deeds:
This is the treasure that pursues a man.
This is that treasure which to gods and men
Bringeth all manner of delights. By this
The things they long for may in truth be won.
A fair complexion, a mellifluous voice,
Comely appearance, figure full of grace,
Power over men, and lengthy retinue,
This treasure can obtain them, every one.
Dominion and o'erlordship of the earth,
The bliss of wide-extended sovereignty
Dear to men's heart, yea, empery in heaven
Over the shining conclaves of the gods,
This treasure can obtain them, every one.
Prosperity on earth and joy in heaven,
The winning of the high Desireless State,
This treasure can obtain them, every one.
Whoso is blessed with goodly fellowship,
By efforts right wins knowledge and release
And self-control: all these are won thereby.
The Highest Wisdom, freedom of the mind,
The topmost summit of discipleship,
Illumination of the self by self,
Yea, ev'n the matchless state of Buddhahood,
This treasure can obtain them, every one.
Such power miraculous this treasure hath,
The treasure of good deeds: wherefore it is
Good deeds are done by wise and learned men.[32]

# LOVING-KINDNESS
## (*KARAṆĪYA METTĀ SUTTA*)

This must be done by one who kens his good,
Who grasps the meaning of 'The Place of Peace'.
Able and upright, yea, and truly straight,
Soft-spoken and mild-mannered must he be,
And void of all the vain conceit of self.
He should be well content, soon satisfied,
With wants but few, of frugal appetites,
With faculties of sense restrained and stilled,
Discreet in all his ways, not insolent,
Nor greedy after gifts; nor should he do
Any ignoble act which other men,
Wiser, beholding might rebuke him for.

Now, may all living things, or weak or strong,
Omitting none, tall, middle-sized, or short,
Subtle or gross of form, seen or unseen,
Those dwelling near or dwelling far away,
Born or unborn – may every living thing
Abound in bliss. Let none deceive or think
Scorn of another, in whatever way.
But as a mother watches o'er her child,
Her only child, so long as she doth breathe,
So let him practise unto all that live

An all-embracing mind. And let a man
Practise unbounded love for all the world,
Above, below, across, in every way,
Love unobstructed, void of enmity.
Standing or moving, sitting, lying down,
In whatsoever way that man may be,
Provided he be slothless, let him found
Firmly this mindfulness of boundless love.
For this is what men call 'the State Sublime'.
So shall a man, by leaving far behind
All wrongful views, by walking righteously,
Attain to gnostic vision and crush out
All lust for sensual pleasures. Such in truth
Shall come to birth no more in any womb.[33]

## SALUTATION TO THE THREE JEWELS (*TIRATANA VANDANĀ*)

Such indeed is He, the Richly Endowed: the Free, the Fully and Perfectly Awake, Equipped with Knowledge and Practice, the Happily Attained, Knower of the Worlds, Guide Unsurpassed of Men to be Tamed, the Teacher of Gods and Men, the Awakened One Richly Endowed.

All my life I go for Refuge to the Awakened One.

To all the Awakened of the past,
To all the Awakened yet to be,
To all the Awakened that now are,
My worship flows unceasingly.
No other refuge than the Wake,
Refuge supreme, is there for me.
Oh by the virtue of this truth,
May grace abound, and victory!

Well communicated is the Teaching of the Richly Endowed One, Immediately Apparent, Perennial, of the Nature of a Personal Invitation, Progressive, to be understood individually, by the wise.

All my life I go for Refuge to the Truth.

To all the Truth-Teachings of the past,
To all the Truth-Teachings yet to be,
To all the Truth-Teachings that now are,
My worship flows unceasingly.
No other refuge than the Truth,
Refuge supreme, is there for me.
Oh by the virtue of this truth,
May grace abound, and victory!

Happily proceeding is the fellowship of the Hearers of the Richly Endowed One, uprightly proceeding… methodically proceeding… correctly proceeding… namely, these four pairs of Individuals, these eight Persons.

This fellowship of Hearers of the Richly Endowed One is worthy of worship, worthy of hospitality, worthy of offerings, worthy of salutation with folded hands, an incomparable source of goodness to the world.

All my life I go for Refuge to the Fellowship.

To all the Fellowships that were,
To all the Fellowships to be,
To all the Fellowships that are,
My worship flows unceasingly.
No refuge but the Fellowship,
Refuge supreme, is there for me.
Oh by the virtue of this truth,
May grace abound, and victory!

# PART II
# COMMENTARIES

# LIVING WITH AWARENESS

# BEGINNING

> Thus have I heard. On one occasion the Blessed One was living in the Kuru country at a town of the Kurus named Kammāsadhamma. There he addressed the bhikkhus thus: 'Bhikkhus.' 'Venerable sir,' they replied. The Blessed One said this:
>
> 'Bhikkhus, this is the direct path for the purification of beings, for the surmounting of sorrow and lamentation, for the disappearance of pain and grief, for the attainment of the true way, for the realization of Nibbāna – namely, the four foundations of mindfulness.'

The term 'mindfulness' crops up in some of the most important formulations of the Buddha's teaching. It is one of the seven factors of Enlightenment, it is one of the five spiritual faculties, and it is also one of the limbs of the Noble Eightfold Path. Here, in the teaching called the *Satipaṭṭhāna Sutta*, the Buddha appears to suggest that mindfulness is nothing less than the whole of the path, the 'direct way' for the overcoming of sorrow and lamentation. This is perhaps one reason why the *Satipaṭṭhāna Sutta* is held in such high esteem in the Theravādin Buddhist tradition which is still practised in many parts of the world today – many Theravādins are able to recite the entire *Sutta* from memory. But in the Mahāyāna tradition also, and throughout the Buddhist world, mindfulness continues to be recognized as fundamental to spiritual growth – and it is the *Satipaṭṭhāna Sutta*, upon which this commentary is based, that gives us the clearest and most detailed account of why this should be so.

The teaching was given, so we are told in its opening words, among the Kuru people, who lived at the time of the Buddha (around 500 BCE) somewhere in the area of what is now Delhi in north-western India. We are given no other clues as to the circumstances in which the discourse was given, but we can guess – going on accounts of similar occasions in the Pāli texts – that the Buddha was probably staying among a small group of *bhikkhus* (itinerant monks) who were dwelling in little huts dotted about somebody's park or garden, or simply living under the trees. In some texts we find the Buddha instructing his companion Ānanda to gather all the *bhikkhus* together so that he can address them – presumably this would have happened when there were a number of them living over a large area. But if there were only a few of them around, the Buddha would probably have called them together himself, and this seems to have been what happened on this occasion, perhaps once the *bhikkhus* had returned from their almsround in the nearby town of Kammāsadhamma.

The Buddha often taught in response to a question put by Ānanda or one of the other disciples, or by someone else he happened to meet. Sometimes a layperson or a follower of another teacher would seek him out to ask him a question or try to catch him out on a point of logic. In some cases the question had to be asked not once but three times. (Apparently the Buddha would always answer a question on the third time of asking, whatever the consequences for the questioner.) But here he seems to call the monks together himself with the intention of giving them what we can infer he considers to be a very important teaching – 'the direct way', as he tells them, 'for the purification of beings'.

This sense of a unified way is emphasized throughout the Buddha's teaching. It is what the path is in principle, as distinct from all the different presentations of it. The Dharma finds expression in many formulations: there is the Noble Eightfold Path, which is the fourth of the four noble truths, and the threefold path of morality, meditation, and wisdom – while in the Mahāyāna tradition the path of the bodhisattva is central, with its vow to liberate all beings and its training in the six or ten perfections. One cannot say that any one presentation of the doctrine, or any one method, is the best under all circumstances and for all people, but for all the diversity of these presentations of the Buddhist path, each in its own way embodies the same spiritual principles.

Of course, there is a view of spiritual development that goes further than this to regard all the world's religious teachings as equally valid paths to the goal, holding that, just as all roads lead to Rome, the truth to which all spiritual paths lead is the same truth, expressed in different ways. Perhaps the image of the path is misleading: although many of the world's religious teachings use it, they are not necessarily using it to describe the same thing. One obvious difference is that unlike Christianity, Islam, and even Hindu Vedic philosophy, Buddhism teaches that the highest being in the universe is not a god but an Enlightened human being, and that the state of Enlightenment – which is the goal of Buddhist practice – is attainable through one's own efforts to transform one's consciousness. This transformation is made possible by the principle which, as the Buddha states throughout the Pāli canon, is the essence of the path: the principle of conditionality, the truth that whatever exists owes its arising to causes and conditions; that is, things change – we change – and we have the capacity to direct that change towards spiritual growth and development. This is the guiding principle of the Buddhist path: it is the means by which our consciousness is transformed, transcended, Enlightened.

The Buddhist outlook is profoundly optimistic. The greed, aversion, and delusion of the unenlightened mind are universal problems, but human consciousness, wherever it arises, also shares the same spiritual potential. From a Buddhist perspective, any religious teaching can be said to lead towards Enlightenment to the extent that it enables and encourages the individual to develop spiritual qualities. And if it leaves some qualities out, or encourages the development of qualities that are inimical to spiritual growth (examples of this readily come to mind, of course), it cannot be regarded as an expression of the path at all, and this must be acknowledged if real growth is to be possible.

From this, we can work out a basic definition of mindfulness. The 'direct way for the purification of beings' is the sum total of the ethical and spiritual qualities that a human being must develop in order to reach what Buddhists call Enlightenment. But mindfulness is more than just a mixture of all these aspects of the path. It is a distinct spiritual faculty – the defining quality of all Buddhist practice – and according to the words attributed to the Buddha in the *Satipaṭṭhāna Sutta*, one learns to practise it by attending to four basic aspects or 'foundations' of mindfulness:

> 'What are the four? Here, bhikkhus, a bhikkhu abides contemplating the body as a body, ardent, fully aware, and mindful, having put aside covetousness and grief for the world. He abides contemplating feelings as feelings, ardent, fully aware, and mindful, having put away covetousness and grief for the world. He abides contemplating mind as mind, ardent, fully aware, and mindful, having put away covetousness and grief for the world. He abides contemplating mind-objects as mind-objects, ardent, fully aware, and mindful, having put away covetousness and grief for the world.'

The term *satipaṭṭhāna* combines 'mindfulness' (*sati*) with 'building up' or 'making firm' (*paṭṭhāna*), and as its name suggests, the concern of the *Satipaṭṭhāna Sutta* is the development of a continuity of mindful positivity across the whole field of human consciousness.[34] To give us a more specific idea of what this means, the *Sutta* classifies this mindfulness according to what are called the four foundations of mindfulness. In Pāli, the ancient Indian language in which this teaching was first written down, these are: mindfulness of *kāya* or body – usually taken to mean one's own physical body; mindfulness of *vedanā*, or feelings; mindfulness of *citta*, which in this context means thoughts; and mindfulness of *dharmas* (Pāli *dhammas*), *dharmas* being in this context the objects of the mind's attention. By establishing these four foundations, one cultivates the conditions for the arising of ever more positive and refined states of consciousness. The same word for this 'establishing' appears in the 'establishment' aspect of the 'relative *bodhicitta*', the *prasthānacitta*, of the Mahāyāna schools. Alongside the bodhisattva vow, this involves the cultivation of the six or ten perfections in a practice which, like that of the four foundations of mindfulness, progressively harmonizes its different aspects into an increasingly dedicated commitment to the path.

While the word 'foundation' gives a good sense of the mental stability developed through practising this teaching, we are not to imagine anything static. These foundations are not to be laid down like blocks of granite; like the motifs of a symphony, or the basic steps of a ballet, they are the essence of a continuous dynamic development.

Mindfulness harmonizes and unifies every aspect of Buddhist practice into a concentrated, responsive awareness of body, feelings, mind, and mental objects. Perhaps the most apt analogy – again from the arts – is to say that being truly mindful is like playing a musical instrument, with oneself as both instrument and player. A violinist doesn't give a bit of attention to the score, then a bit of attention to her fingers on the strings, then a bit of attention to the conductor. To play well, she has to bring about a fusion between herself and what she is doing, a fusion almost between her awareness and its object. Everything must come together in a single, rich experience of energy and expressive skill. She is fully absorbed yet at the same time keenly aware of every movement she makes. This heightened state of awareness is what we need to aim for, body and mind fully engaged in a state of clarity and positivity that saturates and colours the whole of our experience. And it is surely a state much to be desired – not a duty, but a great pleasure.

This is the aim – everything coming together in a smooth flow. But just as the violinist needs to work on the details of her technique to achieve the full effect, so we need to pay careful attention to the details of our mindfulness practice – that is, to each of the four foundations and to further details within each of the four. The Buddha therefore proceeds to elaborate on each foundation in turn, to make the nature of the practice clear.

This detailed and specific approach helps to counteract the tendency to over-generalize the nature of spiritual development. It is sometimes said that the aim of Buddhist practice is to attain insight into the true nature of things, and that is fair enough, in a way. But the nature of that insight is not a general, abstract understanding, and it will not come about by chance. A great deal of preparation is needed – first to clarify one's consciousness and then to develop a state of receptivity into which the essential truths of the Buddha's teaching can be introduced. And according to tradition, much of this preparation is best done through the vigorous and creative practice of meditation. It has become a commonplace of contemporary Buddhist teaching that we can learn to be mindful while eating, doing the washing up, and so on – and we certainly can, indeed must. We can be mindful – that is, we can be preparing ourselves for the attainment of insight – in all the circumstances of our lives, and the *Satipaṭṭhāna Sutta* takes full account of this, as we shall see. At the same time, as so often in the Pāli canon, the emphasis is placed on the practice of meditation as the basis of the whole process.

What kind of meditation? In the Buddhist tradition meditation practices are generally classified as being of two kinds: *śamatha* (Pāli *samatha*), 'calming', and *vipaśyanā* (Pāli *vipassanā*), 'insight'. Through *śamatha* meditation one develops mindfulness of the body and an ardent, energetic one-pointedness of mind, building up an intensity and subtlety of concentration on the basis of which a deeper, more far-reaching understanding can be developed. At this point you broaden the scope of your concentration by introducing some method of insight meditation, designed to help you to experience the truths of the Buddha's teachings not just as religious or philosophical ideas but as tangible realities. As we shall see, the distinction between these two kinds of meditation is not as clear-cut as it is sometimes thought to be – the 'mindfulness of breathing', for example, is far more than a simple concentration technique – and the *Satipaṭṭhāna Sutta* encompasses both types of practice. All this will be the stuff of this commentary. But before we home in on the details – we will be working through the text a section at a time – in the next two chapters we will consider two aspects of mindfulness that are pertinent to all aspects of its practice: memory and mindfulness of purpose.

## 1
# REMEMBERING

The Pāli term *sati* (Sanskrit *smṛti*) is usually translated into English as 'mindfulness', which in western Buddhist circles has come to be associated with a keen attention to one's present experience. This is not wrong – awareness of the present moment is certainly crucial to self-transformation – but mindfulness is not just a spotlight focused on the present. True, learning to develop the kind of concentration that is so intense that you are conscious of nothing outside your present experience is important to spiritual growth, but to attain transcendental insight you need to appreciate the true nature of such intense experiences. While staying receptive to and being enlivened by the whole range of your present experience, you also try to wake up to the true significance of that experience – which involves awareness both of the past and of the future.

This is brought out by the literal translation of *sati*: 'recollection, memory, recalling to mind'. Just as important as the impressions we receive through our senses, including the mind, are the ways we understand those sensations, the knowledge and previous experience that impinge upon the present, colouring it and allowing meaning to arise. Memory is what enables us to 'recollect' ourselves in the present moment, and without it we cannot experience anything fully, however strongly focused we are on the present situation.

One of Charles Dickens's Christmas books called *The Haunted Man* illustrates this very well. It concerns a learned professor of chemistry whose past contains a particularly painful episode, the memory of which weighs continually on his mind, dragging him down into a deep depression. It is Christmas, and as the frost and snow close in upon his lonely room, the scientist's memories somehow coalesce into a ghostly doppelgänger, a mirror-image of himself. Announcing that it has come to make a bargain with him, this figure offers him the power to banish all his recollections and with them the 'intertwined chain of feelings and associations' that depend upon them. After some deliberation the scientist accepts the offer, which brings with it not only the ability to forget his own past but also the power to remove – at a touch of his hand – all trace of memory from anyone he approaches. Thinking this a real benefit to humanity, he begins to go about the city touching various people he knows. Just as the phantom promised, their memories begin to disappear.

The significance of the phantom's bargain is, of course, its moral effect. For each of the people affected, the consequences of losing their memory turn out to be entirely negative. As the recollection of their past life slips away, they start to disintegrate as moral beings, becoming by degrees more and more mean and selfish. So much of what is good in them is bound up with their past that once memory begins to fade, their selflessness and compassion is supplanted by a calculating indifference. Take the Tetterbys, for example, a poor and hard-working couple who are just managing to scrape by and feed their seven children. They are kept going by their strong sense of interdependence and mutual affection. But once the scientist has brushed past them, their sense of themselves starts to disappear, together with their memories of their shared struggles, and their concern for each other and their children. Gone are their memories of their youthful times together, their courtship and marriage. Now they are only aware of what they can see in the present. Mrs Tetterby can only see a shabby, bald old man with no noble or attractive features to redeem his worn-out appearance, while her husband sees only a fat and unprepossessing woman who is well past her prime. Any sense of what they once meant to each other dissolves into a mean-spirited grasping after petty gains and immediate enjoyments. As the scientist comes to learn, without the capacity to recollect the past there can be no real friendship, no real love. Things lose their meaning and our humanity ebbs away. The moral of the story is that the function of memory is inseparably connected with the ability to act ethically towards one's fellow human beings. Our moral responsiveness to the world around us, which is central to our spiritual development, functions by accessing memory through the application of mindfulness, but also through the emotional connections that memory delivers.

Retrieving memories is not a mechanical process like rewinding a tape recorder: our recollections come back to us in the form of emotions which grow stronger as scenes and events re-emerge in our minds. Once those emotions are rekindled, be they pleasant or painful, they illuminate all the small details of the situation that would otherwise have been lost to us. The greater the importance to you of an event, the more vivid will be your emotional associations with it and – generally – the more fully you will be able to recall it. We remember our first deep friendships, the first time we fell in love, the first books or music that made a deep impression upon us, and we have powerful and meaningful memories of events which others who were present at the time might have entirely forgotten because to them they were insignificant. When elderly people recall events from the distant past very clearly, although they can't remember what happened just last week, this is not necessarily due to the diminishing mental powers of old age. It might simply be that, set against the pattern of one's whole life, certain impressions and experiences stand out more distinctly because of their formative influence.

Sometimes, of course, we do forget events that have strong emotional associations, but this bears out the idea that memory and emotions are inextricably linked: we might forget some experiences because we are repressing our difficult feelings about them. It is entirely natural to wish we could forget the sorrow, the wrong, and the trouble we have known. But if we did, how could we learn from life and move on? All our experience, pleasant and unpleasant, is part of who we are now; we need to find ways of recontacting our past if we are to become fully-formed individuals.

Dickens himself was able to use his great powers of imagination to unlock his memories. He once tried to write his autobiography, but quickly became aware that he had lost access to some periods in his early childhood because the memories associated with them were so painful. His solution was to write *David Copperfield*, an autobiographical novel into which he incorporated many of those early experiences. By writing about himself in the character of David Copperfield, and his father in the character of Mr Micawber, he brought up those hidden memories in a way that enabled him to be objective about them and thus at last to liberate himself from them.

Retrieving repressed memories is of course the stuff of much contemporary therapy, but we should consider the purpose of retrieving them. It is a question of our vision of human existence, and here Buddhism goes further than most psychotherapeutic models, although some do have a spiritual dimension. As we recollect ourselves, as we retrieve and integrate what has been scattered, we do so with a sense of where we are going, a sense of a future goal. This also, then, must be included in our definition of mindfulness – and it is the subject of our next chapter.

## 2

# GOAL-SETTING

Mindfulness may begin with calling past experience to mind, gathering together the parts of ourselves that have been scattered across time, but the whole idea of learning from the past implies an orientation towards the future. What we learn from experience will help us anticipate the likely fruits of present action, and this demands a concern for our future life and a sense that what will happen is – at least to some extent – in our own hands. Mindfulness thus involves awareness not only of where we have come from but also of where we are going. A Pāli term associated with this 'awareness of the future' is *sampajañña*, which is usually translated as mindfulness of purpose or clear comprehension – the implication being that everything we do should be done with a sense of the direction we want to move in and of whether or not our current action will take us in that direction.[35]

How can we be aware of the future? I am not talking about developing a kind of soothsaying faculty. We cannot be sure of the exact course that events will take, but we can take our stand on the most basic truth the Buddha taught: the truth that actions have consequences. We can be quite certain that what we do now will have a decisive effect on what will happen in the future. I am talking, of course, about karma, which must be one of the most misused words to have entered the English language through contact with the East. When something unexpected happens, people often say 'That's my karma', as though karma were some sort of bad luck or fate about which nothing can be done. But karma simply means action. It is what you do. When people talk about karma, what they usually mean is what is known in Pāli as *vipāka*, the results or fruits of action which, sooner or later, one inevitably experiences as the result of having done something – performed a karma – in the past.

Karma is more than simple cause and effect, however. It is to do with the moral weight of an action, and this is how it comes to be so important to the spiritual life. Ethically skilful action (Pāli *kusalakamma*) is the foundation of any higher spiritual experience. It is not a completely straightforward matter to determine whether or not any given action is skilful, because it has nothing to do with any external set of rules by which behaviour might be judged; it is determined by the state of consciousness out of which something is done. Things done when you are in a state of neurotic desire, aversion, or mental confusion will have karmically negative effects, while an action performed out of love, understanding, and clarity of mind will lead to happiness. When you act on a skilful volition, that positivity will grow and bear fruit in the form of skilful, inspiring states of mind.

It is not always possible to discern the detailed workings of karma because by no means everything we experience is the result of what we have done in the past. But sometimes when we find ourselves in a strangely familiar situation, we may look back over a period of years and identify a recurring cycle of events – most obviously, perhaps, in the way we conduct our personal relationships. You may have a tendency to blame other people for the way things turn out or to shrug your shoulders and put it all down to circumstances or coincidence, but once it has dawned on you that the same thing is happening again and again, it might occur to you that this might be connected with some aspect of your own make-up. You might even realize that you yourself are setting up that recurring situation – even though it might be very painful – through your own actions. This is clear comprehension at work: you look deeper within yourself, learn something, make amends, and find a new determination to change the way you behave in that sort of situation.

This sense of moral continuity is absolutely essential to the idea of oneself as an individual. Animals, driven by instinct and a sort of habit-knowledge, cannot reflect upon courses of action and make choices in the way that human beings can. To be human is to inhabit a realm in which ethical responsibility is not only possible but requisite. Thus, mindfulness must be understood to be more than simple concentration: we need to be as clear as we can about the nature of what we are doing and why. A murderer intent upon his victim is certainly concentrating, but that kind of single-mindedness is very different from the ethical attentiveness that characterizes a state of true mindfulness.

Recollecting what you have done, what you have experienced, and how you have felt in the past gives you a sense of the effects of your actions on the overall course of your life. If you reflect on what this tells you about yourself, you get a more objective view of yourself as the product of what you have done and said and even thought in the past. You can then begin to see the direction your life is taking – or could take if you were to act differently. As you discern the overall pattern of development, you may glimpse the possibility of further progress, as your ideals and aims begin to stand out more simply and clearly than before.

It is hard to get this objective perspective – to see ourselves as others see us[36] – and this is why friendship is so valuable to spiritual growth. The ways in which our past actions have made us who we are now may not always be clear to us, but they will be obvious enough to a friend to whom we have disclosed something of our personal history. The transactions of friendship always include exchanging information about one another's past, and as a friend one should be prepared to give a sympathetic ear to the recollections of one's companions, as well as tactfully helping them to make sense of their recollections. The past is always present in us, and if you can appreciate what someone has been through – a hard childhood, an unhappy marriage, an unpleasant or demanding job – you can appreciate them better as they are now.

Best of all is to tell your life story as a continuous narrative, whether you write it down or – better still – tell it to your friends. If you can speak in confidence to people you trust, you are free to be frank and take your communication deeper, and to have such open communication received can be a powerful, even cathartic, experience. Communication has a momentum of its own, and you can find yourself saying things about yourself that you had never even thought about before. It is as if the person listening acts as a sort of catalyst. You are not always aware of what is there until it is disclosed; but as a result, you can sometimes find a clear thread running through your life, revealing all your disparate and complex experience as the manifestation of a single developing individuality.

According to the Buddhist way of seeing things, the process by which skilful and unskilful actions bear fruit in our experience is not confined to our present existence. This lifetime represents the tip of the iceberg with respect to our karma – indeed, one's very embodiment as a human being is said to be the result of one's previous karma. If a certain situation seems to crop up again and again in your life for no obvious reason, it could be that you are experiencing the karmic effects of actions performed in previous lifetimes. In the case of a negative experience, it is generally said that it may be the result of unskilful karma if it repeats itself even after you have made every effort to make sure that it doesn't keep happening. However, although you cannot do anything about it directly, you can certainly apply spiritual remedies. You can counteract the future effects of past unskilfulness by creating a counter-balancing weight of ethically skilful action.

In the first place, you can accept and bear the fruits of your unskilful karma mindfully and patiently. Secondly, you can take positive steps to cultivate the skilful above and beyond just avoiding unskilful reactions. For example, if you had some inkling that you had been habitually cruel in some past existence – or if you knew perfectly well that you had been cruel in this one – you would have a particularly strong motivation to go out of your way to be kind and considerate to others in whatever way you could. The interesting implication of this observation is that as a general rule, the more suffering is visited upon someone, the more compelling reason that person has to be kind to others. It is worth repeating that not every painful occurrence is the result of our own actions: other kinds of conditionality may be at work. But the practice of kindly speech and action is going to be the most reliable recourse in any case. Whatever one has to suffer as a result of past action, one can be quite certain that ethically skilful actions will eventually bear positive fruit. It is always worth making the effort to be skilful.

Thirdly, one can create particularly 'weighty' positive karma by the effective practice of meditation. And fourthly, one can become Enlightened, which is obviously the most conclusive answer to negative karma. You are then assured of no further rebirths in the six realms of conditioned existence, and therefore of no further suffering beyond this life, though in the human life remaining to you there will still be the afflictions attendant upon any human life, of sickness, old age, and death. Among these afflictions there may even be some negative *karma-vipāka*. According to tradition, the Buddha himself had to suffer in this way, when his cousin Devadatta tried to kill him by rolling a stone down a hill onto him. Although the stone missed, a splinter from it injured the Buddha's foot, and this was said to be a consequence of an unskilful action in a remote past life.[37]

In extreme cases Enlightenment is the only answer to negative karma, as the life story of the great Tibetan yogi Milarepa confirms. He and his guru Marpa were only too well aware of the gravity of his situation – he had committed multiple murder to avenge the cruel treatment of his family – and realized that his only hope of avoiding rebirth in hell was to gain Enlightenment in this very lifetime.[38] His situation was like that of a driver who has lost control of his car: it is about to crash as a result of his bad driving, but if he can jump out, he stands a chance of surviving. If you can, as it were, throw yourself clear of conditioned existence, as Milarepa did on gaining Enlightenment, then whatever might have happened to you if you had stayed within the six realms is of no concern. The same dramatic escape would seem to have been engineered in the case of the Buddha's disciple Aṅgulimāla, who had been a notorious bandit and murderer, but having seen the error of his ways, became a monk, and eventually an *arhant*. The only negative *karma-vipāka* that he had to endure, which he did patiently, was the harsh treatment of villagers who recognized him and threw stones at him.[39]

Of course, not all the fruits of previous actions are painful. If you have acted skilfully in your previous existences, the consequences will be positive both for you and for everyone with whom you come into contact. The benefits of ethically skilful actions are attested and exemplified by the great Buddhist saints, who may in some cases have walked the spiritual path for many lifetimes. Their biographies, which are traditionally regarded as teachings in themselves, to be recalled and dwelt upon and contemplated to inspire one's practice of the Dharma, demonstrate, in their different ways, how the ideal can be realized in an individual human life, out of often humble – and sometimes very unlikely – beginnings. In the end, looking back through all the strange twists and turns of a lifetime, a noble pattern emerges of a life integrating itself, sometimes apparently against all the odds, around that ideal. The message is that if you have cultivated a strong will to follow the transcendental path, you will be impelled, seemingly inevitably, towards spiritual attainment.

Even hearing about the lives of 'ordinary' Buddhists – and over the years I have listened to the life stories of a good many – can leave one with the distinct impression that their progress towards the spiritual path was inevitable, as though there was a goal implicit in everything they did, a goal that gradually became clearer to them as they experienced more of life and realized what they really wanted to be and do. You might not realize the path your life is taking until you look back on it, but when you do become aware of your purpose, it might seem uncannily as though your life has had a direction of its own, independent of your conscious volition. As that direction emerges into consciousness, with the arising of some degree of clear comprehension, it is intensified and you can pursue it even more vigorously. This might provoke considerable resistance within you, perhaps reinforced by circumstances and by the values of the society you are living in. But when you become aware of your higher purpose, however much you kick against it, you will never be able to forget it entirely. The traditional Indian image for this state is graphic: you are a snake that has swallowed a frog and can neither get it down nor throw it up. But there is a more delicate metaphor: it is said that, just as the flower is implicit in the seed, the goal of spiritual growth is implicit in human consciousness. For all human beings, not only saints and sages, the implicit purpose of human existence is to evolve and develop. To grow in consciousness we just need to look carefully at the past and try to discern that trajectory, so that we can continue to move in that direction. If we look carefully enough, we will always find that thread of meaning running through our lives – and it is the function of the Dharma to help us find it.

Not that it is easy to spot. Some people carry over from the past sufficient strength of purpose and clarity to help them find it, but for others the adverse weight of past karma and the vagaries of life in the world conspire to prevent the pattern from emerging into consciousness at all. Life is not *entirely* determined by karma; so much depends on circumstances and plain chance. Even making contact with the Buddha's teachings might seem to be sheer accident – a matter of glancing at a poster or picking up a book. Of course, such chances depend on whoever took the trouble to put that poster up, or publish that book, which is why it is so important to make the Buddhist path known to others. In ways we cannot know, it can be like throwing a lifeline to a drowning swimmer, and they will eagerly clutch it and haul themselves in if they get a chance.

However it comes about, when we become aware of that sense of direction, we should do whatever we can to dwell upon it, intensify our experience of it, and allow it to permeate and transform us. Once you are conscious of yourself unfolding within the framework of conditionality, you can make a directed effort to strengthen the process of growth and remove obstacles from its path. This is mindfulness of purpose, *saṃprajanya* (Pāli *sampajañña*). Just as when setting out on a journey you might resolve that you are not going to linger or allow yourself to be turned aside or distracted, developing mindfulness of purpose means becoming more and more conscious of the goal of growth and development. Because it is the purpose of your life, it is the implicit purpose of all your activities, and you can aim to let it gradually pervade every aspect of your life.

Traditionally, Buddhism has given the goal a name: Enlightenment. But even the shortest journey can be fraught with difficulties, so it is little wonder if from where we are now Enlightenment seems too vague and remote a destination. Even if one has seen the limited nature of mundane goals – and this is by no means easy to do – the ideal of Enlightenment can still seem very far off. One may have no intellectual doubts about the principles of Buddhism, but translating that rational understanding into lived experience means having a clear idea not only of the goal but also of the steps necessary to achieve it. Without that, we won't make much progress in the spiritual life. We need intermediate goals between the ultimate objective and where we are at present, goals we can actually see in the process of being achieved.

Buddhist mythology tells the story of Amitābha, a Buddha who created an entire realm, a 'pure land' complete with jewelled trees, birds singing the Dharma, and all manner of wonders – perfect conditions for the living of the Dharma life. But although he was able to build a pure land for all sentient beings, Amitābha started out as an ordinary *bhikkhu* called Dharmākara, and he must have moved from one limited goal to another, just as we can.[40] The idea of building a cosmic pure land is no doubt far beyond us. But if someone told you they had managed to get hold of some premises and wanted to turn them into a meditation centre, you would probably be able to envisage what that would mean, and you could summon every particle of faith and determination you had to help achieve it. So long as you were prepared to throw yourself into whatever task needed to be done, you could be confident that the new meditation centre would be opened some day. And having done it, you could set yourself further, more demanding goals and thereby achieve things you would never have dreamed of when you first set out.

So long as you keep that clarity of perspective, a series of proximate, short-term goals stretching into the future can take you all the way to Enlightenment itself, however unlikely that might seem from where you are now. Short-term goals give us something concrete to work on and an effective measure of our progress – the measure being in terms of the spiritual benefit to ourselves or to others. We can approach this just as we would approach anything else we wanted to achieve. If, for example, you were going to embark on a course of study, you might select your reading matter and aim to cover a clearly defined field of enquiry, then write up your conclusions or discuss them with other people within a certain time schedule. That would help you monitor your progress and give you confidence in your ability to achieve the goals you set. The important thing is to enter every activity having formed a clear intention and not to lose sight of your purpose even in the midst of the complexity of life. This is what mindfulness of purpose (sometimes called clear comprehension) essentially is: developing the habit of recollecting one's goal often enough and deeply enough to ensure that one's life is organized around it.

To live with clarity of intention and unity of purpose suggests not only an appreciation of cause and effect but also the moral sensitivity that is fundamental to true individuality. When you lose clear comprehension of purpose you haven't just lost your mindfulness; there is a lapse of your moral character, a break in the continuity of your being. So far as the implicit goal of growth and self-knowledge is concerned, it is a kind of lapse into unconsciousness, and in this state of spiritual unconsciousness your instincts and habitual patterns of greed and aversion will be likely to take over. Whatever kind of worldly sense of continuity you are left with will be antithetical to any real unity of purpose. It is mindfulness in the sense of a recollected, purposive quality that makes us capable of creative action – and without it even reflexive consciousness is impossible because there is no basis other than habit from which to act: a very unsatisfactory and uncomfortable state to be in.

In the *Satipaṭṭhāna Sutta* the Buddha exhorts the monk to apply clear comprehension in all the activities of daily life. Bending and stretching, wearing robes, carrying the begging-bowl, eating, drinking, chewing, savouring, attending to the calls of nature, speaking and keeping silent, are all carried out with awareness of what you are doing and why, so that that aspiration is allowed to permeate everything you do. Any activity, however small or apparently insignificant, can be done with a sense of purpose. You can even fall asleep mindfully, with a sense of when and why your period of rest is necessary. If you have to be up in the morning at 6.30 for meditation, your clear comprehension might take the form of making sure that you get to bed in good time so that you have enough sleep and won't just feel like a lie-in when the time comes to meditate.

If you are serious and passionate about reaching your spiritual goal, it is absolutely necessary to take a regular, disciplined approach to what you do. Success, as in any other enterprise – sport or art or business – depends on establishing a disciplined and committed lifestyle. It is strange that people are often reluctant to adopt regular habits, because these do in fact make life easier. If you live haphazardly, just doing what you feel like when you feel like it, you can end up not finding the time or inclination for things you know will benefit you. But with a regular routine you will still, for example, sit to meditate even when you don't feel like it, because you are aware of the benefits of doing so. You can take the likely outcomes of particular courses of action for granted – you don't have to reassess them every time you think about doing them.

It is equally important, however, not to get too rigid about this. The 'path' is not a set of rules that you can stick to mechanically and be sure of getting the results you want. At dinner time you might be able to get away with shovelling food into your mouth in the knowledge that your stomach will take care of the rest of the process, but it isn't like that with meditation, puja, or Dharma study. These practices are designed to be liberating, but if you lose touch with why you are doing them, they become so many obstacles to your progress. Mindfulness is an intelligent, responsive awareness to ever-changing conditions. If the urgent need to develop insight gets lost in the lacklustre business of keeping everything ticking over, it is time to look again at the balance of your life.

This loss of perspective is essentially what has happened in many of the traditional Buddhist cultures of the East. In some Buddhist countries, the stated aim of spiritual practice for lay people is not to gain transcendental insight but to acquire what is called merit (*puṇya*, Pāli *puññā*) through acts of devotion towards shrines and stupas and acts of generosity towards the monastic order. That merit might bear fruit in an auspicious rebirth but it will not bring about insight in this life – which lets the lay follower off the hook, because anything further in the way of spiritual progress is by definition impossible. If you want to practise effectively – this is the popular belief – you need to become a monk or nun; and if you don't get ordained, there is no need to change the way you live. So long as you observe the five ethical precepts, at least on special occasions, you need ask nothing more of yourself. The monk, on the other hand, can safely assume that he is practising the Dharma effectively simply because he wears the robe. As long as he is visibly worthy of the layperson's offerings through the strict observance of ethical discipline, everything will be fine, regardless of his mental states and motivations.

This unwritten contract between monks and lay people serves to preserve the monastic community and ensure its continuing support, but it entirely fails to acknowledge that there are certain ways of going about your business in life that hold you back in your spiritual development, and there are others that help you to progress, whatever your overall lifestyle. The aim of the Buddhist path – for *everybody* – is the transformation of consciousness, and this requires active choices. Without a positive engagement with the principles of Buddhism and a commitment to living in accordance with them in all areas of one's life, the precepts and practices are devalued to the level of mere group custom, enabling people to settle into social roles which vaguely imply that their spiritual practice is effective. From the perspective of the Buddha's own day, however, there could only be one difference between Buddhists: not between monastic and lay people, but between people who are fully committed to growth and transformation and people who are less willing or less able to commit themselves. Without this commitment the whole edifice of monastic life is liable to turn into a mundane institution preoccupied with its own preservation.

It is easier to fall into the trap of understanding religious practice in this purely external way than we might like to think. These days some western Buddhists work in 'right livelihood' businesses whose aim is for even the most mundane tasks to be carried out with awareness – 'clear comprehension' – of one's true goal in life. But it is all too easy to lose sight of this. The short-term demands of the work can take priority over reflections on your higher purpose, so that you lose contact with it, at least for the time being. Your work is meant to support your spiritual practice; it is not just a job. But if you lose that perspective, the ideal of right livelihood as a limb of the Noble Eightfold Path disappears too, and with it the ideal of Enlightenment to which every aspect of that path is dedicated. As the vision behind your daily work fades, you are likely to find yourself less able to contact any depth of positive emotion, and your capacity for effective meditation might slip away too. You might even start to get annoyed with your co-workers because they don't seem to be pulling their weight or engaging as fully with the work as you are yourself. That is a sure sign that something is wrong.

The problem is that, having lost awareness of the deeper currents in your life, you have allowed mere circumstances to take over. This can happen in any line of work; we all need to review what we are doing from time to time and remind ourselves what we are really trying to achieve. If your short-term goals have begun to assume an importance that makes no sense to anyone else, it may be that you have become too dependent on success and too upset by potential failure. It is of course natural to be upset by failure and uplifted by success, but you must keep a check on it, or you will end up depending on constant reassurance from others. If you are experiencing a desperate need to meet your targets for their own sake, you are clearly attaching too much importance to something that was only ever meant to be a means to an end.

Despite their different emphases, mindfulness and clear comprehension of purpose often appear as a compound term in Pāli, *sati-sampajañña*, and the two words can be considered to be so close in meaning as to be virtually interchangeable. There is no precise word in English for this kind of recollection, and it is difficult to come up with a definition that evokes its spirit. One might say that it is going about one's daily life without ever forgetting one's higher purpose, but that still doesn't quite bring out the full sense of *sampajañña*, because ‘forgetting’ refers to something you are trying to remember from the past rather than the future goal to which you aspire. *Sampajañña* (Sanskrit *saṃprajanya*) has more of a sense of insight about it than the more psychological idea of memory. You know not only what you are doing but why you are doing it. It is in this twofold sense that the Buddha exhorts his followers to be aware – ‘clearly comprehending and mindful’ – of the four foundations of mindfulness.

The subtle interplay between awareness and recollection has the effect of integrating one’s whole experience and continually re-establishing a sense of harmony and direction. *Sati-sampajañña* has a balancing and integrating quality that permeates every area of experience, to bring about a whole way of life concentrated not so much on a future goal as on the dynamic, cumulative nature of the path itself. Once you have learned to recognize and cultivate this precious quality, you will never lose touch with the truth that our existence is not confined to the present, and that what we will become depends to a very great extent on what we do now.

# 3
# BREATHING

> 'And how, bhikkhus, does a bhikkhu abide contemplating the body as a body? Here a bhikkhu, gone to the forest or to the root of a tree or to an empty hut, sits down; having folded his legs crosswise, set his body erect, and established mindfulness in front of him, ever mindful he breathes in, mindful he breathes out.'

Having laid down the four foundations of mindfulness, the Buddha goes on to recommend a particularly accessible method of developing mindfulness: the mindfulness of breathing. The fact that it is *accessible* is very important. The plain truth is – and we had better face this squarely – that awareness of any kind is not easy to develop. The Buddha's method is therefore to start by encouraging us to develop awareness of the aspect of our experience that is closest to us: the body. Even this is not as easy as one might think. The first of the four foundations may be 'mindfulness of the body', but it is hard to focus on 'the body' as a whole; it is such a complex thing, within which all sorts of processes are going on at the same time. To lead your awareness towards a broader experience of the body, it is therefore best to begin by focusing on the breath. Breathing is a simple bodily activity, providing a relatively stable object of attention that is both calming and capable of sustaining one's interest. On this basis, you can go on to become aware of your bodily sensations and even of your feelings and thoughts, which are still more subtle and difficult to follow.

The breath is available to us at every moment of our lives, and becoming aware of it has a calming effect at stressful times, as we know from the received wisdom of our own culture: 'Take a deep breath.' But it is possible to cultivate a more systematic awareness of the breathing through a meditation which is widely practised throughout the Buddhist world: the mindfulness of breathing (*ānāpāna-sati* in Pāli), which some say was the meditation the Buddha was practising when he gained Enlightenment.[41] In the *Satipaṭṭhāna Sutta* the Buddha launches straight into a description of how the *bhikkhu* should go about this practice. He is directed to go into the depths of the forest, or to the foot of a tree, or just to an empty place. Then, sitting down with his legs crossed, he is to keep his body erect and his mindfulness alert or 'established in front of him', and start to become aware of his breathing.[42] Thus we learn straightaway that the right place, the right time, and the right posture are all important for successful meditation.

The right place, we gather, is a place of solitude. In the Buddha's time, of course, there was plenty of space in the depths of the forest for meditators to sit there for long periods without being disturbed, but I think the Buddha's instruction here means something more. We need to imagine what it would be like to take up this practice if you had always lived in the traditional Indian family, which was the core of brahminical society in the Buddha's day. An Indian village, with all its noise and bustle, was hardly conducive to the development of mental calm, and the psychological and moral pull of the family group would have been just as inimical to spiritual practice. Even today in India, if you live in a traditional extended family it can be very difficult to steer your life in a direction not dictated by your family. For anyone seeking an awakening to truth, simply going forth to the undisturbed solitude of the forest, abandoning anything to do with home and family life, at least for a while, was – and continues to be – a major step.

Finding solitude is just as much of a challenge for us in the West today, although for us 'solitude' might mean getting a respite from the world and worldly concerns rather than literally getting away from other people. Indeed, the companionship of other people following the same spiritual tradition as yourself can be a great source of encouragement, especially when you are just starting out. To meditate in isolation, you need to know what you are doing and be very determined. It is all too easy for discouraging doubts to arise about whether you are doing the practice properly, and in the absence of an experienced guide you might lose interest in meditation altogether. While the Buddha's instruction to seek out the foot of a tree certainly suggests finding a place where you are likely to be undisturbed for a while, it does not necessarily mean going off into the depths of the forest or isolating yourself from other meditators.

People didn't always meditate alone even in the Buddha's day. The Pāli *sutta*s contain striking descriptions of the Buddha and his disciples sitting and meditating together, sometimes in very large numbers. We come upon such a scene at the beginning of the *Sāmaññaphala Sutta*. On a full-moon night, King Ajātasattu decides to have his elephants saddled up (five hundred of them) and ride with his entourage deep into the forest in search of the Buddha. It is quite a long way, and the king (who has a guilty conscience) is beset by all sorts of fears as they journey through the darkness. But at last they come upon the Buddha, seated in meditation with twelve hundred and fifty monks, all of them perfectly concentrated and spread out before him like a vast, clear lake. The silence, says the *Sutta,* fills the guilty king – he has murdered his own father to gain the throne – with a nameless dread, making the hairs on his body stand on end. But he is sufficiently moved to ask to become a lay disciple of the Buddha on the spot.[43]

Since those early times, Buddhists throughout the tradition – especially in the Zen schools, which place a particular emphasis on meditation – have well understood the benefits of collective practice. The Westerner learning to meditate is quite likely to do so alone, buying a book on the subject and beginning the practice in the comfort of his or her own home, but this is not to be recommended. It is hard to tell from the printed page how much experience the author has, and in any case no book can cover every contingency. There is also the danger that you will end up just reading about Buddhist meditation and never getting round to doing any. It is certainly possible to learn the basic techniques from a book, but if you can, it is worth seeking out a meditation teacher and other meditators with whom to practise.

As for the Buddha's instruction that the *bhikkhu* should sit cross-legged, this posture is recommended because it spreads the weight of the body more broadly and evenly than any other sitting position, and thus gives stability and enables you to sit comfortably for a long time. However, while it would have come naturally to the people of the

Buddha's time and culture to sit cross-legged on the floor, we might find it more difficult. If so, any posture can be adopted, whether on the floor or on a chair, as long as it is stable and comfortable. Incidentally, this is another reason to go along to a meditation class – to get some help with working out a suitable meditation posture.

Next, the monk is advised to keep his mindfulness 'alert' or 'established in front of him'. Some commentators suggest that this is an instruction to be mindful of the breath, which is in a way in front of you – but the meaning is probably less literal, referring simply to being undistracted. It's rather like the behaviour prescribed for a monk going for alms: he is supposed to keep his gaze on the ground about six feet in front of him, looking neither left nor right. This discipline is a very good preparation for meditation, helping one to be more aware of what one is doing and why, so that one does not let one's mind stray into unskilful thoughts.

> 'Breathing in long, he understands: "I breathe in long"; or
> breathing out long, he understands: "I breathe out long."
> Breathing in short, he understands: "I breathe in short"; or
> breathing out short, he understands: "I breathe out short."'

The precise details of the mindfulness of breathing are not recorded in any text, perhaps because the detailed ins and outs of the practice have traditionally been handed down from teacher to pupil by word of mouth; one can see the teaching of meditation in classes or groups as a continuation of that tradition. But the best method to start with is probably the traditional Theravādin practice of *ānāpāna-sati*. This is divided into four stages, the first two of which involve counting the breaths, to stop the mind from wandering and help you become aware of the breathing's dynamic yet gentle regularity. In the first stage you count at the end of each out-breath; according to the commentaries this corresponds to the phrase in the *Satipaṭṭhāna Sutta* which describes the meditator as knowing 'I am breathing in a long breath.'

There is nothing sacrosanct about this counting – in a sense it doesn't matter what number you count to. In some traditions you don't count at all – for example, there is a Thai method whereby you prevent the mind from straying by combining the inward and outward breathing with the pronunciation of the syllables '*bud*' and '*dho*' ('*buddho*' means 'awake'). Other traditions go to the opposite extreme – some Tibetan yogis count on indefinitely, even into the thousands. The *Satipaṭṭhāna Sutta* itself makes no mention of counting. But the best method for the beginner is probably to count the breaths in groups of ten, as they do in the Theravādin tradition. Counting to five or less tends to restrict the mind unnecessarily, while going beyond ten involves paying too much attention to keeping track of which number you've reached.

Although you should be careful not to become so preoccupied with counting that you forget to concentrate on the breathing itself, it is a good idea to keep counting in these early stages of the practice. Experienced meditators may find that counting obstructs their concentration, but in that case the counting tends to fall away quite naturally. If you are going to modify the practice, you need to be able to recognize the state of concentration you have reached and what to do to deepen it, and that calls for a good deal of experience. If you are a relative beginner, you may think you are concentrating when all that has happened is that you have slipped into a light doze as your thoughts wander to and fro. Some beginners do become deeply absorbed in meditation, but it is rare to be able to stay concentrated. It is best to adopt a systematic method that will help you keep up the momentum of the practice.

Once the first stage has been established, the *Sutta* tells us that the meditator knows that he is breathing in a short breath. This can be taken to refer to the second stage of the *ānāpāna* practice, in which you change the emphasis slightly by counting before each in-breath rather than after each out-breath. Presumably a correspondence between the *Sutta*'s instructions at this point and the first two stages of the *ānāpāna* method is made because the breath has a natural tendency to become a little longer in the first stage and a little shorter in the second. But you don't deliberately make the breaths shorter or longer – you just watch and count them as they come and go, steadily becoming more and more aware of the whole breathing process as you do so.

In the early stages of meditation, much of your effort will be taken up with drawing the disparate energies of your mind and body together, and this involves recognizing the various ways in which the mind resists the process of deepening concentration. Traditionally these forms of resistance are called the five hindrances: doubt, sensual desire, ill will, sloth and torpor, and restlessness. More will be said about this unsettling list of obstacles in a later chapter. Here, it will suffice to say that to begin with, one's effort in meditation is mainly directed towards avoiding them.

Buddhaghosa's commentary on the *Satipaṭṭhāna Sutta* (he was a celebrated scholar of the Pāli texts who lived in the fourth century CE) compares the mind at this stage to a calf which, having been reared on wild cow's milk, has been taken away from its mother and tethered to a post.[44] At first, unsettled and ill at ease in its unfamiliar surroundings, the calf dashes to and fro trying to escape. But however much it struggles, it is held fast by the rope tethering it to the post. The rope of course symbolizes mindfulness. If your mindfulness holds firm, your mind will eventually be brought to a point where, like the wild calf, it finally stops trying to get away and settles down to rest in the inward and outward flow of the breath.

For all its qualities of strength and steadfastness in the face of distraction, mindfulness is neither forceful nor aggressive in its quiet taming of the wayward mind. Like the rope, mindfulness has a certain pliancy. If you fix your attention too rigidly on the object of meditation, subtle states of concentration will have little opportunity to arise. The aim is a gradual process of unification: you guide your energies firmly until they harmonize about a single point without strain or tension, and you are absorbed in the breathing for its own sake. A deep contentment will then lead quite naturally into concentration, as the traces of distraction fade away.

> 'He trains thus: "I shall breathe in experiencing the whole body (of breath)"; he trains thus: "I shall breathe out experiencing the whole body (of breath)." He trains thus: "I shall breathe in tranquillizing the bodily formation"; he trains thus: "I shall breathe out tranquillizing the bodily formation." Just as a skilled turner or his apprentice, when making a long turn, understands: "I make a long turn"; or, when making a short turn, understands: "I make a short turn."'

In the *ānāpāna* method the first two stages of the practice are succeeded by two more, in the course of which your awareness of the breathing becomes increasingly refined. In stage three you drop the counting altogether and give your attention to the breathing process as a whole, experiencing your breath rising and falling continuously and without effort, like a great ocean wave. You follow the breath going into the lungs, you feel it there, and you continue to experience it fully as it is breathed out.

Note that the future tense used here ('I shall breathe in') simply signifies the meditator's intention; it carries no suggestion that the breathing should be controlled in any way. Nor should the injunction to verbalize, even silently, be taken literally: if you become deeply concentrated there will be no mental activity at all. Another possible source of confusion is the expression 'whole body of breath', which means simply the whole breath, not a subtle counterpart of the physical body like the Hindu concept of *prāṇa*. When you are experiencing the whole breath body, it is not just an awareness from the outside, but a total experience – you are identifying yourself with the breath.[45]

After some time this subtle stage gives way to the fourth stage of the practice, which is more subtle still. Now you bring your attention to the first touch of the breath about your nostrils or upper lip, maintaining a delicate, minutely observed awareness of the breath's texture as it enters and leaves your body. Buddhaghosa compares this to a carpenter sawing timber, who keeps his attention fixed not on the saw as it moves back and forth but on the spot where the saw's teeth are cutting into the wood.[46]

The *Sutta* itself provides the analogy of a skilful wood turner who knows precisely what kind of turn – long or short – he is making. For most of us the reference will be somewhat obscure, but this is the kind of rural image the Buddha often used, and it would have been immediately clear to the people of village India in his own time. The basic principle of turning remains the same to this day: the turner shapes the wood by rotating a piece of timber at speed and applying various cutting tools to the surface as it spins. In the Buddha's day this would have been a very simple process, by which a strip of wood would be peeled from the rotating timber in either a long or a short traverse. The turner's whole attention has to be concentrated on the point at which the timber revolves, and this demands steady concentration, because a hesitation would leave a mark which would be hard to remove. Likewise, by means of the meditation technique, your consciousness becomes increasingly refined and you become more keenly aware of the breathing. As you bring your physical and mental energies into a state of tranquillity and dynamic balance, you steadily identify yourself with the breath until there is only the subtlest mental activity around the breathing process. You are simply and brightly aware.

When you are just starting the practice, your experience of the breath will be more or less the same as usual, but as the meditation moves into a different gear you will perceive it more subtly and it will become much more interesting to you, as though it were an entirely new experience. This signals that you are entering the phase known as access concentration, *upacāra-samādhi*, a state in which meditation becomes lighter and more enjoyable and distractions are easier to recognize and deal with. You feel buoyant, as though you are floating or expanding, and everything flows naturally and easily.

This phase of meditation might be accompanied by experiences called *samāpatti*.[47] These are difficult to describe because they vary so much from person to person and from one time to another. They might take a visual form – perhaps a certain luminosity before the mind's eye – or arise as a kind of symbol of your state of awareness. All such phenomena are just signs that your concentration is becoming deeper. Your aim is to concentrate all the more deeply on your breathing, leaving these experiences to look after themselves, not dwelling on them or getting too interested in them.

Gradually, if you keep your momentum, you will be able to go just a little further than access concentration, to enter full mental absorption or *appanā-samādhi*, otherwise known in Pāli as *jhāna* and in Sanskrit as *dhyāna*. In *dhyāna* you enter a crucial stage, passing beyond the psychological process of integrating the disparate aspects of yourself into true concentration. As long as you remain immersed in this state you are no longer dependent on the physical senses for anchorage – a statement which makes more sense in experience than in words, it has to be said. Absorption in *dhyāna* is inherently pleasurable. It is a highly positive state of integration and harmony, which moves consciousness, at least temporarily, into the realm of genuinely spiritual experience. It has longer-lasting effects too: it is what is sometimes called 'weighty' karma – that is, it has very powerful positive karmic consequences.[48] It is a mistake to think of *dhyāna* as passive, mild, and restful in a pleasantly vague way – it is an active, powerful state. But for all its skilfulness, *dhyāna* is by no means the final goal of the mindfulness of breathing. Its main importance lies in the fact that it is the basis for the development of transcendental insight.

> 'In this way he abides contemplating the body as a body internally, or he abides contemplating the body as a body externally, or he abides contemplating the body as a body both internally and externally. Or else he abides contemplating in the body its arising factors, or he abides contemplating in the body its vanishing factors, or he abides contemplating in the body both its arising and vanishing factors. Or else mindfulness that "there is a body" is simply established in him to the extent necessary for bare knowledge and mindfulness. And he abides independent, not clinging to anything in the world. That is how a bhikkhu abides contemplating the body as a body.'

The way Buddhist meditation practices are described can make it seem as though some of them are designed to develop concentration (*śamatha*) while others are meant to develop insight (*vipaśyanā*). In fact, though, all these practices are part of a single system of mental development leading towards higher states of awareness. The aim of all Buddhist practice is ultimately transcendental insight, and there is thus no need to draw too clear a line between *śamatha* and *vipaśyanā* meditation. The process is essentially the same: you start by becoming aware of the aspects of existence most immediately apparent to you – your own body and its functions – and then you narrow the field of concentration in order to cultivate the *dhyānas*. This preparatory stage can take the form of the mindfulness of breathing, or the *mettā bhāvanā* (the development of loving-kindness), or even a practice traditionally thought of as '*vipaśyanā*' – the six element practice, for instance. Whatever the method, you have to develop concentration as a first step if the reflective aspect of the practice is to be effective. Having narrowed the field of your attention to deepen your experience, you expand that field to increase the breadth of your vision, placing your experience of concentration, intensely absorbed as it is, within the broader perspective of *vipaśyanā*. Without these two aspects – the harmonization of consciousness and the cultivation of insight – no system of meditation is complete.

One tends not to think of the mindfulness of breathing as an insight practice, but in principle it is, just as much as practices more usually designated '*vipaśyanā*'. The *Satipaṭṭhāna Sutta*'s description of the practice certainly suggests that it is. *Vipassanā* is presented here as a stage of meditation – that stage of meditation which follows on naturally from the concentration and tranquillity established by the mindfulness of breathing. As this section of the *Sutta* moves beyond the technical description of the establishment of concentration around the breath, it goes into a series of more general reflections concerning the nature of breathing: the contemplation of the breath internally and externally, and of the origination and dissolution factors of the breath. Through these reflections – this is the intention – you eventually come to grasp the essential fragility of the breathing process.

So it is possible to take a reflective attitude to the breath as well as dwelling on the physical experience of breathing. Although these reflections are suggested here in the *Satipaṭṭhāna Sutta*, such a reflective attitude is only occasionally mentioned in the Theravādin tradition, while in the Mahāyāna, *vipaśyanā* practices such as the six element practice may take over where the mindfulness of breathing leaves off.

No doubt the six element practice could be said to provide a more comprehensive method of channelling the same kinds of reflection. But to reflect on the nature of the breath is in essence to reflect on what the Buddhist tradition calls the three *lakṣaṇas* (Pāli *lakkhaṇas*), the three characteristics or 'marks' of mundane existence: that it is impermanent, unsatisfactory, and insubstantial – and what could be more directly related to insight than that?[49] The *Sutta* instructs the practitioner to live 'contemplating in the body its arising factors, or its vanishing factors'. The meaning of this is quite straightforward: you contemplate all the factors or conditions that go to produce the breathing process, and in the absence of which it does not take place. It is essentially a recognition of the breath's contingent nature. As well as bringing to mind the physiological conditions affecting the rise and fall of the breath, you can also reflect that the breathing, as an intrinsic part of the body as a whole, is ultimately dependent upon the ignorance and craving that, under the law of karma, have brought that body into existence.

The very impermanence of the body, you can further reflect, gives rise to its unsatisfactoriness. This is the second of the three 'marks' of conditioned existence: the truth that all conditioned things are unsatisfactory, even potentially painful, because they cannot last for ever. The breath, like the body, arises and passes away, and one day our breathing – and our life – will come to an end. To bring this reflection home, you can call to mind the inherent fragility of the breathing. Like the body, it is a delicate, vulnerable thing that is always susceptible to the unpredictable forces of the natural world.

This inherent instability is something we share with all sentient beings, indeed with everything, which is presumably what is meant in the *Sutta* by the exhortation to contemplate the body 'externally' as well as 'internally'. It could conceivably mean looking at the body from the outside as well as experiencing it subjectively from within, but it is usually taken to mean contemplation of the physical experience of others. In the later stages of the mindfulness of breathing, when you might be concentrating more on the development of insight, you can recollect that just as you are breathing, so too are all other living beings (or at least those that do breathe). In this way you cultivate a feeling of solidarity with all other forms of life. As far as I know, this sort of reflection forms no specific part of the mindfulness of breathing as it is usually practised, but it is the natural result of sustained practice: you realize in a very immediate way that just as you are breathing in and out, so too are other beings. The mindfulness of breathing practised in this way thus provides a corrective against an alienated or one-sided approach to spiritual life. It seems a shame that it is not standard practice.

In reflecting that we share with all breathing beings the same body of air and the same material elements, we approach the third mark of conditioned existence – the fact that the distinction we make between ourselves and others is quite arbitrary. This is the truth of insubstantiality – the fact that the discrete and permanent self is only an illusion. We depend on other people for our existence and we are very much like them. And when we die, the material elements of which we are all composed will disperse across the universe once more. The *Sutta* thus refers to the monk's body not as 'his' body but as 'the' body. There is no question here of 'I' or 'mine'; it's just a body. Reflecting in this way is not meant to alienate you from your body; you are trying to see it as an impersonal process, part of the universal rise and fall of things. It is another move towards a sense of solidarity with other beings.

In this way the *Sutta* leads the meditator through the *śamatha* stages of calming and integrating consciousness around the breathing, through the various levels of absorbed concentration, and on to the contemplation of the inherent truths of conditioned existence, in preparation for the arising of transcendental insight. How the effort to develop insight within meditation is made is quite difficult to explain. You have to look actively for insight into the true nature of things, but without looking for it in any particular direction or in any particular way. It is a sort of active receptivity: you are actively holding yourself open to insight. These two aspects of the practice – receptivity to something outside yourself, so to speak, and an active searching – are equally important. The quest for insight demands exertion – not intellectual exertion, but a meditative, intuitive searching: not trying to think your way to reality but trying to see it directly.

This is not to say that insight will necessarily arise directly as a result of insight practice. Sometimes it happens that you are trying too hard, or not in quite the right way. When you release that effort, the momentum of your practice may continue to build up and insight may suddenly strike you out of the blue when you are doing something ordinary like peeling potatoes. There is no situation, whether positive or negative, pleasant or painful, in which insight may not arise. All that is needed is mindfulness.

This section of the *Sutta* is therefore less about what you do in seated meditation than about what you take away from it. This is perhaps why it is so concise. Perhaps it is not advocating a thoroughgoing practice of *vipaśyanā* at the end of the mindfulness of breathing so much as simply making the point that mindfulness, especially in its more reflective, insightful aspects, is something to be carried over into all areas of our experience. Mindfulness is not just what you do when you are sitting at the foot of a tree in the forest (or wherever you choose to meditate). Having clarified and unified your consciousness by means of the mindfulness of breathing, you are meant to reflect that the breathing is a precarious and fragile thing, and to carry that awareness with you all the time. This section of the *Sutta* prepares the ground for what is to come later on, when the transition between seated meditation and the practice of mindfulness in daily life is addressed. It suggests that a continuity is established by becoming conscious of the body's impermanence, its internal and external qualities and its existence simply as a body, regardless of your mental constructions around it.

# 4
# LIVING

> 'Again, bhikkhus, when walking, a bhikkhu understands: "I am walking"; when standing, he understands: "I am standing"; when sitting, he understands: "I am sitting"; when lying down, he understands: "I am lying down"; or he understands accordingly however his body is disposed....
>
> 'A bhikkhu is one who acts in full awareness when going forward and returning; who acts in full awareness when looking ahead and looking away; who acts in full awareness when flexing and extending his limbs; who acts in full awareness when wearing his robes and carrying his outer robe and bowl; who acts in full awareness when eating, drinking, consuming food, and tasting; who acts in full awareness when defecating and urinating; who acts in full awareness when walking, standing, sitting, falling asleep, waking up, talking, and keeping silent.'

Meditation is widely regarded as a thoroughly beneficial practice, but not many people think of it as something that can or even should result in fundamental change. The idea of fundamental change is in fact not at all inspiring as far as most people are concerned, which is no doubt why many teachers of meditation tend to stress instead the great improvement that it can bring to one's powers of concentration, one's health, one's self-control, and even one's success in one's chosen career. Meditation, it seems, can help you improve your performance in any field of activity, from tennis to trading in stocks and shares. I even heard one guru who was famous in the sixties suggest that a millionaire can expect to grow richer still as a result of meditation. But it is a great mistake to imagine that you can pursue spiritual practice without changing the way you live and work. Transformation is implicit in every aspect of spiritual life – so we need to be prepared to change.

Without question, if you practise the mindfulness of breathing you do become more self-controlled and even more efficient in your activities – at least, those of an ethical nature. As far as unethical activities go, you increasingly come to see how unskilful they are and this makes you less comfortable about continuing to engage with them. As we have seen, mindfulness is inherently skilful, relying upon an understanding of actions and their consequences which goes beyond a petty-minded and worldly need to get ahead. Mindfulness is essentially the cultivation of an uninterrupted flow of skilful states of consciousness. After you have begun to make meditation part of your life, certain kinds of activity might therefore start to upset and disturb you, even if you haven't given them any thought.

But the *Satipaṭṭhāna Sutta* looks at life in a much more detailed way even than in terms of whether or not your activities are ethical. The words of the text are straightforward enough: mindfulness of the body consists in making no movement, assuming no posture, of which you are unaware. When you are standing, you know that you are standing. When you are sitting down, you know that you are sitting down. This might seem so obvious as to be not worth saying. How could we fail to carry out this simple exercise? When we are walking or standing or sitting down, don't we know that we are? Obviously we do in a way, otherwise we would bump into lamp-posts all the time – but we don't really experience our bodily movements because our minds are largely elsewhere. When you come to think about it, you might find that in fact you are not really aware of what you are doing at this basic level for much of the time. And the aim is not just to be aware, but to develop and sustain a certain *quality* of awareness. You are aiming not just to perform any given action in a concentrated and efficient manner, but to sustain a continuously skilful, mindful state of consciousness throughout your waking life.

This is easier said than done, and all too easily mistaken for a state of mind that is simply alienated. This 'alienated awareness' is to be avoided at all costs. It is an awareness of oneself that lacks emotional depth. You are somehow cut off from what you are doing; only part of you is interested in it, while the rest of you is caught up with something else or simply disengaged from the sources of positive emotion that are so vital to spiritual growth. This is the kind of state of mind in which you might be trying to write a letter, have a telephone conversation, and give instructions to someone, all at the same time, and doing none of them with any emotional engagement. The tasks get done somehow, but you are only conscious of doing them at an alienated, superficial level – a deeply unsatisfactory, indeed painful way of living, and one that demands a heavy cost from you as a spiritual being. Even the common habit of combining mealtimes with business transactions or serious conversation involves a damaging conflict of emotional and physical energies that often manifests in the form of indigestion or even ulcers.

With care and planning, you can avoid this sort of situation almost entirely. Ideally, this means doing one thing at a time, so that you can engage your emotions fully with the task in hand. After all, as far as your spiritual development is concerned, the nature of the task itself is unimportant. It is the extent to which it supports the continued cultivation of skilful states of awareness that needs to be your priority.

This is not to say that it is impossible to combine two activities, or think about one thing while doing another. Except when you are seated in meditation, your attention will always be divided to some degree. If you make a conscious decision to think something through while you are walking along, so that you are only minimally aware of your physical experience, there is nothing wrong with that. The main thing is to retain the harmony of consciousness which is characteristic of any skilful state, so that your emotions are fully part of your awareness. You are not just coldly observing the body or aware of it at a superficial level; you are consciously experiencing the way you move as an expression of mindful positivity.

Such clarity of mind is hard to achieve even in meditation, so it is little wonder that it so often eludes us in daily life. Our minds are in a state of almost constant muddle and agitation. Even though we may very much want to become calm and concentrated, all too often the mind goes on turning over and over. Sometimes the reason for this is just that you are not giving yourself wholly to what you are doing, and a determined effort may be needed, or inspiration found, to rally your commitment. By simplifying and clarifying your day-to-day activities, your experience becomes more emotionally rich and – as your interest becomes more focused – your distractions begin naturally to subside.

The mindfulness of breathing is said to be the classic remedy for distraction, and certainly anyone who takes it up will discover before long how incessant and intense mental chatter can be. But the technique of the mindfulness of breathing alone can be strangely ineffective in stilling the wandering mind. Even saying that the mind is 'wandering' does not express the extent of the problem. In fact, the mind is like a bucking bronco: the more you try to control it, the more it bucks. It may be that it will be assuaged more effectively by the *mettā bhāvanā* meditation (in which one cultivates positive emotion) or by devotional practices such as puja and mantra recitation – because the difficulty is not lack of concentration but lack of emotional integration and positivity. Lacking fulfilment, the mind roams incessantly in search of a deeper emotional satisfaction – or in an attempt to hide from an unwanted emotional experience. Mental distraction can be seen as a compensatory activity, an unconscious protest at one's lack of emotional involvement.

Distraction manifests in different ways. For some people it is a purely mental thing. Others fidget and twiddle, twisting rings or buttons, scratching or pulling their nose, drumming on the table with their fingers. In animals, their own versions of this kind of displacement activity are apparently (so the zoologists tell us) signs of severe inner conflict, and the same is probably true for us. Still other people, of course, express their mental chatter in terms of actual chatter. I once got to know an old lady in India who was given to continuous compulsive talking. In spite of her extraordinary volubility, it seemed that she could never get to the point, whatever the point may have been. My sense was that she needed to get something off her chest, and yet she could never bring herself to confess what it was, though she sometimes seemed to get close to doing so. Eventually I did come to understand – though not through the lady herself – what was going on. She was, or had been, a doctor, and had nursed her late husband through a long illness. Whatever the circumstances surrounding her husband's death, it seemed she had yet to resolve that episode in her life and that it somehow held the clue to her compulsive talking. Her endless, restless need to roam from one topic to another expressed an emotional absence which would only be satisfied once she had looked into its real origins. But what she needed was not a determination to concentrate on the topic in hand, but a good friend to confide in, so that she could at last find some peace of mind.

The same goes for inner, mental chatter. Somehow you never seem to be able to get to the point, and forcing your wandering mind to concentrate is not what will get you there. Mindfulness of the body is not about forcing anything, but about finding a deeper source of satisfaction to still that confusion. If you are deeply and fully emotionally satisfied – listening to music and really enjoying it, or absorbed in a book – the problem of mental chatter simply does not arise. It only crops up when you are not enjoying the situation you are in. The traditional image for this is a bee buzzing round a flower: once it alights on the petals and begins to burrow inside to find the nectar, all the buzzing ceases. When you are interested you are concentrated, and when you are concentrated you are happy. If we could only allow this simple analysis to guide our activities all the time, we would be able to live satisfying lives with no room for mental distraction.

When your mind starts to become distracted, you therefore need to ask yourself whether you are really enjoying the situation you are in. If the answer is no, the next question is: what do you need to do to start enjoying it? If you are engaged in conversation when your mind starts to wander, for example, there will be definite conditions, either internal or external, which cause this to happen. Perhaps it is just that the other person is doing all the talking, in which case you can make an effort to take a more active part in the conversation, even interrupting your friend's monologue if need be. Or, if you are not interested in the topic of conversation, you can tactfully change the subject. Whatever the situation, it is usually possible to find a way to change it, though you may have to do some lateral thinking.

This applies to the workplace too. If you don't find your work interesting or enjoyable, mental distraction will arise as a reaction to your lack of emotional involvement with what you spend most of your time doing. This can be quite harmful, especially if you bring that alienated state of mind home with you at the end of the day. Arriving home drained and tired, it can be hard to generate much positivity, even if you want to. You won't be able to concentrate on reading, or music, or anything of a refined nature which you usually enjoy, because you just don't have the energy. As W. B. Yeats says,

Toil and grow rich,
What's that but to lie
With a foul witch
And after, drained dry,
To be brought
To the chamber where
Lies one long sought
With despair?[50]

If you feel like saying that about your work, clearly you need to take the initiative in some way.

If you have chosen to work in a context which is organized to support your spiritual aspirations – some form of right livelihood, as Buddhists call it – you may still feel emotionally unfulfilled, perhaps because you are forcing the pace and not taking care to stay in touch with sources of enjoyment. Of course, you won't be able to keep working skilfully for long if you aren't enjoying it. Everyone needs satisfaction and inspiration if they are to stay in touch with the spiritual path – and not all that is enjoyable is unskilful. One can find great enjoyment in devotional practice, as well as in music and poetry, and especially in communication with one's friends. Meditation, too, should be enjoyable, not a hard grind. If you don't find the spiritual life enjoyable, you might be able to keep going for a while on force of will and intellectual conviction, but you can't rely on this indefinitely. In the end the conflict between the call of duty and the need for pleasure will be too great.

The way to become mindful, therefore, is to learn to enjoy mindfulness for its own sake. Humdrum everyday activities such as eating, walking, and sleeping can give deep satisfaction. Paying attention to how things look, sound, and feel makes them more enjoyable; it is as simple (and as difficult) as that. If we give close enough attention to the aesthetic dimension of daily life, we will be drawn into the simplest activities with interest and enjoyment. It makes all the difference to a mealtime, for instance, if there is a clean cloth and a vase of flowers on the table. Even inexpensive crockery can be well-designed and aesthetically pleasing, and even simple food can be served with genuine care. Simplicity is very important to mindfulness. At mealtimes, you can enrich the experience by focusing on the process of eating. A little gentle conversation is all right, but leave serious discussions until later. As for business lunches, avoid these at all costs!

Mealtimes give us an especially good opportunity to practise mindfulness of the body, both because they arrive with such regularity and because so much energy is aroused by the activity and even the very thought of eating. From a Buddhist perspective the purpose of eating is not to indulge ourselves and assuage our neurotic cravings, but to sustain the strength of the body and keep ourselves in good health so that we can get on with the all-important quest for higher states of consciousness. However, this is not to say that in the interests of spiritual progress we have to give up enjoying our food altogether. If you become attached to the pleasant sensations of eating, food can easily become a distraction, but if you can enjoy eating a meal whatever it is, irrespective of your likes and dislikes, this will be an important breakthrough in your practice of mindfulness. People sometimes imagine that with the arising of transcendental insight we will become completely indifferent to the tastes of food, because we will have gone beyond liking and disliking. But it is more that, freed from the tyranny of our likes and dislikes, we will be able to savour with enjoyment the very experience of eating, whatever we happen to be eating. We know that Milarepa, the great Tibetan yogi, lived for years in the mountains on nothing more than nettle soup – and we can assume that he thoroughly enjoyed his nettle soup every time. Of course, without putting it to the test we can't know whether we ourselves would be able to eat a very simple diet with the relish with which we might tuck into a gourmet banquet. It is worth trying it from time to time.

One could say that eating gives us our very best opportunity to 'contemplate arising and vanishing factors in the body', as the *Satipaṭṭhāna Sutta* advises us to, because our need for food is continuous, which shows us how dependent the body is on causes and conditions for its continued existence. Reflections like these keep our broader aim in view – and they do not by any means have to remain in the realm of abstract theory. You may have your doubts about craving and ignorance, or about karma, but you can't have doubts about food, because it is all too obvious that the body is sustained by and dependent upon it.

> 'In this way he abides contemplating the body as a body, internally, externally, and both internally and externally....'

Mindfulness of the body and its postures need not be confined to one's own body; it can be extended to other bodies too. When we think of other people, we tend to think of them as entirely separate from ourselves. Our feelings also remain separate, and even when we interact with others we don't really empathize with them. But in 'contemplating the body externally' (as the *Sutta* has it) we train ourselves to regard the bodies of others, and the whole material world, as no less important than one's own body and to be treated with as much care and consideration. The spiritual life is not all introspection and self-evaluation. Turning our mindfulness outside ourselves we train ourselves to take delight in the positive qualities of those around us, and in doing this we loosen our identification with the ego, that is, we come closer to developing an awareness of the truth of non-self (*anātman*, Pāli *anattā*). This understanding of the insubstantiality of the self is one of the most famous Buddhist doctrines, but it is often misunderstood. *Anattā* is not a cold, alienated vision of impersonality; it is imbued with all the warmth of the Buddha's compassion. To realize it, we need to be prepared to look after and care for other bodies with the warmth and responsiveness we lavish upon our own.

This is without doubt very difficult to do. We are strongly conscious of the body as being *my* body; it is almost impossible to give as much consideration to other people. We may show care for the bodies of others when they are ill, but most of the time we don't feel enough for other people to go out of our way to help them. The strongest other-regarding feelings we have are for our friends and family, and as a rule we care for these people not because they need care but because we need them. However attentive we may be to our own kith and kin, however much we give to our personal friends, there is rather more that is self-regarding than other-regarding in such gestures. Our nearest and dearest often hold the key to our own security and happiness, so we are giving, in a sense, to ourselves. This is not to say that there cannot be genuine selflessness in the way you feel towards those you love most. But it is only when you can be just as selfless in relation to people from whom you can expect nothing at all that the great obstacle of self-cherishing begins to be broken down.

To go beyond our preoccupation with the needs and interests of our own bodies, we have to generate a much stronger emotional connection with other people. That means looking out for situations in which someone needs help and you can respond, in however small a way.

At mealtimes you can make sure that the people sitting near you have everything they need and like, and when your friends and neighbours are ill, you can look after them, going out of your way to make them comfortable, doing things for them which they had been used to doing for themselves, and taking full account of their objective needs, and even their likes and dislikes (which in their own way are objective too). Even when your friends are perfectly healthy, you can take care of their needs and in this way begin to grow beyond the boundary where your interests end and those of another person begin.

In Tibetan Buddhism this attitude is embodied in the figure of Māmakī, the consort of the Buddha Ratnasambhava (who is the southern Buddha of the five-Buddha mandala). Māmakī's name literally means 'mine-ness'. She shares Ratnasambhava's wisdom of equality, appreciating all things and all beings equally, making none of the distinctions conventionally made between what belongs to 'me' and what belongs to 'others', but regarding everything, including all beings, as her own, even as her self.

Can we adopt this attitude? The real test is what we do in practical terms to overcome the great obstacle of dualistic thinking with regard to other people. A measure of this is the extent to which we are aware of the effect we have on others, through our actions, our words, and even our thoughts. When you start to feel responsible for the effect you have, and to act upon that sense of responsibility, that is the sign that the ethical dimension of mindfulness has begun to emerge.

This is what the *Sutta* means when – according to Bhikkhu Sīlācāra's translation – it says that the monk 'lives detached'. Of course, it is easy to misunderstand this idea of detachment entirely (so that Bhikkhu Bodhi's translation, 'abides independent', is more helpful). Some Buddhists have been known carefully to detach themselves from other living beings and think that they are thereby following the Buddha's teaching. But to be detached really means that your attention is not exclusively directed to the care and nourishment of your own body. You have some care for the bodies of other people too – indeed, for the bodies of beings in general. They may very well be contingent phenomena, but that is no reason not to treat them with care and, up to a point, as though they are extensions of oneself.

'Mindfulness that "there is a body"', adds the *Sutta* in the concluding part of this section, 'is simply established in him to the extent necessary for bare knowledge and mindfulness.' In other words, the body has no absolute reality of its own, however much we like to think it has, and we should cherish it simply as a vehicle for spiritual development. Again, note that the *Sutta* refers to 'the body', not 'my body' – no question of 'I' or 'mine'. It is simply a set of phenomena that have arisen in dependence upon causes and conditions, and seeing it like that helps to reduce our attachment to it. In this way, awareness of the body and its movements allows the practitioner to sustain intensity of mindfulness in situations far removed from seated meditation. Indeed, like awareness of the breathing, such awareness can become a vehicle for reflections that are not feasible in states of deep meditative concentration (even if they derive their force and focus from those states). The effectiveness of these reflections involves carrying them over from meditation into every aspect of day-to-day life, i.e. it involves a continuity of mindfulness.

It is this reflective quality that calls into question our mistaken views about ourselves and about those around us, and so brings about lasting change. By reflecting as best we can between meditation sessions, we develop a conceptual basis from which true knowledge and vision can arise. Such reflections by their very nature have a guiding influence on our conduct, and of course they have a truly transformative effect when animated by the arising of true insight.

# 5
# LOOKING

> 'Again, bhikkhus, a bhikkhu reviews this same body up from the soles of the feet and down from the top of the hair, bounded by skin, as full of many kinds of impurity thus: "In this body there are head-hairs, body-hairs, nails, teeth, skin, flesh, sinews, bones, bone-marrow, kidneys, heart, liver, diaphragm, spleen, lungs, large intestines, small intestines, contents of the stomach, faeces, bile, phlegm, pus, blood, sweat, fat, tears, grease, spittle, snot, oil of the joints, and urine." Just as though there were a bag with an opening at both ends full of many sorts of grain, such as hill rice, red rice, beans, peas, millet, and white rice, and a man with good eyes were to open it and review it thus: "This is hill rice, this is red rice, these are beans, these are peas, this is millet, this is white rice"; so too, a bhikkhu reviews this same body ... as full of many kinds of impurity thus: "In this body there are head-hairs ... and urine."'

We do not normally think of our bodies as intrinsically unpleasant. We might spend a while in front of the bathroom mirror each morning preparing our body for public view, but we generally feel that these preparations are enough to render us inoffensive in the eyes of our fellow human beings. After all, when we look at the bodies of other people, and even when we come into physical contact with them, it is often quite a pleasant experience. But, of course, we don't see the whole picture. When we see or touch the body, we are aware of its surface – but what about all those internal processes, the organs, the fat, the blood and bones? These are not the features that usually spring to mind when we think of bodies, especially not our own, and yet they are as necessary to the body's make-up as anything we can see.

This section of the *Sutta* is designed to give us a more complete perception of the body, a more balanced response to it, and therefore a deeper awareness and understanding of its nature. You are meant to start the meditation by mentally comparing the body to a bag in which various kinds of grain are mixed together, the body's outer skin being imagined as the container of all the thirty-one kinds of bodily substance. Thus far, unpleasantness does not enter into the picture – the analogy is meant simply to enable us to view the body's constituents with the attitude that we would bring to the neutral task of sorting out a bag of mixed grains. This will lessen both our personal identification with the body and our resistance to taking notice of its unpleasant aspects, for, of course, the recollection of the body's 'foulness' is not an abstract, conceptual affair, and the *Sutta* drives this home by relentlessly listing the contents of this 'bag'. When we start to consider them in isolation – the hair, nails, and teeth, organs such as kidney, heart, and liver, and various kinds of pus, grease, blood, sweat, and so on – we are likely to feel a sense of revulsion. And this is the object of the practice: not only to become aware of the body's contents but actively to cultivate a sense that it is revolting.

Why then should we want to cultivate revulsion towards the human body? Is it any more objective to view the body as foul than to view it as fair? Would it not be more positive to cultivate a sense of the beauty of the human form? In fact, the Buddha's intention here is not to tell us what an objective view of the human body would be like, but to restore a balance in our response to it, to enable us to experience it more as it really is. It is because we have a fundamental bias towards wanting to see the body as beautiful that we must acknowledge that it is repulsive as well – although in itself it cannot be said to be either one or the other. It is a case of bending the bamboo the other way, to use a traditional metaphor, or looking at the other side of the picture. We will consider later the extent to which this practice might be appropriate for us; first, let us try to grasp its original purpose.

The things we are enjoined to perceive as impure or unlovely are exactly those aspects of life about which we delude ourselves most compulsively. The body is impermanent – sooner or later it will break down and die, and thus it cannot make us permanently happy, however much time, effort, and money we spend on keeping it healthy and beautiful. It is simply not worth expending energy on pampering the body, adorning it and trying to make it attractive; it will not repay the attention we lavish upon it. The only reason for looking after it is so that it can function as the basis for the cultivation of truer, deeper beauty – the beauty of higher states of consciousness. If we are too attached to the attractive physical aspects of our own body and the bodies of other people, we can all too easily fail to see that deeper beauty.

The main target in cultivating revulsion of the body is of course the huge power over our lives of sexual desire. Followers of the Theravādin tradition commonly recite the list of bodily constituents like a sort of mantra as an antidote to this, the strongest form of attraction of all. In the grip of sexual attraction we can scarcely help relating to other people just as bodies, or even as objects. The more we look to others to gratify our own desires, seeing them as members of a particular sex, the less we can relate to them as individuals. The point of cultivating revulsion towards the physical body of someone whom we find attractive is in fact to give room to the imagination so that we can see that person as an emergent individual rather than just as someone who arouses our sexual interest.

So the aim is not to see ourselves or other people as loathsome. The practice is a corrective meant to help us see through our infatuation with the surface of human existence and learn to adopt a more objective view, so that we can relate more truly and deeply to life's essential purpose. By drawing our attention to those aspects of the body we normally experience as repulsive, and away from those aspects that are attractive to us, the practice encourages us to reflect on what bodies are really like, to see the skull beneath the skin, as Eliot says.[51]

Love is blind, as the saying goes: we simply overlook someone's less attractive features if we are strongly drawn to them. Of course, it is not just someone's body to which we are attracted; we are also drawn to the character inside the body, so to speak – indeed, one may be attracted to all sorts of aspects of a person to which a relationship with their body may give access. These features often – in a way quite rightly – make us oblivious to a person's physical defects. However, there is a difference between freely choosing to look at a person's best qualities and being 'captivated' by them. What the *Sutta* is concerned with here is freedom from sexual craving.

We say that we are 'captivated' or 'charmed' or 'bewitched' by someone when in truth we are in thrall to our own craving. We might think that it is their sparkling eyes or shining hair that attracts us, but it is really what that feature has come to represent in our own mind. If the features of our beloved are less than perfect, our desire will override our direct experience of what is actually there – after all, very few people are perfect to look at. Our capacity to be selective in the way we perceive the loved one shows that what we think of as attractive in someone's appearance is a function of our craving rather than anything intrinsic to that person.

The method offered by the *Sutta* is to reflect on an organ or some recognizable bodily tissue in isolation from the rest, to prevent it from being subsumed in the general perception of the body as a whole as being essentially attractive. A lover is thrilled at the idea of taking his beloved in his arms, but the romance inevitably palls if he starts to think of that alluring figure as a bundle of physiological processes. The technique is to keep focusing on the parts of the body separately – all the traditional thirty-one items. One cannot deny that the thirty-one substances are present in the body, nor that the idea of handling them separately would dampen one's enthusiasm for handling the body as a whole. Thinking of the snot or spittle of one's beloved is hardly calculated to inflame the passions. By reversing our normal view of the body, the recollection of the foulness of the body helps us to look unblinkingly at what exactly we are attracted to. It can be helpful, when you are losing sleep and mindfulness and self-respect over some very attractive person, to ask yourself, 'What really is this thing that I am so obsessed with getting intimately involved with? Let's see, there's head-hairs, body-hairs, nails, teeth, skin, flesh, sinews, bones, bone-marrow, kidneys …'

In the *Therīgāthā*, the verses of the early Buddhist sisters, there is a tale that illustrates in a shocking manner how the list of body parts prescribed for recitation in the *Satipaṭṭhāna Sutta* differs from the infatuated lover's recital of beautiful qualities – 'Her hair! Her eyes! Her lips!…' The story concerns Subhā, a female wanderer of exceptional physical beauty. One day, while walking alone in the forest, Subhā is accosted by 'a certain libertine of Rājagaha' who bars her way and tries to 'solicit ... her to sensual pleasures' in contravention of her monastic vows. ''Tis thine eyes,' murmurs the youth (in Mrs Rhys David's Edwardian translation) 'the sight of which feedeth the depth of my passion.' Subhā, however, is no ordinary woman. She has, so the verse tells us, strengthened her resolve towards Enlightenment under former Buddhas in previous lifetimes, and having received the precepts from Śākyamuni himself, has at last established herself as a 'non-returner' (a very high level of spiritual attainment). This is unfortunate for the young man in our story, whose passion continues to grow despite all Subhā's efforts to help him see sense. She repeatedly points out that the body is an aggregation of foul substances and that no ultimately real self or beauty can be found in it. 'What is this eye but a little ball lodged in the fork of a hollow tree?' she asks. But the youth will not take no for an answer, and drives Subhā to a drastic and dramatic gesture. She gouges out one of her own eyes and offers it to him, to do with as he wishes. The youth, as one might expect, is horrified: his passion withers on the spot and he implores her forgiveness.[52]

Subhā's story shows how craving turns objective truth on its head. Subhā means 'shining', 'beautiful', and also 'auspicious'. But Subhā is not beautiful because of her good looks. Her beauty is not physical but spiritual, even transcendental. When she plucks out her eye, it does nothing to blind her spiritual vision or diminish her loveliness. It is the libertine who, with two good eyes, remains truly blind in the spiritual sense. The concern of this story is not to denigrate what seems to us beautiful but to expose the lack of spiritual vision exemplified by the young man, and thus to encourage us to look beyond mundane beauty. The story is meant to jolt us out of our usual distorted way of seeing things, which is summarized in the Buddha's teaching of the four *viparyāsas* or 'topsy-turvy views'. Firstly, we see things that are impermanent as though they were permanent. Secondly, we see things that are intrinsically painful as if they were pleasant. Thirdly, we see things that are insubstantial as if they had some ultimately real essence, and especially we imagine that we ourselves have some kind of fixed self. And fourthly, we see things that are crude and unremarkable as if they were beautiful.[53] It is especially this last *viparyāsa* that the practice of *aśubha bhāvanā* is designed to put right.

From the upside-down perspective of worldly consciousness, the physical body is the centre of all our activity and interest. We work to feed the body and give it shelter, we clothe it and decorate it, we might even fall in love with other bodies and, in time, bring new bodies into being. According to Buddhism, however, we are determined not by the physical body but by consciousness. Our concern should therefore be less with the quality of what we look at and more with the quality with which we look. By transforming our level of awareness, we can transform not only what we are but also the world we live in. The polarity, if it can really be described as such, is not between the pleasant and the unpleasant, but between the relatively crude and the relatively subtle. Through concentrated meditation, one's interests and desires come to be more and more absorbed in refined states of being and are led upwards towards forms that are purer and more intrinsically beautiful than anything to be found on the gross material plane.

Without direct experience, a tremendous leap of the imagination is required to trust in the possibility of such refined states. Usually, not daring to make the leap, we stay firmly attached to 'the devil we know', the physical body and the material world it inhabits. This, essentially, is the problem faced by Nanda, who was another of the Buddha's disciples, as well as being his cousin. According to a story from the *Udāna* of the Pāli canon, Nanda wants to pursue the spiritual life, but he is held back from committing himself fully by his lack of experience of higher modes of consciousness. Instead, he finds himself longing for his former lover, a beautiful Śākyan girl. He cannot develop faith in the Dharma when the greatest pleasure he knows is the love of a beautiful woman: he can't imagine anything more satisfying than that. The Buddha knows that Nanda will have to broaden his spiritual perspective if he is to commit himself to the spiritual path. By means of his magical powers, he therefore transports Nanda to the Heaven of the Thirty-Three, a '*deva* realm' coterminous with highly absorbed states of meditative concentration. There, Nanda at last encounters a beauty deeper and lovelier than he has ever imagined, enjoying the company of celestial nymphs whose 'dove-footed' beauty far outshines the crude, merely physical beauty of his earthly lover. This is enough to make his confidence in the Dharma unshakeable: he can see for himself that higher states of consciousness exist. From this point onwards he is able to make swift progress on the path, because material objects of desire no longer attract him.[54]

From the perspective of heightened consciousness, the apparent beauty of the mundane world appears grotesque. This is Subhā's teaching to the libertine from Rājagaha: it is not her eye plucked from its socket that is grotesque, but his lust for her 'beautiful eyes'. Her objectivity is not so much about what is beautiful as about what is true. Unable to see how cramped and gloomy, how mediocre, our experience really is, we presume that all we have ever known is all there is to know and form our judgements accordingly.

The traditional teaching as delivered to celibate monks can sometimes give the impression that the repulsiveness of the body is the reality of it and that its attractiveness is purely illusory. But, of course, a sense of the repulsiveness of the body does not constitute a dispassionate view. I am reminded of a doctor friend of mine who once read the passage of Buddhaghosa's *Visuddhimagga* in which the process of digestion is described as part of the meditation known as the 'contemplation of the loathsomeness of food'. Buddhaghosa goes through the whole process with what one can only call gusto, lingering almost lovingly over the way in which great lumps of coarse, heavy matter are tossed into the mouth and from there descend to the stomach, where all sorts of unspeakable things happen to them.[55] It is another example of 'bending the bamboo the other way', of course, but my friend was quite indignant about it. 'It is clear,' he said, 'that Buddhaghosa has not understood the delicate, complex, and miraculous phenomenon that is the human digestive process.' Clearly, attractiveness and repulsiveness are both subjective judgements; my friend's admiration of the digestive system was in its way just as valid as the repulsion advocated by Buddhaghosa.

The approach of the Theravādin monk might be to say, 'You may think this woman is attractive, but she is really just a bag of impurities,' but to take this attitude literally is to make the classic mistake of confusing method with doctrine. It is on some occasions recommended that one should dwell on a certain aspect of something not because it is the absolute, objective truth of the matter, but because to see it that way is beneficial to one's spiritual development. The methodological approach consists in fastening your attention upon one aspect of something – while for the time being ignoring other aspects – for a specific practical purpose. The fundamental Buddhist teaching of *duḥkha* (Pāli *dukkha*), for example, the idea that existence is characterized essentially by suffering, is to be understood as methodological truth rather than 'objective' truth. Obviously there is more to life than suffering, but it is essential to the development of awareness and faith that we keep the truth of *duḥkha* in mind. Likewise, one might choose to reflect on a particular aspect of bodily existence for a particular purpose. The emphasis of Tibetan Buddhism on the preciousness of the human body is an encouragement to make the most of the unique opportunity we have to practise the Dharma – an opportunity that is indeed precious. But it is simply a method of practice, just as much as the Theravādin exhortation to reflect on the body's foulness; in reality, the body is no more precious than it is foul. Neither approach is intended to push home a point about what bodies actually are – they are techniques, not statements of metaphysical truth.

However, perhaps we need to question whether 'bending the bamboo the other way' by contemplating the foulness of the body is likely to have the desired effect in our own case. Most western Buddhists have considerable work to do to establish the basis of healthy positivity necessary for any sort of spiritual life, and this might be made still more difficult if we were to dwell upon ugliness. Viewing each other as bags of manifold impurities is hardly the best way to start developing compassion and empathy and appreciation, particularly at the start of our spiritual career. Better, perhaps, to banish thoughts of all that pus and phlegm and bile, and with them the limited, literal perspective of attraction and repulsion, of mundane beauty versus ugliness, to apprehend an altogether higher beauty, a beauty that is not reliant on physical conditions at all. Lama Govinda made this the theme of a short story called 'Look Deeper!' The narrator is walking along a road with a Theravādin *bhikkhu* when a young village girl passes them by. 'What a beautiful girl!' says the narrator, whereupon the monk, as might be expected, replies, 'Look deeper. It's only a bag of bones.' At this point the bodhisattva Avalokiteśvara manifests before them and in turn tells the monk to look deeper still – to look deeper than the bag of bones and see the living, suffering human being, with all her potential for spiritual development.[56]

The message is that we have to go beyond the superficial appearance of the body, just as we have to go beyond the literal meaning of the words of the *Sutta*, any *sutta*. Bodies as we encounter them are never simply bodies. The most truly beautiful aspect of any human being is the fact that he or she is, potentially at least, a spiritual being. Even though that spiritual potential is sometimes well hidden, we cannot afford to reduce anyone to a bag of impurities if we want to appreciate that beauty. The beauty we experience through the senses is not the highest beauty available to us, and when we have some experience of this higher beauty, we are at last able to shake off the hold that worldly desire has on us. We can begin to transform our habitual attachment to what we think we see and, by extension, to what we think we are.

# 6
# GETTING DOWN TO THE ESSENTIALS

> 'Again, bhikkhus, a bhikkhu reviews this same body, however it is placed, however disposed, as consisting of elements thus: "In this body there are the earth element, the water element, the fire element, and the air element." Just as though a skilled butcher or his apprentice had killed a cow and was seated at the crossroads with it cut up into pieces; so too, a bhikkhu reviews this same body ... as consisting of the elements thus: "In this body there are the earth element, the water element, the fire element, and the air element."'

Much of what is known about ancient Indian society in the days of the Buddha comes from the Pāli scriptures. Quite apart from the many references to issues of religious belief and philosophical speculation current at that time, the *sutta*s are full of interesting details about the way ordinary people lived. The *Satipaṭṭhāna Sutta* is no exception to this, and following the wood-turner and the trader in grains and pulses now appears the skilled butcher, setting out his stall at a crossroads, where presumably he will have good prospect of some brisk trade. So here is evidence that beef was on open sale in ancient India, although a lot of Hindu – especially brahminical – lore vehemently disclaims this, because today the cow is a sacred animal to the Hindus. However, the matter-of-fact way in which the Buddha uses this image suggests that in his day beef butchers were quite common. As in the case of 'the man with good eyes' who is imagined opening up the bag of grain in the previous section, the Buddha is evidently using a familiar feature of Indian village life – if one that will not appeal to the sheltered sensibilities of modern western vegetarians – to illustrate the analytic method, and its meaning would have been immediately apparent to the Buddha's audience.

Thus, we are being called upon to divide the human body mentally into what pertains to each of the four elements, just as the butcher physically divides the carcass of the cow into the various joints of meat. Clearly, the same analytical quality is being applied to the body as in the previous section, but the emphasis here is on one's own body, and we are looking not for the impurity of the body but for the four great primary elements: earth, water, fire, and air.

There is often no direct equivalent for a Pāli term in English, and superficial resemblances between Pāli terms and their English translations can hide deeper and more subtle differences of meaning. This is certainly the case with the word 'element': while it is the only translation available to us, its associations and shades of meaning are quite at odds with the basic concepts by which traditional Buddhist thinking is shaped. To state the difference very briefly, Buddhist thought understands the elements in terms of the changing processes that constitute our world, rather than as basic substances from which the world is made up. In the *Satipaṭṭhāna Sutta* the word translated as 'element' is *dhātu*, but an alternative term frequently used is *mahābhūta. Mahā* means 'great', and *bhūta* comes from the word *bhavati*, which literally means 'become'; so the derivation of the word *mahābhūta* reflects the underpinning analysis: that the elements are not fixed but in a constant process of coming into being. In the *Visuddhimagga* also, Buddhaghosa is careful to define the elements not as substances in their own right, but as tendencies: a tendency towards solidity for *paṭhavī* (earth), motility or undulating movement for *āpo* (water), expansiveness for *vāyo* (air) and radiation for *tejo* (fire).[57] The elements, in other words, are to be thought of as different qualities of physical form.

*Rūpa* is the Pāli term for the physical aspect of our existence, the mental aspect being covered by the term *nāma*; the two terms usually appear together in the compound *nāma-rūpa*, which covers the whole of our psychophysical being, both mind and body. According to the analysis of the Abhidhamma, the four material elements are the first four items on a whole list of subdivisions of *rūpa*.[58] *Rūpa* is usually translated into English as 'matter', but here also there is potential for confusion, because *rūpa* is not matter in the sense of something that exists independently of human consciousness; here Buddhism parts company with western science. In Buddhist philosophy there is no conception of a split or opposition between mind and matter; 'matter' is said to arise in dependence on human consciousness, and there can be no consciousness without some kind of form. Form (to use another possible English translation of *rūpa*) is not just an idea; it has a reality. In our contact with things, there is always a factor that is not under our control. When your body comes up against a solid object, you certainly know about it – and whatever it is that you come up against can be termed *rūpa*. *Rūpa* is – in the words of Herbert Guenther in *Philosophy and Psychology in the Abhidhamma* – 'the objective content of the perceptual situation'.[59] This may seem a dry and academic way of describing experience, but it does explain quite accurately what is meant by the term. A perceptual situation, an experience, comprises two basic components: first, the object of consciousness, and second, what you as the perceiver bring to the situation. When you see a flower, the recognition 'this is a flower' comes from you, not from the flower. Similarly, all the characteristics of the flower – its colour, its fragrance, a sense of its beauty, and so on – arise in you as perceptions. But not everything in this perceptual situation arises from or in you. There is the flower itself, the external object or stimulus to which the act of perception refers, and this – whatever it is – is *rūpa*. I say 'whatever it is' because in a sense it can only be a mystery. We can only know it through our senses, never 'objectively'.

What distinguishes physical form from other aspects of our experience, such as ideas or emotions, is that it is knowable to us through the five physical senses, principally touch and sight, rather than through the mind alone. As we move about in the world and *rūpa* impinges on our consciousness, the senses first of all register bare sensations without interpreting them. But if we are to function, we need to be able to discriminate between these various sensations and work out what they might mean, so the mind rapidly sets about organizing that contact with the objects of the senses into the subdivisions of *rūpa*.

If *rūpa* is the objective component of perception, the four primary elements, the *mahābhūtas*, are ways of classifying what kind of form that objective component appears to take. There is solidity, or the quality of resistance to our touch; there is fluidity and cohesiveness; there is the quality of heat or cold; and there is the quality of lightness and expansiveness. Each of these primary qualities can be further classified, but for our present purposes it will be enough to focus upon this fourfold designation of *rūpa*. The important point is that earth, water, fire, and air are not properties of the objects of which we are conscious, but ways of understanding consciousness itself.

The Pāli commentaries say that a *mahābhūta* is a great feat such as that performed by a magician when he makes you perceive clay as gold or water as fire.[60] In just the same way we perceive *rūpa*, the objective content of the perceptual situation, as if it were literally earth, water, or fire. But this is an illusion born of our limited understanding. We cannot say categorically what is there, but only what appears to us to be there. What earth or water are in themselves, if in fact they are anything at all, we cannot know. Earth and water are just names we assign to particular kinds of sensation. We have no option but to connect up our sensations to form ideas of things that we suppose to be 'out there' in the world beyond our selves, but if we are not careful, that quality of resistance or fluidity takes on a life of its own and we turn what is essentially an experience or a mode of experiencing into a supposedly concrete thing. We make sense of experience through language – this is how we learn to cope with it – but the problem with language is that it almost compels us to treat ever-changing processes as entities. We need to be on our guard against this, especially when we are engaged in conceptual thinking. *Rūpa*, for instance, is a conceptual term which does not refer to any 'thing' we can directly experience. We only experience the things for which *rūpa* is the general term – that is to say, the four elements. But can we even say that we experience the elements directly? We do not experience a thing called earth, but only a sensation of resistance; not water, but only wetness. And we do not experience wetness or solidity as they are in themselves; we only experience them as they seem to us to be. As the *Perfection of Wisdom sūtras* tell us, forms are like dreams, illusions, the reflection of the moon in water.[61] All things are like ghosts: when they appear, we know that we see them, but what they are in reality, we do not know. This is brought out by another meaning of the term *mahābhūta*: 'great ghost', of which more later.

As far as the *Satipaṭṭhāna Sutta* is concerned, the aim of the first part of the practice is to be aware of the four elements as qualities extending through and beyond one's own body. The very fabric of your body is in perpetual change; you are the nexus of all kinds of interactions which are going on as the body powers away, continually renewing itself by taking in foodstuffs, water, and heat, and continually expelling them again. This analysis does not conceive of a finite number of inanimate elements combining and recombining according to fixed physical laws. There is only the awareness of one's body as it impinges upon consciousness according to these various modes of contact. Unlike the elements of science, these great elements are alive. We ourselves are composed of them and it is our own living consciousness that contemplates their incessant flux across the field of the body in the meditation practice called the six element practice.

In practical terms the difference between the elements as conceived in Buddhist philosophy and a more materialist theory has important consequences. It requires us to bring a responsive awareness to what we perceive, because we are active participants in consciousness, not merely receivers of messages from a fixed external universe. This is tremendously significant, calling into question the whole distinction between a living 'me' and a non-living 'not me'. In our modern techno-scientific culture we are able to do all kinds of things with and to the natural world, but as a result we have lost our affinity with it. Alienated from nature, no longer experiencing it as a living presence, we sorely need to recapture the sense that to be human is to be part of nature.

This feeling, of course, came naturally to people in the early days of Buddhism. The Buddha and his disciples lived in the midst of nature, wandering on foot for eight or nine months of the year from one village to another through the jungles of northern India. Their days and nights were spent in forests, in parks, on mountains, or by rivers; out in the elements, sleeping under the stars. Theirs was a world populated not only by human beings and animals, but by gods and spirits of the hills and streams, trees and flowers. The sense of the physical environment experienced as a living presence is a significant theme in all the oldest texts of the Buddhist tradition. For all its factual content, the Pāli canon also reminds us that the supernatural world was a reality for the early Buddhists; and one might say that it was the continuous presence of nature that made it so.

All the episodes of major significance in the Buddha's life history unfolded in close contact with a natural world which actively responded to his presence. He was born in the open air, we are told, while his mother supported herself by holding a bough laden with flowers. He gained Enlightenment beneath the bodhi tree, seated on a carpet of fresh grass. And in the end he passed away between twin *sāl* trees which sprinkled his body in homage with blossoms out of season. This sense of nature as a vibrant and animated presence is often the part of the Pāli canon that is edited out of selected translations into English; the editors tend to leave intact the outline of the Buddha's teaching but include little of the world in which it is set. If some mythic strands are left, the modern reader is likely to skip over the accounts of *nāgas*, *yakṣas*, and other supernatural beings to concentrate on the 'real' stuff, the doctrine. But the gods and goddesses, and all the various kinds of non-human beings, are not there simply as ornamentation. Their presence is itself part of the teaching. They provide glimpses of an ancient mode of human consciousness fully integrated into a universe of value, meaning, and purpose. To miss them is to miss the poetry, and the heart of the Buddha's message.

If we are really to understand the contemplation of the four elements in the *Satipaṭṭhāna Sutta*, therefore, we need to find ways of deepening our understanding of what this elemental imagery meant to the early Buddhists, how they knew those mythic figures and lived in relation to them. To help us do this, we can return to the term *mahābhūta*, whose meaning hints at the living, inherently ungraspable quality of the elements. *Mahābhūta*, 'great ghost', means something that has somehow arisen, or has been conjured up – a mysterious, other-worldly apparition. To think of the four elements as 'great ghosts' suggests that we are dealing not with concepts or inanimate matter, but with living forces. The universe is alive, magically so, and the haunting appearance within it of the four great elements makes that experience inherently mysterious and inaccessible to definitive knowledge. Rather than trying to pin down reality with technical and scientific thinking, the Buddhist conception of the four elements helps to bring about a fusion of objective and subjective knowledge, enabling us, like Shakespeare's King Lear, to 'take upon's the mystery of things'.[62]

This does not mean that the Buddhist conception of the elements is vague or imprecise, nor that the rational faculty is no longer necessary. Concepts are vital – but they do not exhaust the whole of life's mystery. To understand the four elements as psychophysical states rather than as material substances or states of matter undermines the conventional idea of what the body is. It reminds us that the division between inner and outer worlds is a product of dualistic thinking. Rather than any division between a thing called matter and a thing called mind, or a thing called body and a thing called consciousness, there is a continuity running all the way through, a continuity of our awareness patterned in different ways. If we can really understand this, those inner and outer worlds become interfused in a deeper, more meaningful vision of what it is to be alive.

All this runs counter to the way we in the West have been conditioned to experience the body and the world of which it is a part. But it must surely be better – or at the very least more fun – to be an animist and feel that the whole world is animated by spirits, rather than gazing out at a world of non-living matter which occasionally and haphazardly comes to life, and in which even our own life is ultimately reducible to inanimate matter. All the same, it is not easy for us to develop a genuine feeling that the material elements are really living entities. Conversely, it is all too easy to generate a false and sentimental notion that 'the hills are alive' by projecting all kinds of imaginary properties on to the world. We cannot generate a belief in, say, naiads and dryads by force of will; nor can we deny what we know scientifically about the way the universe operates. We have somehow to hunt for a real feeling for the life of things, even from our sophisticated viewpoint. It starts with intuitive knowledge, not a set of beliefs.

There is a hierarchy: rocks are not as alive as plants, and plants are not as alive as human beings. We have to draw the line somewhere – it would be hard to regard, say, stainless steel as a living substance; each of us will have a point at which we stop acknowledging and respecting the life of another being or 'thing' and start simply using it for our own convenience. For some unfortunate people this line is drawn even at certain other human beings – of course this is also unfortunate for the people with whom they come into contact. At the other end of the spectrum, the Tibetans used to refuse to engage in mining for minerals: they would pan for gold but not, as the Chinese are now doing in Tibet, disturb the earth and the dragons that they believe guard the gold it conceals.

I would go so far as to say that a universe conceived of as dead cannot be a universe in which one stands any chance of attaining Enlightenment. (Whether you stand any chance in a living universe is of course up to you.) It may be difficult for us to get back to the view of the world that came naturally to our ancestors, but poets have persisted in seeing the universe as alive: surely no poet could have a totally Newtonian outlook, the kind of attitude that Blake termed 'single vision' and 'Newton's sleep'.[63] Milton, for example, traces the origin of mining to Hell itself: in *Paradise Lost* the devils start excavating minerals in order to manufacture artillery to use against heaven.[64] One could even interpret the whole Romantic movement as expressing a great protest against the Newtonian picture of nature and a reassertion of essentially pagan values.

To get a more vivid sense of the elements, you could think of them in terms of the colours and shapes of the Buddhist stupa, which is said to symbolize the elements. Or you could let your imagination go even further and think of the elements as gods or goddesses (traditionally, earth and water are goddesses and fire and air are gods), building up connections with them that will gradually deepen and enrich your feeling for them, so that you experience them more and more vibrantly, with more and more emotional colour. You could also make use of the mythological system of elements connected with western alchemy, though it offers not single personifications so much as multiple denizens of each element: gnomes in the earth, undines in the water, salamanders in the fire, and sylphs in the air. Suggesting that one should summon up such beings through the imagination is not to say that they are imaginary. Local spirits do not represent a primitive attempt to explain things in a pseudo-scientific way: when people speak of dryads in the trees, they are trying to express their actual experience of these 'things' as living presences.

The elements that we experience as earth, water, fire, and air are represented at the highest, transcendental level by the four female Buddhas of the Vajrayāna mandala of the five archetypal Buddhas (the fifth, central figure representing the element of space) just as different characteristics of wisdom are represented by the male Buddhas. The female Buddhas inseparably united with their male consorts thus represent the highest conceivable sublimation of one's experience of the four great elements. In other words, there is a continuity of experience running all the way through our everyday classifications and categories to Enlightenment itself. Mind and matter, body and spirit, are not separate things but patterns we can recognize in what is really an unbroken continuity of experience.

# 7
# DYING

'Again, bhikkhus, as though he were to see a corpse thrown aside in a charnel ground, one, two, or three days dead, bloated, livid, and oozing matter, a bhikkhu compares this same body with it thus: "This body too is of the same nature, it will be like that, it is not exempt from that fate."...

'Again, as though he were to see a corpse thrown aside in a charnel ground, being devoured by crows, hawks, vultures, dogs, jackals, or various kinds of worms, a bhikkhu compares this same body with it thus: "This body too is of the same nature, it will be like that, it is not exempt from that fate."...

'Again, as though he were to see a corpse thrown aside in a charnel ground, a skeleton with flesh and blood, held together with sinews ... a fleshless skeleton smeared with blood, held together with sinews ... a skeleton without flesh and blood, held together with sinews ... disconnected bones scattered in all directions – here a hand-bone, there a foot-bone, here a shin-bone, there a thigh-bone, here a hip-bone, there a back-bone, here a rib-bone, there a breast-bone, here an arm-bone, there a shoulder-bone, here a neck-bone, there a jaw-bone, here a tooth, there the skull – a bhikkhu compares this same body with it thus: "This body too is of the same nature, it will be like that, it is not exempt from that fate."

'...That too is how a bhikkhu abides contemplating the body as a body.

'Again, as though he were to see a corpse thrown aside in a charnel ground, bones bleached white, the colour of shells ... bones heaped up, more than a year old ... bones rotted and crumbled to dust, a bhikkhu compares this same body with it thus: "This body too is of the same nature, it will be like that, it is not exempt from that fate."'

There are a number of stories in Buddhism and also in the Christian tradition of how the realization that they are going to die has changed the whole course of a person's life. One such story is that of St Bruno, who lived in France during the Middle Ages. The definitive event of the saint's early life occurred when as a young cleric he attended the funeral of his teacher, the canon of Notre Dame, a learned and pious man of the church. On the day of the funeral, the elders of the cathedral and of the city gathered to mark his passing, the corpse was carried in procession to the graveside, and the recitation of the office for the dead commenced in the usual manner. But as the words '*responde mihi*' were intoned, the entire congregation witnessed an eerie interruption to the proceedings. Slowly the body of the dead man half-raised itself and called out in a piteous voice, 'I am accused,' then sank back down onto the bier. Horrified, the priests put off the interment – but on the next day, and the next, the same thing happened. On the second day, at the words '*responde mihi*' the corpse called out, 'I am judged and found guilty' and then, on the third day, 'I am condemned.' Once the body had let out this final cry, the congregation, as one might imagine, was stunned. Nonetheless, the late canon had evidently received his judgement, and since he had been found wanting, the body could no longer be considered fit for Christian burial. The priests, St Bruno among them, could do no more than throw the corpse into an unhallowed grave in a field outside the city. The young man, profoundly influenced by this awful incident, resolved to live the life of a monk and eventually founded the order of Carthusians, perhaps the most austere of all Christian monastic brotherhoods.

Even if we never have an eerie experience like this – and it is very unlikely that we ever will – to come close to a dead body, however it happens, brings us face-to-face with impermanence in its most naked form. The body is essentially a part of the natural world. We have quite literally borrowed our bodies from the universe, and after death they will crumble away into a few handfuls of dust. It is essential to recollect this, and keep recollecting it, if we are ever to come to terms with this unpalatable but inescapable aspect of our existence. This is why the practice appears here in the *Satipaṭṭhāna Sutta*. It is as though we have to engage in these contemplations to convince ourselves that we really will die.

The method of the practice is to go to the charnel ground and there to find the corpse of a newly deceased person. Then you observe its decomposition and putrefaction through all its stages right down to the bare bones that are eventually left. The number and nature of the stages seem to be arbitrary – in his account of the practice in the *Visuddhimagga*, Buddhaghosa cites ten stages (rather than the nine enumerated here), with the grisly addition of a corpse 'swollen and bloated with gases' – but the process is basically the same.[65]

Just reading the description of these stages of decomposition is sobering. Unlike the contemplation of the body's foulness, however, the aim here is not to engender a sense of revulsion but to cultivate an awareness of the inherent impermanence of the body. Nonetheless, the practice will sound alarming to most Western readers and – even more alarming – we can take it that it is not meant to be just an exercise of the imagination. Although the translation says 'as though' or 'as if' one were to see a corpse, it is unlikely that this is hypothetical. You are meant actually to do it.

According to the tradition, these contemplations should be practised in a charnel ground, a place where bodies were simply thrown away and left to rot. These days this has been superseded by the practice of cremation, but in some parts of Asia it is still easy to find opportunities to practise the corpse reflections. Within minutes of your arrival in an Indian city you may well see a corpse, face uncovered, being borne shoulder-high through the streets, en route to its cremation. The body is usually still visible during the cremation itself, burning and disintegrating as the fire takes hold and the logs fall away, and even afterwards the partly destroyed corpse may be left exposed to view if the family cannot afford enough fuel to burn it completely.

In the Tibetan tradition there is usually no cremation at all but a 'sky burial'. The body is chopped into pieces and left in a place outside the city for vultures, dogs, and other animals to dispose of the remains; then, once all the animals have had their share, people gather the bones, grind them into powder and mix them with clay to form little images called *stza-stzas*, which are sometimes found enshrined, hundreds at a time, in wayside stupas. The sky burial may have something to do with the scarcity of firewood in Tibet, but it is also linked with the bodhisattva ideal of sacrificing your body for other living beings, so that even after death your body is not wasted.

An Indian cremation can be a moving occasion. I remember in particular the cremation of the mother of some friends of mine. My friends were Hindus, so – as is the Hindu custom – we took the body down to a sandy beach on the banks of the river. Dusk was falling as we arrived. As we built the funeral pyre I looked up from time to time to the forested mountainside which stretched away behind us towards Kalimpong. On the other side, mirrored in the river's surface, were the wooded slopes of the Darjeeling hills. Above us hung the deep blue of the early evening sky, and as we got the cremation under way the smoke rose and disappeared into the half-light. As the stars began to come out one by one far above us, a sense of peace seemed to settle all around our little group, faintly lit by the glow from the funeral pyre beside the silent river. You could hardly have a more inspiring ceremony to mark the body's dissolution back into the natural world. By contrast, the system by which the body arrives packed away in a box to be invisibly disposed of in the municipal crematorium seems to lack so much. It's a far cry even from the hearses drawn by plumed black horses that I remember from my boyhood in south London.

Some of my experiences of the physical realities of death in India were inspiring in a rather less agreeable way. During my early days in Kalimpong I was involved with the deaths of several people whom I knew quite well and this caused me to reflect deeply, especially as in each case I saw the corpse itself, and some of them were in quite an unpleasant condition. For example, there was Prince Latthakin, with whom I had stayed for a while shortly after my arrival in the town. Had Burma remained a monarchy he would have been its king, but as things turned out he died in poverty and obscurity, and in the end there wasn't even enough of his fortune left to pay for the funeral. When the old man died, I was no longer in close contact with him and was only called some four days later, by which time his body was in quite a dreadful state. Since I was to perform the funeral ceremony, I felt it was my duty to persuade the authorities to cover the cost of his cremation, which – reluctantly – they did. It was thus brought home to me – I was still a young man then – that death shows no respect for earthly privilege. Whatever his royal ancestry may have been, Prince Latthakin's was simply a lifeless body like any other.

> Imperious Caesar, dead and turned to clay,
> Might stop a hole to keep the wind away.[66]

In the secularized culture of the modern West, for many people the body's physical decease signals an end to everything, which is perhaps why an encounter with death sometimes raises fears of nightmarish proportions. Not wanting to die, unable to face the fact that everything we hold dear will one day just be snuffed out, we hide the realities of death away from view. In many parts of the East, people – at least those with a more traditional outlook – tend to accept the idea of death far more readily, due to their confidence that bodily death is not the end. For them, ancestral spirits and realms of rebirth remain very much a reality. The emphasis is not on what might happen after death – they know they will be reborn – but on what kind of rebirth they can expect.

In western societies these days comparatively few people have even seen a dead body. At an English funeral, the only suggestion that a corpse is involved is usually the sight of a shiny black car containing a coffin discreetly covered with flowers – hardly a basis for reflecting on death in the way the *Satipaṭṭhāna Sutta* suggests. Even if we go down to the local cemetery, it will be nothing like a charnel ground of the Buddha's day; all those gravestones in neat rows cannot bring the fact of physical decomposition before the mind's eye.

If one were serious about doing this practice, one would therefore need to seek out opportunities to see corpses in the process of dissolution. Some kinds of work – that of hospital porter or care home worker, for example – do of course involve very close contact with the realities of death. One could also conceivably arrange to visit a crematorium and ask to see a body being cremated. Of course, it is important to be aware that such experiences can be disturbing. In its full form the contemplation of the stages of the decomposition of a corpse is a practice for the spiritually mature; you have to know what you are letting yourself in for.

But most of us, sooner or later, will have to face a version of this practice with the death of someone close to us. Bereavement, dreadfully painful though it often is, provides a special opportunity to come to terms with our own impermanence. It is definitely not a good idea to do this meditation practice in relation to the body of someone you were close to. You might be able to contemplate the body of a stranger with equanimity, but the sight of a friend or relative literally deteriorating before your eyes can be terribly upsetting. In any case, when somebody close to you dies, the shock alone is enough to concentrate the mind. Death is an existential situation, and you don't have to sit down and meditate on impermanence at a time like that – you just need to maintain a clear awareness of what is happening in and around you, observe your reactions and responses, and try to understand why you think and feel the way you do. One thing you will almost certainly feel is fear. By its very nature, death threatens one's whole being. The instinct for survival is so strong that when death comes close, it is a terrifying experience, because one identifies so completely with the body.

One of the unnerving aspects of death is the inherent mystery of it. It is impossible to be sure what happens to consciousness after we have died. It is not even easy to be clear about the point at which death can be said to have taken place. One hesitates to use terms like soul or spirit, but there is clearly something that holds the physical functions together and organizes them into a sentient human being. At death, as this underlying consciousness begins to dissociate itself from the body, the process of physical decomposition also begins, but how the actual moment of death is to be identified is not fully agreed among medical professionals. And there are other medical traditions – the Tibetan Buddhist tradition is one – which hold that the dying process takes effect over a long period, longer than is usually recognized by Western medicine, in a definite series of stages, as the processes of body and consciousness break down and disperse.

The subtlety of the relationship between consciousness and physical form makes dealing with the body of someone who has just died a delicate matter. If you were still around, as it were, hovering close to your body after death, what effect would it have on your consciousness if the body were to be opened up for the purposes of autopsy? You might still feel something, although not necessarily physically, even after the point of medical death. If you take this seriously, you might feel a need to intervene, if possible, in the normal course of events following the death of someone you know, as the various medical officers and coroners become involved in disposing of the remains. It is a good idea to include in your will a statement of your own wishes if such a situation were to arise in your own case.

Indeed, it is important to make a will that includes whatever instructions you want to leave – especially if you consider yourself to be a Buddhist and want a Buddhist funeral. If you die intestate, things might not go as you would have wished. This is what almost happened after the sudden death of a woman I knew in Kalimpong. I had been away, and arrived back in town to find a scene not unlike something from the *Iliad*. On one side, the local Christians were claiming her body for a Christian burial. On the other, my own students were insisting that Miss Barclay had been a Buddhist and should have a Buddhist cremation. And in the middle were the police, who had been called in because she had died an accidental death, trying to make sense of the whole situation. Luckily I arrived in the nick of time and was able to produce documents signed in Miss Barclay's own hand to show beyond doubt that she had indeed been a Buddhist.[67] This settled the matter, and she was given a Buddhist funeral. So if you are a Buddhist and want to make sure you are disposed of in the proper Buddhist manner, you should make a will, appointing Buddhists as your executors if you can.

Making a will can also be considered to be a form of the practice being recommended here by the *Satipaṭṭhāna Sutta*. Even if you don't have the opportunity, or indeed the wish, to study the decomposition of a corpse at close quarters, just sitting down and writing your own will is a very good way of recollecting death. Not only are you acknowledging, objectively in black and white, the fact that you are going to die; you might also stipulate what you wish to happen after your death. People are often reluctant to make a will until quite late in life, as if by putting it off they are somehow keeping death at bay. Given the precarious nature of our existence, this is short-sighted, to say the least. We cannot afford to forget the fact that human life is essentially an unstable, fragile thing. Without a real sense of that impermanence, we cannot free ourselves from the idea that there are at least some things that we can depend upon never to change. Reflecting upon bodily death reminds us that everything is changing – our families, our homes, our country, even ourselves. There is nothing we can hang on to, nothing we can keep. Perhaps this is what we are really afraid of. Awareness of impermanence can be terrifying at first – it seems to deprive you of everything. But if you become fully convinced, both intellectually and emotionally, that the body will come to an end one day, and if you have sufficient positivity to make real changes to your priorities in life as a result, surely this is the way to the arising of transcendental insight.

Reflecting on impermanence is so important because through it we begin to break down the tendency to over-identify with the body, and thus the delusion of a fixed self is weakened. This is the heart of the matter. An experience of bereavement, for all its pain, is a precious opportunity to grow. If everything changes, indeed must do so, then you can change too. You can develop and grow; you need not be confined to what you are at present, or have been in the past. Impermanence is what makes the path possible, for without it there could be no transformation or creativity. You would be stuck with your old self for ever, with no hope of release. Think how terrible that would be! You might be able to put up with it for quite a while, but eventually life would become truly unbearable. Yet, paradoxically, here we are, clinging to this fixed view of self for all we are worth.

Impermanence is what enables us to turn our whole lives towards the ideal of Enlightenment. To speak of death is not necessarily to lapse into pessimism – it is just being realistic. Old age, grief, lamentation, and death are after all just facts. But life can still be positive, even though it sometimes involves having to face things we find unpleasant. If we are to grow, we will need to face those things, acknowledge them, and go beyond them. The overall process is positive, and the Buddhist vision expresses that positivity without seeing everything through a rosy mist or refusing to face unpleasant facts.

The recollection of death should therefore be as familiar to the Buddhist as it is strange to the person who hasn't given any thought to the fact that they will one day die. If you have never reflected on impermanence in any serious way, you will be in a difficult position when the time of your own death draws near. You won't suddenly be able to intensify your mindfulness if you haven't already developed sufficient momentum in your practice of it. This is when you will need to call your spiritual friends around you, to give you help and moral support. But although they will be able to help you to some extent, the best and wisest thing is to keep up your spiritual practice as an integral part of your life when you are free from sickness and danger. Do not leave it too late. One does not wish to be morbid, but we are reminded sometimes that we never know when we are going to be run over by the proverbial bus. The best policy is to concentrate your energies and pour them wholeheartedly not just into your practice of meditation or study, but into the whole of your spiritual life.

# 8
# FEELING

> 'And how, bhikkhus, does a bhikkhu abide contemplating feelings as feelings? Here, when feeling a pleasant feeling, a bhikkhu understands: "I feel a pleasant feeling"; when feeling a painful feeling, he understands: "I feel a painful feeling"; when feeling a neither-painful-nor-pleasant feeling, he understands: "I feel a neither-painful-nor-pleasant feeling." When feeling a worldly pleasant feeling, he understands: "I feel a worldly pleasant feeling"; when feeling an unworldly pleasant feeling, he understands: "I feel an unworldly pleasant feeling"; when feeling a worldly painful feeling, he understands: "I feel a worldly painful feeling"; when feeling an unworldly painful feeling, he understands: "I feel an unworldly painful feeling"; when feeling a worldly neither-painful-nor-pleasant feeling, he understands: "I feel a worldly neither-painful-nor-pleasant feeling"; when feeling an unworldly neither-painful-nor-pleasant feeling, he understands: "I feel an unworldly neither-painful-nor-pleasant feeling."'

Judging from what one reads about them, one gets the impression that the people of previous times experienced their feelings in a much more full-blooded way than we do in the urbanized, modern world. What stands out in the accounts of ancient and traditional societies is their sheer emotional energy. Take the ancient Greeks, for example. In the days of Plato and Socrates, it seems that people took their friendships very seriously indeed.

If they loved you, they would love you without reservation and do anything for you. But they hated unreservedly too, and made fearsome, even ruthless, adversaries. Life today might be more comfortable, but in comparison with the people of earlier times, we seem to live it in a very flat, lifeless emotional state. Going to work on the bus, or packed into a crowded train, our emotions are for the most part disengaged as we simply try to get through the day. One might well say that in this tepid, unresponsive state, we are 'out of touch with our feelings'.

Why is this? One obvious fact of life these days is that it is very complicated. The traditional society, in which one was born, lived, and died in the same place among the same people, is a thing of the past. Many people move every few years, and have to build up a new social network time after time. In these circumstances they have little chance to build up strong friendships outside the nuclear family, and the weakness of their connections with others makes it difficult for them to respond emotionally to the people around them.

However, as Western psychology tells us, those strong feelings do not go away, but remain repressed on a subconscious level. One of the aims of psychotherapy is to bring them to the surface and restore a full awareness of oneself as a whole personality. When Buddhist psychology refers to developing mindfulness of feelings, however, something rather different is meant from the 'getting in touch with one's feelings' with which psychotherapy is concerned – something less complex, though perhaps more useful. Indeed, being able to identify feelings (in the sense of *vedanā* as defined by Buddhist tradition) is what makes it possible for us to follow the Buddhist path.

The Pāli and Sanskrit term *vedanā* refers to feeling not in the sense of the emotions, but in terms of sensation. *Vedanā* is whatever pleasantness or unpleasantness we might experience in our contact with any physical or mental stimulus. To understand what we would call emotion, Buddhism looks at the way in which that pleasant or painful feeling is interwoven with our reactions and responses to it. In Buddhist psychology, *vedanā* is said to combine with *saṃskāra*, a volitional quality involving a tendency towards action. It is this combination of sensation with volition that approaches what we would recognize as fully developed emotion.

Feeling – whether pleasure or pain – is passive: that is, it arises as a result of all sorts of conditions. We can change feelings that arise in various ways by changing the conditions that give rise to them – opening the window when we're hot, to take the simplest of examples. But there is a certain kind of painful feeling against which we can do nothing to protect ourselves: the feelings that arise as a result of our past unskilful karma. These must simply be borne, although of course we can protect ourselves from future pain by making the effort to create fresh positive karma, even while we are experiencing pain.

It is very important that we learn to do this. Feelings of pleasure and pain are not themselves productive of fresh karma, but when we allow ourselves to react to them in the form of some emotion, and when that emotional reaction is negative, negative karmic consequences will follow. The practice of recollecting feelings is intended to help us be aware of our feelings before an emotional reaction to them sets in. If we can distinguish between the feelings we receive as impressions and what we then make of them, we will be able to take more responsibility for our emotions, while not suppressing our feelings. We need to know what we feel if we are to direct the flow of our emotional life in a positive way.

This is quite difficult because most of the time our feelings get lost in our emotional reactions to them. If you are meditating, for example, and you feel an itch or hear an ugly sound, the simple experience of feeling tends swiftly to be overlaid with an emotional reaction – in this case, of aversion. Our natural tendency is to want to get away from a feeling if it is painful and to want more of it if it is pleasant. Before we know where we are, we have thus shifted from the simple experience of pleasure or pain into some form of craving or hatred. The practice, therefore, is to keep returning to the bare feeling, allowing no space for these habitual reactions to establish themselves.

We do not always know when we are experiencing a feeling. Sometimes we might not feel much at all because our feelings are such a mixture of pleasure and pain that we do not register anything in particular, and sometimes our attention is elsewhere – we may be eating something tasty, for example, but be unaware of the pleasure of it because we are in the grip of an emotion unconnected with it. On the other hand, if we are not aware of the effect of pleasant or unpleasant feeling on our mental state, our awareness of that state may also be muted. Our feelings and our emotions are so closely linked that if our awareness of either is blunted, our level of awareness as a whole will be low. It is thus very important to be aware of our feelings: if we are not aware of the feeling quality in our experience, even as a component of a more complex mental state, our contact with phenomena will not affect us as it could, and emotionally speaking our consciousness will remain at a low ebb. This is the significance of the third, 'neutral' category of *vedanā* listed in the *Satipaṭṭhāna Sutta*. 'Neither-painful-nor-pleasant' is not really a distinctive quality of feeling (although it is so categorized here), but an absence of feeling altogether, a response so low in energy, so faintly felt, that you simply cannot tell whether your experience is pleasurable or painful. It is not quite accurate to speak of not being in touch with your feelings in this case: it is more that there aren't any feelings there to be in touch with. If you are trying to live a spiritual life, this needs urgently to be changed: neutrality of feeling provides a poor basis from which to pursue spiritual aspirations, because if it is to be effective, our practice must be impelled by a strong and positive emotional drive.

To feel strongly calls for energy, so if we are to experience real positivity and depth of emotion, we need to know how our energy arises and how we use it. Emotional energy is aroused when we are inspired, but no one, not even the most creative of artists, can be inspired all the time. Dickens was an immensely gifted and prolific writer, but he still needed time for eating and sleeping, at the very least. So perhaps the first thing that has to be said is that our capacity for positive emotion, like our physical energy, is necessarily limited. We can aim to be positive all the time, but our reserves of energy will not support a continual state of intense emotion. Spiritual energy, like the capacity for physical work, needs to be cultivated and periodically renewed.

Modern living seems almost designed to drain away energy and dissipate positivity. Continual contact with the day-to-day stress of ordinary life tends to damp down one's responses: walking through the city, you pass many people in quite negative mental states, and you can feel your energy being drained away just through warding off those influences and keeping all the noise at bay. City life seems to draw out energy and waste it senselessly, not just through noise and worry, but also through the mechanical and electronic devices that dictate the pace of life. Our senses are bombarded by all manner of powerful messages, both crude and subtle, and all demanding our attention. Another feature of modern life is the extraordinary range of superficial enjoyments available to us. Although many of these little outlets of energy are not harmful or unethical in themselves, if our attention is spread thinly across all of them, we will be unable to have any single experience of real depth.

If we are to make any progress spiritually we therefore need to intervene positively in the way we feel and the way we experience the world. In our own interests, we need to shield ourselves from negative influences. Feelings do not arise of their own accord; they come about in dependence on conditions and disappear when those conditions are removed. By being aware of how we are liable to be influenced by our environment and activities, we can manage the feelings that are likely to arise and cultivate a reserve of positive energy upon which to draw in the pursuit of stronger, brighter states of awareness.

This is all common sense, and easily verifiable in our own experience. If you are feeling depressed, for example, you might decide to spend a day in the country to put you in a more positive mood. If you feel uninspired, making contact with someone who shares your ideals and aspirations will give life a much more positive aspect. By taking a more active role in handling our sense impressions we can bring our feelings more effectively under our control. One might say that this is the purpose of going on retreat. A retreat centre is an environment dedicated to concentrating one's energies and directing them towards the attainment of higher states of awareness and more positive and refined emotion. It might take a little time to adjust to the absence of distractions to which you are accustomed in everyday life, but as you get used to it, your state of mind becomes much more contented, even blissful, just through simplifying your sensory impressions and cutting down on the activities through which your energy is usually frittered away. Sometimes on retreat one is asked to observe regular periods of silence, and people are often amazed to find that as a result they have much more energy than usual, with, strange to say, no diminution of their level of communication with others – a good basis from which to tap deeper sources of inspiration through meditation. One invariably comes back from retreat charged with energy. (Incidentally, this is also one reason for observing celibacy. Even athletes are said to conserve their energy in this way and some would say that it is essential if one intends to explore the deeper levels of meditative experience.) The stillness and simplicity of a retreat provides the ideal basis for a heightened and consistent emotional positivity. When you are not on retreat, one of the most effective ways of banking up your energies and preventing them from leaking away is a regular lifestyle which keeps energy flowing continuously through the same channels. Regular sleep, diet, working hours, and meditation all help to clarify and concentrate one's energies, harmonizing them in the service of one's higher aspirations.

But external conditions are not everything. Even if you went on solitary retreat and placed yourself in ideal conditions, free from any external factors that might dissipate your energies, even if you had plenty of time in which to meditate and reflect, you might still lack the inspiration to do it. Obviously you couldn't blame your surroundings; the reason would have to be subjective. You might look for a clue by investigating what does seem to stimulate an emotional response. You might discover that while higher thoughts and aspirations leave you cold, when your mind wanders towards visions of a succulent meal or some beautiful sexual partner, you are much more interested. Food and sex, after all, are likely to arouse almost everyone's interest, and the energy to pursue them is more or less ever-present.

So it is inaccurate to talk about having or not having energy in absolute terms. Emotional energy can't be measured in terms of a fixed quantity like water or heat or even the capacity to perform physical work. It is all about one's level of inspiration. The question is not how much energy you can muster, but how refined that energy is. Energy arises in connection with objects of pleasure and interest, and your relationship to those objects says a great deal about the kind of person you are. One way of thinking of the spiritual life is that it is about shifting the focus of your emotional energy from, say, food or sex, or watching football or boxing, to the more refined pleasures of art, music, friendship, and meditation.

Sometimes it is only when we are on retreat and our everyday supports and pleasures are removed that we find out what is really keeping us going from day to day. We may have an idea or even a conviction that higher pleasures are the most fulfilling, but our ability to enjoy them is unlikely to be as fully developed as our intellectual understanding that they are a good thing. In other words, our spiritual ideals may not have filtered very far into our deeper emotions and volitions, so that we continue to seek pleasure in the same old places. This is the usual pattern of spiritual life: our intellectual understanding will always be some way ahead of our emotional involvement. It is quite usual to find oneself oscillating between relatively crude pleasures and a rigid determination to engage with spiritual practice which has little of the warmth and ease characteristic of truly positive emotion.

But in the end this is not sustainable. If spiritual practice is to transform your life, you need to think of it as something you can enjoy, not just a hard grind, and this means making sure that there is not too much of a contradiction between 'spiritual' activities and the activities of daily life – and looking for enjoyment in both. If there is at least an element of enjoyment in our daily lives, we will be able to bring that positive attitude to puja, our study of the Dharma, and our meditation. The alternative – a dreary day followed by a meditation that is nothing short of a struggle – is hardly an inspiring prospect.

It is not that all enjoyment is compatible with progress in the spiritual life, of course. Satisfying one's appetite for sex or food certainly involves intensely pleasurable feeling, but the experience will not stir the higher emotions, and it will be short-lived. One might be intensely in love, for example, but the feeling might not last more than a week. On the other hand, one might love so deeply that that depth of emotion continues steadily for many years, even throughout one's life, because it is so firmly rooted that it cannot be shaken by mere circumstance. There is conviction and purpose in it, from which deep emotion flows.

Everybody is subject to craving and attachment in one way or another, because we all tend to look outside ourselves for something that can only be developed from within. But we can begin to draw on our own deep resources of positivity by focusing our energies on the quality of our responses to experience, instead of keeping on drawing in more and more sense impressions from the external world. Enjoyment is passive, but emotion is active (the very word emotion suggests a sense of outward movement), expressive, even creative. The kind of positive emotion we need to cultivate comes from directing that active energy in conscious pursuit of the good.

In the *Majjhima Nikāya* of the Pāli canon the Buddha reminds the *bhikkhus* that they are his heirs not in worldly things but in those things that are free from the realm of the bodily senses.[68] The Pāli word the Buddha used, *nirāmisa*, literally means 'not dependent upon meat' but in this context it can be taken as an idiomatic expresson that we can translate as 'spiritual', while in the *Satipaṭṭhāna Sutta* the same word is used to indicate a mode of feeling which has gone beyond the closed polarity of pleasure and pain that characterizes feeling on the physical and mental level.[69] This is the realm opened up to us through beauty and through meditation, in which we learn to experience rapture and bliss without need of any sensory stimulus, and in which painful and even neutral feelings play no part at all.

Absorption in the *dhyānas* is characterized by an abundance of blissful feeling, an access to a deeper and hitherto unknown source of energy, like some underground reservoir of inspiration. It brings to mind the simile the Buddha used to illustrate the second *dhyāna*: a vast lake of energy that is continuously refreshed from below by some hidden spring.[70] This seems to be how inspiration works: not a single moment of breakthrough into an infinite lake of energy – such a highly charged state of positivity would be exhausting – but a continuing process, a whole series of interconnected reservoirs of inspiration, each deeper and vaster than the one before. From time to time it is as if the highest reservoir runs dry, so that we have to wait for it to be replenished from a deeper source of inspiration currently hidden from consciousness. In this way we gradually evolve, following a steady path of refinement and concentration, going further and further – even going beyond the senses altogether – in the direction of an ideal beauty.

Another passage from the Pāli canon describes how, near the end of his life, the Buddha fell seriously ill. His physical pain was intense, but he overcame it, as he explained, by entering deeply into meditation.[71] Most people would be prevented from entering *dhyāna* by such severe pain, but not the Buddha (nor indeed any advanced meditator). He was able to go beyond it, leaving the *kāmaloka* (the 'realm of desire' in which we live much of the time) to pursue more blissful states of consciousness, free from bodily pain. The distinction made in the *Satipaṭṭhāna Sutta* between worldly and unworldly feeling – *sāmisa* and *nirāmisa* – suggests a higher dimension of pleasurable feeling than we are used to, echoing a distinction found elsewhere in the Buddha's teaching between *kāmacchanda*, the desire for sense objects, and *dhammachanda*, the desire for higher states of consciousness. Desire for the Dharma does not eliminate craving altogether, but transforms it into a mode of enjoyment that helps the process of growth rather than standing in its way.

So it is not enough just to 'get in touch' with our feelings. If we are to refine the quality of our consciousness and build bridges between worldly and spiritual experience, we need to be able to recognize the ethical content of our emotions, distinguishing between the positive and the negative, in order actively to develop ethically skilful, positive emotions. It is impossible to jump from preoccupation with worldly pleasures like food and sex straight into meditative concentration. If you don't have strong emotional experiences when you meditate, it may be because there is too big a gap between the way you relate to meditation and the way you relate to your habitual sources of emotional fulfilment. To bridge the gap you need to find a way – your own way – of coaxing your feelings up to a more subtle level, and from there into meditation. Each of us will have our own approach to this, but it is the role played by nature and also by the arts in many people's lives. The appreciation of beauty draws consciousness upwards into realms of greater brightness, steadily refining one's crude volitional energies, and that more refined energy can then be directed towards the object of one's spiritual aspirations. In the modern world, in which everyday activity lacks any clearly spiritual dimension, we need to recognize more than ever the tremendous value of the love of art and culture for the cultivation of positive emotion. We might perhaps have been brought up to think of classical music – to take that example – as being difficult to appreciate – especially for young people; it doesn't have the same appeal as music you can dance to. But you don't have to have a conceptual understanding of music before you can enjoy it. You could start off by listening to popular pieces and gradually progress to more profound works. As your emotions become more refined, you may find yourself naturally drawn to Mozart or Beethoven. It isn't a question of giving up your present sources of pleasure, but growing beyond them. Without denying what is of value in your present enthusiasms, you can work gently but persistently to raise your interests to higher levels. If you have been interested in Śākyan maidens, Buddhism leads you to contemplate the heavenly nymphs – and once you get tired of those, you can really begin to contemplate reality.

Whatever you decide to focus on, make sure that you are actively appreciating it. You have to be prepared to get really carried away. Listening to a Beethoven symphony or a Handel oratorio, one can have experiences of extraordinary intensity, occasionally extending even as far as the *dhyānas* for short periods, and this is how the mind is gradually attuned to the enjoyment of an altogether higher order of delight than anything one has experienced before. There might be some negative conditioning to clear away to begin with – you might not want to be seen enjoying classical music because you don't want people to think you stuffy or pretentious. But we can't afford to ignore the potential of works of art for raising our states of consciousness; we owe it to ourselves to bring them into our quest for higher enjoyment. The greatest art, through its sheer intelligence and beauty, can nourish our efforts to grow beyond the cramped confines of more worldly enjoyments.

Of course, many people would have to confess, even after years of attempting to lead a spiritual life, that their most intense emotional experience is still connected with food or sex rather than with Shakespeare or Mozart. But if our level of consciousness is to be decisively and permanently elevated, we have to keep challenging ourselves to move beyond our habitual sources of pleasure towards things that extend the scope of our being. If we cannot entertain that possibility, we devalue the love of art and nature to the level of merely minor pleasures. But the wonders of art, like the wonders of nature, have the power to draw awareness to them, to delight, fascinate, and nourish us, to impel our whole being towards higher states of consciousness – if we will let them.

Pleasure – even sensuous pleasure – is, after all, not in itself unskilful. Enjoyment is an essential element in the spiritual life, helping one to sustain a sense of vitality, enthusiasm, and interest. Once you begin to draw consciousness upward and outward into brighter, more expansive states, pleasure plays an increasingly important part in your experience – pleasure that will not tip over into pain and grief, as worldly pleasure inevitably must. These subtle enjoyments do not arise in the same way as the evanescent pleasures of worldly life. They are the fruits of a positive effort to transform consciousness. The key is decisive action. The message of this section of the *Satipaṭṭhāna Sutta* is that the motivation to pursue the path of spiritual development is dependent upon specific conditions and situations. The Buddha is saying emphatically that your present state of consciousness is not fixed, not an absolute 'given'. It has come about in accordance with certain causes and conditions, all of which are constantly arising and passing away – but not at random. If we are in the habit of finding our enjoyment in ephemeral pleasures, we will just need to take a new approach, actively pursuing sources of positive feeling rather than just allowing ourselves to be affected by whatever stimulus happens to come along. As we become more aware of our feelings, it will be clearer to us which factors conduce to the arising of positive emotion and energy. It might be the inspiration one finds in a conversation with a good friend, or the fruit of a period of effective meditation. It might come about through reading an inspiring and stimulating book, or even just a good night's sleep. But however it happens, it doesn't happen by accident.

Once we start taking responsibility for our feelings, then we really begin to transform our emotional life and open up the way to escape from the world of material enjoyments, with its ceaseless ebb and flow between pleasure, pain, and a dreary neutrality. Such a state is not necessarily harmful in the sense of having negative karmic consequences, but in it, we are missing so much. Our lives are far too precious an opportunity to be wasted in a relatively comfortable but ultimately meaningless twilight zone.

# 9
# UNDERSTANDING

> 'And how, bhikkhus, does a bhikkhu abide contemplating mind as mind? Here a bhikkhu understands mind affected by lust as mind affected by lust, and mind unaffected by lust as mind unaffected by lust. He understands mind affected by hate as mind affected by hate, and mind unaffected by hate as mind unaffected by hate. He understands mind affected by delusion as mind affected by delusion, and mind unaffected by delusion as mind unaffected by delusion. He understands contracted mind as contracted mind, and distracted mind as distracted mind. He understands exalted mind as exalted mind, and unexalted mind as unexalted mind. He understands surpassed mind as surpassed mind, and unsurpassed mind as unsurpassed mind. He understands concentrated mind as concentrated mind, and unconcentrated mind as unconcentrated mind. He understands liberated mind as liberated mind, and unliberated mind as unliberated mind.'

What distinguished the early Buddhist conception of the path was its analysis of the mind. Even among the other Indian systems of thought at the time, some of which were extremely rigorous, Buddhism was unparalleled in its exhaustive approach to the nature of mind and mental events. This line of development culminated in the Abhidhamma, a sequence of texts that was eventually included in the Pāli canon. The Abhidhamma teachings are not direct records of the Buddha's discourses, but a presentation of those teachings in a more systematic form than is found in the other books of the Pāli canon. They contain much material whose usefulness to the non-monastic world would have been negligible even at the time it was written down: tables and lists of terms which sometimes make the Buddha's thinking appear stereotyped, his intimations of sublime mystery obscured in the mechanical repetition of fixed formulas. The texts may be venerated for their antiquity, but it must be admitted that they show little imagination and fail to draw out the spiritual meaning of the *sutta*s. It is as though over time people became so convinced that the analytical understanding of existence was the key to transcendental insight that they neglected other approaches, even meditation.

There is, however, a great deal of value in an analytical approach properly applied. The section of the *Satipaṭṭhāna Sutta* on the mind and mental objects can be seen as the basis of the whole Abhidhamma project. Although many of the Abhidhamma's analytical categories were added to the original discourses of the Buddha at a later date, we can be fairly sure that the classifications outlined in the *Sutta* originate from the earliest days of Buddhism. For one thing, the *Satipaṭṭhāna Sutta* appears in the *Majjhima Nikāya*, which we know is a collection of early discourses. The fact that all these categories can also be found elsewhere in the earlier strata of the Pāli canon further supports the view that they are original teachings, not later scholastic elaborations. Be that as it may, given the overall emphasis of the Buddha's teaching, it seems likely that he would have had something to say on the subject of the contemplation of consciousness. If so, he would surely have introduced at least a few rudimentary categories, although he is unlikely to have elaborated or intellectualized the teaching in the way the Abhidhamma did later. As we have already seen, the essence of the Buddha's teaching is quite simple: consciousness is not fixed but subject to change, and if we can learn to trace the way it changes, we can direct that change towards positive growth.

This section thus represents a next step from the last one. Having noted whether the feeling you are experiencing is pleasant, unpleasant, or neutral, you now move on to acknowledge its ethical status and karmic significance, trying to ascertain what has brought it into being and judging whether or not you want it to continue. This corresponds to a basic psychological fact: we are generally aware of the simple and immediate reality of being happy or unhappy before we go more deeply into the matter to consider why and with what justification we feel that way. You might be able to say straight away that you are feeling happy, but you would probably have to give more thought to the question of what sort of happiness it is. Is it associated with skilful or unskilful mental states? Has it arisen because of your morning meditation, or because you had a good breakfast, or because you are gleefully contemplating doing something unskilful later in the day? The mindfulness called for here thus involves *sampajañña* as well as *sati*, right from the start. You are gathering information on how to proceed, ascertaining the level of consciousness on which your experience of pleasure or pain takes place, its ethical significance, and how it relates to other states of mind.

Perhaps the most striking aspect of this section of the *Sutta* is the detail of the analysis – it is concerned with the identification of very specific states of consciousness – but it begins with a more broad-brush, general approach, with the 'three roots'. This is the most elementary classification of all: analysing whether one's consciousness is with or without lust, with or without hate, with or without delusion. This threefold formulation, which appears very early in the Buddhist tradition, might be quite generalized, but it is not to be overlooked because it gives us a benchmark, a basic measure of mindfulness. Examining consciousness from this point of view is a whole practice in itself.

The *Sutta* goes on to describe a very wide range of states of consciousness; perhaps no other system of mental analysis has ever come up with quite so many. At one end of the spectrum are the familiar states of everyday consciousness, while at the other are states of *samādhi* and insight so highly refined that they are seldom experienced by anyone. And not far from the bottom of the range is what the *Sutta* describes as the 'contracted' or 'shrunken' state (Pāli *khitta*). In this rigid state, the mind has settled into a fixed position from which it is reluctant to budge. One example of the way such a state comes about is in the field of academic study. Say you were studying English history: you might narrow down your research to a particular town, then to that town in the eighteenth century, then to the study of local by-laws at that time, until you ended up devoting your whole life to some minutely specialized field of study, perhaps at the expense of a wider understanding. There might be an undercurrent of fear here: anxious for certainty, the scholar narrows the terms of reference until certainty is assured – or so he would like to think. Of course, an astonishing amount of controversy can arise even within a very limited field. You can be quite sure that if you did become an expert on the history of Norwich city council during the eighteenth century, there would be some other specialist in the field who would take issue with you on every point.

The way the Abhidhamma scholars subdivided the Buddha's teachings in such minute detail would suggest that they themselves were in the grip of the 'shrunken state' of consciousness. The fact that the Abhidhamma cites three different kinds of Stream Entrant, for example, suggests a confinement to narrower and narrower terms of reference at the expense of a deeper understanding. Such a state of mind also seeks the security of belonging to a group, whether a gang or a club, a movement or school. This contracted or inflexible mental attitude is at the opposite extreme from another, equally limited state of mind, the distracted mind, which has a tendency to be over-expansive and over-flexible, far too easily diverted, and always keen to explore new avenues. It throws up generalizations, hypotheses, and speculations without running the risk of choosing one thing and sticking to it. If the shrunken mind seeks the security of a narrow field of reference, the distracted mind tries to escape into one so broad that no one mind could ever hope to encompass it, thus avoiding responsibility and commitment.

Once you have overcome whichever of these two opposite mental tendencies you are prone to, the developed or 'exalted' state – *mahaggata* – can emerge. *Mahaggata* literally means 'become great', and it refers to the expanded consciousness of meditative concentration, or *dhyāna*. The dhyānic mind is more integrated, more serenely blissful, and much more far-reaching than the ordinary mind. And yet it is still only relatively more luminous, only relatively clearer and more enjoyable; beyond it there are the various levels of transcendental consciousness. Getting a sense of how far consciousness can be expanded, exalted, and ultimately liberated places our experience in the broadest possible perspective. When we are unenlightened, in other words, we need to be aware that we are unenlightened, so that our efforts have a worthwhile goal. If you wrongly imagine that there is no mental state superior to the one you have reached, you are stuck. We need to be aware that there are states of consciousness that we have not yet attained, and keep reminding ourselves that they are attainable. Fortunately, we are not restricted to contemplating these states in the abstract; they are made vividly real for us in the lives of those Enlightened individuals who have left autobiographies, like Milarepa, Huineng, and of course the Buddha himself.

> 'In this way he abides contemplating mind as mind internally, or he abides contemplating mind as mind externally, or he abides contemplating mind as mind both internally and externally. Or else he abides contemplating in mind its arising factors, or he abides contemplating in mind both its arising and vanishing factors. Or else mindfulness that "there is mind" is simply established in him to the extent necessary for bare knowledge and mindfulness. And he abides independent, not clinging to anything in the world. This is how a bhikkhu abides contemplating mind as mind.'

As with the breath, one can contemplate these factors 'both internally and externally' – and as before, one can take this to mean turning one's attention outwards to consider the mental states of other people. Of course, this is notoriously difficult. A prose poem by Baudelaire illustrates the degree to which we can be unaware of other people's feelings and thoughts even though we might think we are close to them. A young man takes his beloved to a restaurant and, as they sit together at a table by the window, he feels that their souls have merged and that they share every thought and feeling. Just then, he notices a wretched old man begging in the street outside. He is about to express his feelings of sympathy and concern when his beloved suddenly gives vent to her indignation that such ugly old beggars should be allowed to come so close to the window. So much for the merging of souls![72]

It goes to show that while you might think that because someone is near and dear to you, you know them very well, in truth, the nearer and dearer they are, the more attached to them you are likely to be, and consequently the less truly you will be able to see them. In a sexual relationship there might be intimacy but not necessarily much honesty. Each is living in a dream world of their own – a comforting dream and one that might release hidden energies for a while, but a dream nevertheless. True receptivity to other people requires us to see them as they really are, not just in terms of what we want from them or what we think we see.

We can move towards this with the help of the traditional Buddhist practice of rejoicing in merits, whereby you make yourself more and more aware of the positive qualities of others. What the *Satipaṭṭhāna Sutta* can be thought to advise is that we should contemplate an aspect of our inner experience and then expand that focus to encompass other beings. This is clearly somewhat akin to the method of the four *brahma vihāra* meditations, which are designed to develop loving-kindness, sympathetic joy, compassion, and equanimity. In the first of these, the *mettā bhāvanā*, you develop loving-kindness towards yourself, then towards a good friend, then towards someone you scarcely know, and so on. But – at least in my reading of it – the *Satipaṭṭhāna Sutta* is here suggesting something rather different: not so much the cultivation of a particular emotional response to others, but the contemplation of *their* mental states. The idea is not that you imagine or infer their state of mind from their appearance or from the circumstances, but that you cultivate a direct awareness of it. One might say that this is, strictly speaking, impossible (unless you happen to possess the supernormal power of telepathy), but you certainly can get so close to someone that you are aware of their changes of mental state in much the same way that you are aware of your own – and it is at the very least possible to cultivate the habit of avoiding making assumptions about what someone's state of mind 'must' be. One person might respond with anger to a certain situation, while another might respond to it with patience or distress or a sense of irony. With practice, you will find that you don't have to infer someone's state of consciousness from their behaviour; you can experience it intuitively, sometimes even picking it up when they are in another room.

How does one learn to be aware of other people's mental states in this way? We have already come across the idea of telling one's life story as a way of recollecting and integrating one's past experience and also moving closer to other people. But listening to the life stories of others is also a very good way of learning to 'contemplate mind externally'. We have all done things in the past that are part of our present selves. They have had an effect on us, though this might not always be obvious. If you know what other people have been through, you can understand them better as they are now. In Dharmic terms, you understand the *vipāka* (the fruit of karma) better if you are aware of the karma (the action) that was the seed of that fruit.

'Contemplating mind externally' becomes a matter of course within a closely-knit spiritual community; you quickly become aware of other people's states of consciousness without anything being said. You begin to notice not only changes in an individual's mental state but also the development on a collective level of a greater tendency towards mindfulness, or towards distracted or restricted states. Of course, it is not always easy to know what to do with your awareness of another person's mental state. There may be times when you feel a need to say something to them about it, and there is always a risk of getting it wrong or misinterpreting it. But you have to take that risk. Most people find it difficult to be aware even of their own mental states; in a way, it's *all* difficult. So even though contemplating mind externally might sound challenging, we should not let that put us off. There is much to be gained in terms of empathy with and sensitivity to others.

The descriptions of mindfulness of feelings and of consciousness in the *Sutta* show how the various classifications overlap – because, of course, they are describing different aspects of the same experience. Despite the complexity of its classifications, the *Sutta* is not really concerned with clear-cut, mutually exclusive divisions, or with a finite number of states of consciousness to be crossed off the list as they are encountered. The intention is to encourage us to be constantly aware of our states of consciousness as they arise and fall away. When a state of consciousness of whatsoever nature arises, you note that it arises. When it ceases you note that it ceases. You know the liberated state of consciousness as the liberated state, the unliberated state as the unliberated, and so on. The *bhikkhu* establishes mindfulness of consciousness in this way and 'abides independent, not clinging to anything in the world'. He sees nothing permanent, or unchanging, or of the nature of a self, but only a stream of states of consciousness, constantly arising, constantly passing away.

Discriminating between states of consciousness is not an end in itself. The point of the practice is not just to notice them as they come and go, but to transform them. You are not saddled with your present state of consciousness: if you don't like it, you can do something to change it – so long as you know what steps to take. This ability to discriminate between mental states and follow certain mental avenues in preference to others is what makes meditation possible.

In contemplating consciousness as a conditioned phenomenon, as distinct from thinking in terms of a soul or fixed identity, we are picking up a thread leading all the way back to the Buddha. The essence of the teaching is that we must constantly be aware of our states of consciousness, and be prepared to use that awareness to fuel growth. In contemplating mind and mental objects, you are turning subjective experience into an object of your awareness, and therein lies an immediate transformation. As soon as you become aware of your self you have in some sense changed: you have gone a bit further, become a bit more creative. Of course, we are constantly escaping from our own knowledge of who we are, and in any case there is always more of our being than we have knowledge of. But we need not be too concerned about this. Provided we remain mindful, the process of transformation will continue of its own accord.

# 10
# REFLECTING

'And how, bhikkhus, does a bhikkhu abide contemplating mind-objects as mind-objects? Here a bhikkhu abides contemplating mind-objects as mind objects in terms of the five hindrances. And how does a bhikkhu abide contemplating mind-objects as mind-objects in terms of the five hindrances? Here, there being sensual desire in him, a bhikkhu understands: "There is sensual desire in me"; or there being no sensual desire in him, he understands: "There is no sensual desire in me"; and he also understands how there comes to be the arising of unarisen sensual desire, and how there comes to be the abandoning of arisen sensual desire, and how there comes to be the future non-arising of abandoned sensual desire.

'There being ill will in him.... There being sloth and torpor in him.... There being restlessness and remorse in him.... There being doubt in him, a bhikkhu understands: "There is doubt in me"; or there being no doubt in him, he understands: "There is no doubt in me"; and he understands how there comes to be the arising of unarisen doubt, and how there comes to be the abandoning of arisen doubt, and how there comes to be the future non-arising of abandoned doubt.'

We normally think of an object as a solid thing whose existence is objectively, verifiably real, as opposed to those 'unreal' things that exist only in the mind. But in Buddhism the mind too is considered to be an organ of sense. Just as the eye responds to forms and the ear to sounds, so the mind responds to ideas. Of course, the mind is a different kind of sense organ from the other five, the difference being that sight cannot see itself, taste cannot taste itself, but mind can contemplate mind. The ability to make consciousness reflexive – to become aware that we are aware, to know that we know – seems to be a specifically human characteristic. Animals, driven by instinct, graze or hunt or work things out apparently without any self-questioning – and human beings do this too, much of the time – but the human mind has the capacity to turn its attention back on itself and take a questioning attitude even to consciousness itself.

In other words, as we have seen, although your state of consciousness is subjective, when you think about it, you make it into an object – that is, a mental object, a *dhamma*, to use the Pāli word. You can turn 'you, the subject' into 'you, the object'. You don't just experience sensual desire; you know that you experience it. Your desire for sensuous enjoyment is a part of your subjectivity; but when you become aware of this desire, you make it into an object. In the *Satipaṭṭhāna Sutta* these *dhammas* or mental objects are divided into five sets – the five hindrances, the five *skandhas* (Pāli *khandhas*), the six senses and their bases, the seven factors of Enlightenment, and the four noble truths – and these form the basis for the remaining chapters of this commentary. All these ways of categorizing mental experience are very useful to us: only with a clear way of understanding what a given state of consciousness really is can we interpret what the mind is dwelling on at any given time and thus transform our mental state. The contemplation of mental objects thus relies strongly on an ability to think in a purposeful and directed manner.

States of consciousness are far from simple; in any state of mind, there is always a lot going on. To 'contemplate mind-objects' – such as the hindrances – is therefore in a sense to simplify, taking a cross-section of a state of consciousness so that one can discriminate between those aspects of it which could lead to subtler modes of awareness and those which will obstruct one's efforts to develop those subtle states. In the section on the contemplation of mind, the Buddha suggested using the three roots of conditioned existence, greed, hatred, and delusion, as a measure for mental states. This same classification very broadly underpins the one presented in this section, the list of the five hindrances, but here one is considering these conditioning factors in a more specific way.

The nature of the mind is to go wherever it wants to go, but when we meditate, our task is to persuade it to move in the direction of skilful modes of mental and physical activity. In his commentary on the *Sutta*, Buddhaghosa associates meditation with *sammā vāyāma*, perfect effort. This is described as being fourfold: the effort to prevent the arising of unskilful mental states; the effort to eliminate unskilful mental states that have arisen; the effort to cultivate positive mental states; and the effort to maintain positive mental states that have arisen.[73] This is a good description of the aims of meditation: as a method of cultivation it enables one to develop blissful and radiant concentration, while as a process of prevention and elimination it banishes and stills distracting thoughts. The quicker we can respond to what is happening in our mind, feeding skilful impulses and starving unskilful ones, the better. But to do this, we have to become aware of the mental state in the first place; this is the function and practice of mindfulness.

A mental object – sensual desire, for example – does not arise in the abstract; it comes in a specific form – a desire for food, say. It is then up to you to recognize that that is what is going on in your mind: hence the *Satipaṭṭhāna Sutta*'s instruction that one should ascertain 'how there comes to be the arising of the unarisen sensual desire'. The usual generalized explanation for this is 'unwise attention': it is because you have thoughtlessly indulged in this sort of mental state in the past that it is able to arise now. Probably, though, by the time you have become aware of the distraction, you will have no idea where it has come from. It has apparently arisen out of nowhere. For example, you might be sitting trying to meditate when you become aware that for quite a while – you're not sure how long – you have been sitting there thinking about food. You might be able to brush this distraction aside, but it is still important to acknowledge that it hasn't popped up out of nowhere – it has a definite origin. Tracing the origins of your mental states helps you to discover more about their background, so that you can make adjustments to the way you live your life and specifically to the way you prepare for meditation.

The intention of dividing unskilful states into those characterized by sensuous desire, by ill will, by sloth and torpor, by restlessness, and by doubt – this is the list commonly called the five hindrances – is to give us the opportunity to transform them. The *Sutta* says that the monk knows 'how there comes to be the abandoning of arisen sensual desire'. But how do you 'know'? If you are being plagued by a mild form of a hindrance, just becoming aware of it will usually be enough to dispel it. Sometimes, however, you might need to change your external conditions to influence your mental state for the better. If you are sleepy in meditation, for example, you might need to check your posture, making sure that you are sitting upright so that energy can flow through your body without obstruction. You might also try finding a brightly lit place in which to meditate, or perhaps even sit in the open air. *Dhyāna* is a state of brightness and clarity in every sense, so light, even the light of a candle, will stimulate brighter states of consciousness. You could also freshen your face with cold water, or walk up and down for a while before returning to your meditation seat. If on the other hand you are experiencing distraction, worry, and restlessness, you will need to set up calming conditions, perhaps by making the lighting softer. There are all kinds of things you can do. However, even the most perfect conditions are of little use if you are in a state that seeks distraction. The mind works incredibly fast. The smallest external stimulus – the distant rattle of cups, the sound of conversation outside the meditation room – can trigger trains of association that draw the mind far away from the object of meditation in next to no time.

If awareness of a hindrance is not enough to shift it, you can bring to mind the various antidotes recommended by the Abhidhamma tradition for dealing with the hindrances as they arise. They are all described in Buddhaghosa's *Visuddhimagga*, and include the cultivation of the opposite quality, considering the consequences of allowing that mental state to continue and so on.[74] The antidotes are useful as a sort of first-aid measure during the meditation session itself. If your states of awareness are to be radically transformed, however, you will have to do more than that. The relatively small amount of time spent in meditation will not on its own outweigh the consequences of a life lived without a consistent level of mindfulness. Our experience in meditation is influenced – for better or worse – by our whole way of life. We experience the hindrances because this is our usual state in daily life. By the same token, the more we can simplify and unify the mind, whatever situation we are in, the closer our mental state will naturally be to meditative concentration.

In other words, we cannot rely solely on the first aid of the antidotes. A systematic course of treatment is what is required: a consistent practice of mindfulness outside meditation will do far more to overcome the hindrances than anything we do once we have started to meditate. Achieving concentration depends on establishing a way of life that is more harmonious, contented, energetic, confidence-inspiring, and other-regarding, and less restless, grasping, and doubtful – and this requires us to understand the way we are affected by things. In the *Sutta*'s words, we need to know how 'there comes to be the arising of unarisen sensual desire' – or the arising of the unarisen irritation, or whatever it is. We have to make a habit of watching out for the hindrances in daily life and setting up conditions in which they are unlikely to occur, or will occur only in a weakened form.

Once you get to know your habits of mind, you can avoid situations that tend to stimulate recurrent patterns of behaviour. All that is required is a little foresight. If you are going out for a run, you won't eat a large meal beforehand because you know that if you do, you will end up with a stomach-ache. The hindrances are similarly linked to their causes. If you stay up late, for example, it is not realistic to look forward to a concentrated and alert meditation first thing in the morning. At the very least, you are likely to be setting yourself up for an extended battle with sloth and torpor – a battle that could have been avoided by planning ahead, organizing your time around the things that matter to you most in the long term.

When you do give way to the temptation of the moment, usually you know full well that you will regret later what you are doing now – sometimes you regret it even while you are doing it. (Perhaps this is an especially English trait, if we are to believe the Duc de Sully, who remarked that 'the English take their pleasures sadly'.)[75] It is understandable that one might occasionally decide to sacrifice one's morning meditation for the sake of something one thinks is worth such a sacrifice. Our real failing when we indulge ourselves in this way is our unwillingness to take full responsibility for our actions, our failure to make a clear choice between long-term goals and short-term distractions, and be clear which we are choosing at a particular time.

Hindrances tend to arise when we react mechanically to situations – when we grab things without thinking, when we react to things, fidget, daydream, or dither without really being aware of what we are doing. If the television is in the room, we switch it on, and if it is on, we change channels rather than switch it off. Learning some self-discipline in matters like this will support your meditation practice. If you just let yourself follow semi-conscious impulses, this will undermine your intention to become more conscious, whereas if you can learn to pause and consider quietly whether an action is skilful or not, you will inhibit the tendency to give in automatically to your impulses and this will help you to stay focused when you are meditating.

Traditionally, virtuous conduct (*śīla*) is said to cast out craving and distraction, and it does this by inculcating a habit of self-control. This is the point of many of the practices of the orthodox *bhikkhu*, including that of not taking food after noon. If you do not allow craving for food uncontrolled expression, that hindrance is gradually weakened. (It can be eliminated altogether only with the arising of insight.) If we do not observe such rules ourselves, we have to exercise extra vigilance instead; with a wider range of possible courses of action before us, we still have to be prepared to take responsibility for our mental states, acknowledging that certain avenues of thought and action lead to certain kinds of consequences.

The *Sutta*'s advice to 'set up mindfulness in front of you' which we came across in the section on breathing, was taken quite literally in the Buddha's day, and in some Buddhist countries the monks still follow the practice of walking looking straight ahead or with their eyes downcast as they go about their daily almsround. The *Satipaṭṭhāna Sutta* might well be the inspiration for this practice, whose aim is simply to prevent the mind from being led astray into unskilful thoughts. In the modern city there is obviously even more need for such a practice. Not that there is any kind of virtue in looking at the floor, and this practice would be too drastic for most of us. Perhaps more effective, and in a way more radical, is the cultivation of the mental attitude of *apramāda* (Pāli *appamāda*) or 'non-heedlessness' – that is, an overall vigilance that takes into account a broad range of conditions, both within and outside us, enabling us to be active and open to what is going on around us while still maintaining mindfulness.

It is a tremendous challenge to sustain this combination of openness and vigilance. In the media-free India of the Buddha's day, you would not have known about events in the neighbouring kingdoms until perhaps years after they had happened – much less about floods in China or earthquakes in Peru. On the whole life was very peaceful, because there were so few things to occupy the mind. We on the other hand have more information – and input generally – available to us than we can possibly keep up with, and we therefore need to develop some kind of filter. We cannot cut ourselves off from the society in which we live, but we can try to give such attention as we devote to issues of the day mainly to matters within our own sphere of influence. We should not surrender our initiative to the torrent of information coming at us, which is presented as hugely important today only to be replaced by something else tomorrow. As Thoreau says, with a little exaggeration, 'All news, as it is called, is gossip, and they who edit and read it are old women over their tea.'[76] When we switch on the television or pick up a newspaper or log on to the Internet, we have to consider not only the value and interest of what we find there but also the cumulative effect of developing a habit. If we have regular recourse to these resources when we are bored, we get used to adopting an unduly passive attitude towards our sensory input. We drift from one thing to another, exercising less and less critical judgement and becoming less and less capable of dealing creatively with those times when we are at a loose end.

When it comes to the hindrances, it is essential to keep the initiative. This is largely a question of taking responsibility for the situations we find ourselves in. Unfortunately, we tend to shrug off responsibility by disguising as a practical necessity what is really our personal choice. We present our decisions as being dictated by circumstances or by other people, as though the whole matter were out of our hands. It is a useful way of diverting blame; it allows you to present yourself as the victim when you feel resentful about something, and to do what you really want to do while pretending you are only doing it because you have to. Even if we cannot help deceiving others in this way, we should not deceive ourselves. In reality there are very few occasions when we can truthfully say, 'I had no choice.' Every moment of awareness, indeed, presents us with an opportunity to choose what to do, or at least how to do it. It isn't 'the world' or 'life' that draws us away from the path, but our own motivation. Sooner or later we have to acknowledge that we are influenced not by external distractions in themselves but by our own tendency to become enmeshed in them. The fact that we succumb does not let us off; we are still making an active choice to succumb. If you are dissatisfied with your circumstances, you need to remind yourself that you are really dissatisfied with your own decision not to change them. You may then decide that you don't want to do anything to change things, but at least you will be able to stop feeling dissatisfied about the state of affairs. By refusing to be the victims of circumstances we begin to steer circumstances towards our goals.

The ability to be decisive and single-minded is rare enough but it is especially so with regard to any spiritual objective. The conditions of modern living seem almost to conspire against it, and most of us are only too willing to join the conspiracy. However, we can decide to change our attitude at any moment. We will no doubt forget our decisions as often as we make them, but there is no need to despair – changing habits takes time. Being ready to assume full responsibility for the decisions one makes, consciously or not, is perhaps the defining characteristic of the true individual: one's continuity of intention might have to take into account some inner conflict, but should not be undermined by it.

We need a strong sense of initiative, responsibility, and decisiveness if we are to counteract the hindrances. But the taking of this kind of initiative might itself be obstructed by one of the hindrances: doubt (Pāli *vicikicchā*). This is not intellectual doubt, but an unwillingness to make up one's mind and clarify one's thinking. It is a deliberate muddying of the water to avoid facing up to the truth of a situation, a culpable refusal to take responsibility for one's view of things and for the things one does based upon that view. To give an example, when I lived in India, I would from time to time challenge some brahmin on the subject of 'untouchability', almost invariably to be fobbed off with mystical obfuscation. 'Truth is one, God is one,' he might say. 'Who, then, is touching whom? There is no toucher, no touched, only God.' As this smokescreen settled over the whole issue, any discussion of the moral dimension of the caste system would successfully be avoided. It is one thing to experience doubt in the struggle towards the resolution of a genuine intellectual difficulty, but it is quite another to be doubtful in order to avoid any decision that might involve a definite course of action. In the case of the brahmin, whether he was conscious of it or not, his refusal to acknowledge the fact of untouchability meant that he could continue to benefit from an unjust system he would rather not question.

To take a less controversial example of doubt and indecision as moral muddle, someone might say, 'What do you mean, that was a selfish thing to do? Everyone is ultimately selfish.' Or again, you can always tell when someone doesn't want to do something but won't admit it. They turn the issue into a mass of imponderables: yes, a walk this afternoon sounds like a nice idea – but it is going to depend on the weather, and there might not be time, and do you think you should go for a walk when you haven't been very well?

If you keep your options open indefinitely, you avoid having to do anything. Doubt is a kind of camouflage: if you don't take up a clear position, no one can attack you – you are beyond criticism, or rather you haven't yet reached a point where you can be criticized. You might not be certain, but at least you can never be wrong, and this is a comfortable position – or non-position – to be in. Once you eliminate doubt, you have to act, you have to stand up for something – or if you don't act upon your conviction, you are obliged to admit to your own shortcomings. You have to say, 'Well, I'm just lazy,' or 'I'm afraid'; you know where you stand, you aren't pretending.

Doubt is essentially resistance to the positive, forward-looking spirit of the path. As soon as you are convinced that the Buddha was Enlightened, you have to take what he said seriously enough actually to do something about it. If, on the other hand, you give yourself the luxury of doubting whether the Buddha was really Enlightened at all, or at least postponing committing yourself to a view until you are 'really sure', you don't need to take his teaching so seriously and, best of all, you don't need to do anything about it. The ideal way to free yourself from doubt is thus to clarify your thinking, not necessarily in a bookish or abstract way, but simply by reflecting on what you know of the spiritual path.

While it is good to learn to be vigilant and aware within the jumble of impressions and opinions that is modern life, we do need some respite from the bombardment. Even within the most positive and inspiring spiritual community, it is easy to start functioning as a group member rather than as a true individual, becoming dependent on other members of the community in one way or another and to that extent using them, albeit not consciously. This is why it is important to get away on your own from time to time – on solitary retreat, if you can. When you are on your own you can take stock of things and assess your relationship with other people. Can you get by on your own? Can your spiritual practice survive without the support of other people? What happens when you are setting your own programme? A solitary retreat shows you the extent to which you are dependent on the company of other people for your positivity and your sense of who you are, including your attitudes and views. If you can demonstrate to yourself that you can function at least for a while without support, you will be able to interact much more positively with other people.

Setting up the conditions for a solitary retreat is simple. You seek out a place to stay in a quiet and preferably remote part of the country, take a supply of food, and spend your time meditating, reflecting, and studying your reactions to being on your own. Community or family life needs such a counterbalance of self-reliance to make it work. On solitary retreat you can meditate or read or do whatever you want whenever you want, without reference to anyone else. You can let your energies flow freely, not just in the predetermined channels of habit or circumstance. A solitary retreat doesn't have to be long – a month is fine, or a week, or a weekend if that's all you can manage.

Even if you find that blissful meditations elude you, there is still much to be gained from a solitary retreat. As well as giving you the chance to experience what it might be like to be truly self-sufficient, both physically and mentally, it also gives you time and space to think creatively about the situation to which you will be returning and in particular to consider what distractions are most likely to arise. For one person the major distraction might be work: they might work so much that there is not enough time left for meditation, study, or contact with spiritual friends. For another person it might be the excitement of city life, while someone else might end up slumped in front of the television. All these things can be insistent and seductive in their appeal. If you don't plan your strategy in advance, they will catch you unawares and rob you of a week's hard-won mindfulness in a day. But if you are realistic about your weaknesses and go back into the world with a positive attitude, this need not happen.

You do need to be vigilant, but there is no need to be too defensive. You don't have to hole yourself up like a rabbit in a burrow cowering from a fox. The best method of defence is attack: why not use the challenge and stimulation of ordinary life to cultivate even more positive states of mind than those you enjoyed on retreat? The whole point of spiritual practice is to be able to operate in difficult and challenging circumstances. Just be aware that the gains of meditation can easily be dissipated, and aware, above all, of the nature of your own reactive mind. If you live among spiritual friends you have a very good base upon which to take your stand.

This somewhat military-sounding approach is as traditional as anything in Buddhism. Our battle with the hindrances is personified in the tradition in the figure of Māra, the wily adversary who so often appears in the stories of the Pāli canon to tempt and taunt Buddhist practitioners as they strive for mindfulness and positivity. Māra is not to be underestimated: he is cunning and resourceful. That is the nature of the reactive mind – to get its own way by underhand means. But there is no need to assume that Māra will inevitably get the better of you. If you know what you are doing and keep one step ahead of what he is up to, if you are prepared to give him a good hammering, he is not going to have it all his own way. No doubt we should be wary of Māra, but we can remind ourselves that he is just as wary of us. We may even be able to give him a bit of a fright. He is called 'the lord of life and death' and is thus said to have a vested interest in keeping us in the world of distraction and delusion, since if we escape it, he loses his power. But that power is illusory. In the many encounters between Māra and the Buddha's followers recounted in the *sutta*s, the punchline is always the same: 'Māra retreated, sad and discomfited.'[77]

Whatever the distraction, it doesn't appear in the mind at random; it arises in dependence on definite causes and conditions. And – this is the important thing – you don't have to put up with it. The list of hindrances helps us to identify the many kinds of thoughts and feelings that interfere with the process of unifying and concentrating the mind, and by becoming familiar with the list we can become aware of the arising of our unconscious habits of mind before they have really taken hold. However subject one might be to the five hindrances, there is always this measure of hope. The essence of the matter is not complicated or intellectual. It is simply the fact that phenomena arise in dependence on causes and conditions – in other words, we are back to the plain fact of impermanence. Everything changes – everything can change – and mental states are no exception. Your state of mind is within your control, and to be convinced of that is more than half the battle.

# 11
# ANALYSING

> 'Again, bhikkhus, a bhikkhu abides contemplating mind-objects as mind-objects in terms of the five aggregates affected by clinging. And how does a bhikkhu abide contemplating mind-objects as mind-objects in terms of the five aggregates affected by clinging? Here a bhikkhu understands: "Such is material form, such its origin, such its disappearance; such is feeling, such its origin, such its disappearance; such is perception, such its origin, such its disappearance; such are the formations, such their origin, such their disappearance; such is consciousness, such its origin, such its disappearance."'

The traditional phrase 'Thus have I heard' with which the *Satipaṭṭhāna Sutta* opens tells us that this is one of the discourses that the Buddha's companion Ānanda is said to have recalled from memory at the First Council, the first gathering of monks after the Master's passing away. Ānanda stands at the beginning of a long tradition of teaching and translation of the Buddha's message, which now spans some thousands of years. Yet despite the increasing availability of texts from all parts of the Buddhist tradition, the fact remains that the Buddha himself committed nothing to writing. He gave discourses and engaged in dialogue with many people, but it was his disciples who passed down to succeeding generations what they had heard and understood. And this, of course, meant memorizing it all.

The First Council was the first major step towards addressing the problem of how to maintain the authentic teaching once the Buddha had passed away, a problem which was to become a major preoccupation for the Buddhist community as the tradition grew and spread. For several hundred years the energies of the Buddha's followers went into simply preserving the teachings as they had been handed down by the oral tradition, and this is why the Pāli *sutta*s appear so formulaic and repetitive to the modern reader. They were not intended to be *read* at all; the idea was to lodge them in the mind through oral recitation. Originally the word-schemes of the Pāli canon were regarded as supports for meditation, helping the practitioner to make the fact of, say, impermanence more real by reciting a list: feelings are impermanent, perceptions are impermanent, and so on. A more abstract or general statement might wash over the mind, but this breakdown into specific detail gives a variety within the steady repetition of a constant pattern, and the idea is thus hammered home.

This technique was not the invention of those who began the tradition of recitation and memorization; it goes back to the Buddha himself and to his identification of what are called in Pāli the five *khandhas* (Sanskrit *skandhas*). From the very beginning he urged his followers to recognize the impermanent and conditioned nature of existence. But it is very difficult to acknowledge this fully; powerful measures are needed to help one break through one's resistance to the hard reality behind this simple idea. As we have seen, one way is to seize the opportunity of those times when the fact of impermanence is painfully impressed upon us by circumstances. But even such sharp reminders are dulled by the passage of time. One has to find a way of keeping one's awareness fresh and alive. Clearly just saying to oneself that all things are impermanent – even repeating it over and over again – is not going to do that. But one can take it further by breaking one's experience of things down into its constituent parts and considering that each and every part is not fixed but ever-changing. Thus the apparent solidity of things is revealed as illusory, and even the very idea of personal existence, the notion of a 'self' or 'soul' which is somehow impervious to change, is challenged. Reflection on the five *khandhas* shows that one's experience and indeed one's self is complex and fluid, never for an instant to be thought of in terms of fixed identity. It is no doubt because of the power of these reflections to change one's perception of existence that the *khandhas* are one of the most frequently cited classifications in the whole of Buddhist literature, both in the texts of the Pāli canon and in centrally important Mahāyāna scriptures such as the *Heart Sūtra*.

The term *khandha* (translated here as 'aggregate') is often translated simply as 'heap', and according to the Buddhist analysis, everything in existence can be understood to be composed of a collection of these 'heaps', inextricably mixed together. The word heap, though, suggestive as it is of something concrete and substantial, does not capture the ever-changing nature of the five *khandhas*: form (*rūpa*), feeling (*vedanā*), recognition (*saññā*), volition or formations (*saṅkhāras*) and consciousness (*viññāṇa*). In the normal course of things we experience the *khandhas* all together – as one big heap, one might say. But for the purposes of this practice – which is meant to help us break the chain that seems to hold them together and thus prevents us from seeing that our experience is composite – we are given the challenge of contemplating them as separate items in a systematic way. They have already been considered as objects of mindfulness – mindfulness of the body, mindfulness of feelings, and so on: now you reflect on their very nature.

You start by becoming aware of your physical body as *rūpa* or material form, which as we have seen stands for the 'objective content of the perceptual situation'. It is what we seem to come up against in our basic relationship with the world. The exercise involves being mindful primarily of sense contact, noticing the particular qualities of things before you have started identifying what they represent to you or having feelings about them. You just watch them arise and pass away.

With the arising of *vedanā* or feeling, the second of the *khandhas*, this awareness of stimulus is coloured by some kind of attitude towards it, a response of pleasure or pain emanating from within our own consciousness. We either like, dislike, or remain unaffected by the stimulus and this leads us into acting – even if only mentally or emotionally – in some way in relation to the object. However, in the context of reflecting on the *khandhas* you are mindful primarily of the feelings in your experience, and if you can manage not to get carried away by thoughts and desires based on those feelings, you can note how they arise and how they disappear.

Our response to those feelings involves perception (*saññā*), the third *khandha*, which is a sense of recognition of the perceptual situation and its basic meaning for us. So the third stage of the practice is to be mindful of your perceptual activity as far as you can, being conscious of a world of objects which you can identify and seeing that one perception gives way to another.

This is quite a delicate operation, as it must be carried out at the very point at which the fourth *khandha*, volitions (*saṅkhāras*), comes into play, as the desire arises for a particular kind of new experience towards which we direct our action. So the fourth aspect of the practice is to be mindful of these volitions, observing impulses, drives, acts of will – whether of attraction or repulsion – as they arise and disappear. This is perhaps the most crucial part of the practice, concerning as it does the very workings of karma. These volitions will generally produce effects of some kind in the future, particularly in terms of creating habits, whether positive or negative. However, in this specific practice the task is not to try to do something different but simply to be mindful of those volitions, to note how they come into being and pass away.

Lastly, one is aware also of being conscious of the whole process: this is *viññāṇa*, consciousness itself. So in the final stage of the practice you try – and again, this is something of a challenge – to be mindful of your own consciousness, to be aware of the space, so to speak, in which objects of consciousness arise.

> 'In this way he abides contemplating mind-objects as mind-objects internally, externally, and both internally and externally.... And he abides independent, not clinging to anything in the world. That is how a bhikkhu abides contemplating mind-objects as mind-objects in terms of the five aggregates affected by clinging.'

As in the other sections, the *Sutta* exhorts us to contemplate the *khandhas* externally as well as internally – a reminder of the other-regarding perspective that we always need in order to counterbalance what is inherently 'internal' or self-regarding about the practice. We can also apply the principle of conditionality to the practice – 'contemplating arising and vanishing factors in mind-objects' – and we can keep reminding ourselves of our ultimate goal, so that we don't get caught up in worldly or limited aims.

This last perspective seems especially relevant to the five *khandhas*, at least historically speaking, because it is quite easy to see how limitations in relation to them did begin to arise within the tradition. Contemplating the *khandhas* encourages one to see one's personal existence in dynamic terms, as a complex of interrelated processes rather than a fixed entity, or even an entity made up of a collection of smaller entities such as organs or substances. The keynote of the whole formulation is impermanence. But of course it is human nature to try to pin things down, and this applies to the *khandhas* themselves; we might start to think of *them* as fixed entities. To guard against this, the tradition further subdivided these components of the self into smaller fragments still. *Rūpa*, for example, was broken down into twenty-eight subcategories, the first of which were the four material elements, which were themselves classified into subjective and objective aspects. Indeed, the more you look into this complex system, the more complex it becomes.

And there's the rub. Although this method of classification was specifically set up as a means of understanding individual existence as the product of conditions, the very development of a procedure to reduce everything to constituent, subsidiary processes seemed to imply that in the end you could arrive at a finite number of ultimate elements of existence. Over time, under the influence of scholastic elements within the Buddhist tradition, particularly in the Theravādin and Sarvāstivādin schools, there emerged a tendency to reify the elements, or *dhammas*, into which the *khandhas* were subdivided as really existent things in themselves.

We should not underestimate the subtlety with which the early schools of Buddhism sought to understand the mystery of impermanence: these schools were not talking about *dhammas* as if they were the objective constituents of the universe like the 'atoms' of Democritus or the periodic table of twentieth-century chemistry. Nonetheless, they did show a tendency to treat *dhammas* as ultimate, even without creating an actual philosophical theory of their ultimacy. The mind, it seems, can cope with certainties, even irrelevant certainties, much more easily than with incommunicable truths.

When some members of the dominant school in India in the early period of Buddhist history, the Sarvāstivādins, stated explicitly that *dhammas* were ultimate, it was realized by the people whom we might call the earliest Mahāyāna Buddhists that it had become necessary to reaffirm the Buddha's original teaching. The question was, how to get back to the original point that the five *khandhas* were meant to illustrate? Among all the early schools there was general agreement that while questions regarding the path were of utmost importance, more speculative questions and philosophical views did not affect one's progress to Enlightenment. But the Mahāyānists took the view that the reification of *dhammas* – that is, the view that the constituents of existence had some unchanging reality – limited the level of one's insight to that of *pudgala nairātmya* or 'no self in the person'. Progress to the realization of *dharma nairātmya*, 'no self in the *dhammas*', would occur only when that wrong view was abandoned. Not that the Sarvāstivādins would have agreed that what they were doing was reifying *dhammas*, but clearly the Mahāyānists felt that the point had to be made.

Before we look at the Mahāyāna perspective on the five *khandhas*, it is worth reminding ourselves of the history of that perspective. Clearly it differs in some ways from the recension of the Buddha's teachings found in the Pāli canon – but we need not assume that what we think of as 'Mahāyāna' was therefore a later development. Indeed, it is evident that Mahāyāna-type views had their antecedents very early in Buddhist history. The Pāli scriptures cannot be regarded as the only version of the Buddha's original dispensation, handed down exactly as received from the Enlightened master himself. For one thing, the form in which the Pāli canon has come down to us clearly owes much to succeeding generations of recorders of the oral tradition. In order to evaluate or even understand the Pāli canon, we must view it as a collection of disparate texts with different histories. But also, it is pure chance that it is this version of the teachings that was written down and preserved. It seems that from very early on the Dharma found expression in a great diversity of schools. One gets the impression that the Buddha's teaching was many-sided to begin with and that quite soon after the Buddha passed away a whole spectrum of schools emerged, interpreting and presenting different facets of the original dispensation. These traditions grew up gradually in an organic way and continued to flourish side by side at least until the reign of the emperor Aśoka in the third century BCE. Aśoka's accession to power was perhaps the most significant influence on the growth of Buddhism in India. A convert to Buddhism himself, one of his decrees was that messengers of the Dharma should go out into the world beyond the imperial frontiers. According to Sinhalese tradition it was Aśoka's son Mahinda who took the Buddha's teachings to Sri Lanka in oral form, and it was there that the teachings were eventually committed to writing shortly before the beginning of the Common Era.

With the Muslim invasions of mainland India in the eleventh and twelfth centuries, the extensive Buddhist culture that had prospered for some sixteen centuries was wiped out within a few short years, and Buddhism in India died out almost completely. No Pāli Buddhist texts and very few Sanskrit ones have subsequently been found there; those few that did survive have been taken out of ancient stupas in Nepal and Kashmir, or dug from the deserts of Afghanistan and central Asia. Only the Theravādin teachings were written down in Sri Lanka and thus escaped the obliteration of Buddhism in India, so that they have been preserved down to the present day in the form of the Pāli canon. When in the nineteenth century European scholars came upon this ancient work, there was no knowledge in the West of any other Buddhist canon to rival it. Thus what we now know as the Pāli canon gained its status as the major source of the Buddha's teaching for modern scholars through an accident of history rather than as a reflection of its original status within the tradition as a whole.

And the Pāli canon is itself a glorious mixture, a mishmash of mnemonic schemes organized for use in monastic instruction, reported sayings, additions and omissions by centuries of narrators. We can guess that the teachings as communicated by word of mouth had far more life and fluency than these written versions, which sometimes seem rather dry. Admittedly the Pāli canon is our main source of early Buddhist teaching, but given what we now know about the history of the Sangha in India, we can no longer take it as the definitive record of the Buddha's dispensation. Such records as we have of the schools that grew and flourished on the Indian mainland at around the same time as the Theravāda show a diversity of interpretation of the *Buddhavacana* (word of the Buddha) which is not to be found in the Pāli canon.

In a text called the *Mahāvastu*, for example, a very different spirit prevails. The *Mahāvastu* belongs to the *Vinaya* of the Lokottaravāda, an offshoot of the Mahāsāṃghika school. Although some of the material contained in it overlaps with the Pāli canon, its joyful and poetic tone contrasts markedly with the atmosphere of austere composure of many of the Theravādin texts. The *Mahāvastu* is ostensibly a book of monastic discipline, but unlike the Pāli Vinaya it contains practically no information on the rules of the order or their origin. It suggests a kind of Buddhism that emphasizes not codes, lectures, and prohibitions, but myths, stories, and celebrations of the heroic deeds of the great personalities of Buddhist history and legend. The exploits of the Buddhas of the past stand side by side with those of the Buddha Śākyamuni in his previous existences, stretching back into endless past aeons.

In short, the *Mahāvastu* gives a rather different impression of early Buddhism from that which we associate with the Pāli canon, indicating that significant sections of the early Buddhist sangha continued to follow practices and propagate teachings that were not to find their way into the Theravādin canon and that show – although at this stage relatively undeveloped – Mahāyāna characteristics. The Mahāyāna was evidently not just a movement of reaction to what it called the 'Hīnayāna': the *Mahāvastu* alone reveals the pre-Mahāyāna Buddhist scene as a far more diverse landscape than is commonly assumed. Early Buddhism, we can conclude, like the Mahāyāna later on, was more a broad spiritual movement than a particular school with a clear-cut scheme of doctrines and practices.

Nonetheless there was, of course, something of a transition from the first phase of Buddhist history to the second. And – this is where we return to the theme of the *khandhas* – it could be said that the transition from mainstream 'Hīnayāna' teaching into early Mahāyāna Buddhism turned upon the conception of *śūnyatā*, or the inherent emptiness of all phenomena. It was the *śūnyatā* doctrine that posed a direct challenge to the Hīnayāna's conception of *dhammas* as having some kind of ultimate nature. According to the Mahāyāna view, the belief in a plurality of ultimately existent *dhammas* is what prevented the Hīnayāna schools from entering into what might be called the deepest dimension of insight. It is a start to realize that the so-called personality is made up of subsidiary qualities, even of atoms or *dhammas*, but obviously it is no use if the 'start' is regarded as the end of the story, if these *dhammas* are not themselves seen to be without inherent existence. The truth the Mahāyānists perceived was that not only could these supposedly indivisible elements be broken down into even smaller parts, but this process could logically be extended indefinitely, so that the whole idea of a plurality of ultimate *dhammas* was therefore inherently absurd. This provided a clue to the significance of the concept of *śūnyatā*. Viewed from the perspective of *śūnyatā*, any term or concept is an *upāya* – a means to an end, not a fixed entity or ultimate truth. However hard we try, we cannot analyse everything to a conclusion, not even if we call that conclusion 'emptiness'.

This is why we have to be very cautious about even trying to say anything about *śūnyatā*. However much the mind desires certainty, words can only take us so far. It has been said that intelligence consists in the creative use of concepts; one might say that this definition must include the awareness that concepts cannot encompass the whole of reality. The great sages of the Mahāyāna, such as Vasubandhu and Asaṅga, taught that the doctrine of *śūnyatā* can only be perceived in a state in which all previous modes of thinking have been abandoned and the very concepts and symbols introduced by the various schools of Buddhism are understood to be no more than provisional aids to the attainment of Enlightenment. The doctrine of *śūnyatā* does not remove the need for other Buddhist teachings, for provisional truths, or for examination of the nature of the self and the mind along the lines of the five *khandhas* or the fuller analysis of the Abhidhamma. All it is meant to do is remind us that the ultimate point of our practice is not to be found in the means we employ to realize it.

The analysis of the thirty-one constituents which, through the analogy of a bag of mixed grains, are said earlier in the *Sutta* to make up the human body, can hardly be said to be adequate to the complexities of our physical condition. How much less adequate still is the doctrine of the five *khandhas* to the even greater complexities of the whole psychophysical organism. The five 'heaps' are sometimes less specifically divided, into two: *rūpa* or form being one, and *nāma* – comprising feeling, perception, volition, and consciousness – the other. When the Sarvāstivādin Abhidhamma scholars set to work, though, they came up with a far more sophisticated and systematic schema. This was based on three main categories – *rūpa*, *citta* (mind), and *cetasika-dhammas* (mental events) – each of which they subdivided in various ways.

But for all this elaboration, the Abhidhammists continued to base themselves on the same fundamental model. In the end it was never a very imaginative exercise. Even though some of the analysis throws useful light on the workings of the mind, the real point was somehow lost along the way. It could not help giving the impression that the mind is finally nothing more than a very complicated machine, made up of all manner of cogs and levers, pulleys and springs, which can be numbered and laid out in front of you in easily defined groups.

Such an impression is really inevitable, however sophisticated your model. The problem is more in our own minds than in the models we use: we tend to take ideas literally, to take models of things for the things themselves, to take the picture of what is going on for what is going on. Even with an aspect of ourselves that is clearly observable, the physical body, the precise nature of its workings is almost impossible to envisage: we might abandon the static image of the bag filled with thirty-one kinds of grain, but if we analyse the body down into organs, glands, systems, and all the various kinds of tissue, it still seems that we cannot help thinking in terms of bits and pieces rather than interacting processes. In the same way, *dhammas* remain essentially components, and useful as they may be in identifying the nature of our mental states; they do not do justice to the way the psychophysical organism works as a whole, any more than do the five *khandhas*. If we cannot stay aware that the five *khandhas* are not separable components but five sets of processes that are inextricably involved with one another, no amount of further analysis will make this any clearer.

Historically, the five-*khandha* classification is a very important teaching, and for this reason alone one cannot ignore it. As a Buddhist one needs to be very familiar with the list of the *khandhas*, at least in English and preferably in Pāli as well. If the classification of the *khandhas* is fundamental to the Buddhist tradition, however, it may seem rather less so to contemporary Buddhist practice as a modern practical proposition. Although it may help to overturn the illusion of a fixed personality, it still gives no more than a hint of the way in which the many activities of consciousness are interrelated at any given moment.

In short, the fivefold breakdown of our experience into form, feeling, perception, volition, and consciousness is not the only possible – or even necessarily the best – formulation of the principle that it is meant to convey. One might well decide that it is time to give the five *khandhas* – and all the *dhammas* into which they were subsequently divided – a well-earned retirement. It could even be that some modern formulation might be better: one of the advantages of Freud's analysis of human experience, for example, is that it does explicitly take account of the essentially dynamic nature of the psyche.

With some ancient Buddhist teachings, one might just about be able to see what they are getting at, but they need so much careful explanation that it might be more helpful to go back to the drawing board, try to reformulate the basic principle involved, and come up with an entirely fresh way of bringing the principle home to people. A modern Abhidhamma might be able to make use of developments in psychology, neuroscience, and anatomy, for example. Whether or not such an analysis was ultimately judged to be adequate, it would be useful because it would make us look more carefully at what the Buddha was trying to convey through the doctrine of the five *khandhas*. It might even be in the end that – for all our knowledge – the contemplation of the five *khandhas* would still prove to be the most effective practice to help us come to realize the conditioned, composite, dynamic, and insubstantial nature of things.

# 12
# INTERLUDE: ON FURTHER REFLECTION

One gets the impression that, far from having time on their hands, the monks in the Buddha's day were more or less fully occupied. There is a good day's work in just making one's way through a couple of sections of this teaching – considering what is involved, examining the operation of your own mind in the light of its analysis, and reflecting on your observations – let alone the lifetime's work of perfecting the practice. Once the monks had bathed, gone on their almsround and come back, eaten, and rested, the remainder of the day would have been spent in meditation, the sessions of seated practice would be interspersed with periods devoted to the regular, rhythmic exercise of what is called in Pāli *caṅkamana* – that is, walking up and down, or ambulating, as the practice is termed in the Christian tradition. (The cloisters of medieval monasteries and cathedrals were designed for this purpose.) I used to do this practice myself when I lived in Kalimpong, walking up and down the veranda every evening, and sometimes after lunch as well, to avoid the drowsiness that might have set in if I had sat down to meditate.

*Caṅkamana* not only provides physical exercise and relaxation; it is also a great aid to contemplation or reflection. The rhythmic quality characteristic of walking seems to be especially conducive to the purposive application of one's thinking to the investigation of a particular subject. This might be a doctrinal, philosophical, or spiritual question, or even some quite ordinary practical matter. A slow and measured walking pace seems to help bring one's mind to bear on that point of doctrine or that practical issue, isolating it from other concerns.

*Caṅkamana* as a Buddhist practice involves thinking of a very different kind from the aimless, more or less involuntary mental activity of ordinary daily life. One is thinking in a highly directed and specific way about the Dharma, the truth as experienced and taught by the Buddha. To be committed to this truth involves dwelling upon it in some depth – hence the importance of developing the ability to think clearly and directedly. To reflect on the Dharma is to reflect on the expression of fundamental truth in terms only barely accessible to human thought; without intellectual clarity we will be unable to grasp the essence of the teaching in all its subtlety and depth. If we are to practise Buddhism effectively, in short, we will need to learn to reflect.

It is not easy, however, to concentrate the mind and direct one's thoughts undistractedly for sustained periods. When you are engaged in a discussion or absorbed in a book, you might be able to hold your mind to a train of thought, but if you leave it to its own devices you are likely to find your attention wandering and your concentration starting to flag. You might set yourself to reflect undistractedly for an hour on, for instance, the three *lakṣaṇas* (Pāli *lakkhaṇas*), but it takes a lot of practice to manage more than a few minutes. (Anyone who doubts this should try it and see what happens.)

Thinking should be under one's control, and when it isn't objectively necessary one just shouldn't engage in it. The Buddha used to exhort his disciples to maintain a noble silence (Pāli *ariya-mona*) rather than indulge in unprofitable talk, and one could say that the same should go for thought-processes. The alternative to clear and mindful thinking should not be idle mental chatter; one should be able to maintain inner silence. Again, it is obviously a lot easier to say this than to do it – but it is possible.

One way to improve one's ability to think in a directed way is to plan time for thinking. One can learn to take up and put down one's thinking according to one's own needs, not just circumstances. Why not plan thinking time just as you schedule other activities? This is in effect a practice of *sampajañña*, mindfulness of purpose. We all have plenty to think about but our trains of thought seldom reach a conclusion. We are forever dropping one thing and picking up another, then when we sit down to meditate, unfinished business resurfaces and hinders our concentration. Such muddled mental activity is an obstacle to action of any kind and means that we often end up making decisions on the spur of the moment rather than thinking them through. If it is necessary to make a decision it is best to sit down, apply oneself to the matter in hand, and come to a well-considered conclusion. But if we sit down to reflect at all, we often turn the matter over in our mind in such a half-hearted way that quite soon our thoughts have wandered away to irrelevant topics. Unable to come to any clear conclusion, we just make the decision on the basis of how we happen to be feeling at the time, or in response to some quite incidental external pressure. We cannot afford to do this if our decisions are going to count for anything.

We should think about things when we have time to do them justice. Just as mealtimes, meeting friends, and making time for exercise and meditation involve making definite arrangements, mental activity can also be planned. You could apportion, say, an afternoon each week for thinking about things that really matter, things that are of much more consequence than day-to-day practicalities, although they might not be so pressing. If you keep yourself free of thinking about your deeper problems until the appointed time, you might also find everyday difficulties easier to deal with. If you try this out, though, make sure you are going to be free from interruption for however long you need – half an hour or an hour, or even weeks or months together. A chain of sustained and directed thinking can be very subtle, and to have it snapped by untimely and trivial interruptions is painful. The idea of planning in a period of thinking at two o'clock on Tuesday afternoon might come as a shock, but anyone with a busy life already has to do this to some extent. There are always urgent matters to attend to, but these should not be allowed to push the really important questions to the margins of our consciousness.

Whether planned or not, the best way to improve one's directed thinking is simply to think more. Just as physical exercise is the way to become fit, so thinking is the way to improve the capacity for thought. It is a good idea to take any opportunity you get to consider views and opinions with a logical, questioning attitude. Reasoned discussion with a friend or in a small group – the smaller the better – gives different angles on an issue and brings an enjoyable stimulus to thinking. Because our views tend to be emotionally based, if you are thinking about something on your own, there is always the temptation to come to a premature conclusion and resist thinking along lines that run counter to that conclusion. Collaborative thinking forces you to be more objective, to look for a truth that does not necessarily suit you. There is something about the physical presence of another person that generates interest and a keenness to get at the truth, and if you are talking with someone whose intellect is quite active, you might find that you have to get used to organizing and articulating your thoughts more carefully, to avoid non-sequiturs and short-cuts in your argument. Your friends might convince you, or you them. You might even end up convincing yourself, if you were not sure at the outset of the discussion what you really thought. Writing also helps to develop clear thinking – your argument has to be more rigorous than when you are speaking to people you know, and you have to be more careful to make logical connections between the ideas you present.

From the point of view of learning to think clearly, argument is better than agreement. If you only ever have discussions with people whose views you share and read books you agree with, you will never be obliged to address any faulty reasoning that might underpin your view of things. A valid conclusion does not guarantee the logic of any and every argument used in its support. A statement based on a poor line of argument – or no argument at all – might go unchallenged because everyone agrees with the conclusion anyway, regardless of how it is reached. It can therefore be a good idea to seek out a bit of opposition: there is nothing like meeting criticism for improving one's ability to frame a logical argument and make it watertight. Even though sound arguments are unlikely to win over someone with a deep emotional investment in the views they hold, trying to win that person over can make you aware of the strength or weakness of your logic. On the other hand, if your arguments do hold water, the confidence this gives you will help you to be more open to new ideas, because you will know that you have the ability to sift through them without getting muddled or feeling threatened.

The capacity for directed thinking is a characteristic of the truly integrated personality, and the more highly developed an individual is, the more capable of sustained and directed thought he or she will be. All too often, falling back on a romantic view of how thoughts arise, people believe there is some special faculty that makes a certain person an originator of new ideas, a 'genius'. This idea that you've either got genius or you haven't is of course a convenient excuse to disguise one's unwillingness to make the effort to think things through. Genius, the old saying goes, is an infinite capacity for taking pains, and chief among the qualities of someone who has it is sheer creative energy. When the whole person is integrated around a creative vision, the energy that arises can be tremendous. The works of Dickens, for example – a genius if ever there was one – are full of tremendous zest, and the same is true of those of Shakespeare, Mozart, Titian, and Rembrandt. Another quality that marks such geniuses out as special is their refusal to be caught up in the petty details of everyday life at the expense of a higher goal. Instead, they dedicate all their energies to the production of a truly great body of work.

In modern times people seem to desire to be 'original' at any cost, as though originality signified genius. But being different is not the same as being original. Original thought is always an extension of what has been thought by others in the past; originality thus requires you to interpret the tradition, and to do that you need to understand it. People would often rather not acknowledge their debt to tradition; they want to start being 'original' without troubling to master what has gone before them. But if you are really interested in a subject, you will want to know what others have had to say about it, and you might then see a way to move further in the same direction. That is the point at which original thought begins.

Most of the time, of course, our thoughts and ideas are far from original. They are also far from being directed; they arise haphazardly, stimulated by random external events and wandering from one thing to another. This kind of associative thinking does have its value. Just as your dreams – proceeding as they do by way of free association – can tell you something about yourself, so too can patterns of associative thought, if you can become aware of them. One thing leads apparently arbitrarily to another, but the connection is never as arbitrary as it seems. If you allow the mind to free-associate, it will still be choosing which direction it takes, though you will not be conscious of its choices. Wherever your thinking process starts, you will generally keep returning to much the same sequence of thoughts. To take the classic psychoanalytical scenario, you might find that your thoughts are always coming back to some aspect of your childhood, in one disguised form or another, and once you have realized this, you might be able to see a link between those early events and certain patterns of behaviour in the present. As you begin to understand your conditioning better, you free yourself from it.

Thus, associative thinking has its place in reflection, especially if you want to uncover something on an emotional level. Suppose, for example, that you are prone to anger: rather than following a strictly logical process of deduction, you might use associative thinking to feel your way closer to the source of your problem. And we are in a sense thinking associatively every time we use metaphor or symbol. Literature, especially poetry, often helps us to appreciate truths that could never be fully communicated in a logical way. But you have to keep an eye on the direction in which your thought is moving so that your associative thinking takes place within a broader sense of purpose. Despite its associative, impressionistic tone, you are not merely wool-gathering. It is still directed thinking in a sense, although it is being directed from a distance. Just as the recollected, purposeful aspect of mindfulness brings the mind back to the breath when you become distracted, so directed thinking draws your awareness back to the purpose of your mental activity. All your thinking should have an aim, even if that aim is sometimes best served by thinking associatively. Associative thought might help us to unearth resemblances and patterns hidden from rational thought, but this is only valuable if it helps us to arrive at a correct conclusion – that is to say, a true conclusion. Very often associative thinking arrives at no conclusions at all.

If your thinking has to lead somewhere, to solve a problem or explain something to someone, the connections between your thoughts must be logical, not private, arbitrary, or symbolic, however significant the latter kinds of connection might be. If you can't put an argument together, even if you are right, you will not be able to convince anyone else that you are. It is fine to pay attention to your intuition and feelings within the context of your own reflections, but it is not so reasonable then to dress up your feelings as objective facts. When someone says 'How do you know?' it is no good replying, 'Well, I just know,' however confident of your knowledge you feel. Either something is capable of demonstration or it isn't. You might have a well-developed intuitive faculty which you know you can rely on, but it is unreasonable to expect someone else to accept your views simply because you feel them to be true.

Of course, strong feeling has tremendous power to convince, especially if it is forcefully expressed, but it is all the more convincing if it is backed up by reason. For example, you could give a talk on compassion by evoking, in poetic and symbolic language, the figure of Avalokiteśvara, the bodhisattva who is the embodiment of that sublime quality. You might paint a vivid and appealing picture in the minds of your audience, but your communication would only be fully effective if you were able to demonstrate that the image corresponded in some way to some external reality – otherwise you would be left with a kind of extra-terrestrial, science-fictional figure. There is, in other words, a big difference between a compelling image of the ideal and the reality of that ideal. The Christian evangelist falls into a similar trap if he opens up his Bible and says, 'It must be true, it's written here,' – because, of course, the fact that certain assertions are printed in a book does not prove them to be true. He will have to demonstrate that the Bible has that kind of authority, and if he cannot do so, he will have no reason to be annoyed if other people cannot accept what he says.

One way to make your case is to refer to the experience of the person you are talking to. They might never have had dhyānic experience, for example, but you can give them an idea of what the *dhyānas* are like by referring to experiences that *are* familiar to them. Pleasure, for instance, is part of dhyānic experience and everyone has experienced at least some pleasure, so if you ask the person to imagine the pleasure they have experienced magnified ten or twenty times, they will get some sense of the intense pleasure of *dhyāna*. Likewise, we have all experienced at least short periods of creativity and positivity. If we were to imagine that positivity continuing unbroken for a whole day at a time, what would it be like? Imagine waking up in the morning with that positive feeling already there, so that you were happy and cheerful, and glad to jump out of bed and begin enjoying the day ahead. That mood would grow – you would become blissful, even rapturous, and certainly inspired – and that inspiration would have all sorts of consequences. You might be inspired to write a poem, or help a neighbour, or any number of things. Then imagine what those few hours of positivity would be like extended into a whole day, and another, and another, indefinitely, into a whole lifetime, week after week, month after month of creativity, building to ever higher and more positive levels of awareness. This is the kind of life to which the Buddhist aspires. Thus one might conclude if one were trying to describe the goal of Buddhism in terms with which someone else could identify. Starting from an everyday experience of positivity, you would use simple logic to suggest how the state of Enlightenment might be compared to it, if only very approximately. People are not always convinced by an image – metaphor and symbol hold different associations for different people – but reason is a language we all have in common.

But you don't always need to find a logical argument to show that something is true. If you have experienced the benefits of something, you can demonstrate them simply by being able to speak about them with confidence – or even just by being the way you are. For example, the fact that a Buddhist right livelihood business exists and thrives shows that it is possible to reject an economic system geared to material gain and still have a viable means of supporting oneself. If you are living contentedly in a single-sex community, this is direct evidence that true happiness does not depend upon being part of a nuclear family with the statutory number of children. The reality of your life is its own argument. This was especially true of the Buddha. If someone living at the Buddha's time had said they did not believe that the Enlightened state was possible, they only needed to observe the Buddha to see that it was indeed possible. His immense kindness, his intelligence, his very existence, was living proof of the possibility of Enlightenment.

For all its subtlety and rigour the Buddha's teaching is not in essence intellectual. For Buddhism the heart and the mind are not separate: the term *citta* refers to both, so that, for example, *bodhicitta*, the 'will to Enlightenment' which is the central aspiration of the Mahāyāna tradition, is not just a thought about Enlightenment in an abstract intellectual sense, but a heartfelt aspiration to emancipate oneself and all other beings from suffering.

In the early Buddhist tradition represented by such texts as the *Satipaṭṭhāna Sutta*, wisdom is also seen not as an intellectual pursuit but a spiritual one, to be realized through reflection, meditation, and direct experience. After all, there can be no intellectual clarity without an awareness of one's emotions. Even the most rigorously intellectual disciplines are taken up on the basis of some emotional motivation, and if this goes unacknowledged any pretensions to rationality are vitiated from the outset. By the same token, you will never be able to convince someone by rational argument if you fail to take their feelings into consideration: 'He that complies against his will,/ Is of his own opinion still', as Samuel Butler says.[78] This is the potential flaw in academic scholarship, even in the field known these days as Buddhist studies. Good scholarship is usually measured in terms of the strictness of its objectivity, and this is thought to mean setting aside one's own emotional responses to the material being studied – but this is not possible. There is no such thing as a 'pure' intellectual who is not influenced by the emotions. What, after all, is the reason behind one person's choice to take up, say, Tibetology while another chooses marine biology or nuclear physics? There is always some subjective element at work, and if it is not acknowledged it will make its presence felt by indirect means. Indeed, there is nothing wrong with an emotionally engaged argument, as long as those emotions are acknowledged. Problems only arise when you try to present your pet hobby-horse or deeply held conviction as unbiased logical thinking.

When it comes to mindfulness, what we are aiming for is an ability to think conceptually in a way that is infused with positive emotion. Thought cannot be separated from emotion; effective thinking is wholehearted, with the whole person focused on the activity and integrated around it – 'a man in his wholeness, wholly attending', as D. H. Lawrence wrote.[79] As with everything, we are looking for a middle way. We don't have to be intellectuals to be Buddhists – rather the opposite. We don't have to get bogged down in the minutiae of Abhidhamma philosophy; very often those who make the most spiritual progress are those who concentrate on the basic teachings. But although the intellectual study of Buddhism has its limitations, we cannot afford to underestimate its importance to the cultivation of insight. Whatever aspect of the teaching we decide to focus on, we must know it and practise it thoroughly, and for this a clear understanding of the tradition is essential. There is no substitute for a committed and clear effort to think things through. Any rational grasp of truth is provisional and we will have to venture beyond rational thinking in the end – but the end may be further away than we think.

# 13
# SENSING

> 'Again, bhikkhus, a bhikkhu abides contemplating mind-objects as mind-objects in terms of the six internal and external bases. And how does a bhikkhu abide contemplating mind-objects as mind-objects in terms of the six internal and external bases? Here a bhikkhu understands the eye, he understands forms, and he understands the fetter that arises dependent on both; and he also understands how there comes to be the arising of the unarisen fetter, and how there comes to be the abandoning of the arisen fetter, and how there comes to be the future non-arising of the abandoned fetter.
>
> 'He understands the ear, he understands sounds.... He understands the nose, he understands odours.... He understands the tongue, he understands flavours.... He understands the body, he understands tangibles.... He understands the mind, he understands mind-objects, and he understands the fetter that arises dependent on both; and he also understands how there comes to be the arising of the unarisen fetter, and how there comes to be the abandoning of the arisen fetter, and how there comes to be the future non-arising of the abandoned fetter.'

Like any other phenomenon, consciousness owes its arising to conditions and passes away when those conditions disperse or change. In the *kāmaloka*, the realm of sensuous desire, consciousness cannot arise without some kind of physical basis – in our case, the human body. This combination of mind and body, known in Buddhism as *nāma-rūpa* (which, as we have seen, is an abbreviated version of the five *skandhas* (Pāli *khandhas*), appears among the twelve links of dependent origination on the Tibetan wheel of life in the form of a boat with four passengers, one of whom, the one representing the mind, is steering. Further round the wheel, in dependence upon name and form come the six sense bases, represented by a house with five windows and a door – appropriately, because the six senses are the six ways in which external phenomena enter or impinge upon our awareness. Consciousness is not fixed but changes from moment to moment as the sense organs, including the mind, meet their objects. Sight-consciousness, for example, arises when the external object impinges upon the eye and that object is brought into the field of visual awareness. Then, when a different object comes into view, a new mode of sight-consciousness arises. It is this interaction between internal and external sense bases, combining again and again, that brings about a continuous flow of awareness.

Buddhism calls these internal and external factors of sense experience the twelve *āyatanas*. Since we have six sense bases and six kinds of object – sight, hearing, and so on, including the mind – the forms of consciousnesses that arise when they meet are also of six kinds. Add these six kinds of consciousness to the twelve *āyatanas* and you get what are known collectively as the eighteen *dhātus*. They give us a closer analysis of experience than the hindrances or even the *skandhas*, and through them we can become aware of how mental states emerge into consciousness time and time again. In the case of the root negative mental states – greed, hatred, and delusion – they emerge in the form of what are known, tellingly, as fetters: the various kinds of habitual and reactive behaviour that prevent us from being able to experience consciousness in its pure form.

The act of sensing is in itself quite innocent; the mere fact that you happen to see something or think of something has no karmic repercussions. What is karmically significant is the state of consciousness that arises in dependence on that sensory contact. For instance, when you look at a flower, there is no craving present in that simple looking, but it may be that in dependence upon the sight of the flower, you develop a craving to pick it, to possess it, to make it your own. This state of consciousness, arising in dependence upon the sensory event, defiles that pure awareness, and thus begins sensual desire. But this chain of events is not inevitable. Indeed, the aim of the contemplation of the six sense bases and their objects is to prevent the arising of that unskilful mental state, to leave a pristine, non-deluded consciousness of reality.

This state of pure awareness might seem a long way from our everyday experience, but it does sometimes happen that we are able to be aware of things in this way, at least briefly. At the end of a session of meditation, when you have just opened your eyes, you might be content just to sit for a moment, before your mind starts to tick over and desires take hold. Or you might sometimes look at nature with a comparatively innocent eye, not wanting to make use of what you see or even take a photograph, but appreciating it for its own sake. But it is only when one has entered upon the path of transcendental insight that this state of mind becomes a regular feature of life.

A Hindu *yoginī* once suggested to me that the pleasure one experiences upon attaining the object of one's desire is produced not, as it might appear, by the obtaining of the object, but by the fact that, for a moment at least, desire has ceased to operate, and you are no longer looking outside yourself for contentment. If you have satisfied your hunger by eating an enjoyable meal, for example, you might be able to look at a lovely bunch of grapes with no desire to eat even one. At that moment, with your appetite satisfied for the time being, desire has all but disappeared from consciousness and you can for once look at something without wanting anything from what you see. But until you have attained insight, such purity of awareness can only be a temporary respite. It will only be a matter of time before you will start to look at those grapes with a different eye because, after all, it would be such a pity to waste them....

However, the fact that we have occasional moments of freedom, when the power of craving has been attenuated and we can look at things in comparative innocence, shows that there can be sensuous enjoyment without sensual desire. There is nothing wrong with seeing and hearing, with a sense organ coming into contact with a sense object, nor indeed with the feeling that arises in dependence upon that contact. It is only when craving – or one of the other fetters – arises in dependence upon feeling that our problems start – and also where the solution to those problems is to be found. At the very beginning of the *Sutta* we learned that the *bhikkhu* 'abides … having put away covetousness and grief for the world', and the laconic conjunction of these two makes the nature of the problem plain. Suffering is the inevitable fruit of craving. It is in our actions, whether of thought, word, or deed, that we are skilful or unskilful, not in what we experience. It is how we go about choosing our experience that determines the ethical weight of any situation in which we become involved. It is when we want a bit more out of our sense experience than the sense experience itself that we get into trouble.

In the *Udāna*, the 'verses of uplift', the Buddha gives exactly this teaching to the mendicant Bāhiya:

> 'Then, Bāhiya, thus you must train yourself: in the seen there will be just the seen, in the heard just the heard, in the imagined just the imagined, in the cognized just the cognized. Thus you will have no "thereby".'[80]

In other words, if you see something, just see. Don't read anything into the experience – just see what is there. In the same way, just hear, just touch, just taste, just smell, just imagine. If thought is needed, go ahead and think. But think and have done with it – don't wander off along the way. And if you become aware that you have wandered off, don't make a drama out of it; let the critical moment of awareness be what it is, no more and no less. The moment of awareness is a time to be aware, not a time to speculate about the whys and wherefores of the situation. Give up the mental commentary, the ego-based, interpreting 'thereby'.

Just see. Just think. It sounds simple enough. But if you have ever tried to achieve such mental clarity, you will know exactly how difficult it is. Once it is accomplished, the awareness created is like a mirror, reflecting everything without distortion. Crucially, however – and this is what makes it so difficult – it should not be cold like a mirror, it should not be an alienated awareness that stands back from its objects, coolly looking on without really experiencing them. It is a truly unfettered consciousness, known in the Vajrayāna tradition as the wisdom of Akṣobhya, the imperturbable deep blue Buddha of the five-Buddha mandala. His 'mirror-like' wisdom is not a cold hard surface from which experience bounces away, but a deeply responsive awareness which has no need to force its own views onto what arises in its depths. This pure unadulterated experience is like that of the skilled musician immersed in a beautiful symphony. If he were to linger in playing any of the music, to savour and enjoy it more, the music would be ruined. Yet that is what we so often want to do. We won't let the music continue. We want to play one little passage again and again, refusing to let the symphony of life go on. But if we could be a living mirror (or echo), happy to appreciate phenomena just as they are, we would be content simply to experience and let go.

The Buddha spoke of the mental states that hold us back from that pure awareness as fetters. He probably didn't have a particular list of fetters in mind when he gave this teaching. The *Satipaṭṭhāna Sutta* does not list them all, and indeed there is no single definitive list in use throughout the Buddhist tradition, but one example is the list of ten fetters put forward by the Abhidhamma, which includes belief in a fixed self, doubt about the truth, attachment to rules and rituals as ends in themselves, hatred, various kinds of desire, conceit, and ignorance.[81] Any of these fetters will tend to arise whenever an external sense base impinges upon one or more of the corresponding internal bases. Ideally one would learn to exercise such vigilance that the fetters didn't have a chance to get a grip, but would be broken very quickly – but this is much easier said than done. One can suppress the hindrances temporarily in meditation, but to break the fetters once and for all, one has to develop insight.

The overlap between the hindrances and the fetters – sensual desire, doubt, restlessness, and ill will appear in both formulations – indicates that the two groups of negative mental states are not distinct classifications. Various groupings of positive states overlap similarly – indeed all the groups of 'mental objects', from the hindrances to the four noble truths, consider the same states of consciousness from different angles. The fetters and the hindrances in particular are two ways of understanding what are basically the same drives, the difference between them being a matter of the breadth of one's perspective. If you are trying to overcome the hindrances, the aim is the practical one of absorbed meditation, while the attempt to break the fetters is made with the aim of attaining insight. You eradicate the hindrances temporarily every time you attain states of *dhyāna* in meditation. When sensual desire arises as a hindrance, for example, you can put it into a kind of temporary suspension in order to concentrate and unify your mind, but this doesn't conduce directly to insight as it would if the corresponding fetter had been broken: the potential for the hindrance is still there and it could still re-emerge into consciousness in any situation in which the internal and external sense bases come together.

Both the fetters and the hindrances are cyclical in nature; they will come around again and again in dependence on the particular ways in which you habitually seek satisfaction. You might perhaps hear a sound in the kitchen and in dependence on this the thought of food might enter your mind, swiftly followed by a memory of some sweet taste. Before you know it, through sheer force of habit you are beginning to hanker for something to eat. The fetter of sensual desire has arisen due to the hearing faculty, in a sense, but it is not really the sound that made it arise – the chief conditioning factor was the accumulated force of your own karma, resulting from having given what is called 'unwise attention' to sense-objects in the past. Perhaps you have always greedily enjoyed eating sweet things, so that your mind continually looks for an opportunity to have that sensation again. This is where the development of awareness comes in: when you become aware that this is happening, you can file away at that fetter just a little more, before it disappears again out of your conscious awareness.

The metaphor of the fetter is rather misleading. A single decisive moment of mindfulness will not be sufficient to break a fetter: the fetters are deeply entrenched in our psychophysical make-up, not to be broken without the continuous and long-term application of mindfulness. Sensual desire, like the other fetters, is an extension of the body's functions, inherited from the lower evolution; it is written into the very fabric of body-and-mind. If you feel hungry you might start searching for something to eat without even being aware you are doing so. You have the drive of sensual desire because you have a body – and the body is itself the product of your karma, your past habitual action. Through the deep-seated will to 'be', you have provided yourself, in the form of your present body, with the means of giving expression to all those fetters, including the belief in a separate self that underpins them.

We cannot look back to a time when we were free of the fetters. It is sometimes considered that children are innocent. In modern times ideas of impurity and immorality have tended to be associated almost exclusively with sexuality, and in that sense children are innocent; they are also innocent in the eyes of the law, which does not hold them responsible for their actions. But interestingly, the more we are socially conditioned to think of children as innocent, the more they seem to become selfish little monsters. Innocence is not something we have lost, to be rediscovered. The fetters are there from the beginning: they are beginningless, self-renewing, and thus potentially endless.

The aim of spiritual practice is to redirect this cyclic flow of semi-conscious volitions. By bringing awareness into the fetters as they arise from sense contact, we send the energies involved in them onto a more creative path, thus adding a fresh dimension to our experience, like a three-dimensional spiral emerging out of a two-dimensional circle. Every time we break out of the cycle of reactivity, every time we choose not to turn in upon ourselves in a reflex of greed or cynicism, ill will or restlessness, we are opening up to a new way of being or, in other words, embarking on what is often called the spiral path. And every time we fail to make this creative shift away from unreflective habitual action, we reinforce the fetters and reduce the strength of our will to break free of them. Spiritual practice is always a decisive act; conversely, the fetters, being the product of the whole cyclical mode of reactive consciousness, are perpetuated by our just going with the flow. This is the anguish of the ghost of Jacob Marley who, in Dickens' *A Christmas Carol*, appears before Scrooge fettered by a terrible chain and curdles his former business partner's blood with a fearful admission: 'I wear the chain I forged in life. I made it link by link, and yard by yard; I girded it on of my own free will, and of my own free will I wore it. Is its pattern strange to *you*?'

Maintaining enough vigilance to stop the perpetual reforging of the fetters is very demanding, at least at first. But if you sustain that directed effort, in the end it is sure to bring about the arising of transcendental insight. 'If the doors of perception were cleansed,' says Blake, 'everything would appear to man as it is, infinite.' When in the seen there is only the seen, consciousness ultimately opens out into a non-dual awareness. When your vision is as clear as this, you see impermanence not as something marked off in steps and stages – the impermanence of particular things – but as an unbounded, unbroken flow, so that you have no need to hang on to an idea of an unchanging sense of self to connect all these supposed fragments together. This goal of seeing everything as 'infinite' can seem alienating, as if one is supposed to become something one isn't or even no one at all. But the reality is simpler: when the doors of perception are cleansed, you perceive more clearly and brightly than ever before – though it is difficult to say *what* you see and realize.

Through the practice of mindfulness, as the obscurations to perfect vision are progressively removed, insight begins to unfold of its own accord. The first stage in this process culminates in the point of 'entering the Stream', or what is also known as the opening of the Dharma eye. According to the Pāli texts there are ten fetters holding us back from perfect insight and one enters the Stream when the first three of them have been worn so thin that they finally break. These three fetters are: belief in a fixed self, doubt about the truth, and attachment to moral rules and rituals as ends in themselves – and each of them has to be removed before we can make any real progress. The fact that they are all broken together at the point of Stream Entry suggests that they are in a way one and the same fetter, viewed from different angles. They certainly share a characteristic that marks them out from the other seven: they are each 'intellectual' – that is, they consist essentially in an attitude of mind. However much we have to take into account their emotional underpinning, they each consist ostensibly in an explicit view, a consciously formulated attitude. They represent the way we usually look at things on the conscious level and can thus be addressed and seen through in conceptual, intellectual terms – hence the usefulness of developing the ability to pursue directed thought.

One might object that our view of the self as unchanging is based on emotions rather than being an intellectual conviction – but this view is still amenable to intellectual examination. We have already considered the impermanence of the physical body in connection with the cemetery contemplations: a dead body changes very quickly indeed. Nor does death provide the sole evidence for physical impermanence: just standing regularly on the bathroom scales will show that your body changes from week to week, and changes in others are even more perceptible, especially when you haven't seen someone for a while. However, even though most people will be prepared to admit, albeit reluctantly, to being physically impermanent, they will still claim to find something unchanging amid this ceaseless bodily and mental change. This is what is meant by the belief in a fixed self or ego identity. To know something – indeed, to know anything – seems naturally to call for a 'knower' as well as something that is known. But the Buddhist position runs counter to this intuitive 'knowledge': it asks us to note what we observe in our actual experience from moment to moment and then ask ourselves whether we can really deduce, from the stream of sense impressions alone, the presence of a permanent self that 'has' all these experiences. Obviously, this is a question to which a negative answer is expected. According to Buddhist philosophy, all we can say with certainty is that consciousness exists. The unchanging self or soul that is supposedly the source of that consciousness is something we have added on, an illusion produced by the very activity of dualistic thinking. It is our belief in its existence that ultimately holds us back from insight into the nature of things as they really are – and if we can convince ourselves through our own observation that this 'self' is an illusion, the fetter will be broken.

The fetter of doubt will also eventually give way under the pressure of clear understanding, close observation, and sustained reflection. It is not thinking the wrong thoughts or asking awkward questions that constitutes the kind of doubt meant here. Doubt binds us as a fetter when we do not investigate those thoughts and questions deeply enough but take up an inflexible attitude of scepticism and indecision. As for the third fetter, 'reliance on rites and rituals as ends in themselves', this is in a sense at the opposite pole from doubt: it is a fidelity to one's practice that is not questioned enough. It is not the observances and rituals themselves that bind us; they are an essential support for spiritual practice. The fetter consists in simply going through the motions of religious activity but forgetting its true purpose.

The more you consider your experience in the light of the doctrines and practices taught by the Buddha, the clearer a sense you will get of what freedom from these fetters might mean. This is what is called by the Buddhist tradition 'right view'. With further practice, as you put more and more energy into the whole process, backing it up with meditation, that understanding will eventually produce a decisive change of direction in the whole current of your being. From that point onwards it is impossible to fall back. Once you have made this decisive break with the cycle of death and rebirth, a breakthrough which the Buddhist tradition calls Stream Entry, you are no longer a victim, dominated by and trapped in these deeply-rooted tendencies, and you can expect to be reborn in the human realm no more than seven times before the attainment of complete Enlightenment.

Although the breaking of the first three fetters calls for particular effort on the intellectual level, you can break them only if the whole of you is involved. Reason and emotion are not separate: challenging your most cherished assumptions about the nature of things and looking deeply into your habits of mind calls for a strongly positive emotional drive. Insight cannot be achieved by rational means alone. You are attempting to shift the basis of your entire life, and to do this demands a powerful and positive – even joyful – emotional commitment. The fetter of dependence on rules and ritual observances as ends in themselves, for example, is more than just a superficial approach to ritual practices. It is a lack of wholeheartedness throughout your spiritual life, a holding back from total involvement, a reluctance to bring your deeper emotions into play, a lazy wish to believe that going through the motions will be enough to see you through.

The first three fetters are called 'intellectual' in part by way of contrast with the remaining seven, which are more clearly emotional, involving as they do deep-seated attitudes that make them even less accessible to conscious transformation. The next phase in this gradual process of awakening involves breaking the fetters of sensuous desire and ill will, both of which persist in subtle forms even beyond Stream Entry. And one has to be a considerable way along the transcendental path before one becomes free of the fetter of *bhava-rāga*, the desire for continuing existence. We have a natural urge to go on living: even someone who is very ill may cling to life although there is no pleasure in it. *Bhava-rāga* means that you want to exist on whatever terms are possible: it runs very deep in us and indeed continues to be present in consciousness well beyond Stream Entry. It manifests particularly in the *dhyānas*: at those refined levels of meditation, one's experience is so satisfying that one would be quite happy for that state to carry on for ever. Desire for such refined states is a positive thing, but attachment to them becomes a fetter, because you have ceased to look beyond them towards transcendental insight. This happens on a more subtle level still in relation to immaterial existence in the even more sublime state called the *arūpaloka*, and it happens until such time as the seventh fetter is broken.

As one gets deeper into meditation the variety of subtle mental impressions, hitherto overlooked, begin to stand out more clearly, and very subtle forms of the fetters become apparent: the fetter of restlessness, for example. It may be experienced in a subtle form as a mental sensation which troubles you even when your meditation is apparently going very well. You might be quite deeply absorbed and then, for no apparent reason, the idea might suddenly arise that you should end the meditation and get back to mundane consciousness, even if you have no need to do so. Or perhaps a breeze begins to blow outside and although your meditation is becoming more concentrated, the thought 'It's going to be a windy night' arises in your mind. There might be no craving present, no hatred, no sloth or torpor, but still a thought will just quietly float into the mind as a slight anxiety, a subtle failure of confidence, a wisp of self-concern. Restlessness rises from deep within the psyche. On the threshold of Enlightenment it is obviously not merely a psychological fidgeting. One might call it a sort of oscillation between the most subtle mundane experience and the transcendental, a last flicker of attachment to the conditioned.

If it seems strange that this hindrance should recur so far up the spiral path, we can remind ourselves that these lists and categories are not to be taken too literally. Doubt, for instance, is listed as one of the first three fetters to be broken, and certainly a substantial degree of sceptical doubt, the wilful indecisiveness that stops us from entering on the transcendental path, disappears at Stream Entry. But even when such doubt is out of the way, there is still the possibility of doubt arising with regard to that which, for the time being, lies beyond one's own experience. At any stage you can entertain doubt with regard to what a higher stage might be like and what you have to do to get there. You might even wonder whether there is a higher stage at all; you might think you have got as far as it is possible to go, a doubt which is clearly linked to the fetter of desire for continued existence in the realm of immaterial form. Thus, even though doubt is one of the first three fetters to be broken, you cannot abolish it conclusively until you have abolished ignorance, the very last fetter to be broken, according to the Pāli canon.[82] In other words, only an *arhant* or a Buddha is absolutely free of the fetter of doubt. Inasmuch as you do not have actual knowledge of the transcendental, because it is beyond your present experience, you are to that extent ignorant, and where there is ignorance there must be at least a degree of doubt.

Indeed, one might even say that ignorance is the only fetter and that all the others are different aspects of it. All the fetters, gross and subtle, imply the continued presence of the conception of a separate self: the self-view eliminated when the first three fetters are broken is only a relatively gross form of that mental attitude, which recurs in subtler forms in the fetters that are broken at more advanced stages of development. Conceit, the idea of oneself as being in some way comparable to other people (whether as superior, inferior, or equal), is the most obvious example, but even this is not the subtlest self-view of all.

Dualistic consciousness is what splits our experience into 'me' and 'the world' – and this, according to the Buddhist analysis, is our fundamental mistake. Subject and object arise in dependence on each other – there is no continuity of an unchanging person. The 'ego', with its likes and dislikes, views and opinions, is a self-perpetuating illusion, arising in dependence on our previous actions, our ingrained habits of consciousness. But although in reality there is no separation between subject and object, we are unable to plunge into that realization because of the mind-made fetters that hold us back. Herein lies the importance of contemplating the six sense bases and their objects. When the internal sense base comes into contact with the external object, if you give very careful attention to what happens as a result, you will in the end come to see how the mind fabricates from that interaction a self and a world, unable to stay open to the ever-changing flux of things. Human kind cannot bear very much reality, said T. S. Eliot.[83] But we can learn to bear it – indeed, it is the wellspring of freedom and joy – if we train ourselves to see it steadily and see it whole.

The Buddha's last words, we are told, were *appamādena sampādetha* – with mindfulness, strive.[84] *Appamāda* is a kind of zeal that never lets a single opportunity go by, a keenness to get on with the things that really matter in the knowledge that there is no time to waste. If you mean to attain Stream Entry in this lifetime, everything of which you become conscious is significant and you cannot afford to let it slip past. Conditions change continuously and as they change, any of the fetters, or a combination of fetters, is likely to get a grip on us. We have to strive constantly to be aware of whether our responses to input through the six senses, including the mind, are conducive to freedom or to bondage, whether our efforts (or lack of them) are making the fetters stronger or weaker, and whether or not our states of consciousness are conducive to our ultimate liberation. If you go for a walk, you have to be aware of the thousands of impressions that come crowding in on you and know just what effect they are having on you. And you have to keep this up from instant to instant, minute to minute, hour to hour, all day and every day throughout the weeks, months, and years. There can be no holiday, no time out from mindfulness. You have to be ever-vigilant. And you must be vigilant not because any authority tells you that you must, but because the price of slackening off – an endless succession of rebirths in the six realms of existence – is simply not worth paying.

# 14
# ENLIGHTENING

'Again, bhikkhus, a bhikkhu abides contemplating mind-objects as mind-objects in terms of the seven enlightenment factors. And how does a bhikkhu abide contemplating mind-objects as mind-objects in terms of the seven enlightenment factors? Here, there being the mindfulness enlightenment factor in him, a bhikkhu understands: "There is the mindfulness enlightenment factor in me"; or there being no mindfulness enlightenment factor in him, he understands: "There is no mindfulness enlightenment factor in me"; and he also understands how there comes to be the arising of the unarisen mindfulness enlightenment factor, and how the arisen mindfulness enlightenment factor comes to fulfilment by development.'

'There being the investigation-of-states enlightenment factor in him.... There being the energy enlightenment factor in him.... There being the rapture enlightenment factor in him.... There being the tranquillity enlightenment factor in him.... There being the concentration enlightenment factor in him.... There being the equanimity enlightenment factor in him, a bhikkhu understands: "There is the equanimity enlightenment factor in me"; or there being no equanimity enlightenment factor in him, he understands: "There is no equanimity enlightenment factor in me"; and he also understands how there comes to be the arising of the unarisen equanimity enlightenment factor, and how the arisen equanimity enlightenment factor comes to fulfilment by development.'

The Buddhist path is essentially a creative process, transforming something positive into something more positive, and creating from that something more positive still. We are given a powerful illustration of that progressive positive vision in a teaching called the *bojjhaṅgas* (Sanskrit *bodhyaṅgas*), the seven factors of Enlightenment, and it is this vision which we are now urged to contemplate. The value of this series consists in its communication of a clear sense of accumulation and development. And the point of departure, the first of the seven factors, is our old friend, mindfulness.

### MINDFULNESS (*SATI*)

We can take it that under the heading of mindfulness is included everything we have learned about it from the *Sutta* so far, but the especially important factor here is the recollection of the need to be mindful at all. There is a curious circularity to the text here: it says in effect that the monk is aware that he is aware, or aware that he is not aware. This makes more sense than may at first appear: the dawning of awareness is usually the result of becoming aware that one has been unaware – all too often as a result of the painful consequences of that lack of awareness. For instance, you might be walking unmindfully along the pavement with the result that you bump into a lamp-post: this is the moment at which you become aware that you have been unaware. Awareness is often forced on us in this way. A less painful way of becoming mindful is to trust the judgement of our spiritual friends, who, if we let them, will perhaps be able to nudge us into mindfulness before we bump into a metaphorical lamp-post. When the monk in the *Sutta* is aware that 'there is no mindfulness enlightenment factor in me', which on the face of it sounds contradictory, that awareness presumably comes from a limited, intermittent mindfulness that might be more fully developed and sustained.

It is so easy to lose touch with mindfulness, especially when things are going well. Success tends to make us over-confident, and that is when we start to make mistakes. It is what the ancient Greeks called *hubris* – the rashness that comes when you are riding the crest of a wave. It is therefore precisely when you feel most successful that you need to take most care to stay mindful: your very success can betray you, with disastrous consequences. Of course, if you don't realize what is happening in time, you will eventually be overtaken by the results of your karma and thus be forced to recollect yourself as you suffer the unexpected and painful consequences of your lack of awareness. The Greeks had a word for this, too – *nemesis*, the punishment of the gods whose wrath you have incurred, which will overtake you sooner or later. By ensuring that you know when the factor of mindfulness is not in you, as the *Sutta* puts it, you can avoid that pain, quickly regaining your mindfulness in any situation in which it might temporarily have disappeared.

The whole series of enlightenment factors thus begins with a simple question: 'Am I being mindful?' That question implies a degree of achieved mindfulness, but also an awareness that this mindfulness may be lost. Indeed, it is safe to say that it will certainly be lost; our job is to make the most of each moment of mindfulness, not waste it in fruitless regrets about the period of unmindfulness it has succeeded or in grandiose fantasies about the transformed life it is heralding. At the same time, our mindfulness should include an awareness of the conditions that will support mindfulness and those that will undermine it. We need to see clearly where our mindfulness comes from and where it disappears to, and actually do something about whatever promotes it or banishes it. As we know by now, there is more to mindfulness than being aware: it is an intelligent and active awareness.

This is where *sati-sampajañña*, clear comprehension of purpose, comes in: you need to be clear about what kinds of situation help you keep the goal firmly in mind. But it works the other way round too; your *sampajañña* can rescue you from sticky situations. Suppose you have become involved in something without much awareness, and then – when you think about it – you realize that what you are doing is rather unskilful. You might choose to turn a blind eye to that realization, of course, but prompted by a sudden recollection of purpose you might ask yourself, 'Why on earth am I doing this?' and at once your eyes will be opened. Bringing mindfulness of purpose to any activity always has the effect of reminding you of your original intention to cultivate more awareness. On a loftier level, it is also the impetus to escape the round of rebirth by attaining transcendental insight. Whether simply in day-to-day living or in the fulfilment of your life's ambition, *sati-sampajañña* steers your consciousness towards your true heart's desire and away from any distractions or obstacles, and the spark that lights the fire of *sampajañña* is mindfulness. Reflexive consciousness, the awareness that you are aware, is what sparks off the whole process of spiritual growth. This is where it all starts. In the *Satipaṭṭhāna Sutta*'s confident words, the monk 'understands how there comes to be the arising of the unarisen mindfulness enlightenment factor, and how the arisen mindfulness enlightenment factor comes to fulfilment by development'. That is, he understands not only how to establish the conditions for the arising of mindfulness but also the conditions that will support the arising of a faculty of mindfulness that is independent of conditions and will therefore never be lost, whatever happens.

### INVESTIGATION OF STATES (*DHAMMA-VICAYA*)

The second stage in the sequence, *dhamma-vicaya*, takes this self-reflexive awareness one step further. While mindfulness is becoming aware of the contents of one's consciousness, *dhamma-vicaya* is differentiating between the mental objects revealed by that mindfulness – in other words, sorting out the contents of one's consciousness. While *dhamma-vicaya* may be translated as 'the investigation of the Buddha's teaching', it is more appropriate in this context to take *dhamma* – without the capital letter – to mean 'state of consciousness', so that *dhamma-vicaya* means 'investigation into one's own states of consciousness', or introspection. Dharma knowledge will certainly help you to classify and evaluate your mental states, but the other enlightenment factors in the list, like mindfulness and energy, suggest that the terms of reference here are psychological and spiritual rather than intellectual: one is not just investigating things in a purely philosophical sense. It is the faculty of *dhamma-vicaya*, with which we sort out our states of consciousness into the skilful – which we need to cultivate – and the unskilful – which we need to transform.

Just as mindfulness involves knowing how to stay mindful, we need to be clear about what helps or hinders the arising of the quality of *dhamma-vicaya*. It might be the advice of your spiritual friends, for example, as they apply their clear comprehension of purpose for your benefit. It might be a certain intellectual curiosity, an interest in psychological processes that helps to bring you back to a critical awareness of your mental states. Perhaps more helpful still is to see for yourself the need to keep up that sort of investigation, both with your general well-being in mind and in view of your overall spiritual purpose. You remind yourself that some mental states are truly fulfilling while others just dissipate your energies, and that it is a good idea to spot them as they crop up rather than waiting until you are suffering their consequences.

### ENERGY (*VIRIYA*)

Dwelling on any skilful state of mind makes it grow. As a consequence of *dhamma-vicaya* you will naturally turn more and more of your attention towards the positive aspects of your experience, and at the same time you will find you are withdrawing energy and interest from things that hold you back – which will result in a tremendous release of positive energy. Often, much of our energy is tied up in internal conflict, one impetus cancelling out another so that we stultify ourselves and very little of our energy is freely available to us. But as – through *dhamma-vicaya* – our priorities become clearer, conflicts are resolved and energy is released. Like someone who leaps up when he sits on a hot radiator, your energies are activated when it becomes blazingly obvious that unskilful actions *are* unskilful, being bungling and unhelpful, and that skilful actions are something of an accomplishment, calling for resourcefulness, finesse, and the ability to discriminate.

Energy as a *bojjhaṅga* – *viriya* (Sanskrit *vīrya*) – is different from what we usually mean by the word. Indeed, there is no Pāli word for our concept of energy, which derives from western science and has been co-opted by psychology. *Viriya* is not just the measure of our capacity to work or play: it is 'energy or vigour in pursuit of the ethically skilful', an active state of being which is developed specifically by the practice of a combination of mindfulness and *dhamma-vicaya*.

Working with energy is progressive. First of all, you have to be aware of the quality of your energy: whether it is blocked by inner conflict or draining away in unskilful activity; whether you are sluggish or shallow or restless, boiling with intense anger or idly distracted, bubbling with *joie de vivre* or overflowing with sympathy. As you become sensitive to more subtle energies, you can learn to work with them directly – which is one of the concerns of the Buddhist Tantra. It is useful to think of the hindrances and even to try to experience them as energy that is going to waste or getting stuck. In meditation you gradually gather your energy together and then direct and channel it, so that it is intensified, refined, and transformed. You can also bring this perspective into the practice of ethics, seeing it as the effort to avoid blocking, misusing, manipulating, exploiting, appropriating, or poisoning the energy of others – or your own energy. This can be a useful way of contacting the spirit of the practice, as long as it goes hand in hand with a consistent effort to fulfil the letter of it. Through mindfulness you become aware of the various ways in which *viriya* gets lost – in craving, worry, watching television, desultory reading, gossiping, parties, romance.... And you also know where it can be found. That same energy is aroused and expressed through friendship, the arts, devotional practice, reflection, work, and many other ways. There are also many ways of containing it: regularity of lifestyle, a strong ethical practice, retreats, silence, stillness, celibacy, meditation....

Expressing positive energy is always pleasurable, and that in itself makes for more integration and therefore yet more vigour – and so these states accumulate and spiral upwards, each supporting the others. The *Sutta* describes the *bhikkhu* as 'ardent, fully aware, and mindful', and it might well be said that one's energies, all working together, impart a healthy spiritual glow. Like the Pāli word it is translating, *ātāpa*, the word 'ardent' has connotations of warmth, suggesting not a cool, cerebral approach to life, but an iridescent mindfulness, an emotionally committed, passionate awareness. This incandescence, this *tejo* or fiery energy, will be sure to arise if all your energies are going into skilful mental states, and that vigour or energy, so long as it is not obstructed, will build up steadily in a kind of chain reaction, drawing into it energy that was hitherto locked up, and giving rise to the next enlightenment factor: *pīti*.

### RAPTURE (*PĪTI*)

With rapture or *pīti* (Sanskrit *prīti*) the unmistakably cumulative and creative nature of the *bojjhaṅgas* really emerges: here we experience the snowballing quality of spiritual development most spectacularly. In the process of becoming more mindful, you draw your energies together and a fragmented sense of self becomes an integrated individuality. As a result, more and more energy is liberated, and joy or rapture starts to bubble up. 'Rapture' is perhaps the best translation of *pīti*, because this surge of subtle but intense emotional and physical pleasure has the quality of something welling up, overflowing, superabundant, even a little out of control.

Free-flowing energy is pleasurable in itself, but *pīti* goes beyond that; it is a release that comes from a deeper source of energy that has been blocked until then. This blocked energy is caught up in the current of moving energy and released until – needing an outlet – it manifests in various physical ways. It is what happens when a beautiful piece of music stirs something so deep in you that you have no words to express what you feel. The hairs on your neck might stand on end or tears might come to your eyes. The more dramatically energy blockages are released, the more pronounced will be the experience. If your blocked energy has had no outlet for a long time, the sudden ecstatic thrill of *pīti* can take you by surprise. All at once you have more energy than you know what to do with and it simply overflows into bodily expression – you might find yourself weeping and shaking, even for hours at a time. At such times you need to hang on to your mindfulness; the experience can be so transporting that – overcome by having more energy than you know how to use – you may want to dance and sing and laugh and roll on the ground. On the other hand, if you are no stranger to states of integration and bliss, *pīti* might be so familiar to you that you experience it as just a slight lump in the throat from time to time, or a few shivers or goose pimples.

Of course, not every release of pent-up energy is skilful. The fierce burst of energy you get when you lose your temper, although it may be enjoyable, is not *pīti*, nor is wild hilarity or hysterical excitement. Although fiery anger might get your energy going for a short time, it soon recedes, and then you are left feeling drained, because ill will is a total waste of energy. *Pīti*, by contrast, is a positive state grounded in mindfulness which doesn't leave you with the exhaustion that follows a loss of temper or hysterical outburst, but gives you a lasting sense of buoyancy and energy.

*Pīti* can affect the whole personality: it is certainly noticeable that some people are more rapturous, enthusiastic, effervescent, and inspired than others. But experiencing dramatic symptoms does not necessarily signify any great spiritual attainment, nor does a more low-key experience of *pīti* indicate some kind of deficiency. *Pīti* is only a sign that energy is on the move. It is a very positive sign, indicating that you are transforming your energies and thus weakening the fetters, but it is a temporary phenomenon, because there is only so much blocked energy to be released. There is no need, therefore, to feel that you have to hang on to *pīti*, or that you have lost something when it subsides. *Pīti* will only occur for as long as there are aspects of yourself that are as yet unintegrated, and if it subsides, that may be to allow the arising of a state which is more positive and enjoyable still.

As one might expect, the Abhidhamma tradition found ways of classifying the various intensities of *pīti*. Buddhaghosa gives five different levels, from goose pimples and little spasms of rapture like flashes of lightning to waves of rapture and flooding rapture.[85] The less intense kinds can be experienced in the course of ordinary waking consciousness, but if you are going to tap into the very deepest reservoirs of blocked energy you need to sit very still and meditate. The most intense form of *pīti* – presumably the 'coming to fulfilment' described by the *Sutta* – is levitation, when the meditator is seen to rise in the air from the meditation seat.

*Pīti* may be a temporary stage, but it is a necessary one, and it will always manifest in some physical way, however subtle. If you are experiencing what seems to be a very calm state of mind but you have not experienced any kind of *pīti*, it is likely that rather than your having progressed to the state of bliss into which *pīti* is transmuted, your calmness is the result of repressed energy. A complacent lethargy is not to be mistaken for the blissful peace to which the path leads – it may be that you will need to stir things up a little, to break up that false peace and give your energies a chance to emerge. You might experience a certain measure of peaceful contentment, but you cannot experience bliss in the full sense without the integration of *all* your unconscious energies.

### TRANQUILLITY (*PASSADDHI*)

*Passaddhi* (Sanskrit *praśrabdhi*) is a kind of calming down; it is the necessary transition from the highly energetic state that precedes it to the state of intense bliss that follows. The bodily manifestations of *pīti* subside as one's consciousness turns deeper into itself, withdrawing from the physical senses into the realm of the mind alone. As the grosser energies become absorbed into a more refined state of consciousness, a state of intense positivity and integration develops. But *passaddhi* is not exactly tranquillity in the sense simply of a state of calm; it is an active state of increasingly concentrated energy. This is what appears in the twelve positive *nidānas* (see pp. 229–30 below) as *sukha*, or bliss, which has no explicit mention in the *bojjhaṅgas* but can be understood as being synonymous with *passaddhi*. The term *sukha* sometimes refers simply to pleasurable feeling but in this context it suggests a very different order of pleasure. Here the physical excitement of *pīti* has subsided and the energy that was present in the earlier stages becomes steadier and more focused, so that the whole being is progressively unified in an experience of joy and delight. It feels less like a state of consciousness than a state of being, because it is much more consolidated and profound than were the earlier stages. Whereas you can have a momentary experience of *pīti*, *passaddhi* involves the whole being over much longer periods of time: there is more of a sense of having arrived somewhere. *Pīti* is in a way anticipatory of – though not impatient for – the bliss to come, whereas *passaddhi* feels much more like the thing itself. One becomes immersed in a deeply blissful state that retains all the energy of the earlier stages intensified into a subtle yet concentrated state of true happiness, a keenness and subtlety of concentration that is born of a great strength of positivity.

Rapture and bliss can be developed systematically in meditation but they can also arise spontaneously in the normal course of life. You might be out for a walk in the country on a fine morning and suddenly find yourself full of rapture. This is more likely to happen if you are in the habit of meditating but it can be the very fact that you are *not* preoccupied with the possibility of the arising of such states that helps them to arise. By the same token, you can be surprised by the quality of your concentration when you are not in the mood for meditation but do it anyway: you are not *expecting* anything. Mindfulness is about being honest with yourself and acknowledging what your actual experience is. It is easy to get caught up in what you are experiencing in meditation, and you do obviously have to monitor what is going on, but the monitoring process can undermine the whole exercise. You have to keep reminding yourself that the exercise consists in simply trying to be aware and mindful within your present state of mind, whatever that may happen to be. 'In the seen, only the seen....'

Once you have reached the stage of *passaddhi*, however, your meditation practice should be quite stable and you should be able to dwell in *dhyāna* more or less every time you sit down to meditate. The effects of dhyānic bliss are such that your daily state of mind will tend to become one of steady cheerfulness and optimism, with a freedom from internal conflicts and a general sense of well-being and serenity. This is not to say that your life will suddenly become free of problems or that you will no longer experience pain in one form or another; but within the painful experience, paradoxically, there will be a deep happiness. Once you sit down to meditate, such a state of mind will be heightened into *dhyāna* quite easily, for once a regular experience of bliss has been built up, there is a shift in one's whole being that makes *dhyāna* much easier to maintain.

### CONCENTRATION (*SAMĀDHI*)

A lot of Buddhist practice can seem very self-absorbed and in a way it is, especially at this stage of the path (*samādhi* means 'one-pointed concentration'). But there is no healthy alternative, if one is to be effective in the world. Buddhist meditation is a clearing of the decks for action, a transforming of unskilful and unexamined mental states into integrated and refined energy, for a purpose beyond self-absorption.

As the Buddha states elsewhere in the Pāli canon, concentration is the natural outcome of spiritual bliss.[86] It increases with pleasure, and as pleasure turns into rapture and then bliss, this process of deepening and refining pleasure has the effect of deepening one's concentration even more. *Samādhi* is thus inseparable from *sukha* just as *sukha* was inseparable from *passaddhi* in the stage before. *Samādhi* is what arises naturally when you are perfectly happy; when you are not, you go looking for something to make you happy. In other words, to the extent you are happy, to that extent you are concentrated. This is a very important characteristic of *samādhi*, and should be clearly distinguished from the forcible fixing of attention that is often understood by the term 'meditation'.

It is a question of motivation. If you are looking for an experience of pleasure or excitement or bliss in meditation, the result is going to be as superficial as the motive. It is rather like the difference motivation makes to sexual relationships. There is a famous passage in Malory's medieval romance *Morte d'Arthur* in which the author bewails how times have changed: once upon a time, he says, a lover and his beloved would be faithful to each other for seven years with no 'likerous lust' between them, whereas now all a lover wants is to whisk his beloved into bed. Clearly not much has changed on that front since the fourteenth century. And something quite similar can happen in the case of meditation: people grab at the end result they want without working through the whole process – and so, of course, never get the desired result at all.

Probably this was what the Buddha realized when, recollecting his childhood experience of spontaneously entering the first *dhyāna*, he came to understand that this was the key to Enlightenment. This is a turning point in the story of his quest for Enlightenment. Having tried all kinds of methods and practices, having meditated and fasted and performed austerities, the Buddha-to-be remembered an experience he had as a boy. He had been sitting under a rose-apple tree out in the fields when he had spontaneously entered a state of meditative concentration. He sat there all day, absorbed and happy. And it was the recollection of this when he was on the very threshold of Enlightenment that gave him the clue he needed.[87] One might wonder what such an elementary spiritual attainment might signify to one who had advanced in meditation even as far as the formless *dhyānas* under the guidance of his teachers. But he knew that he had still not attained the goal to which he aspired, and now he understood why. What he realized was that his previous mastery of meditation had been forced, however subtly; this was why it was in the end useless. Progress had been made but only part of him had been involved in that progress, because it had been produced through sheer will-power. It was not so much the first *dhyāna* itself that was the answer, but the natural manner in which he had entered into that state. The answer was to allow a natural unfolding of the whole being to take place, through the steady application of mindfulness.

We too can make use of this important insight. The states of mind we have produced through our actions during the day and during the course of our life in general, whatever they are, will be the states of mind we have to address in our meditation. Meditation is not about pushing parts of yourself away in order to force yourself into a superficially positive mental state. If you are distracted, unreflective, self-indulgent, and reactive in your everyday life, you might as a novice meditator force yourself in the opposite direction to some short-term effect, but in the long run meditation is about transforming mental states, not suppressing or ignoring them.

With the integration and calming of all bodily sensations, as your consciousness becomes clearer, you enjoy states of increasing brightness, expansiveness, and harmony: these correspond to the stages of *dhyāna* encountered earlier in the *Sutta*. But if you are to proceed to the goal of the Buddhist path, the blossoming of insight into the nature of reality, the practice of *samādhi* has to be understood as far more than the cultivation of *dhyāna*. The intensely positive experience of *dhyāna* has to be invested with the clear recollection of your purpose, so that this intense experience of well-being can be refined still further, to produce a firm foundation for the final stage in this series of enlightenment factors: equanimity.

### EQUANIMITY (*UPEKKHĀ*)

Equanimity – *upekkhā* (Sanskrit *upekṣā*) – appears elsewhere in the Pāli canon as one of the four immeasurables, the meditation practices known as the *brahma vihāras* whereby one cultivates the other-regarding qualities of compassion, sympathetic joy, loving-kindness towards all living beings, and equanimity itself. The transformation of bliss into equanimity is also said to be characteristic of the fourth *dhyāna*. But *upekkhā* in the context of the seven *bojjhaṅgas* is even loftier than these exalted forms of equanimity. These are after all the seven factors of Enlightenment, and if one considers them as a series it will surely be in this last one that a truly transcendental quality will be found. Understood in this transcendental sense *upekkhā* marks the arising of an entirely new quality, the direct experience of insight into the ultimate meaning of things. This steadily deepening realization emerges here as a state of equanimity that reorients all the preceding factors, becoming the transcendental axis about which they revolve.

In this state of equanimity in its perfected form you no longer make any distinction between yourself and others, because that duality has been transcended. Before insight has been fully perfected there is always some oscillation, however subtle or refined, between pairs of opposites. One oscillates between pleasure and pain and even, at a level so subtle that it can barely be comprehended, between existence and non-existence, even between Enlightenment and non-Enlightenment.

But a fully perfected equanimity has gone beyond all dualism, even the dualism of being and non-being. This is *samatā-jñāna*, the wisdom of equality, whose archetypal embodiment is the Buddha Ratnasambhava. In this consummate equanimity all the *bojjhaṅgas* are present in their most highly developed form as they merge with *upekkhā* and are permanently stabilized by that quality so that they truly become aspects of the transcendental.

> 'In this way he abides contemplating mind-objects as mind-objects internally, externally, and both internally and externally.... And he abides independent, not clinging to anything in the world. That is how a bhikkhu abides contemplating mind-objects as mind-objects in terms of the seven enlightenment factors.'

Strictly speaking, contemplating the seven factors of Enlightenment 'externally' – that is, in other people – is only possible if one has oneself experienced the factors in some depth; one may then be able to have a direct apprehension of someone else's experience of them. In any case, contemplating other people's positive qualities is much more worthwhile than dwelling on their ethical and spiritual shortcomings. Appreciating people's qualities and rejoicing in their merits is an expression not only of *mettā* but also of faith in the teaching. If we can look at someone's behaviour and observe that they are cultivating a certain quality successfully, this will encourage us to do so ourselves – and if we are thus encouraged, it doesn't really matter whether or not we are right in our assessment of the other person's qualities. For all these reasons we should rejoice in and wish for the cultivation of the factors of Enlightenment by others while also cultivating them ourselves; each of the factors therefore has an external dimension.

The question of origination and dissolution factors in respect of the *bojjhaṅgas* is more complex because, like the twelve positive *nidānas*, the *bojjhaṅgas* are meant to represent the unfolding process of the mind rather than a cross-section of it. These two formulations resemble each other quite closely. The *nidānas* start to wind out and away from the closed circle of reactive consciousness through the arising of faith and the satisfaction arising from ethical observance. As the fourth *nidāna*, rapture, leads into tranquillity, the *nidānas* and *bojjhaṅgas* come together. *Sukha* (bliss) is absent from the *bojjhaṅgas* as a separately listed quality, but it is implicit in the series; then *samādhi* is common to both systems, after which the *bojjhaṅgas* culminate in equanimity. This final stage in the *bojjhaṅgas* could be thought of as a developed state of *samādhi* and thus equivalent to the point at which the *nidāna* chain moves from the mundane creative path to the transcendental path. The transcendental is implicit in the very nature of the spiral path, and we can take it that as far as the *bojjhaṅgas* are concerned the cumulative spiral does not stop there, even though the final transcendental stages of the *nidāna* path are not explicitly set out.

Although the series of Enlightenment factors brings out the positive and progressive spirit of the path, it need not be thought of as seven discrete stages ranked one above the other like the rungs of a ladder. In moving from *viriya* to *pīti*, for example, you do not leave the preceding factor behind. It is more that when *viriya* reaches a certain point it becomes possible to build on that energy and refine it into something more positive, more dynamic still. Or – like the aspects of the Noble Eightfold Path – the Enlightenment factors can be thought of as emerging like the petals of a flower from the bud. With the unfolding of each petal a state of greater refinement and beauty arises, until eventually all the petals of the flower of Enlightenment stand complete around the centre.

Perhaps the most straightforward way to think about developing the *bojjhaṅgas* is to consider that they are simply the states that arise from establishing mindfulness more and more firmly. This is why they are found throughout the Pāli canon. The more you cultivate the four foundations of mindfulness, the more these factors of Enlightenment can be expected to grow. Thus, the factors make a useful checklist: you can ask yourself: 'To what extent is mindfulness present in me? And *dhamma-vicaya*? And energy?' – and so on. Indeed, if – taking up the *Satipaṭṭhāna Sutta* – you were to concentrate on the mindfulness of breathing, the four foundations of mindfulness themselves, and the seven factors of Enlightenment, leaving out all the sections on the corpse meditations, the *khandhas*, the elements, and so on, you would have a condensed form of the practice which would be entirely in the spirit of the teaching and very effective. The important thing is to get the feel of this gradual progression, the sense of everything coming together, energy welling up, and a continuous upward movement running right up to the attainment of transcendental insight and beyond.

This is what the *Sutta* describes (in the section on the contemplation of mind) as the liberated state of consciousness. In his commentary on the *Sutta*, Buddhaghosa presupposes that the term 'liberated' cannot be applied to the Enlightened state, following the later interpretations of the doctrine according to which *nibbāna* is understood to be a state of complete cessation, in which things can neither arise nor disappear. Although the *Sutta* applies the contemplation of origination and dissolution factors to the 'liberated' state, just as to all the lower states of mind, Buddhaghosa can only explain the liberated state as referring to temporary absorption in *dhyāna* or partial insight resulting from reflection, a state of temporary freedom from the five hindrances.

Following Buddhaghosa's line, some Buddhist traditions say that the idea of a progressive and continually intensifying state of Enlightenment is a contradiction in terms. However, it seems entirely possible that the cumulative process does not end even at the point of Enlightenment. Just as on the spiral path *sukha* arises and passes away only for an even more intense degree of *sukha* to take its place, the same might be said of knowledge and even emancipation. The fact that one lives contemplating the origination and dissolution factors even of the freed state does not necessarily mean that the liberated state is temporary, any more than it implies that it can only be mundane. There could be a passing away of a creative nature from consciousness in its liberated state into a state of consciousness that is even more free, and so on indefinitely. No doubt there is something analogous to *pīti* at the enlightened level – as well as to a kind of *viriya* at the very highest level, manifesting in the form of spontaneous acts of compassion towards sentient beings trapped on the wheel of birth and death.

After all, the Buddha himself was by no means inactive after his Enlightenment beneath the bodhi tree. He continued to travel the villages and towns of northern India for many years, coming into contact with hundreds of people from all walks of life, as well as with *devas* and other beings. We can imagine that in his contact with each new and unique set of circumstances, his insight would have been broadened and enriched even further, each meeting illuminating a new facet of the enlightened consciousness. In such a way might the experience of an enlightened being constantly expand and unfold.

# 15
# SUFFERING, AND CEASING TO SUFFER

> 'Again, bhikkhus, a bhikkhu abides contemplating mind-objects as mind-objects in terms of the Four Noble Truths. And how does a bhikkhu abide contemplating mind-objects as mind-objects in terms of the Four Noble Truths? Here a bhikkhu understands as it actually is: "This is suffering"; he understands as it actually is: "This is the origin of suffering"; he understands as it actually is: "This is the cessation of suffering"; he understands as it actually is: "This is the way leading to the cessation of suffering."'

Buddhist tradition makes a distinction between those teachings that require interpretation and those that do not. The Buddha's statement in the *Dhammapada* that hatred never ceases by hatred is literally true, and the truth of it can be seen quite clearly in everyday life (except, of course, by those who are blinded by the desire for revenge). There are other teachings, however, that require us to go beyond the literal meaning, demanding a prior knowledge of the Dharma before we can understand them. A good example is that of one of the Buddha's most famous teachings, the four noble truths, to which the *Satipaṭṭhāna Sutta* now directs our attention. It is not often realized that when the Buddha speaks of suffering, its origin, and its cessation, he is using that as an *example* of how things arise and cease. It is not a definitive statement; in terms of another traditional distinction, it is method rather than doctrine.

It is worth giving careful thought to this. Hearing these truths, people often conclude that Buddhism is suffering-oriented, inward-looking, and self-centred, as though the idea was to become immersed in one's own suffering and how to alleviate it. But this is not what the Buddha is saying. What is usually translated as 'suffering' is the Pāli term *dukkha*, which points to the fact that conditioned existence, taken as a whole, is unsatisfactory and frustrating. But this does not mean that Buddhists view life as unremittingly painful and unpleasant, which it obviously is not. On the other hand, we can be sure that the Buddha did not choose this example of the workings of conditionality at random. It is salutary to reflect on the inherent unsatisfactoriness of things; like reflecting on the loathsomeness of the body, it is an example of 'bending the bamboo the other way'. We are not being asked to stop finding life agreeable, if that is our experience, but to acknowledge that however agreeable it may be, it is never wholly so. *Dukkha* is pain and sickness, but it is also lack of complete fulfilment; it is anxiety and loss, bitterness and cynicism, a sense of lengthening shadows. It is also the truth that even pleasant circumstances cannot last for ever, inasmuch as they arise within conditioned existence.

The possibility of escaping suffering through a 'cutting off' of conditioned consciousness is illustrated in detail by the teaching of the twelve *nidānas* which map out the cycle of conditionality that so often characterizes our existence. It is possible, however, to withdraw from unskilful states of consciousness by disengaging from the reactive cycle at certain all-important points, and this is the aim of our practice. In the absence of any given link in the chain, the succeeding link cannot arise, and eventually this will have the effect of removing suffering altogether. The method of reflection here is one advocated throughout the Pāli canon. You begin by observing an object and noticing how it has come about due to definite conditioning factors. The object of your scrutiny might be *dukkha*, which arises through desire and attachment, or anything else – food, for example. Then you see that by removing those originating factors you can make it impossible for the object itself to arise.

And this method can be applied to conditioned existence as a whole. In the Pāli canon Enlightenment is associated with the cutting-off of cyclic conditionality, so as to stop the spinning of the wheel of life and go utterly beyond future rebirth; in other words, Enlightenment is described in terms of what it is not. The term *nibbāna* (Sanskrit *nirvāṇa*) literally means extinction, an extinguishing or 'blowing out' of the flame of conditioned existence, and the Pāli texts also describe it as uncreated and unending, uncompounded, indiscernible and so on. Given the inadequacy of language to exhaust transcendental meaning, it is little wonder that, when faced with the task of communicating Reality, the early Buddhists, and perhaps even the Buddha himself, hesitated to say too much about it. But this use of 'negative' terms has had its consequences in modern times. When the Pāli canon first began to be known in the West, the description of Enlightenment in terms of cessation, like the idea that life is suffering, had a profoundly negative influence on the popular conception of Buddhist thought. Lacking a wider understanding of the doctrine, the early translators could only take these terms literally and thus propagate a view of the Dharma as a teaching of almost unrelieved pessimism, emphasizing giving up the world and cutting off the karma-producing reactivity of the mundane mind, while giving little sense of the positivity and expansiveness to which the path leads.

The attainment of *nibbāna* certainly represents a decisive and permanent shift away from cyclical conditionality, but it is not a snuffing-out of the life principle. *Nibbāna* is not annihilation. This is in fact made quite clear in the Pāli texts: the Buddha frequently speaks the language of development, characterizing the path as a way of progressively refining one's state of consciousness and thus bringing about an ever-increasing experience of positivity and well-being. This finds most detailed expression in the teaching of the twelve positive *nidānas* or links – the counterpart of the *nidānas* of the Tibetan wheel of life – which describes spiritual life not as a cutting-off of the negative cycle of mundane conditionality but in terms of the cultivation of the seeds of positivity that are also to be found within mundane existence. The positive *nidānas* show the growth of consciousness as it moves upwards from the wheel of life to describe a spiral of ever more positive and insightful states, leading all the way to Enlightenment. Its method is to place a positive interpretation on the shortcomings of conditioned existence, pointing out that in dependence upon birth there arises not only the sequence of old age, decay, and death, as depicted on the wheel of life, but also the potential realization that birth, old age, and death are inherently unsatisfactory. This leads to faith in the path, and from this point onwards consciousness continues to expand, through faith to joy, rapture, serenity, bliss, concentration, knowledge and vision of things as they really are, liberation, and finally the knowledge that the poisons have been destroyed. This is effectively Enlightenment itself.

But even this version of the path can make it sound rather schematic and alien from the felt experience of our ideals as human beings. It might be better to imagine a day of unfettered inspiration and free-flowing energy, a day in which you were able to be completely true and clear in your communication, a day in which you felt so real a connection with others that your own concerns ceased to loom so balefully over your life, a day in which you never felt as though you were banging your head against a brick wall or getting stuck in a rut. Imagine such a day of creative freedom and then imagine that freedom doubled or trebled, and continuing to expand, and you will start to get an idea of the nature of Enlightenment.

So although the Buddha did sometimes express weariness with conditioned existence, especially in the days before he became Enlightened, a full account of his teaching needs to place the doctrine of cessation side by side with its positive counterpart, or even give the latter more emphasis. It is hard to conceive of a process or path without a final goal, but to think of *nibbāna* as a fixed state at which one arrives and settles down is just as mistaken as any other way in which the dualistic mind might try to grasp and tie down the ineffable in words and ideas of its own devising. The Buddha's reluctance to provide a substantial description of the Enlightened state points only to the inadequacy of dualistic language; in any case, given the vitality that characterizes the path of awareness, the notion of some final state in which one remains, perfected and immutable, does seem strangely inadequate. Literal-mindedness is a great handicap in the spiritual life and we have to remember that we are prone to it. We simply cannot afford to think of Enlightenment as the elimination of the ego without putting anything positive in its place, because if we take this 'elimination' literally, as we are likely to do, we will be left with the idea of annihilation, which is just as untrue to Enlightenment as any other idea might be. It is unthinkable that the state of Enlightenment could be merely a snuffing out of all dynamism, or a quiescent state of inactivity, however refined or contented that state might be.

But there is a long way to go (although it is no distance at all) before we experience that for ourselves. We have to start where we are, and when it comes to reflecting on the four noble truths, we do well to pay particular attention to the second one: that of the origin of suffering. *Dukkha*, we are told, arises in dependence upon craving, and – crucially – dissolves when craving ceases. This merits careful reflection because the idea that there could be a direct connection between suffering and craving runs counter to our instinctive response to *dukkha*. We tend to think of craving not as the root of the problem but as the pointer to its solution. Our natural tendency is to look for something that will solve our problem by satisfying our desires – and of course this works in some situations. When we are hungry we want food, and food does indeed satisfy us, refreshing our body and keeping us going. That is perfectly healthy. But craving is the hunger not of physical need but of emotional emptiness. When we are experiencing craving we want something, anything – something to read, someone to talk to, something to eat – that will fill that gap, mop up that moment of discomfort. In the grip of craving, we wolf down our food to keep misery, shame, and emptiness at bay, or try to snatch happiness from sex or power or money to assuage our aching emptiness. We can even have a craving for meditative states, looking for quick results and getting impatient when they don't materialize. We crave company, looking to other people to make us happy, using them to plug the gap in our positivity. We crave annihilation, even, imagining that oblivion will solve our problems. The object of craving is not the issue: craving is craving. An important aspect of mindfulness is the understanding that this sense of emptiness or incompleteness arises in dependence on definite causes and conditions. At any one time we are reaping the fruits of past actions and performing the actions that will produce fruits in the future.

The discomfort of neurotic attachment, itself produced by craving, produces further craving. In order to break this vicious circle it is therefore necessary, at least at the start of our spiritual life, to be prepared simply to experience that craving, or stifled energy, or inner void, and not try to satisfy it or release it or fill it. This sense of insufficiency or inadequacy goes very deep and it will take us a lot deeper into our experience if we can resist the lure of superficial pleasure. The third noble truth, that of the cessation of *dukkha*, or *nibbāna*, will never be achieved through trying to avoid *dukkha*; likewise, the cultivation of positive mental states will never be achieved through bypassing difficult ones. It is wrong to romanticize suffering – which rarely ennobles, and often degrades and brutalizes. But if you are attempting to lead a spiritual life, you are going to experience a certain amount of suffering simply because you are no longer papering over your discomfort with distractions.

When the text says that the *bhikkhu* understands each of the four noble truths 'as it actually is', this means that he understands them as part of his experience – that is, he has some real insight into them. But how can we approach this? What does this practice actually feel like? When you practise mindfulness of the unsatisfactory nature of conditioned existence, moment by moment, you notice that *dukkha* is only part of any experience; there is always more to what is going on than simply *dukkha*. You notice, too, that the forms in which *dukkha* arises change moment by moment. You might become aware of a pull towards reacting to your experience with craving at one moment, then with aversion the next. You might recognize *dukkha* within very pleasant feeling, in the form of some slight wisp of dissatisfaction, and then see where that dissatisfaction comes from, noticing that it arises from a desire for that pleasant feeling to continue, or from a slight anxiety or conceit or restlessness or doubt. Having noticed this, you may then be able to let go of it, or put conditions into place that will allow you to let go of it. Alternatively, you might notice that when you are experiencing craving, it always comes with a feeling of distress, and that if you stop feeding the craving, that distress will give way to a sense of freedom.

You might then contemplate your experience of the absence of craving, at least in its more obvious forms, as well as the consequent experience of the cessation of suffering, however temporary and partial this might be; and you could go on to contemplate whatever understanding of the principle of conditionality might then arise. Finally, you could contemplate whatever understanding you have of the Noble Eightfold Path as the way to the cessation of suffering. You could take account of the degree to which you are giving attention to the constituents of the Path, the extent to which you are treating your practice as a full-time occupation rather than an occasional quick fix.

You can also bear in mind the general nature of the Path. Taken as a whole, it represents a combination of realism and positivity. Even though our working method needs to be directed to the eradication of unskilful states, the Path itself is positive and progressive. True, we are aiming to stop the wheel of life revolving, that is, to put a stop to our own unskilful states of consciousness; but that is only half the truth. We also want to develop our potential as human beings and to feel confident that the Dharma will help us grow. In other words, the *Sutta* is describing the Path as a creative process.

And the 'Path' is not something outside of ourselves; it is the creative mind itself. Whereas the reactive mind drifts in a desultory way from happiness to misery and back again, depending on circumstances, the creative mind changes this process into a progressive path; indeed, it *is* that progressive path. Instead of drifting on the winds and tides of the world you fix upon a clear goal and, even against a head wind, you tack back and forth, sometimes obliquely, but maintaining a steady course.

*Dukkha* is placed at the heart of Buddhism because it is what stimulates us to act, to do something about our situation, to alleviate our discomfort. Of course, time after time we act mistakenly; we do the wrong thing and we fail to escape that discomfort – but at least we want to do something about it. The second and third noble truths show us where we have been going wrong, and the fourth suggests how we can act in a way that is more in tune with the way things are. In other words, we are exhorted to look at the unpalatable facts of life not in a spirit of 'dismal Jimmyism' but so that we can do something about them. *Dukkha* comes from the fruitless search for permanence in a world where everything is impermanent, but impermanence is painful only as long as we insist on treating the things and people we like as if they were going to last for ever. In contemplating the truth of *dukkha*, we should be careful not to confuse the form of the teaching with the reality that it is designed to reveal to us. It is indeed the truth that will set us free.

> 'In this way he abides contemplating mind-objects as mind-objects internally, or he abides contemplating mind-objects as mind-objects externally, or he abides contemplating mind-objects as mind-objects both internally and externally. Or else he abides contemplating in mind-objects their arising factors, or he abides contemplating in mind-objects their vanishing factors, or he abides contemplating in mind-objects both their arising and vanishing factors. Or else mindfulness that "there are mind-

> objects" is simply established in him to the extent necessary for bare knowledge and mindfulness. And he abides independent, not clinging to anything in the world. That is how a bhikkhu abides contemplating mind-objects as mind-objects in terms of the Four Noble Truths.'

We owe the original compilers of the Pāli canon an enormous debt of gratitude. For several centuries a vast literature was preserved with (as far as we know) a reasonable degree of accuracy, entirely by word of mouth. But because the *Satipaṭṭhāna Sutta* was not primarily a literary text, it is difficult, even impossible, to determine what of the material we now have is original and what was added later, although there are some clues that suggest that the text we have is a hybrid dating from more than one period. The version of the four noble truths in the *Sutta*, for example, is strikingly brief compared to the more detailed version in the *Dīgha Nikāya*, being little more than a simple statement of the existence of the truths and an instruction to contemplate them.[88] Moreover, the absence of any further explanation is in contrast to the detailed descriptions of the parts of the body and the Enlightenment factors given earlier in the *Sutta*. It does not follow the same pattern, and this raises questions as to its place in the text as a whole. One might guess that it was included in the *Sutta* almost as an afterthought.

It is easy to imagine reasons for this. In the course of the centuries after the teaching was first given some material will inevitably have been added and some removed. Teachers in successive generations of the oral tradition might have sought, in good faith, to fill out their explications of the *Satipaṭṭhāna Sutta* by adding more categories of mental objects and their attendant formulations. The *Sutta* would have been passed on in that form, and then when the doctrines were eventually committed to writing, such additions would have become an accepted part of the written tradition. Some scholars think that the original discourse was simpler and had fewer categories, perhaps only the mindfulness of the body and breath, the contemplation of feelings, mind and mental objects having been included at a later date.

The fact that the teachings were handed down orally may have had another consequence: some features of the *Sutta* could have been carried forward mechanically from one section to another with little or no sense of their deeper significance. To have arranged and catalogued these thousands of teachings from memory was a tremendous feat and it would not be surprising if the monks should sometimes have been more concerned with the preservation of the oral tradition than with any penetrating insight into its meaning.

For all their brevity, the four noble truths are still accompanied by the usual repetitions of internal and external contemplation and the factors conditioning their arising and dissolution. But how are we to understand the contemplation of the noble truths in these ways? They are not quite like the other sets of mental objects listed in the *Sutta*. The hindrances, the fetters, and even the *khandhas* all arise and pass away in dependence on conditions, but the noble truths are statements of principle, not factors of consciousness, and as such they are not subject to origination and dissolution in the same way: one can only contemplate them as statements of fact. However, the contemplation of the four noble truths is still a useful exercise. As already suggested, one can contemplate the extent to which one has experienced the truth of suffering, the extent to which one has realized the truth of its origin, and the extent to which one is following the Noble Eightfold Path that leads to the cessation of suffering. But this is not what the text actually says. It seems likely that this passage has been added as a matter of course in the form in which it appears in the earlier sections of the *Sutta*, virtually word for word, regardless of whether or not it is really appropriate.

One might further conclude that the inclusion throughout the *Sutta* of the contemplations of mental objects 'externally' and 'internally' is symptomatic of the same mechanical approach. The recurrence of this phrase in such a variety of contexts, with no explanation as to its precise meaning, makes it difficult to be sure what is really meant by it. In his commentary on the *Sutta* Buddhaghosa has no trouble explaining the external contemplation of the foulness of the thirty-one parts of the body or of the decomposing corpse – by definition practices that take an external object as their point of reference – but when it comes to the breathing he skirts around the whole issue. We are left to infer either that the external aspect of the practice was so familiar that it needed no comment or that it had been lost by the time the commentary was compiled, some eight hundred years after the Buddha gave the discourse, or – and this is perhaps most likely – that the instruction to contemplate the breathing externally was just added to the *Sutta* at some point for the sake of completeness, with no thought as to what such contemplation might involve.

It does seem entirely possible that over the years less attention came to be paid to the 'external', other-regarding aspects of Buddhist practice, the emphasis instead coming to be placed on familiarity with the categories of the Abhidhamma. After all, anyone can practise the *mettā bhāvanā*. You don't have to be a scholar; you don't even have to be able to read and write. Some Theravādins, even today, tend to look down on the practice as being essentially for lay people. Even though the *Karaṇīya Mettā Sutta* is one of the most frequently recited texts, it is not necessarily taken seriously any more than the commandment to love your neighbour as yourself is taken seriously by all Christians. Such is the effect of many hundreds of years of institutionalized religion. Although everyone might agree that loving-kindness is a good thing, it seems that the editors of the *Sutta* did not see the need to spell out the importance of this other-regarding attitude.

But the further back you go in the history of the Buddhist tradition, the more significant this attitude seems to be. Buddhism, in other words, was never as individualistic as people sometimes think. It may well have been that the other-regarding aspect of the practice was second nature to the early Buddhists and hence did not receive so full an emphasis in the oral tradition. The *Sutta* contains only the most perfunctory references to anything beyond one's experience of oneself, the fourfold establishment of mindfulness apparently having come to be regarded as an all-sufficient method.

It is easy to imagine how this might have been so. The Buddha's early followers would not have experienced the alienation from nature that characterizes the lives of so many people today. For them the natural world was ever-present, and the forest glades and parks in which the monks and nuns meditated were highly conducive to the cultivation of enthusiasm and *mettā*. These days we have to shut ourselves off from the clutter and disharmony of modern urban life, in which the cultivation of positive emotion is continually undermined, and in these circumstances we are likely to find it difficult to contact our feelings in meditation. A relatively integrated and balanced person practising the mindfulness of breathing will naturally and spontaneously feel good will towards other people, and for them the method of the *Satipaṭṭhāna Sutta* as it has come down to us will be quite sufficient. However, it is unlikely to be so for all of us. We have to make sure that we pay specific attention to the other-regarding aspects of spiritual practice, both for their own sake and because they involve the deeper energies that remain untapped by simple concentration. There is a dreadful lack of positivity in many people's lives, and to be positive is absolutely essential to spiritual life and growth. As modern Buddhists we need all the help we can get from devotional practices and the *mettā bhāvanā*.

As well as meeting the needs of our own age, this approach has a sound basis in Buddhist thought. Whether or not they were part of the original teaching, the *Sutta*'s references to the external aspect of practice serve to remind us that the Buddhist path has a double emphasis. However important our subjective experience might be and however much we need to work on our own growth and development as individuals, the other-regarding aspects of Buddhist life are just as important. If your aim is ultimately to transcend the subject–object duality, you have to transcend the object just as much as the subject, the two being mutually dependent. The teaching of the four noble truths is not just about getting rid of your own personal suffering; it is about getting rid of suffering itself, wherever it exists in the universe. As Śāntideva says in the *Bodhicaryāvatāra*, whether it is you that happens to be suffering or somebody else doesn't matter in the light of that aim.[89] Any approach to the non-dual calls the whole idea of 'individualistic' versus altruistic motivation into question: the more we progress in our individual growth and development, the more positive and creative will be our effect on everyone with whom we come into contact.

# 16
# CONCLUDING

'Bhikkhus, if anyone should develop these four foundations of mindfulness in such a way for seven years, one of two fruits could be expected for him: either final knowledge here and now, or if there is a trace of clinging left, non-return.

'Let alone seven years, bhikkhus. If anyone should develop these four foundations of mindfulness in such a way for six years … for five years … for four years … for three years … for two years … for one year, one of two fruits could be expected for him: either final knowledge here and now, or if there is a trace of clinging left, non-return.

'Let alone one year, bhikkhus. If anyone should develop these four foundations of mindfulness in such a way for seven months … for six months … for five months … for four months … for three months … for two months … for one month … for half a month, one of two fruits could be expected for him: either final knowledge here and now, or if there is a trace of clinging left, non-return.

'Let alone half a month, bhikkhus. If anyone should develop these four foundations of mindfulness in such a way for seven days, one of two fruits could be expected for him: either final knowledge here and now, or if there is a trace of clinging left, non-return.

'So it was with reference to this that it was said: "Bhikkhus, this is the direct path for the purification of beings, for the surmounting of sorrow and lamentation, for the disappearance of pain and grief, for the attainment of the true way, for the realization of Nibbāna – namely, the four foundations of mindfulness."'

That is what the Blessed One said. The bhikkhus were satisfied and delighted in the Blessed One's words.

Short of Enlightenment, the two great turning points – so far as this concluding section of the *Sutta* is concerned – are the point of Stream Entry, when one has gone beyond any possibility of falling back into a lower form of existence upon rebirth, and the point of 'non-returning'. In the early Buddhist scheme of things, the non-returner is said never to return to life as a human being, but to be born in a group of worlds called the *suddhāvāsa*, the pure abodes, which are situated at the highest point of the realm of form, the *rūpaloka*. Beyond these lies only the realm of infinite space. Buddhist cosmology correlates these various 'realms' with the stages of meditative absorption or *dhyānas*. One might think of meditation as being simply an internal, subjective experience, but the Buddhist position is that once one has become absorbed in these subtler modes of consciousness, one also gains entry to an external world which is their objective correlative – not any material world, but one that is subtle and more ethereal. One can bypass this model and say simply that as your consciousness becomes more refined, discriminative awareness rises to ever higher levels, but according to Buddhist tradition it is no less valid to say that with entry into the *dhyānas* you enter what are called the *deva* or god realms.

Initially you enter the *rūpaloka*, the world of pure form, where your experience is purely an awareness of light. The mystical writings of many religious traditions contain references to this. Sometimes the image of light is used symbolically, but sometimes it is an actual description of the mystic's perception of a kind of subtle brilliance, and corresponds with many people's experience of *dhyāna*. The pure abodes are five in number: the not-great (*avihā*), the unscorched (*atappā*), the clearly-visible (*sudassā*), the clear-visioned (*sudassī*), and the greatest or highest (*akaṇiṭṭhā*), said in the *Laṅkāvatāra Sūtra* to be resplendent with light.[90] Having left the gross material plane behind, the non-returner moves upwards from one subtle plane to another until the goal of Enlightenment is reached, never taking another human birth.

In the devotional Buddhism of the Mahāyāna Pure Land schools the figure of the non-returner appears in a slightly different form. Through devotion to Amitābha, the Buddha of Infinite Light, one aspires to be reborn in the pure land of Sukhāvati, the realm over which Amitābha presides. From here, as from the pure abodes, one attains Enlightenment directly, without being born again in any of the lower realms. According to the Pure Land schools, however, the devotee attains rebirth not due to his or her own merits, but due to the power of Amitābha's original vow, as contrasted with the non-returner of the early Buddhist tradition, who reaches the pure abodes by virtue of the momentum of spiritual practice generated during his or her last human existence. This is the essential doctrinal difference between early Buddhism and the Mahāyāna Pure Land schools.

Inasmuch as the Pure Land is inhabited by beings on the transcendental path, it is not really part of the mundane world system at all. And although the *dhyānas*, however refined they may be, are still within mundane experience, even a substantial experience of the fourth *dhyāna* is insufficient to assure one's rebirth there. In fact, *dhyāna* is a feature only of the pure abodes in that, as the product of *śamatha* meditation, it provides the concentration necessary to break the remaining fetters and gain transcendental insight. But even though it is difficult to see how the pure abodes can be thought of as mundane in the sense of being worlds in which beings are born and from which they pass away, in early Buddhism they are said quite clearly to be a subdivision of the *rūpaloka*, the world of form. Thus it is difficult to say whether the pure abodes are mundane or transcendental.

But we need not get too caught up in questions of cosmology. The important thing is to get some sense of the nature of the further reaches of the Buddhist path. Buddhism can seem to be all lists – the five of this, the six of that – and the stages of the path beyond Stream Entry can seem like just another one: Stream Entrant, once-returner, non-returner, *arhant*. Furthermore, this list might create the impression that these stages are quite close and follow easily one upon another. Nothing could be further from the truth. Words can scarcely capture the immense distance between Stream Entry and the higher stages of the transcendental path. In the Buddha's original teaching, at least in its earlier phases, what afterwards came to be known as Stream Entry constituted the real turning-point in one's spiritual life: subsequent stages of attainment seem to have been elaborated later and were not defined so precisely. Even the *arhant* ideal does not emerge very clearly at that stage of the teaching, no doubt because it is unimportant compared to the overriding need to break the first three fetters and thus enter upon the transcendental path.

Characteristically, very little is said about the goal in this final part of the *Sutta*. 'Either final knowledge here and now' is to be attained, or 'if there is a trace of clinging left, non-return'. This suggests that while it is necessary to have a clear sense of the goal, the Buddha placed greater emphasis on the path as a means to Enlightenment than on descriptions of the goal to which that path led.

According to the Mahāyāna text called the *Aṣṭasāhasrikā-prajñāpāramitā Sūtra* or *Perfection of Wisdom in Eight Thousand Lines*, one of the hallmarks of an irreversible bodhisattva – that is, a bodhisattva who can never fall back from spiritual progress – is the fact that they are not concerned about whether or not they have reached that stage. Whatever your level of spiritual attainment, you don't have to be constantly analysing your progress. As the days and weeks go by you will feel intuitively that you are becoming spiritually more alive: you will see the little knots of habit and attachment breaking up as you become steadily less attached to material things, less easily upset by what others say, and so on.

Here at the conclusion of the *Sutta* the reiteration of the point that 'the way of mindfulness is the direct way' takes on a new significance. It is as though by its very nature mindfulness ensures a gradual acceleration of the whole spiritual process, if you put enough effort into it. One should not forget that the Buddha is speaking here to a group of monks who have gone forth from the household life and have very good conditions for spiritual practice: some of his listeners would no doubt be able to make swift and effective use of this teaching. At the same time, the Buddha says 'if anyone should develop these four foundations of mindfulness in such a way' rather than 'if any *monk* should,...' thereby implying that although they are a full-time exercise, it is possible for anyone to practise them, whatever their circumstances. There is no reason for a layperson to hold back from so doing. Whether you are male or female, a member of the monastic community or not, how soon you arrive at the goal will depend entirely on the intensity of your effort.

The important message is that you don't necessarily have to spend years working away at developing mindfulness to get anywhere; indeed, the *Sutta* seems to suggest that seven years is rather a long time. By intensifying your effort you can reduce the length of time required to reach the goal. Even seven days is not too short a time, it would appear. The recurrence of the symbolic number seven suggests that it is not to be taken literally, but we can take it that substantial spiritual progress can be made, more or less from scratch, within a few years and certainly within the present lifetime. There is no limit to the progress you can make if you are single-minded – which is to say, if you can resist the myriad obstructions that the world places in the path of anyone who wants to be single-minded.

Ultimately, all the teachings of the *Satipaṭṭhāna Sutta* have one end in view: transformation. This goal is approached on the basis of the defining principle of Buddhism: that states of consciousness never arise haphazardly, but are always the product of definite conditioning factors. To bring about certain results we have to know the right way to go about changing those conditions. Sometimes this hardly seems possible, and indeed, no amount of pious determination to experience more positive states of mind will achieve it. If we want to bring about certain mental states, we have to be clear about how those states actually arise. Our habitual modes of mental activity seem to plough on through the waves of life like some enormous ocean liner, regardless of our best intentions. But even the supposedly unsinkable *Titanic* sank, though it took an iceberg to sink it. In the same way – even the same drastic way – mindfulness can bring a halt to our unskilful mental and emotional states.

We need to learn to monitor our states of consciousness much more closely and in much greater detail than people usually do. It isn't enough just to keep up a vague general awareness: we need to scrutinize our mental state almost from moment to moment, and we can use the classes of mental objects outlined by the *Sutta* to help us do this. You can call to mind, say, the seven *bojjhaṅgas*, and ask yourself whether in your mind at this moment there is greed, aversion, or delusion, or investigation of mental states, or mindfulness itself. (These latter two qualities are obviously present to some extent, given that you are asking yourself these questions – an encouraging thought.) In this way you can cultivate the conditions for a continuous development of awareness. Work on the mind really is work, and full-time work too, both in meditation and outside it. The *Sutta* advises us to carry on contemplating our minds whatever we are doing – walking, standing, or lying down – and this is no mere pious exhortation; the Buddha left nothing unclear. The *Sutta* provides everything we need; we are told exactly what to do, and exactly how to go about doing it.

If we have learned anything from the *Satipaṭṭhāna Sutta*, we have surely gathered that maintaining mindfulness is no easy task, especially to begin with. But once you are on your way mindfulness becomes steadily easier to sustain, especially if you have the moral support of your spiritual friends and indeed the whole spiritual community. As you go on, mindfulness demands progressively less effort. In contrast to the slow painful process it is sometimes made out to be, you find yourself treading a path of ever-growing clarity and delight. Immersing yourself in a flow of positive and creative states, you come to get a feeling for the 'direct way' towards which this *sutta* steers us, and thus focus and refine your efforts towards growth.

By remaining sensitive to the nature of the path and the extent to which our mental states help or hinder our spiritual growth, we can direct our consciousness towards skilful states of mind. Once we have acknowledged that mundane consciousness is an ever-changing, conditioned phenomenon, through the practice of mindfulness we can steer that change in the direction of the highest spiritual and moral perfection. And the key to all this is provided by the succinct words of the *Satipaṭṭhāna Sutta*, in which we can hear an echo of the Buddha's original intention when he addressed the *bhikkhus* on that day in Kammāsadhamma. Like the *bhikkhus* on that occasion, we have every reason to be satisfied and to delight in the Blessed One's words.

# LIVING WITH KINDNESS

# THE *KARAṆĪYA METTĀ SUTTA*

He who is skilled in his good, who wishes to attain that state of calm (Nibbāna), should act thus: he should be able, upright, perfectly upright, of noble speech, gentle, and humble. Contented, easily supported, with few duties, of light livelihood, with senses calmed, discreet, not impudent, not greedily attached to families.

He should not pursue the slightest thing for which other wise men might censure him. May all beings be happy and secure, may their hearts be wholesome!

Whatever living beings there be: feeble or strong, tall, stout or medium, short, small or large, without exception; seen or unseen, those dwelling far or near, those who are born or those who are to be born, may all beings be happy!

Let none deceive another, nor despise any person whatsoever in any place. Let him not wish any harm to another out of anger or ill will.

Just as a mother would protect her only child at the risk of her own life, even so, let him cultivate a boundless heart towards all beings.

Let his thoughts of boundless love pervade the whole world: above, below, and across without any obstruction, without any hatred, without any enmity.

Whether he stands, walks, sits or lies down, as long as he is awake, he should develop this mindfulness. This they say is the noblest living here.

Not falling into wrong views, being virtuous and endowed with insight, by discarding attachment to sense desires, never again is he reborn.

# INTRODUCTION: THE MEANING OF *METTĀ*

> The great secret of morals is love; or a going out of our own nature, and an identification of ourselves with the beautiful which exists in thought, action, or person, not our own. A man, to be greatly good, must imagine intensely and comprehensively; he must put himself in the place of another and of many others; the pains and pleasures of his species must become his own.[91]

The question of happiness – or the problem of unhappiness – is fundamental to Buddhism. If we could be sure that we would never experience sorrow or disappointment, we would have no need of the Buddha's teaching. But, things being as they are, we need to find a way to deal with our human predicament; and this is what the Buddha himself sought to do, and succeeded in doing. Having solved the problem himself, he spent the rest of his life explaining to others the nature of the solution and how it is to be achieved.

The Buddha's problem-solving approach finds expression in one of his most famous teachings, that of the four noble truths, a teaching which offers a kind of blueprint for Buddhist practice. The first of these truths states quite simply that unhappiness exists as a feature of human experience. This is to state the obvious, no doubt. But the second noble truth, the cause of suffering, gives more food for thought. The essential cause of suffering, the Buddha says, is craving, the natural but painful desire for things to be other than they are. If we can let go of that desire, if we can accept the rise and fall of experience as it is – not just in our heads, but in our heart of hearts – the problem of suffering will be solved.

Of course, this is far easier said than done. But it *can* be done. The third noble truth is the truth of Nirvāṇa, the truth that the end of suffering can be achieved, not through elevation to some heavenly state in some other place or time, but in this life, through one's own efforts to transform one's experience. What the Buddha is saying is that every human being has the capacity to become not just happy but Enlightened. The figure of the Buddha himself, the man Siddhārtha, whose own spiritual progress is charted in the texts of the Pāli canon, is the enduring example of such self-determination. He embodied the sublime potential that can be activated in the human mind when it is turned resolutely towards the positive. The method of this transformation is outlined in the fourth of the noble truths, the Noble Eightfold Path, each step of which, all the way to Enlightenment, is based on the truth of conditionality, the principle of cause and effect that underlies every aspect of the Buddhist approach to human growth and development. All things change, as we know to our sorrow, but this very fact becomes the source of joy when we realize that we ourselves have the power to change ourselves and our experience.

People sometimes prefer to think of Buddhism as a philosophy, or even a system of rational thought, rather than a religion. Buddhism does not, after all, rely upon divine aid as the means to happiness, but instead emphasizes the value of transforming one's experience in the light of a clear understanding of the nature of change. As such, it is a highly systematic teaching. But if we are not careful, we can end up thinking of the Buddha as a rather scholarly intellectual delivering lists of terms and definitions, an image which does justice neither to the depth of his wisdom, which goes far beyond words and terms, nor to the all-embracing breadth of his compassion. There are some forms of Buddhism in which a somewhat cerebral idea of the Buddha persists, and in which, consequently, little emphasis is placed on the emotional aspect of the Buddhist life. One might get the idea that we are supposed to keep our emotions firmly in check and concentrate on applying logic if we are to pursue insight into the nature of reality. There may even emerge a picture of the ideal Buddhist as someone who has gone beyond any kind of emotion, as though all strong emotions were unspiritual, or even unethical; and this view does suit some people.

But a close look at the early Buddhist texts reveals a different picture. Throughout the ancient scriptures of the Pāli canon it is made clear that the way to Enlightenment involves the cultivation of the emotions at every step, most often in the form of the four *brahma vihāras* (the Pāli words can be translated as 'sublime abidings'). This series of meditations is designed to integrate and refine one's emotional experience so as to produce four different but closely related emotions: *mettā* or loving-kindness, *muditā* or sympathetic joy, *karuṇā* or compassion, and *upekkhā* or equanimity. *Mettā* is the foundation of the other three *brahma vihāras*; it is positive emotion in its purest, strongest form. In this commentary we will be exploring in detail the Buddha's account of how this positive emotion is to be cultivated, as laid out in a text called the *Karaṇīya Mettā Sutta*. But first, let us examine the term *mettā* itself a little more closely. Of course, an emotion cannot be conveyed fully by verbal explanation, though poetry sometimes comes close to doing so. Then, we have the added complexity of translation, as there is no exact English equivalent of the Pāli word *mettā*. But nonetheless, let us try to get at least a sense of the nature of this very special emotion.

### AN ARDENT GOOD WILL

The Pāli word *mettā* (*maitrī* in Sanskrit) is related to *mitta* (Sanskrit *mitra*), which means 'friend'. *Mettā* can thus be translated as friendliness or loving-kindness. Developed to its full intensity, *mettā* is a down-to-earth care and concern directed to all living beings equally, individually and without reservation. The unfailing sign of *mettā* is that you are deeply concerned for the well-being, happiness, and prosperity of the object of your *mettā*, be that a person, an animal, or any other being. When you feel *mettā* for someone, you want them to be not just happy, but deeply happy; you have an ardent desire for their true welfare, an undying enthusiasm for their growth and progress.

The friendliness of *mettā* doesn't necessarily involve actual friendship in the sense of a personal relationship with the person towards whom you are directing it. *Mettā* can remain simply an emotion; it doesn't need to become a relationship. Nevertheless, when you feel *mettā*, you will want to go out to other beings, to help them and express good will towards them in everyday, practical ways, and thus friendships can easily develop out of *mettā*. If two people develop *mettā* towards each other, their *mettā* is likely to blossom into a true friendship – a friendship with a difference. The same goes for an existing friendship into which an element of *mettā* is introduced. The *mettā* will tend to take the self-interest out of the friendship, so that it becomes something more than the cheery camaraderie or emotional dependency that is the basis of most ordinary friendships. Friendship infused with *mettā* becomes *kalyāṇa mitratā* – spiritual friendship – which flourishes not on the basis of what each party gets out of the relationship, but by virtue of the mutual desire for the other's well-being that flows unreservedly in both directions.

Thus there is no rigid distinction to be drawn between 'worldly' friendliness – or the worldly friendships that may come of it – and *mettā*. As we shall see, in its most highly developed form *mettā* is akin to insight into the very nature of things (insight with a capital 'I', as I sometimes say). But as a developing emotion it remains for a very long time more akin to ordinary friendliness. *Mettā* is friendliness as we know it, carried to a far higher pitch of intensity than we are used to. In fact, it is friendliness without any limit whatsoever. *Mettā* is present in the feeling you have for your friends, but it includes the intention continually to deepen and intensify whatever element of disinterested good will there is within it. Any friendly feeling, any friendship, contains the kernel of *mettā*, a seed that is waiting to develop when we provide it with the right conditions.

There is by definition something active about *mettā*. We call it a feeling, but it is more precisely described as an emotional response or volition rather than a feeling in the sense of a pleasant, unpleasant, or neutral sensation. (This distinction between a feeling and an emotion is basic Buddhist teaching.)[92] It includes the desire to act on our positive feelings, to do something practical to help the object of our *mettā* to be happy, to look after their welfare and encourage their growth and progress, so far as lies in our power. As well as friendliness, therefore, *mettā* includes the active, outgoing sense of good will or benevolence.

So why don't we translate *mettā* as love? Love, especially romantic or parental love, can have the intensity and strength to move mountains, and this vigorous concern is one of the most important characteristics of *mettā*. The problem with the word love is that it can be applied to almost anything that takes your fancy, including simple objects of appetite: you love your children or your boyfriend, but also the scent of orange blossom and many more things besides. *Mettā*, on the other hand, is directed only towards living beings.

Moreover, when it is based on appetite or possessiveness, love always has the potential to turn sour, because that appetite may be thwarted, that possession may be taken away. The feelings of jealousy or resentment that derive from romantic – that is to say, dependent – love can be more powerful than the most positive feelings of love in full bloom. And even parental love can turn bitter when it is felt to be unreciprocated – when one's child's ingratitude is 'sharper than a serpent's tooth', as King Lear describes it.[93]

### AN ECSTATIC ENERGY

While being careful to differentiate *mettā* from all sorts of other emotions, we need not be so precious about it that we refine it out of existence. In the *Itivuttaka*, a collection of sayings from the Pāli canon, there is a passage in which the Buddha says of *mettā* that 'it burns and shines and blazes forth',[94] suggesting that it is closer to incandescent passion than what we usually think of as 'spiritual' emotion. The English terms friendliness, loving-kindness, and good will don't come close to expressing this sort of intensity and expansive energy.

Indeed, the words we tend to use for the more spiritual emotions – that is, the more refined and positive ones – are usually understood in a rather weak sense. For example, the words 'refinement' and 'purity', which refer to the quality of being free from impurities, and in that sense concentrated or powerful, suggest quite the opposite – something effete and diluted. When it comes to the more positive spiritual emotions, words seem to fail us. By contrast, our words for harmful and unrefined emotions – hatred, anger, jealousy, fear, anguish, despair – make a much more vivid and powerful impression.

*Mettā* as I have described it may seem pure but rather cool, aloof, and distant – more like moonlight than sunshine. We tend to have the same sort of idea of angels. These celestial beings, for all their purity, usually come across as rather weak and lacking in energy by comparison with devils, which tend to be both physically and spiritually powerful and full of vigour. Rather like the angelic realm, *mettā* or 'loving-kindness' is for most people ultimately just not very interesting. This is because it is difficult to imagine developing positive emotion to anything like the degree of intensity of one's experience of the passions. We rarely experience purely positive emotion that is also strong; if we do experience any really intense emotion, there is usually an element of possessiveness or aversion or fear in it somewhere.

It is not easy to get rid of emotional negativity and develop the strong and vigorous positive emotion that is true *mettā*. To do so, we have somehow to bring to the refined and balanced emotion of universal good will the degree of energy and intensity of lower, coarser emotions. And to begin with, we have to acknowledge that this goes against the grain. If we are to do justice to *mettā* as an ideal we have to be realistic about the kind of strong emotion we actually experience. It may seem strange, but this is the basis upon which a higher emotional synthesis may be achieved.

In our desire to be near the object of our passion, in our need to possess it and our longing for it to be part of us, we experience the energy and intensity that will eventually characterize our experience of *mettā*. Similarly, when we achieve the object of our passion we may for a brief moment experience the blissful calm, the balance and harmony, that also characterize the genuine *mettā* state. *Mettā* brings together the contrasting emotional reactions of dynamic energy and calm repletion into a single quality of emotion, completely transforming them in the process. Although when it is fully developed, *mettā* is a feeling of harmony, both in oneself and with all beings, it also has a fiery, full-blooded, even ecstatic quality. Ecstasy literally means a sense of standing outside oneself, and this is how *mettā* can feel: it is marked by such an intensity of positive emotion that when purely felt, it can carry you outside yourself. *Mettā* is blissful, ecstatic, a naturally expansive desire to brighten the whole world, the whole universe, and universes beyond that.

## A RATIONAL EMOTION

*Mettā* is clearly a good thing in itself. But there is another reason to practise it, apart from its obvious merits as a very positive state of mind. It makes clear sense in terms not only of subjective feeling, but also of objective fact. This is brought out very clearly by the philosopher John

Macmurray. He distinguishes first of all between intellect and reason, designating reason as the higher, or integrated and integrating, faculty. Reason, he says, is that within us which is adequate to objective reality.[95] When reason, thus defined, enters into intellect, you have an intellectual understanding that is adequate or appropriate to the objective situation, to reality. This definition of reason comes very close to the Buddhist understanding of *paññā* (Sanskrit *prajñā*), or wisdom.

Next, he goes on to point out that reason may be applied not only to intellectual understanding, but also to emotion. A brief example should illustrate the point. If, when you see a small spider, you fly into a panic, jump up, and run to the other end of the room, this is an irrational reaction: the emotion is not appropriate to the object, because the spider is not really harmful. But when reason, as defined above, enters into emotion, your emotional responses will be adequate or appropriate to the objective situation, the real situation.[96]

We can see *mettā* in the same way. Unlike emotions like mistrust, resentment, and fear, *mettā* is the appropriate and adequate response to other human beings when we meet or think of them. That is, *mettā* is a rational emotion. When we think of others the most reasonable response is that of *mettā*. We will wish all other beings happiness and freedom from fear, just as we wish ourselves these things. To understand that one is not so very different from any other human being, and that the world does not revolve around oneself, is an example of an intellectual understanding that is adequate to reality. To proceed from such a basis provides an appropriate foundation for our interactions with others.

*Mettā* is the norm or measure of our human response to others. This term 'norm' does not mean average or ordinary: it is closer in meaning to words like template or pattern or model. It is an ideal to which one seeks to conform. It is in this sense that Mrs Rhys Davids and other early western scholars of Buddhism sometimes translated Dhamma as 'the Norm'.[97] For all its shortcomings, this translation does bring out the sense of the Buddha's teaching as being the template of the spiritual life. Likewise, in the true sense of the word 'normal', a normal human being is someone who accords with the norm for humanity, and a normal human response is the response to be expected from that positive, healthy, properly developed, balanced human being. *Mettā* is the response to be expected, as it were, from one human being encountering another. There has to be that fellow feeling if we are to experience our humanity to the full. It is what Confucius called *jen* or human-heartedness: the appreciation of our common humanity, and the behaviour or activity that is based on that feeling.

*Mettā* is an emotional response to others that is appropriate to reality, and to that extent it has the nature of insight. That insight is likely to be fairly mundane to begin with – insight with a small 'i', one might say – but eventually it can become Insight with a capital 'I': *prajñā* or wisdom in the full sense. In other words, through the development of *mettā* you can eventually transcend the subject–object duality – and this is the ultimate goal of the wisdom-seeker.

## THE SUBLIME ABIDINGS

In cultivating *mettā*, we are trying to develop what one might call the higher emotions, that is, those emotions that provide us with a means of bringing together our everyday consciousness and something more purely spiritual. Without such a possibility we have no way of approaching either the higher ranges of meditative experience – called *dhyāna* – or Enlightenment itself. It is as though *mettā* in the sense of an ordinary positive emotion stands midway between the worldly and the spiritual. First, we have to develop *mettā* in ways we can understand – just ordinary friendliness – and from there we can begin to take our emotions to a far higher degree of intensity.

As should now be clear, *mettā* in the true sense is different from ordinary affection. It isn't really like the love and friendliness we are used to; it is much more positive and much more pure. It is easy to underestimate *mettā* and think of it as being rather cosy and undemanding. It is difficult, after all, to conceive what it is really like; only when you have felt it can you look back to your previous emotional experience and realize the difference. The same goes for each of the four *brahma vihāras*. When we begin to cultivate compassion, for example, we have to take whatever seed of it we can find within ourselves and help it to grow. As time goes by, our experience of it will deepen, and if our efforts to develop it are accompanied by a keen appetite for studying the Dharma and a willingness to bring our ideals into our everyday activity, we can come to experience a very pure, positive compassion which is quite different from what we usually understand by the term. In the same way the pure experience of sympathetic joy, *muditā*, is, because of its intensity, entirely different from the ordinary pleasure we might take in knowing that somebody else is doing well.

*Upekkhā*, equanimity, is a spiritual quality of a particularly elevated kind. There are traces of it in ordinary experience, perhaps in the tranquillity that can be found in nature, in the experience of standing alone in a forest when the air is still and the trees stand silently around you. But *upekkhā* goes far beyond even that kind of stillness; it has an intense, definite, even dynamic character of its own. And that is only to describe *upekkhā* in its mundane sense. The fully developed *brahma vihāra* is peacefulness of an indescribably subtle and intense kind. Infused as it is by insight, it is as though there is nothing but that peace. It is truly universal and utterly immovable. It is not just an absence of conflict; it has a magnitude and a solidity all of its own. Since it partakes of the nature of reality itself, no kind of disturbance can affect it in any way.

Through cultivating *mettā* you lay a strong foundation for the development of transcendental insight. In other words, the more adequate to reality your emotional responses become, the closer you are to insight. In the Mahāyāna this fully realized *mettā* is called *mahāmaitrī*. '*Mahā*' means 'great' or 'higher', and *maitrī* is the Sanskrit equivalent of *mettā*, so this is *mettā* made great, made into its ultimate, Enlightened form. *Mahāmaitrī* represents a Buddha's or bodhisattva's response to the reality of sentient beings, though that response is not quite emotion as we understand it. For one thing, it is suffused with a clear and rational awareness. Sentient beings are suffering, so what reason can there possibly be not to feel sympathy? How can I not feel compassion? How can I not try to help them?

In a completely healthy person feeling and thinking are virtually identical. You think and feel at the same time; there is no gap. But in most people thought and feeling are distinct and even alienated from each other. If our thinking is over-objective to the point of being calculating, while our feeling is over-subjective to the point of being sentimental, our inclination will be to shrink from that over-objective thought back into that over-subjective feeling.

D. H. Lawrence refers to the activity of thought as 'Man in his wholeness wholly attending',[98] which brings out the integrated, emotionally alive quality of the awareness we should aim for in our intellectual life. William Blake describes the relationship between reason and emotion in another way. Reason, he says, is the bound or outward circumference of energy, the bounding or limiting factor that is necessary if the expression of energy is not to degenerate into formlessness and muddle.[99] So reason is what gives emotion its form. Significantly, it is not imposed from without by force, so as to cramp or constrict the emotion. It grows with the emotion, enabling it to express itself and body itself forth in beauty and truth.

Likewise, when we generate *mettā* and compassion, this involves mental, rational activity, not just feeling. We deliberately prepare the appropriate conditions from which we know that the feeling will arise. For example, we call to mind images of the people towards whom we want to direct love and happiness. *Mettā* is the synthesis of reason and emotion, right view and skilful action, unobstructed spiritual vision and the bliss of a warm and expansive heart.

Perhaps the earliest and certainly one of the most outstanding examples of the Buddha's teaching on *mettā* is to be found in one of the earliest surviving scriptures of the Pāli canon: the *Karaṇīya Mettā Sutta*. Scholars have determined that collection of teachings called the *Sutta-Nipāta*, from which the *Karaṇīya Mettā Sutta* is drawn, is in large part an early scripture, but by no means entirely so, containing a good deal of comparatively late material. It has also been established that the *brahma vihāras* are not only early but also central teachings in the Buddha's dispensation.

The *Sutta* occurs twice in the Pāli canon, once in the *Sutta-Nipāta* as the *Mettā Sutta*, and once in the *Khuddaka-pāṭha*, where it is given the title that has become its more popular name, the *Karaṇīya Mettā Sutta*. The form of the *Sutta* is not a prosaic discourse, but a series of stanzas composed in quantitative measure – that is, in lines of a fixed number of syllables. Perhaps we could even think of it as a poem inspired by an intense experience of *mettā*.

The text consists of just ten verses. To begin with, it refers to the goal to be pursued and the clear-sighted and healthy ambition that one needs to pursue it. It goes on to set out the general moral character required as a basis for the development of *mettā*. Following this, we are introduced to the specifics of how to practise the *mettā bhāvanā* meditation, with a suggestion in the seventh verse of the degree of intensity to be achieved in our experience of *mettā*. Finally, the *Sutta* sets out the fruits of the training, indicating the close connection between the cultivation of *mettā* and the development of insight into the nature of reality.

The translation we are using, which is just one of the very many that have been made, is by Saddhatissa.[100] Before we look at it in detail, line by line, word by word, you could perhaps read it through to yourself a few times. As I said, the text is really a kind of poem, and as with the reading of all poetry, but especially such meaningful poetry, just reading it is a kind of meditation, whose atmosphere should pervade all that follows.

# I
# THE WAY OF *METTĀ*

He who is skilled in his good, who wishes to attain that state of calm (Nibbāna), should act thus:

*Karaṇīyaṃ atthakusalena*
*yan taṃ santaṃ padaṃ abhisamecca*

## THE GOAL

The practice of Buddhism has a clear purpose: to bring about insight into the true nature of things. It is not surprising, therefore, that in the *Karaṇīya Mettā Sutta* the Buddha places that purpose right at the forefront of his exposition of – or paean to – *mettā*. The point of cultivating *mettā* is to bring you closer to reality. Kindly or benevolent thought or action, while it is of course good in itself, is an expression of *mettā* only in so far as it conduces to a realization of the true nature of things.

The Buddha makes this point in two ways here. First, we learn that *mettā* is to be cultivated by someone who knows what is good for them, who is 'skilled in his good', *atthakusalena*. The Pāli noun translated as 'good' is *attha*, which means not only 'good' but also 'goal'.[101] This makes sense in that something can hardly be your goal or aim if it is not also to your good. In this case the term is used to signify one's *ultimate* good or ultimate aim, in the light of which all lesser goals, all lesser goods, are to be valued.

Buddhism has a clear conception of what that ultimate good or aim is, as indeed do all religious teachings, though their conceptions of that good may differ widely. It is not one's good in the vague sense of what might be to one's general benefit, not just something that will make one feel better. For Buddhism, the good, or *attha*, usually called Enlightenment, offers the only lasting solution to the universal human problems of disappointment, frustration, and unhappiness.

*Attha* is the ultimate good towards which all skilful activity leads. It is the motivation on account of which one might leave home and go forth into the wandering or monastic life. It is the goal for the sake of which one decides to live the spiritual life. It is the reason one takes up meditation. The beauty of the term *attha* is that it suggests something higher, better, more beautiful, more real, without putting a limit on it by being too specific. It leaves everything to the imagination. Without being vague, it simply conveys the sense of something ultimately beneficial, towards which all your highest aspirations lead. This aim is filled out by other well-known Pāli terms such as *bodhi*, or awakening, and *nibbāna* (Sanskrit *nirvāṇa*), traditionally defined as the final snuffing out of ego-clinging. However, the great Edwardian Pāli scholar, Mrs Rhys Davids, says that early in the Buddha's teaching career he was less inclined to use these vividly descriptive terms when referring to the ultimate goal of his teaching. Instead, he preferred to call the goal just that – the goal, the good: *attha*.

## PEACE

If *attha*, the good or the goal, does seem too vague a term, the *Sutta* goes on to qualify it a little – and here we come to the Buddha's second point. Some translators include the term *nibbāna* in this verse to make it clear that the ultimate good is a transcendental, not a worldly, goal. However, the expression that occurs in the *Sutta* itself is *santaṃ padaṃ*; there is no mention of *nibbāna*. *Padaṃ* is 'state' or 'abode' (we find the same term in the title of the famous collection of the Buddha's sayings, the *Dhammapada*), but here the abode is not truth, or wisdom, or even Enlightenment. It is the abode of peace – *santa* being synonymous with the Sanskrit *śānta*.

It is possible that the word *santa* is used simply to fit the metre of the poetry. But leaving that aside, why should peace be set forth in this context as the primary characteristic of the ultimate goal or good of Buddhism? The answer is perhaps to be found in what *santa* is not. In Buddhist literature, it is the positive counterpart of the state of unease known as *dukkha*, the state of turbulence, dissatisfaction, and frustration from which – in pursuit of our goal – we are moving away. When *dukkha* is permanently eradicated, when its roots are torn out, when all that conflict is over, what is left is peace. *Santa* is thus that aspect of our ultimate goal or good that is most immediately relevant and appealing to us, inasmuch as we are in a chronic and habitual state of dissatisfaction or even suffering. So important is this idea of the goal as peace that the Buddha is sometimes described as *śāntināyaka* (Sanskrit), 'the one who leads to peace'.

### SKILL IN TRAINING

The term translated as 'wishes to attain', *abhisamecca*, is more literally 'having attained, grasped, understood', so it implies really knowing and understanding the way to attain that state. It is a question of skill, and therefore to some extent one of training. The unenlightened state of dissatisfaction and muddle that we call *dukkha* is the outcome of our past failure to act skilfully, and if we are ever to eradicate that *dukkha*, we shall have to become skilful in whatever conduces to that end. We shall have to undertake the appropriate training. This is how Buddhism works: it is a matter of training, a practical development of skills that will help you move towards your ultimate goal or good. And it begins when you become aware that there is some higher goal or good to realize.

The expression *atthakusala*, 'skilled in his good', represents an important spiritual principle, at least in Buddhism. As far as I am aware, there is nothing that corresponds to it in the Christian tradition, for instance, but as far as Buddhism is concerned, the spiritual life is a question not so much of goodness or piety as of skill. Of course, the idea of training is implicit in any religious practice. But as a training, the Buddhist path is unlike most other ideas of religious practice. There is no sense of obligation about it, no imperative to be more holy. Instead, one will simply need to develop certain skills and subtleties of action, much as might a musician, a cook, an architect, or an athlete. The *Karaṇīya-Mettā Sutta* does not speak of 'the good person' or 'the holy man'. It simply offers itself to one who knows what constitutes his or her true good, who knows what is truly good for a human being and the right way to go about realizing it.

Being able to undertake this training requires a degree of intelligence, but also a practical capacity, an ability to do things. You don't rest content with theory. If you are skilled in your good, you may not know precisely what the ultimate goal might be like, but you are nevertheless quite clear about what will take you towards it. *Kusala* is a straightforward term meaning literally 'skill' in the ordinary sense of doing the thing that will bring about the results you want, just as one might speak of someone being skilled in handicrafts, the use of language, driving a car, or playing a musical instrument. In the present context, however, the skilful or the good refers to that which is *morally* skilful or good.

Perhaps the defining characteristic of skilful action, speech, or thought is its freedom from narrow self-interest. Skilfulness is essentially a state of mind that is one of equanimity, steady and clear-sighted in its recognition of the impermanent nature of things. If you are a morally skilful person you see the suffering and disappointment that arise from narrow and deluded self-interest, especially your own, and you try to act, speak, and think more in accordance with reality. It is axiomatic for Buddhism that the self we guard so jealously is really no more than an idea. More than that, Buddhism teaches that it is precisely our guarding of the self, and our habitual grasping at things to reinforce this fixed sense of who we are, that is the root cause of all our difficulty and suffering in life.

Unskilful states always seek to drive the wedge of self-interest between things, obstructing the flow of life with the thought of our own benefit or gain. Moral skilfulness on the other hand lies in the avoidance of harmful emotions like envy, hatred, and greed, and the cultivation of positive emotions such as *mettā*, together with clarity of vision (traditionally called right view). In skilful states of mind, we act out of an awareness of things. We are able to put ourselves in another person's shoes and attempt to understand their troubles and difficulties, as well as their ideals and aspirations. We feel happy at the happiness of others. We are patient when others annoy or threaten us. We are generous with our possessions, our time, and our energy. We are willing to be helpful in any way we can.

Above all we think, speak, and act in ways that are intended to benefit the situation as a whole, rather than just to further our own aims. To be skilled in one's good is to aim for states of consciousness that are free from the dead weight of self-interest and recrimination. It is to know also how to go about achieving those mental states. On such a basis one will begin to enjoy one's experience with a lighter touch and a more discriminating eye, in the knowledge that this approach will lead one towards one's ultimate goal, towards one's real benefit and happiness.

### THE BUDDHA'S VOICE: CONDITIONAL, NOT IMPERATIVE

*Karaṇīyaṃ* means literally 'what is to be done'. If someone wishes to attain that state of calm, they should do this. The sense here – conditional rather than imperative – is very characteristic of the Buddha's teaching and appears time after time in the Pāli scriptures. The Buddha is not issuing commandments, but clarifying the implications of possible courses of action. If you wish to see a certain outcome, says the Buddha, you will need to act in a certain kind of way.

The conditional statement appeals to one's intelligence, whereas the categorical or imperative statement can be said to appeal only to a desire to be relieved of personal responsibility. The imperative voice suggests a haste, almost an impatience, to see someone act in a particular way. You might offer rewards for compliance with your orders or threaten sanctions for non-compliance, but you don't want to waste time on unnecessary explanation. The imperative voice is the voice of all authority figures, from military commanders to busy parents. It is the voice of Jehovah, the God of the Old Testament, with his ten commandments, his plagues of locusts and boils, his fires and his floods.

During my days in India, I was once staying in Poona with my friend Dr Mehta when a Seventh Day Adventist couple turned up to visit him.[102] The husband was an enthusiastic proponent of his religion, and almost as soon as they were inside the door he started trying to bring about the doctor's conversion to their own faith. Dr Mehta was a man of considerable intelligence, and the Christian preacher's approach proved entirely inadequate to this task. Apparently incapable of offering an argument based on reason, he sought to rely upon the persuasive power of the Bible, a power which came in his view not from its capacity to provide rational argument, but simply from its claim to be the word of God. 'But don't you see?' he kept saying, 'Here is what the Bible says. God is speaking to us directly through this book.' And he held the book up for Dr Mehta to see, as though its very existence was sufficient to forestall any possible doubt. It was as if we were rather dense in not letting go of our rational objections. His argument, which was in effect, 'It must be true, because it is true,' was like the one offered by harassed parents everywhere: 'Because I say so.' Eventually, it fell to the preacher's wife, who seemed to understand the nature of reason better than he did, to tug his sleeve and say to him, 'But, dear, the gentleman doesn't believe in the Bible.'

The conditional statement, by contrast, expresses calm, patience, and a respect for the individual's responsibility to assess the situation for him or herself and choose what course of action, if any, to take. As for the imperative statement, unless there is an emergency it suggests that the person issuing the directive has an axe to grind, an emotional investment in the outcome. The imperative statement always contains a veiled threat of sanction and for this reason we should always be wary of it. If someone is unwilling to clarify why they want you to do or think or believe something, it is possible that they do not themselves know what those reasons are, and that they do not want to examine them for fear of being left with doubts. Any impatience with rational objections on their part, any tendency towards anger when their will is obstructed, suggests it would be wise to question their motives.

By contrast, Buddhism teaches that there is nothing wrong with doubt, and Buddhists are encouraged to think things through and come to their own conclusions. We might be surprised by the calmness and equanimity of even the most unsophisticated Buddhist monk in a traditional Buddhist country on encountering someone who does not share his religious outlook. His easygoing attitude is not born of intellectual woolliness, doctrinal carelessness, or the kind of relativism that sees all views as ultimately the same. It comes from the fact that he doesn't take things personally. He will be very happy to explain something of the Buddhist outlook to you if it seems appropriate to do so, but he will not feel threatened if he learns that you follow a different faith. He may privately think that you are not quite on the right track, but he will not allow that view to disturb his equanimity and friendly attitude to you.

The Dharma, the Buddha's teaching, is an appeal to one's intelligence in the broadest sense, not to one's willingness to believe. You have to be able to understand, for example, the connection of unskilful actions and states of mind with suffering, and of skilful actions and states of mind with happiness. The Buddha himself is represented in the scriptures as saying, 'Whether Buddhas come or whether they do not come, one thing is fixed and sure: out of craving arises suffering.'[103] This is something you can verify yourself, with reference to your own experience. Whether Buddhas come or whether they do not makes not the slightest difference.

The figure of the Buddha, although central to Buddhism from a historical and inspirational point of view, is not central in a doctrinal sense in the way that belief in the figure of Christ as the son of God is central to the Christian tradition. Buddhism is founded not upon the will or even the personality of the Buddha, but upon the Dharma, the teachings of the Buddha, and the truth to which these teachings are a guide, and which the Buddha himself reveres.

The Buddha does claim to have experienced for himself the truth of what he teaches, and this is the source of his spiritual authority. But that is all the authority he has. It has no claim on us unless we choose to submit to it. If you are truly to develop, you have to make up your own mind about whether or not your life is satisfactory. And if it isn't, it is up to you to decide what to do about it.

Buddhists down the ages have glorified the Buddha, and have gone so far as to make him – in the Mahāyāna *sūtras* – a symbol of ultimate reality itself. But even when he is seen in this way, that achievement is still only what any human being is capable of achieving. Buddhists believe that any individual can become an enlightened human being if they only make the effort and follow in the footsteps of the Buddhas. In doing so, you follow not commands or orders but an example. You see what the Buddhas have done, and that it is the most skilful thing to do; that it has brought those human beings in the past to their ultimate well-being, and that it can do the same for you.

It is one thing to accept the authority of a teacher, or to decide to take on a precept or rule; it is quite another thing to be expected to obey commandments. Inherent in the use of the imperative – the commandment rather than the precept – is a sense of coercion, and where there is coercion there cannot be any spiritual teaching worthy of the name. The spiritual life is dedicated to the development of the individual, especially the development of awareness, of your own consciousness, your own sense of responsibility. How can you be forced to do that? It would be a contradiction in terms.

This is why the *Sutta* says that 'he who is skilled in his good, who wishes to attain that state of calm (Nibbāna), should act thus'. If you are not skilled in your good and don't particularly feel the need to attain *nibbāna*, all well and good; this teaching isn't for you. Although the Buddha might reason with you, he would not attempt to coerce you into doing something that you were unwilling to do. To deny someone their ordinary human freedom or to threaten or cajole them is not to communicate the Dharma. A presentation of spiritual principles that appears to come from a position of power or coercive authority is not really true to those principles. It is a secular statement, not one that comes from a position of spiritual authority.

So the conditional or hypothetical statement is the most appropriate way to communicate the Dharma. If the Buddha is the *śāntināyaka*, the one who leads beings to peace, this is in a sense all he does, perhaps all he is capable of doing. Nobody is threatening you with hellfire and brimstone if you decide you are quite happy as you are. The Buddha simply shows the way. It is up to you to decide whether or not you want to follow it.

## 2

# THE ETHICAL FOUNDATIONS OF *METTĀ*

> He should be able, upright, perfectly upright, of noble speech, gentle, and humble.
>
> *Sakko ujū ca sūjū ca*
> *suvaco c'assa mudu anatimānī*

The Buddha's conditional statement – that if you want this, you will need to do that – is more than an invitation, it is also a challenge. How ready are we to follow the path of peace? In the opening lines of the *Sutta* we are introduced to the level that our ordinary human development needs to have reached if we are to embark on the path of the Higher Evolution, as I call it – that is to say, the path of conscious self-development by which we can realize our full spiritual potential. Leaving aside the spiritual qualities needed for this, do we have even the basic human qualities that such an undertaking calls for? At this stage, before attempting to develop the ideal response to others that we call *mettā*, we need to clarify how we relate to others at a basic level, perhaps by becoming more straightforwardly ethical. Until we have done this, our ideas about *mettā* will bear little or no relation to our ability to bring it into being in our everyday experience. Having told us what the one 'skilled in his good' is really aiming for, the *Sutta*'s first verse therefore goes on to tell us how such a person should act, not specifically but in general.

It is worth noting that the first quality mentioned is one that most people would never think of associating with the spiritual life at all. *Sakko*, the word translated here as 'able', means just that: 'able to do', vigorous and adept. It suggests that the Buddhist approach to the spiritual life is quite practical and matter-of-fact. The *Sutta* is not looking for signs of incipient piety. It is not saying that you need to be a sensitive soul or a spiritual person. It is simply saying that you need to be capable.

An example from the Pāli canon shows us that some of the Buddha's very earliest disciples were anything but pious, at least to begin with. These young men were what one might today call playboys, looking for a good time and experiencing a measure of frustration and disillusionment in the process. They came from wealthy merchant families and, so the story goes, they were out picnicking one day in the countryside. They had all brought their wives along with them – all except one young man who had no wife but who had brought along a courtesan. This young woman then rather spoiled the outing for everyone by disappearing with some ornaments, and when the Buddha came across them they were busy searching for her.

Having set out to enjoy themselves, it all turned rather sour, and the Buddha seized this moment of disillusionment to suggest to the young men that there was a more reliable source of enjoyment to be found in the Dharma. Why waste your time searching for this woman, asked the Buddha, when it could be put to better use searching for yourself? Eventually, inspired by the Buddha's teaching, these playboys became what we would nowadays call monks.[104]

The episode has much that is worthy of reflection, but the point to be noted in this context is that these men were not obvious candidates for the spiritual life. They were not the types to be especially interested in religion or meditation. However, they were clearly able to know their own good, and to know what was even better when it was pointed out to them. They were psychologically sound, able to look after themselves, capable.

A person who is truly capable can turn their capability in almost any direction. You can go out to work or choose not to. You might know how to do a bit of gardening, you might know how to do a bit of carpentry, you might be able to look after a baby, or cook a meal from any bits and pieces left over in the kitchen. In fact, confronted by any given situation, difficult or otherwise, you can cope, you can manage, you can get by. You know how to look after yourself, and you can look after others if need be. This is the capable human being, the product of the long march of evolution, and the kind of person one will need to be in order to embark on the path of spiritual development. It doesn't matter whether or not you are interested in religion, philosophy, spirituality, mysticism, high art, or even Buddhism itself. None of this counts for much if you are not first of all a capable human being, someone who is able to be an effective member of society in the ordinary sense, to look after themselves, manage their own life, and make their own way in the world.

It should be said that being capable is not always a matter of one's own efforts alone. Some qualities are the result of all sorts of deep-seated conditions that stretch back through your life or that may simply be inherited. If you have had a supportive upbringing – that is, one in which you have been surrounded by people who care about you, who have helped you grow and learn effectively – the necessary qualities may come to you quite easily, especially if, because of your personality, you have been able to make full use of these opportunities. In all likelihood you will have the resourcefulness and stability of mind to begin the path of self-directed spiritual practice.

Without these advantages you may find it hard to muster the ordinary human capability to take you forward in the spiritual life. If your upbringing and life experience has been particularly difficult, if there are psychological or emotional factors that stand in the way of spiritual progress, you may need time to overcome these and to integrate the various aspects of your personality into a single-minded clarity of purpose. You may be inspired by the Dharma but lack the practical human qualities and the mental toughness necessary to make a success of practising it. If you realize that you are psychologically frail or emotionally dependent, the best thing to do to begin with is to work steadily at that level. Not everybody who comes along to a Buddhist meditation class possesses the self-assurance, self-motivation, and independence of mind which are not only associated with successful human endeavour, but which also give the necessary drive to spiritual practice. If you are in this position you will have to devote your energies first to building up your basic psychological strength. You may benefit from therapy or analysis, but it may be even more helpful to work on your friendships and to learn to do a job of work competently and reliably.

Spiritual teachers have a responsibility not to push their students into a more demanding spiritual practice than they are ready for, or allow their students' enthusiasm to lure them into biting off more than they can chew. Meditation can help to sort out one's problems at this straightforward psychological level, just by introducing a little peace of mind, while ritual and devotion help to generate more energy and positivity. Retreats can deepen and stabilize one's practice. But even someone who meditates regularly and is definitely getting something from it will not necessarily be capable in the sense of remaining emotionally positive through all the ups and downs of a life dedicated to spiritual practice. Not everyone can form a resolution to act in a certain way and stick to it, for example. Becoming a healthy, capable human being takes time. I myself know people who have been meditating regularly for many years but who do not seem to have got very far spiritually. In some cases work and friendship are more effective ways of building up self-confidence and an ability to engage effectively with the world.

The *Sutta* makes it quite clear that one has to be capable to begin with. Being capable is nothing extraordinary. It doesn't mean being perfect or infallible. It means being adequate, competent, able to make a reasonable success of your work. As such, it may seem a small thing. But being capable may not be something you can achieve immediately. If you do come to see that you are *not* yet capable in this way, this need not stop you from further spiritual endeavour. There are plenty of other qualities that may be more accessible, and the *Sutta* goes on to tell us what they are.

### UPRIGHT

As well as being able, the one skilled in his good needs to be 'upright'. The Pāli word is *uju*, a term which does not specifically refer to ethics but is more commonly associated with archery, being used to refer to the shaft of an arrow. It means quite simply 'straight'. Just as the shaft of an arrow needs to be straight if it is to hit its target, the follower of the Dharma needs to be straight in order to be true to their aim. This quality of being upright or straight typically shows itself in our dealings with other people. It concerns the social sphere, the sphere of economic relations and daily work.

In a sense, it follows on naturally from the first quality, being capable. There is a certain clean practicality in the attitude of one who is straight. If you are capable, you will do things in a straightforward, open, uncomplicated way. You don't need to resort to anything underhand or devious. You don't need to duck your responsibilities. You know what you think and you are honest in communicating it, without playing games or hiding behind half-truths. You are upright.

Being straightforward is often the key ingredient in Buddhist practice. It is so easy to compromise, to equivocate, to fudge the truth and dilute your intention. 'On the whole I'm pretty honest,' you might say, 'So there surely can't be any harm in softening the harsh reality a bit, covering up the raw truth, bending the bare facts a little, just to help things along.' It is true that equivocation can sometimes appear to prevent upset, at least in the short term, and avoid hurting people's feelings – even if your *own* feelings are the ones you are most concerned to protect. There is also no doubt that being straightforward can land you in trouble, and in business dealings it can create complications. Even from a worldly point of view, however, these difficulties will in most cases be offset in the longer term by a positive dividend of trust and respect from colleagues and clients.

And from a spiritual point of view, we have to consider what the avoidance of confronting people or situations is really about. If you are watering down the truth of what is really going on, you are watering down your ability to apply the Dharma to your life. If you habitually mask your true feelings out of fear of confronting people with the truth of yourself as you really are, you are hardly likely to be able to confront that truth yourself. You need to be able to see the real danger in being woolly and vague, to see that avoiding the truth of the immediate situation fatally undermines your practice of the Dharma. Being upright in this context involves being clear about your aims and honest about how they are to be achieved.

The upright and straightforward person knows his or her own mind and is not afraid to speak it. Freedom from fear and anxiety is a natural consequence of this willingness to be honest. If you are genuinely straightforward, you will not attempt to conceal whatever negative emotions might arise. Even if you are prone to anger or lust or fear, you can acknowledge these tendencies, and so avoid the guilt and alienation that go with dissimulation and pretence. You will be emotionally engaged, self-confident, and uninhibited. The *Sutta* is itself unequivocal and uncompromising in advocating this virtue: 'He should be able, upright, perfectly upright.' The only way to be straight, the *Sutta* seems to be saying, is to be perfectly straight, straight without any qualification or rationalizing: *sūju*, 'perfectly and happily upright'. Let there be no doubt about it.

It might seem from this that being straightforward is a very straightforward virtue. However, one needs quite a degree of psychological integration if one is to have the kind of emotionally positive, trusting nature that can deal with others without feeling the need to obfuscate, dither, or beat about the bush. On the other hand, you may think you have no problem with being straightforward when in fact your plain speaking is close to boorishness. There is a difference between being open and candid and being simply blunt and crude. Harshness of speech can masquerade as honesty and openness when it really expresses a closed attitude towards others, a lack of awareness of the effect upon them of one's speech and manner. Some people pride themselves on being outspoken – 'I speak as I find' – when really it's just an excuse for being insensitive to other people's feelings. A straight approach can turn into a bludgeon if it goes with a lack of awareness of the complex differences in people's sensitivities, and an assumption that the consequences of your straight talking are not your affair.

So a further human quality that the *Sutta* recommends to one who wishes to attain the state of peace is that of gracious speech, speech that is good, appropriate, and pleasant. We cannot afford to be abrupt or uncaring in our communication with others if we want to make progress towards that ultimate goal.

### FLEXIBLE

A quality that offsets the unhelpful connotations of straightforwardness or perfect uprightness in speech is *c'assa*, a word that seems to have caused translators a few problems. *C'assa* is simply 'and he should be'. The dictionary translation of the next adjective in this line, *mudu*, is 'soft, mild, weak, and tender'. Clearly, we can rule out 'weak' in the present context. We are left with a sweet temper, a mild and gentle manner, a tender responsiveness. It is a quality that emerges naturally out of the previous one: *mudu* suggests a pliancy, a suppleness of mind, without any sense of being weak or easily led. There is plenty of elasticity, plenty of 'give' in your attitude. Where flexibility is required, you can be flexible. You can adjust. You are adaptable and even-tempered.

Finally, there is *anatimānī*. It is translated here as 'humble', a word which carries some rather unfortunate connotations. Someone who is 'skilled in their good' is not going to adopt the obsequious, hand-wringing posture of one of Charles Dickens' more repellent characters, Uriah Heep, who repeatedly declares himself to be 'ever so 'umble'. Buddhism calls not for cringing self-abnegation, but for heroic altruism. *Māna* means 'pride', and *anati* 'not high' or 'not extreme', so *anatimānī* means an absence of high-and-mightiness, arrogance, or conceit. It does not preclude a proper pride or self-respect.

We now have a composite picture of one 'skilled in his good'. Such a person is capable, completely straightforward, gracious in their speech, flexible, and lacking any conceit. What is perhaps most significant about this initial impression of someone who is proficient in the means of attaining the state of peace is that if you were to meet such a person they would not necessarily strike you as religious, certainly not as pious or holy. These are simply positive human qualities. The *Sutta* seems to be saying that the practice of Buddhism consists, first and foremost, in the conscious development of the ordinary virtues of the happy human being.

> Contented, easily supported, with few duties, of light livelihood,
> with senses calmed, discreet, not impudent, not greedily attached
> to families.
>
> *Santussako ca subharo ca*
> *appakicco ca sallahukavutti*
> *santindriyo ca nipako ca*
> *appagabbho kulesu ananugiddho*

*Santussako*, or contentment, the first-mentioned quality of the second verse, presupposes a degree of individuality. Firstly, the contented person knows how to find satisfaction with what they have. Of course, only a Buddha or bodhisattva or *arhant* would be content in absolutely any situation, but in most circumstances a contented person will have an inner peace, a brightness or warmth or harmony within, that tends to obviate the need for stimulation from outside. The person who is contented is thus one who leads a simple life; conversely, one who leads a simple life will become contented. Contentment is linked to individuality in that if you are an individual, you don't need anything special to compensate for some lack within yourself. You have a being of your own; you are not unreasonably dependent on external circumstances or on the approval of others. You find a certain sufficiency or fulfilment within yourself, in the experience of your own being. It is in this sense that you are contented.

But in trying to be self-sufficient, and choosing not to expose yourself to much in the way of stimulation or excitement, aren't you shutting yourself off from others and closing your mind to life in general? In fact, contentment is the opposite of a closed or fixed state of mind. It is a state of openness and freedom. Contentment is a generous state of being wherein you have no need to cling to anything, or gain anything, in order to be happy. When you are content you have a healthy enjoyment of your state of being, free from caginess or undue reserve.

Depending on your inner resources does not mean cutting yourself off from other people. That would suggest not so much contentment as complacency. As the near enemy of contentment, complacency betokens a superficial satisfaction with things as they are, particularly with yourself. If you scratch the surface of this self-satisfaction, you are likely to find blind attachment to your present state at almost any cost. You inwardly – and perhaps not so inwardly – congratulate yourself on being the way you are, with no thought of ever becoming anything different, anything more. You regard your present state as final. You do not look beyond it, and underneath you are clinging to it for dear life.

Complacency is related to a fault referred to more directly in the first verse of the *Sutta*: *atimānī*, or arrogance. The arrogant person, like the complacent person, does not want to go too deeply into anything that might threaten their fixed idea of who they are. Yet, ironically, complacency and arrogance stem from a lack of contentment with who you *really* are. Your apparent contentment is with who you *think* you are. You know – or you feel – that the real you is simply inadequate. Perhaps you are unwilling even to get to know the real you, and to explore your real identity, for fear of the shortcomings and inadequacies you may find. So instead, you climb up on to your high horse and create a false self in place of the real self.

If you do that, you fend off any real communication, because true communication always involves opening yourself to others. An arrogant or complacent person would rather not know the truth about themself, which in turn means that they cannot really be receptive to others. Only by learning to feel *mettā* towards themself and others can such a person move on from his fixed, and therefore false, view of themself.

Stillness, simplicity, and contentment can be said to be the positive counterpart of the third precept, abstention from sexual misconduct. Without contentment, for example, a married person will perhaps experience dissatisfaction with their situation and start to look around for a new sexual partner. But when you are emotionally more self-sufficient – that is to say, more contented – you are aware that a sexual relationship cannot bring complete fulfilment, but only a certain level of satisfaction. You will then be more likely to be able to keep to the terms of the marriage contract, not looking outside it for some special experience that seems to promise greater fulfilment. You realize that contentment is found in what you are and what you have, not in what you could be and what you might have.

Our desire for the things we crave seldom bears any relation to the capacity of those things to satisfy that craving. People usually eat sweets not because of their flavour but for the temporary experience of reassurance they give. But reassurance is intangible, and certainly not to be found in a plastic wrapper, so we are more or less certain to be disappointed. Then, having failed to assuage our craving for reassurance, and in the absence of any more creative option, we are likely just to eat another sweet. It is as if we suffer from some constant niggling need, some nameless lack, some ever-present void that we try to fill with something, anything – a sweet, a special treat, a flick through the pages of a magazine or the television channels. This is the repetitive nature of neurotic craving. We cannot enjoy what seem to be the things we desire because what we really want is insubstantial. Although we see it in the object, it is not really there. The sweet, after all, does not contain reassurance; it only contains sugar. Reassurance is a subjective experience, and one can only find it by looking inwards.

One's contentment, or lack of it, is basically always with oneself. All our attempts to get satisfaction from external objects, all the hankering and scheming and yearning, come from this restlessness, this refusal to accept ourselves and our condition. If we are to become contented, therefore, there will need to be a radical shift of direction in our search for satisfaction. Trying to arrange the world to suit our desires will never produce the stillness and simplicity that characterize true contentment, but only the irritation and disappointment that come from dependence upon external conditions. Contentment can come only from our inner resources, from creating the appropriate conditions within our own mind. We are dissatisfied with our experience, but we look in the wrong place for the solution. We look out into the world for the remedy, in the form of desired objects and people, when we really need to be looking inwards, into the hidden treasure of the mind itself. To be contented, then, you need to have a positive appreciation of yourself. This is why the *mettā bhāvanā* meditation practice begins with the cultivation of *mettā* towards oneself. So you need to have a degree of contentment to practise the *mettā bhāvanā*, but then the practice itself will strengthen that sense of contentment.

We can begin to see that the practice of the *mettā bhāvanā* meditation can be an example of what is sometimes known in the Buddhist tradition as the path of irregular steps.[105] According to the *Sutta*, we need to have all these human qualities if we are to be able to feel and express *mettā* fully and effectively; but we will be greatly assisted in the development of qualities like contentment by our attempts to develop loving-kindness towards ourselves and others.

### EASILY SUPPORTED

In the first verse, the *Sutta* sets out the qualities of the healthy human, one who is able to take responsibility for making their own way in the world. The second verse brings a transition, suggesting a more specifically mendicant lifestyle. The term *subharo* – 'easy to support' – refers to the economic situation of the monk. The suggestion seems to be that we renounce work and commit ourselves to a life of contemplation, relying on the support of others to give us the necessities of life. The quality we have just been discussing, contentment, clearly also supports this. If they are not contented within themselves, the monk or nun will not be able to sustain their chosen lifestyle.

The fact is that in the Buddha's time, the monks were completely dependent upon lay people, who provided them with food, clothing, and even sometimes with shelter. With the basic necessities of life taken care of, the monks and nuns were free to devote their energies to meditation, study, and devotional practice. This being the case, it was the responsibility of the monks to be easy to support, and not to make life difficult for those who were considerate enough to provide them with their material needs.

The tradition of the homeless wanderer being supported by society at large was not instituted by the Buddha; he inherited it, it existed in Indian society already. In the Buddha's day, the renunciation of social identity was a common and accepted practice all over northern India, and the homeless wanderer or *paribbājaka* (Sanskrit *parivrājaka*) was thus an accepted outsider. When the Buddha started out on his journey to Enlightenment, he too left the home life to become a *paribbājaka*, and after the Enlightenment many of his disciples came from that same casteless social category, or rather non-category, and continued to go on foot from village to village with their alms bowls, accepting whatever food they were given. In the early days of the Buddhist community, the sangha, the priority was to establish a spiritual community on principles that transcended the worldly concerns of the wider society. As the figure of the itinerant spiritual practitioner was already a feature of Indian society and the support of such individuals by the wider community an accepted tradition, the Buddhist sangha adopted this model quite naturally.

The withdrawal of the monk or nun from the world of work went with an attitude to work, particularly manual labour, which still persists in Indian society today: the view that it is inherently unspiritual. The ancient Indians had a similar view to that of the ancient Greeks, except that whereas the Athenian state relied on a class of slaves to carry out any manual labour that might be necessary, Indian society depended on a number of lower castes. The Greeks have of course given up slavery, but to a large extent India continues to run on the basis that physical work is inherently degrading, and that no respectable person would do such work if he or she could possibly avoid it.

Thus in the India of the Buddha's day the possibility of taking up the spiritual life and continuing to do physical work simply did not arise. You could not be a full-time spiritual practitioner and continue to support yourself. But by virtue of the same attitude, you could rely on the lay people to support you. Indeed, the religious renunciant was almost compelled to depend for alms on the lay community if he was to form any kind of socially acceptable relationship with them. Nor did the Buddha think it worth challenging this convention. It is not after all such a bad thing in principle for the more spiritually committed to be supported by the less committed, and he accepted the customary division between monks or wanderers and lay communities as a reasonable way to make this happen, and a way of propagating the Dharma in the process. But as Buddhism developed and spread, the range of activities that the full-timers were able to take up expanded. In the beginning, they were expected to devote all their energies to meditation, study, and teaching. For the first 500 years the teaching was passed on entirely through oral transmission, so a good deal of the time would have been spent learning the *sutta*s by heart and chanting them communally to impress the doctrine on the memory of every monk. Then, when the *sutta*s began to be written down, a great deal of literary activity ensued. Later still, with the building of the great monasteries, monks would have been involved in the sculpting and gilding of images, as well as in the design and decoration of the monasteries and temples themselves.

Later, when Buddhism, especially in its Mahāyāna form, travelled to China and Tibet, whose cultures had a more practical inclination than that of India, monks began to take up everyday physical tasks. Tibet, for example, has no cultural prejudice against manual labour, and in a Tibetan Buddhist monastery you will find monks energetically engaged in all manner of necessary activities according to their various abilities. In the Chan and Zen schools, work is considered to be an integral part of a fully committed spiritual training. As in Tibetan monasteries, monks are expected to throw themselves wholeheartedly into every task that needs to be done, from cooking, cleaning, chopping wood, and drawing water to the printing of Buddhist *sūtras*.

So we have to be careful not to be trapped by our respect for ancient texts such as the *Karaṇīya-Mettā Sutta* into thinking of practical, physical, and even economic activity as being necessarily worldly or unspiritual. A human being is not only a mind, but also a body inhabiting a sensory, physical universe. We need productive activity for our physical and psychological well-being. If our mind is the only part of us that gets any real exercise, whether through study or teaching, or at an office desk or computer, there will be an imbalance in our being as a whole, and we will be in need of physical work and exercise to bring it back into balance.

I know from my own contact with Buddhist monks in South-east Asia (admittedly as far back as the 1950s) that they can get into quite an unhealthy state – not just physically or psychologically, but also spiritually – from lack of exercise. Their dependence upon the laity, who in most cases looked after them extremely well, was such that even though the monks would have liked to have done more for themselves, the lay people would not let them. As I remember it, the lay people felt embarrassed, or even affronted, if the monks tried to do things for themselves. It is after all through service to the monks that lay people traditionally express their devotion to the ideal of Enlightenment.

On the face of it, the dependence of the full-time spiritual practitioners on the laity ought to contribute to the simplicity of their lifestyle, enabling them to concentrate more of their energy on purely spiritual matters. But in reality it can hinder them from engaging their energies at all. Perhaps in the early days of Buddhism this unequal distribution of labour between monks and laity was necessary. The dawn-to-dusk burden of physical labour was no doubt so heavy that a degree of freedom from such duties was essential if one was to have the time and energy for reflection and other higher pursuits. It is understandable that a conflict emerged between the demands of farm and field on the one hand and those of spiritual pursuits on the other, and an outright separation of the two was probably the most straightforward solution. However, the cost was a certain alienation: from worldly affairs on the part of the monks, and from any real spiritual life on the part of the laity.

It would seem then that this concept of *subharo*, 'easy to support', owes its appearance in the *Sutta* to the social conventions prevalent in India at the time of the Buddha. In view of this it would be a mistake to interpret the term as suggesting that someone committed to leading the spiritual life must be materially supported by others, and should not get involved in practical or economic activity. In the market economies of the modern world, we are very fortunate in being able to be full-time Buddhists while at the same time involving ourselves unashamedly in straightforward, practical tasks. We should take that opportunity. In our practice of the Dharma there is invariably a healthy tension between the need to be involved in the sphere of worldly human activity, and thus practise the other-regarding aspect of the Dharma, and the need to withdraw from worldly activity for the purposes of meditation and reflection. As modern Buddhists we have a unique opportunity to decide for ourselves how this balance may be struck in our lives. In doing so, we need to return to the basic principles of Buddhism, and specifically to the principle of right livelihood, that is, ethical work.

To practise right livelihood, we may have to question our overall attitude to work. Like ancient cultures, industrialized societies have their own conventional attitudes to work, these attitudes being based in the case of the latter on the strict division between paid work and leisure. For many of us, work is an activity we don't *want* to do but *have* to do in order to support ourselves, and leisure time is 'our own time', in which we are free to pursue our personal interests. This unhappy distinction seems to affect much that we do. Jobs, tasks, physical activities with some practical purpose or end in view, like cleaning or cooking, are considered a burden, a chore, and resented as such; and we imagine that when we are not working we should be continuously diverted. We certainly don't want to have to do 'chores'.

However, all human beings, even spiritual full-timers, need work, in the sense of some productive, useful activity, whether paid or unpaid, that is beneficial to themselves and to others; and simple, practical physical work may be better than intellectual work from the point of view of fulfilling this human and spiritual need. If you are able to devote all your time and energy to meditation, study, teaching, and writing, all well and good. But not everyone is able to meditate or study the Dharma day in, day out. Many people, including many monks, are quite unsuited to teaching or writing. So, for them, an injunction to refrain from working and physical activity would be quite unhelpful. Of course, this means that we have to be able to carry out such work without resentment, without considering it demeaning or a burdensome imposition.

Today we have the opportunity to reappraise the whole question of work and financial support. We do not necessarily have to accept the traditions as they have come down to us, especially when these are influenced by Indian social and cultural conditions of some 2,500 years ago. In modern post-traditional societies, you can renounce family life and worldly occupation without having to rely for your livelihood on those who have chosen to engage with them. You can choose to work with other Buddhists – that is, others who share your aspirations – in such a way as to support one another's spiritual development and at the same time provide for the material needs of each one of you. The necessity to support oneself financially can become an opportunity to deepen communication, share skills, and learn new ways of cooperation and mutual support. Working in such a situation you can take full account of individual temperaments and attitudes to allow each person to work in a way that is appropriate to their spiritual needs. Some people might find it suited them best to do mainly manual work, while others would benefit from gradually taking on more managerial responsibility. Of course, everyone would need to have time for meditation and Dharma study.

In today's world, it is up to the individual to choose their own way, to make their own decisions, according to whatever principles they wish to live by. There can no longer be blanket rules for spiritual life and practice. What is appropriate at one time and in one place may not work in another. We need a new kind of Buddhist culture in which economic relations can be constantly recreated to meet a constantly changing world. This is probably as close to the Mahāyāna ideal of the Pure Land – the perfect environment for spiritual practice – as we can hope for.

### GIVE WHAT YOU CAN, TAKE WHAT YOU NEED

Taking the *Sutta* at face value, therefore, we can interpret the term *subharo*, 'easy to support', as referring to how a monk should behave in terms of his economically dependent role with respect to the laity. But there is a deeper and less historically specific principle at work in this part of the *Sutta*. Whether we are monk or lay, or neither one nor the other, we are supported by society at large, and dependent on the labour of innumerable other people for the necessities of life. We do not grow all our own food or draw our own water; we do not build and furnish our own houses or weave and sew all our own clothes.

If we reflect on how it is that we can enjoy so many consumer products for so little outlay – if we think of the hours of cheap labour that go into what we are able to buy for next to nothing – we will find that we are not at all easily supported. There are also environmental and ecological considerations to take into account. The natural and human resources available to our society should not be expended heedlessly or needlessly. The fact that we have the financial resources to help ourselves to what we fancy does not justify our consuming the wealth of the world without consideration for the claims of others – both in the present and in the future – on those same resources. We owe it to the society that supports us to give what we can to support others. There are very few people who would benefit spiritually from being entirely supported by others in the way the traditional monastic sangha was.

The principle behind this term *subharo* therefore comes down to taking from the world and from society no more than you need, and freely contributing whatever you can. You are entitled to rely on others for the help and support that one human being can be reasonably expected to give another, but you also need to be prepared to stand on your own two feet, as far as you can. You cannot expect to be propped up by others as a right.

This principle operates on all levels of exchange, not only on the material and economic level. We need the emotional support of others, for example, but we should not expect from our friends what we are capable of providing for ourselves with a little effort. Once they have helped us back on our feet, we shouldn't expect them to prop us up indefinitely. If you are emotionally needy, you are clearly not yet 'capable', and as such you are not 'easy to support'. You are therefore unlikely to make much progress in meditation. Of course, if you are such a person it is quite possible that you will not understand that you are making undue emotional demands on others, and that their time and energy might be better spent in other ways. In that case it is up to your friends to help you to see the truth of your situation, and perhaps direct you towards getting some therapeutic help, rather than offering 'support' that will just perpetuate the problem.

## SIMPLIFYING

If you are aiming to be easy to support, the way to do it is to keep your wants and needs to a manageable level, however you manage to do so. This is the ideal to which the term *sallahukavutti* refers: a livelihood, *vutti*, that is *lahuka*, literally 'trifling' or 'lightweight'. It suggests a basic simplicity in one's attitude to life, a determination not to be weighed down by a multiplicity of wants and desires or onerous material commitments. Clearly a taste for hard work, and a relish for the challenge of practical tasks and problems to be overcome, is a virtue, but it is possible to like these things too much for one's own good, especially if they become distractions from more spiritually pressing challenges. So the *Sutta* goes on to say that one should be *appakicco*, 'with little work' or 'with few duties'.

The fact is that one can become too busy even with religious or spiritual activities. Again with reference to the monastic context of early Indian Buddhism, the *Sutta* warns against giving yourself too many things to do. The monk shouldn't be too occupied with performing ceremonies for the laity or running errands for his teachers or preceptors, or even with teaching his own pupils. He should allow himself enough time for study, meditation, reflection, and just spending time quietly by himself – all the things that the lay people in fact support him to do.

Work, in the sense of pleasurable, productive activity, is a necessary part of life for most people. But there is a difference between this and a kind of neurotic, compulsive activity that masquerades as work but is really a way of keeping the deeper emotions at bay. Work can be an unhealthy means by which to escape from being alone with oneself and one's feelings. We should beware of feeling that we have to keep busy, that we can never be without something to do. So yes, by all means work, but don't let busyness be an escape from your true self. Be occupied only with those activities that are really necessary.

### MODEST

The division of labour between monk and lay person has other disadvantages. Relying completely on other people for your support puts you in a passive relationship with regard to them. There is a suggestion of this danger in the *Sutta*, in which the Buddha now enjoins the monk to be *apagabbho kulesu ananugiddho*. Like *subharo*, the term *apagabbho* clearly has to do with the relationship between wandering monks and the lay people upon whom they depend. It is the negative form of *pagabbho*, which means 'impudent', 'over bold', 'tending to push oneself forward', and Saddhatissa translates it quite neatly as 'modesty'. Together with the term that follows, *kulesu ananugiddho*, 'not greedily attached to families' it would seem to refer to the danger of monks insinuating themselves into special relationships with particular families. It could happen that a family would end up adopting a particular monk and in a way 'domesticating' him. To avoid this, the *Sutta* directs the monk to avoid making strong connections with anyone or soliciting special favours from them when on his almsround, as this is against the whole spirit of renunciation for which he stands.

Reading between the lines of the *Sutta*, we can see that even the homeless wanderer of the Buddha's day was not necessarily free from attachment to the things that came his way, few as these must have been. He might well be tempted to secure creature comforts and a certain sense of belonging by getting to know certain families, out of a yearning for the approval and acceptance of ordinary people. To guard against this, he is counselled to cultivate a sense of identity based on inner stability and contentment.

But how should we ourselves interpret this exhortation? After all, we don't knock on doors for alms. For us, perhaps, the danger is of depending for our sense of identity upon the acceptance or approbation of others, being afraid of exclusion. The possible result of such dependence is that one is unable to make decisions, hold opinions, dress, eat, or do all manner of other things without reference to the norms of the group whose approval one seeks. To protect ourselves from this, we should avoid making ourselves too much at home in any one human grouping, or identifying with a group too rigidly. We should avoid 'getting our feet under the table' in the course of our involvement with groups, systems, and ideologies. If you are skilled in your good and wish to attain Nirvāṇa, you cannot afford to be too attached to the approval of any group, whether it is your biological family, your cultural or ethnic group, your caste or nationality. A mature individual has an existence, as it were, in his or her own right, without needing to have recourse to the affirmation of any group, be it a family, a community, or even a religious movement. Such a person is capable of finding a sense of fulfilment within the experience of his or her own being, independent of external circumstances.

The clarity of purpose discussed thus far finds expression in a particular kind of mindfulness suggested by the term *santindriyo*. This is often translated as 'with senses controlled' or 'with senses disciplined', as though the senses were like wild horses to be reined in and brought under control. But this is not an accurate reflection of the nature of the bodily senses, or an accurate translation of the Pāli word. The literal meaning of *santi* is not 'disciplined' but 'calmed', and it is not to the wild horses of the eyes and ears that it refers, but to the wild horse within, the wild horse of the mind.

It is traditional in Buddhism to speak not of five senses but of six: not just the senses of sight, sound, taste, smell, and touch, but also that of the mind. And of all six senses it is the mind that is the origin of craving and attachment. It is only as a mental experience that we need to address the issue of sensory experience at all. The physical senses are in themselves quite pure. Their nature is just to register stimuli. They are being stimulated all the time we are awake, as all kinds of phenomena impinge on them and present themselves to our consciousness. In fact, the physical senses are not so much wild horses as windows or mirrors: they may be obstructed or closed or stained, but they do not determine what degree or quality of light passes through them or is reflected by them. They are themselves incapable of mischief. There is nothing inherently wrong with seeing forms and colours, nothing wrong with hearing sound or tasting food. If our minds were pure, if there were 'in the seen only the seen, in the heard only the heard' (to quote another famous Pāli *sutta*),[106] there would be nothing to pacify, no conflict to resolve.

If, for instance, you were to look at a flower, you might experience an intense perception of colour, scent, perhaps movement, and you might simply appreciate that sensory experience. If you didn't appropriate what you saw or smelled, if you didn't react to it with craving, no unskilful mental state would have arisen from that sense contact. Likewise with a disagreeable or fearful object: if you could respond creatively to the experience, without reacting to it with revulsion or horror, no unskilful mental state would arise. Ideally, this is what we need to be cultivating: the ability to appreciate any sort of sense experience simply for what it is, free from the imposition upon it of our likes and dislikes.

Appreciation is very much part of this activity of mindful awareness. Even though we cannot rely on sense experience for lasting fulfilment, it is nonetheless to be enjoyed on its own level. You need food that is wholesome and nutritious, for example. If it tastes good as well, so much the better. If someone offers you some succulent fruit, for example, you will appreciate it as both nourishing and delicious. On the other hand, if there is no fruit today, but only porridge, that's perfectly fine too. You remain content, because your good humour is not dependent on having that fruit. This is how the peaceful mind operates in relation to sense experience.

It was once seriously suggested to me that high spiritual attainment made all food taste the same. The person who suggested this – clearly he had quite a high opinion of his own level of attainment – claimed that he no longer tasted rice or potatoes or tea, but simply food and drink in a general sense. This is of course nonsense. When you are free from greedy or anxious grasping at objects, you can become aware of them in all their colour, depth, and vitality as never before. You are free to enjoy them fully. The more aware you become, the more sensitive you are to subtle differences of taste, sound, and so on. This is the middle way between hedonism and hair-shirt asceticism. You don't have to avoid good food, but if your ability to remain happy is too dependent on what you are given to eat, then some degree of renunciation is clearly in order.

To be aware of what is pleasant is fine. It is when we move on to forming a desire for that pleasant experience to stay as it is, and therefore the desire to possess it, that we sow the seed of future dissatisfaction. Likewise, unpleasant sensory experience need not inevitably produce dissatisfaction. It is the mind reacting with ignorance, craving, or revulsion that produces the sense of dissatisfaction. All the objects of the senses – things, people, and experiences – are impermanent, always changing, and when the mind is calm you are able simply to let them be as they are, without the anxious desire to grasp at them or to push them away.

Having said that, we do need to limit the sense experience to which we expose ourselves. The movement from the bare perception of something into the desire to possess it (or move away from it) is taking place all the time, but at such a subtle level that we need a certain degree of mental stillness to be aware of it. By exercising choice over our sensory experience, we aim to calm the mind, withdrawing, in a relative sense, from worldly activity, as a way of simplifying and deepening awareness. There are a thousand and one sensory distractions ready to impinge on our awareness in everyday life, and any one of them can quickly engage our interest in an unguarded moment. Modern forms of publicity and mass communication are expert at seizing the attention and manipulating the emotions so as to induce states of greed, craving, and aversion. They make use of the fact that there are certain ideas, images, sounds, and even smells that will affect most people's minds in a particular way. Popular forms of entertainment, for example, rely on violent or erotic images to hold our attention and keep the mind excited and spellbound. For the average person at least it is thus not advisable to give free rein to sensory stimuli. The best time to visit the supermarket or pastry shop is when you are not feeling hungry, and thus more likely to be drawn into a greedy state of mind by the cleverly arranged displays of tempting titbits on offer.

Our aim, however, is not to shut down perception, blinker the senses, or rigidly control input. Isolating ourselves from experience in this way would produce a brittle, artificial contentment that could not withstand the knocks of ordinary life. When calming the mind's response to the world through the senses, you still act, think, make decisions, and engage with people and with things; but you don't allow your choice of actions to reflect a neurotic and rigid adherence to personal likes and dislikes.

Training the mind may well involve restraining the eye from contact with certain visual objects, and the ear from taking note of certain sounds, but with practice your contentment will not be *dependent* on your living simply. It is fundamentally the mind that has to be pacified, so that it can become more aware of its own movements. Once your mind has become calm, and as your awareness broadens and deepens, you become more sensitive than before to your experience – a sensitiveness that begins to shine through with greater vitality and warmth.

### DISCREET

The ability to find contentment in one's own resources depends on one's having a certain degree of psychological integration in the sense of self-knowledge. You have to get to know the conditions, both internal and external, that tend to produce discontent, and how to bring to the fore the inner qualities and resources that support contentment. In other words, you have to be what Saddhatissa translates as 'discreet' and Chalmers as 'quick-witted'. The Pāli term *nipako* suggests intelligence in the sense of prudence, the ability to adapt means to ends. It is a practical kind of wisdom. There is also a sense of being able to forestall trouble. The prudent person knows what is likely to result from certain kinds of action within a given situation.

As we have noted, it is the mind that has to be calmed, not the senses. Nonetheless, external conditions are still important. When we make decisions and choices about the kind of environment in which we allow our senses to operate, we therefore need to exercise *nipako*. We owe it to ourselves to look for circumstances that will inspire and support our cultivation of higher states of consciousness. To settle for less when we can do something to change our circumstances is a kind of false contentment that is more like lethargy. Most of these will be circumstances that everybody will find helpful, so it should be a relatively simple matter to find out what they are.

Where discretion becomes particularly necessary is in judging where you as an individual should draw the line in any situation. Rather than falling back on a set of inflexible rules about what you should or should not do, you need to exercise your own judgement, based on what you know about yourself. Whereas one person might find that a certain situation quickly brings about an unskilful mental state, another person might find they can handle the same situation quite skilfully.

In all likelihood a bodhisattva or an *arhant* could encounter crude images and noisy environments and still sustain mental states that were just as skilful as those they would have when looking at beautiful and peaceful scenery. But for the rest of us, the guarding of the senses is a crucial aspect of the practice of mindfulness. Thus one's practice of ethics involves observing for oneself what one's reactions are likely to be. The mark of a morally responsible individual consists in knowing the kind of environment he or she really needs and trying to bring it about.

This is especially true if you are living or working with other people. It is part of your responsibility towards others to take care of yourself, to make sure that you can bring enough contentment into the situation. If you aren't able to be positive, you aren't really pulling your weight, spiritually speaking, and somebody else is going to have to make up for that. Your mental state will impinge on others unless someone else takes up the slack. If you put yourself in a situation in which you are bound to feel discontented, you are being irresponsible with regard to your own welfare, and letting others down as well.

Doing something about this is easier said than done. Somehow you need to cultivate contentment even while you are trying to turn an unsatisfactory situation around. For the ordinary human being, with all their quirks and inconsistencies, their habits, their likes and dislikes, their longing for approval, comfort, sympathy, and all the rest, this is no small thing to ask. In any situation that does not place us under extreme or prolonged pressure, contentment is certainly an achievable goal, but the ability to maintain contentment and inner harmony in absolutely any situation is one of the defining characteristics of a Buddha, *arhant*, or bodhisattva. While it is a goal to aim for, it should not be an expectation placed on a practising Buddhist as a matter of course.

And Buddhas and bodhisattvas, contented as they may be in themselves, will not be 'content' as far as others are concerned. They will see where the situation and circumstances of others can be improved or transformed, and will do something about it. They will recognize how unskilful states of mind and unskilful actions are brought about by certain conditions, and out of compassion will draw attention to that fact and try to remedy the situation.

Such is the contentment and practical wisdom of a bodhisattva. Of course, this is a far cry from the ordinary human contentment required as one of the preliminary qualities for the development of *mettā*. This more achievable form of contentment is simply a relative freedom from the inner dissatisfaction that compels us to seek pleasure and fulfilment in external things. Likewise, the practical wisdom called for here is no transcendental quality, but simply the ability just to keep out of trouble, spiritually speaking.

The key characteristic of one who is self-aware is that they are able – indeed find it necessary – to act in accordance with their aspirations and make their own judgements rather than comply with the norms and requirements of any group. If you are an individual, you are able to take responsibility for yourself, for what you do, and for what you think. However, you still need to form relationships with other people. In fact, taking responsibility for your own decisions and experience will make you more truly responsive to the needs of others. Being independent, you are better able to relate to others than if you were to rely on external affirmation and approval for your sense of well-being. That is, you are more able to be ethical.

Morality understood in the Buddhist sense is not so much about rules as about personal growth and progress, both your own and that of those around you. In the spiritual community the group and its norms are ideally replaced by the subtle relationship of *kalyāṇa mitratā*, spiritual friendship based on that which is wise, skilful, morally beautiful, and true. The spiritual community has as its goal the highest possible development of each of its members, as well as that of the spiritual community itself as a whole. Indeed, it aspires to contribute, at least indirectly, to the ultimate welfare of all beings.

Beyond certain broad categories it is impossible to reduce morality in this sense to a matter of observing rules, of doing some things and not doing other things. Relying on the strict application of rules and regulations seems to work satisfactorily only in the case of simple, straightforward situations. Most circumstances are so complex, and human beings themselves so various, that what is a skilful and beneficial course of action for one person may not help another person – or even that same person at another time. What is right in one set of circumstances might not be right in other circumstances, and what is right for one person might not be right for someone else. This is not to suggest a complete ethical relativism. The point is that given the complexity of real-life situations, it is difficult to judge exactly how even carefully agreed moral principles will work out in practice, or whether what you are doing is really good for you or for others. Once you begin to sharpen your ethical awareness, situations that had formerly seemed entirely straightforward may begin to raise knotty moral problems.

If you cannot rely on the rules, and, as is often the case, you cannot fall back on a reliable intuitive sense of the skilful thing to do, what is left for you to rely on? The traditional answer is that in this kind of situation it is the opinion of the *viññū* – literally 'those who know' – that is your best guide. In other words, you can place your faith in the informed judgement of those in the spiritual community with more spiritual experience than you. Hence the next verse of the *Karaṇīya Mettā Sutta*.

> He should not pursue the slightest thing for which other wise men might censure him.

*Na ca khuddaṃ samācare kiñci*
*yena viññū pare upavadeyyuṃ.*

## THE WISE – WHERE DO WE FIND THEM?

So the person who is skilled in his good and wishes to attain the state of calm, who has the very positive qualities set out in the first two verses of the *Sutta*, should not do even the slightest thing on account of which those members of the spiritual community who are wise might have cause to find fault. This is a necessary and important criterion for ensuring that your actions are taking you on the right path: to know that those who understand how unethical actions are followed by consequences will not censure you.

But how do you know that they really are wise and that you are not just seeking the approval of the more powerful and influential members of the group? This is a question that is not always easy to answer. In extreme cases, it may be easy to see the difference between conformity to group values and reliance upon the advice of the spiritual community. But obviously there will be intermediate cases where you might not be so sure. Situations may arise in which you are uncertain whether you are acting on the advice of 'the wise' because you want to be accepted by the group and fear rejection, or because you respect the greater spiritual maturity of those you are consulting. Either way, their opinion will matter to you. But a reliance on the opinion of 'the wise', in the sense that the term has in this *sutta*, is really a question of how far you regard your spiritual friends as being a truly spiritual community, rather than just another social group.

The wise have to be those in whom you have real confidence, those whom you know have your best interests at heart. But such trust can come only from experience, in other words from giving them some provisional trust. You may have taken their advice on trust in the past and found from experience that in some circumstances their judgement is more reliable than your own. You may also know and trust other people who have found them trustworthy. However you garner this testimony of experience, it takes time to discover whether or not the members of what you have identified – again provisionally – as the spiritual community have a degree of vision, skill, and maturity that you yourself do not yet possess.

If we are going to be sceptical about those who appear to be 'the wise' we have also to be sceptical about our own objectivity. Perhaps it should not come as too much of a surprise to discover that we are inclined to doubt the judgement of the wise. They have, by definition, a different perspective from our own. The fact that they really do know, and we do not, means that we cannot see things quite as they see them, because we lack their vision and their level of understanding.

In order to be receptive to the advice or censure of the wise, you therefore have to have a personal relationship with them. Only by knowing your spiritual friends well can you be sure that they know you well also, and have your best interests at heart, indeed may understand your interests better than you do yourself. You can then accept their judgement even when it does not correspond with your own. A spiritual friend is someone who knows you well and cares about you. They won't see your welfare in quite the same way as you do; they will see beyond what you want for yourself – almost as a parent sees that the welfare of their child does not necessarily lie in what the child wants. But the spiritual friend will be at the same time disinterested. They won't be upset if you don't do what they suggest; they don't have an emotional axe to grind.

## SPIRITUAL FRIENDS: OUR MORAL TOUCHSTONE

In the spiritual community, the rigid application of rules is replaced by something far more subtle: a living network of friendship and communication centred on the highest shared ideals. Essentially, friendship within the spiritual community is based on *mettā*, on an appreciation of the other person's virtues and faults alike. Feeling *mettā* does not blind you to the facts. If someone is greedy or stupid, you see that they are. But with *mettā* you can always see through that greed or stupidity to the beauty of the human being: it is through *mettā* that you can hold the two together, the ugly truth and the beautiful reality. Indeed, if you don't see the one, you won't really see the other, not clearly anyway.

So feeling *mettā* does not mean seeing the inner beauty of people while deliberately blinding yourself to their weaknesses and imperfections. Nor is it about *appreciating* their weaknesses, or even appreciating them in spite of their weaknesses. It's more subtle than that: it's more like an aesthetic appreciation, or the clear-sighted love of a parent for their child. You see the child's faults and weaknesses, and the qualities he or she needs to develop, but your knowledge of these frailties has no effect on your love. Indeed, it is in the nature of real love to nurture the loved person without cherishing any illusions about them.

The wise have an ethical sensibility that is the product of their own experience and transcends the legalistic application of rules. They don't look at your actions in isolation, but in the context of your emerging individuality. It is like the aesthetic sensibility of someone who really understands painting or literature. They know what painting or literature is quite intuitively. Someone who knows what writing is can start reading something and know after a few paragraphs whether it is worth continuing or not. And a person too is all of a piece. (Of course, the difference between a book and a person is that it is always worth continuing with a person.)

Also, when our spiritual friends become aware of certain of our actions, they may not know all the circumstances, but they will have an accurate sense of whether those actions are skilful or not. For our own part, as the *Sutta* says, we would do well to give the spiritually mature the respect they deserve, and heed their opinion. That opinion will not necessarily come in the form of censure. It is generally more subtle than that. You may detect some change in them, or they may detect some change in you. Either way, you begin to be conscious of some disharmony between you – not in a dramatic, obvious way, but more a sense that you are no longer on the same wavelength, no longer really communicating.

It may well be that your spiritual friends are oblivious to any change in the relationship between you. They may have said nothing to you. Nonetheless, you may start to get the uncomfortable feeling that they are displeased with you, even angry or reproachful, and you may begin to feel resentment and even anger towards them, even though they have no idea what is going on. Surprisingly, perhaps, this sort of misapprehension is one of the more useful products of spiritual friendship, for it shows that your ethical sense, your sense of shame, is developing. You know in your heart of hearts that you have started to go astray, to slide a bit, and this is your way of allowing your guilty conscience to make its presence felt. In time, if they are at all mindful of their relationship with you, your spiritual friends will begin to notice that something is amiss, that you seem rather uneasy, perhaps a little sullen or unforthcoming. When they probe gently and kindly for an explanation of your changed demeanour, you may start wondering how this has happened, and how you can re-establish communication and harmony and put your friendship back on track. Once they are able to say that they are not angry with you and that you have done nothing to displease them, you can take the opportunity to say that well, actually, you do have something on your conscience, if only they knew.

Clearing the air with your friends in this way, you come back into harmony with the spiritual community, all through your openness to the possibility that your spiritual friends, those who really know you, might disapprove of what you're doing, even, as the *Sutta* says, on account of 'the slightest thing'. The essential element is your own sensitivity to the ethical sensibility of others, not your fear of punishment or disfavour. If you feel that your spiritual friends are beginning to disapprove of you, that they are not quite at ease with the way you are, the chances are that you should take special care. It is not your spiritual friends who have changed and started to drift out of contact. It is you.

Outside the spiritual community, people are not as a rule committed to this expansive aspiration to grow and to see others grow. Without spiritual friendship and *mettā*, what masquerades as helpful criticism may be no more than a thinly veiled form of one-upmanship. If the effect of your 'helpful' criticism is to leave someone feeling downcast, it is not an expression of *mettā*. Outside the spiritual community (and sometimes, despite our best efforts, within it) the emotional basis for interpersonal communication is so fraught with competitiveness, not to say aggression, that even a well-intended criticism can hurt and be wide of the mark.

In the context of a genuine spiritual friendship, however, I would go so far as to say that if you were to point out to someone that they had acted unskilfully, even if this was painful for them to hear, they would feel better for your having told them. Perhaps these difficult situations, in which openness and honesty are likely to involve a certain amount of pain, are the real test of *mettā* and of the depth of our friendship. If your straight talking expresses a sense of moral superiority – however justified – and a wish to put someone down or make them feel small, you are clearly not motivated by *mettā*. But as long as your communication is illumined by a genuine feeling of *mettā*, your friend will feel not crushed but liberated by what you have said, and the friendship will become stronger as a result.

How you stand in relation to your spiritual friends is a very good touchstone of where you stand ethically. Whether or not your friends are happy with how you are progressing tells you whether or not you need to be concerned about your spiritual practice. However, it must be emphasized that the censure of the wise is not an authority to be followed blindly. Whatever you do must be your own clear choice, for which you take full responsibility. Group censure is essentially a demand on the part of the group elders that you conform to the standards and norms of the group. By contrast, in the spiritual community, the criticism that you receive ideally comes from a different kind of attitude – though of course even within the spiritual community censure and advice is sometimes offered and received in the spirit of the group.

# 3
# CULTIVATING *METTĀ*

> May all beings be happy and secure, may their hearts be wholesome!
>
> *Sukhino vā khemino hontu*
> *sabbe sattā bhavantu sukhitattā*

We have now come to a natural break in the *Sutta*. Up to this point, the teaching has been about setting up preparatory conditions for the effective cultivation of *mettā*. One might even say that if you fulfil these conditions – if you are capable, straight, upright, and so on – you will be in such a skilful, healthy frame of mind that you can't help wishing others well. It will be the natural thing for you to do, not only when you sit down to meditate but all the time. Your mental and emotional state will be so positive that, quite spontaneously, you will wish for others to enjoy health, happiness, security, and peace of mind.

The next section of the *Sutta* begins with a phrase that sums up the generosity, the sincere and heartfelt regard for others, in which the cultivation of *mettā* consists. We wish simply that beings may be happy and secure and that their hearts may be wholesome. *Khemino* means secure, that is, free from danger, free from disturbance, free from fear. *Sukhi* simply means happy. *Sukhitattā* is translated here as 'their hearts be wholesome', but the suffix *atta* means 'self' or 'being', so the Pāli term literally means 'of happy self' or 'happy-hearted'. To be precise, the whole phrase could be translated as 'May they be those whose self is happiness.' This makes it clear that you want that their happiness, their bliss, should be entirely within themselves, not dependent on external circumstances. In their essence they should be happy. Happiness is not something they should *have*, but something that they should *be*. It is happiness in this sense, together with the *mettā* that produces such happiness for oneself and wants it for others, that characterizes the spiritual community. If you don't find a greater degree of *mettā* and happiness in the spiritual community than you find in the world generally, it isn't really a spiritual community.

The broad message of the first section of the *Sutta* is that if we want to enjoy positive mental states, we must pay attention to our everyday activities – our thoughts and volitions, our speech and actions, throughout the day. We should raise our consciousness in the only way that can generate a genuine transformation of being, by living out our ideals, by turning skilful actions into skilful habits, to the point where our mind naturally tends towards states of clarity, concentration, and happiness.

This opening section of the *Sutta* has essentially been a preparation for what is to come. The wish expressed in this verse, that all beings may be happy and secure, is more than a vague hope. It introduces the section of the *Sutta* that is concerned with the technique of meditating on loving-kindness, and thus designed to help us develop that aspiration for the well-being of others in a very real way. It is in the practice of formal meditation, when the mind is brought to bear directly on the mind, that *mettā* is cultivated most intensely.

The next section, again of two-and-a-half verses, sets forth the means by which we can develop that *mettā*. It does so through what is effectively a description of the *mettā bhāvanā* practice, the meditation on loving-kindness taught by the Buddha himself, which is, as we have seen, an indispensable aspect of the path to the attainment of the state of calm, or Nirvāṇa.

> Whatever living beings there be: feeble or strong, tall, stout or medium, short, small or large, without exception; seen or unseen, those dwelling far or near, those who are born or those who are to be born, may all beings be happy!

*Ye keci pāṇabhūt' atthi*
*tasā va thāvarā vā anavasesā*
*dīghā vā ye mahantā vā*
*majjhimā rassakā aṇukathūlā*

*Diṭṭhā vā ye vā adiṭṭhā*
*ye ca dūre vasanti avidūre*
*bhūtā vā sambhavesī vā:*
*sabbe sattā bhavantu sukhitattā.*

## THE WHOLE WORLD OF BEINGS

The aim of any meditation practice is to train the mind and thereby to heighten and transform consciousness. In the *mettā bhāvanā* meditation this training takes the form of various explicitly formulated aspirations and wishes for the welfare of different classes of beings, and for their abstaining from various forms of unskilful behaviour. Calling to mind those categories of beings and directing thoughts of loving-kindness towards them, you engender loving-kindness towards real people, as many of them as possible. In the course of your meditation you bring to mind all the weak, helpless beings, all the strong and healthy ones, and then beings of various shapes and sizes, right down to those beings who are too small to be seen at all – which presumably refers to microbes and single-celled organisms, as well as to those beyond human perception in other ways. You call to mind those who are as far away as you can possibly imagine, and those nearby. So this is one systematic way of developing *mettā*. In other forms of the practice you concentrate on the geographical differentiation of beings by directing your *mettā* towards all beings in the eastern quarter, all those in the south, the west, and the north, and finally all those above you and below you. You then call to mind those born and those unborn, thus reminding yourself that your *mettā* is not limited by time or by space.

In this way the *Sutta* addresses the central problems of cultivating *mettā*. Firstly, there is the sheer scale of its reference. If you sat down to meditate and found yourself immediately full of *mettā*, you could no doubt direct that *mettā* towards any class of beings that you wished. But probably very few people would find themselves in that position.

A methodical approach is therefore necessary if you are going to get anywhere with the practice. Otherwise, you would wish for all beings without number to be well, and after a brief but mind-boggling attempt to visualize them all, you would pass on to the next meditation.

The second problem is that *mettā* is impersonal in the sense that it has no specific object, while at the same time it is not at all 'woolly'. A vague sense that you wish everyone well together with a generalized impression of 'everyone' won't do. Ultimately *mettā* may be without an object, but to begin with you have to develop it in relation to actual specific persons, otherwise your emotions will not get involved. You have to begin closer to home. The same goes for other reflective practices: the contemplation of impermanence, for example.

Another practical reason for the *Sutta*'s detailed roster of the recipients of *mettā* is to counteract any irrational dislike you may have for certain categories of people. One would do well to draw up a list of one's own prejudices to make the list as inclusive as possible. You might have a prejudice against tall people or fat people, or men with beards, or blonde women. Since there is no accounting for taste, or indeed distaste, it is as well to include these in the practice formally, as well as trying to become aware of those categories of beings you have overlooked altogether.

### THE *METTĀ BHĀVANĀ* PRACTICE

There are many variations of the *mettā bhāvanā* practice, including the one outlined by the Buddha here and a version contained in the *Visuddhimagga*, Buddhaghosa's fifth-century exposition of the Buddha's teaching as found in the Pāli canon.[107] But all the variations share their working method with other Buddhist contemplations and meditations for the cultivation of particular kinds of awareness or understanding. In the contemplation of impermanence, for example, you call to mind a number of things that can be identified as impermanent, some quite easily, others with a little more difficulty. This helps you to deepen a fundamental awareness of impermanence as being in the nature of all conditioned existence. The general methodology is the same in the case of the cultivation of *mettā*. Universal loving-kindness is not the easiest of emotions to cultivate, but there do exist various effective stage-by-stage ways of doing it.

The more or less standard way of practising the *mettā bhāvanā* is in five stages, each of which takes your *mettā* deeper. First you generate *mettā* towards yourself, then towards a good friend, thirdly towards a 'neutral' person – someone whom you know but for whom you have no particularly strong feelings – and fourthly towards an 'enemy' – someone you find difficult for some reason. In the fifth stage you try to feel *mettā* for all four persons equally, then conclude the practice by radiating your *mettā* outward in wider and wider circles. The main thing is to get your *mettā* flowing, and bringing to mind the four different persons and then 'equalizing' the *mettā* seems to do that most effectively.

Thereafter, you can either go all round the world in your imagination, country by country, continent by continent, or you can take up the traditional method of dividing the globe into the four directions or quarters – north, south, east, and west – and radiating your *mettā* in each direction in turn. Another method is to consider variations on the *Sutta*'s different categories of beings – say the rich, the poor, the well, the sick, the young, the old, animals, birds, fish, and so on. You can try any combination of these approaches to the fifth and last stage. It doesn't really matter which method you follow once you have got the *mettā* flowing as long as you include everyone, indeed all beings, everywhere. The technique of the *mettā bhāvanā* is based on the principle that the more strongly you feel *mettā* towards one person, the easier it will be to experience the same emotion towards someone else who is less obviously a candidate for your affection. By bringing all those categories of beings to mind, one after the other, you give yourself the best possible opportunity to amplify and deepen your experience of *mettā*.

> Let none deceive another, nor despise any person whatsoever in any place. Let him not wish any harm to another out of anger or ill will.

> *Na paro paraṃ nikubbetha*
> *nātimaññetha katthaci naṃ kañci*
> *vyārosanā paṭighasaññā*
> *nāññamaññassa dukkham iccheyya.*

Having established the scope of the practice, the *Sutta* moves on to further explore the quality of *mettā* we are aiming to develop. Although the form of the practice in five stages is not explicitly mentioned here, each stage presents its own challenges when it comes to keeping the flow of *mettā* going. Before we look at these in turn, we can get from the text a general sense of what we are aiming to do. This verse shows us the response of *mettā* to the betrayals and slights, the abuse and malice, that come to us from other people, and also, by implication, the positive spirit in which we should acknowledge our own unskilful actions. To begin with, if you truly desire the happiness of others as much as you desire your own, there will be no question of misleading them or lying to them. Any attempt at deception is almost always motivated by calculated self-interest, which is the very antithesis of *mettā*. Even when no calculation is involved, it is dreadfully easy to belittle or humiliate someone with a few casual words. But although it is so easily done, it is no small matter: it betrays a terrible failure of *mettā*, a thoughtless discounting of another person.

This translation unusually renders *dukkha* as 'harm'. The term generally refers to misery, unhappiness, or even simple disappointment, none of which unpleasant or painful states of mind are necessarily connected to physical harm. *Dukkha* can also be understood to mean the opposite of peace or *santa*, the ultimate goal or good which is our real aim in life and towards which the Buddha, the *śāntināyaka*, directs us through his teaching. *Dukkha* is the fundamental experience of unease inherent in conditioned existence. In this context, however, *dukkha* refers specifically to suffering wished upon us by someone else, out of anger or ill will. As such, it can indeed be translated as 'harm'.

To be angry is not necessarily to wish harm upon someone. The Pāli term translated here as 'anger', *rosanā*, is the momentary flash of rage that might cause you to lose your temper. It is the result of frustrated energy: you want to do something, have something, or see something happen, and when your wish is blocked in some way, the energy that has been restricted or frustrated bursts through in an explosion of bad temper. Anger is an emotion of the moment. If there is a desire to cause harm, it is momentary and instinctive.

*Paṭigha*, on the other hand, translated here as 'ill will', is more sinister, involving a conscious, even calculated, desire to do harm.

*Paṭigha* is thus a much stronger term than simple ill will. At the very least it means 'violent malice', and it usually refers to a state of rage: an uncontrolled, unreasoned, almost mindless determination to wreak harm and suffering on another person. *Paṭigha* can be taken to stand for all those deeply unskilful states that are antithetical to *mettā*. As well as malice there is cruelty, a gratuitous pleasure in inflicting harm, which in its extreme form becomes sadism. The key difference between these deeply unpleasant mental states and anger is that whereas malice, cruelty, and sadism continue over time, indeed are sometimes nursed for years, anger is an emotion of the moment. But if anger remains unexpressed, it will turn into something that settles down and anchors itself, to become resentment or even hatred. It is hatred, not anger, that is the real enemy of *mettā*. It is the conscious, fixed, and settled desire to do harm which we have to guard against, and which is hatred's defining quality.

Negative emotions are more closely connected than we might think; they are all expressions of the fundamental wish to do harm to others. Hatred can arise in many forms, in many kinds of situation. It is when some everyday occurrence sparks off a momentary sense of ill will that the deeper, darker residue of hatred emerges. When we get angry, our sudden anger can toss a match into a kind of tinder-box of hatred, sparking off cruelty, rage, or malice. If we are prone to anger in the sense of *rosanā*, it can be difficult to rein it in, because once we have lost our temper we are no longer susceptible to reason. We need to be especially on our guard when we feel our anger is justified, as a sense of righteous indignation opens the gates for more destructive emotions. All the same, compared to *paṭigha*, anger is a relatively healthy reaction. Sometimes letting off a bit of steam in an innocuous context is better than bottling it up.

## WHY DO WE HATE?

Hatred is the antithesis of human growth and development. With craving and ignorance, it is one of the three 'unskilful roots' (*akusala mūlas*) that feed and sustain our lower nature. It is perhaps strange to reflect that hatred is a uniquely human quality. Animals may compete to the death for natural resources, fighting one another, feeding upon one another, even killing for amusement, and yet as far as we know they do not harbour any conscious intention to do harm. So why do humans have this particular capacity for evil?

Although we share a common ancestry, human beings have a quality that animals do not: the capacity for reason. It can lead to great good, of course, but unfortunately it can also lead to hatred. We experience suffering as animals do, but we also have an ability to seek and find causes for our unhappiness, and to extrapolate from knowledge of our own motives in such a way as to attribute motives to other beings. According to the seventeenth-century Dutch philosopher Spinoza, if you have a feeling of pain accompanied by the idea of the pain's external cause, your response will be hatred towards that external cause.[108] Hatred, in other words, is as much an idea as a feeling. We hate whatever or whomever we see as responsible for the unhappiness we feel.

But this still does not really explain what happens. Indeed, there seems to be no rational explanation. After all, if you were suffering and realized that another person was the cause, and if you were able to keep out of their way or to stop them from hurting you, there would be no reason for your wanting to inflict harm upon them. Unfortunately, however, when you are suffering you don't just want to remove the instrument of your unhappiness; you also have an urge to retaliate by inflicting a degree of suffering on them that will satisfy you emotionally – an urge that has no basis in reason.

Another thing that marks us out from animals is our consciousness of the passing of time, and this also plays a part in the arising of hatred. Every time we allow the memory of a supposed wrong to run through our mind, hatred accumulates until a fixed attitude develops. From then on, whatever our enemy does we interpret their actions according to that fixed view, and they simply cannot do anything to please us.

While emotions are essentially active, we nonetheless create them from the raw material of feelings, and these come to us passively, to be taken up and given meaning and direction by the activity of the mind. Feelings in themselves, whether pleasant or unpleasant, are karmically neutral; they are the results of our previous actions. As such, it is how we deal with them, not the fact of our feeling them, that is of decisive importance. If you have a painful experience, you need not manufacture hatred out of it, and if you do, you render yourself liable to further painful feeling in the future because by reacting with anger you have created fresh – and unskilful – karma. So hatred is not something that just happens to you. Like any other emotion – craving, say, or *mettā* – it is something you do. Feelings are presented to you, you experience them; but whether you create harmful or helpful emotions out of them is up to you.

The point is that our dislikes and resentments are often not based on anything people have actually done. They may come from our own irrational expectations, or they may be a matter of interpersonal chemistry. There is such a thing as hate at first sight. Someone may have an emotional quality that you pick up and react against without your even knowing them, or they may unconsciously remind you of someone else, perhaps a parent or sibling, an ex-lover, or someone else from your past with whom you have had difficulties. This is what psychologists call projection. Likewise, a small incident can spark off an outburst of anger or irritability, awakening an emotion connected with some suppressed incident or series of incidents long ago and far away.

A great deal of our latent tendency towards ill will is likely to stem from our early conditioning. It is easy to recognize people whose early life has been comparatively untroubled, as they are relatively straightforward, open, and receptive in their attitude towards others. Others are much more suspicious, reserved, and wary, and this may be a result of their early experience. It seems that many of us have a certain residual resentment, or even hatred, that lingers from our childhood and tends to attach itself to objects and people as we make our way through adult life.

Sometimes these negative feelings are found to be attached to close relatives, if we are prepared to look for them there, although many people are shocked at the idea of feeling animosity towards their nearest and dearest. When such feelings do come out into the open, the resulting family disturbance can be particularly painful. If you think there is no one you dislike, it might be revealing to try putting one of your relatives in the fourth stage of the *mettā bhāvanā*, in which *mettā* is directed towards an 'enemy', and see what happens. If we live with someone, or work closely with them, or share a circle of friends with them, and have no particular reason to dislike them, we often fail to realize that, all the same, we *do* dislike them. It seems to be a sort of rule that there will always be someone we dislike among our acquaintances or colleagues. When that person leaves, another person with whom we have previously been on good terms may well take their place, to be the next object for the residue of hatred that is so difficult to shift from the human psyche. This is why removing someone from a situation of conflict rarely solves the problem in the long run.

We should try not to feel discouraged by all this. It is true that to wake up in the morning with an overwhelming wish for the happiness and bliss of absolutely everyone is highly unusual even if one aspires to do so. Even after a great deal of intense effort in meditation, a tidal wave of universal love is unlikely to sweep us off our feet and carry us away. We shouldn't really be surprised. In trying to cultivate *mettā* we are swimming against the current of our human nature as it has evolved over millions of years from its animal origins. Sometimes we simply feel like a rest. As we struggle against the stream of our habitual negativity, *mettā* seems just too much to ask of ourselves. The tendency to feel hatred for others, even for people who pose no threat, comes all too easily to us. It is a basic human trait. It should be no surprise that the world is so full of conflicts, wars, and fatal misunderstandings. As beings with reflexive consciousness, with a sense of ourselves as continuous identities moving through time, our defences are naturally directed against the threat of attack, not just upon our bodies but also upon our fragile sense of who we think we are. This is why cultivating *mettā* is such a challenge. It is an attempt to reverse our usual way of experiencing the world and ourselves.

If hatred is a specifically human reaction to a threat, in its most primitive form it originates from any threat to your specifically human sense of self, the most basic sense of who you are. Indeed, to identify with a 'self' in that limited sense is to open yourself up to that primal threat. Thus to identify with a self is to be susceptible to the arising of hatred. If we think in terms of karma and rebirth, we have been prone to hatred for as long as we have been embodied human beings. It is as though hatred was woven into the very fabric of our being. Since our first human birth we have reacted with hatred to all those situations that threatened the integrity of our continued existence. When a human being experiences this sense of being threatened, there is more at stake than territory or physical safety. We are afraid for our personal identity, our very sense of self, the sense of 'I' that enables a human being to interact and form relationships in much more complex ways than animals can. A threat to the self is a threat not just to our physical well-being but to our psychological security.

If you succeeded in perfecting the practice of the *mettā bhāvanā*, it would suggest that you no longer felt any threat from anybody and therefore that you no longer identified your being with your contingent personality. But for as long as you are a worldly personality, the potential for hatred will always be there. You can detect it in yourself sometimes – a little flash of undiluted hatred, often when you least expect it.

### THE ENEMY WITHIN

It is painful to realize that a mind dogged by hatred or irritability continues to harbour a stock of resentment regardless of circumstances, a residue of ill will that will always seek out an object in order to express itself. But such apparently irrational reactions are not necessarily a bad thing. If we never catch sight of our projections, how will we learn to see through them? Psychological projection is unconscious, but by bringing our unconscious reactions into awareness, we can begin to act more appropriately and put down the psychological burdens we have been carrying.

To transform emotions we need to feel them, but in doing so we have to take into account an external reality with which our feelings and urges are not necessarily in touch. We should take care to do this especially if, as is likely, that external reality involves other people. No one can dispute that we feel what we feel, but we need to ask ourselves whether our feelings correspond to reality, whether they are adequate to the situation. From the authoritative way in which many people speak about how they feel it would seem that they believe that invoking their feelings excuses them from considering objective reality, and that their feelings about it constitute a fully adequate assessment of the situation. Of course, no one should be allowed to get away with this. By all means have emotions – be as emotional as you like – but let them be true to the situation. Don't dress up peevishness or fury as clear thinking and straight talking. If the intellect is to support the emotions, the emotions have to return the favour and support the intellect.

When we are indulging in a subjective and perhaps negative emotion, we very often know in our heart of hearts that our response is not really true to the way things are. When we get angry with someone for a trivial reason, we know – if we are even just a little aware – that the situation does not justify that emotional reaction. When this happens, instead of thinking, 'Oh, I must get rid of my negative emotions,' ask yourself, 'What is the objective situation? Are my emotions appropriate to what is really going on?'

The harmful states that are the enemies of *mettā* can arise in many different forms, gross and subtle. If you are in a happy, upbeat mood and you mix with people who are not, they may want to share your happiness, but it is also possible that they will prefer to see you as being no less unhappy than they are themselves. They may resent your happiness and feel they have to resist it, even destroy it, as if it were an affront or a challenge to them. Perhaps they want you to show their misery a little respect, or suspect that you are feeling superior and smug. Humans are contradictory beings. How strange it is that we do not quite naturally and wholeheartedly wish others the deepest happiness and bliss! It's as if we feel that there is only so much happiness to go round, and that if others are happy there is less happiness left over for us. Certainly people often feel they have a limited quantity of love, to be preserved for close friends and family. But of course the happiness of others cannot do us or them anything but good. Our task in practising the *mettā bhāvanā* is to learn to extend our *mettā* beyond this small circle, bit by bit, until it encompasses all beings. And – in the five-stage version of the practice – we begin very close to home indeed: with ourselves. This makes perfect sense. If, as we have seen, the enemy is within, it is within that the enemy needs to be tackled – indeed, needs to be transformed from an enemy into a friend.

### DOING THE *METTĀ BHĀVANĀ*: FIRST STAGE – *METTĀ* FOR ONESELF

You simply cannot develop much loving-kindness towards anyone else if you are on bad terms with yourself, or if you are uncomfortable with what you find out about yourself when all your external supports and comforts are removed. This is why in the first stage of the *mettā bhāvanā* meditation you begin by cultivating *mettā* towards yourself. Most people find that this is not at all easy. Only too often the residue of hatred within us is directed towards ourselves.

The solution for many of us lies in our relationships with other people. One way to learn to feel *mettā* towards yourself is through becoming aware that someone else feels good will towards you, and in this way coming to feel it for yourself. This is rather tricky. When you don't have *mettā* for yourself, you experience an emptiness, a hunger, and you look for love from someone else to fill that void and make you feel better, at least for the time being. You clutch at love, demanding it as compensation for the unconditional acceptance that you are unable to give yourself. But this can only be a substitute for the real thing. You try to squeeze as much love as you can get out of others even though that love is something only you can give yourself. It is as though you need them to do it for you. And being dependent on their love, you cannot care for their welfare except in relation to yourself; you cannot feel *mettā* for them because of your own neediness. For many people this is surely a depressingly familiar picture.

But if you find yourself in this situation, all is not lost. By calmly reasoning with yourself, you can begin to turn that misapprehension around, using the 'substitute' love shown by others to help you develop *mettā* towards yourself. If they can feel good will towards you, you can learn to feel the same positive emotion towards yourself, and thus gradually learn to stand on your own feet emotionally. Even though you may have begun with the assumption that you were not worth much, you learn from the other person that you were mistaken and thus begin to appreciate your own worth. You allow the knowledge that another person feels that you are genuinely worthwhile to percolate through your mind. You can learn to love yourself, in other words, by realizing that someone else really values you.

Feeling *mettā* for oneself is often simply a question of dropping the habit of self-criticism and allowing the objective reality of the situation to arise. Whatever you have done, however great your failings, the honest intention to develop *mettā* towards yourself and all living beings can be a source of happiness in itself. Feeling *mettā* for oneself is the keystone of contentment – and when you are contented, you can maintain your equanimity no matter in what circumstances you find yourself. It is a resilient, deeply-rooted state of peace, a source of energy and confidence. Contentment is, moreover, an inherently active state, with nothing of the resignation or passivity that is sometimes associated with it. The contented person is both inspired and an inspiration to others. It isn't a question of just gritting your teeth and grinding your way through some awful situation. There is a place for selflessness in Buddhism, but not for acquiescence in the face of ill-treatment or a grey and unrewarding environment. Human beings need food, light, space, periods of peace and quiet, human companionship, friendship, and so on. We are naturally geared to look for delight in the world. But if you are contented, you can find delight in the world around you, even when you don't have everything you would like.

The way to cultivate contentment is to bring a lighter touch to your experience. It is to enjoy what is enjoyable in it, but not to become attached to your pleasures, nor overwhelmed when things appear not to be going your way, in the knowledge that both the pleasures and the pains of life are impermanent. Contentment comes from being aware that as long as you depend on external objects for a sense of well-being, your happiness can never be guaranteed.

Developing *mettā* consists in large measure of finding contentment in oneself and living by that. Once it becomes a way of life, one stands a good chance of communicating that peace of mind to everyone with whom one comes into contact. Thus, the first stage of the *mettā bhāvanā* practice flows naturally into the second.

### DOING THE *METTĀ BHĀVANĀ*: SECOND STAGE – *METTĀ* FOR A FRIEND

In the second stage of the practice we bring to mind a good friend and direct our *mettā* towards them. But if our ultimate aim is to feel *mettā* for everyone, doesn't this stage carry with it the danger that we will get this far and no further? Isn't it rather exclusive? Here we need to take a pragmatic approach. Although we can do our best to respond positively to everyone, if we are going to explore friendship to any great depth we can do this in practice with only a limited number of people. Friendship requires a level of trust and intimacy that can arise only through spending a lot of time with a person, becoming a significant part of their life, and allowing them to become a significant part of one's own. We need not think of our circle of friends as being exclusive; it is simply a fact that we cannot develop depth and intensity in our relationships without making a firm decision to deepen our friendships with just a few people. This remains true even when one has a great deal of spiritual experience. Perhaps after years of practice you will no longer experience partiality in your friendships, and will be able to be equally friendly towards anyone you happen to meet, taking life as it comes and relating to everyone equally warmly and with an equally genuine desire for their well-being. But with the best will in the world, your capacity for friendship will still be limited by the number of people with whom you are realistically able to come into contact.

Thus one can cultivate *mettā* as a universal and ever-expanding care for all beings, whether near or far, while at the same time enjoying substantial relationships of trust and affection with those with whom one has chosen to enter into a closer relationship. Committed friendship demands personal contact, and that requires both time and opportunity. But a friendly disposition is another matter. There is no limit to the number of people towards whom we can feel genuinely friendly, and with whom we could potentially be friends. And that friendliness, however strongly felt, can only improve the depth of our existing friendships.

Committed friendship obviously involves openness, and this calls for patience and empathy when what our friends reveal to us turns out to be difficult or even hurtful. A trusting and open friendship is an excellent context within which to bring our fears and antagonisms to the surface and begin to lay them aside. But if this is to happen, the friendship must have a spiritual dimension, because hatred is far more than the psychological phenomenon that we have been examining so far. Just as *mettā* is a spiritual rather than a psychological quality, so its antithesis, hatred, is not just a psychological state, but a spiritually destructive force operating within us.

It is perhaps not surprising that when we start to practise the later stages of the *mettā bhāvanā* we can find the going difficult. We may even discover, if we are honest with ourselves, that despite our good intentions we do not as a rule experience much desire for the happiness and well-being of even our closest friends. A famous moralist once observed that 'in the misfortune of our best friends, we always find something which is not displeasing to us'.[109] It would seem that even our friends represent some kind of threat. Perhaps this is why ex-lovers are able to do each other so much harm, and why the break-up of a marriage can be so acrimonious: both partners know each other's weak spots only too well. It is the person with whom you have fully lowered your guard who can do you the most damage if the relationship changes. It is all about power. If some misfortune befalls our friends and they are brought down a peg or two, or suffer some disappointment, they are made, as it were, less powerful in relation to us, and the threat is to some extent removed. Sometimes we cannot help finding pleasure in that, however fond of them we might be. If you are very observant and honest with yourself, you will notice these little flashes of pleasure from time to time at the adversity suffered even by your dearest friends. It is sad but true.

At the same time – and this is an encouraging thought – we don't have to act on our feelings. Our task is to experience our negative emotions and then find a way to change them. If we never get to know these emotions, if we indulge them unthinkingly or try to deny them, no transformation will be possible. One of the skills you need to develop as a meditator is thus to learn to broaden the scope of your emotional awareness, without allowing completely unmindful expression of what you start to feel. This is by no means easy: it requires experience, patience, the clarity and kindness of your friends, and gentle persistence in the *mettā bhāvanā* practice.

### DOING THE *METTĀ BHĀVANĀ*: THIRD STAGE – FEELING *METTĀ* FOR A NEUTRAL PERSON

In the third stage of the *mettā bhāvanā*, you direct *mettā* towards someone you know hardly at all, someone who has only a very minor walk-on part in your life – perhaps the man who sells you your newspaper in the morning, or the woman you pass in the park when you're walking your dog. To see the point of this stage, we need to examine our emotional life a little further. Although we may not like to think so, in the usual run of things our experience of what we imagine to be positive emotion is likely to be sketchy and intermittent. Whether or not we are aware of it, this is partly because we tend to limit our affection to those we deem deserving of it, usually those who are likely to return the favour. But the chief characteristic of *mettā* is that it is entirely without self-interest. It is not possessive or selfish, and has nothing to do with appetite. This is why 'friendliness', although it may seem insipid, translates *mettā* more accurately than 'love'. Being applied only to other sentient beings, and having an inherently outgoing quality, friendliness is more likely to be relatively free of self-interest.

I say 'relatively' because a great deal of what we think of as friendliness and even friendship involves a need for something in return. When we give affection we want something back, and when a little intensity develops in our friendships we can end up with a dependency that has something of the nature of an unspoken contract. The Pāli term for this mixture of honest affection and an expectation of some return is *pema* (Sanskrit *prema*). It is usually translated as 'affection' in the limited sense of ordinary human fellowship, and it is contrasted with *mettā*, which is the corresponding, more spiritual emotion.

*Pema* is often understood to be the natural affection and good will that arises within the family group, and it is undoubtedly a positive emotion. Indeed, it is the cement that holds social life together. Expressing warmth and affection to your family members and close friends is a very good thing. Through your affection for them you learn to set aside your own narrow self-interest and get a sense of yourself as being involved with other people in a real and tangible sense. But your family, your circle of friends, the supporters of your football team, the members of your ethnic or cultural group, are only a tiny fraction of the universe of living beings. What might it be like to feel the same warmth towards everyone you met, whether known to you or not? This may seem a naive dream, a well-meaning fantasy that could never be realized, but before we give up the whole idea, we could consider the implications of one of the essential tenets of Buddhism – that in reality there is no separate self, and that we are related, directly or indirectly, to everyone else. If we reflect on this, we will come to see that unlimited friendliness is not a dream at all. It is we who are in a dream when we imagine that only our close ties with friends and family are important, while relationships between other families and other groups are of little or no consequence.

When we look at things in this way, we have to admit that our relationships contain more than a little self-interest. Indeed, the very warmth of our relationships with family members and close friends can be what makes the rest of the world seem cold, unfriendly, and uninteresting. Through our relationships we are seeking security; we want things to stay the same; we want the relationships we build to provide a refuge against the difficulties and uncertainties of life, thus guaranteeing the stability and security of our own small, inward-looking world. We need those people, those relationships, if we are not to feel terribly alone and vulnerable. We are, in other words, desperately attached to them, an attachment that is entirely bound up with *pema*.

*Pema* is essentially a social emotion, concerned with preserving the human group, rather than with transcending boundaries and reaching out to all life however it manifests. If *pema* is love or friendliness that expresses attachment, *mettā* is love or friendliness that is not self-referential at all. Both are positive in their own way, but *mettā* is positive in the spiritual sense whereas *pema* is a more worldly emotion. *Pema* is love and affection for others in the ordinary, human way, ranging from erotic desire to a simple warm fellow feeling, a sense of human solidarity with others.

*Pema* provides a useful contrast with *mettā*, as the two words are close enough in meaning to be confused with each other, so that *pema* is sometimes identified as the 'near enemy' of *mettā*. *Mettā* is much more than the warmth of good fellowship, or a gregarious feeling of togetherness. Unlike *pema*, *mettā* includes no attachment, no self-interest, no need even to be near its object, much less to possess it. *Mettā* is not necessarily a reciprocal emotion. As already mentioned, you can cultivate *mettā* or friendliness towards someone without that person knowing about it – indeed, without your having any connection with them at all. You can even express your *mettā* in practical ways – by putting in a good word for someone, say, or helping them financially – without there being any personal contact between you.

Ordinarily we feel affection more or less exclusively. Indeed, the more intense the affection, the more exclusive it tends to be. When we use the word 'love' to describe our strong feeling for someone, the someone in question is usually just that – some one: a single individual. It is a strong partiality for that one person over anyone else. But when you feel *mettā*, a strongly developed feeling of good will towards one person will tend to spread more and more widely. Being without self-interest, *mettā* is impartial. Just as the sun is not selective in the giving of its light and warmth, when you feel *mettā*, you don't choose its recipients or keep it for those you deem worthy of it. *Mettā* is love that breaks out of the narrow confines of self-referential selectivity, love that does not have a preference, non-exclusive love.

If we are going to use the word 'love' at all, we could describe *mettā* as disinterested love. It is of course 'interested' in the sense of 'concerned' – it is not *un*interested – but it is *dis*interested in the sense that when you feel it you have no thought of what you might get back in return. There are a number of English words that include a quality of disinterested love or appreciation in their meaning. Philosophy, for example, is the love of wisdom for its own sake, not for what is to be gained from it. Wisdom is essentially useless. Whatever practical purpose it might have is incidental to what it is really about: the direct realization of the truth of things. Similarly, *mettā* is concerned with its object purely for the sake of that object in itself.

There is in *mettā* no desire to impress, or to ingratiate oneself, or to feather one's nest, or to gain favours. Nor is there any expectation of emotional reciprocity. Being friendly or offering friendship to someone in the spirit of *mettā* is something you do for their sake, not just for yours. *Mettā* is not erotic love, or parental love, or the love that seeks the admiration and esteem of a particular social group. It is a cherishing, protecting, maturing love which has the same kind of effect on the spiritual being of others as the light and heat of the sun have on their physical being. And we really can learn to love in this way. This is the value, and the challenge, of the third stage of the *mettā bhāvanā*.

### DOING THE *METTĀ BHĀVANĀ*: FOURTH STAGE – FEELING *METTĀ* FOR AN ENEMY

We have already seen that to practise the *mettā bhāvanā* effectively we need to learn to detach the emotion of which we have become aware from the person towards whom we are feeling it. Success in the meditation depends in large measure on how pliant one's mind can be in this respect. You probably won't be able to do it straightaway; it takes quite a lot of practice. The challenge is particularly great in the fourth stage of the meditation, when we try to maintain our feelings of loving-kindness in the 'presence' of someone who is perhaps intent on doing us harm.

The method of the *mettā bhāvanā* is systematically to coax the habitual reactive mind into the first glimmerings of positive emotion by concentrating one's thoughts and emotions on real individuals, with all their virtues and failings. However, sooner or later you will have to detach the emotion from these particular individuals. *Mettā* is essentially objectless, and in the course of the practice it should come to depend less and less on the nature of the object and more and more on itself. This is what it means to say that *mettā* is ultimately impersonal. It is no less an emotion, but it is less dependent on particular persons. You feel the same *mettā*, the same emotional response, towards the so-called enemy as towards the so-called friend.

This does not mean eradicating the particularity of our emotions. *Mettā* expresses itself in different ways according to the differing nature and degrees of intimacy of our different relationships. What *mettā* does is infuse our positivity with the heightened energy that previously arose when we felt anger or hatred towards an enemy. The *mettā bhāvanā* is fundamentally a practice of transformation, not annihilation; the aim is not so much to obliterate our negative emotions as to redirect them. There is energy in anger, and if we are to attain the ultimate good – Nirvāṇa – all our energies, all our emotions, positive and not so positive, have to be released in the direction of that goal. Rather than suppress negative emotions when we can and allow them to run riot when we can't, the aim is to transform the energy in them and integrate it into the existing stream of our positive emotion, thereby making that positive stream of emotion stronger.

Here again there is an important role for reflection, as Śāntideva advises in his *Bodhicaryāvatāra* or 'Guide to the Bodhisattva's Way of Life'. Reminding us of the central Buddhist insight of conditionality, he points out that people who do us harm do so on the basis of conditioning factors over which they have no control: 'A person does not get angry at will, having decided "I shall get angry."'[110] Anger and hatred arise due to factors outside our conscious control, and the anger with which we respond to anger is also irrational. There is no justification for anger, and no point to it. Anger and hatred are states of suffering that can lead only to further distress, so there is nothing to be gained from perpetuating them. Śāntideva goes on to encourage us to reflect on the painful consequences of our anger or hatred, and to inform our emotional life with the only rational conclusion to draw from these reflections: that unhelpful emotions should be abandoned for more positive ones. This is the only effective way to help beings, including ourselves.

Such reflections may help a little, but our emotions are rarely susceptible to reason alone. It is relatively easy to acknowledge that we feel ill will, and certainly easy to talk about turning it into love, but it is not at all easy actually to bring about the transformation. If the kind of reasoning that Śāntideva proposes is to be successful, we need to ensure that *all* our emotions are lined up behind our spiritual aspirations. If they aren't, anger and hatred, for example, will make their presence felt in a way that obstructs those aspirations (in the guise of 'righteous indignation', for example). We may then find that we simply cannot get started on feeling *mettā* for our enemy.

It is an unfortunate fact that our emotional life very often tends to lag some way behind our intellectual development. We can analyse our situation indefinitely, but without a fair degree of self-knowledge our feelings will tend to remain tied to their old familiar objects in an ever-recurring cycle of craving and dissatisfaction. Directed thinking is important – indeed, essential – but we also need to find a way of working directly on and with our emotions. Our task is to unlock the energy uselessly tied up in harmful feelings and channel it into positive and productive mental states.

If the object of your attention brings up intensely negative feelings, it can be difficult to get any grip on *mettā* at all. Positive emotion no longer seems even a remote possibility; just for that moment you seem to have forgotten what *mettā* might even feel like. If you are beset by strong feelings of resentment, anger, jealousy, or craving, you may feel they are just too much for you to handle at present. If you have presented your emotional positivity with too great a challenge, it may be best to withdraw temporarily and retrace your steps, dwelling for a while longer on someone towards whom your feelings are more straightforwardly positive before returning to this most difficult but vital stage.

We need to be able somehow to grapple with the very idea we have of this person as an 'enemy'. We have probably designated them as such because they have upset us in some way, and now we are maintaining this fixed view of them by dwelling on the injury they have done to us. The solution is simple: concentrate on their more attractive qualities. In order to draw your attention away from someone's irritating habit of always arriving late, for example, you can direct it towards some mitigating factor that you may have overlooked: they may perhaps be turning up late because they are devoted to looking after their young family, for example. You focus on their positive human qualities, or at least the problems with which they are faced. At the very least, you can reflect that they are not always performing injurious actions, or at least not towards everybody. In this way you learn to paddle against the stream of your ill will.

You can even begin to like your enemy, just a little. But while such a shift in your feelings is a very positive development, it should not be taken for the arising of *mettā* itself. Liking someone is not the same as feeling *mettā* towards them. Our usual attitude towards someone perceived to have done us some harm – which is what an 'enemy' is by definition – is to feel hatred towards them. But in this stage of the practice you try to make that person the object of your *mettā* not on account of anything they have done or not done but simply because they are there. Irrespective of whoever is around, or whether there are any people around at all, you are aiming to be entirely equanimous in your attitude of loving-kindness. You are not so much feeling love for your enemy as simply being undisturbed in your attitude of *mettā* towards all beings by the thought of someone who has done you an injury.

Although *mettā* is in a sense the rational response to reality, in the end it is produced without cause or justification. When we practise the *mettā bhāvanā*, our feelings of good will towards beings arise not on account of anything those beings may have said or done. We simply wish them well. If it were otherwise, *mettā* would be no more than a psychological thing, coming and going in dependence on whom we bring to mind at any one time. As a spiritual quality, *mettā* is not bound by any kind of stipulation or qualification or condition. It is not meted out according to whether beings deserve it or not.

According to Buddhism there is no entity corresponding to the idea of an unchanging self underlying all that we do and say and experience. If there were such a thing, then one might approach the fourth stage of the *mettā bhāvanā* with the thought that underneath all the bad that one can see in someone, there is something good that is still lovable. To view a person as essentially good despite their unskilful actions suggests there is an underlying person there to begin with. Buddhism, on the other hand, sees a person not as an entity that can become sullied by unskilfulness and then cleansed of impurities, but as the sum total, and nothing more than the sum total, of their actions, bodily, verbal, and mental.

If we are trying to direct loving-kindness towards somebody of whose actions we do not approve, what is it, then, towards which we are really directing our attention? As far as Buddhism is concerned, a person is not any kind of fixed identity. There is no underlying 'self' that is somehow capable of performing actions while remaining essentially unchanged. Those actions are precisely what that human being ultimately is. Hence it is self-contradictory to speak, for example, of hating a person's actions but not the actual person, because the person includes the action that you have just said you condemn. The villain of Shakespeare's *Measure for Measure*, Angelo, who asks with rhetorical sarcasm, 'Condemn the fault and not the actor of it?' is quite right.[111] It cannot be done.

In this penultimate stage of the *mettā bhāvanā*, you deliberately call to mind someone who has hurt you not in order to change your opinion of them, but to test and strengthen your attitude of *mettā*. If your *mettā* is genuine, it will not be disturbed even by your thinking of a so-called enemy. Taking in their bad qualities with their good qualities you direct *mettā* to the person as a whole, good and bad.

This is very much the sense in which we speak of the limitless compassion of the Buddhas towards living beings. A Buddha's compassion – which is the response of *mettā* to suffering – does not emerge in the form of isolated acts of loving-kindness that we somehow earn by our devotion or some other 'deserving' action. A Buddha has the same attitude of *mettā* towards beings whatever they do or don't do, because his *mettā* is beyond time and space; it exists both before and after those beings committed any action or exhibited any quality, skilful or unskilful. This is not to say that a Buddha condones your unskilfulness, only that his *mettā* is unaffected by it and he does not threaten to withdraw his limitless care and concern. Indeed, as it is limitless, you will not get more of it by behaving better. His *mettā* is rather like that of a loyal friend whose attitude does not change even though you have done something to upset them. You may apologize to your friend and beg forgiveness, but they will continue to feel – and perhaps say – that there is nothing to forgive.

The *mettā* of the Buddhas is unwavering; they are entirely compassionate, before, during, and after whatever might have taken place. For this reason we need never approach them with the slightest fear or apprehension. To sit in judgement forms no part of a Buddha's business. Nor therefore is there any need for us to ask for their forgiveness or mercy. Buddhas do not, after all, administer the law of karma. Conditionality will go on operating, come what may, and nobody, not even a Buddha, can save us from experiencing the consequences of our foolish actions.

The unconditional love of a Buddha takes place on a plane altogether beyond such concepts as 'enemy' or 'person' as these terms are generally understood. You can love someone unconditionally, as a Buddha does, only in so far as you believe, unconditionally, that they can change, however apparently hopeless the state they are in; it means being unconditionally willing to help them evolve, irrespective of the point at which they have at this present moment arrived. If they have abused you, you fully take in what they have done and still you wish them well. Truly loving someone does not mean seeing them as perfect or their moral weaknesses as unimportant. Quite the opposite: the more you care about someone the more you are concerned for their spiritual welfare. With the warm and unflinching gaze of *mettā* you see them as they are, warts and all.

# 4
# THE CULMINATION OF *METTĀ*

> Just as a mother would protect her only child at the risk of her own life, even so, let him cultivate a boundless heart towards all beings.
>
> *Mātā yathā niyaṃ puttaṃ*
> *āyusā ekaputtam anurakkhe*
> *evam pi sabbabhūtesu*
> *mānasam bhāvaye aparimāṇaṃ.*

## HOW MUCH *METTĀ*?

So here we are, poised at the beginning of the fifth stage of the practice, about to gradually extend our *mettā* beyond all bounds. It seems an appropriate point at which to bring in the next verse of the *Karaṇīya-Mettā Sutta*, in order to strengthen our sense of the kind of emotional depth we are aspiring to develop. This verse seeks to give us an idea of this, by means of the analogy of a mother's love for her only child. It is an image that seems to stand out from the rest of the *Sutta*, communicating the kind of commitment with which you develop the 'boundless heart', the 'limitless mind', towards all beings. It is a compelling image, although this translation mutes somewhat the full force of the original verse. The Pāli words are more emphatic, repeating the word for child, *putta*: 'her child, her only child', to show us the picture of the loving mother concentrated on a single, utterly vulnerable human being. It's a deliberate paradox: the intensity of such love directed towards one person turned outwards to shine upon all living beings.

Maternal love is a particularly appropriate image for *mettā* not so much because it is a stronger love than other kinds – romantic love, for instance, can be very powerful – but because it is nurturing love. The love of a mother is concerned to help a child grow and thrive, and *mettā* has the same quality of support and tender care. A mother seeks her child's well-being in every possible way, preparing and educating them to grow and become strong, healthy, and fulfilled. In the same way, *mettā* seeks to nurture all living beings, seeking their welfare, wanting to help them to be happy and fulfilled.

A mother will lay down her own life for her child, and *mettā* is imbued with the same spirit of selflessness, though obviously to go as far as to sacrifice your life for another is the tallest of tall orders. Making that sacrifice on the basis of *mettā* would not betray a lack of care for yourself, but would express the value you placed on your own potential for future growth (the future as far as you yourself were concerned being a future life, obviously). You cannot truly value yourself as long as you persist in putting yourself before others. To counteract this tendency you may need to make a point of putting others before you, but the aim of this is to value others *as* yourself, not more than yourself.

The quality of impartiality in *mettā* has a degree of wisdom in it. It is a kind of equanimity that enables you to be quite unbiased in your appreciation of a situation. It has a touch of the objectivity and selflessness of insight. If you see that the best outcome for everyone might involve a risk to your own life, then you are happy to take that risk. Buddhaghosa gives an illustration of this in his *Visuddhimagga*. You are to imagine that you, your best friend, a 'neutral person', and an adversary are held up by bandits while travelling, and the bandits offer to spare the lives of just three of you. It is up to you to choose which one of you is to be sacrificed. Buddhaghosa says that if you had developed perfect equanimity, you would be unable to express a preference.[112] You wouldn't automatically opt to save yourself, but neither would you automatically offer to give up your own life. You would consider the situation with an even mind, no less concerned for the fate of others than for your own fate. This is equanimity, an attitude that in its profound objectivity values all – including one's own self – equally highly.

As well as being self-sacrificing, the love of a mother also involves a willingness to take responsibility for her children. The gratitude we feel towards our mother is for the affection she has given us but also for the fact that she has taken responsibility for us: she has thought for us, planned for us, taken our long-term needs into consideration before we had any idea what we would need to get through life. The role of thinking for others that a mother assumes for her children is also taken by other people in our lives: nurses and doctors, for example, have to ensure their patients' needs are met, whether or not the patients themselves know what those needs are. Medical professionals make it their business to be aware of the medical conditions that affect their patients and take responsibility for guiding their recovery. It is a kind of compassion that includes an intelligent objectivity. And the same objectivity is found in *mettā*.

If you really seek the good of others, you must have an understanding of what that good actually is. If you do not, you may turn into a do-gooder, relentlessly interfering in people's lives in a way that involves no awareness of their wishes and needs, however helpful and benevolent you may wish to appear. For an example of this sort of thing I'm afraid I must fall back on the old joke about the boy scout who reports that he has done his good deed for the day by helping an old lady across the road. 'That doesn't sound very difficult,' says the scout leader. 'Oh yes it was,' replies the boy, 'She didn't want to cross.' Good intentions alone are not enough, and even the well-intentioned love of a mother is not infallible, although her instincts are usually reliable enough. Likewise, the objective intelligence of *mettā*, if it involves some element of insight or wisdom, is intuitive in its own way – intuitive, not thoughtless.

*Mettā* is like a mother's love in that it is intense, selfless, nurturing, and even intuitive. But it is quite unlike the mother's love in one crucial respect: a mother's love – perhaps especially if she has only one child – is limited to her own offspring, whereas *mettā* is universal and unlimited. A mother views her child as a kind of extension of her own being, and it is as natural for her to love her baby as it is for her to love herself. But that does not constitute a real transcendence of self, because the scope of her intense concern is so circumscribed.

The expression of *mettā* certainly does not involve smothering people with sticky affection or drawing them into a dependent relationship.

A mother's love may even cause her to act unskilfully for the benefit of her own child, even at the expense of others. She may, for example, become fanatically competitive on behalf of her family, with ruthless disregard for the well-being of other children. A mother is fierce in defending her young, but when it comes to encouraging the child to become a person in his or her own right, mother-love can hinder the child's development and place unnecessary obstacles in the way of their emerging individuality. Of course, a mother may feel, or develop, *mettā* towards her children, as indeed may a father.

From an Enlightened point of view, all beings are helpless. However capable they may be in mundane matters, spiritually speaking they are like helpless children. In this sense a Buddha or a bodhisattva is very much like a mother, helping beings to grow up spiritually. But the analogy of the mother's love is no more than an analogy. *Mettā* is in some ways quite different from maternal affection. It is perhaps significant that the verse following the analogy with the love of a mother for her only child should emphasize the unbounded quality of *mettā*. It is as though the possibility of misunderstanding the analogy has been anticipated, and the qualities of *mettā* that a mother's love does not necessarily share have been brought quickly forward to guard against such a possibility.

> Let his thoughts of boundless love pervade the whole world:
> above, below, and across without any obstruction, without any
> hatred, without any enmity.
>
> *Mettañ ca sabbalokasmiṃ*
> *mānasam bhāvaye aparimāṇaṃ*
> *uddhaṃ adho ca tiriyañ ca*
> *asambādhaṃ averaṃ asapattaṃ.*

### *METTĀ* FOR ALL BEINGS

The Pāli phrase translated here as 'without any enmity' can be translated more literally and precisely as 'without any enemy'. This is a subtle difference, but significant in that if you declare yourself to be 'without any enemy' you are in effect saying that you regard nobody as being beyond the reach of your good will.

In the fifth stage of the *mettā bhāvanā* we try to remove the barriers we habitually raise between ourselves and others by extending an equal concern and regard towards ourselves, our friend, the neutral person, and the enemy. Then we extend our *mettā* beyond these individuals to encompass all beings everywhere. This idea of 'all beings' is not meant to refer to a finite and limited number of beings, but at the same time we can't really conceive of there being an unlimited number of beings. If this seems like a dilemma, the nature of *mettā* supplies the solution. *Mettā* cannot settle down and stop at a given number of beings. Your benevolence and compassion continuously expands, taking in more and more people all the time. The natural tendency of the mind is to set limits and settle down, but positive emotion goes against this tendency.

This is especially clear at the beginning of the last stage of the *mettā bhāvanā* meditation when, having equalized your loving-kindness towards the four individuals from each of the previous stages, you allow your *mettā* to open out completely, to become free of any specific reference. You no longer consider individual beings, but the *mettā* goes on, and as your thoughts fall on each person the *mettā* naturally expresses itself towards them. Outside the context of meditation, too, your *mettā* will have no particular object, but as you encounter individuals it will express itself in terms of your feeling and behaviour towards them.

*Mettā* is ultimately a state of mind or heart. This means that in the final stage of the *mettā bhāvanā*, although you may be concentrating now on this, now on that aspect of the totality of living beings, your attention, your concentration, remains constant. Although you cultivate that state in reference to a specific person or succession of people, once it really starts flowing you don't need to direct it towards anybody in particular. In this respect *mettā* is like the sun. The sun goes on shining whether or not anything is there to receive its rays. If a planet happens to be in the path of the sun's rays, it is bathed in that light; otherwise, the sunlight just continues to stream through space. In the same way, if someone comes into the orbit of your *mettā*, your *mettā* falls upon them. If no one is there to receive it, *mettā* just carries on infinitely throughout space, as it were.

Thus, strictly speaking, it is not that you *direct mettā* towards someone. Nor do you literally imagine all the beings in the world in front of you and then make them the collective object of your *mettā*. Nor can you possibly be aware of every single one of them individually. But there is an infinitely expanding flow of *mettā* that goes on and on, arising and expanding, and anyone who comes into your mind is lit up by its warmth and brightness. Looking at it in this way, we can begin to form an idea of *mettā*, not so much as a state of mind, as a movement within consciousness, or a medium within which consciousness can move.

Clearly it is too much to expect that your positive emotion will be universal and unlimited at the outset. This is a progressive practice of cultivation, not instant Enlightenment. But your developing experience of *mettā*, if it really is *mettā*, will show in a tendency for you to become more and more inclusive of others, and less and less tied to your own narrow interests. The seed of Buddhahood is there in every small, everyday thought or word of generosity or act of friendliness. Indeed, this naturally expansive, other-regarding tendency is the quality common to all truly positive emotions, whereas negativity shuts us down, closes us in upon the private, self-regarding 'I'.

## THE IMMEASURABLES

The first four stages of the *mettā bhāvanā* are there to help you get the *mettā* flowing. Once it is in full flow, you can let it spread in any direction you like, strengthening it and extending its flow more and more widely. You can send it in the direction of animals, towards sick people, old people, famine victims, evil dictators, wherever your thoughts take you.

The same goes for the other *brahma vihāra* meditations: the *karuṇā bhāvanā* or development of compassion; the *muditā bhāvanā* or cultivation of sympathetic joy; and the *upekkhā bhāvanā* (Sanskrit *upekṣā*) or cultivation of equanimity. Each of them shares with *mettā* the same limitless object. This is perhaps most obvious with *upekkhā* or equanimity. To speak of an equanimity that was somehow restricted to a few people would be a contradiction in terms, because the essential nature of equanimity is to not make distinctions but to have an even mind towards all.

The *brahma vihāras* are all closely interconnected. Indeed the basic emotional state underlying them all is the same: it is *mettā*. If you experience *mettā* and that *mettā* encounters someone who is happy, it is transformed into sympathetic joy, *muditā*, the state of being happy in the happiness of others, rejoicing in their merits and positive qualities. The inherently outgoing quality of *muditā* reaches its peak when you are able to recognize and rejoice in the merits of people who perform positive actions even when they seem to be set against you. You are still as happy to rejoice in their merits as in the merits of your friends.

If you could appreciate only the skilful actions of people you liked, or who liked you, this would be a very limited form of *muditā*, and if you could appreciate only those actions that benefited or gratified you in some way, *muditā* would not come into it at all. *Muditā* is the appreciation of the true happiness of others. If you can't rejoice with others, if you can't feel happiness in their happiness, then you can have no real *mettā* for them.

But suppose your *mettā* encounters someone who is suffering. *Mettā* is then transformed into *karuṇā*, the strong and practical desire to do whatever one can to relieve suffering. Like *muditā*, *upekkhā*, and *mettā*, the natural tendency of compassion is to reach out and to go on expanding its field of activity ever further and more powerfully. Indeed, any positive emotion has this tendency. We look upon not just one person, but anyone we meet, with the love a mother feels for her own helpless child. All the time the same light of *mettā* is shining through. Then, according to whether people suffer or whether they are happy, this same basic positive emotional attitude will be mantled with the sober shades of *karuṇā* or clothed in the bright, dancing colours of *muditā*.

To the four *brahma vihāras* one could arguably add other positive mental states which have become non-exclusive and expansive, which as positive mental states they will indeed do. Devotion, for example, might appear to be necessarily limited and exclusive in its frame of reference, but this is not really the case. Devotion is the emotion that arises when our *mettā* touches upon something much higher and nobler than ourselves. When you look up with love, your love becomes reverence and devotion – *śraddhā* and *bhakti*, to use the Sanskrit terms. Conversely, the *mettā* of the Buddhas looking upon all beings who are not yet Enlightened of course becomes *karuṇā*, compassion.

Devotion in Buddhism is usually considered in terms of the Indian idea of *bhakti*, the pleasure felt in connection with the contemplation of spiritual objects. Although this plays its part in Buddhist devotion, it is not really about showing formal respect towards the symbols of religious authority. It is an aspect of faith, and includes a degree of certainty that the path you follow is the sure path to your goal, your ultimate good. It contains a strong element of insight, the direct knowledge that certain practices will lead to certain results.

As a Buddhist you are drawn to the Buddha, the Dharma, and the Sangha, confident that these represent the ultimate values of life, that they symbolize humanity's highest goal. Being intent upon the Three Jewels in this way brings a clarity to the mind over and above whatever pleasure you may or may not feel. To be devoted in the true sense is to acknowledge and to resonate spiritually with any representation of your goal. If devotion is limited to only some of its forms – those exclusively connected with a certain school of Buddhism, for example – it is scarcely devotion in the true sense. Even though the images as cultural objects may not be familiar, or even particularly attractive, the devoted Buddhist still recognizes in them the goal that is common to all Buddhists. This is because the goal itself is beyond language, beyond culture. It does not find full expression in any particular set of forms.

Positive emotion, whether it is devotion or *mettā* or anything else, is expansive by its very nature. If one's sense of devotion is not broadening its scope, it is thus not really a positive emotion at all. Like *mettā*, its tendency is to become universal. *Mettā* should go on expanding, renewing itself, growing brighter and stronger as it does so. If it really is *mettā* you are feeling, you will never feel you have had enough.

> Whether he stands, walks, sits or lies down, as long as he is awake, he should develop this mindfulness. This they say is the noblest living here.
>
> *Tiṭṭham caraṃ nisinno vā*
> *sayāno vā yāvat' assa vigatamiddho*
> *etaṃ satiṃ adhiṭṭheyya;*
> *brahmam etaṃ vihāraṃ idha-m-āhu.*

### HOW YOUR *METTĀ* AFFECTS OTHERS

Of course, *mettā* is not just a meditation exercise; it's a way of life. The phrase 'whether he stands, walks, sits or lies down' is found in almost identical form in the verse on mindfulness of the body in the *Satipaṭṭhāna Sutta*, the discourse on the four foundations of mindfulness.

Like mindfulness, *mettā* is something you never lose sight of, and clearly this verse of the *Sutta* envisages it as a form of mindfulness. If you really want to attain the 'noblest living', you will need to practise *mettā* in every moment of the day and night, not just when you are seated on your meditation cushion. This is *mettā* in the full or true sense.

The qualifier 'as long as he is awake' can be taken in different ways. It refers to being awake in the everyday sense, but if you are going to be truly awake in the sense of *sati*, mindfulness, then you can take such wakefulness in connection with *mettā* into your dream life. In fact, in any state of consciousness, *mettā* will stand you in good stead, as long as you remain attentive. So the phrase can refer to a physical state or a spiritual state, but it can also refer to a more general state of alertness or vigour.

*Etaṃ satiṃ adhiṭṭheyya*, which Saddhatissa translates as let him 'develop this mindfulness', could perhaps also be rendered as let him 'radiate this mindfulness', thus implying that by this stage of the *Sutta* you are no longer in the process of developing the 'power' of *mettā*. That power has now been developed, and you are just extending its influence, radiating *mettā* for the benefit of all beings everywhere.

But while your *mettā* may have a powerful influence on others, an influence that you are now able to extend and to radiate, it is in no sense your own. We do speak of 'developing' *mettā*, but this is not a kind of power technique whose aim is to manipulate other people to one's own advantage. *Mettā* is certainly powerful, but it is not a coercive power. For example, if you cultivate *mettā* towards an 'enemy', there is at least a possibility that this will have a positive effect on their behaviour towards you, but you are not to think of *mettā* as a force or power, to be used so that others will have no choice but to fall under your spell and like you. This would not be *mettā*, but an assertion of your ego over that of another person. It is of course skilful to direct *mettā* towards people who seem to be trying to do us harm. But if we do so just to stop them giving us a difficult time and making a nuisance of themselves, it probably won't be the real thing. If we then start getting irritated because we have tried to be full of *mettā* towards them and they do not respond positively, then our mental state will be not unlike theirs.

Other factors being equal, your practice of the *mettā bhāvanā* will have a positive effect on others. The expansive quality of *mettā* is by no means confined to meditation. One of the sure signs of *mettā* is that you will quite naturally have a lightening, encouraging, even tonic effect on those around you. But others must be allowed the freedom to resist that influence if they want to. In the end we are all responsible for our own mental state. A positive emotion cannot be imposed.

There is also the possibility that some people may not be sensitive to your *mettā*, particularly if they are used to relationships based on a kind of emotional quid pro quo, in which everything one is given has to be paid for. *Mettā* is entirely unconditional, and when people are used to emotional dependency in a relationship, they may think you are rather uninterested in them, or even that you don't care about them, simply because you seem not to want anything from them in return. The *mettā* coming from you is a little too rarefied; it isn't quite on their wavelength. Even though you may be clearly concerned for their welfare, good will is not what they want: they want some kind of commitment and surrender, some dependency, to fill the aching void left by their incapacity to feel *mettā* towards themselves. Your *mettā* may mean very little to them if they interpret your unwillingness to enter into a dependent relationship as meaning that you are rather distant and impersonal.

The idea that *mettā* is something expansive comes through again in the last line of the verse, in the expression *brahmam etaṃ vihāraṃ*. Here, the word *vihāraṃ* means 'abode', 'state', or 'experience', while *brahmam* means 'high', 'noble', 'sublime' – exalted, that is to say, almost to the point of divinity. According to some authorities, the word *brahman* comes from a root meaning to swell, grow, or expand. The brahmin was thus originally the inspired sage, the priest or holy man who, having 'swelled' under the pressure of divine inspiration, released it to the community as holy teachings. So *brahmam* is something divinely great in the sense of 'expanded', and in this way comes to approximate to the idea of 'the absolute'.

*Idha-m-āhu* – 'This, they say' – comes at the end of the verse to give a further clue as to how we should understand this phrase *brahmam vihāraṃ*. It is as though this expression, although it describes the ultimate outcome of the training, is in the final analysis only a figure of speech. The experience is ineffable, so to call it 'the Sublime Abiding' is only a metaphor, a poetic turn of phrase. There is, however, no implication of any kind of doubt or disclaimer: rather the opposite. It is affirming that this is not just personal experience, but the experience of many others. It is an appeal to tradition, in other words, to the experience and testimony of the spiritual community of those who are truly wise.

Just as a mother's nurturing love for her child helps the child to grow, our *mettā* for others helps them to develop, as well as being the means of our own growth and development. *Mettā* is not only expansive in itself; it is also a cause of increase and expansion in others, and of the joy that comes with such expansion. It brings a lightness to your being, taking you beyond narrow, purely personal concerns. You start to become receptive to other people, happy to open yourself up and let them in, unafraid to pay them more attention and give them more of yourself.

*Mettā* is not just metaphorically expansive. You *feel* expansive; you feel an airy and weightless joy. This quality is characteristic of positive emotion generally, hence expressions like 'up in the clouds' and 'walking on air', and *mettā* is the brightest and most positive of emotional states. You feel carried outside yourself, warm, sunny, uplifted. If you want to develop the joy of *mettā*, look for this sense of lightness. If your devotions are heavy and cheerless, and your faith is a dull and dismal piety, *mettā*, which has the taste of freedom and delight, will be very slow in coming.

Of course, freedom and delight are not emotions usually associated with religion, especially in Europe, where an uplifting legacy of tapering Gothic spires and sublime church music is accompanied by the whiff of brimstone and the promise of eternal damnation for the unbeliever. Anxiety and guilt may be the traditional flavours of established religion in our culture, but they are the antithesis of *mettā*. It is a dreadful pity that our emotions are so often a source of misery rather than joy. No wonder that we try to suppress, constrict, and crush them! But in doing so, we compound our unhappiness. We become more and more downcast, we go about with head bowed and shoulders drooping, and of course it spreads. When we meet someone who starts to tell us about their difficulties, we can't wait to start putting in a word about our own troubles, looking for an audience for our complaints.

But just as we tend to want to pass on our misery, the generosity of spirit that comes with *mettā* makes us want to confer our happiness on everyone we meet. While intention is the starting point of *mettā*, its culmination is a matter of conduct, the 'noblest living' of Saddhatissa's translation.

No doubt if everyone throughout the world were to cultivate genuinely expansive positive emotion as a way of life, human society would be entirely transformed. But even though this is hardly feasible, at least for the time being, it should be possible to experience such a thing within the sangha, the spiritual community. The sangha is the expression, across time and space, of that practical commitment to transforming self and world which is inherent in the life and teaching of the Buddha. Through *kalyāṇa mitratā* or spiritual friendship, through which one connects with and encourages the best in one's friends, one generates and intensifies positive emotions in a continual reciprocity of good will.

In the sangha, everyone is committed to the cultivation of *mettā* as a way of life, *mettā* being experienced as a practical reality through friendship. You may well profess great feelings of *mettā* towards all sentient beings, and even perhaps try to put *mettā* into practice in the way you behave with colleagues and acquaintances. But how far are you really living out your ideals? If you never experience *mettā* in the closeness and reciprocity of friendships that are essentially spiritual rather than collusive, you will never experience the full possibilities of *mettā*. Spiritual friendship enables us to be true to our individuality and on that basis bring about an authentic meeting of hearts and minds. It is very difficult to develop *mettā* as a purely individual experience. You need other people.

# CONCLUSION: THE REALIZATION OF *METTĀ*

Not falling into wrong views, being virtuous and endowed with insight, by discarding attachment to sense desires, never again is he reborn.

*Diṭṭhiñ ca anupagamma*
*sīlavā dassanena sampanno*
*kāmesu vineyya gedhaṃ*
*na hi jātu gabbhaseyyaṃ punar-eti.*

## A FINGER POINTING TO THE MOON

The opening verses of the *Sutta* laid down the necessary foundations of the practice. Now the closing verse describes the results of one's perfecting it. The term *dassanena*, translated here as 'insight', is more literally 'sight' or 'vision', as in 'seeing the true nature of things'. Both *dassana* and the first word of this verse, *diṭṭhiñ*, come from the same root: *diṭṭhi* (Sanskrit *dṛṣṭi*), which means 'view', commonly occurring in the expressions *micchā diṭṭhi*, 'wrong view', and *sammā diṭṭhi*, 'right view'. Whereas *dassana*, like vision, the English equivalent, always has positive connotations, *diṭṭhi*, a view, can be positive or negative depending on how it is qualified. However, the word *diṭṭhi* on its own, without a qualifier, is always negative. It is understandable, therefore, that this phrase has been translated as 'falling into wrong views' – but this does change the meaning. The implication of the Pāli word is not only that one should avoid falling into wrong views, but that any view at all ultimately gets in the way of true insight. Even right views are to be given up eventually, in the sense that, though still holding them, one is not attached to them.

By a view is meant any conceptual formulation to which you adhere as if it had absolute value as a truth-statement. 'I exist' is a view, and so is 'the moon is in the sky.' Such views are necessary for communication, and conventionally speaking we need to label some as true and some as false. From the point of view of the Dharma, too, we need to distinguish between views that are helpful to the attainment of our goal and those that point us in the wrong direction, spiritually speaking. But from the point of view of the goal, reality itself, all views are inadequate. No view is capable of expressing that reality. They are expedient means, only representations of things, not the truth.

Thus, on many occasions, not only in the Pāli scriptures but also in the Mahāyāna *sūtras*, the Buddha states that the Tathāgata (another term for Buddha) is free from all views. Even though he spent some forty years treading the roads of ancient India, giving discourses, making careful distinctions between right views and wrong views, in reality, as a Buddha, he has no views.

This paradox reminds us that we need to hold our views lightly. As the Zen tradition puts it, they are a finger pointing to the moon, not the moon itself. The Buddha uses words like 'self', 'person', and 'Enlightenment', for example, but he doesn't have a view of self, or person, or Enlightenment; that is, he doesn't adhere to any conceptual formulation of any kind as having absolute validity. Not falling into views means not 'absolutizing' any conceptual construction. However useful a set of concepts might be for the purposes of communication, if you adhere to them as anything more than useful markers, you have fallen into a kind of literalism, or even fundamentalism. Any concept relies for its meaning on its relationship with a whole string of other ideas and concepts which are equally relative. No view, no concept, is independent and therefore fixed. In fact, as soon as you start to take your conceptual constructions too literally, and hold on to them too tightly, they cease to function effectively as a means of communication.

We tend to think of a concept as the content of our communication; it is easily forgotten that it is more fundamentally a *means* of communication. A concept is the means of communicating something that is essentially incommunicable. Concepts do not exist on their own; they come as part of a package that includes the way they are presented. To communicate, they must be offered in the right spirit, at the right time, in the right place, and in the right way. Above all, they have to be put across with the right feeling.

An idea of *mettā* that lacks the corresponding emotion only muddies the waters when we try to communicate it to others. Indeed, this is true of any Buddhist doctrine. If you want, for example, to communicate the teaching of *anattā* (that there is no unchanging 'self' or 'soul'), you have to be aware that to insist on the idea of no self and argue belligerently, not to say self-assertively, with those who hold a different view undermines the very point you are trying to make. In the name of a view that is meant to pull down the barriers between yourself and others, you are, through your self-assertion, building up those barriers more strongly than ever.

As a Buddhist you need to be familiar with the concept of *anattā*, but you should not cling to any particular formulation of that concept. It is there to be used simply as a vehicle of thought and communication. We need Buddhism as a system of doctrines and practices to be used appropriately, not so that we may have something to hide behind. If you use Buddhism as a collection of ideas to mark you out as a 'spiritual' and perhaps rather interesting or mysterious person, this is at the expense of a deeper emotional engagement with the truth towards which any conceptual formulation can only point. A view of Buddhism, in other words, is an essentially alienated version of Buddhism, and a very different thing from Buddhism itself.

## *METTĀ* AND INSIGHT

The final words of the *Sutta* – 'never again is he reborn' – suggest that the goal of *mettā* is a depth of transcendental realization that frees the practitioner from the suffering of repeated rebirth. So how might this be the case? Simply put, in developing *mettā*, we are deepening our emotional involvement with the truth of *anattā* or no-self.

The unenlightened person takes the self, specifically their own self, as the fundamental and absolute reality of things, and this has a profoundly negative effect on every aspect of experience. At the back of all negative emotion is the thought 'What's in this for me?' Even in our cultivation of positive emotion, the sense of self acts as a kind of gravitational pull that prevents us reaching the heights to which our *mettā* would otherwise take us and makes it very difficult for our friendliness and kindness towards others to be truly selfless. Cultivating *mettā* is like launching a satellite. It may look as though it is tracing a straight line away from the earth into space, but in fact it remains tied to the earth's gravitational field, and rather than disappearing off into the blue, it comes to maintain a steady orbit around the earth, and never fully breaks away.

*Mettā* behaves similarly. It is inherently expansive, but however strong our feelings of warmth and friendliness, the very fact that we still think of ourselves as being separate from others will have a limiting effect on our experience of it. At some point those good intentions reaching out across the universe will start to deviate from their perfectly straight trajectory and slowly curve round so as not to lose contact with the self entirely. How far your ability to experience genuine *mettā* carries you before you settle back into a comfortable orbit around the self is a measure of the quality of your practice. The affection between ordinary friends might produce quite a low orbit, while the intimacy and trust of a spiritual friendship would trace out a wider trajectory. And the more powerful positive emotion experienced in the deep meditative states called *dhyāna* would take your course a good deal further out still. *Dhyāna* is clearly a vast improvement on everyday self-interest; it is a far wider, more elevated reach of consciousness. But however wide its circle of influence may be, it continues to be self-referential, albeit more and more subtly. Only when *mettā* is permeated by insight, or a deeper understanding of the truth of *anattā*, do our emotions finally go beyond the range of the self.

This is of course an analogy. When we practise *mettā* it isn't that there are literally beams of *mettā* radiating out from us as we sit and meditate, even though the image might be a useful one. Moreover, that central point of reference, that 'core' of the self, is in reality only a fiction. It is more useful to regard *mettā* as an outward movement *of* the self rather than *from* the self. As we continually expand the scope of our care and concern, the self is universalized, one might say, or expanded indefinitely. This does not mean that we have to transform our sense of who we *are* according to an idea of how we *should be* that is quite alien to how we experience ourselves. It is rather that our direct experience of ourselves should be that we are continually going out to be aware of and concerned for the well-being of others, not fixed on any single point of identity.

This directly experienced insight into the truth of no-self (*anattā*) is the first real breakthrough on the journey towards Enlightenment. It is traditionally known as *sotāpatti*, 'entering the stream'. The 'Stream Entrant' is one who has broken the fetter of self-view, who understands directly and intuitively that the separate self, the 'I', is no more than an idea – an idea that is the ultimate source of our unhappiness and lack of fulfilment. This insight is not merely cognitive, not a matter of intellectual assent to a logical proposition. The Stream Entrant *lives* his or her knowledge, experiencing it in the form of a fully developed positivity. Once one has reached this point, one will never fall back into mistaken, worldly ways, and one will have to undergo no more than seven 're-becomings'.

If we could really see that there is no difference between our own true interests and those of others, *mettā* would come naturally. As our capacity for positive emotion grows stronger, self-reference becomes ever more difficult to detect, because it becomes harder for us to tell just where the boundaries of the self lie.

The Buddhist tradition offers yet another way of understanding the situation. According to the analytical psychology of the Abhidhamma, while the *brahma vihāras* are positive and highly skilful mental events, they lack any element of transcendental insight. They are thus classified as *śamatha* practices, dedicated to calming and concentrating the mind, rather than as practices devoted to the development of *vipassanā*, or transcendental insight. As such they are mundane (*lokiya*), not transcendental (*lokuttara*), inasmuch as they are temporary emotional states, and cease to exist once the factors that have provided support for them – such as regular meditation, spiritual friendships, study, retreats, and right livelihood – are removed. This said – again according to the Abhidhamma – the *brahma vihāras* can be transformed by the insight generated by sustained reflection (itself supported by the basis of *samatha* that they provide). They will then arise naturally from the clear knowledge that there is no real difference between self and others. But as cultivated states they are not themselves capable of that transformation.

As a result of this kind of analysis it was said – and perhaps Buddhaghosa bears some responsibility for this – that *mettā* doesn't take you very far along the path to Enlightenment. The traditional Theravādin view is that you cannot gain Enlightenment by practising the *mettā bhāvanā* alone because the *mettā bhāvanā* is essentially a *samatha* practice. Indeed, it came as a surprise to me when I lived among eastern Buddhists to find that the *mettā bhāvanā* was often regarded as a simple little practice that anybody could do, two minutes of it at a time being considered more than enough.

The Theravāda's relegation of *mettā bhāvanā* to the *samatha* side of things seems to be an example of a general methodological undervaluation of positive emotion, associated with a preference for expressing spiritual perspectives in negative terms. In the Pāli canon, and in the Theravādin tradition that is based upon it, Enlightenment is generally spoken of as a state in which the self has been eliminated or – to translate the term *nibbāna* literally – 'snuffed out'. But in the *Karaṇīya Mettā Sutta* the same aim is envisaged in positive terms: not as the elimination of the ego but as a deeply realized attitude of even-mindedness towards all.

There are other sections of the Pāli canon that make it abundantly clear that just as there are negative emotions that bind beings to the wheel of rebirth, there are positive emotions that are not just conducive, but absolutely necessary to the attainment of transcendental insight. This insight is, after all, a realization of – among other things – a state of egolessness, and this is the aim of the *mettā bhāvanā*. You succeed in the practice of the *mettā bhāvanā* when in the fifth stage you can genuinely feel equal love towards all. If your care for others is made genuinely equal to your care for yourself, your whole attitude is egoless.

## TAKING *METTĀ* TOWARDS INSIGHT

The traditional Theravādin attitude rests on the distinction it makes between the emotions and the intellect, with insight being seen as an essentially intellectual realization. But fully developed *mettā* is inherently more than an emotion pure and simple, and insight is inherently more than just cognitive. If your experience of *mettā* is straightforwardly emotional, and not based on much reflection, then it is the emotional equivalent of insight, not insight per se. But even the deepest insight need not be experienced cognitively – i.e., it need not take the form of a logical proposition. You simply live it, experience it, as a fully developed positivity and selflessness that is neither emotional nor cognitive.

A common misapprehension is to think of insight and egolessness in abstract, even metaphysical terms rather than as comprising concretely-lived attitudes and behaviour. But realizing the truth of egolessness simply means being truly and deeply unselfish. To contemplate the principle of egolessness as some special principle that is somehow separate from our actual behaviour will leave it as far away as ever. If we find it difficult to realize the ultimate emptiness of the self, the solution is to try to be a little less selfish. The understanding comes after the experience, not before.

When it is less than fully developed, *mettā* may lack the clear awareness that is characteristic of insight arrived at through reflection on the Dharma. Nonetheless, it is always heading in the direction of a brighter and clearer awareness, as its nature is to grow and expand beyond the limits set by the self. In short, *mettā* and insight are not separate aims. Indeed, *mettā* is a necessary aspect of insight, and with reflection on the real nature of *mettā*, insight will shine through. Having developed *mettā* in a limited sense as an equal kindness towards others, you can go on to reflect on whether there is really any difference between yourself and others and, if so, what that difference might be. Thus reflecting, you will begin to see that the idea that 'I am I' and 'he is he' is no more than a delusion, and in that way *mettā* begins to blend with insight.

It isn't that you drop the *mettā* in order to start developing insight. If in the course of your meditation you were to develop *mettā*, and then were to begin *vipassanā*-type reflection on that basis, it would represent a continuity of experience, not a shift from one kind of consciousness to another. The Mahāyāna expresses this poetically, saying that the cultivated emotions of the *brahma vihāras* pass through the fires of *suññatā*, or emptiness – that is, non-self or non-duality – thus giving rise to the *bodhicitta*, or wisdom heart. Of course, in practice one's experience of *mettā* is likely to flag, to be revived by again bringing to mind and heart other living beings before *vipassanā*-type reflection is resumed. In this way one's practice alternates between concentration and reflection, *samatha* and insight, perhaps for a long time, until eventually the two merge as clear transcendental insight rooted in powerful positive emotion.

It is in terms of insight that the expansive aspect of *mettā*, its tendency to break through any sense of exclusivity, is so important – though it is easy to overlook this because *mettā* has no conceivable end-point. But to miss the link between *mettā* and insight is to miss the point of *mettā* entirely. For example, people sometimes talk about doing things 'for the sake of my spiritual development', which seems a grotesque reduction of any truly spiritual practice, especially in the case of the *mettā bhāvanā*, *mettā* being essentially good will that is free from self-interest. That one should aim to develop that disinterested good will in one's own interest clearly undermines the whole enterprise.

While the *mettā bhāvanā* begins with a cherishing of oneself, this is meant to be the springboard for the practice, not an end in itself. Of course, you do benefit yourself when you help others; even if you give a beggar some money because you think the giving will be good for you, at least you have parted with the money, and both parties are happier as a result. It is difficult to stop yourself from thinking of the ways you are going to benefit from what you do, but you just have to try to focus on your altruistic intention and keep the knowledge of what you will get out of your action in the background, as it were. If you are practising the *mettā bhāvanā* chiefly for the sake of its beneficial effect on your own mind, that benefit will be diminished, as will any benefit to others, because the practice was vitiated from the outset by self-interest. The more heartfelt your intention to do the *mettā bhāvanā* entirely for the sake of others, the more beneficial the practice will be, both to you and to them. The idea is gently but persistently to expand the boundaries of your *mettā* and therewith the boundaries of your own self.

When *mettā* is experienced in this fully expansive mode and is universal in its scope, there is no experience of a self that is separate from anyone or anything else. To speak of 'oneself' at this stage is almost a contradiction in terms. Just as a circle that has expanded to infinity is not really a circle any more, having gone beyond any distinguishable shape, so the mind that has expanded to embrace all beings has gone beyond definition. Forgetting the self as a reference point, no longer asking what any given situation means for you alone, you can go on indefinitely and happily expanding the breadth and depth of your interest and positivity. The self is replaced by a creative orientation of being, or rather – since 'being' is not a very Buddhistic expression – a creative orientation of becoming.

This is the essence of the spiritual life: to bring about a state in which the whole movement and tendency of our being is expansive, spiralling creatively outwards and upwards. If, on the other hand, we remain fixed in the circularity of reactive consciousness, returning again and again to a fixed and finite idea of the self as the central point of reference, even spiritual achievements can become fetters, by remaining our own 'property'.

Stream Entry – after which, according to tradition, one is not reborn more than seven times – is the point at which the balance of skilful and unskilful energies is decisively shifted towards the positive. Until that point is reached there will always be some degree of conflict between our skilful aspirations and our unskilful resistance to change. For this reason we will sometimes get tired of practising the *mettā bhāvanā*. But to the extent that we succeed in raising some genuine *mettā*, it will, we shall find, generate its own energy and expansiveness and depend less on our efforts, at least until we again experience the resistance of some aspect of ourselves that is not behind our skilful intention. Indeed, with repeated application, the *mettā* we develop will gradually integrate the energy of our resistance into the outward flow of our beneficial energies.

*Mettā* has the taste of freedom. If you are able to act out of *mettā* – if you treat others just as you treat yourself – you are acting as if the distinction you unthinkingly create in your mind between yourself and others simply did not exist. In doing so, you free yourself from the power of the illusion of a separate self. This is insight, and though you might not experience it in a cognitive way, the fact that you have developed *mettā*, the emotional equivalent of insight, means that you have developed insight nonetheless. It is a mistake to approach the practice of the *mettā bhāvanā* as though it were an elementary exercise, a mere preparation for 'proper' insight practices. The *Karaṇīya Mettā Sutta* is dedicated to a very high ideal: the cultivation of *mettā* as a path to insight.

## HOW FAR DOES *METTĀ* GET YOU?

The concluding line of the *Sutta* seems to suggest that the culmination of the perfection of *mettā* is Enlightenment itself. Taken literally, however, the line does not exclude further rebirth. The Pāli says 'For him there is no re-becoming in any womb (*gabbhaseyyaṃ*),' which would seem conclusive if it were not for the fact that according to the Buddhist tradition birth via the womb is not the only possible mode of birth. In fact, four modes – birth from a womb, birth from an egg, birth from moisture, and apparitional birth – are mentioned in Buddhist texts of all kinds. So for the traditional Buddhist, although this verse means that they will not be reborn in the human or animal realms, this does not rule out the other three kinds of rebirth. In the higher heavenly worlds, for example, the gods are born by apparitional birth – that is, they just appear – as the result of their previous karma. This is the mode of rebirth of the 'non-returner', or *anāgāmin*: he or she is reborn in the Pure Abodes and dwells there surrounded by the golden light of the Buddha's teaching until such time as supreme Enlightenment finally dawns.

This Theravādin doctrine has an approximate parallel in the Mahāyāna Buddhist teaching of the Pure Land, the main difference being that the bodhisattva may take further rebirth out of compassion, to help beings still suffering in impure realms of existence. The bodhisattva Kṣitigarbha, for instance, vows to refrain from becoming Enlightened until every region of hell has been emptied of tormented beings. However, the bodhisattva consciously chooses to be reborn, even though in a sense it is an inevitable choice, flowing naturally from his compassion. Thus, like the non-returner, the bodhisattva does not undergo the involuntary rebirth that conditioned beings must endure in consequence of their actions in previous lives.

Whether or not we are prepared to take this distinction between kinds of rebirth as applicable to the text we are studying depends to some extent on how we take the text itself. We can be fairly sure that early on in the transmission of the Buddha's teaching certain expressions will have had a metaphorical rather than a literal significance. Then, as the Abhidharma tradition developed through the centuries, particular terms did come to acquire a more precise meaning. The heaven realms and the different kinds of rebirth, like the *dhyānas* and the fifty-one mental events, came to be mapped out in scrupulous detail. It may be that this reference to the end of further rebirth from a womb was originally meant to be understood in a general, literary sense, rather than in a technical one. If we wish, we can certainly take this last line as meaning that one does not take rebirth in any form ever again – that one is fully Enlightened. It is hard to be certain either way. What we can be sure of is that it at least expresses complete confidence in the connection between the cultivation of *mettā* and highly skilful states of mind.

### AN INHERITANCE OF JOY

It is good to contemplate inspiring images of the consummation of *mettā*, as we struggle to awaken a little of it in meditation. But it may sometimes be more helpful to refer back to the starting point of this whole process of spiritual expansion. The transformation begins with trying to lead a principled and upright human life, and if this preparatory achievement seems a distant goal for most people, clearly it is there that we have to put most emphasis.

We know that an intellectual understanding of selflessness is not enough. But how do we go about integrating that knowledge into a deep and mature emotional awareness? In modern life, especially in the western world, we are not adept at dealing with strong emotion, perhaps especially strong positive emotion, and it is not surprising that we underestimate the power of *mettā* and hence the importance and spiritual status of the *mettā bhāvanā*. We prefer to equate the goal with a cool appraisal of the true nature of existence rather than with an ardent and unremitting dedication to bringing all beings into the infinite light and limitless bliss of Nirvāṇa.

*Mettā* requires strong positive energy. If your positive emotion does not last long in the bright glare of daily life, if you are restless or irritable and unable to be friendly after you have risen from your meditation seat, you will clearly need to go back to the basics of the practice. Before you start meditating, it makes sense to take a good look at how you behave in daily life. I sometimes think that people are not nearly kind enough to one another, either in their actions or in their general attitude. Any unkindness or quarrelling reveals a basic lack of *mettā*, and unless you are willing to cultivate *mettā* in your everyday dealings with people there is little point in trying to cultivate it on the meditation cushion. Allowing ourselves to descend into acrimony and rancour displays a fundamental lack of faith in *mettā* as a path of regular practice. It is as though we leave it in the shrine-room and walk away without it, even though we may have experienced it quite genuinely while there. If that happens, our *mettā* evidently doesn't have enough strength for it to be carried over into our daily interactions with people.

*Mettā* is a high ideal, so high that it includes being ready to sacrifice life and limb for others, and it is very difficult to achieve it in its fullness. We must therefore be prepared to appreciate a more limited achievement of *mettā* as entirely genuine as far as it goes. On the other hand, even our embryonic *mettā* should not be too delicate. It should be able to survive transplantation, to bloom at least for a few hours in the cold and busy world outside the meditation room. In meditation you may sometimes feel that you are radiating *mettā* from a safe and rather aloof distance. In that case, you could try introducing a greater sense of imaginative identification with others, as is customary in the *karuṇā bhāvanā*, for example, in which you aim to feel with others, putting yourself in their shoes. And that warmth and empathy should be carried over into your actual relations with people. It might be worth asking yourself if there is enough warmth in your various relationships, especially with those who also practise the *mettā bhāvanā*.

The Buddhist path is one of regular steps. The foundation of our practice has to be securely established in mindfulness and *mettā* before we move on to anything else. For most people, as I hope I have shown, the *mettā bhāvanā* asks more than enough of their spiritual aspirations, and it hardly needs to be supplemented by anything except the practice of mindfulness. If we are dissatisfied with the *mettā bhāvanā*, to ask for higher and more advanced practices is self-defeating. Naturally we would like something different for the sheer novelty of it, and we may even persuade ourselves that we are ready for more advanced training. Of course we are in a hurry to move on to the next stage. But all this grasping after the next attainment, the next spiritual goody, is little more than craving and conceit. If we are dissatisfied with the *mettā bhāvanā*, or if we are not getting on with it very well, it isn't because we have outgrown it, but rather the opposite. It probably means that we have not prepared for the practice adequately, or that we need to be more imaginative, perhaps more intuitive or devotional in our practice. It may just mean that we need to do it for longer periods or more often. The *mettā bhāvanā* is not a kindergarten practice.

If we follow the path of regular steps, as Buddhists in traditional, pre-modern cultures have done for many hundreds of years, we shall begin by cultivating a happy, healthy, human existence, and we start to practise *mettā* from that foundation. These days it is much more likely that we will be on the path of irregular steps. Only once we have learned to meditate do we think of attending to the ethical foundations necessary for successful meditation.

Quite soon we are likely to find that our meditation has ground to a halt, and that we have to start cultivating the essential human qualities of uprightness, amenability, contentment, simplicity, and so on in a more purposeful way before we can make further progress. This happens again and again: you run out of steam and have to retrace your steps to consolidate the ethical basis of your practice. It is difficult to tell which qualities are missing from that basis until you try to build on it and find that it lacks the strength to support you. This is how the path of irregular steps rather haphazardly winds its way.

It is fundamental to Buddhist practice that if you prepare yourself thoroughly, you are already practising. If you have all those positive human qualities, if you are capable, straight, and so on, the chances are that your emotional attitude towards others will already be so healthy and positive as to be akin to *mettā*. For most people, the task in hand is not chasing after some lofty idea of transcendental insight, but establishing this basis of positive emotion. Without developing love, compassion, faith, joy, delight, rapture, we won't get very far. There has to be a firm, quiet ground of positive emotion to our life all the time. And this is well within our reach. It is the normal human state. There is nothing extraordinary, nothing even particularly spiritual about it. We just happen to have sunk below that level, at least for the time being. Thus the way of *mettā* is not only a path of ever-increasing positive emotion leading to Enlightenment. It is a guide to recovering our basic human inheritance of joy.

# LIVING BEAUTIFULLY

Based on a seminar on *Dhammapada* chapter 9: 'Evil', held at Padmaloka, 12–13 March 1983

The *Dhammapada* is an anthology, some of the verses being found in other parts of the Pāli canon, but others only in the *Dhammapada*. Judging from the terminology and the kind of Pāli it is written in, it would seem that it is one of the older portions of the Pāli canon, though probably not as old as the oldest parts of the *Sutta-Nipāta* or the *Udāna*. A Sanskrit equivalent called the *Udānavarga*, which has many verses in common with the Pāli *Dhammapada*, has been translated into English, Tibetan, and Chinese. We know that the Buddha encouraged his disciple Vaṅgīsa to put the teachings into metrical form so that they could be more easily remembered, and there could well have been others among the Buddha's disciples with this gift who versified his teachings and made them into ballads that could be recited and chanted as people went around. Perhaps the Buddha himself sometimes produced verses, though no doubt when he gave a more lengthy and detailed exposition he spoke in prose.

So we can regard the *Dhammapada* as reflecting a quite early stage in the development of the Buddha's teaching, and reflecting much of the teaching of the Buddha himself. It is one of the best known of the Buddhist scriptures. There are many English translations, including one I made myself, having found the existing ones unsatisfactory. They're either pseudo-literary, or not literal enough, or clumsy. Radhakrishnan's isn't bad, though it Hinduizes a bit, and Buddhadatta's is quite a good translation, though the idiom isn't quite English, so it's a bit awkward.

A translation to be avoided is the Mascaro one published by Penguin. That is dreadful. It's not even a paraphrase. Narada Thera's is not bad, it's quite accurate, but the English is quite flabby and dead; there's no bite in it, whereas the Pāli text is very pungent and pointed; it has punch, so if the translation doesn't, it misses one of the most vital features of the original text.

> Be quick to do what is (morally) beautiful. Restrain the mind from evil. He who is sluggish in doing good, his mind delights in evil. (116)

This translation is my own, and I have translated this first sentence a little differently from the way in which it is usually translated, though not in any way eccentrically, but completely literally. The word I have translated as beautiful is *kalyāṇa*. An even more literal translation would be 'Be quick in the beautiful', that is the Pāli idiom, but the meaning is to be quick in the doing of that which is morally beautiful. The word *kalyāṇa* is quite important, as in *kalyāṇa mitratā*. We usually translate it as 'spiritual friendship', but we could just as well speak of beautiful friendship, or lovely friendship. So we could translate this as 'Be quick to do what is lovely' – lovely in the moral sense.

In bringing out the fact that what is usually spoken of as the good is also the beautiful – not so much in the purely aesthetic sense, but in the sense of the morally beautiful – I am making the point that ethics is not a question of dos and don'ts. It is basically a question of being attracted towards an appealing ideal. That assumes that you have some sensitivity to what is *kalyāṇa*, that you are capable of being affected by it, responding to it. If someone has no sense of what is morally beautiful, perhaps he has to be restrained by dos and don'ts, but if one can simply feel the beauty of the ethical ideal, that is a much better way of going about things.

What exactly do we mean by moral beauty? Well, what do we mean by beauty? An important element is attractiveness. The beautiful appeals to us, and the morally beautiful appeals to our ethical sense; an action seems to us fine, noble, lovely, beautiful. One could think of Socrates' voluntary death for the sake of standing by the principles which he believed in as ethically beautiful. But why does it impress us in that sort of way? It is moving to read, but it also seems fitting, appropriate. One might say that that appropriateness has a sort of elegance. Sometimes mathematicians talk about an elegant mathematical demonstration. It has an element that appeals to an aesthetic sense, not just to the sense of truth. In the same way, the morally beautiful action doesn't just appeal to the moral sense; it also appeals to the aesthetic sense. It seems to be elegant, fit, appropriate. There is something in human nature that derives deep satisfaction from contemplating the good, a satisfaction that is almost aesthetic in nature, like the satisfaction that you get from great art, as though a great ethical action has an artistic value.

But even if we are attracted by the morally beautiful, we tend not to do it very quickly. Sometimes we have an impulse of generosity, but unless we act upon it immediately, we have second thoughts. Someone might be in need of money and your immediate response is to give them ten pounds, but if you don't give it on the spot, after a while you'll start thinking that maybe they could manage with five. If a further period elapses, you might think that they don't need it all that much, but you'd better give something, so you give two. You quickly perceive the moral beauty of the ethical action when it is suggested to you, but if you don't act upon that response, that can have fatal consequences. So you must be quick to do what you perceive as being the morally beautiful thing to do; otherwise all sorts of other forces and factors may arise and prevent you from carrying out your original intention.

And then, 'restrain the mind from evil'. More literally, that would be 'hinder the mind from evil'. The word is *nivaraṇa*, which is connected with the *nivaraṇas*, the hindrances; it means 'hinder', 'restrain', 'prevent'. This obviously suggests there is a tendency of the mind to go in the direction of evil that needs to be restrained. People are not wholly unskilful, but they certainly are not wholly skilful. It is very difficult to dismiss people as either good or bad, and your opinion about them may change from time to time.

Very often what happens is that the mind, in the sense of the reason, though reason has many good qualities, gets in the way. Your impulse may be towards a state of emotional positivity, but it's obscured or distorted by all sorts of wrong ideas as to what constitutes happiness, what constitutes the good, and how to go about realizing it. You start thinking that some external object can give it to you, so you go in pursuit of that external object. This is why the Buddhist term *kusala*, skilful, is so useful: it makes it clear that some element of intelligence is required to be what we usually call good. In Buddhism there is no such person as the holy fool of medieval Christianity.

'He who is sluggish in doing good, his mind delights in evil.' Here, the word for good is *puñña*. It is as though the mind needs to be occupied with something. Perhaps under certain circumstances the tendency to evil is stronger than the tendency to the good, so if you don't make a determined effort to do what is good, the chances are that your mind will get into the habit of delighting in evil. It's like the well-known proverb, 'Satan finds work for idle hands to do.' The best way of keeping out evil is to have something positive and good and inspiring and beautiful to do. It is like the small boy who hasn't anything to do or anyone to play with and gets bored, so he starts tormenting the dog.

The 'mind delights in evil' is a simple little phrase, but it represents a terrible thing. It is a very terrible thing for a human being to be in such a mental state that he takes pleasure in doing, saying, and thinking things which are evil, which do not conduce to his own development, happiness, and welfare, or to that of other people. Everybody must have had this experience of delighting in something which, at least in your better moments, you recognize as unskilful. Take a simple example: idle or malicious gossip. I think everybody at some time has taken pleasure in this, even though they know that it is very unskilful. So what is it that virtually compels us not only to engage in unskilful activities but to enjoy engaging in them? It suggests that there is a sort of underground fountain that is struggling to find an outlet. If you don't open a positive channel for it, it will find a negative channel. I mentioned the small boy tormenting the dog, but there are people who take delight in inflicting pain and suffering on other living beings on a quite enormous scale. You want to feel something, and that need is so great that if for some reason you cannot feel something positive, you would rather feel something negative than not feel anything at all, or you may mistakenly regard that negative feeling as something positive.

It isn't just a question of a neutral feeling of delight that can be attached either to skilful or to unskilful actions; the quality of the delight varies. People say that they feel exhausted by gossiping, whereas you wouldn't be exhausted after a delightful session of meditation or positive communication or reading. The delight that you experience in connection with skilful activities would seem to be nourishing, whereas the feeling of delight attached to the unskilful would seem to be just an ego-satisfaction. If you have had experience of both, you come to know that they are quite different things, even though we use the same word, delight.

In the case of the delight we take in doing good, it is much more wholehearted and genuine because it has the approval of our conscience. There are people who seem to take a wholehearted satisfaction in doing what is unskilful, but it is difficult to believe that they're in the same state of delight as someone who is performing a skilful action. They don't look as though they are. If you are doing what you know to be morally beautiful, you can feel that you are putting your shoulder to the wheel of Higher Evolution, that you are on the side of life, on the side of progress in the true sense. In this verse it is as though the Buddha is saying, 'Allow yourself to be attracted by the good, you are capable of it.'

People who get into negative states seem to work themselves into more and more negative states. You might try to help them, but it is like trying to extend your hand to someone who is being sucked under in a whirlpool; you may be dragged down with them if you are not careful. Sometimes it seems they are much happier dragging you down than allowing you to pull them up. They seem to derive a sort of satisfaction from their suffering, or at least from the point they are making. Sometimes the point is, 'Look what you have done to me, look how miserable I am, look what a terrible state I am in. I am in such a bad state that no one can help me.' The reasons for that no doubt go quite deep in their psychology. One has to be quite careful how one handles such people, otherwise you start getting disappointed or even angry that they are not responding to your efforts, which means that you have switched from the love mode to the power mode, assuming that you were operating in the love mode to begin with.[113]

If we are born to develop, presumably we'll be naturally attracted by whatever represents the next stage in our development, but it is quite important that ethical ideals should be embodied in aesthetically pleasing forms. This is a great feature of the best Buddha images, which embody the ideal of Enlightenment in an aesthetically attractive and inspiring human form. An example from Greek history is that of Alcibiades, who could always sway the Athenians. He had only to make a speech and they would follow him, because he was the tallest and the most handsome of the Athenians and exercised great influence over them, though unfortunately he didn't always give them good leadership. He seems to have been a rather slippery customer, even though he had been associated with Socrates in his younger days.

Ethical actions which are unskilful, unbeautiful, are sometimes performed in a superficially beautiful way. Even though they were doing things that were quite unbeautiful, their style could be beautiful, they could act with a sort of elegance, and that might take in someone whose perception of beauty didn't go very deep. For instance, there was the late Madame Chiang Kai-shek, the wife of Generalissimo Chiang Kai-shek. She was a very elegant lady, one of the famous Soong sisters. Apparently at a dinner party in New York, someone asked her how it was that she and her husband had no trouble with the opposition. Apparently she gave a beautiful smile and drew her elegant gloved hand across her throat. What she was saying was unethical, unbeautiful, and although she did it with a certain style, a beautiful gesture, it was quite hideous, and the fact that she did it with style made it worse because the glaring contrast between the ugliness of what she was saying and the superficial elegance with which she said it was so shocking.

Conversely, someone can do a beautiful action, but clumsily. It might be that you are in need of money, and someone comes and gives you some. They have no social graces, they do it inelegantly, but you can see the generosity there, so the beauty of the action shines through that lack of superficial elegance, that lack of manners or culture. In the same way, you should be able to see the ethical ugliness of an action manifesting itself despite the superficial charm. One mustn't be misled by someone's smart suit or beautiful car. The fact that someone has a beautiful Oxford accent shouldn't prevent one from perceiving that what he is saying is quite ugly, though that can be difficult to spot.

It seems to be important to instil early in life the idea that the good is the beautiful, that the ethical life is attractive and inspiring, not dull and depressing. You might even say, to use the current idiom, that it is fun to be good. Very often it doesn't sound like fun. When I was in Crete, we looked in quite a few antique shops and there were a lot of icons of saints of the Orthodox church for sale. It was amazing how grim and forbidding their features were. Their faces were long and thin and mournful, sharp, angular, frowning, disagreeable, as though they were suffering from theological indigestion. The corners of their mouths were turned down, and their lips were thin, and tightly pressed together.

No doubt there is an element of effort, even of suffering, in the spiritual life which needs to be taken into consideration, but it is, after all, only an element. Most of those saints were people whom one wouldn't like to meet on a dark night. There have been saints of another kind, like St Francis, who was by all accounts a joyful person, but joy is not the characteristic note of Christianity, despite their protestations. It is quite important in the case of Buddhism that whatever embodiments of our spiritual and ethical ideals we have around us are beautiful, that their form does justice to their content. I don't mean that we should prettify the ideal, but we should make sure that the genuine beauty of the ideal is allowed to manifest. This is the importance of heroes. In the lives and actions of heroes there is an element of nobility which appeals to people, especially when they are young, an element of heroism which is clearly of an ethical nature, at least in principle. The image of Siddhārtha when he was fasting conveys the impression that he was making a tremendous effort, but not that he was deliberately inflicting suffering upon himself. One feels that the suffering is incidental, not an end in itself. The Buddha made it clear that the suffering was not an integral part of the spiritual life. He said, 'Some have it hard all the time, others have it hard at the beginning, but not at the end, and vice versa and others who have an easy, pleasant time from the beginning to the end of the spiritual life.'[114] Well how fortunate they are.

It is not only a question of embodiments of the ethical ideal in wood and marble and metal; real live people embody it too. If you are officiating at a Buddhist centre, you are the leading embodiment of the ethical ideal, and a lot will depend on your smile or your frown. If someone comes along for the first time, and the first real live Buddhist that they see is a happy person, at once they will get the message that the Buddhist ideal is a happy, beautiful, attractive ideal. So one has to be extremely careful to make sure that one remains in a positive, healthy state, so that one does not convey the impression that Buddhists are tired, overworked, disagreeable people; otherwise, how can one expect other people to see the beauty of the ethical ideal that one is supposedly dedicated to?

> Should a man (once) do evil, let him not make a habit of it; let him not set his heart on it. Painful is the heaping up of evil. (117)

It is as though the Buddha is saying that anybody can make a mistake once, anyone can commit an unskilful action once, but you should be careful not to allow it to become a habit. It would seem to be a sort of rule that whatever you do, the fact that you have done it, even once, means that you have got a greater tendency to do it again. So if you do something once, you must be very careful – if it is an unskilful thing – that you don't do it again. It is very easy to slip into habits whether good or bad, skilful or unskilful, even with regard to simple things.

Suppose you had two cups of tea this morning at breakfast (assuming that you've never had tea at breakfast before), the chances are that tomorrow you'll have two cups again, and in a course of a week, a habit will have been confirmed. The chances are that if you come here tomorrow, you will sit in the same place you sat in today. It doesn't matter – it is a quite neutral thing – but if it is a question of skilful or unskilful, you have to be very careful the first time that you do anything to make sure it is a skilful thing to do. Once you have started doing something it is easy to continue. One finds this with writing. Don't bother about the fact that you have got a hundred pages to write. Just think in terms of doing one page today, and another page tomorrow, and in that way you will finish the hundred pages. You have only got to start and to keep on, to get into the habit of doing something. Human beings seem to be creatures of habit, so make sure that whatever habits you form are skilful ones that help you in your development. One sees this in the case of relationships. If you see someone once, you want to see them again, and if you see them a third time, the chances are that you will start seeing them regularly. So think very carefully the first time. Try to ascertain whether the habit that you're likely to get into is skilful or not.

You see the sequence: you do a thing once, then you make a habit of it, and then you set your heart upon it. The habit becomes confirmed. The fact that you do that thing becomes almost part of your identity. You are determined to do it. You don't want not to do it. And the last sentence reminds one of the consequences: 'Painful is the heaping up of evil.' Notice this term, 'heaping up', 'piling up'. By doing something unskilful and making a habit of it, then setting one's heart on it, one is heaping up unpleasant consequences for oneself.

But, let's consider this principle in positive rather than negative terms. Let's go on to the next verse:

Should a man (once) do good, let him make a habit of it; let him set his heart on it. Happy is the heaping up of good. (118)

It is often easier to change one's habits or to set up fresh habits after you have been away for a while and then come back into your original situation in some different capacity or just determined to do things differently. We all know that there is a resistance to doing something new. Once you have done it, it is quite easy. Do it two or three times and after that it is often plain sailing. The most difficult thing is to make the change in the first place. One can make quite dramatic changes if one is sufficiently determined. You may have had cornflakes for breakfast every day since you were a child, and if you have muesli tomorrow it may be difficult, but after a while you will feel as though you have had muesli for breakfast all your life. It is as simple as that. It just requires that little bit of determination to make the change. If it involves deep-seated resistances which start coming into operation, even resistances can be overcome. You have a greater depth than where they come from. People can change much more than they think they can: much more quickly, much more easily.

Things are connected; there can be little groups of habits, and if you change the leading one, a lot of other bad habits can be discarded at the same time. So the formation of habits is a very important thing. We cannot live without habits – otherwise we are constantly having to make decisions about all sorts of petty matters. You want to settle those things once and for all, so that you are able to do them without thinking about them and devote your thoughts to more important matters. So it is important to set up positive habits with regard to the time that you get up, when you do your meditation and for how long, what you have for breakfast, and so on. You don't want to have to endure agonies of indecision every breakfast time. Make up your mind once and for all. Even if you decide that it doesn't matter and you'll just reach out for whatever happens to be nearest, that is also a habit.

One must take care to avoid habit as an end in itself, as I once described one of the three fetters. One must constantly review one's habits. It is not sufficient reason for doing something that you have done it every day for the last forty days, or even ten years. You must constantly ask yourself, 'Are my habits helping me, are they functioning in a skilful way?' There is a tendency to keep up habits for the sake of keeping them up, because we derive comfort and security from them, so we need to keep our habits under review, and sometimes change them just for the sake of changing them, so that we don't become attached to them for their own sakes. Skilful habits are meant to help us to change, not to be hindrances to change, and we shouldn't hesitate to give them up if the larger interests of our personal development require it. A time may come when we have to be ready to drop any cherished or useful habit at the drop of a hat, and do something completely new and unexpected, though not too soon, otherwise we will be unsettled in a negative way. We need enough routine to be able to grow and develop, but not so much that we start settling down in a worldly, pseudo-spiritual way. Our spiritual community shouldn't start to become our home, to which we are attached in much the same way that one might be attached to a conventional home, and we resent ever being away from our community because it is so cosy and convenient. But it may take quite a few years to get into that sort of state of mind. For the time being one is concerned with settling down in one's spiritual community in a positive way and developing skilful habits and forming skilful friendships which become stronger and stronger.

I think at present we need an emphasis on the formation of skilful habits and in a sense settling down, and developing friendships on a long-term basis and pledging oneself to a particular centre and a particular community for several years. There has been so much moving around on the part of a number of people that they have not been able to put down roots anywhere. It is true that a rolling stone doesn't gather any moss, but the trouble is that it may not gather anything at all, and far from polishing itself by rolling around, may only chip a few more bits off.

One can see the value of forming positive skilful habits, at least provisionally, and certain habits may make it very convenient for you to lead your life, but they may make interaction with other people virtually impossible if you follow them so strictly that you won't drop them for anything or anyone, even in an emergency. That means that the habits have become ends in themselves. You may have developed the perfectly good habit of meditating every morning at seven o'clock, but if, just as you're going to enter the shrine-room someone staggers up bleeding and needing immediate attention, but you say, 'No, I have got to go and meditate,' and you go straight into the shrine-room and leave the injured person on the doorstep, you are making your admittedly skilful habit an end in itself, rather than allowing it to be overridden by other considerations. It isn't always easy to judge whether something is important enough for you to break your skilful habit for its sake, though there are cases where it is glaringly obvious. You must not be too open to disturbance, otherwise you end up not developing any habits at all, and a life without habits is a very difficult life indeed. A life with no regularities can only be a chaotic life, and I think that only a quite spiritually advanced person could stand a life of that kind.

Assuming that one's habits are at best a mixture of skilful and unskilful, the next step is to create habits that are only skilful. There is a further stage, a long way on, where one gets rid of even skilful habits, where one is able to act completely spontaneously according to the needs of the moment, but that isn't easy to do, and perhaps one shouldn't aim to do it immediately. What most people need to do now is form habits which are entirely skilful and keep them under review. For instance, you might have developed the good habit of getting up at six o'clock every morning, but if you have to stay up very late every night for valid reasons, getting up at six every morning may no longer be the best thing for you to do. A good habit is never an absolute; its goodness is relative to circumstances and to your present stage of development. But there is certainly an advantage in forming provisional good habits; then a lot of matters look after themselves. Our systems like rhythm. If you always went to bed at a different hour and got up at a different hour, it would have a jarring effect on your system. One can take advantage of that rhythm, developing positive habits and basing one's spiritual life upon a positive habitual programme, without allowing it to become rigid or an end in itself. You should be prepared to interrupt your programme for valid reasons, but they must be valid.

> As long as it bears no fruit, so long the evildoer sees the evil (he has done) as good. When it bears fruit (in the form of suffering), then he recognizes it as evil.
>
> As long as it bears no fruit, so long the good man sees the good (he has done) as evil. When it bears fruit (in the form of happiness), then he recognizes it as good. (119–20)

Here a very important principle is indirectly enunciated: that actions have consequences. It is as simple as that. One of our friends went up to Kalimpong to see Dhardo Rimpoche not so long ago, and asked him, perhaps a little naively, whether he thought that all the children being educated at his school would leave it with a sound understanding of Buddhism. Dhardo Rimpoche said that he would be quite satisfied if they left with an understanding of the fact that actions have consequences. This sums it up. If you understand that actions have consequences, you can act in a responsible manner. You cannot be an individual, cannot be truly mature, unless you realize that actions have consequences for yourself and other people and therefore that you should be careful of what you do, for your own sake and for the sake of other people. Very often people don't realize that. For instance, people driving recklessly, taking risks, overtaking vehicles in a foolhardy way, don't seem to realize that actions have consequences. This is an extreme example, but it holds good all along the line. It suggests the ability to look ahead, to exercise foresight, to think about the future, not to be simply overwhelmed by the present.

There is a difference between theoretical understanding and actual insight. You may think that by good luck or by chance you'll escape whatever consequences of your actions there might have been. Many people only realize that actions have consequences when they suffer. Very often the situation is so complex that you are unable to see what is producing what, what you're responsible for and what other people are responsible for. In order to understand what is going on, sometimes you have to simplify the situation, as you do when you go on solitary retreat. You may not know whether certain mental states of yours are the result of circumstances, external conditions, or of factors within you, so you remove yourself from your original circumstances, you go on solitary retreat, and then you find out whether your mental states are coming from without or within.

Some people only learn when they suffer, though the next verse envisages the opposite state of affairs, as we will see. Even if you mean well, you may not be sure that you are doing the right thing; it is only when you experience positive results that you can be sure. Our hold on this law of cause and effect, this principle that actions have consequences, isn't always very strong. Even those whose actions are quite skilful cannot be sure what is going to happen as a result. Sometimes it is like that with meditation. You may not be sure whether it is doing you any good, because you don't seem to be seeing changes in your level of consciousness. You peg away at it more or less out of blind faith. But after a while you do start perceiving, or other people start perceiving, that positive changes are taking place, and then you start feeling that meditation does work, that actions – in this case the action of meditating – do have consequences.

We may have difficulty in extrapolating ourselves into the future, and this is bound up with the weakness of our reflexive self-consciousness. I have made a general distinction between simple consciousness and reflexive consciousness, as it is sometimes called, or self-consciousness. Can you be aware of yourself in the future, experiencing the consequences of actions that you have done in the past, without reflexive consciousness? You cannot. If there is in you a preponderance of simple consciousness over reflexive consciousness, you will find it quite easy to live in the present, but you will find it very difficult to imagine yourself as living in the future and as experiencing then the consequences of what you are doing now. Only an individual can be ethical, an individual by definition being, among other things, one in whom there is reflexive consciousness as distinct from simple consciousness. If our reflexive consciousness was sufficiently developed, we would have a genuine apprehension that actions have consequences, and we could not refuse to see that fact, but we are able to close our eyes to it because our apprehension of it is so weakly developed that it is hardly more than a theoretical consideration. We lack imagination.

The drive for satisfying an instinct can be stronger than the desire to develop the imaginative faculty. This applies to the spiritual life generally; there is a force that is holding us or even pulling us back all the time. As the first verse makes clear, 'He who is sluggish in doing good, his mind delights in evil.' This doesn't mean that we are evil in a theological or metaphysical sense, but we have to reckon with the fact that the tendency to act unskilfully is very powerful, and sometimes we deliberately close our eyes to possible consequences. That also means that we don't see them clearly enough to begin with, otherwise we couldn't close our eyes to them. If our sight amounted to insight, there would be certain things we just could not do, however strongly we were tempted, because we would see their consequences so clearly. A further stage would be where you saw the undesirability of doing them so strongly that you could not even desire to do them.

This is why it is very important to be able to see the ethical ideal in positive terms, so that there is something that at least begins to attract you strongly. It is not just a question of restraining yourself from the unskilful, but allowing yourself to be drawn towards the skilful, seeing it as attractive and appealing and desirable. There were two phrases that we didn't go into very much in the previous verses: 'painful is the heaping up of evil', and 'happy is the heaping up of good'. When you reap the positive consequences of your skilful actions, that can be exhilarating, but until that has happened, you can be doubtful whether you are on the right path at all with respect to meditation, or study, or the spiritual life generally. Sometimes it seems dull and dry and nothing much is happening, and you start wondering whether you've been a fool. If you hadn't got involved with the spiritual life, you could have had your own house by this time, and a car, and all the rest of it, and instead of that you have spent the last two or three years slogging away in a co-op. You might wonder whether it was worth it, whether you have benefited from it at all. You may have an intermediate period where you have serious doubts about everything, because the great heap of good that you have been piling up all this time hasn't yet come into view.

The spiritual life is a happy life, but the struggle to get into the spiritual life isn't necessarily happy. It is a question of defining exactly what one means by the spiritual life. In the *Dhammapada*, the Buddha's disciples are represented as saying, 'Happily indeed we live, we who call nothing our own.'[115] But do we call nothing our own? And if we do call this our own and that our own, how can we expect to be happy in that way? The spiritual life is indeed a happy life, but are you leading the spiritual life? You may be *trying* to lead it, but that is different. It's difficult to imagine within a Buddhist context someone genuinely leading a spiritual life and being miserable. They might face difficulties, and even undergo suffering, but they wouldn't be miserable, they would be basically happy and content.

There is a formal aspect of mindfulness or awareness called 'mindfulness of purpose' – that is to say, awareness of the reason why you are doing something – and this is an integral part of awareness or mindfulness in general. It is not enough to be aware of what you are doing; you must also be aware of why you are doing it. If you are walking along the road, it is good to be aware of yourself as walking, but you must also be aware of where you are walking to, and to what purpose, because you could be quite mindful of the process of walking, and yet be walking somewhere to do something quite unskilful. Likewise, you can overeat mindfully in the sense of being aware of every mouthful, but if you are aware of why you are eating, which is to maintain health and strength so that you can lead the spiritual life, that awareness of purpose would stop you from overeating. It is not enough simply to be aware of what you are doing; you must ask yourself, 'Why am I doing this?' And the reasons for doing it may change, so you have to keep that activity under review.

If you are doing something simply for the sake of the reward that you get out of it, one could say that you are not really involved with the doing of that thing. Quite often people do a job just for the sake of a wage packet, but if you are working in a co-op, your work is your life. You are giving everything you've got to it because you believe in right livelihood, and in the whole situation in which your right livelihood takes place. If someone says, 'If you work extra this afternoon, I'll give you extra money', the whole co-op situation has been undermined. You are giving what you can and taking what you need, that is the principle in a co-op.

It's a bit like meditating to achieve a positive state of mind, rather than just meditating, though in a sense the distinction is an artificial one, because meditation *consists* in that positive state of mind. If you say that you are meditating in order to achieve a positive state of mind, that is no more than saying that you are meditating in order to meditate, because the positive state of mind is not extraneous to the process of meditation in the same way that money and the goods that money can buy are extraneous to the work that you do. Otherwise it would be as though your recompense for doing the work is being given more work to do, but clearly it is not like that. You are not committed to doing something when your reason for doing it is extraneous to the activity itself, whether you are doing it for money or reputation, or a sort of ego-satisfaction.

I believe that everybody in the long run does what they want to do, not that what you want to do is necessarily always pleasurable in a superficial sense. You may want to write, but you might not find it easy. It may be a struggle just to put down a few words on paper, but even though it might be very difficult, even painful at times, you accept that that is what you deeply want to do, and what, despite the difficulty, you most enjoy doing. But doing things that you find painful out of a sense of duty to which you don't subscribe is a different kind of situation.

If all this sounds like common sense, quite a bit of Buddhism is just common sense. That is why the Buddha said, 'Let any reasonable man come to me and I will teach him the Dharma.'[116] He doesn't say that the person has to be half-Enlightened already. Let him just be reasonable, that is all that is required. Sensible might be a better word than reasonable. What you need is a sensible person to talk to.

> Do not underestimate evil, (thinking) 'It will not approach me.'
> A water-pot becomes full by the (constant) falling of drops of water. (Similarly) the spiritually immature person little by little fills himself with evil. (121)

Do not underestimate the power of evil. Do not underestimate your tendency to form habits. Don't think, 'What does it matter even if it is unskilful? It is just this once.' It is very tempting to make an exception 'just this time', but if you do something unskilful once, the chances are that you will do it again and again. In that way you will, in the words of the *Dhammapada*, fill yourself with evil. You will just be a mass of unskilfulness. So don't think that you can afford to allow exceptions. You shouldn't think, 'Oh well, if I go out and get a bit drunk one night, it won't make all that much difference', because you might do it again the next week, and the next. You might allow yourself to forget that you are likely to do it again and develop a habit. You may believe that it is only going to be this once, though in your heart of hearts you may know very well that you are setting up a habit, and perhaps you even intend to. You bluff yourself as well as other people – usually it is easier to bluff yourself than other people. One doesn't want to go to extremes; a strong-minded person might be able to do it 'just this once', but you would have to be very clear and sure about what you were doing. Don't underestimate evil; don't underestimate the power of habit; and don't think that you are the exception: that rules are all right for other people but in your case it doesn't matter. There is that tendency too. We underestimate evil, and we also underestimate good, as the next verse makes very clear.

> Do not underestimate good, (thinking) 'It will not approach me.' A water-pot becomes full by the (constant) falling of drops of water. (Similarly) the wise man little by little fills himself with good. (122)

We are sometimes discouraged by the fact that our admittedly feeble efforts to pursue the spiritual life don't seem to be bearing much fruit. It is a very gradual process, usually; there aren't any dramatic breakthroughs or overwhelming revelations. You aren't snatched up into the seventh heaven; you remain with your feet planted firmly on the earth, or even sunk in the mud. You need to constantly remind yourself that it is a slow and gradual process of constantly repeated increments of the good. But good is accumulated. If you go on performing skilful actions on however humble a scale, you will in the end transform yourself. Maybe people you haven't seen for years will notice the difference, even if you don't.

This is one of the benefits of spiritual friendship. A friend may tell you that five years ago he was neurotic and miserable and he nearly committed suicide, and you see that he must have changed because he is in such a positive state now. The spiritual life must work, because it has changed him. One starts to see that the methods like meditation, and communication and institutions like spiritual communities have an effect for large numbers of people. To give a simple example, I can look back on people who not so many years ago were so nervous that they couldn't stand up in public and speak even a few words, and they are now giving beautiful lectures on the Dharma. There has been such a change, such an increase not only of knowledge of the Dharma, but of self-confidence. People who were very scattered, one sees becoming more concentrated; people who were negative, one sees becoming emotionally positive. Over a period of five or ten years big changes can take place, even though the individual steps might have been almost unnoticeable.

On a three-month ordination retreat sometimes one sees the change taking place from one day to the next, especially from the day before people are ordained to the day after. If one hadn't seen it, one might hardly have believed that such a change could take place. The work hasn't all been done in those twenty-four hours; there has been a build-up. But it is as though the change becomes manifest, and when people have new names that seems to underline the fact that they are new people, or at least one experiences them very differently from how they were before. So one can change, sometimes more quickly than one would have believed possible. A lot depends on circumstances and conditions. A positive environment helps; a lot can happen even on a weekend retreat. Dr Johnson quoted a poem about someone who had been killed as a result of a fall from his horse: 'Between the stirrup and the ground,

Mercy I asked, mercy I found.'[117] Just at that instant of falling, his whole mental attitude had changed from being an irreligious to a religious man; he had been converted in that instant, in the face of death. That sort of thing is possible, ignoring the Christian context and language, but taking the principle. You can change instantly, even dramatically, though it may require exceptional existential circumstances.

After a meditation you need to be quiet for a while, because sometimes the results do not come immediately. You might have been struggling to get concentrated, but even after you have come out of the shrine-room the momentum set up by that effort continues, and if you stay quiet you may start experiencing that. So after meditation don't jump into things, if you can help it. I am quite sure that when you go on retreat you start experiencing the results of things that you have set in motion earlier on but whose consequences you were prevented from experiencing due to unfavourable conditions. You have put effort in and that will bear fruit, if not now, then later.

Sometimes one gets discouraged, thinking, 'Well, what is the use of half an hour of meditation every morning and maybe half an hour in the evening, and a bit of study now and then, and a bit of communication? I'm not getting anywhere.' But the fact is that you are doing it every day of every week, every week of every year, and it is having an effect. You are filling yourself with good, little by little, and sooner or later, especially as circumstances become more favourable, that will be manifest. It is encouraging if we get quick results. Nothing is so encouraging as a good experience in meditation. But people can very quickly forget their experiences. That is one of the reasons some spiritual teachers recommend the keeping of a spiritual diary, because you can browse through it during a dry or miserable period, and remind yourself of your positive experiences.

Also, we don't always appreciate the progress made by other people. We have to be careful to see other people as they are, not as they were, keep open to the possibility that they have changed, and be willing to acknowledge that and treat them differently. If you are always expecting that people will do foolish things, the chances are that they will, but if you manage to convey to them that you are expecting something good from them, the chances are that they will rise to the occasion. Your feeling must be genuine, not just a ploy. You mustn't say, 'Oh, I am sure you would never do such and such a thing.' It mustn't be a species of emotional blackmail. You must have a genuine confidence in that person's potentiality, and that can be very encouraging and inspiring. It is a question of emphasizing the positive.

It is also important not to underestimate the facilities at one's disposal. Sometimes I think that within the FWBO people don't appreciate the facilities they have got, and thus don't make full use of them – using the word, 'facilities' in the widest sense. One has got a healthy human body and one is young; these are extraordinary advantages. One has come into contact with the Dharma, one has leisure, one is free from painful disease, one has strength, one has spiritual friends, one has facilities for study and for practising meditation. What more could one want? Sometimes we forget how rare these things are in the world. Think how easy it is today to get hold of the scriptures translated into one's own language. A few hundred years ago literacy wasn't general, there was no such thing as printing, and books were very rare, so the chances of getting hold of a book and being able to read it was very remote indeed. Nowadays, some people seem to think of leisure almost as a curse, but that seems strange. They have got leisure, which they could use creatively. The unemployed, or the potentially unemployed, don't seem to have woken up to that fact yet. They have got a wonderful opportunity. Here they are, being supported by the state in a way that people in many parts of the world would regard as lavish. They are not even being paid to look for a job, because they know that there are no jobs.[118] They are being paid to do anything they please. You could say that it is the greatest achievement of our civilization that we have got three million people being supported to do whatever they want to do. I don't know much about economics, in fact I probably don't know anything at all about it, but it does occur to me that under modern conditions full employment may be an impossibility. Maybe full employment is only possible when you have got an enormous market which you are exploiting, so if there is no market for you to exploit, maybe full employment is not possible for everybody all over the world, and maybe the Western industrialized countries have reached a higher level of development, economically speaking, whereby they can support several million people who are unemployed, but potentially occupied doing higher things. This has happened in the past on a more modest scale, because countries like India and Burma and Tibet have supported masses of monks in monasteries, who were unemployed in the sense of being non-productive in the economic sense, but were supported to meditate and study and maintain the higher culture of that civilization. Should we not feel blessed that our economic system is so strong that we can support three million people who don't have to work and pay them to live fairly decently? Far from apologising for it, we should be proud of it. This is what civilization is all about, that you can support people who have sufficient leisure to be able to devote themselves to higher pursuits, and can thereby have an extremely healthy and positive effect on the whole community. Maybe we Buddhists should inculcate this point of view and even make it a feature of our advertising: 'Unemployment is an opportunity. Learn to meditate.'

A lot of the people who are living, as we say, on the dole think that they are very hard done by, and that they want more money for more material goods, but people should realize that by world standards they are quite well off, they have got their basic needs of life, and they should build on that basis in cultural and spiritual terms, not in terms of getting more in the way of material goods and services. You are not a human being if you are not working on something, if you are not putting your energies into something, if you are not growing and developing, but the economic side of it is secondary. Even if you can get a particular job, is that job worthy of the efforts of a human being? You don't just want a job, you want right livelihood.

> As a merchant (travelling) with a small caravan and much wealth avoids a dangerous road, or as one desirous of life shuns poison, so should one keep clear of evil. (123)

This is pretty straightforward. The image is of the journey. The merchant travelling with a small caravan through the desert avoids a dangerous road. This perhaps suggests that when you are travelling on the journey of life with your little load of merit, you have got to be on the watch for the unexpected attack. So what in our own experience corresponds to this ambush that may be sprung at any moment? Logically one ought to be always expecting to be ambushed by Māra. But what is it that lulls one into a sense of false security? You start forgetting, or you may be in a quite positive state and maybe feeling exhilarated, and because of that you become a bit unmindful, or sometimes the unexpected can just strike you. It suggests that one should always be on one's guard. You are like 'a merchant (travelling) with a small caravan and much wealth'. 'Much' is a relative term, but it is quite a lot so far as you are concerned. You have accumulated quite a bit of merit, and you don't want to dissipate it.

One of the things that can dissipate merit more quickly than anything else is a sudden outburst of anger. Quite a lot of people feel quite shattered after such an experience, as though whatever merit they have accumulated, whatever emotional positivity they have built up over years, is dissipated in minutes. People coming off retreat find the same sort of thing. Someone wrote me a letter recently saying that they came off retreat in a quite positive state, went back to their own centre and community, but almost immediately, for reasons that they couldn't understand, started behaving in a foolish way, and within a day all their emotional positivity was blown. That can happen. You need constant mindfulness to safeguard your gains because until you reach the point of no return, the point of Stream Entry, they can be dissipated at any moment by apparently quite trivial things. If you get into an argument with somebody, if you are not very careful to watch every step in the argument and everything that you say, you can find yourself getting into a very negative state. The discussion develops into a rather nasty argument and the argument can end in disagreement and even in blows. Sometimes you are at a loss to understand in retrospect at exactly what point things started to go wrong. So you have to watch quite carefully. There are thousands of Māras lurking in ambush all over the place.

Next, 'as one desirous of life shuns poison, so should one keep clear of evil'. Obviously if you are desirous of life you will shun poison, but here are people desirous of happiness and not shunning evil. If you want to be happy, if you want to progress, shun evil, in the same way that someone who is desirous of life shuns poison. Evil is poison. It may taste very nice, but the effects aren't so pleasant. One has to realize that unskilful mental states, unskilful actions, and unskilful words are dangerous things. They are going to have a dangerous effect, a mortal effect. Ethically speaking, spiritually speaking, you are going to do yourself real harm.

> If one has no wound in one's hand one may (safely) handle poison. The unwounded hand is not affected by poison. (Similarly) no evil befalls him who does no wrong. (124)

This seems pretty obvious, but there are possibilities of misunderstanding lurking in the expression 'handling poison'. The only way you can avoid being harmed by evil is to have nothing to do with it. You might expect the Buddha to say that just as 'if one has no wound in one's hand one may (safely) handle poison', likewise, if you reach a certain spiritual state, you can do those things which might be unethical in the case of less developed people. But the Buddha doesn't draw that conclusion. He goes on to say, '(Similarly) no evil befalls him who does no wrong.' It is a slightly unexpected twist. In India, there is in some spiritual circles an antinomian tendency; that is, if you reach a certain level of spiritual development you can act either in what appears to be an ethical or an unethical way, you have gone beyond good and evil. But the Buddha is denying that you can go beyond good and evil in that way.

The English term 'evil' can denote either an unskilful mental state or an unpleasant experience of suffering. The fact that no evil befalls him who does no wrong does not mean that the innocent person will never have to suffer, even unjustly, but that suffering will not affect your mental state. Evil may befall you outwardly, you may suffer, you may even be killed, but the fact that you are doing no evil means that your mental state remains skilful. You are suffering evil but not doing evil; that is the important thing. This point is discussed in the Socratic dialogues, in which Socrates maintains that the good man cannot in a sense suffer, because his mind remains inviolate. He can only suffer externally, which is in a sense not suffering at all.

But if someone treats you badly, they can change your mental state, and if you are not of a sufficiently high level of development, their persistence can gradually wear you down. However much you may try to keep your temper, you may lose it and explode. So we have to be very careful about what sort of situations and people we allow ourselves to get involved with, because people can affect us quite deeply in a positive or a negative manner. People can get at us, and even destroy or at least weaken our positivity for the time being, like robbers lying in ambush, or like pseudo-friends who are supposedly travelling with us as part of the caravan, but only so that they can rob us.

When you get to a certain level of spiritual development, that sort of attack will not affect you in the same painful way. If someone was to beat you, you would feel it, but you wouldn't react. We are told that the Buddha suffered physical pain when a splinter of the boulder rolled down on him by Devadatta pierced his foot, and he suffered physical pain when he had an attack of dysentery shortly before his death, but it did not affect his mental state.[119] A less developed person, for example when being berated by another person, may be able to refrain from reacting for a time, but in the end they will retaliate. If you are not spiritually developed your mental state is in the power of other people, so you have to be extremely careful with whom you associate. You may know that you can take one glass of wine without its affecting your mental state, if you take two it is going to start affecting it, and if you take three glasses you will have no control over your mental state, so you must take steps to ensure that you never reach that third glass. Similarly, it is in your control with whom you associate, but once you are in the company of a certain kind of person – perhaps someone you know will irritate you – you have surrendered your mental state into their keeping, so you should avoid such a situation. Spiritual friendship becomes all the more important, because your spiritual friends are people to whom you can entrust your mental state. It is not that people affect us just a bit. Sometimes they can affect us totally. They can rob us of our skilful mental state and replace it with something very different. So if you find that the company of a certain person perpetually rubs you up the wrong way, it is best if you are a beginner in the spiritual life to avoid that person. The same applies to situations in general. Run away as quickly as possible! It may be escapism but it is a healthy, skilful escapism. Don't imagine yourself to be a sort of spiritual hero who can battle on. Before long you will be on your knees and defeated, and a dead hero is of no use to anybody. 'He who fights and runs away lives to fight another day'! In spiritual life as in biological existence survival is the important thing – spiritual survival in this case.

One can imagine a situation in which someone who is a Stream Entrant is in a thoroughly unsuitable situation. He will not lose his skilful mental state, but the conflict may be so great that he may die. He won't succumb mentally or spiritually, but he may lose his will to live. Even if he is spiritually positive and incapable of falling back, he may not feel it worthwhile to go on living under those circumstances. If he loses the will to live, the chances are that he will die, but that doesn't matter because for him the only point of going on living would be to go on developing even further. If that has become difficult, why continue to live? What cannot happen is that he falls back mentally or spiritually. Anything can happen, but not that.

Even though you are in a highly skilful mental state, that doesn't mean that only pleasant experiences are going to befall you. This is where theists sometimes get into difficulties, because they think that God is looking after everything, and protecting the righteous. When something unpleasant befalls such a person, say when they are bereaved, they are likely to say, 'Why should God do this to me? I have led such a good life. I go to church every Sunday. I have never harmed anybody. I have been a teetotaller all my life, I have been faithful to my wife,' – as if living a good life is a sort of insurance policy against accidents. But the web of existence is so complicated that sometimes the good also have to suffer. Perhaps you will get your just deserts in the long run, but at least you can be sure that if you are leading a genuinely ethical and spiritual life, your mental state will not be affected by what befalls you. The main thing is that you preserve your own skilful mental and spiritual state. You shouldn't need the satisfaction of a reward to look forward to. In a sense, virtue is its own reward, or at least that is how you should feel about it.

The law of cause and effect is there, but it works itself out in a complex way. It may or may not be that in ten thousand years' time in some future existence you will be exactly recompensed for what is happening to you now, but you may have forgotten all about the sufferings of the present existence by that time, and have no time to bother with trivial recompenses. It is rather like, on the ordinary level, if you have a minor accident and there is some small sum due to you from the insurance people, it may take a long time coming through, and maybe a couple of years later you will get a letter and a small cheque, but by then you may have forgotten all about the little trouble that you had years earlier. You can find sufficient recompense in virtue itself. Otherwise, it is like expecting to be paid for meditating. The fact that you meditate and that you enjoy it, and that you get into a higher mental state, is surely enough in itself. Under the law of karma, a recompense may eventually come, but if you are genuinely into the spiritual life, you will not be concerned with recompense other than that of the experience of the spiritual life itself. You won't be concerned with recompense in the form of material blessings, for example.

The next verse approaches the matter from the other end: not from the point of view of the innocent person whom the evil befalls, but from that of the evil person who offends the innocent person:

> Whoever offends against an innocent man, one who is pure and faultless, to that spiritually immature person the evil (he has committed) comes back like fine dust thrown against the wind. (125)

So what sort of situation does this verse envisage? You cannot harm another. You are doing harm to yourself. Well, in a sense you can harm others, but it depends on their degree of purity and faultlessness. You cannot harm a Stream Entrant in any way. You can inflict physical suffering upon him, even perhaps a certain amount of mental suffering, but you cannot harm him in the sense of interrupting his spiritual development. In the case of a lesser person, you can hold him back by inducing unskilful mental states in him, but you cannot do that in the case of one who is truly pure and faultless. In that case, the evil that you have been trying to do to him will come back to you. Even in the case of being able to influence and affect the mental state of another person in an unskilful way, that evil will come back as well. Perhaps it will come back doubly because you have succeeded in your evil attempt and that is even worse than attempting and failing. It is a terrible responsibility to bear, not only to be in an unskilful mental state yourself, but trying to induce unskilful mental states in others.

One is reminded of that episode of the Buddha's encounter with Tālapuṭa. Tālapuṭa was an actor manager in the Buddha's day, who approached him and said, 'I have heard there is a tradition that we actors, when we die, go to the heaven of the laughing gods, because during our lifetime we make people laugh.' The Buddha asked him not to press him on this point, but Tālapuṭa did press him, and in the end the Buddha said, 'No, actors go to hell when they die, because, themselves subject to greed, hatred, and delusion, they induce mental states of greed, hatred and delusion in other people through their acting.'[120] This wouldn't be true for all actors, no doubt, but it is true that quite a lot of popular entertainers induce states of greed, hatred, and delusion in other people, and this is a very terrible thing to do. If you become aware that you are in that sort of mental state, like a person with an infectious disease you should isolate yourself from other people and not spread your mental state. Sometimes people almost deliberately spread it, and that is the height, or rather the depth, of unskilfulness, the exact opposite of the bodhisattva, who wants to share his skilful mental state with as many beings as possible. The person concerned may genuinely believe that he is doing good, but that only makes things worse. What about people who perpetrate sick jokes? I cannot help regarding those Monty Python films as quite unskilful, for example. Some people might argue that such things give people an outlet for their unskilful mental states, but does it mean that the unskilful mental state is discharged and you are freed from it and can rise above it? No, what it usually means is that you have indulged in it and it has become, if anything, stronger than it was before. People who produce and direct and act in and write scripts for films have a lot to answer for.

But how can humorous films be unskilful? It depends what you're humorous about. If you make a joke of violence, that is the height of unskilfulness, because you are suggesting that violence doesn't matter, it is just a joke. You are finding pleasure in the contemplation of the suffering of other living beings, even though only as depicted on the screen. If you are not careful, the transition from the screen to real life, especially as what appears on the screen is so life-like, can be very easy. Even things like cartoons make violence funny. You have to be careful about any sort of humour that is based on cynicism or ridicule because of the negative emotional element that is involved. I am sure that there is such a thing as innocent humour, but perhaps it is significant that it seems very rare. Humour only too often seems to have a streak of ill nature. It is always at somebody's expense, putting somebody down. Maybe humour is one of those ambushes where the unskilful is lurking. It is a rather unfair way of getting at someone, because if he objects, you say, 'Oh, can't you take a joke?' In the same way you are allowed to get away with a cynical remark because it's a joke, but the point that is being made may be deeply negative. The nature of humour requires investigation. Freud wrote a book on the joke, and it seems as though the joke represents a sort of energy release, but it can be under negative circumstances. You can take pleasure in somebody else's suffering.

On one occasion the Buddha said, according to the Pāli canon, 'Laughter which shows the teeth is madness. If you have cause to show your pleasure, it is enough to smile.'[121] Maybe he was thinking of those hearty guffaws which are not very elegant. But you can often tell what people are laughing about from the quality of the laugh. A laugh in response to a dirty joke is quite different from the laugh when it is just innocent fun, not at anybody's expense. So often there is an element of near sadism in a lot of our laughter. Here again, it is an ambush-type situation. You are not necessarily in a positive state because you are laughing; it depends what you are laughing at and how you are laughing. So watch how you react next time a person tells a joke; maybe it is not very funny if you think about it, or shouldn't be funny.

> Some (beings) arise (by way of conception) in the womb. Evildoers
> are born in a state of woe. Those who do good go to heaven.
> Those who are free from defilements become utterly 'Cool'. (126)

Presumably by 'womb' is meant the human womb. This verse suggests that if you are born as a human being, it is because your karma is rather mixed. You seem to have four classes of beings: those whose karma is mixed, both good and evil; those whose karma is evil, who have committed unskilful actions; those whose karma is good, those who have committed skilful actions; and those whose karma is neither good nor bad, nor a mixture of both, but neither, in the sense of higher, something that transcends karma altogether. But the more basic principle still is that actions have consequences. If one doesn't want to think in terms of heaven and hell, at least one has to think in terms of skilful actions having positive consequences, unskilful actions having negative consequences, and those actions which are utterly skilful or positive having no reactive consequences at all, but only cumulative or creative effects. The fourth kind of person goes beyond both good and evil, from good to greater good, up the spiral.

We have to translate this line *parinibbanti anāsavā* rather clumsily, and Buddhadatta translates it as 'The undefiled ones become extinct', which introduces endless misunderstandings. The goal of Buddhism is to become extinct? Well! It would be more correct to say 'transcendentalized' because the Pāli word is a verb, not a noun. If you say 'attain Nirvāṇa', you weaken it because you separate Nirvāṇa as a static goal from the process of 'its' attainment which the text doesn't do. 'Those who become free from the *āsavas*' is a very clumsy paraphrase – they 'nirvanize'. They ascend the spiral. It could also be translated 'the unbiased nirvanize' – to coin another rather clumsy phrase.

If you want to study a text seriously you need to be able to consult the original, or at least to know what the key terms in the original are. If you knew no Pāli at all and you read 'The undefiled ones become extinct', would you be able to guess from that that the word in the original was Nirvāṇa as a verb? No, you'd just take it that Buddhism teaches extinction as the goal. Some early translations of the *White Lotus Sūtra* speak of 'extinct Buddhas', and then the 'extinct' Buddhas appear on the scene and speak! They're dead but they won't lie down! It's not surprising that non-Buddhists – even relatively sympathetic ones – think that as a Buddhist you believe that the goal of the spiritual life is a state of the extinction not only of suffering, but of life itself, existence itself, that your goal is a void in that sense. And when they come across *śūnyatā* translated as 'the void' it becomes perfectly obvious to them that Buddhism is a philosophy of the Void, of nothing, nihilistic.

> Not in the sky, nor in the midst of the sea, nor yet in the clefts of the mountains, nowhere in the world (in fact) is there any place to be found where, having entered, one can abide free from (the consequences of) one's evil deeds. (127)

This verse states the inexorability of the law of karma, but what does that mean? How is it that one can't escape from the effects of one's deeds, good or bad? Well, is the deed separable from you? If you act differently, you become different. Your actions of body, speech, and mind are not detachable from you. It is not that you remain in the middle of them all and they are extraneous, just as the branches of a tree are extraneous to the trunk. You don't remain unaffected by what you do, because you *are* what you do, and everything that you do modifies your being – maybe not at once, but in the long run, if you perform certain actions a sufficient number of times. There is a very good example of this in Oscar Wilde's novel *The Picture of Dorian Gray*.[122] I always regard Wilde as a very moral writer, and this story is about a handsome young man who wished to remain always handsome and was granted that wish. But the changes brought about in his appearance by his actions all registered on his portrait, so while he remained even after fifteen or twenty years the same carefree, handsome, innocent-looking young man, the features of the portrait changed and in the end became hideous and repulsive. That is what happens. Your actions affect you, your thoughts affect you. You cannot escape from the results of your actions because you cannot escape from yourself.

That is not the whole of it, because the fact that you are a changed person means that things affect you differently from how they would have done if you hadn't done or thought those thoughts. But we need not see the law of karma as something operating external to us, like the police. You *are* karma. It is not that the recompense is outside of you, waiting to pounce. It is there with you all the time, it is another aspect of the action itself, because it is changing you, it is having an effect upon you. How can you escape the consequences of your actions, wherever you may go? You carry yourself with you. So how can you ever not be rewarded for the good that you do? The good is its own reward in the sense that by that good action you have modified your being in a positive manner. What greater reward could there be? Your actions, good and bad, are all that you can take with you.

I remember seeing during the war a staging of a ballet of a medieval morality play called *Everyman* which illustrates this beautifully. The story is that Everyman, the hero of the story, is at the point of death. Death, God's messenger, has summoned Everyman to go on a journey to be judged. In the play, Everyman goes from one person to another desperately seeking someone to accompany him. He goes to his kinsmen, but they can't accompany him; he goes to his friends, but they can't accompany him. His wealth can't accompany him. He discovers there is only one thing that can go with him, and that is his good deeds, so he looks around for his good deeds and he cannot find them. 'Good Deeds' are personified as a female character. He reaches a point where he exclaims, 'My Good Deeds, where art thou?' And a faint voice comes from below the stage and says, 'Here lie I close in the ground, your deeds have me sore bound, that I can neither stand nor stir.' So he hastens to undo all the ropes in which he has tied himself. It is powerfully dramatized in this way, that only your good deeds can go with you, or your bad deeds, as the case may be, because they *are* you. We speak of our actions as though they are separate from us, like our house or our children or our money, but they are not. They are us. We cannot but take them with us, and that is all that we can take with us, wherever we go. This medieval morality play was written by some anonymous monk in the Middle Ages,[123] but in some ways it is a remarkable anticipation of Buddhist teaching. It doesn't bring in God and all that. It isn't especially Christian; if it was, Everyman wouldn't bother about taking his good deeds with him, he'd just get a papal indulgence to take along, and make sure that he had had the Last Sacraments. That would dispense with any necessity for good deeds. But it's like Lady Macbeth trying to wash the bloodstains from her hands: 'Out, out damned spot'. You would have to cut out a piece of your own flesh, because you have done the action, it is your action, it adheres to you, it is part of you. This is one of the basic teachings of Buddhism, that you are your actions. Actions are not stuck on to you from the outside. You cannot shake them off. They are not just yours, even; they are you.

The last verse is slightly different:

> Not in the sky, nor in the midst of the sea, nor yet in the clefts of mountains, nowhere in the world (in fact) is there any place to be found where, having entered, one will not be overcome by death. (128)

Do people try to escape death in the same way that they try to escape from the consequences of their own actions? Do people think that they *can* escape death, obviously not consciously, but in some other way? When you are young death seems quite remote, especially when people who are older than you are still going strong. You may only start thinking seriously about it when the majority of your contemporaries have passed on. But the fact that people who are older than you are still alive is no guarantee that you are going to be alive even tomorrow, whatever the statistics might suggest. There is no refuge from death, as the verse is saying, and you will have to face it one day, whether in a palace or a hovel, in sickness or in health.

I have found that quite a lot of very old people don't mind dying. It is as though your will to live fades away after a certain age, and you just carry on from day to day. I know several people in their eighties and nineties who say quite cheerfully, 'Well, I don't know if I'm going to live till tomorrow, but I'll just carry on.' They don't seem to be bothered by it at all, and this seems perfectly natural. I don't think it is just that they know that it is going to happen. I think that there has been an actual change in their being; they have withdrawn from full participation in the world, they don't have any ambitions left. They just accept that they are going to die, in an almost animal-like way, but nonetheless in a positive way.

At the end of your life you can afford to speak the truth, because, after all, there are not going to be any consequences. You can say things that you hadn't dared to say before. What prevented you from saying them? Fear, ultimately the fear of death. But now you are dying, what is there to fear? You can say what you like. No one can come back at you, no one can punish you, you are going to elude their grasp. So sometimes people do speak the truth on their deathbed, if not before. Very old people are sometimes much more outspoken than younger people, because they have nothing to gain, nothing to lose. Extreme old age, assuming one is in good health, can give a sort of freedom.

Death is the paradigm of the inescapable situation. There are lots of situations that we would like to avoid if we could. You can put off an unpleasant experience like going to the dentist or having to give someone bad news, but you have to face death whether you like it or not. Death represents the archetypal unpleasant situation which many people aren't willing to face, even though very old people seem to reconcile themselves to facing it, perhaps by not thinking about it very much. You might even look forward to death as a quite interesting experience to find out what it is like, having heard so much about it and yet knowing so little.

# AUSPICIOUS SIGNS

A seminar on the *Maṅgala Sutta* held at Broomhouse Farm in May 1976

Those present: Sangharakshita, Lokamitra, Sagaramati, Mark Barrett (later ordained as Ratnajyoti, later named Maharatnajyoti), Gary Hennessey (later ordained as Ratnaguna), Richard Hutton (later ordained as Padmavajra), Graham Steven (later ordained as Harshaprabha).

## Introduction

SANGHARAKSHITA: First of all, about the title. Hare translates the '*maṅgala*' in *Maṅgala Sutta* as 'luck', indeed as 'the greatest luck',[124] and Woodward translates it as 'blessings'.[125] So why do you think there is this difference between the two versions? What is a *maṅgala*, really? I myself, when translating this *sutta*, have translated *maṅgala* as 'auspicious sign', which I think gets much nearer to the real meaning of the word. *Maṅgala* is not only 'auspicious sign', however, but also an 'auspicious performance' in the sense of a good luck ceremony. In ancient India they had all sorts of beliefs, and even practices, that we would regard as superstitious. For instance, if you saw a certain kind of bird flying in the sky it was a sign of good luck, whereas if you saw a certain other kind of bird it was a sign of bad luck. The bird that meant good luck was a *maṅgala*, an auspicious sign, and if you saw it you knew that something good would follow. Similarly, if you performed the auspicious ceremony, the auspicious rite, you would know that something good would follow. Do you get the idea? A *maṅgala* is an auspicious sign in the sense that it indicates something good coming along. In the *Maṅgala Sutta* it's as though the Buddha takes up this idea and asks, in effect: What is the *real* auspicious sign? What is the sign that you must *really* look out for? What is the sign that will *really* assure you that something good is coming? And the answer is, it's your own skilful action. That's the best auspicious sign, because if you perform a skilful action you know quite certainly that in the future some happiness will accrue to you, some progress and development, even Nirvāṇa. So the good deed is the best auspicious sign, the greatest luck.

We find throughout the Pāli canon that this kind of attitude is typical of what, so far as we can make out, is the teaching of the historical Buddha. He tried very hard to give existing beliefs, practices, customs, and traditions a positive twist, as it were.[126] He didn't condemn outright all those auspicious performances, all those good luck ceremonies and good luck signs. He said, 'Look out for the real sign of good luck, perform the real auspicious ceremony' – the good action which you yourself perform. If you perform that, then you can be really certain that happiness and progress and individual development will follow. It's this idea that he is enlarging upon in the *Maṅgala Sutta*. There's a sort of sequence in it, you'll notice, a cumulative development. He proceeds from very simple and ordinary things to quite advanced states and levels, even though both language and method of treatment remain very simple indeed. Whether the Buddha himself actually spoke this *sutta* in these very words, we can't really know after 2,500 years; but we can be pretty certain that these are the kinds of ethical and spiritual principles the Buddha insisted upon. Maybe one of the disciples put them together in this sort of ballad form, or maybe the Buddha himself summarized his own teaching in this way and spoke these verses in this very form. We don't know. But certainly the eleven verses of the *Maṅgala Sutta* represent the substance of his simple, straightforward teaching, to and for ordinary people, put in this very concise and simple way.

First, let's go through the prose introduction.

> Thus have I heard: Once, when the Master was dwelling near Sāvatthī in Anāthapiṇḍika's park at Jeta Grove,...[127]

Sāvatthī was the capital city of the kingdom of Kosala, which was one of the two leading kingdoms of North India in the Buddha's day. (There's an interesting description of the Indian 'middle country' and of the commercial, cultural, and political importance of Sāvatthī in the sixth century BCE in Trevor Ling's *The Buddha*, which I've been reading recently.)[128] Jeta Grove was situated outside the city, at a convenient distance, and had been acquired by the merchant Anāthapiṇḍika for the use of the Buddha. After acquiring the property from Prince Jeta by covering the area with gold coins Anāthapiṇḍika put up what we mustn't call monasteries; they were rest houses for the monks – though we shouldn't really call them monks: they were the Buddha's full-time followers.[129] The Buddha himself spent altogether twenty-six rainy seasons staying either in the Jeta Grove itself, which was situated to the south of Sāvatthī, or at East Park, which was situated to the east of the city and had been acquired for his use by the well-to-do lay patroness Visākhā.[130] So far as we can see, Sāvatthī was the Buddha's headquarters. He spent more time there, and seems to have given more teachings there, than in any other single place. It's therefore not surprising that it is the setting for this *sutta*. According to Buddhaghosa's account,[131] when the Buddha was in residence anywhere, as distinct from wandering from place to place, he used to divide his day into five periods: going in quest of almsfood in the morning, assigning the *bhikkhus* topics for meditation in the afternoon, and so on. During the second of the three watches of the night he would lie awake, and during this period *devas* and other spiritual beings would visit him, and he'd give teachings to them in the same way that he gave teachings to human beings during the daytime. We therefore find the text saying:

> A *devī* of surpassing beauty, lighting up the whole of the Jeta Grove, approached him, as night waned;...

The text actually says *devatā*, which is grammatically feminine, but it could mean a divinity of either sex. Perhaps it was the fact that the *devatā* was 'of surpassing beauty' that misled the translator. Perhaps he thought that only someone of the female sex could be described in such terms. Be that as it may, the divinity 'lighting up the whole of the Jeta Grove' approached the Buddha 'as night waned'– in other words, just before dawn. That hour of the day is a very mysterious time, neither light nor dark, with a faint glow in the sky, and a very definite atmosphere. According to Buddhist tradition it was at this particular time that non-human beings – or superhuman beings – used to approach the Buddha.

> ...and drawing near she saluted and stood at one side. Thus standing she spoke this verse to the Master:
> 'Devas and many men have thought
> On luck, in hope of happiness:
> Tell me the greatest luck!'

If you don't know much about the law of cause and effect, the law of conditionality, you're very dependent upon good luck, on 'signs'. Primitive people didn't have a very scientific understanding of things. They didn't always understand why certain things happened. They saw that the sun rose every morning, but they didn't know why. But then some people might have noticed that the cock crew every morning and concluded that it was the crowing of the cock that *caused* the sun to rise. The cock crew, then the sun rose: it was obvious. It was the old logical fallacy of 'subsequent to, therefore because of'. A lot of things that we think of as superstitious are in fact observed sequences that are not really cause-effect sequences, but were thought of as such by primitive people. They were always on the lookout for things that would tell them that certain other things can be expected, as in the traditional verse 'Red sky at night, shepherd's delight. Red sky in the morning, shepherd's warning.' More specifically, people were always on the lookout for signs, indications, hints, from nature or other sources, that something *good* was on its way. In Britain, even today, when a black cat crosses your path it's a good luck sign. Among the Nepalese it's just the opposite: if a black cat crosses your path it's a sign of *bad* luck. In Hindu India it's bad luck to meet a widow. In losing her husband she's lost everything, and she's in a very miserable state. If she's an orthodox Hindu she's got a shaven head and wears plain white garments. Unless she can devote herself to the spiritual life she's certainly not a very happy person. So to meet a widow is a sign of ill omen. To meet a woman of bad character is also considered very ominous. In Kalimpong there was a woman – a local Tibetan, born in Darjeeling – who was notorious, having been married no less than thirty-seven times, besides having numerous affairs – all mixed up with shady business and financial transactions, and transfers of property, jewellery, etc. She had such a bad name in the Kalimpong bazaar that if a merchant met her in the street in the morning he would avoid doing any business that day. She was regarded as such a bad omen on account of her bad character.[132]

The *devatā* is therefore saying that many *devas* and men 'have thought / On luck, in hope of happiness'. They want to know how to tell when happiness is coming. Gods are no better than human beings in this respect. Both are equally ignorant, equally unenlightened. What auspicious signs are they to look out for? What auspicious performances should they engage in, so that they can be sure that happiness will come? As I've already said, primitive people just didn't know how things worked. To them it seemed very much a matter of luck, or the simple association of one thing with another. At one time there might be a terrible epidemic, at another time no epidemic. Why, they just didn't know, but they wanted to know, so they'd look out for signs. Some of the signs they observed might be causally connected with the phenomenon in question, but others might be completely fortuitous. Their attitude was scientific, but not their method. The *devatā* is therefore saying that people want to be happy. They want to feel, they want to know, that happiness is on its way, so they're looking out for the signs that will assure them of this. 'Please tell us these signs' – this is what the *devatā* is saying. 'Please let us know what we need to look out for, so that we may be sure that happiness is coming.' Everyone wants to feel that they are going to be happy, that something good is coming.

### Serving the Wise

So what does the Buddha say? With a smile, as it were, he says, 'Serving the wise, not serving fools...' Woodward's translation says: 'Not to follow after fools, but to follow after the wise...' 'Follow' is also good. *Sevanā* means to associate with, to follow, to serve: in India they don't separate these ideas. Associating with, serving, following, are cognate ideas, and all are expressed by the term *sevanā*. If you're associating with the wise, and not associating with fools, then happiness is on its way. The Buddha at once indicates an ethical-cum-spiritual – or even a common sense – sequence rather than a superstitious one. He answers the question in ethical and practical terms, not in pseudo-scientific or magical terms. You associate with someone, especially with a teacher or elder, you wait upon him and attend to his personal needs, and you follow him, i.e. accept his teachings and put them into practice. To associate with, or to serve, or to follow, the wise, and not associate with, not serve, not follow, the foolish, is a good luck sign. If you're doing the one, and not doing the other, you can be sure that good luck, happiness, is on its way.

The word for 'the wise' here is *paṇḍita*. In later Indian literature *paṇḍita* acquired the slightly derogatory meaning of the mere scholar, but in Pāli it signifies a wise man. In the *Dhammapada* there's a 'Paṇḍitavagga', a section or chapter on 'The Fool', and one gets the same contrast between the *paṇḍita* or wise man and the *bāla* or fool. In my own translation of the *Dhammapada* I render *bāla* as 'spiritually immature'.[133] The *bāla* is the young, immature, foolish person. In Pāli and Sanskrit the immaturity of youth and foolishness are connected. The fool is simply the man who's not grown up yet. He's not matured. He's not wise. The *paṇḍita*, as the opposite of the *bāla*, is therefore not just the wise man but the spiritually mature person. So if you follow after, associate with, and serve the wise man – the spiritually mature person – then you can look for happiness in the future. But if you associate with, if you follow, if you serve, the fool – the spiritually immature person – then you can only look for suffering. In the *Dhammapada* there is a definition of the fool, the spiritually immature person: *Putta m'atthi, dhanam m'atthi*. These sons are mine, this wealth is mine, *iti bālo vihaññati* – thus the fool torments himself. In other words, the foolish person is the egoistic person, the self-centred person, the person who grasps at things thinking that they are their own. This is the essence of being spiritually immature, being a fool. The fool is one in whom the I-sense and mine-sense is strong. 'Fool' doesn't mean simply the country bumpkin, the uneducated or unintelligent person. A fool in the Buddhist sense can be highly intelligent, highly intellectual – but spiritually speaking he's a fool, a spiritually immature person, a *bāla*, because his 'I'-sense is strong and he thinks in terms of 'me' and 'mine'. Conversely the wise man, the spiritually mature person, doesn't think or feel in that way, doesn't have a strong 'I'-sense, doesn't grasp at things thinking 'These are mine.'

GRAHAM: Could this go back to Chintamani's new article about the will – that it's very much the will that people function with. They keep the will rather than giving themselves up to the path.

SANGHARAKSHITA: Yes, the spiritually immature person is the wilful person rather than the powerful person. The wise man, the *paṇḍita*, is the spiritually powerful person, whereas the fool, the *bāla*, is the wilful person, the person motivated by egoistic will. It's interesting that the Buddha puts this particular *maṅgala* right at the beginning, as this means that he is emphasizing the importance of *kalyāṇa mitratā* or spiritual fellowship. The real spiritual fellowship is with the wise. You can't have spiritual fellowship with a fool, with a spiritually immature person: it's impossible. The Buddha is therefore putting 'serving the wise, not serving fools' right at the beginning of his enumeration of the signs of good luck, or the auspicious signs. He gives *kalyāṇa mitratā* the first place.

MARK: Forming a basis for all the others, presumably.

RICHARD: It seems to me that those auspicious signs, those signs of luck, are chancy. The Buddha's saying, 'This is auspicious', but one gets the impression that this is what you ought to be doing.

SANGHARAKSHITA: Yes, it is. It's not only an auspicious sign, it's an auspicious *performance* that is required. You *provide* the sign, you *create* the sign, you make the sign for yourself. That's the Buddha's original twist:

that one should be not just passively wait for a sign but create it. To believe in signs and omens in the ordinary way tends to create a rather passive attitude, such as you in fact find in India, but this is quite opposed to the Buddha's attitude, which is that you should create the signs for yourself and bring about your own so-called 'good luck' in the future. In India people really do rely upon auspicious signs. If you go to the bazaar you will find men sitting there with little birds in cages for fortune-telling. Lots of people get their fortune told every time they go to the bazaar, which might be every day. A few grains of rice are scattered inside one of the cages, and according to the way in which the little birds peck at them the fortune-teller will predict your luck for the day or for the week. You will also find palmists and astrologers in the bazaar. Whatever the method, lots of people stop for a few minutes and get their fortune told, because then they'll know what to do, or what to expect, in the course of the day. They tend to have this very passive attitude. Moreover, there are various almanacs telling you which are good luck days and which are bad luck days. Even the Tibetans have this sort of thing, more as an inheritance from ancient Indian and Chinese belief than as anything to do with Buddhism. The Buddha's attitude is not to encourage you to sit around waiting for good luck signs or looking out for good luck signs. Rather, he encourages you to create your own good luck signs by your own auspicious performances – in other words, by your own skilful actions of body, speech, and mind. Then you can be *really* sure that happiness is going to follow. In this way the Buddha gives an 'activist' twist to the whole thing.

RICHARD: I must admit that sometimes, when I pick up a paper and look at the stars and see that I've got a good day or a good week ahead, I really feel sort of secure. I really feel, 'Cor, that's good, that.'

SANGHARAKSHITA: Well that's all right provided that if you find a bad prediction you don't let it upset or discourage you. Believe it when it's good, ignore it when it's bad! Or, if it's bad, be all the more determined, and say, 'The stars don't determine everything. I'll just prove the stars wrong!' Or, if the prediction is good, say, 'If the stars help, so much the better, but even if they don't, never mind!'

SAGARAMATI: Going back to what you said about being passive, and relating that to the sense of 'I', I usually see three levels. Some people, I find, can be passive in the sense that certain things happen to them. This might be annoying to certain other people, on account of the 'I'-sense, but it doesn't annoy them, because of their natural passivity. I don't know whether that's a good thing in that it indicates a lack of 'I'-sense or whether…

SANGHARAKSHITA: What the Buddha was against was passivity in respect of the good. The good is something you have to bring into existence in your own life through your own efforts. When you're meditating you are, in a sense, passive, but by your actual practice of meditation – by the fact that you've at least sat down, at least folded your hands, at least closed your eyes – you've brought yourself into a state or condition where you can be not inactive but passive in the sense of opening yourself up to, being receptive to, higher spiritual influences. You're not completely passive the whole way through.

SAGARAMATI: What I meant was that the passivity can appear to have not so much of an 'I'-sense. I'm thinking of certain people I know…

SANGHARAKSHITA: Like the Indians I mentioned who go to the bazaar and have their fortune told. They are very dependent upon what they hear. In a way they're passive, but it's not that they don't have egos.

SAGARAMATI: No, it's things that happen to people, as when they experience disappointments, or have things stolen. It's almost like they don't care, in a sense, but the feeling one gets off them is very passive and cow-like. In such cases you don't know whether that's a skilful state or whether perhaps it might be a step up for them to say something by way of protest, or even do something, from more of an 'I'-sense.

SANGHARAKSHITA: Very often such people are merely blocked,[134] which is quite a different thing from being passive in the positive sense. Many of the Hindus in India have this cow-like passivity, this lack of initiative. Yet it was these same people who, during the Hindu–Muslim riots, were slaughtering the Muslims. Some of my friends – including Hindu friends – who witnessed the riots said that it was amazing to see the way these people were transformed, and became so violent and bloodthirsty, when things that they were sensitive about – that is, their religion in the communal sense – were touched. When they felt threatened, they reacted with real violence. So the ego, the 'I'-sense is there, underneath, even in the cow-like, passive sort of person. They're not really calm, they're not really gentle. They're either blocked or just slothful or dull. But they can be aroused, and sometimes in a very extreme way, as was shown during those riots. It's important to distinguish genuine calm from that sort of negative passivity.

LOKAMITRA: It's often a blocked fear, I think. I've noticed this with one or two people at the centre. There is very definitely a blocked energy – sort of not wanting to admit something, not wanting to confront something. And often it really is blocked: they're just not aware of this emotion in them.

SAGARAMATI: People say that they're very detached and unegotistical and things like that, but sometimes you just feel there's something there that's not quite right.

SANGHARAKSHITA: Well, as I said, it's not so much that they're non-attached: they're just blocked. During the time I was at Sukhavati there were at least two people there who seemed very quiet at the time of my arrival but who started coming out of themselves a bit after a while.[135] One of them ended up by expressing a certain amount of aggressiveness which didn't seem to be there at the beginning at all. But that did seem to be an improvement. Passivity, to be genuine, mustn't be this blocked or inert state, much less still a state of bovine stupidity. It's like the cat. He might appear to be very gentle and contented, purring away on the hearthrug, but just pull his tail and he can turn on you and give you a nasty scratch: it's all there. Sometimes you find this with women. So long as they've got all the things they want – home, husband, and so on – they appear very contented, very docile and peaceable. But just you suggest taking away any of those things, and the woman can become an absolute wildcat, ready to tear your eyes out. Pseudo-passivity of this kind must be distinguished from the real thing.

After associating with and following the wise, and not associating with and following fools, the Buddha speaks of:

The worship of the worshipful...

Here there is a difficulty in translation. The word *pūjā*, which we translate as 'worship', has a much wider connotation in Pāli and Sanskrit – not only worship in the specifically religious sense but also 'paying respect', 'reverencing', or 'revering'. For us worship is exclusively religious, though there is a slight suggestion otherwise in expressions like 'his worship the mayor'. Etymologically speaking, worship is 'worth-ship', which as a verb means to ascribe worth or value to something, or to treat it as possessing worth or value. This is what worship really is. It hasn't got a narrowly religious connotation.

MARK: People in the West seem not so much to want to acknowledge that anybody is worth praise – other than God, I suppose.

SANGHARAKSHITA: Except that they don't believe in God, so that doesn't leave anybody!

RICHARD: People aren't open to the idea that there's somebody better than them in a spiritual sense. In the West we're all brought up democratic. Everybody's equal. Everybody's the same.

SANGHARAKSHITA: Nobody has more worth than you have yourself.

RICHARD: Often I should think it would be quite a treat when somebody comes along who is worthier than you are.

SANGHARAKSHITA: But what about the phenomenon of pop stars or famous footballers who receive an enormous amount of adulation? What is happening there? Is it a case of people ascribing worth to them in the present sense, or what is it?

GRAHAM: It is almost at that level, I feel.

SAGARAMATI: Well, that's certainly energy…

SANGHARAKSHITA: What is it, then? What is happening there? Is it a genuine worship, an ascribing of worth – or something else?

RICHARD: I think often it's a projection. It's wanting to be like that person – you know, really wanting to be what you think that person is. Often you can think of what a pop star is and imagine he's got a perfect life, but he's probably not like that at all. So I don't think that's the same thing as genuine worship.

SANGHARAKSHITA: He's like what you think he is simply for your benefit – and his own benefit too in other ways. There's some truth in that statement of yours, that this is projective. When you genuinely ascribe worth to someone you're not just projecting onto them. You're really seeing them as they are, seeing them as better than you, and this is a genuine insight. You're not merely projecting any unrealized potential, any unfulfilled wish, of yours onto them. That is the difference, I think. You're not really worshipping the pop idol or the footballer. You're not really ascribing worth to them; you can't, because you don't *see* them. They have no worth really, in themselves, for you. They're just a hook for your projections.

RICHARD: It suddenly occurred to me – the difference between Buddhist worship and worship in a theistic sense! Maybe worship in a theistic sense is one massive projection. In the case of worship in the Buddhist sense, on the other hand, you're saying, 'Look at all these wonderful qualities! Let's rejoice in them. Let's pay respect to them.'

SAGARAMATI: I think you'd have to be quite developed to worship the Buddha, in a sense.

SANGHARAKSHITA: Yes, you really would.

SAGARAMATI: Worship represents quite a high level of development. It means you're not projecting and you feel in contact with something almost transcendental.

SANGHARAKSHITA: That's right. It's certainly not true that worship is for the beginner, which is very often the point of view that one hears expressed.

SAGARAMATI: It's for the masses.

SANGHARAKSHITA: That it's for the masses, for the non-intellectual majority – the unintelligent, the undeveloped; it's a sort of crutch that they need until they're intellectually developed enough to throw it away – this is the sort of language that one hears, and it's totally wrong. This is why some people have been rather surprised that someone like Śāntideva, who had evidently such a deep understanding of the Dharma, could at the same time be so devotional.[136] Yet this is what you find. This is what I found in India: that wise, and deeply learned and profound people were at the same time highly devotional. The two seemed to go together. According to popular belief, when you become really wise you are supposed to leave your devotion behind, but I never found that at all.

SAGARAMATI: From that point of view it definitely makes sense that the more understanding you have the more devotional you will be.

SANGHARAKSHITA: Yes, I think that's very true.

RICHARD: I remember you saying in a lecture once that in Tibet it's only the rimpoches or 'incarnate' lamas who performed the longer and more complex rituals, so it's all on that same level.

MARK: Maybe there's something about projection tied up with the idea that you only worship until you can do something better – almost, I suppose, until you've achieved that state yourself.

SANGHARAKSHITA: Except that there's the intermediate state of being a real worshipper. First you're the projector, then you're the worshipper, and then you are worthy yourself.

RICHARD: So, to start with, worshipping is projecting.

SANGHARAKSHITA: Sometimes not even projection, because it's not all that easy genuinely to project. You can't do it by force of will; it's an unconscious process. Quite a lot of people, when they come along new to the Buddhist centre and are confronted with the shrine with its Buddha image, lighted candles, and so on, just feel completely cold, completely uninvolved, because (1) they don't project, (2) they've no genuine feelings of devotion, and yet (3) they're not 'worthy' themselves. They're not even able to project, never mind worshipping! In some cases, of course, there may be a negative projection, as when the shrine is mistakenly associated with some of the less pleasant features of Christian faith and worship.

RICHARD: Do you think there might be the odd case, though, that somebody comes along and worship is the thing that turns them on? Because I remember the first time I came along I did a puja, and that was it so far as I was concerned.

SANGHARAKSHITA: Yes, this does sometimes happen. John St John was very powerfully affected by the puja. He's written about it in his forthcoming book *Travels in Inner Space.*[137]

So, 'The worship of the worshipful', or 'the reverencing of those deserving of reverence' is 'the greatest blessing', as Woodward puts it.[138] We might say, 'This is the greatest luck!' But you can see what the Buddha is talking about in this first verse of the *Maṅgala Sutta*. He is concerned with the twin ideas of *kalyāṇa mitratā* or spiritual fellowship and puja or reverence. In my lecture on 'The Path of Regular Steps and the Path of Irregular Steps' I quoted Coleridge,[139] who had detected, all those years ago, a decline in reverence – reverence being the feeling or attitude you have towards something or someone acknowledged as being genuinely superior to yourself and therefore beyond your understanding.

## A Congenial Environment

In a fair land to dwell...

Or, as Woodward renders *Paṭirūpadesavāso ca*, 'To dwell in a pleasant spot.' *Paṭirūpa* could be interpreted as beautiful, even attractive, but it really means suitable or appropriate. For instance, when someone who wants to be ordained as a *bhikkhu* asks an elder *bhikkhu* to act as his preceptor, the latter may give his consent by saying '*Paṭirūpaṃ*', meaning 'It's suitable', or 'It's all right', or, translating the expression more colloquially – 'That's fine.' *Paṭirūpadesa* is thus 'a fine spot'. But why is to dwell in a fine spot a *maṅgala*? It is because of the importance of environment. The Buddha's approach is simply common sense. First of all he talks about spiritual fellowship, then about a feeling of reverence towards those who are more developed than ourselves, and then comes 'To dwell in a fine spot' – that is, in a good, suitable environment. We know how important this is from our experience of the retreat situation, when we go away for a period of meditation and study, either on our own or with other people. We know how the mind changes according to the change in environment, how we are helped by dwelling 'in a fine spot'. This is something quite basic, even elementary. But the Buddha – adopting a slightly different point of view – is reckoning it here as a blessing, an auspicious sign.

SAGARAMATI: Because only good can come of it.

SANGHARAKSHITA: Because only good can come of it. But it does raise the question, 'What is really a fine spot?' We shouldn't jump to conclusions. It is not necessarily a peaceful place in the country. The *Sutta* doesn't say that. It says 'a fine spot'. So what is 'a fine spot'? Among other things, it is where you can meet 'good friends'.

MARK: And from that point of view...

GARY: Pundarika[140] or Sukhavati!

SANGHARAKSHITA: Right. We mustn't jump to the conclusion that the fine spot necessarily means somewhere peaceful, or easy, or even pleasant. As you get more advanced and more experienced, the fine spot might be a quite difficult situation.

RICHARD: It's relative, then.

SANGHARAKSHITA: Yes. The fine spot, or the suitable spot, is not just the spot that makes everything easy for you, because if everything is easy there may be certain sterling qualities you just don't develop. Hakuin, the great Japanese Rinzai Zen master of the eighteenth century, firmly maintained that the best time to meditate and to make spiritual progress is when you are sick and suffering, and this is very true.

GRAHAM: That's when it comes to discipline, you know, if you discipline yourself on all occasions, in all situations.

SANGHARAKSHITA: When you are a beginner, conditions can get you down, and sometimes you just can't practise at all, so you need 'good', pleasant, and agreeable surroundings. But as you get more experienced, and more firm within yourself, you should quite freely expose yourself to what are, in a sense, more difficult situations, and even live in more difficult surroundings. That's the bodhisattva spirit: not to look out for easy, comfortable, attractive, agreeable surroundings, and nice, pleasant people all the time. It may be much more stimulating, and much more beneficial in the long run, to be in what may seem to be difficult conditions.

RICHARD: Padmasambhava and the cremation ground springs to mind: a sort of crucial situation.[141]

SANGHARAKSHITA: Right. For the beginner it will certainly be the pleasant, quiet spot that will be 'fine': where you can meditate and have good friends, and where there aren't too many interruptions, perhaps a place in the country. For beginners, you may therefore say, the retreat situation is the best. But for someone who is a bit more advanced the city centre may be the best situation.

GRAHAM: It's quite a test to be able to sit through noise and disturbance. Maybe it's not even meditation then, but you're practising...

SANGHARAKSHITA: You're perhaps practising patience, if nothing else.

LOKAMITRA: The importance of solitary retreats has come back to me recently very strongly. Working in the city seems to be a very good situation for a lot of people, but recently I've been finding myself becoming very conscious of having a sort of defiled consciousness. After a while you're affected by the noise, the building work, the greyness.

SANGHARAKSHITA: Yes, of course. You're not really able to get on top of it. You're only able to bear it. Even to be able to bear it is a good thing, but you can't do that indefinitely. You need a respite. That is why for the majority of people, for quite a long time, it's good, even best, to alternate between town and country. Most people won't benefit from being indefinitely on retreat. They'll stagnate in the end. And hardly anybody would benefit from being indefinitely in the city, because they would be worn down. But to alternate between the two can be very fruitful.

Hakuin maintains that to be in difficult situations gives you a lot of energy – if you face the difficult situation in the right sort of spirit. Well, Hakuin was Hakuin. What he says is true, but it isn't necessarily true for everybody indefinitely. Just as it doesn't follow that the longer you meditate the better your meditation becomes, in the same way it doesn't necessarily follow that the longer you stay in the city the more energy you get. There may be a point beyond which there are only diminishing returns, and when you reach that point, you have to break off and go into the country for a while.

GARY: I should imagine that's quite a difficult situation anyway: going into the country after being in the city.

SANGHARAKSHITA: Some people feel very restless because there's nothing to do. But anyway, dwelling in 'a fair land' is certainly very good for the beginner, but we have to be careful that we don't assume too much about what the 'fair land' is like. It varies according to our level of development. At the beginning it may be a very easy situation: quiet and peaceful. Later on it may be a much more difficult and demanding situation – which is more positive and creative for us at that stage.

...good wrought in past...

Or, 'To have done good deeds in former births' (Woodward) – *pubbe ca katapuññatā. Pubbe* means 'in the past, formerly', and *katapuññatā* means good deeds done. In other words, this *maṅgala* is that of meritorious works performed in the past, 'past' being understood traditionally as referring to one's previous existences. Why do you think the Buddha mentions this? It's because if you've done good deeds in the past you can be sure that some happiness is on its way, even if you are not experiencing it now.

RICHARD: Has this got anything to do with the idea that you need merit to develop spiritually?

SANGHARAKSHITA: You mean a store of merit.

SAGARAMATI: This seems to be a tricky one in the West. I feel that it's going to be very tricky.

SANGHARAKSHITA: 'Tricky' because it's connected with the whole idea of karma and rebirth, which some Western Buddhists have difficulty in accepting?

SAGARAMATI: Yes.

SANGHARAKSHITA: Having a store of merit means having a solid, positive human base for your spiritual development, especially in the form of positive emotions like friendliness, compassion, sympathetic joy, and equanimity, i.e. the four *brahma vihāras*. It's very important to have that base.

SAGARAMATI: The positive emotion almost always seems to be the result of something done in the past. Even when you're practising, say, *karuṇā bhāvanā*, you don't actually experience compassion at the time, but you're working towards it. If you can believe, or have a feeling, that there is this karmic process going on then I suppose you can believe that in the future some results of your practice will come about.

SANGHARAKSHITA: I've talked about this idea of *puñña* (Sanskrit *puṇya*) quite a bit lately. *Puñña* is not just good action: it's a bit more than that. It's the aura almost, or the vibration in you, which is set up by good action. When you strike a certain note on a musical instrument the sound of that note goes on vibrating in the air, and the more often you strike that note, the more strongly does the sound go on vibrating at that pitch. Similarly, the performance of a good deed sets up a vibration in you – a vibration which is you. If a person is always performing certain good deeds, or thinking certain good thoughts – and deeds here includes thoughts – in fact, thought is a deed even more than external physical action – then a certain vibration is set up. The individual, the person himself, is vibrating in a certain way: a certain aura is created. He produces, therefore, a certain impression: he has a certain effect on other people, and on his surroundings. So it's as though the Buddha is saying that it's a very good thing, it's a blessing, a sign of good luck, if the quality of your being is such that you are vibrating in this positive way – in the way which, according to Buddhist teaching, is brought about by good deeds done in the past.

But in any case, regardless of whether or not it is accepted that it is the result of 'good wrought / In past', it is a good and lucky and auspicious thing that you 'vibrate' in this positive way in the present. This is what the Buddha is saying. This word *puñña* is very significant here. For instance, someone who is really happy and cheerful, maybe attractive to look at as well, and very agreeable, creates a very pleasant atmosphere, sets up a very pleasant vibration. Why is this? Well, you may or may not believe that it's the result of good deeds done in the past, but the fact is that this particular person sets up this particular kind of vibration, which is a very good thing. Certainly it augurs well for him in the future, because it's very attractive. With it he makes friends: he wins friends and influences people. So *puñña* is not just the good deed. It's the good deed plus the vibration that the good deed sets up, and the aura it creates around the person who has performed it and is still performing it. On a very much higher, transcendental level, this is connected with the Buddha's subtle *rūpakāya*, what in Mahāyāna Buddhism is called his *sambhogakāya*.

LOKAMITRA: Can you say a bit more about that?

SANGHARAKSHITA: In the course of his career as a bodhisattva the Buddha accumulates throughout innumerable lives boundless good deeds which gradually set up more and more powerful vibrations which cling about him as his *sambhogakāya*, his 'body of glory'. This is what the *sambhogakāya* is: a sort of *puṇyakāya* on the transcendental plane. So far as I know, the expression *puṇyakāya* is never actually used in Sanskrit Buddhist texts in this sense: but it is an intelligible expression nonetheless. Certainly there is mention of the *puṇyasambhāra*, or accumulation of merits, and the *puṇyasambhāra* is sometimes said to correspond to the *sambhogakāya*, just as the *jñānasambhāra*, or accumulation of knowledge, corresponds to the *dharmakāya*. Thus you could conceivably speak of a *puṇyakāya*. I also compare the *sambhogakāya*, and the *puṇyakāya* too, to the works of the artist or the writer. There are pictures of Dickens at his desk, or Shakespeare with his quill pen in his hand, and all around them are the characters that they have created. Around Dickens there is Mrs Gamp and David Copperfield and Martin Chuzzlewit and Mr Pickwick, all hovering in a sort of cloud. Around Shakespeare there is Romeo and Juliet and King Lear and Hamlet and all the rest of them, a bit like an aura. Dickens and Shakespeare created this, they produced this. It's their *puṇyakāya* in a way. Do you get the idea? In the case of the Buddha and his *sambhogakāya* the connection is very much like that.

RICHARD: If the Buddha, through his good deeds in previous existences, created this sort of aura, then how do the archetypal bodhisattvas like Avalokiteśvara and Mañjughoṣa come into the picture?

SANGHARAKSHITA: Well, if you don't regard the archetypal bodhisattvas as real individual personalities, you can regard them as different aspects of the total *sambhogakāya*. Each bodhisattva has a specific function – one is wisdom, one is compassion, and so on – but the *sambhogakāya* is all of these together. Anyway, that takes us a long way from the Pāli canon! Richard's cunningly luring us onto Tantric territory [Richard snaps his fingers in 'Tantric fashion'], edging us nearer and nearer to it. But you can see that the seed of the later developments is in the Pāli canon, because the *Maṅgala Sutta*'s idea of *puñña* was what we started talking about.

So back to 'Good wrought in past ...' *Puññakamma* in the past means *puñña* now. *Puññakamma* is merit-producing action – not just the good deed itself but what I call the vibration that the good deed sets up, the aura that it creates around you. This is what the fact that you have done all these good deeds really is. When you see the Buddha in the flesh, unless you are a bodhisattva you don't see the *sambhogakāya*. In the same way, when you meet the great writer you don't actually see all the works that he has produced, but they are there. They are just as much a part of him as they would be if they were visible. If you'd met Shakespeare you wouldn't have seen or felt Lear and Macbeth and so on, but they would have been there in his mind. He produced them, he created them; they are part of his invisible *rūpakāya*. You see the visible *rūpakāya*, i.e. the physical body; you don't see the invisible *rūpakāya*, i.e. the *sambhogakāya*.

LOKAMITRA: It seems that *puṇya* can also refer to the mundane aspects of the spiral of spiritual/transcendental development, i.e. to the first seven out of the twelve positive *nidānas*.[142]

SANGHARAKSHITA: Yes, very much so.

LOKAMITRA: This goes back to what you said about establishing a healthy base for one's spiritual development.

SANGHARAKSHITA: Yes, a healthy, solid human base, especially by way of cultivating positive emotion. If someone has positive emotions you feel that, don't you? – just as you feel the negative emotions.

SAGARAMATI: Because they're also part of the cyclic process, as well as part of the spiral, you can fall away from good actions. Is this because you just sit back, as it were, and ride out that good *puṇya* you've built up?

SANGHARAKSHITA: It's also the active gravitational pull from the rest of your being. You're not a totally integrated person. You have performed good actions, but not with the whole of yourself. There's still a large part of you that isn't involved, perhaps doesn't want to be involved, and that large part – or larger part – starts asserting itself sooner or later. You have to struggle against it to preserve and extend that more positive part.

LOKAMITRA: Recently I thought in terms of the first stages of the spiral as creating and accumulating more and more merit.[143] When seen like that it's quite a difficult process. It's not just a matter of making offerings and so on, but of really bringing into play all one's emotional energies and making them positive. That's very much where the merit is.

SANGHARAKSHITA: It's a matter of being a positive person.

SAGARAMATI: Also, if you have got a lot of charisma, or whatever you call it, you are more open to temptations than you would be if you didn't have a charisma.

GRAHAM: What do you mean?

SAGARAMATI: Well, if you're really good-looking, and have a good personality and so on, you're going to attract a lot of attention.

SANGHARAKSHITA: You can be carried away by it. You can become a bit intoxicated with your own success, your own popularity, your own influence.

Let's go on to the next *maṅgala*: 'to have high aims for self...' *Attasammāpaṇidhi ca*. Woodward translates this as 'To have set oneself on the right path', which is not quite so literal, but faithful enough to the spirit of the word. Chalmers translates it as 'aspiration high'.

MARK: To decide that the path of the Dharma is the one you actually want to follow, and not something of merely passing interest.

SANGHARAKSHITA: Right. Actually to have set yourself on it, to have started following it. You do this because it naturally follows from the *maṅgalas* so far enumerated. First of all you associate with the wise and avoid the unwise, the fools. Next, you have the benefit of spiritual fellowship. Then you recognize that there are others more developed than yourself and adopt a worshipping or reverential attitude towards them. After that you live in a suitable environment. Finally, you have a stock of merit from the past, Well, having come so far, what do you do next? You set yourself on the right path. You start actually practising. One could say that this *maṅgala* consists in setting oneself on the path of the Higher Evolution, the Eightfold Path, the path of regular steps: setting oneself to practise regularly and systematically. You realize what advantages you have had, whether accruing from karma or not.

LOKAMITRA: All the *maṅgalas* not only set up the right conditions for the future – if you like, for Enlightenment – they also make one feel good at the time.

SANGHARAKSHITA: Right.

SAGARAMATI: How would merit fit into the Higher Evolution? Last Sunday, or the Sunday before, someone at the Centre commented that it was good that we have this concept of the Higher Evolution, because then we don't have to bother about things like merit. This is why I brought that point up earlier.

SANGHARAKSHITA: The Higher Evolution is a process that can be considered within the context of this present life. This is presumably what that person was referring to. But it can also be considered from the Buddhist point of view within the context of karma and rebirth, because the process of the Higher Evolution can span a number of successive lives.

SAGARAMATI: That brings in the question of karma, and karma brings in the question of merit.

SANGHARAKSHITA: Certainly. But merit can also accrue within the span of a single lifetime. If you give *dāna* now, merit accrues to you now. You don't necessarily have to wait until a future life.

LOKAMITRA: I see the Higher Evolution as a process entirely to do with merit.

SAGARAMATI: The person I mentioned was quite glad that in the Higher Evolution we don't bring in anything like karma and merit.

LOKAMITRA: I think that's because people see merit in a very materialistic way, but it doesn't have to be seen that way.

SANGHARAKSHITA: *Puṇya* is that quality of your being which is brought about by your regular performance of skilful actions. It's a modification of your being. Inasmuch as the skilful action doesn't proceed from wisdom in the transcendental sense it's not a permanent modification. That would be Enlightenment, or a measure of Enlightenment. But *puṇya* is at least a temporary modification of your being which provides you with a very strong, powerful, and positive basis for the development of insight and wisdom.

LOKAMITRA: Would that be a necessary basis?

SANGHARAKSHITA: A necessary basis too.

SAGARAMATI: What they call a working basis.

SANGHARAKSHITA: Yes, a working basis. This is why traditionally in Buddhism great importance is attached to earning or making merit.

GRAHAM: Does this mean action as opposed to words or both together?

SANGHARAKSHITA: Both together. Though action is understood as including thinking.

LOKAMITRA: To perform certain actions requires a corresponding emotional attitude which encourages the further development of that emotional attitude.

SANGHARAKSHITA: It's a cumulative process.

LOKAMITRA: I see this very much in working for the Movement.

SANGHARAKSHITA: Well, the more you do, the more you are able to do.

LOKAMITRA: But not only that. You need a certain emotional approach to be able to do it, and to continue with it; and to go on and on requires further emotional development.

RICHARD: Do you mean a sense of confidence in taking things on? You know, like being stable.

SANGHARAKSHITA: It's partly that, but it's more too. Doing things not only expends energy but gives you energy.

LOKAMITRA: Also, you are in conflict, as it were, with the gravitational pull.[144] You may want to go off and do something of your own or have a rest, but there's something drawing you on; it draws out the positive emotions, and the heroic qualities, almost.

SANGHARAKSHITA: It's as though Māra the Evil One was saying, 'Come on, take it easy. Take the day off.' And the voice of the Buddha says, 'No, you don't need to take the day off. You can carry on quite easily.'

LOKAMITRA: When things get difficult you can quite easily think, well...

SANGHARAKSHITA: ...Māra was right after all.

LOKAMITRA: But when things get 'dry' there are opportunities for bringing up new life.

SANGHARAKSHITA: I think Hakuin was getting at this sort of thing. He even said you could have particularly good meditations under difficult conditions. You drew extra energy from that – which I'm sure is true of people who are a bit more advanced.

RICHARD: One thing that keeps coming to my mind in this context is this business of the 'crucial situation'. I remember that when I moved to London from Brighton I was pretty frightened. I didn't know what was going to happen. But the energy that I got from it was tremendous.

SANGHARAKSHITA: Eveline was pretty frightened of moving *to* Brighton! It does seem ridiculous, doesn't it?

RICHARD: It was just the energy that was produced from that situation.

SANGHARAKSHITA: You produced energy by resisting inertia. Energy is required to overcome inertia, so if you overcome inertia, you feel more full of energy, more confident, more potent.

### Education and Elucidation

> Learning and skill and being trained
> In discipline, words spoken well:
> This is the greatest luck.

This is the next verse, which contains four *maṅgalas*. The first is 'learning' (*bāhusacca*) or, as Woodward more accurately renders it, 'much learning'. *Bāhusacca* is a well-known term. *Bāhu* is 'much' and *sacca* is 'learning' or 'knowledge', literally 'hearing'. In the Buddha's day knowledge was transmitted entirely by oral means, so that the learned man was the man who had heard much, the man of much hearing. Sometimes the term is translated 'much understanding'. It's certainly not learning in the book sense: that is the main point to be understood here. There were no books at that time anyway.

RICHARD: Could it be wisdom?

SANGHARAKSHITA: No, it is knowledge, understanding: understanding of things heard, especially.

RICHARD: Woodward's translation has 'much learning and much science'.

SANGHARAKSHITA: 'Science' translates *sippa*, the second *maṅgala* of the verse. This gives us a clue to the real meaning of *sacca*. It is learning and knowledge in the more cultural sense, the traditional arts and sciences. Perhaps 'culture' would be a better word, in view of the context, though this is not a literal translation. *Sippa* (Sanskrit *śilpa*) is not so much skill as craft, or even handicraft. In ancient Indian literature there are works called the *Śilpa-śāstras*, which are sort of text books of architecture, sculpture, and so on. Thus, whereas *sacca* represents the more theoretical, mental side of things, *sippa* represents the more practical, even mechanical side.

To pass on now to this second *maṅgala*, *sippa* or craft, it's quite important that it is included by the Buddha as an auspicious sign. In ancient India, as in ancient Greece, manual work – including handicraft – was regarded as much inferior to mental work. The Greeks had a prejudice against physical work, feeling that it was the sort of thing that should be left to the slaves. Similarly, in India manual work was the sort of thing you left to the lower castes, and the attitude is still widely prevalent. In orthodox Hindu society blacksmiths and goldsmiths – even artists – have a quite lowly caste status. It is therefore significant that the Buddha should have regarded *sippa* as an auspicious sign, a source of future blessing. By speaking in terms of learning and skill he gives a place to the arts and sciences and a place to the handicrafts, to culture, and to the more practical side of things as well. Such an emphasis was badly needed in ancient – as in modern – India.

SAGARAMATI: Going back to the Greeks, it's a bit like Socrates explaining morality in terms of the carpenter's skill. They called it *arete*, I think.

SANGHARAKSHITA: *Arete* is virtue, excellence. You find exactly the same line of thought in the *Sāmaññaphala Sutta* of the *Dīgha Nikāya*. The King of Magadha, Ajātasattu, comes to see the Buddha and says that there are a number of craftsmen – mahouts, horsemen, weavers, basket-makers, potters, and so on – all of whom enjoy, in this very world, the visible fruits of their craft. 'Can you, Sir', he asked the Buddha, 'declare to me any such immediate fruit (*phala*) visible in this very world, of the life of a recluse (*samaṇa*)?' The Buddha replies that he can, and to this end puts a question to the king.[145] Clearly Socrates and the Buddha are following the same line of thought. In the case of Socrates, the reasoning is from the particular to the general. The good wheelwright is the man who makes a good wheel. The good shoemaker is the man who makes a good shoe. But what is the good man? What does he produce? He 'produces' virtue. In the case of the Buddha he reasons from one particular case to another particular case. Just as the mahouts and so on enjoy the fruits of their craftsmanship in the form of a livelihood for themselves and their families, so the recluse enjoys the fruits of his recluseship in the form of the personal experience of the four *jhānas* (Sanskrit *dhyānas*) or states of 'higher consciousness'. In the *Sāmaññaphala Sutta*, of course, the practice of the crafts is only *compared* to the living of the spiritual life. In the *Maṅgala Sutta* it is apparently an integral part of it, at least at a certain stage.

LOKAMITRA: Could it be also that as one progresses along the spiritual path, one will be prepared to turn to whatever is needed at the time?

SANGHARAKSHITA: Yes, it's also that, but principally it's that the Buddha is going step by step. You've got associating with the wise, worship of the worshipful, dwelling in a fair land, having done good deeds in the past and having, therefore, an accumulation of *puṇya*, having set oneself on the right path. But having got them, what do you actually *do*? The Buddha starts with very simple things. You get into the arts and sciences: that at least represents a step forward in ordinary human terms. You become a more cultured and knowledgeable individual. You become culturally productive. In other words, at this stage you fulfil certain specifically human norms, and in this way lay a solid foundation for your future spiritual development.

... and being trained in discipline ...

*Vinayo ca susikkhito*. Woodward says, 'and a discipline well learned'. So what is *vinaya*? We are familiar with the word in relation to monastic rules, but it doesn't necessarily have that narrow meaning. A popular traditional (not scientific) explanation is that *vinaya* is that which leads (*nayati*) away from (*vi*) all that is unskilful. The word really means discipline, though not in the narrower sense, or something like skilful behaviour. *Susikkhito* means 'well learned'. So again there's a sequence. First comes culture – the arts and sciences – and then there's the matter of your own behaviour. First of all, there are all the good external conditions, all the advantages and facilities in the midst of which you find yourself. Then, having found yourself thus favourably situated, you make up your mind to set yourself on the right path. And to go about this, first you achieve a certain level of cultural development, and then you start regulating your behaviour, you start practising *sīla*. In this way you gradually progress.

There then takes place an extension of your *sīla*:

... words well spoken ...

*Subhāsitā ca yā vācā*. The *sīla*, the 'being well trained', might consist, for instance, in your abstaining from harming living beings, or from taking what did not belong to you, and from this you come onto right speech, to 'words well spoken', *subhāsitā ca yā vācā*. *Su* is good, happy, appropriate; *bhāsitā* is '(what is) well spoken', or 'pleasant utterance', as in Woodward's translation. First of all you start with the opportunities and facilities; then comes your decision to set yourself on the right path; next there's your practice of the arts and sciences, and becoming a cultured person; and after that you proceed to matters of personal ethical discipline, including right speech, even perfect speech.

SAGARAMATI: I suppose in that sense you're beginning to express something.

SANGHARAKSHITA: Yes. There's further 'expression' in the next verse:

**Family and Occupation**

> Service to parents, care of son
> And wife, a peaceful livelihood:
> This is the greatest luck.

Clearly one is concerned, at this stage, with the householder path. You haven't yet become a *bhikkhu* or monk, you haven't yet gone forth: you're still functioning within the ordinary social and domestic framework. You could also look at it in terms of heredity. First of all there's the advantages you are born with – the fact that you're born in a good country, among good people. Then you have the benefit of a good education: you become knowledgeable, and are well trained. Then the question of your parents and your attitude towards them comes in. You could look at it like that.

GRAHAM: Even though you've gone forth, should you still...?

SANGHARAKSHITA: At this stage you haven't gone forth, you've only set yourself on the right path in a very preliminary and basic, even elementary way. You're still practising that part of the path that comes in before your going forth from home into homelessness: 'service to parents, care of son and wife, a peaceful livelihood', and various other things. For quite a long time – for several verses of the *Maṅgala Sutta* – one is concerned, certainly within the ancient Indian context, with practising the Dharma as a householder, as one who has not yet gone forth. Thus there comes 'service to parents': *mātāpitu-upaṭṭhānaṃ*. The word *upaṭṭhānaṃ* really means something more like 'support', as in Woodward's translation. But why do you think support of parents comes in? It's partly because of the general nature of ancient Indian social life. In those days there was no such thing as state insurance, pensions, and all that. Parents relied on their sons, and even daughters perhaps, to look after them in their old age and repay their debt to them, as it were. You're supposed to reflect that when you were young your parents looked after you, so that it's only right and natural that when they are old you should care for them and support them.

MARK: Could it perhaps have a slightly different meaning, so far as we are concerned? Could it not mean that even though you leave home, and leave your parents behind, you're not rejecting them or pushing them out of existence: you still respect them.

SANGHARAKSHITA: In ancient India you didn't leave home and set up a separate household. If you remained a lay person, i.e. did not go forth as a wanderer, you brought your wife into the family and your children were born and grew up there with your unmarried sisters and your brothers and their wives and children as part of a single extended household. Eventually you would take over your father's work. If he was a blacksmith, you would become a blacksmith. Indeed, he would have taught you the work when you were small.

MARK: When he died, the cycle would just continue.

SANGHARAKSHITA: Right. Father would take a back seat, and you would look after him – feed him and support him – just as he had done with you when you were a child. It was a natural cycle. You didn't leave home and then, after finding a wife, set up a separate household. In the case of very bad sons, the worst criticism that could be levelled against them is that they drove out their old parents, who had to wander from place to place as beggars.

MARK: And the sons kept the house for themselves.

SANGHARAKSHITA: The sons kept the house for themselves. Even now the Hindu idea is that the sons have a right to the family property. This is quite an important conception, quite different from our own. As soon as the sons are born they automatically have a share in the property and the father can't disinherit them, because it's joint family property, not his personal property. The law has now been changed in India, I believe, or at least modified, but all through the British period the law governing joint family property fully applied. But if the grown-up sons ganged up against the father they could drive him out of the house and force him, and even their old mother, to wander from place to place as beggars – and occasionally this did happen, though such unfilial conduct was very much looked down upon. So it wasn't so much a case of the son leaving home and setting up his own separate establishment: occasionally it might mean the father being driven out.

Inasmuch as the whole family was living under the same roof, and as the son had taken over the father's trade or profession, and was now the earner, he supported his old father and mother and maybe the younger dependent members of the family as well. This was quite natural: it was the decent thing to do. But going a bit more deeply – a bit more psychologically – into the matter, this *maṅgalam* indicates something I've talked about quite a lot over the last two or three years: the importance psychologically, and therefore, in the long run, spiritually – inasmuch as the psychological provides a positive basis for the spiritual – of a positive relationship with your parents. I've sometimes said that you can't *not* have a relationship with your parents, and if it isn't positive then it must be negative. From the psychological and ultimately spiritual point of view it's in your own best interests to have a positive relationship with your parents, not to be on bad terms, as very often people are these days. A bad relationship with your parents means a sort of emotional breach in you, because the natural relationship with the parents is very close, especially with the mother. If you feel negatively even towards your parents it means the emotional breach must be very deep indeed. In ancient India, and in Buddhism generally, it's considered particularly bad to kill your father or your mother – worse than killing anybody else, because you must be more negatively motivated to kill your parents than to kill anybody else, in order to be able to overcome the strong natural attachment to and love for your parents. Killing them means doing huge violence to your own natural feeling. If you feel negative towards your parents you feel very, very negative indeed.

RICHARD: My parents used to be quite nearby when I lived in Brighton and obviously I used to see them fairly regularly. Since I've moved to London I haven't wanted to go and see them even when I've been in Brighton, but I don't feel it was negative. It was just that I didn't want to go. When my mother phoned the other day, really wanting me to go and see them, I said, 'Well, I just can't; I'm too busy.' But I didn't feel particularly negative.

SANGHARAKSHITA: There is another aspect of the matter: a sort of cutting free. Almost always nowadays, I think, the son has to cut free and maybe not have much at all to do with his parents for a year or two – not because he has any negative feelings towards them (at least ideally it shouldn't be for that reason) but just because he wants to make a clean break and be psychologically independent. How can you feel really positive towards your parents unless you *are* independent? If you feel dependent you'll only feel resentful. So if they don't have the sense to chuck you out, by the time you're 18 or 19, you must leave, if you've got enough common sense to understand the situation. Under a decent cultural system, and a decent tradition, you would have left. If you had been brought up in a tribe, by people who understand these things, you would have been taken away from your mother and father as a boy and kept with the wise old men for a while, and weaned from mother. Chintamani has written about this in his article 'Leaving Mother and Initiation into Manhood'.[146]

RICHARD: The trap I fell into was that when I was feeling ill, or had the blues, I used to go straight back and spend a day with my parents. It used to be awful: even worse.

SANGHARAKSHITA: You should go back when you feel really good, when you feel you can relate to them in an independent way. You should bounce back, not collapse in a soggy heap on the doorstep pleading, 'Mum, take me in!'

LOKAMITRA: This cutting off is something that is going to hurt them quite a bit, but it doesn't mean to say that one is being negative.

SANGHARAKSHITA: No, one isn't really being negative in doing that. One is being positive.

LOKAMITRA: Even though it might hurt them, in a way.

SANGHARAKSHITA: It can't really hurt them. It may go against their neurotic feelings of attachment to you, but it can't really hurt them. It's very important to get things emotionally straight with one's parents.

RICHARD: One can also fall into the trap – I know I've done this – of thinking, 'Oh well, I'll go home. It'll please them.' Really I'm just rationalizing.

SANGHARAKSHITA: Well, that's not much good, if it doesn't please you. If you're glad to see them in a genuine, healthy way, by all means go home. But if you aren't, probably it's better not to do so until you can feel more positive. If you don't enjoy your visit to them the chances are that they won't really enjoy it either. They'll certainly pick up on how you're feeling, at least unconsciously. In almost all cases the break needs to be made, and if they can't push you out you must leave, since there's no tribe to arrange it all for you.

RICHARD: I left when I got into Buddhism, actually.

SANGHARAKSHITA: Later on, when we have a bigger movement, maybe with children growing up within it, there will have to be someone appointed to go round plucking the children from their parents as soon as they reach a certain age: taking them off on permanent retreat, or at least for a camping period for a couple of years somewhere. They could take them off to Australia! Or anywhere away from their parents! We should be sending shiploads of them every year!

RICHARD: With the elders.

SANGHARAKSHITA: There was a saying I used to quote: 'Few misfortunes can befall a boy which bring worse consequence than to have a really affectionate mother.'[147] I've seen some of these loving mothers! You can have a really positive relationship with your parents only if you are emotionally mature and can relate to them simply as another individual, not just as their son or daughter. Parents – especially mothers – have this terrible tendency to see you as little Johnny, aged about 5 or 6, when you're 25 or 26, or even 35 or 36.

LOKAMITRA: You may be able to relate to them as an individual, but they still may not be able to relate to you as such.

SANGHARAKSHITA: Unfortunately this may happen. You may then have to limit your contact with them, because two-way communication on that basis isn't possible, and to insist on it may upset them. If they refuse to accept you as an individual you can't really do anything about it.

RICHARD: One thing that I got into when I used to go and visit my parents was hugging my father – really going up to him and giving him a big hug, like a mate. At first he was really cold, but in the end he started really getting into it. I see that sort of behaviour very much as a way of relating as an individual and both of you being very affectionate.

SANGHARAKSHITA: There's an admirable verse in the *Manusmṛti*, the great Hindu law book. Though there is much in this ancient work that Buddhists can't agree with such as the laws regarding caste, there are certain other things which are very basic and commonsensical and universally acceptable. The verse in question advises the father that when his son reaches the age of 16 he should cease to regard him as a son and regard him as a friend. This is very sound advice, and represents the tribal attitude. The child is regarded as belonging not to the father but as being a member of the tribe, and this gives him an identity apart from his identity as the child of his father. The tribesman's position in the tribe is just like that of the son in the Hindu family, who is not just his father's son, but a member of the family, and has rights as a member of the family, independent of his rights as the son of his father. Do you see the reasoning? When a brahmin boy becomes a brahmin on being invested with the sacred thread, he is just as much a brahmin as his father is: in a sense he's equal to his father. If it comes to speaking up in the brahmin assembly they've got equal voice. Maybe the father will speak first, and because he's an older man people may even listen to him a bit more, but the son has also got the right to speak up. It's much the same on a spiritual level in the Buddhist sangha. Even the youngest monk has a perfect right to pipe up in the monastic assembly and say what he thinks, even if he was ordained yesterday, and everybody has to listen to him, just as much as to the seniormost monk. When someone is ordained his position is not just that of the disciple of his teacher but that of a member of the sangha. In a sense by virtue of his ordination he becomes the equal of his teacher, even though the teacher is still his teacher. You see here a rather different attitude from our own. In the West, traditionally, all your rights in the family follow from the fact that you are the son of your father, though modern legislation has changed this to some extent. Your father can disinherit you. It's his property, and you've no rights apart from what he graciously gives you. This may be connected – though perhaps the notion is a bit far-fetched – with the idea of God and his supreme despotic will. In the West the father is a sort of little God. But in India, it's not really like that. There the son is also a member of the family, and a member of the tribe – even of the caste – independently, almost, of his affiliation to his own father. Your rights do not derive exclusively from your affiliation to your father or, in the case of Buddhism and the sangha, exclusively from your spiritual affiliation to your teacher. You are also, equally, a member of the group or the spiritual community, as the case may be. I think that's quite an important point.

SAGARAMATI: This sort of attitude is so much less narrow. It's almost as if God narrows everything down… But in the case of the Indians, their perspective is so much broader, just like their cosmology.

GRAHAM: You mentioned in a talk how, as children grow older, the family put them down. If they speak out too much they are snubbed, and so the sense of awe about everything disappears.

SANGHARAKSHITA: I noticed a bit of that tendency to snub the young among the Nepalese. Some of my young Nepalese friends used to get quite annoyed at this. They'd come to me and say, 'When I said what I thought about such-and-such a member, my grandfather said, 'Keep quiet, you egg!' He hasn't even been hatched yet, so how dare he speak up in front of the old roosters? But maybe that's enough about parents.

> … care of son
> And wife …

Or 'Cherishing child and wife' (Hare): *Puttadārassa saṅghaho*. You notice that 'son' comes first, which is perhaps a bit significant. The wife is only the means to the son. This again is something we don't understand much – or maybe have lost – in the West: that the son is more important to the father than his own wife. In the traditional East you marry for the sake of progeny, to continue your ancestral line and produce a son in your image. This reminds me of an interview given by Muhammad Ali.[148] He was interviewed by an English woman journalist who asked him if he had ever thought of marrying a white girl. The interviewer obviously expected him to think it a grand idea: interracial harmony and all that. But he answered quite indignantly, 'Why should I marry a white girl? I want a son that looks like me.' That is the natural feeling. The father wants his son to look like – to *be* like – him, to be a continuation of him. The Indian idea – the traditional idea all over the world – is that you marry for the sake of getting a son. That is what marriage is all about: not to get you a soulmate, or a life companion, or your missing other half, or anything like that. No, you marry for the sake of a son, for the sake of progeny. That's why in the *Dhammapada* the fool says, 'This son is mine', not 'This wife is mine.'[149] She is not important enough – she is not the subject of a very strong attachment. The strong attachment is to the son and wealth. If anything, the wife is included in wealth, in possessions.

SAGARAMATI: It seems to have been the same with the ancient Greeks. In the *Symposium*, I remember, the lowest form of seeking immortality was to produce a son. There didn't seem to be any mention of women at all.

SANGHARAKSHITA: Right. I think many men in the West have lost this very primitive and basic feeling for the son.

SAGARAMATI: Somebody said that you thought that in time some of the men in the Order would, when they 'grew up', settle down and have families.

SANGHARAKSHITA: I didn't think any such thing. That's a gross misrepresentation – though there's *some* truth in it, as there usually is! What I said was that in the future, having sorted out their emotional problems, some male Order members might decide, quite objectively and conscientiously, to get married and produce a few children and – by way of setting an example – bring them up as children ought to be brought up. There is no reason why a mature and responsible individual should not be able to take on that sort of responsibility, in the right sort of way, if on proper reflection he decides to do so. If he knows what he is doing, and if he can handle the situation, and if, all things considered, it is the best thing for him to do, well, he's a responsible person and that's his decision. Most men would not be in a position to do that. Blinded by passion, pricked by the goad of their desires, they blunder into something they don't know anything about, find themselves with a wife and two or three children – all without knowing what they're doing. But if you've been an Order member for ten or fifteen years, if you've got over your emotional hang-ups, you're not emotionally dependent, if you're a responsible person and know what you're doing, if then you decide to get married, that's quite a different situation. You might think, 'Marriage would be quite a positive situation for me. I'll have two or three children. There's no question of my bringing them up as Buddhists, but I'll lay a positive foundation so that if ever they do wish to be Buddhists – and conceivably they might want to be – they'll have a good foundation on which to build. I'll give them that sort of opportunity, that sort of training.' That is quite a different thing from blundering into matrimony in the way most people do. That's what I was getting at – that you mustn't exclude that possibility, thinking, 'No one in the Order is ever going to get married: it's impossible.' No, marriage as I have described it must be left open as an option for the mature, responsible person.

GRAHAM: But it would be so difficult to try and find that sort of woman, though!

SANGHARAKSHITA: Don't make things more difficult than they actually are! We'll be training up the women too! With luck there'll be one trained woman for every ten trained men.

GRAHAM: Not the reverse?

SANGHARAKSHITA: At least one in ten men could be sure of a suitable trained woman partner. That is the sort of ratio – very roughly – that I was thinking of. Anyway, be very careful about believing what I am supposed to have said. Track it down to the source and find out what I really did say.

So, 'Care of son and wife.' If you've got a son and a wife, they're your responsibility; you should look after them. And 'a peaceful livelihood', *Anākulā ca kammantā*: peaceful, non-contentious right livelihood. There is quite a lot that could be said about that, obviously. It's a livelihood that does no harm to other living beings, and no harm to oneself. I've gone into this in the course of the lecture on perfect livelihood in the series 'The Buddha's Noble Eightfold Path'.[150]

**Generosity and Good Deeds**

> Gifts and by Dharma wayfaring …

*Dānañ ca dhammacariyā ca. Dāna* is generosity. Here we come to something very positive and outward-going. With *dhammacariyā* we go even further, and come on to the specifically spiritual path. The word *dhammacariyā* is quite important for early Buddhism. It is a key term: you get *dhammacariyā* and *brahmacariyā*, and later on in the development of Buddhism you get *bodhicariyā*, which is the specifically Mahāyāna equivalent. Literally *dhammacariyā* is 'practising the Dharma.' It is following the path of the Dharma, following the spiritual path.

RICHARD: Woodward has: 'Giving of alms, the righteous life'.

SANGHARAKSHITA: It's more than righteous in the purely ethical sense. 'Righteous' suggests the ethical life; but *dhammacariyā* is the Dharma life in the full spiritual sense. It's the Dharma faring, the Dharma practice. *Cariyā* means a going, a walking, therefore also a practising, a living. *Dhammacariyā* is a faring, or a walking, or a practising in accordance with the Dharma. It is living the Dharma life, putting the Dharma into actual operation.

> … the care of kin …

Or 'to cherish kith and kin.' (Woodward): *Ñātakānañ ca sangaho. Ñātaka* means a relative, a kinsman. It has been suggested that the word 'kind' came from 'kin'. Kind behaviour was the behaviour you naturally used towards kinsfolk, towards people who are related to you by blood and in other ways – not towards people outside the group, outside the tribe. Later on such behaviour was extended to other people as well. In the course of the spiritual life it's gradually extended to everybody: everybody becomes kin, so you are kind to everybody.

> … blameless deeds …

*Anavajjāni kammāni.* That's quite interesting. Who blames your deeds?

A VOICE: Karma?

SANGHARAKSHITA: No, it's a bit more straightforward than that. It's other people. Other people blame you. But why should you bother what other people say? Why does the Buddha speak of blameless deeds, not just of good deeds or spiritual deeds?

GRAHAM: 'Blameless' is maybe stirring something up in people to bring out the negative emotions.

SANGHARAKSHITA: It's more the opposite of that.

RICHARD: It's just being good to people, I suppose.

SANGHARAKSHITA: No, it's more than that. Maybe we should refer here to the Abhidharma. Do you remember the list of skilful mental states, according to the Yogācāra tradition?[151] First was *saddhā*, and then what comes next?

SAGARAMATI: It's *hiri*, isn't it?

SANGHARAKSHITA: Yes, it's *hiri-ottappa*, as those two mental states would be called in Pāli. So what are these? *Hiri* is usually translated as shame. *Ottappa* is more like not doing something because it goes against your own conscience and you would feel remorse if you did it. *Hiri* is your ethical response to the expectations of the positive group. It's considered a very important quality. It presupposes the existence of a supportive and emotionally healthy group within which you were brought up, or within which you find yourself. You do not want to be blamed by the group because you trust the judgement of the group. After all it's a positive group and is concerned with your genuine well-being. If you do something wrong, if the group blames you, you must be wrong you think: you've got that sort of faith in the group and its norms. So you don't do any deeds for which the group might blame you. In the case of the sangha it's not, of course, a group in the ordinary tribal sense, but a group in the spiritual context, i.e. a spiritual community. Elsewhere in the scriptures the Buddha says quite frequently that one who is a worthy disciple does not do anything for which others who are wise will blame him. One does not wish to be blamed by the wise because if you're blamed by the wise you really have done something wrong. At the same time you don't always know for yourself, directly, what is wrong and what is right, so you go by the reactions of the wise. You try to live up to their expectations of you in a positive and healthy way. This is considered a very important ethical determinant: your sensitivity to the judgement passed upon you by those who are wise, those with whom you're in positive contact, i.e. the healthy group on the social level and the spiritual community on the spiritual level. Such a judgement is a judgement not in any hard or negative sense, but in a kindly sense. In the case of the Western Buddhist Order, if any Order member feels that something that he is doing is being blamed by the whole Order, the chances are that it's wrong. Under exceptional circumstances, it could be that the whole Order is wrong, and that the one individual is right, but I think that that would be very rare. It's much more likely that the individual is wrong, i.e. one individual as compared with a number of other individuals *qua* individuals, not with a number of other individuals falsely conceived as a corporate entity. It's not that the Order comes down heavily on you, but that there is a sensitivity and awareness on your part that by virtue of something you have done or left undone you have put yourself out of harmony with the Order and that, whether overtly expressed or not, the attitude of the Order towards you is in that respect one of blame.

RICHARD: I was reading about *hiri* today in *Mind in Buddhist Psychology*, and it suddenly occurred to me, where does this idea of being a good boy come in? You know, as in the article on 'Leaving Mother and Initiation into Manhood' by Chintamani.

SANGHARAKSHITA: Mother, mother! That's where the good boy bit comes in. You want to please mother, and just mother. But it's not a question of pleasing mother. You've got to please the elders of the tribe: that's where the positive group comes in. Just pleasing mother makes you a good boy. Living up to the expectations of the elders of the tribe, which are realistic expectations, makes you a man.

RICHARD: Presumably if you were to put a mother projection onto the elders of the tribe then they would let you know what was going on.

SANGHARAKSHITA: Yes, indeed they would. If you try your boyish tricks with the old men they are just not interested. They don't react – they're not impressed – or they take you down a peg or two.

LOKAMITRA: In trying to live up to the expectations of the rest of the group, or of the Order, it's sometimes hard to know whether we are simply transferring a mother projection onto them or whether we are acting as individuals.

SANGHARAKSHITA: The difference between the two is as the difference between the attitude of mother and the attitude of father. Mother is pleased whatever you do, because you're unconditionally her little boy, but father wants you to grow up. Father's got more objective norms for you which mother usually doesn't have. Whether you're a criminal or a saint, mother feels towards you the same way. It doesn't make any difference to her whether you're the one or the other: you're still her son. Father will not feel like that, and if you commit really serious misdemeanours, he may refuse to have anything to do with you. Mother will never go to that extreme – not unless she's very much influenced by father. Mother will forgive you and in a sense accept whatever you do. Father will not. If he's a real father in a healthy, objective way, he will insist that you live up to certain standards, that you develop and be a man, that you behave properly, i.e. like a real human being. That is the difference. So if, in the case of the Order, a certain Order member is acting like a small boy and the Order is approving what he does, regardless of its nature, they're behaving like mother. But if they apply objective criteria, and are pleased with him when he does well, and displeased with him when he does badly, then they're being more like father, and therefore their attitude is more spiritual. Of course they're not being like a heavy, repressive father. I'm using the word father in a positive sense, as basically it should be used. Mother will forgive you anything; but father won't, and he shouldn't.

SAGARAMATI: Until you do something about it.

SANGHARAKSHITA: Until you do something about it. Mother will let you get away with anything. Father won't. When you are a small child you need mother's love, otherwise you don't grow properly; you need to be unconditionally accepted. But as you grow older you must be conditionally accepted. You're accepted by the men on condition you become a man. The men will not accept a little boy into their ranks. Mother will accept you. If you remain a little boy till you're 50, 60, 70, mother doesn't mind: she's all the more mother, then. That's how you tell the difference. Father is much more difficult to deal with for the child, for a son especially. Father imposes certain objective demands. Mother doesn't. That's why the boy has to be taken away from mother, otherwise he won't develop. The mother's part is not to be underestimated: it's indispensable for the baby and for the small boy. But the father's part is indispensable too, and the part of the tribe, or the positive group, the positive community – and later on the spiritual community.

GRAHAM: Does the spiritual community take over from father?

SANGHARAKSHITA: You could say that as father takes over from mother, the spiritual community takes over from the ordinary social community.

SAGARAMATI: One can still see little vibrations of these things. Although they've almost passed away, you feel as if they're there on the verge…

SANGHARAKSHITA: Vibrations of what?

SAGARAMATI: Of this sort of development from mother to father. I remember being at home and how, when you were seventeen or whatever, you were suddenly dragged out into the pub.

SANGHARAKSHITA: Right. I remember this sort of thing too. When I was very young, when I was 7 or 8, and then when I was ill, I was much more with my mother and my aunties, and my granny. But when I reached my early teens I started spending more time with my father. He took me out quite a lot: I was quite lucky in that way. He was out of work for a while, so he used to take me walking on Wimbledon Common. When I was a little older he took me to the pub and I met his friends. Then I was evacuated, and then I left school of my own accord and got a job. In this way I started getting out into the wider world, and met a lot of other people. Then, of course, I was called up into the army, which meant an expansion of another sort, and after that, eventually, I came into contact with other Buddhists and, in a sense, with the spiritual community. Very often there is that sort of natural progression, even now. It may be that it happens in an uninstitutionalized way, but it does happen, because at certain levels of society there's a residue of that basic, healthy, almost tribal, primitive human attitude.

SAGARAMATI: I feel there's a danger in the way people like us live – not people like us in the FWBO community but people who are wandering round a big city like London and who haven't even got the tribal thing.

SANGHARAKSHITA: Right. They're completely rootless, so they'll try to use us for the wrong purpose sometimes. In a way that's all right – we can be big enough to have these different levels – but we must be quite clear to which level people are attaching themselves. They may be asking for ordination when what they really want is to be accepted by the group, or by father or even by mother. We must be able to sort out that sort of thing. We must make sure that this person really wants to commit himself or herself individually – that they're not looking for father, much less still looking for mother, but that they want to commit themselves individually, with all that that implies. I think that cases of people attaching themselves to the Movement mistaking one level for another are happening less and less. The different levels are anyway quite well sorted out, at least in some people's minds.

So much then, for the *maṅgala* of 'blameless deeds'.

## Restraint

> To cease and utterly abstain from wrong ...

*Ārati virati pāpā. Ārati* is simply abstaining and *virati* is altogether removing yourself from *pāpa*, that is to say evil, wrongdoing. The first is the result of the temporary cessation of unskilful mental states, as in *śamatha*, the second the result of their permanent cessation, which occurs only with *vipaśyanā*. This *maṅgala* represents the 'negative' side of ethical life. It consists in altogether disentangling yourself from everything that is evil or unskilful.

... Restraint in drink and zeal for things ...

*Majjapānā ca saṃyamo appamādo ca dhammesu*. Woodward translates these two *maṅgalas* as 'To shun intoxicants; and be steadfast in righteousness', but this is a bit interpretive. *Saṃyamo* is restraint or control, especially control of the senses: not allowing the senses to go blindly towards their objects. It thus implies awareness (*appamādo*), which comes up in the next part of the verse. *Majja* is anything intoxicating, especially any intoxicating drink. *Majjapānā ca saṃyamo* therefore means restraint in the drinking of intoxicants. You notice that it doesn't say complete abstention, but only restraint, which is interesting. If it is argued that restraint here does in fact mean complete abstention, it could be replied that it no more means that than, for instance, restraint of the senses means complete abstention from the use of the senses. 'Zeal for things' is a very poor translation of *appamādo ca dhammesu*, and 'steadfastness in righteousness' is not really any better. 'Awareness in the midst of *dhammas*' or 'mindfulness in the midst of *dhammas*' (that is, with regard to *dhammas*) would be a more accurate rendering – *dhammas* in the sense of mental states, as in the first verse of the *Dhammapada*: *Manopubbaṅgamā dhammā manoseṭṭhā manomayā*, that is, 'All mental states are preceded by mind, dominated by mind, made up of mind', or, in Abhidharma/Abhidhamma terms, *caitta dharmas / cetasikas* are preceded by *cittas* as is the *citta*, so are the *caitta dharmas / cetasikas*. This was the interpretation given by my teacher Jagdish Kashyap. One could also understand *dhammas* (in 'awareness in the midst of *dhammas*') as 'things,' as in the penultimate verse of the *Maṅgala Sutta*. Thus the verse as a whole speaks of (1) abstention from, complete dissociation from, everything that is evil, (2) restraint with regard to intoxicants, and (3) mindfulness in the midst of mental states, that is to say, with regard to mental states.

LOKAMITRA: Thinking about the fifth lay precept, the positive version of which is really mindfulness, it seems that it's not only abstention from drinking intoxicants but also from certain mental states that can have the same sort of intoxicating effect.

SANGHARAKSHITA: There's a list of three intoxicants in the earlier Pāli texts – intoxicants in a more metaphorical sense. There's the intoxication of youth, the intoxication of health, and the intoxication of life.[152] The word for intoxication here is *mada*, which is from the same root as *majja*. It can also be rendered infatuation, or pride. The later Abhidhamma texts give a longer list, including the intoxication of birth, i.e. caste, intoxication of clan. You can see, therefore, what intoxication means. Suppose you're intoxicated with youth. You may even look down upon older people. You think that if you're not young you're nobody. You've had it. It's the young who are where it's at! The fact that you're young takes possession of you, and that makes you a bit reckless, inconsiderate, unmindful, and unaware. You're intoxicated by your own youthfulness. You forget that you too are going to grow old one day. In the same way you may be completely possessed by the fact that you're an attractive and handsome, good-looking, even beautiful person. You find this with some actors and actresses who are very much into their own good looks, very much into their own powers of fascination and the effect that they have on other people. They're really carried away by all that. This intoxication is, in fact, very much like being carried away by something.

RICHARD: Is it a sort of infatuation?

SANGHARAKSHITA: Yes, it is. You can also be intoxicated by the fact that you're healthy and vigorous, or by your social position or by your possessions.

SAGARAMATI: What about beauty? Beauty can be both subjective and objective. You can be intoxicated by someone else's beauty as well as by your own.

SANGHARAKSHITA: Yes, but in a different sort of way, I think. As regards intoxication or infatuation by possessions, there's a well-known Indian story about a frog who found a farthing. A frog found a farthing, and was very pleased with himself indeed on this account. He hid the farthing in his hole, and sat proudly at the entrance, thinking, 'I'm very rich. I'm the possessor of this farthing.' While he was sitting there an elephant came walking towards the frog and his hole, and of course he didn't even see the frog. The frog called out to the elephant, 'Stop! Don't you dare walk over my hole. Don't you dare walk over me. Don't you know that I am the possessor of a farthing?' But the elephant didn't even hear the frog, and just walked on over the hole. The frog was so enraged, the story goes, that he hopped along behind the elephant, trying to kick him! He was so infatuated by his own wealth that he lost all sense of proportion. This is the effect that infatuation has upon you. You become completely blind. It's like Shakespeare's

> ...man, proud man,
> Dressed in a little brief authority,
> Most ignorant of what he's most assur'd,
> His glassy essence, like an angry ape
> Plays such fantastic tricks before high heaven
> As make the angels weep.[153]

People become puffed up by their position, but it's purely external to them. It has nothing to do with their own innate powers.

GRAHAM: What if the frog had used what he had in a positive way? I was thinking of people in the Friends, and how they should be using what they have, rather than putting it down.

SANGHARAKSHITA: To depreciate yourself, and not appreciate – or not use – your own good qualities, that's the other extreme. You depreciate yourself when you think, 'What can I do? I'm perfectly useless. I can't do anything.' There was a lot of that sort of thinking around in the early days of the FWBO. Alcohol intoxicates in a certain sense, but there are other things that intoxicate you even more – of which, in a way, you should be even more careful. This is the significance of the four sights, or rather, of the first three sights. The Buddha says that when as a young man, before the Enlightenment, he saw the first sight, that of the old man, the intoxication of youth faded in him. He realized that he too would grow old. When he saw the sick man, the intoxication of health and strength faded in him, and he realized that he too was liable to sickness. When he saw the dead man the intoxication of life itself faded and he realized that he too must die one day. In this way the first three sights brought him up against the facts of life with a sharp jolt and made him more aware, more mindful, and more open to the possibilities of the spiritual life, as represented by the fourth sight.[154]

**Reverence and Gratitude**

Reverence, joy, meekness, gratitude.

*Gāravo*, the first *maṅgala* of this verse, is 'reverence,' as both Hare and Woodward translate it. It's even more than reverence. It's not only giving to others but also giving weight (*garuka*) as it were to them. Giving consideration out of respect – it's more like that.

GARY: How does it differ from worship?

SANGHARAKSHITA: In the case of worship (*pūjā*) you realize the worth, or the value, of something but in the case of reverence (*gāravo*) you realize its importance, its seriousness, its gravity. There's that element too. This is probably why Chalmers has translated *gāravo ca nivāto ca* as 'reverent awe', taking *nivāto* not as humility but as reverence and apparently not as a noun but as an adjective modifying the preceding noun, *gāravo*, which he takes not as reverence but as awe. In this way he makes one *maṅgala* out of two. *Gāravo* consists in your being impressed by the seriousness, the weight as it were, of what you are valuing and ascribing worth to. In a way it's a more weighty word than *pūjā*. It consists in your being genuinely impressed, in really *feeling* the worth of something – not simply recognizing its worth but actually feeling it as something of great importance that is almost weighing on you, as it were. Chalmers' 'awe', with its suggestion of the numinous, is therefore probably a better translation than Hare and Woodward's 'reverence'.

SAGARAMATI: It's more like something from the outside that comes in to you.

SANGHARAKSHITA: Right. In the case of worship it's you going out to acknowledge its value; but in the case of *gāravo* or reverence it's more like that valuable thing impressing its value on you in a weighty way, so that if you are open to it at all, you are forced to recognize it.

RICHARD: Is it not also being moved by something?

SANGHARAKSHITA: That too one can say.

LOKAMITRA: It's a spontaneous feeling towards something coming from outside, as it were.

SANGHARAKSHITA: The English word reverence, though a good word, is rather weak in this context. It's more like the feeling you get when you look up at a great mountain: you feel that it is very high, very sublime, and you're quite overpowered, quite awed. You're not just thinking, 'What a wonderful mountain! How high it is!' It's more than that. It's as if the mountain weighs on you, dominates you. You're actually forced to recognize its height and grandeur.

GRAHAM: I think the awe is even more powerful if you intend to try to climb that mountain.

SANGHARAKSHITA: Oh yes, it becomes a challenge. You realize what you are actually up against. There's that mountain, and you're going to climb it.

MARK: Would 'veneration' be more suitable word for *gāravo*?

SANGHARAKSHITA: Yes. Veneration is a stronger word than reverence. *Nivāto* is more like humility, as Woodward translates the term, because it complements reverence or veneration. It's not humility in the grovelling sense. If you recognize the value and the weight of something, and really *feel* that as it were weighing upon you, then how do you feel about yourself? You feel humble. Even though you're going to scale the mountain, you still feel humble. It's a bit like in the Sevenfold Puja, where you get first the worship and the salutation and the Going for Refuge and then the confession of faults. You recognize the sublimity of the ideal, so you worship and salute it; but having done that, you look at yourself and think, 'How far short do I fall! And why? Because of this – and this – and this', which you proceed to confess. The confession is complementary to the worship and the salutation. In the same way this *gāravo ca nivāto ca* is being impressed by the weight and grandeur of the ideal and therefore feeling yourself to be correspondingly humble – as if you were being dwarfed by the mountain. But that's taking the analogy in a very limited sense, because you're also capable of climbing the mountain; you're also capable of becoming a mountain. So there's a certain confidence in the humility too. You're not crushed, even though you feel humble. You could even say it's a sort of proud humility: you know you're going to be a mountain too one day.

RICHARD: Is it having no illusions about where you are at this particular time?

SANGHARAKSHITA: Yes – but it's also being confident about where you can be, if you only make the effort. So that's *gāravo ca nivāto ca*. Next comes *santuṭṭhi*. *Santuṭṭhi* is 'content', the positive counterpart of *kāmesu micchācārā* or sexual misconduct. I was thinking quite a bit about contentment recently, after Chintamani read us his latest article, in which he stressed the importance of receptivity, and pointed out that there was a connection between contentment and receptivity; if one was receptive, one could also be content. If you're not content, what happens? Well, first of all, what is the state of not being contented? Let us try to understand that. It's when you're dissatisfied with the present, or dissatisfied with yourself as you at present are: you feel a sort of inner emptiness, an inner void, so you try to fill that, and the discontent therefore leads to craving. You also start thinking about the future, and thinking about the past – to fill up the emptiness of the present. Thus time comes in too. You can't be receptive, because you're not even in the present: your mind is straying back towards the past or reaching out into the future. You find, therefore, that if you're contented you're receptive, you're in the present, you're 'filled', whereas if you're discontented you're in a neurotic state of inner emptiness and frustration, and therefore craving develops – you start thinking about the past and anticipating the future, and you can't even receive in the present – you're blocking that too. So contentment seems to be a very important quality. Very few people are content with what they have now, with what they are now. Contentment isn't complacency, which is common enough. It is a full and genuine acceptance of what you are now and where you are now. If you accept that, then you can be receptive to what you are able to receive in the here and the now. So if you feel discontented or bored, don't start trying to fill that emptiness and remove that boredom: just stop and experience it, but stay with it. If you do that, at least you're in the present. If you can stay with it, and stop trying to remove the boredom by filling the void with something or other, then the boredom and discontent will slowly dissolve, and you'll feel more at peace with yourself, more at ease, and then you can receive, or you might feel that there is something that you would like to do. I think that contentment is quite important. If you're contented you're very much in the present, but consciously in the present – because you're always in the present, anyway.

GARY: If you were bored and you didn't remain with the boredom but just looked for something to do you'd become alienated.

SANGHARAKSHITA: Yes: you are alienated from your boredom. You haven't really got rid of the boredom: you've simply cut yourself off from it, or covered it up. So if you feel bored, that's good: you're right down to brass tacks, as it were. Just sit down and be bored! Feel very bored. Sooner or later the feeling will pass off, and you'll feel 'I'd like to do this,' or 'I'd like to do that.' But to start thinking, 'What can I do to get rid of the boredom?' is fatal. You won't be able to get rid of the feeling of boredom in that way.

LOKAMITRA: I find that if my energies are dissipated, I tend to put myself into a situation where positive energies are drawn out. I suppose I have been with the boredom and dissipation for a bit, but in my case I find that it isn't doing nothing, but doing something, that helps.

SAGARAMATI: There is a boredom due to a stagnation of energy, in a sense.

SANGHARAKSHITA: Yes, that's true, but even then I think that usually you just have to stay with it until you get an impulse to do something or other. But you shouldn't think what to do, i.e. shouldn't force yourself to do something on purely rational grounds before the impulse to do it has arisen.

GRAHAM: One of the things that I've found is quite easy to do in situations like that is to turn to something like music. It had a fairly instant effect, but afterwards I still didn't feel very good; often I felt worse.

SANGHARAKSHITA: Another healthy thing to do is just to do the next thing to be done. If it's the washing up, just finish that off. Or go and wash your shirt, or say to yourself, 'Let's tidy things up.' Just do the next thing to be done, in a very elementary, basic way. If you have been feeling bored and you just sit down until you feel a genuine impulse to do something, very often the first thing you feel like doing is something like that; but then that leads to something else, and that to something else. In that way you start losing the sense of boredom, and your energies start flowing again. But if you start thinking, 'What wonderful, interesting thing can I do to get rid of this feeling of boredom?' you can pick up the most interesting book, or go to see the most interesting person, but it won't work. The book will seem quite dull, and the person likewise. You must just give yourself time.

LOKAMITRA: Productive situations would be better than positive situations, because they would get the energies going again.

SANGHARAKSHITA: Yes, there's an objective need, where you're not doing the thing just to get out of the state of boredom, but doing it because it needs to be done.

LOKAMITRA: Yes. And it does manage to stimulate something.

SAGARAMATI: There's a connection between that and the first stage of the *mettā bhāvanā*. I feel that some or even most people – or I do anyway – find the first stage of this practice the most difficult, and that seems to be connected with this tendency not to accept where you are, your own emptiness, at the actual time. It sounds as if in the first stage you have to start from exactly how you feel at that present moment, not try to grab after some occasion in the past when you've been happy.

SANGHARAKSHITA: Perhaps you have to start by actually feeling yourself, experiencing yourself, accepting yourself, and then gradually start feeling good and positive towards yourself; but not think, necessarily, that you can switch on the positivity right away. You have to feel yourself first – and it may be quite a negative, unpleasant self that you feel for a while.

LOKAMITRA: That's why it's quite good before the *mettā* starts to be mindful of the body, just to get one physically in touch: I find it very helpful, with the class especially.

SANGHARAKSHITA: Yes, I've done this sometimes. Just mindfulness of the body, starting from the tips of the toes and the tips of the fingers, and working one's way right up to the head. Then you're feeling yourself, you're in touch with yourself. You can't feel good will towards yourself if you're alienated from yourself, and don't even feel yourself. It may be a very angry self that you have to feel and experience first.

SAGARAMATI: That's another connection I've found, from taking the Sunday class – a connection between that and the stage of developing *mettā* towards the enemy. It's always the same people who have the same difficulties: it's those who can't love themselves who don't have enemies! Everything's a bit too neutral.

LOKAMITRA: They just don't feel.

SANGHARAKSHITA: Or just don't *allow* themselves to feel. In the early days of the FWBO, when we were doing the *mettā bhāvanā*, some people would say, when I gave my preliminary talk explaining the practice, 'But I don't have any enemies. There's no one I dislike, no one I hate.' Sometimes I used to say, 'Well, in that case just look around within the family circle. It's probably there that you'll find someone that you dislike.' And you could see from their expressions, in the case of some people, that they knew at once that there was somebody within the family circle – even somebody quite near and dear – whom they didn't like or whom they really hated. That's where the enemy was. You usually take it for granted that you like those who are near and dear to you, but it isn't necessarily the case. One of our friends told me that when he was in his teens he and his brother used to hate their father so much that when he had his afternoon nap, they used to creep up behind him and go through the motions of smashing the top of his head in with an axe. They used to really enjoy letting out their feelings in this way. They felt so violent towards their father that when they saw his bald head resting on the back of the chair, they couldn't resist it. Another of our friends, in fact an Order member, discovered that he really hates his mother. In the light of these and a few other facts, I rather mistrust people who say, 'I don't have an enemy in the world. There's no one whom I dislike.' In the very last resort it may be their own unfortunate self that they really dislike and take it out on.

RICHARD: It seems that there's not enough black-and-whiteness around: there's not enough hate.

SANGHARAKSHITA: Neither hot nor cold.

RICHARD: There's just this wishy-washy, grey sort of feeling that you have towards people. But I find that if I really hate someone I really start to love them, in a way, because there's something there, something tangible.

SANGHARAKSHITA: Well I have sometimes said that it is easier to transform hatred into love than to transform indifference into love. At least when you hate someone, there's some feeling there.

GARY: It's funny, the hate and the love part of the *mettā*, the friend and the foe, swap pretty frequently.

LOKAMITRA: You often don't start to hate until you start to love, and vice versa. When the *mettā* really gets going you discover lots of enemies.

SANGHARAKSHITA: Very often there isn't enough oomph (for want of a better term) in people's emotions, whether positive or negative. They're not full-blooded enough. They're neither full-blooded friends nor full-blooded enemies. They'll never do you down, but they'll never help you out, either.

RICHARD: What's that quote from George Bernard Shaw you showed me? Something like, 'The worst feeling you can have towards somebody is indifference.'[155]

SANGHARAKSHITA: That's very true.

SAGARAMATI: You're just not acknowledging the person at all by being indifferent to them.

SANGHARAKSHITA: Right. It's an emotional ignoring. That's why small children who have got very active, physically demonstrative mothers are very often in a healthier psychological state. Even if the mothers do slap them sometimes, or are a bit short-tempered, there's this emotional contact all the time nevertheless, whereas a mother who does her duty but is a bit indifferent and not very demonstrative leaves the child a bit cold and not very energized.

RICHARD: When a kid hates he hates and when he loves he loves. There's no two ways about it.

SANGHARAKSHITA: Yes. Very small children, especially, will say, 'I don't like you!' And you can see that they don't; they don't try to hide it at all. And if they really like you they climb on your knee and show it in no uncertain terms. When I was 15 or 16 I was staying in Torquay with some friends of the family, and the woman there had a little girl aged about 4. For some reason or other, the minute this child set her eyes on me she took an absolute fancy to me. She was always wanting to sit on my knee and talk to me. I just couldn't understand it. At 15 or 16 one isn't very interested in small children, and it was a bit of a nuisance. But that was how it was. Whenever she saw me she would start laughing, she was so pleased, and want to sit on my knee. I wanted to read my book! It might just as well have been an instant dislike, in which case she would have shown it just as readily. Children have got that sort of directness and adults, unfortunately, lose so much of it. You end up by not feeling. You become a bit atrophied in your feelings: you don't really respond or react. D. H. Lawrence has quite a bit to say about this, though he does go rather to extremes. He says things like, 'Smack the child's little bottom and let the child feel your clean, healthy, hot anger.'[156] That's taking it a bit too far.

LOKAMITRA: Perhaps that takes us back to what Sagaramati was saying about indifference earlier. Equanimity, which is a sort of spiritual indifference, comes after developing *mettā* and the rest.

SANGHARAKSHITA: Exactly. It's a state of equilibrium. This is a very important point. Equanimity (*upekkhā*) comes when you've developed your *mettā* (friendliness), *karuṇā* (compassion), and *muditā* (sympathetic joy) equally towards all. If you like someone very much but dislike somebody else, then there's a bit of wavering and to that extent no equanimity. If the person you like comes into the room you'll be happy.

If the person you dislike comes into the room you'll be unhappy. In this way there's an oscillation between the two states. But if you like everybody equally, you'll be happy whoever is around. Your state will not change, there won't be that oscillation, and that is equanimity. If you like everybody intensely – if you've got very strong *mettā* towards all equally – how can there be any mental wavering? It's the same with the *karuṇā* and the *muditā*. The state of equanimity is that state of equilibrium and even-mindedness that comes about when you have the same positive feelings towards all, so that you have no preferences. You like everybody equally, you're kind to everybody equally, and you rejoice in the happiness of all beings equally. By concentrating on the development of that equality, feeling *mettā* towards all equally, you develop equanimity. You don't develop equanimity by cutting down on *mettā* and trying to love fewer people, but by taking the love you have for this person or that and trying to love everybody as much as that. That is the difference.

Anyway, so much for *santuṭṭhi*, content. Fourthly, there's *kataññutā*, which is gratitude. Again, this is a very important virtue. Obviously gratitude should be a matter of spontaneous feeling. You shouldn't say to anyone, 'Well you ought to feel grateful!' though often this is what we hear. Gratitude should be a natural thing, and not as rare as it seems to be. In the early days of the FWBO people who came along to meditation classes and lectures didn't seem to feel any sort of gratitude. Some people said that they were under the impression that there was some big wealthy foundation behind the FWBO that was paying for everything and therefore it was all supplied for free, and nothing was expected from those who came along. They were the consumers, as it were, the FWBO was just something set up for their benefit, and they had no obligation towards it.

LOKAMITRA: I think we must be quite careful not to give that impression still.

MARK: Especially when we've got things like Sukhavati and centres all over the place.

SANGHARAKSHITA: What I call the consumer mentality is very strong nowadays in Britain. Everything is to be supplied. All you do is open your mouth, and whatever you want will be piped into it.

RICHARD: Even if there was a big foundation behind the 'Friends', that's still no reason for not feeling grateful.

SANGHARAKSHITA: No… Even if there is a big foundation, we should pretend there isn't! I did remark, when I was at Sukhavati, 'Just imagine. Suppose some wealthy donor had come and said, 'Here's your £50,000. Just give the contract to a building firm and get the work done.' It just wouldn't have been the same, would it?

LOKAMITRA: It wouldn't! Raising the money and building a place has broadened out the energy required to run something like that. If we'd been given it, we wouldn't have been able to use it.

RICHARD: Well, this is what happens. You see these gurus coming over. They have lots of money, they set up these big organizations, and they're just five-minute wonders.

SANGHARAKSHITA: Also, it's being goal-orientated rather than process-oriented. You're grabbing at the goal, or trying to buy the goal; but the process is as important as the goal. In a way, the process *is* the goal. Even when you've got your Sukhavati, what are you going to do? You're not going to just stand there and admire it. It's got to function. By your working on it and creating it, it is in a way already functioning – and then it can continue to function. There isn't a day when everything is done and there's nothing to do after that. That's just an imaginary dividing line. You might have an opening day to mark the achievement of a certain stage, but the process is still going on.

LOKAMITRA: The process of becoming …

SAGARAMATI: We always tend to think that some time in the future there is this pensioned-off heaven. You sort of drop off somewhere, and then there's nothing else to do.

SANGHARAKSHITA: As I said to Subhuti, the people working at Sukhavati don't realize they're not working for it: they've got it already! They don't know that – that's why they're enjoying it so much – but actually they've got it already. Their getting it is in the working for it.

LOKAMITRA: You said that generosity should be spontaneous. But *dāna* is a practice to encourage that, to bring that out.

SANGHARAKSHITA: That is true. But it's very difficult to have a practice for gratitude. You can, of course, express your gratitude verbally, and say, 'Thank you very much.'

SAGARAMATI: You can intellectually acknowledge the fact that you have something to be grateful for and do something, even if you don't actually feel it because you're a bit blocked.

LOKAMITRA: You have said that it's not only negative feelings that are blocked but often positive ones, and that it's necessary somehow to bring those out.

GRAHAM: Sometimes the negative ones are not even negative. They're things that are put on us because of the society we live in, and we are told that they're negative.

SANGHARAKSHITA: Several people have remarked on the fact that many criminals, especially younger ones, seem quite healthy people. They're rebelling against certain things, and maybe in a sense they've done wrong, but there is a healthy energy in them which is just dashing itself against certain limitations.

SAGARAMATI: I often think that about John – one of the kids who throws stones through the windows of the Archway centre. He always seems a lot healthier than most of the people who come to the centre for classes and lectures.

SANGHARAKSHITA: A devil rather than an angel, in the Blakean sense of these terms.

SAGARAMATI: Yes, with a glint in his eye.

SANGHARAKSHITA: Anyway, in the first two lines of this verse there are these four qualities enumerated as *maṅgalas* or auspicious signs: reverence (that'll do for *gāravo*), humility, content, and gratitude.

They all seem to run together, don't they? They seem very much associated.

> Dharma to hear in season due:
> This is the greatest luck.

This is *Kālena dhammasavanaṃ*, 'timely hearing of the Dharma', or as Hare translates it, 'Dharma to hear in season due'. This is mentioned next because the hearing of the Dharma links up with contentment and receptivity. 'Hearing' is very, very important in early Buddhism. The disciple is the *śrāvaka* (Pāli *sāvaka)*, the one who hears. The word we translate as 'learned person' is *bahuśruta*, the one who has heard much, listened much, taken in much. *Dhammasavanaṃ* is just 'hearing the Dharma' – or better still, 'listening to the Dharma'. When you listen to the Dharma you're taking in, you're being receptive. This is one of the reasons why ceremonial chanting is so beneficial in its effect. If you hear the Pāli texts chanted and understand the meaning, it's quite an experience – particularly if they are well chanted. It's like some archetypal voice uttering these timeless truths and you just hearing them, just taking them in. You don't have to think about them. You just take them in: just receive. Such truths sound quite different when heard in that sort of way – or they feel quite different. There's a recording of the *Dhammapada* and other verses made under the direction of Dr Ambedkar by leading North Indian musicians and singers. It's really beautifully done. I wish I could get hold of that recording. The verses are so beautifully chanted – half chanted, half sung. It really is as though some archetypal voice is enunciating the truths taught by the Buddha and you are just listening and taking it in completely passively and absorbing it. You don't have to think: thinking isn't necessary.

SAGARAMATI: That's why the readings from the scriptures on festival days, in the context of the puja at the end of the celebrations, are so much more potent.

SANGHARAKSHITA: Right. But this sort of chanting is even more effective than a reading.

SAGARAMATI: Even though you don't understand the language?

SANGHARAKSHITA: No. I did say, 'If you hear the Pāli texts chanted, and understand the meaning'. If you don't understand the meaning, there's some effect, but it's much greater if you understand what is being said. Otherwise you only hear the sounds, not the meaning – and it's the meaning that's more important. In all Buddhist countries the lay people like to listen to the monks chanting, sometimes all night. They sit there quite contentedly, hour after hour, listening to the sound of the chanting. They may not always understand the meaning of the words, but it has a beneficial effect nonetheless. In Sri Lanka the chanting of *suttas* by monks is a regular feature of the daily radio programme. Even in this country we can listen to chanting on tape. I remember Sanghamitta telling me that she played the tape of the Sevenfold Puja every evening, and just sat and listened. Sometimes she might feel a bit depressed, but the tape would always help. She didn't have to make any effort. All she had to do was switch it on, sit back, and just listen. Even in the case of reading you have to make a slight effort, but you don't have to make an effort to listen, if the volume of sound is adequate, so you can be totally receptive in that situation. It's *hearing* the Dharma that is important: you hear it before you understand it. If you don't really hear it, don't really take it in, there's no question of understanding it either. Just to hear, just to listen, just to receive, is very important.

RICHARD: It says here, in the Woodward, 'To hear the Norm at proper times…'

SANGHARAKSHITA: *Kālena* is 'timely', or 'duly' (Hare) or, as Woodward has it, 'at proper times'. This brings up another important point. There's a right time and a wrong time for listening to the Dharma, apparently. So what would be the wrong time? Could there be a wrong time?

RICHARD: Yes, could there?

SAGARAMATI: I think if you were in a negative state…

SANGHARAKSHITA: Clearly according to the text there can be a wrong time!

LOKAMITRA: When you are not receptive.

SANGHARAKSHITA: When you are not receptive, and when you are not really going to be hearing it. When you're not in the mood, as it were.

LOKAMITRA: You must be prepared to open yourself. A few years before joining the FWBO I used to go to a meditation teacher. Once, I remember, a lad who was quite new to the class just sort of sprawled out on the floor, just lay right back. I felt quite angry and told him to sit up. I was quite shaken by the rudeness of his behaviour.

SANGHARAKSHITA: When you behave like that you're not really being receptive. It's not that you're lying back to take it all in. You're lying back to show that you don't care, that you're not impressed. I've talked about this in the excerpt 'On Formality and Informality', from the Huineng seminar.[157] The 'informality' is a pseudo-informality, an attitude adopted to show that you are not impressed. This means that you're not being very receptive.

RICHARD: You're just sort of super cool.

SAGARAMATI: The super cool is also tied up with the indifference. All these things seem to fit together.

SANGHARAKSHITA: Yes. Alienation. Discontent. Lack of receptivity. Ungratefulness... The whole lot!

SAGARAMATI: If we ever have a Western Abhidharma the list of the negative emotions is going to be incredibly long.

SANGHARAKSHITA: It's long enough even in the Eastern Abhidharma.

SAGARAMATI: We'll completely outstrip them. This means we'll have to find more positive qualities to counteract the negative ones.

SANGHARAKSHITA: Right. So this *maṅgala* is *kālena dhammasavanaṃ*, 'listening to the Dharma at proper times', or 'in a timely manner'. It doesn't mean that if you were really listening to the Dharma you could be doing it at the wrong time, but you could be going through the motions of listening to the Dharma while in fact you were not really listening. When you're only able to go through the motions, that is not the time to be doing that sort of thing.

RICHARD: There are supposed to be certain times – I'm thinking about meditation here – when it's particularly auspicious to meditate. Has that anything to do with this?

SANGHARAKSHITA: It could be brought into connection with it, though I don't think there's any connection intended. When you're in a highly meditative state it's good to call to mind the words of the Dharma, because in that state you are particularly susceptible and impressionable and receptive. You can then turn those words over in your mind: that is a particularly good time to 'hear' them. This could be considered a more timely hearing of the Dharma. It's more timely because you're more receptive.

### Forbearance and Conversation

> Patience, kind words, to see good men,
> Duly on Dharma to converse:
> This is the greatest luck.

*Khanti* is here translated as patience, but it's more like forbearance. There's the famous example in the *Jātakas* – referred to also in the *Vajracchedikā Sūtra* – of the monk Khantivādī, 'Preacher of Patience' or 'Preacher of Forbearance'. When his limbs were severed from his body by the enraged king of Kāsī he did not feel any anger; he practised forbearance.[158]

GRAHAM: What is forbearance?

SANGHARAKSHITA: Absence of retaliation. Somebody does something to you, or against you, which would normally make you angry and cause you to retaliate, or at least want to retaliate, but you don't feel any anger, you've no desire to retaliate. Instead of retaliating you forbear.

GRAHAM: When I was quite young I never used to retaliate. Could that be forbearance?

SANGHARAKSHITA: It's only forbearance if you don't have any anger to express. If you feel angry but nevertheless don't act it is not forbearance in the Buddhist sense, though it may be in the ordinary worldly sense.

RICHARD: It's not that you're gritting your teeth and saying, 'I'm not going to hit you. I'm practising patience.' In a sense there is no reaction at all on your part.

SANGHARAKSHITA: There is a reaction, but it's a positive reaction. You feel good will towards that person. That is forbearance. Śāntideva has a great deal to say about this in the *Bodhicaryāvatāra*. He regards *kṣānti*, forbearance – or patience, as you could possibly translate it – as the antidote to anger.

RICHARD: It's called the greatest asceticism, isn't it?

SANGHARAKSHITA: Yes. *Khantī paramaṃ tapo titikkhā*. This is *Dhammapada* verse 184.

SAGARAMATI: How would you start to practise in that way? Suppose you are in touch with your anger, you are not emotionally blocked, and you come across a situation where your anger is really aroused.

SANGHARAKSHITA: According to Śāntideva there are various reflections that you can encourage. 'Why should I get angry? Suppose someone has struck me: what does that mean? Two things are involved. There's his stick, and there's my body. These two things coming together produce the pain and suffering which I feel. He has taken up the stick, so he is responsible for that half of the transaction; but who has taken up the body? The body that I have taken up comes into collision with the stick that he has taken up. He's no more to blame than I am. I am no less to blame than he is. How ridiculous of me to be angry with him!' Śāntideva has a number of such reflections which make you realize how foolish and stupid it is to be angry with somebody.[159]

SAGARAMATI: Gritting your teeth wouldn't be a practice, would it?

SANGHARAKSHITA: It would be the first stage. You have to go step by step. When someone hits you, first of all you feel anger and you retaliate; you hit back. But once you've realized that that isn't the right thing to do, you can at least check your anger midway. You may have seized the stick and be ready to beat him, but then you think in time and check yourself – or at least you don't hit him as hard as you might have done otherwise. Well, this is some improvement. Then at a later stage you come to a point where you feel quite angry but know very well you are not going to do anything about it: you just don't allow the anger to express itself. It's not that you're repressing it, but the anger runs its course in your own mind. After a while, you feel only a little anger, and maybe in the end you don't feel any anger at all. You just think, 'Poor chap! Never mind. His action is understandable.' You just don't mind at all.

That's *khanti* then, the antidote to anger. The next *maṅgala* is *sovacassatā*. Hare translates this as 'kind words', but it's really more like 'good speech', or even sweet speech'.

RICHARD: Woodward has 'soft answer'.

SANGHARAKSHITA: Perhaps he's thinking of 'the soft answer that turneth away wrath'.[160] It's pleasant speech, soft speech – not soft in the sense of weak, but in the sense of gentle, kindly. It's the quality of being well spoken. The meaning of this *maṅgala* is obvious.

'*Samaṇānañ ca dassanaṃ*': 'the sight of the *samaṇas*'. 'To see good men' is much too general. The *samaṇas* are the ascetics, the mendicant monks, the Buddha's full-time disciples who have gone forth as wanderers. The very sight of them is a blessing, a sign of good luck. The word *dassana* (Sanskrit *darśana*) is a very important one in India. It means just looking, just being inspired by the sight of somebody. In India they go and see the holy man: they just go and sit and look at him. In India it's not considered at all impolite to look at people. Sometimes people pass you in the street and if they're a bit interested, without any hesitation they can spend a couple of minutes just staring at you. They gape at you, and gawk as you pass, standing in the middle of the street and doing it at leisure. You can see their jaws dropping and their eyes popping. When they've fully satisfied their curiosity they turn away, shaking their head. You can actually see what they're thinking – they make no attempt to hide it whatever. In the same way – but in a very different spirit – you go and take *darshan* of the holy man. The holy man just sits there. Sometimes you have professional holy men who do nothing else: they just sit there for you to look at them. In the case of a genuine holy man the *darshan* is an actual spiritual experience. There is no need for words, no need for discussion. You just sit and look. The most famous exemplar of that kind of *darshan* in modern times was Ramana Maharshi. (I've spoken of this a number of times.)[161] He just sat on his *gaddi*, on his cushion, for about forty years. People would come and just look at him and take *darshan*. This sort of contact is considered very important.

MARK: This could inspire you to realize what actual physical benefits could be gained by following the Path. 'See what it's done for somebody!'

SANGHARAKSHITA: Right. But it's not only that. *Darshan* sets up a sort of communication between you. In connection with one of the first Tantric initiations I had, one of my teachers told me that according to the *sūtra*s the disciple, when in front of the teacher, must look down, at the time of the ordination especially. It is considered rather bold and presumptuous on the part of the disciple to look up on such occasions: he should keep his head well down out of humility. But in the case of Tantric initiation, he should look the teacher in the face.[162] You see the difference of approach? This is because it is a sort of communication, even a sort of initiation, just to look. Hence this *dassana* or *darshan* of the *samaṇas* is also an auspicious sign.

GRAHAM: Can't looking sometimes be a bit of a strain? I often feel I strain people by looking at them.

SANGHARAKSHITA: Assuming it isn't their own fault, it's sometimes that you are staring. Looking is not staring. It's not giving them a prolonged suspicious stare. It's looking in a relaxed way, not fixing them with your gaze.

LOKAMITRA: It's not just looking at them either. It's taking them in, and feeling, and sort of experiencing them.

SANGHARAKSHITA: You may not have your eyes actually focused on them. It's not that you try to fix them with your hypnotic stare and 'hold' them – as I sometimes say in connection with the communication exercises.[163] You just look, and sometimes, quite naturally, you look away. But you're still aware of them even when you look away. You still feel them there.

RICHARD: I see what Graham means, though. It's not just a question of staring. After all, you can look at beautiful scenery: why not at a beautiful human being? But often if you say, 'Oh, look at that!' the person you're drawing attention to sort of shrinks away.

SANGHARAKSHITA: Perhaps that's an element of self-consciousness coming in. Ramana Maharshi certainly didn't react in that way. When you looked at him it was like looking at a mountain – except that the mountain looked at you and smiled. He wasn't in the least self-conscious.

SAGARAMATI: Lawrence goes into this type of self-consciousness in his *Fantasia of the Unconscious*.[164]

SANGHARAKSHITA: He also goes into it in connection with education – with the mother prematurely stimulating in the young child what he calls the personal consciousness, which is self-consciousness in this sort of sense.[165] You get this more with little girls than little boys. 'Oh, isn't she pretty! Isn't she sweet! Come and do your little dance, darling!' You know, things like that: making the child very self-conscious, making her a real little Shirley Temple. I remember when I was a boy all the mothers wanted their daughters to be like Shirley Temple. They used to have Shirley Temple frocks and Shirley Temple curls and all sorts of things. There were thousands of little Shirley Temples all over London.[166]

Then *kālena dhammasākacchā*. *Kālena* is, again, 'timely', and *dhammasākacchā* is 'discussion of the Dharma', Woodward has a really dreadful translation of this *maṅgala*. He renders it 'pious talk in season due'. *Sākacchā* is simply conversation, talk, discussion, and the addition of *dhamma* doesn't make it 'pious'. It's talk about Reality, discussion about the Truth. 'Pious talk' is a classic example of the completely wrong type of translation that gives, a completely wrong impression of the Buddha's teaching.

GARY: What does pious mean?

SANGHARAKSHITA: Pious means religious in a goody-goody sort of way. At least, that's what the word means for people nowadays. It wasn't the original meaning of the word in Latin. In classical times *pietas* was a quite important ethical and spiritual quality, a bit like reverence. But in modern English parlance piety means a rather pseudo, rather affected, goody-goody sort of religiosity – the sort of thing you associate with old ladies and prayer books. 'Wasn't it a lovely sermon, dear? I liked that bit about the flowers and Jesus. It was really nice.' That's pious talk. 'And what a lovely hymn! I do like that bit about the blood of Jesus. I feel so clean and pure afterwards.' I heard people talk like that in my younger days. 'Now we must all be good children!' You hear it on the radio sometimes in religious broadcasts. *Dhammasākacchā* is not that sort of thing. It is something very searching, very deep, very real. It is discussion about the Truth, about Reality, about the Norm.

RICHARD: There's a text – isn't there? – the *Kathāvatthu*, that is translated 'Points of Controversy'.[167]

SANGHARAKSHITA: Yes. *Kathā*, which is similar in meaning to *sākacchā*, is translated as 'controversy' here, though maybe 'discussion' would have been better, because as Mrs Rhys Davids, one of the translators, points out, there's no violent argument in the work: just discussion between the followers of different schools of Early Buddhism about certain topics, certain 'points' (*vatthu*). *Kathāvatthu* is therefore 'points of discussion', or 'topics of discussion' rather than 'points of controversy'.

SAGARAMATI: There aren't any conclusions, even, to many of them.

SANGHARAKSHITA: No, there aren't. In many cases the topic of discussion is left unsettled. The Pubbaseliyas think this, the Sarvāstivādins think that, but the Theravādins think something else. Full stop.

RICHARD: What you said about what *dhammasākacchā* really means reminded me very much of the *Perfection of Wisdom in Eight Thousand Lines*, where Subhūti is discoursing...[168]

SANGHARAKSHITA: In modern India there's a particular kind of Hindu religious performance called *kathā*, where someone gives his own version of an episode from the *Rāmāyaṇa* or the *Mahābhārata*. He gives it at great length and with much elaboration, taking the parts of all the different characters in the story in turn. Every now and then he bursts into song, a chorus joins in, and when they have sung together for a while he goes back to the telling of the story. This sort of performance is very popular, especially in north-western India.

GRAHAM: He just sings about anything whatever?

SANGHARAKSHITA: No. He sings about what he has been discoursing on. Suppose it was the story of Rāma and Sītā. At great length – much greater than in the original text – he'd describe how Rāma came back to his hermitage and found that Sītā was missing. He'd describe how he looked this way and that, searching for Sītā, and he'd act the part of Rāma a bit to make the audience feel Rāma's grief at the loss of his beloved wife. Then he'd burst into song – Rāma's song for the loss of Sīta. The rest of his party would come in with the chorus, and if the song was a popular one the audience might join in too. This part of the performance would go on for perhaps ten or fifteen minutes, then it would die away and the *kathākāri* would come back to the story and relate what happened next, interspersing his discourse with various subsidiary stories, anecdotes, and jokes – even with comments on political affairs – all of which are very popular with village audiences. (In Buddhist countries much the same sort of thing is done with the *Jātaka* stories.) Some *kathākāris* are very highly skilled: they keep the whole thing going hour after hour, and everybody gets very absorbed. The more professional of them travel around with highly trained choruses, complete with drums and cymbals. When they all come in at the right moment – very dramatically – they quite carry the audience away. People listen to this sort of thing at night for six or eight hours at a time. There will be tens of thousands of people, even, if there is a famous performer of *kathā*.

In Thailand the *bhikkhus* sometimes teach the Dharma in this way. There are two *bhikkhus* at a time, and they sometimes go on all night, one questioning the other alternately. Some *bhikkhus* are highly skilled at this sort of thing and do it in a slightly farcical, knockabout manner, almost like a double comedy act, to make the Dharma interesting to ordinary people. If they are telling a *Jātaka* story, one *bhikkhu* will ask, 'Well, what happened next? What did the bodhisattva do then?' This is to create interest and suspense. The other *bhikkhu* then says, 'He did this, and he did that', to which the first *bhikkhu* replies, 'Oh no, surely not! But wasn't that wonderful!' In this way telling of the *Jātaka* story proceeds. I haven't witnessed this type of performance myself, but some of my Thai *bhikkhu* friends have described to me the scene in the temple where it takes place. The two *bhikkhus* are seated on thrones at the far end of the hall, on either side of the altar, and the talk is tossed like a ball between them. Everybody follows with great interest and attention. Where the whole population is Buddhist, as it were, and people are on different levels of intelligence, you need different kinds of presentation of the Dharma. The *bhikkhus* have therefore introduced this sort of thing. They don't have songs in between – that's not permitted – but the Hindus have them, and that makes their performances even more effective. The Tibetans, of course, have their so-called mystery plays, many of which are based on *Jātaka* stories, and these too are very effective. All this can be regarded as coming under the heading of *dhammakathā* or *dhammasākacchā* – talk or discussion about the Dharma.

### A Godly Life

> Ardour and godly life, to see
> Truths Ariyan, to know the cool:
> This is the greatest luck.

The Pāli phrase translated here as 'ardour and godly life' is *tapo ca brahmacariyañ ca*. Looking back over the ground covered so far, you notice that from verse to verse there's been a sort of progression. If you look back at verses 1–7, including the *devatā*'s question, this becomes all the more evident. With the present verse we come to the more specifically 'monastic' life (for want of a better term). Even a lay person who lives at home with wife and family can practise forbearance and right speech, can have the sight of mendicant monks, and can discuss the Dharma. With *tapo ca brahmacariya*, however, we come to the more specifically spiritual life, which it is difficult for the layman to lead. The word *tapo* or *tapa* (Sanskrit *tapas*) is from a verb meaning 'to heat'. It's a sort of incubating psychic heat that you generate within yourself by the intensity of your spiritual, especially meditative, practice and which causes the hardness and rigidity of your psychological conditioning to melt, as it were, so that something new is brought forth, hatched. The implied analogy is with the hen sitting on her eggs and generating a lot of heat and in that way hatching the eggs so that the chicks burst forth. We usually translate *tapo* or *tapa* as asceticism, but basically it means heat and represents the same kind of inner experience as the Tibetan *tummo* or 'psychic heat' (Sanskrit *caṇḍālī* or 'fiery one'). Where there's heat, there's energy, and where there's sufficiently powerful energy, there's heat, a sort of radiant energy. It's very interesting that the Indians think of what we call asceticism in this way. I talked earlier about *puñña* as the 'vibration' set up by a good action. It's very much like that. It's as though the intensity of your effort radiates, as it were, or is incandescent, just like an electric bulb. You 'light up'. The English word asceticism conveys a completely different idea, doesn't it? ''Tis strict austerity' – this is the translation Chalmers gives. Hare translates it as 'ardour', which is quite good, because like *tapa* it is a word basically meaning heat. Yes, ardour will do. The word is not quite strong enough, but *tapo* is certainly ardour more than asceticism or austerity.

LOKAMITRA: I've always associated with austerity a withdrawing from outside activities and concentrating on yourself, so as to build up this sort of inner heat.

SANGHARAKSHITA: But that isn't the meaning the word has in ordinary parlance. If you say of someone that he is an austere sort of person you mean that he is a bit dry and grey, a bit hard and unsympathetic, even aloof and forbidding, not that he is working on himself and generating inner psychical or spiritual heat. We speak of the traditional Scottish minister as being an austere man.

*Brahmacariya* (Sanskrit *brahmacarya*) is quite an interesting word. It's often used in the sense of celibacy, i.e. chastity, but this is only its secondary or applied meaning. *Brahma* is 'high', 'noble', 'sublime', even 'spiritual'; and *cariya* is 'walking', 'faring', 'practising'. *Brahmacariya* is therefore the 'noble faring', or the 'lofty course', or the 'sublime practice', especially in the sense of the faring or coursing in, or the practice or experience of, the noble or lofty states of higher meditative consciousness. There are these three terms: *brahmacarya*, *dharmacarya*, and *bodhicarya*. *Brahmacarya* is the more general 'Hindu' term, the term current in the Buddhas's day, which the Buddha took over for the spiritual life. The more specialized Buddhist term, which he and his disciples may have started using later on, was *dharmacarya* in the sense specifically of the practice of his spiritual teaching. *Bodhicarya* was the practice of the more specifically Mahāyāna form of Buddhism. *Brahmacarya*, *dharmacarya*, and *bodhicarya* are thus progressively more specialized terms. *Brahmacarya* denotes the practice, or the life, which is based upon high or noble states of consciousness and expressive of those states, especially the states we experience in meditation. It is the spiritual life as distinct from the worldly life. *Dharmacarya* is not just the living of the righteous life. It's the practice of the Dharma in the sense of the practice of the Truth, the practice of Reality. It goes beyond the *brahmacarya*. It is the transcendental life as distinct from the spiritual life. As for the *bodhicarya*, it goes even beyond the *dharmacarya*. It is the practice of Buddhahood, i.e. the practice of the bodhisattva ideal as distinct from the *arhant* ideal.

The next phrase, 'to see Truths Ariyan', *ariyasaccāna dassanaṃ*, ties up very much with the *dharmacarya* and the *bodhicarya*, because it is the *ariyasaccāni*, or Noble Truths, of which you have the vision (*dassana*), as you are walking and practising, whether that walking and practising is *dharmacarya* or *bodhicarya*. In the case of the *bodhicarya*, however, one also 'sees' *śūnyatā* or emptiness. There's quite an important point to be dealt with here in connection with the first noble truth, that is to say the truth of *dukkha* or suffering. It is important because it is quite often raised by beginners. People say, 'According to Buddhism everything is suffering. But everything isn't suffering. I lead quite a happy life. I don't suffer.' This supposedly disproves Buddhism, because 'Everything is suffering' is the first noble truth. What do you say in reply to this?

SAGARAMATI: It's potentially suffering. If I talk about it, I talk about limitations. Like a rubber ball in a room, worldly existence is pretty limited and you tend to bounce around.

SANGHARAKSHITA: Ah, but Buddhism doesn't say anything about potential or actual. It says everything *is* suffering.

LOKAMITRA: In its ultimate sense it's unsatisfactory.

SAGARAMATI: From the point of view of the Transcendental...

SANGHARAKSHITA: Yes, from the point of view of the Transcendental. This is where the *ariyasacca* comes in. The first noble truth is how you see things when you have that transcendental vision. It's not how you experience things through the senses and the sense-consciousness. It's not the feeling but the 'seeing' of existence. Even if you have a happy experience you see that as ultimately *dukkha*, because you see its limitations.

SAGARAMATI: It would be much better to use another word than 'noble' for *ariya*.

SANGHARAKSHITA: *Sukha*, or pleasant experience, is painful not in the sense that it is a painful experience, but that it is seen to have its limitations. So it's the *ariyasaccāna dassanaṃ*, the sight or vision of the *āryan* truths that we are concerned with here, the word *ariya* (Sanskrit *ārya*) indicating that transcendental level of awareness. You can only 'see' the noble truths if you are a noble person, an *ariya*: that is, you can only see them with insight. This is a very important point. Buddhism doesn't say that everybody experiences everything as suffering all the time and that this is the noble truth of suffering. Obviously they don't. But in the ultimate perspective, as disclosed by or to insight, it is seen that nothing conditioned is completely satisfying. You can have the experience of something quite pleasant, like eating a sandwich or a cake, and quite enjoy it. The experience is pleasant, it's *sukha*; but at the same time you see with your insight that it is *dukkha*. The universality that is posited of suffering is in the insight, not in the actual feeling of *dukkha*.

GRAHAM: This could be a point for action: to see that life in itself is not perfection.

SANGHARAKSHITA: Well, then you won't be bothered unduly about things, even though you do enjoy them. You know they have their limitations – they don't last for ever – so, all right, you enjoy them, but you're not attached to them. They end; you don't expect them to last.

RICHARD: It seems that things like *dukkha* are interpreted really wrongly, e.g. 'You've got to suffer to develop.'

SANGHARAKSHITA: Oh yes, 'suffering is good for you. I shall help you, I shall make you suffer.' You get a touch of that in Zen, don't you? 'It must be doing me good: it's really hurting.'

MARK: I noticed that attitude very much at the Buddhist Society the one time that I went there. The bloke who was taking the Zen class seemed to be infatuated with the idea of whacking you on the back with a stick.

SANGHARAKSHITA: I think it's a leftover from the Christian tradition of guilt, and wanting to punish yourself. If you are interested in Buddhism you go along to the Zen class and get your punishment there!

LOKAMITRA: The interpretation that suffering is good for you is one of the major things which holds back Buddhism in the West at present. There are so many so-called Buddhists, or people who claim to be Buddhists, who give this sort of impression.

SANGHARAKSHITA: It was certainly the impression around the Hampstead Buddhist Vihara when I arrived in 1964. It was really terrible.

LOKAMITRA: So many books give it too, and it's this which gives the name of pessimism to Buddhism.

SANGHARAKSHITA: This is also why people sometimes get baffled by Buddhism: because of their own assumptions. They go to a Buddhist country and they find that everyone is cheerful and happy, and they think, 'But they're not supposed to be happy! They're supposed to be Buddhists. They're supposed to believe that everything is suffering. They even tell you that everything is suffering – with a big, beaming smile.' Western visitors just can't understand it. The Christian missionaries can't understand it. 'These people are always happy, but they're supposed to be pessimists – radical pessimists. They are the gloomy Buddhists.' Actually, it's the Christians who are the gloomy people – and they're supposed to have heard the Good News! They're supposed to be rejoicing in the Lord.

One must therefore remember in connection with *ariyasaccāna dassanaṃ* that the fact that in the ultimate sense everything is suffering is a truth that discloses itself only in the perspective of the transcendental vision.

*Nibbānasacchikiriyā ca. Nibbāna* is of course Nirvāṇa, and *sacchikiriya* is realization, so this *maṅgala* consists in the realization of Nirvāṇa. Hare renders it 'to know the cool', which is rather misleading. There's a Pāli idiom for the attainment of Nirvāṇa which is 'to become cooled', *sīti-bhavati*, and Nirvāṇa itself is 'coolness', *sīti-bhāva*. This is a beautiful metaphor in a hot country – to think of Nirvāṇa as coolness and the attainment of Nirvāṇa as the cooling down of the heat of passion, the heat of rage, the heat of anger. Nevertheless, the term used here is not *sīta* but *nibbāna*, which is literally a 'blowing out', an extinction, but with the implication not of annihilation but of a reversion to a previous, more subtle state. The Buddha himself used the analogy of the flame of the lamp: when fuel and wick are exhausted, the flame goes out. The attainment of Nirvāṇa, he said, is like that. When the five grasping *skandhas* are no longer there, no further mundane existence is produced: the 'lamp' goes out. This was read by some Western scholars as meaning that on the attainment of Nirvāṇa there was total extinction for the individual concerned, forgetting the old Indian belief that when a fire went out it didn't cease to exist but reverted to a subtle state. After all, when you kindled fire, where did it come from? It had to come from somewhere! The Indian idea was that there was a subtle fire which manifested itself when you struck the iron against the flint and produced a spark. But the fire was there behind, as it were, all the time. When a fire goes out it just reverts to that latent or invisible state. That was the Indian way of looking at things. So the extinction of the flame of the lamp did not suggest to the ancient Indian an absolute and complete extinction but simply a reversion to a previous, more subtle state. This sort of idea would have been at the back of the Buddha's mind when he spoke of Nirvāṇa as extinction. Not that he meant that when you gained Nirvāṇa you went back to a more subtle state of existence that you had enjoyed before you were incarnated, as it were, but there was the definite implication that what took place was not complete annihilation. The 'extinction' was relatively superficial: it was the extinction of greed (*lobha*), hatred (*dveṣa*), and delusion (*moha*). There was a substratum, as it were, which was pure, and which remained. Nirvāṇa wasn't a state of total annihilation.

**Free From Grief**

> With mind unmoved when touched by the world,
> To be grief-freed, dust-freed, secure:
> This is the greatest luck.

This is an expansion of the last *maṅgala* of the previous verse, i.e. the realization of Nirvāṇa. *Phuṭṭhassa lokadhammehi cittaṃ yassa na kampati* is not quite 'With mind unmoved when touched by the world'. A more literal translation would be 'he whose mind (*citta*) is not made to shake by the *lokadhammas* (plural)'. So what are the *lokadhammas*? There are supposed to be eight of these, the traditional list being success and failure, glory and disgrace, praise and dispraise, happiness and suffering. These are sometimes called the pairs of worldly opposites, and the mind oscillates between them. If you experience success you become elated; if you experience failure you become sad and downcast – and so on for the rest of the *lokadhammas*. The mind oscillates because your experience is changing all the time. Sometimes you experience happiness, sometimes suffering, sometimes you're elated, sometimes depressed. All the time you're oscillating between one or another pair of opposites, or between all of them at once. This is the sort of state that you're in. So the Buddha says, 'He whose mind is not made to shake' (*kampati*), or oscillate, or quake – it's the same word as earthquake (*paṭhavī-kampa*) – whose mind is not upset or disturbed when touched by, when experiencing, the *lokadhammas*, or eight pairs of worldly opposites, but whose mind is, on the contrary, *asokaṃ virajaṃ khemaṃ* – this is the greatest *maṅgala*, the greatest good luck or the most auspicious sign. *Asoka* is 'free from grief'; *viraja* is 'free from the dust of the defilements'. *Khema*, which is quite an important term, is more difficult to translate. It's patience, but in a rather special sense that I find quite difficult to define. The best I can say is that it's the patience of the artist with his material. It's also connected with love. When the artist is moulding his clay he's very patient. He loves his material. He works it very slowly and patiently into the shape that he wants. In the same way you're working on your own life, and you're working on or with other people. You don't get upset, you don't get ruffled, you don't react: you just carry on, very patiently, in this sort of way. That is *khema*. It's not patience in the sense of persevering and sticking at something. It involves that too, but it's more like the patience of the artist who is patient with his material and understands it. One could translate this whole verse by saying: 'He whose mind does not shake or quake when touched by the eight worldly *dhammas*, or pairs of opposites; he whose mind is on the contrary free from the dust of the defilements, and patient – this is the greatest blessing' – i.e. that sort of mind is the greatest blessing. We have come now to the very greatest of all blessings, the greatest of all auspicious signs. We can't go any further. The Buddha therefore continues:

## Undefeated

They who live thus see no defeat,
And happily go everywhere:
Theirs is the greatest luck.

*Etādisāni katvāna sabbattha-m-aparājitā.* Those who do thus, who see the auspicious signs enumerated in this *sutta*, are everywhere undefeated. Undefeated by what or by whom?

SEVERAL VOICES: Māra.[169]

SANGHARAKSHITA: Māra, you could say. They are certainly not defeated morally or spiritually by the world. *Sabbattha sotthim gacchanti.* 'They go happily everywhere.' Māra can't overcome them. Wherever they go, they are perfectly happy. They experience – they receive – the real good luck. They've seen the real auspicious sign. Happiness is really coming their way – has come their way: they've already got it. *Taṃ tesam maṅgalam uttamaṃ.* 'Theirs is the greatest blessing, the greatest good luck.' Progressing from one *maṅgala* to another, they've come all the way up to Nirvāṇa, the ultimate *maṅgala* – to the perfectly calm, stable, and pure mind. They're now perfectly happy, perfectly free.

There's quite a lot in the *Maṅgala Sutta*. There are said to be thirty-two *maṅgalas* in all. I've never actually counted them, but I take that to be correct. You could have a whole series of talks on it, couldn't you? One talk on each verse or even on each *maṅgala*.

LOKAMITRA: It's tremendous, this *sutta*! It's so rich, for study and so forth.

SANGHARAKSHITA: It also chants very well, by the way.

# SALUTATION TO THE THREE JEWELS

# PREFACE TO THE FIRST EDITION

The *Tiratana Vandanā* or 'Salutation to the Three Jewels' – i.e. the Buddha, Dharma, and Sangha – is a short Pāli devotional text widely used throughout the Theravādin Buddhist countries of South-east Asia. Since this text – minus its third stanza, which may well be a later addition – is also used throughout the FWBO, I selected it for study on a study retreat that was held at Mill Farm Cottage, Hintlesham, near Ipswich, during the weekend of 13–14 May 1978. The retreat was held in celebration of the first anniversary of the ordinations of Dharmacharis Kulananda, Kulamitra, Kuladeva, and Kularatna, all of whom were present. In the quiet depths of the Suffolk countryside, with the birds twittering in the trees, the four Dharmacharis and I spent two memorable days together exploring the meaning of the *Tiratana Vandanā* and discussing some of the important spiritual issues it raises. Feeling that our discussions may well be of general interest I have asked Dharmachari Ashvajit to bring out the edited transcript of the seminar in his Ola Leaves series for wider circulation among Order members, Mitras, and Friends.

Sangharakshita
Padmaloka
Surlingham
Norfolk
22 October 1978

*Namo tassa bhagavato arahato sammāsambuddhassa*
*Namo tassa bhagavato arahato sammāsambuddhassa*
*Namo tassa bhagavato arahato sammāsambuddhassa*

*Iti'pi so bhagavā arahaṃ sammāsambuddho*
*vijjācaraṇasampanno sugato*
*lokavidū, anuttaro purisadammasārathi*
*satthā devamanussānaṃ*
*buddho bhagavā ti*

*Buddhaṃ jīvitapariyantaṃ saraṇaṃ gacchāmi*

*Ye ca Buddhā atītā ca*
*Ye ca Buddhā anāgatā*
*Paccuppannā ca ye Buddhā*
*Ahaṃ vandāmi sabbadā*

*N'atthi me saraṇaṃ aññaṃ*
*Buddho me saraṇaṃ varaṃ*
*Etena saccavajjena*
*Hotu me jayamaṅgalaṃ*

Such indeed is He, the Richly Endowed: the Free, the Fully and Perfectly Awake, Equipped with Knowledge and Practice, the Happily Attained, Knower of the Worlds, Guide Unsurpassed of Men to be Tamed, the Teacher of Gods and Men, the Awakened One Richly Endowed.

All my life I go for Refuge to the Awakened One.

To all the Awakened of the past,
To all the Awakened yet to be,
To all the Awakened that now are,
My worship flows unceasingly.
No other refuge than the Wake,
Refuge supreme, is there for me.
Oh by the virtue of this truth,
May grace abound, and victory!

*Svākkhāto bhagavatā Dhammo*
*sandiṭṭhiko akāliko ehipassiko*
*opanayiko paccataṃ*
*veditabbo viññūhī ti*

*Dhammaṃ jīvitapariyantaṃ saraṇaṃ gacchāmi*

*Ye ca Dhammā atītā ca*
*Ye ca Dhammā anāgatā*
*Paccuppannā ca ye Dhammā*
*Ahaṃ vandāmi sabbadā*

*N'atthi me saraṇaṃ aññaṃ*
*Dhammo me saraṇaṃ varaṃ*
*Etena saccavajjena*
*Hotu me jayamaṅgalaṃ*

Well communicated is the Teaching of the Richly Endowed One, Immediately Apparent, Perennial, of the Nature of a Personal Invitation, Progressive, to be understood individually, by the wise.

All my life I go for Refuge to the Truth.

To all the Truth-Teachings of the past,
To all the Truth-Teachings yet to be,
To all the Truth-Teachings that now are,
My worship flows unceasingly.
No other refuge than the Truth,
Refuge supreme, is there for me.
Oh by the virtue of this truth,
May grace abound, and victory!

*Supaṭipanno bhagavato sāvakasaṅgho*
*ujupaṭipanno bhagavato sāvakasaṅgho*
*ñāyapaṭipanno bhagavato sāvakasaṅgho*
*sāmīcipaṭipanno bhagavato sāvakasaṅgho*
*yadidaṃ cattāri purisayugāni*
*aṭṭha purisapuggalā*

*Esa bhagavato sāvakasaṅgho*
*āhuneyyo, pāhuṇeyyo, dakkhiṇeyyo*
*añjalikaraṇīyo anuttaraṃ*
*puññakkhettaṃ lokassā ti*

*Saṅghaṃ jīvitapariyantaṃ saraṇaṃ gacchāmi*

*Ye ca Saṅghā atītā ca*
*Ye ca Saṅghā anāgatā*
*Paccuppannā ca ye Saṅghā*
*Ahaṃ vandāmi sabbadā*

*N'atthi me saraṇaṃ aññaṃ*
*Saṅgho me saraṇaṃ varaṃ*
*Etena saccavajjena*
*Hotu me jayamaṅgalaṃ*

Happily proceeding is the fellowship of the Hearers of the Richly Endowed One, uprightly proceeding ..., methodically proceeding ..., correctly proceeding ..., namely, these four pairs of Individuals, these eight Persons.

This fellowship of Hearers of the Richly Endowed One is worthy of worship, worthy of hospitality, worthy of offerings, worthy of salutation with folded hands, an incomparable source of goodness to the world.

All my life I go for Refuge to the Fellowship.

To all the Fellowships that were,
To all the Fellowships to be,
To all the Fellowships that are,
My worship flows unceasingly.
No refuge but the Fellowship,
Refuge supreme, is there for me.
Oh by the virtue of this truth,
May grace abound, and victory![170]

## Introduction

SANGHARAKSHITA: We'll start with the opening salutation, because we might as well understand things in complete detail, and go through it word by word. *Namo* means homage or veneration or salutation, the suggestion being, within the context of Indian tradition, that it is a salutation with folded hands. The word for that is an *añjali*, but *namo* means basically that – not just verbal salutation, but a physical salutation as well. *Tassa* means 'to him'.

*Bhagavato* is usually translated 'to the Blessed One', but there is quite a bit to be said about this translation, because there are several ways of looking at the meaning of *bhagavant*. It's probably the term most often used to refer to the Buddha, in the Pāli texts at least, by his disciples. In its undeclined form it's *bhagavantu*. Here it is in the dative case, *bhagavato*, and means 'to the Blessed One', so the whole phrase means 'Salutation (or homage) to him, to the Blessed One'. *Bhaga* originally meant something like luck or good fortune, and *bhagavant* was therefore one who possesses all luck, good fortune, and blessing, and therefore, by extension, one who possesses positive qualities. In this way the significance of the term grew. *Bhaga* has a short 'a', but the word is also interpreted as though it had a long 'a'. That would make it *bhāga*, which means a share, so that *bhāgavant* means 'one who possesses a share' – that is to say, one who possesses a share in good qualities, or who shares in good qualities. Whether one interprets it with the short 'a' or the long 'ā', it comes to the same thing in the end. *Bhagavant* suggests one who possesses all positive, auspicious, fortunate characteristics, especially of a spiritual nature, and who is outstanding on that account.

It's not a very technical term: it's a popular word which has been taken over by Buddhism, as we'll find was also the case with the term *arhant*. Originally, a person who was *bhagavant* was simply someone who was lucky or fortunate in the ordinary sense and who stood out from the rest, stood out from the group, because of that. But gradually the associations of the term came to be more psychological, more spiritual, until in the end the Buddhists used it to mean someone who possessed spiritual blessings and good qualities – in other words, the Buddha himself. *Bhagavant* is an emotional rather than an intellectual term, and suggests something both positive and impressive. For this reason it is sometimes translated as 'the Sublime One'. The *bhagavant* is someone who impresses one on a lower level, as it were, by being lucky or fortunate, by standing out from everyone else, by possessing positive qualities, spiritual qualities, by being awe-inspiring, sublime. The term has all these connotations, but not a very precise doctrinal meaning. It's a popular, even devotional, term. It can be given all sorts of doctrinal interpretations, but that's a later development. Consequently, the English translation of the term as 'Blessed One' is not too bad, because 'blessed' can mean blessed with good luck, blessed with good qualities, or spiritually blessed.

The translation 'Lord', with its connotations of the British social system, isn't very fortunate. Following the interpretation of *bhāgavant* as having a long 'ā' I've translated it recently as 'the Richly Endowed One', which gives one more of the feeling of the thing, but it is much more a devotional term than anything else, and as such cannot really be analysed or explained. In the Pāli scriptures it's the term the disciples generally use when addressing the Buddha. They say *bhagavan*, which is the vocative case. In modern India *bhagavan* has been taken over by all the saints and mahatmas: we have Bhagavan Ramana Maharshi and Bhagavan Rajneesh. It's as though they, or their disciples, are trying to steal a little of the reflected glory of the Buddha. But we won't go into that now. *Namo tassa bhagavato* therefore means 'salutation to him, to the Blessed One', or, if you like, 'to the Sublime One' or 'to the Richly Endowed One'.

Then *arahato* or 'to the *arahant*'. This, too, is an epithet of the Buddha, and the word has a similar history. *Arahant* means 'worthy', or even 'worshipful': this is the literal meaning. It was pointed out by early English translators of the Pāli texts that in ancient India before Buddhism the term was used as an honorific title for high officials and meant something like the English 'his worship', as when we speak of 'his worship the mayor'. This term too was gradually upgraded and acquired spiritual connotations, until in the end *arahant* came to mean someone who was spiritually worthy in the highest sense. It came to be used for an Enlightened disciple of the Buddha who had gained his Enlightenment not as the Buddha did, without a teacher, but by following the path shown by the Buddha: one who had destroyed all ten fetters or *saṃyojanas*. There's a popular etymology which explains *arahant* as *ari-hanta*, *ari* meaning 'enemy' and *hanta* 'destroyer', so that *arahant* means one who has destroyed all enemies, the enemies being the defilements, the passions, and so on. This is not a scientific etymology, but it reflects the meaning that the term came to have in Buddhist tradition. So *namo tassa bhagavato arahato*: 'salutation to the Blessed One, to the Spiritually Worthy One'.

*Sammāsambuddhassa*. The meaning of the word Buddha, as we know, is from a root meaning 'to understand'. Once again there was an upgrading. Do you see what tends to happen? When you have an experience that goes beyond previous experiences, or goes beyond the normal experience of people, then you've no word to describe that, because the terminology currently in use doesn't extend to your experience, which goes beyond it. You can then either coin a completely new term, or stretch the old term to cover the new experience. The latter is what, on the whole, the Buddhists tended to do in those early days. They stretched the old Hindu or Vedic terms to cover their new Buddhist meanings. This gives rise to a great deal of confusion, because if you're not careful, you may read into the terms used by Buddhism the meanings that they have in a Hindu or non-Buddhist context. Lokamitra was mentioning after his return from India that there were all sorts of what we would regard as Buddhist terms – terms taken from Sanskrit or Pāli – which have cognate forms in modern Indian languages but completely different meanings. Take the word *samādhi*. In Hindi and other North Indian languages *samādhi* often means a tomb, or the place of somebody's death. A saint's *samādhi* is the place where he died, or where he was buried, or the monument erected over his remains. *Dharma*, which in Buddhism has its own very definite meaning, in Hinduism means your caste duty. In North India this is the general usage of the word. If a woman says, 'I'm doing my best to keep up my *dharma*', she means her caste duties, i.e. not eating with certain people, not touching certain people, not taking water from a well that is used by people of a lower caste. That's her *dharma*, she thinks. Or a professional thief may say, 'Why do I steal? To steal is my *dharma*.' In modern India you have to be very careful teaching Buddhism, because you will use words from the Buddhist scriptures in your Buddhist sense, but they'll be understood in their current Indian meaning.

KULARATNA: Even *parinirvāṇa*, Lokamitra was saying, just means to die.

SANGHARAKSHITA: Right. This is among the ex-Untouchables. They know that the term *parinirvāṇa* is applied to the final passing away of the Buddha, so they think that it's just a polite way of saying that the Buddha died. One day, when I was in India, going around among the ex-Untouchables, someone came up to me and said, 'Would you please come to my house tomorrow morning? My father's just had his *parinirvāṇa*.' Thus there are many pitfalls in using Sanskrit and Pāli Buddhist terms in modern India.

So *buddha*, to come back to *sammāsambuddhassa*, originally meant 'one who has understood', that is to say, understood in a spiritual sense – understood the truth, understood ultimate reality – or someone who is Enlightened, as we now say in English. But even in English you have to be very careful using this word enlightened, because it can have connotations of the eighteenth-century rationalist enlightenment. When speaking about Enlightenment in the Buddhist sense, therefore, you must make it clear that you mean a spiritual enlightenment, not a purely rational one. The *sam* in *sambuddha* indicates fullness or completion. *Sammā* and *sam* are connected and have basically the same meaning, so that to say *sammāsambuddha* is heaping superlative upon superlative. One could render *sammāsambuddhassa* as 'to the Fully and Perfectly Enlightened One' or as 'to the Supremely and Perfectly Enlightened One'.

This brings us to something quite basic: the question of whether the Buddha's Enlightenment was the same as that of his disciples or whether it went beyond it. As far as we can see was the case in the Buddha's own lifetime, there was not felt to be any difference between the content of the Enlightenment gained by the Buddha and that of the Enlightenment gained by the disciples. At a later date there was a term for the disciples' Enlightenment which was *anubodhi*. *Anu* means 'going after' or 'following', so that *anubodhi*, the *bodhi* or Enlightenment of the disciple, was the Enlightenment attained by the disciple by going after or following the Enlightenment of the Buddha. There was no 'internal' difference between the two experiences, the earlier one of the Buddha and the later one of the disciple. In several passages in the Pāli texts the Buddha himself is represented as making no difference between himself and his Enlightened disciples. When he sent out the first sixty disciples, he said, 'I am released, *bhikkhus*, from all bonds, those that are divine and those that are human. Ye also, *bhikkhus*, are released from all bonds, those that are divine and those that are human.'[171] On the whole it seems that in the Buddha's own lifetime it was not felt that there was any difference between the content of the Buddha's spiritual experience and that of the disciples. The only difference was that he had attained Enlightenment first and, having attained it, had shown them the way. Having seen the way they followed it and attained the same – one might almost say exactly the same – spiritual experience as he had attained.

But in later generations it seems that people became more and more aware of the fact that the Buddha must have had something that the others didn't have. The Buddha was after all the teacher of all the *arhants*, at least originally. He had rediscovered the path to Enlightenment, whereas others had merely followed it after him. So the feeling or belief grew up – and there may have been traces of this even during the Buddha's own lifetime – that though the disciples were also Enlightened, in some mysterious way the Buddha was more Enlightened. Eventually this feeling of belief hardened into definite doctrinal distinctions, and it was more or less explicitly stated, in some schools at least, that the Buddha had a particular kind of Enlightenment which went beyond that of the disciples. Three kinds of Enlightenment were distinguished: that of the *arhant*, that of the *paccekabuddha* (Sanskrit *pratyekabuddha*), and that of the *sammāsambuddha* (Sanskrit *samyaksambuddha*). Whether one can take these distinctions as actually denoting different kinds of Enlightenment is a bit doubtful, but certainly one might say that on the human level, as a personality, the Buddha was felt to be particularly impressive and that he seemed to have an influence or an effect beyond that of the disciples. This may have been simply on account of his human qualities – because it is also one of the beliefs of Buddhism that for your spiritual qualities to make themselves fully manifest you need a certain equipment of human qualities, otherwise your spiritual vision doesn't get through. You need a 'language', and that language can include your own physical and mental qualities. This is why it was considered very important in the Mahāyāna that, as a bodhisattva, you should accumulate great merits and be born, in your last life, with a perfect, beautiful body – a very attractive appearance – so that your Enlightenment experience, when you've gained it, has the most perfect possible vehicle through which to manifest. One could at least say, therefore, that it was felt that even if the actual content of the Buddha's

Enlightenment was not literally superior to that of the disciples, he at least had a more perfect vehicle through which it could manifest, and that it was on account of that more perfect vehicle – including those more heroic qualities which had enabled him to find out the truth when nobody else had been able to do so – that he occupied a particularly eminent position even among the disciples. Even though they too were Enlightened, he still remained the teacher.

KULARATNA: It's quite interesting that even among Enlightened beings there are differences, and individual characteristics.

SANGHARAKSHITA: In discussing this whole question one must bear in mind one important assumption or limitation. When one raises the question of whether the Buddha's Enlightenment was higher than that of the disciples you're assuming Enlightenment as a sort of fixed point that you can attain to, but that is only a manner of speaking. If you look at the series of the twelve positive *nidānas*,[172] you find that in dependence upon suffering (*dukkha*) there arises faith; in dependence upon faith there arises joy (*pāmojja*), and so on. There's a whole progressive sequence of experiences. Finally, when in dependence upon freedom (*vimutti*) there arises knowledge of the destruction of the biases (*āsavakhayañāṇa*), you stop there. But do you need to stop there? This question was raised even in the Buddha's own lifetime.[173] In a sense you don't. You can think of Enlightenment not in terms of your finally arriving at a fixed state, but as a kind of endless progression in this direction. In other words, you can think of Enlightenment in temporal rather than in spatial terms. If you look at it in that way then the question of whether the Buddha's Enlightenment was different from, or superior to, that of the disciples becomes a bit meaningless. They're all going in the same direction, as it were. Within each one of them there is this creative process going on: that in dependence upon something positive, something still more positive arises; in dependence upon that, something more positive still. And this is not a process that ever comes to a halt. This would seem to be a truer, and in a way more Buddhistic, way of looking at the matter.

KULARATNA: But when is the point in time when somebody is said to be Enlightened?

SANGHARAKSHITA: One can again look at this in several ways, bearing in mind that the doctrinal distinctions that were made later on were not made in the early days of Buddhism. The term for the point beyond which you don't regress is Stream Entry, and it would seem that in the very early days of Buddhism the conception was more of someone who had 'gone upstream' (*uddhaṃsota* is the term), that is to say, one who had passed the point of no return and 'gone upstream' from there. At that stage, it would seem, there wasn't too much inquiry as to how far he had gone. The great point was that he had passed the point of no return and gone further on. He couldn't fall back: he would only progress after that. So that is the basic distinction: whether you've reached the point of no return or not. In a way you could say that it's the point of no return which is the crucial point, and not even the point of Enlightenment. The point of no return is where you switch from the cyclical to the spiral. After that you just go on and on and on without possibility of regression: you needn't think of reaching a definite full stop anywhere. Later on in the history of Buddhism they distinguished between the once-returner, the non-returner, and the *arhant* and then maybe between the *arhant* and the fully Enlightened perfect Buddha. But the really crucial point is this point of entering the stream and going upstream.

KULARATNA: Is that what happened to the Buddha under the bodhi tree?

SANGHARAKSHITA: This is usually spoken of as Enlightenment in the later sense, i.e. not in the sense of Stream Entry but in that of a point very much further on which is regarded more or less as a fixed point. But I think it shouldn't be regarded as a fixed point in too strict a fashion. I've pointed out in a lecture that it's as though there isn't a fixed point in time when the Buddha became Enlightened.[174] There's a whole series of experiences spread out over a period of several weeks. This is illustrated by the famous request by Brahmā Sahampati, the 'Lord of Ten Thousand (Worlds)'. The Buddha says that originally, after gaining Enlightenment (*bodhi*, he may not be using the term here in a very specialized sense), when he had 'understood' things, he was inclined *not* to share his understanding with others, because he felt they wouldn't be able to grasp it. It was then, according to the traditional account, that Brahmā Sahampati appeared and said, 'People are perishing through lack of this teaching: please teach.' Then the Buddha looked out over the world, saw all the different beings in different stages of development like a bed of lotus flowers, and *then* he decided to teach for the sake of those whose eyes were covered with only a little dust.[175] Compassion arose in him, you could say. If you say that the Buddha was definitely and fully Enlightened, and yet decided not to teach, you suggest that compassion is *not* part of the Enlightenment experience: you can't have one without the other. If you take the traditional account literally, it's as though compassion is something added to the Enlightenment experience, not essential to it, as though the Buddha need not have taught; he would still have been the Buddha. But certainly the Mahāyāna, at least, would say that a Buddha who does not teach is not a Buddha. An Enlightened being who has no compassion is not an Enlightened being. Therefore you cannot but regard Brahmā's request and the Buddha's response as being a continuation or extension – a further unfolding – of the whole Enlightenment experience. It seems a bit unrealistic to believe that it all happened at a particular moment, or even on a particular day. After all, it was a very overwhelming, even a very shattering, experience, so it seems more reasonable to suppose that together with all its repercussions the total experience spread itself over quite a period. The impression we get when we read the texts is that the Buddha's Enlightenment experience spread itself over a period of some weeks.

We could therefore say, though this is a little hypothetical, that during that period, the Buddha entered the Stream and went further on, and that this process had various repercussions throughout his whole being which resulted in him being completely transformed. But exactly how far the process went it's very difficult to say. How can one dogmatize and say that it went so far and *that* was the point of Enlightenment? Certainly he didn't just enter the Stream: he entered the Stream and went quite a way up; or one could also say that even during the Buddha's lifetime, i.e. after his 'Enlightenment', the process was still going on. In relation to ordinary human beings it may seem that the Buddha is, as it were, static, because the situation in which the Buddha finds himself rather limits the possibility of expression; but within himself he may be going on and on way beyond human sight – even beyond the sight of the *arhants*. So it's better to think of Enlightenment more in these terms. It's the continued progression of an irreversible process, not a fixed state in which you settle down. Life is constantly changing: your conditions are constantly changing. If you are Enlightened, your Enlightenment does not consist in maintaining a fixed state of mind, but in responding creatively to all the different circumstances that may arise and in the midst of which you may find yourself. The more 'practice' you get, the more and more creative becomes your response. It's a cumulative process, as the whole conception of the spiral path and the creative mind suggests. It's not a fixed position from which you operate.

KULARATNA: It's more a way of operating.

SANGHARAKSHITA: A way of operating in which you become more and more highly skilled. You could use a medical comparison here. When you qualify as a doctor, that's like entering the Stream. But then, with that same stock of knowledge, you go on functioning as a doctor, and as a result of your contact with your patients you become more and more skilled as a medical practitioner. Though it remains basically the same, your original stock of knowledge may be modified by your experience, and in any case you deploy it ever more skilfully. It's not that you operate with exactly the same body of factual knowledge all through your medical career.

KULANANDA: Because existence must be infinitely subtle. You get more and more in touch with the subtleties of it.

KULARATNA: I suppose what tends to give the other impression – that Enlightenment is something static and fixed – is the Zen stories in which you hear about people suddenly gaining Enlightenment and then it's all over: they might as well go home and relax.

SANGHARAKSHITA: Sometimes they do go home, as it were!

KULAMITRA: Is it to do with the terms we use? For example, we use the term infinity as a point of reference just because it's useful, but that doesn't mean that it's a set number.

SANGHARAKSHITA: Right. One could therefore paraphrase *namo tassa bhagavato arahato sammāsambuddhassa* as 'Salutation to him, to the Blessed One, to the Emancipated One, to the Infinitely Creative One'. *Sammāsambuddhassa* means something more like that than 'Fully, Perfectly Enlightenment One'.

KULANANDA: Could you say that total Enlightenment was a sort of hypothetical pole? Just a tendency …

SANGHARAKSHITA: Yes, you could. A hypothetical pole – it being understood that that pole is not located anywhere. Do you see what I mean? You could think of it 'mathematically' as a pole which is infinitely far on and which, therefore, is never attained and which you are ever in process of attaining. But again, that's just a way of looking at it. To account for your continual, uninterrupted, ever-increasing, ever more and more cumulative creativity you posit that infinitely distant hypothetical pole.

KULANANDA: Because then there is still direction.

SANGHARAKSHITA: Yes, but on the other hand it's not a 'pole' which has an opposite. It's not a one-sided pole because, as one could stress here, there is the *sammā* aspect of Enlightenment. *Sammā* means whole, total, perfect – not in the sense of spatial completeness but in the sense of absence of one-sidedness or, in terms of its functioning, an absence of reactivity.

KULANANDA: That's the gravitational pull.

SANGHARAKSHITA: Yes, the gravitational pull here being exercised by the Transcendental, with a capital T, which again is hypothetical. There's not a thing called the Transcendental standing out there and exercising an actual pull. One could say, though this is a bit interpretative, that *namo tassa*, 'salutation to him', represents a salutation to the three 'aspects' of the Buddha. *Bhagavant* represents the Buddha as the supreme object of devotion, i.e. as the embodiment of compassion, because it's through his compassion that he comes into relation with the disciple. The disciples call him *bhagavan*. *Bhagavant* therefore suggests the object of the disciple's devotion. *Arahant* suggests the wisdom aspect: the destruction of all the 'enemies', i.e. the overcoming of defilements, annihilation of delusion, and so on. *Sammāsambuddha* – the complete perfect Buddha – suggests the first two aspects, the compassion aspect and the wisdom aspect, coming together. One could look at it like that.

Thus the *Tiratana Vandanā* begins with a salutation directed to the

Buddha. On the historical plane he is saluted out of gratitude for being the originator of the spiritual tradition of Buddhism. On the plane of immediate spiritual experience he is saluted as the living embodiment of the highest spiritual ideal towards which one is oneself striving, the ideal of infinite spiritual creativity.

### Salutation to the Buddha

Now let's go on to the *vandana* itself.[176] We've really dealt with the first line of the Buddha *vandana* or 'salutation to the Buddha' already, because the same terms occur in it as in the opening salutation: *Iti'pi so bhagavā arahaṃ sammāsambuddho*. Such indeed is he, the Blessed One – he is the Worthy One, the Fully and Perfectly Enlightened One'. *Iti* is 'such', '*pi*, i.e. *api*, is an emphatic participle, and can be rendered 'indeed', and *so* means 'he'. 'Such indeed is he, the Blessed One'. So what is it that he, the Blessed One, indeed is? He is the *arhant*, the *sammāsambuddha*. These epithets we've already explained.

KULARATNA: Such *indeed* he is. That's quite a nice way of putting it, isn't it?

SANGHARAKSHITA: And then comes a whole string of epithets. Incidentally, the same string of epithets occurs quite frequently in the Pāli texts when the Buddha is being referred to or described, and likewise the epithets for the Dharma and the Sangha.

*Vijjācaraṇasampanno*. *Sampanno* means 'fully and completely endowed with'. So what is the Blessed One fully and completely endowed with? *Vijjā* and *caraṇa*. *Vijjā* (Sanskrit *vidyā*) means knowledge or science or lore. Again, this is a word the meaning of which has been upgraded. The Buddha is endowed with knowledge. There are subtle distinctions between the two, but the *vijjā* or *vidyā* with which he is endowed is essentially the same as *bodhi*. I was going to say that there is perhaps a more intellectual flavour to the former, but this is not the case in later Buddhist traditions, e.g. in the Vajrayāna. You may remember that the negative or privative form of *vijjā* or *vidyā* is *avijjā* or *avidyā*, which is the first of the twelve ordinary *nidānas*.[177] In dependence upon *avijjā* or *avidyā* arise the *saṅkhāras* (Sanskrit *saṃskāras*) or karma formations. So *avijjā* or nescience or ignorance is a very basic category of Buddhism and *vijjā* is the opposite of this. There's a discussion about *vidyā* in one of the recent study seminars, in which – following Guenther to some extent – we went into the meaning of the term quite deeply and saw that it consisted in an appreciative – almost an aesthetic – understanding of things.[178] It was a total – a *perfect* – understanding, whereas *avidyā* was the opposite of that. Broadly speaking, therefore, *vijjā* or *vidyā* represents *bodhi* or Enlightenment. *Caraṇa* literally means walking about, but it also means practising or living. It's from the same root as the word *carya*, as in *brahmacarya*, *dharmacarya*, and *bodhisattvacarya*. They are all from the same root, meaning to move, to walk, to go, to practise, to live. *Vijjācaraṇa* is usually translated 'knowledge and conduct', but 'conduct' especially is a very weak translation. 'Understanding and implementation' would be nearer the mark. You could even say theory and practice, except that *vijjā* is not just theory but actual realization. Thus you have the two sides of the spiritual life. There is the inner realization and there is the external – the outer, practical – exemplification; and the Buddha is fully endowed with both. He has the inner realization of the truth, or ultimate reality, and outwardly he fully exemplifies that truth in his conduct, in his whole way of life. Thus he is equally endowed with *vijjā* and *caraṇa*. This suggests that at all levels of spiritual development – all levels of the development of the individual – there must be a balance between what you know and what you do. One could say that nowadays in the West the tendency is to accumulate lots of *vidyā*, but very little *caraṇa*. The two must be kept in equipoise.

KULANANDA: What about *pratyekabuddhas*?

SANGHARAKSHITA: *Pratyekabuddhas* are more a doctrinal category than anything else. One never actually encounters *pratyekabuddhas*, or people claiming to be *pratyekabuddhas*, in Buddhist history as distinct from Buddhist legend. Theoretically, or doctrinally, a *pratyekabuddha* or 'privately Enlightened one' is one who gains Enlightenment without a teacher, but who does not impart what he has gained. It's a rather odd category. It seems to have been introduced for reasons of neatness, i.e. to have an intermediate category between the *arhant* and the Buddha – which presupposes that you've already distinguished the *arhant* from the Buddha – rather than to correspond to an actual possibility in the Buddhist spiritual life.[179]

It is a very important point, this keeping your *vijjā* and your *caraṇa* more or less equal. If you have too much *vijjā*, or pseudo-*vijjā*, and very little *caraṇa*, you become what they call dragon's head and snake's body. Nowadays it is possible to read so many books: Buddhist texts, Hindu texts, and so on. You can have a fair intellectual understanding of these things, but your life can remain completely unchanged: you live just like everybody else. This seems to be happening in the United States, especially in Buddhist circles. People belong to Buddhist groups, go along to gompas, and so on. They read all about those things. Perhaps they even write books about them, or translate texts from the Tibetan. But their way of life remains the same as that of any other middle-class professional American. They live like an American lawyer or doctor or psychoanalyst or therapist: there's no difference. That's because there's very little *caraṇa*. But the Buddha is fully endowed with both *vijjā* and *caraṇa* on the highest possible level – though you could say that no *caraṇa* fully expresses your *vijjā* because your *caraṇa* exists within a very limited context, whereas your *vijjā* may be unlimited. But even so, your *vijjā* should find the fullest possible expression that the objective nature of your circumstances permits.

KULAMITRA: It's a funny kind of understanding that doesn't have any practical application, isn't it? When you're talking about people who understand something and don't practise, they haven't *really* understood.

SANGHARAKSHITA: They haven't really understood. Their understanding needs to be deepened, and also to be balanced by practical application. That's one of the reasons I think it's so important that there must be a new lifestyle set up in the FWBO. That's why I attach great importance to the communities. Unless you've got something like that, something that breaks up the existing social order, your involvement in Buddhism remains academic, virtually, or just pietistic. But if you set up communities, particularly men's communities and women's communities, there's a different sort of social setup immediately. You abolish the family at a stroke, and everything that that implies. The whole family-based way of life is just abolished, broken down, and that's a very big thing to have done. A really massive source of conditioning is removed. Unless one does something like this, there's no real *caraṇa*: it's all quite empty pseudo-*vijjā*. With the possible exception of team-based right livelihood, which we have yet to develop properly,[180] the single-sex community is probably our most powerful means of frontal assault on the existing social setup, because it changes so many things. It changes your whole pattern of domestic life; it changes your whole pattern of work; it changes the whole rhythm of your day-to-day existence. It changes your psychological attitude, and your emotional attitude. It corrects your emotional dependence on the opposite sex and gives you a completely different environment and context within which to function. Suppose each one of you were to project yourself into a situation where you had a full-time job, 9 to 5, where you had a wife, and one or two children. What do you think your state of mind would be like? What do you think your prospects would be like? They'd be very, very different! And what do you think you'd make of your Buddhism? What do you think you'd do with it? With luck you'd get in a short meditation before you went to work, or in the evening when you got home – if you weren't too tired, and if the wife didn't want you to do something else – and with luck you'd get along to a class once or twice a week. Even that would become more and more difficult as your life at home became more and more demanding, especially if you had more children. It would be difficult to go away for retreats because you would have to take the family on holiday, and you couldn't do both, perhaps. Well, it doesn't bear thinking about, does it?

KULARATNA: It sounds almost as big a commitment as being at Sukhavati!

SANGHARAKSHITA: In a sense, yes. In a sense, no. The difference is that in the family it's all on your shoulders, but at Sukhavati responsibility is spread out over so many broad backs. I really feel that if we set up a substantial number of communities of this sort we can achieve almost anything. Mixed communities, i.e. communities made up of both men and women, won't do. The mixed community, though it may be calling itself a spiritual community, except under very exceptional circumstances is only the family writ large. So mixed communities are almost out. It is the single-sex communities that are going to be the revolutionary spearhead of the movement. Set those up all over the place, and very radical changes will come about in so many individuals, and through them in quite large sections of society.[181]

Anyway, that's all emerged from *vijjācaraṇasampanno* – from this equilibrium of *vijjā* and *caraṇa*, theory and practice, insight and activity.

KULAMITRA: It seems to me that unless you have some practice you can get away with theoretical knowledge that won't stand up to practice.

SANGHARAKSHITA: One might even say, taking the word 'practice' in the narrow sense, that practice is not enough. You've got to have a whole way of life and a whole objective social context. It's not enough to have a personal practice. Your family man could have a personal practice, and he could even keep it up, but it would be just like the prisoner sitting in his cell and reading a book about freedom. Yes, he'd read it every day quite faithfully, but he's still a prisoner; he can't break out. The family man who does his practice regularly is very much in that sort of position. It's good that he does it, and it certainly has a beneficial effect on him, but even that is not really enough. The prisoner in the jail may be put in charge of the library instead of breaking stones, but he's still in prison.

KULARATNA: But isn't being imprisoned more a state of mind than whether you live in a family or a single-sex community? Just because you live in a single-sex community it doesn't mean you're automatically going to start leading a creative spiritual life.

SANGHARAKSHITA: No, it doesn't; it still requires your cooperation. But the facilities are all at hand, and the cramping conditions of the small nuclear family setup are no longer there. You have the opportunity: you have the freedom. The more I come into contact with family situations the more I feel that they're so stuffy. They're really claustrophobic. They hem you in all round. You can hardly stir hand or foot, especially if you're permanently there, in the sense of having long-term commitments of that nature. The lay devotee or the lay follower in the strict sense is a very rare bird indeed. There's so much room for rationalization here. In the spiritual community you may not be up to scratch, but there are people to help you keep up to scratch, and the situation itself is like that.

KULARATNA: What do you think the rationalizations are that the family situation opens you up to?

SANGHARAKSHITA: The main one that I've encountered is this. Someone who is married claims he is leading a very unselfish life. The unmarried man, the single man, the bachelor – even the spiritual bachelor – is selfish, only thinking about himself and his own pleasure, whereas the family man has taken on the responsibility of looking after others. He's looking after a wife and children; he's working very hard for them; he's leading an unselfish life. Now obviously unselfishness is a spiritual quality, and a spiritual person should be unselfish, so the family man, being the embodiment of unselfishness, may say that he is in fact leading a highly spiritual life, just by devoting himself to his wife and children, and doing everything for their sake. You'll meet this rationalization in India: you'll hear it from brahmins especially. Now what would you say to this?

KULARATNA: What would *you* say to it?

SANGHARAKSHITA: I try to sort out the mess in this sort of way. I ask, well, why has that person entered into that situation? Why did he get married? Was it out of purely objective reasons that he had this disinterested desire to support this woman, with nothing in it for himself? He was being purely selfless; is that it? The claim to unselfishness is based on a rationalization. The family man gets himself into a situation like that for the most purely subjective reasons. That's why he has got the wife and the children. From a purely biological point of view that's fine; it's quite normal, quite healthy, there's no criticism of it on that level. But he's certainly not looking after them out of motives of spiritual unselfishness. He's landed himself in that situation as the logical – or the biological – consequences of following certain desires which, healthy though they may be from a natural point of view, certainly couldn't be described as unselfish, and he's not acknowledging the fact. That's where the rationalization – the hypocrisy even – comes in. So sometimes I say, look, if some young woman was willing that you should marry her, and look after her, but not that you should ever sleep with her, would you go into it? Or if you were to adopt children, or if she was to have children who weren't yours, would you unselfishly go on labouring for them, supporting them, looking after them? The married man's claim that he is leading a more unselfish life than the unmarried man is a pathetic piece of rationalization. Of course, one has to admit that even in that sort of situation some small qualities of unselfishness may be needed and may be developed. But the basis of the whole thing is just natural desires. One need not find fault with those desires but they need not masquerade as high spiritual unselfishness.

When you hear some householders speak, especially in India, it's as though they've gone sailing into married life, and into family life, from purely bodhisattva-like motives. They'll tell you that they're just as much a monk as anyone living in a monastery, that their house is just like a monastery, etc. 'I'm leading a purely unselfish life,' they say. 'I have no self-interest. I think only of my wife and children.' You won't tend to find this attitude among the new Buddhists in India. I think that would be most unlikely. It's a very sophisticated attitude, the sort of attitude that develops when spiritual life, or religious life, has become something respectable, and something everybody feels they ought to follow or live up to – but basically they don't want to. It's like the Englishman who thinks that to serve king and country is being religious, so what more could you do? What more could you expect of anyone?

So a personal implementation of the principles of spiritual life is not enough. There needs to be a change in the whole social order to which one belongs, because you're being affected by that all the time. You may be the most backsliding member of the community at Sukhavati. You may get up late, and you may not meditate very often, but it still has an effect on you; you are still changed to some extent by being there. I've noticed that with some men who have been up at Padmaloka.[182] In a way Padmaloka is nothing to boast about, but I've seen people coming up there and in the course of a month there is a definite positive change, even though it's so easygoing there, and even though, perhaps, those people haven't made much of an effort. But you wouldn't have seen that change if you'd sent them home to stay with their mum and dad.

KULANANDA: It's just removing limits.

SANGHARAKSHITA: Removing limits. So the whole series thus far reads, 'Such indeed is he, the Blessed One, the One Perfectly Endowed with Knowledge and Practice', and then comes *sugato*. *Sugato* or *sugata*, usually translated 'the Happy One', literally means 'the one gone to a happy state' or 'gone to a happy destiny'. *Gati* (literally 'goings') is the term used for the five (or six) realms of conditioned existence: the world of the gods, the world of the *asuras*, and so on. In a very general sense, one who is *sugata* is one who has gone to, or who is likely to go to, a good state, a good rebirth, that is to say, a rebirth in the realm of the gods or in the human realm. In the case of the Buddha, however, *sugata* means one who has 'gone well', or who is 'well gone', in the highest sense, that is to say, gone to Nirvāṇa or Enlightenment, and who is therefore happy. This draws attention to a very important aspect of spiritual life and spiritual development, which is, of course, the fact that it is emotionally positive, that it is a path of increasing happiness.

KULAMITRA: Going back to families, I think that's one of the biggest drawbacks of family situations. When I stayed with my parents in Zambia it was a constant struggle to be positive, against almost the karma of negativity they'd built up in that situation.

SANGHARAKSHITA: But I wonder why this is. Is it inherent, do you think, in the family situation? If the family life is not a happy one, what makes it that way? Is it only the nuclear family? Could the extended family be better? There seems to be somewhat less tension in the extended family, though there's a lot of squabbling nonetheless, especially among the womenfolk.

KULANANDA: There's no higher ideal, necessarily, in the family.

SANGHARAKSHITA: It's all very much on the animal level.

KULANANDA: On a survival level, and possibly the survival of the family as a whole, not even so much on an individual level.

KULAMITRA: I think that if there are any remnants of ideals from earlier days, as they fail to develop in that situation, the fact that people feel they've stagnated is quite unpleasant too.

SANGHARAKSHITA: Well they might see it simply in terms of not having succeeded – and very few people do succeed in life, even on their own terms. A few may, those who attain eminence in some profession or skill, and you do get a quite definite satisfaction from that. They feel they've made something of their lives; but they're a minority.

KULANANDA: Even so, can that feeling be anything but hollow, really? That's the thing I feel in families: that life is so hollow because it's so immediate. It's these seventy puny years, and nothing beyond.

KULARATNA: It's all sort of preordained, isn't it? It's not open-ended. There's no excitement. I suppose that's why marriages break up in England – because people get so bored that they start quarrelling for something to do.

SANGHARAKSHITA: They get bored even on the most mundane level: they even get sexually bored after a few years within a strict monogamous context. But acting as devil's advocate for a moment, and trying to argue the case for the family, one could take the line that the family is the base from which you operate. You don't expect much from the family, but it's your safe, secure basis, in the case of a man. You've got your job, your professional career, and you can still expand from that in all sorts of ways.

KULANANDA: Yes, your job would be your area of operation.

KULARATNA: It sounds all right in theory, but in practice it rarely seems to work out that way.

SANGHARAKSHITA: Presumably because to really succeed in your job you've got to give yourself to it completely, which means you spend very little time at home. Your wife gets dissatisfied, and complains that you treat the place like a hotel. She's got nothing to do, and she's bored, so she starts looking around. First of all it's the women's clubs, and then she starts going out with somebody else....

KULANANDA: Can you imagine the treacherous boredom of being a housewife today? It must be incredible.

SANGHARAKSHITA: Being a housewife without getting bored was more possible in the old days when there was a bigger, more extended family, and there were other people at home.

KULANANDA: And there was work to do. Nowadays it's all machines.

SANGHARAKSHITA: That's true. In India a woman is busy all the time, and usually she's – I won't say happy, but she's contented in a dumb cow-like way. She goes and draws water and she has to light the fire every morning. You can't just switch something on: you light the fire, you blow it for half an hour, and then you go and get the water and put it on, and you cook, and this fills in the day.

KULANANDA: Imagine just having to open a packet of this or that and then switching on the washing machine.

SANGHARAKSHITA: In India you have to go to the river and pound your clothes. You go with other women; you have a good old chat. At least it fills life up. But the modern wife, living at home, surrounded by her gadgets, can quickly and easily get bored and bang goes your safe base. Well, can anything be said for the home? For the family life?

KULARATNA: It gives you a chance for rearing children.

SANGHARAKSHITA: Yes, this is the only thing. Presumably the generations have to go on. But is the modern nuclear family the best way to do that?

KULARATNA: I'm sure it isn't.

KULANANDA: What would the alternative be? The extended family or the large community?

SANGHARAKSHITA: You could have an extended family, which I think would be more positive, though not ideal. In a more ideal situation you could take the boys away from their mothers when they were 7 or 8 and maybe put them in a special kind of men's community where there were men who would devote themselves to looking after them, and educating them, in a more 'tribal' sort of way. That would probably be better.

KULARATNA: I think that would work out if everyone was living in a fairly small area.

SANGHARAKSHITA: That means an extended colony.

KULARATNA: Yes, a real community.

SANGHARAKSHITA: With constituent units of various kinds, including a women's longhouse and ...

KULARATNA: We don't want to get too institutionalized.

SANGHARAKSHITA: A large-scale community probably would have to be a bit institutionalized, because it's only possible for it to be otherwise when people are really individuals. At present what happens is that the individual who has begun to feel that he is an individual just opts out and sets up his own structures, i.e. the single-sex communities. Probably for quite a long time to come that will be the tendency. When you've got a really large number of such communities, then perhaps you can think in terms of setting up a more extended structure for larger numbers of people who are not so committed, but who would benefit nonetheless. But what I feel about the family situation, whenever I encounter it, or go back into it for a few minutes, is that it's so stuffy. Maybe it is due to the lack of opportunity, lack of excitement even. Family life is so repetitive.

A VOICE: I went to visit my brother last weekend. He's fairly well married, with one child and another one on the way. I went out for a drink with him in the evening, and he just said that he'd given up the fight: he'd just resigned himself.

SANGHARAKSHITA: So what did you say?

A VOICE: Well I've spoken to him about the Friends and Buddhism before, but he feels limited by his situation.

SANGHARAKSHITA: But what do you think impelled him into that situation? Why does a man get married? This is the basic question.

KULAMITRA: Sometimes they just can't think of anything else! I had a lift from a lorry driver who said, when I told him about our men's community, 'Why didn't someone tell me about this sort of thing before I married?' Particularly in Norfolk, where it's still very traditional.

KULANANDA: Some men get married to leave home.

SANGHARAKSHITA: That's true. They don't see any other way of getting away from home except to another home. They take it for granted that they can't look after themselves.

KULANANDA: Right, and they can't possibly build a decent family on that basis. It's defeated from the beginning.

SANGHARAKSHITA: There was a karate teacher called George, who was first of all a pupil of Terry Dukes. Anyone remember him or meet him? He was a very nice chap indeed. Anyway, he lived at home with his mother, and his mother used to say – so he told us – that she'd never allow George to leave home. He'd leave home when he got married, and go straight off to some good woman. From one good woman to another. She'd never allow him to live on his own, she said.

KULANANDA: That's an odd word, 'allow', because it assumes some sort of power which one person has over another.

SANGHARAKSHITA: This has its roots way back in civilization. In the Old Testament, and in Roman law, you find that the father was not just the head of the family, but head of the tribal group-cum-family. He was a sort of king-cum-magistrate, and had the power of life and death. Even in historical times, a patrician Roman father had the right to put his son to death. But this is logical, in a way. Just as today a woman has the right to have an abortion, and she can say, 'The child is mine! I can do with it as I like', in ancient times you produced the child and so he belonged to you: you did as you liked with him, the idea being that the child was produced by the seed of the man. Until recent times it was not known that the embryo was produced by the union of the spermatozoon and the ovum. It was thought that the female only produced nourishment, and that the seed originated entirely from the father and that it was planted in and nourished by the body of the female just as the earth nourishes the seed that is sown in it. And because life came entirely from the father, the father had complete right over his progeny. He'd given them life, and he had the right to destroy them. They were his seed.

KULANANDA: That shows how scientific ideas go hand in hand with social values.

SANGHARAKSHITA: That's right. We now know that the male and the female play an equal part in the process of conception and this has evened things up to some extent, but it has also to some extent gone to the other extreme, with some women claiming total right over the products of their wombs, denying any rights of the father.

KULAMITRA: Far from being a place where unselfishness is practised, families are hotbeds of selfishness, with people making demands on each other and insisting that other people do what they want.

SANGHARAKSHITA: This is certainly the sort of complaint that parents usually make about children. I encountered it among the Nepalese, who are a very traditionally-minded people. Fathers would often come to me and complain about their sons, who were in their early twenties – you know, the excitable age – and the gist of the complaint was that the impudent young so-and-so wants to do what he wants to do! He won't do what he's told. 'I want him to do this' or 'I want him to do that'. (It's taken for granted that this is absolutely right: 'I mean, I'm his *father*'.) 'And he won't do it. Please bring him to his senses. Please *reason* with him.'

KULARATNA: What did you say?

SANGHARAKSHITA: I knew it wasn't much use saying anything to the father. So I'd say something like, 'The way things are nowadays, young men are hard to handle. I'll just do what I can. I'm not very hopeful. Yes, he's very headstrong. I'll talk to him.' The boy would come along and we'd have a good heart-to-heart talk. I'd see quite clearly what was happening. (Usually they felt that I was more on their side than their father's.) They just wanted to make their own choices, their own decisions. Sometimes they were a bit rash, but usually not. Father always played safe. Father had a nice cosy little job already lined up near where he worked, so he could keep an eye on his son, and see him two or three times during the day and make sure he wasn't going with women before he was married. Mother would have been getting ready a nice wife for him, of her choice – the sort of daughter-in-law she'd really like. And he was just trying to get away: 'I want to go to Calcutta.' 'What?' the father would say, 'What will you do in Calcutta, that big dirty dangerous city? You probably won't get any work. You'll become a lounger and a loafer. You might even have to beg.' But the boy wouldn't care if he had to beg. He just wanted to get away from home. There'd be such rebellious feelings, sometimes, in Nepalese young men, and the fathers and grandfathers really used to put them down. Sometimes we don't appreciate the strength of the old-style traditional family, and the extent to which it imposes conformity. One must understand that such conformity is not bad in a strictly biological sense: it does make for the survival of the group, the survival of the species. But when individuals start developing, values change completely.

KULAMITRA: It's also quite hypocritical in the family, isn't it? I've heard that selfishness talked about as 'That's love, that's a marvellous thing.' You know, 'Of course we want you to do what we want; we love you!'

SANGHARAKSHITA: 'We want you to make the right choice because we want you to be happy!' Probably there comes to be less and less of this as one goes up the social scale, where people are accustomed to a bit of mobility. But in ordinary families they're very concerned that the son should make the right choice. So it is important that we should not just run the family down, but be able to show people a living alternative which is an actual option.

Anyway, we are supposed to be dealing with *sugato*, and we're getting off the track a bit. But it is relevant, isn't it? Maybe a few words about India in this connection would be appropriate. In India family life is very strong. All the ex-Untouchable Buddhists you meet will be firmly embedded in families. The only accepted alternative is the life of the monk, in the strict ascetic sense. There's no such concept as the young man-about-town, the happy bachelor, or anything like that. That just does not fit into their scheme of things at all. If they hear of such a monster – a young man who goes around with women who isn't married – well, they've seen things like that on some American films, but in their eyes it's an enormity, something that doesn't fit. So far as they are concerned, young men of that type exist on the fringes of society: they haunt brothels and places like that. They've no idea about someone who is relatively free in a social sense. A few Western- or English-educated people may be a bit familiar with that sort of possibility, but it's far from being an effective possibility for the average young Indian.

KULARATNA: It's incredible when you think about it, isn't it?

SANGHARAKSHITA: Yes. Maybe there's a little bit of social freedom in the Western sense for the university student, but not much. It's a very different kind of social setup. It's either 100% family life or 100% asceticism. There's nothing in between.

KULARATNA: Do they know about Western culture, though?

SANGHARAKSHITA: They know about it, broadly speaking, but they think of it in terms of morality and immorality, and they like to think that in the West there's lots of immorality because the West hasn't got the culture that India has got. You must remember that the vast majority of Indians have got just one big label for anything outside the orthodox social system, i.e. getting married when you're young, etc. Any sort of sexual irregularity is just plain, straightforward immorality, and totally inconsistent with any religious or spiritual life. This is the way the vast majority of people see things. Leave aside spiritual considerations, there's no idea of the socially free individual, certainly not in the case of women: that is utterly unthinkable. They've only one word for women who deviate in the slightest degree from the accepted standards of conduct for respectable women: prostitute. If they see an unmarried woman talking or laughing with a man, it's 'Look at that prostitute!' That is exactly how they see things.

KULARATNA: What's their morality built upon?

SANGHARAKSHITA: One could say custom, just custom. Just the sheer inertia of that society, which functions quite well for the majority of people within it but allows very little scope for the individual. That is why, if you want to be free from it, the only thing to do is to break away totally, i.e. become an ascetic. You cannot be free within secular society: you have to go outside it altogether as a sannyasin or a *bhikkhu*.

KULARATNA: So that's why, in the East, you can't really have a committed lay follower. If they're committed they have to be a *bhikkhu*.

SANGHARAKSHITA: Right. One of the things that I'm not happy about is this hard and fast distinction between the lay follower and the *bhikkhu*. That itself, I think, is something to be broken down. I don't want that when the FWBO goes to India we have yellow-robed *anagārikas* – who are assimilated to *bhikkhus*, and who are pure and holy and outside social life – and *upāsakas* with their white *kesas* from whom nothing much is expected. 'Well, they're just worldly people....' I don't want that sort of division developing. When you and Lokamitra go to India you'll see a gravitational pull exerted on the pair of you by Indian society and Indian culture.[183] He will be pulled towards the *bhikkhus*: they will feel he's one of them and he'll fraternize with them; you will be pulled more towards the lay people: they will feel that you're more one of them, just because you're not in yellow robes. But you must both resist this sort of gravitational pull, and insist on the fact of the common spiritual commitment, the Going for Refuge. But the FWBO as a whole will be subject to this pull in India.

KULADEVA: I thought all Order members who were going out to India to do any work there were going to have the *anagārika* ordination.

SANGHARAKSHITA: Yes and no – if you can really say yes and no. But if all of them are *anagārikas* it plays into the hands of the existing system. People will think that 'monks' have come out and therefore they will get the idea that what really matters is the external things, not the actual spiritual commitment.

KULAMITRA: It lets them off the hook.

SANGHARAKSHITA: Exactly. This is what you hear from so many Buddhist lay people: 'Well, *we* are not *bhikkhus*....' The *bhikkhus* lead the spiritual life for them vicariously, and they're very particular about keeping the *bhikkhus* up to scratch. If you say, 'Look, don't you think you should be a vegetarian? After all, you're a Buddhist', they will reply, 'Oh, I'm just a humble lay follower. What can be expected of *me*?' Or if you reproach them for telling a lie, they'll say, 'Oh, I'm just an *upāsaka*.' So yes, if we send out just *anagārikas*, who look like *bhikkhus*, it'll let them off the hook. But with *you* around that won't happen. Obviously there is a difficulty inherent in the situation. For instance, they might be a bit shocked if you go to the cinema. They'd certainly be shocked if I went to the cinema, unless the film was definitely labelled 'Life of the Buddha' or some such thing. They regard cinema-going as very worldly and they wouldn't be able to understand why, being a spiritual person, I engaged in such a worldly activity. They've no experience of the film as a medium for ideas or anything of that sort. They'd not be too surprised if *you* went to see a film, but they'd be quite surprised if Lokamitra went in his yellow robes. You see what you're up against?

KULARATNA: There seems to be a separation of the spiritual life from the 'real' life. They seem to be making a hard and fast distinction between two completely different kinds of life.

SANGHARAKSHITA: This preserves 'worldly' life in its worldliness. It lets it off the hook.

KULARATNA: In fact they're not taking responsibility for their own actions.

SANGHARAKSHITA: Spiritual life is something you live *outside* society.

KULANANDA: It's quite useful for somebody who really does just want to do nothing to be able to think like that.

KULAMITRA: It's almost like *Brave New World*, where they take the difficult ones and put them on an island.[184] They don't affect the main community, so they let them be.

SANGHARAKSHITA: What we've got to do, on the contrary, is to remain in society but insist on being different from society. The sangha should not be just a monastic body totally separate from society at large, but a sort of model within society of what society as a whole could ultimately become. You find much the same sort of thing in the case of Christianity. Society at large, though calling itself Christian, isn't expected to practise Christianity. This is relegated to the monasteries – if they have any monasteries. It's the monks who turn the other cheek, not ordinary

Christians. So the sort of problem we'll be up against in India, socially speaking, is rather different from what we're up against here. In a way we're in a better position in England. Do you see what I mean? We are free to function within society, because it's possible to be more of an individual within Western society. In the context of Indian society you've either got to be the complete family man or you've got to be completely a monk in a strict and rather narrow way. Other possibilities virtually do not exist. You do find a few artists who are pretty free in their ways in the big cities, but they're few and far between, and frowned on by a lot of people. Conditions aren't the same everywhere, of course, India being such a vast country, but I'm sure you'll find traces of these attitudes in at least some of the people you meet when you go out there.

KULARATNA: Hearing you talk about India and the strongly traditional society in which people live there, and also having heard that lecture on the Axial Age a few days ago, I was wondering about the arising of individuals and the strength and stability of societies.[185] Would it be true to say that you'd be more likely to have people thinking for themselves, and therefore the arising of more true individuals, in societies in which there is quite a lot of social change and upheaval going on?

SANGHARAKSHITA: For the ordinary person, the ordinary group member who is not yet an individual, traditional society is very good. He has his place. He knows exactly where he stands, exactly what his duties are; he knows what is expected of him. There is stability, security. All his natural needs are fulfilled and looked after. But once people start developing as individuals they become quite a disruptive influence, and very often we find that people start becoming individuals when two or more groups come into juxtaposition, or into contact, or even into conflict, because then you have two or more absolutes confronting each other. Formerly you were brought up within one particular group, one particular society, one particular tradition, and that was it for you. You never thought there was any other way of doing things: it was unthinkable. But then you come into contact with another kind of group, another kind of society, who do things completely differently, and that has an unsettling effect. You start thinking: people in this society do things in this way; people in this society do things in that way. A sort of relativism creeps in. Who is to decide what is right and what is wrong? The individual. That's the way it seems to develop. Therefore it seems that you get individuals developing – though this is not the only way, or the only reason – when, for instance, you get one political group conquering other groups and creating an empire. Within the empire there's a great deal of mobility, just because it is one empire. You get court officials going from one part to another, or travellers like Herodotus going around sightseeing.[186] They see that in different parts of the empire people do things in different ways, even live differently. A certain relativism then grows up, which can be a source of individuality in the true sense, but can also be just a source of social decay and confusion, especially for ordinary people. Ordinary people just get bewildered.

KULARATNA: Aren't the two connected in that in a time of unrest there will be more responsibility thrown back on the individual? If the individual is able to respond to that he'll grow into a true individual, but if he's not able to do so he'll just find himself bewildered, the same as the others.

SANGHARAKSHITA: And more likely to become unintelligently conservative, which means *consciously* conservative. Before, he was *un*consciously conservative, because he didn't see any other possibility, but now he becomes consciously conservative, even violently so. This is what happened in the case of Socrates. Why was he condemned to death? Because he came up against these forces of conscious conservatism. The present time in world history is a time of intense relativism, and therefore – perhaps for that reason – more 'individuals' are being produced, but there are also stronger retreats into various kinds of groups: more and more abject submission to authority of various kinds: intelligent people like T. S. Eliot becoming Anglo-Catholics, Chesterton and Belloc actually becoming Catholics.[187] You get movements like Nazism, where the emphasis on the group is very strong. You get loyalty to the firm becoming a way of life. And then there's the socialist state, which becomes the be all and end all of people's lives.

KULARATNA: And ultra-left-wing and ultra-right-wing groups.

SANGHARAKSHITA: Or all these different pseudo-religious groups, where you get people totally dedicating themselves, becoming totally group members of things like the Divine Light Mission and Ananda Marga[188] – not giving themselves, just giving themselves up. And in the midst of all that, you get just a few people struggling to be individuals, struggling to make sense of it all.

KULADEVA: So that the emerging group undermines the value of the traditional group?

SANGHARAKSHITA: What happens is that at times of social change, or where it becomes evident that there's a great deal of cultural relativism in human life, individuals emerge. At such times, the truly stronger people are more likely to become individuals, and the weaker ones more likely either to retreat into existing groups or join new authoritarian groups – or the 'stronger' weaker people start new groups. Some weak people get their security from having followers. That can also be a reaction to unsettling social change. I remember that when Guru Maharaj had his big celebration up at Alexandra Palace some of our friends went there.[189] Several of these friends reported back to me that they had noticed that the followers, the 'premis', were definitely and distinctly of two kinds: a majority that were completely sheep-like and did everything they were told, and a minority that were clearly in charge and had what one of our friends described as a completely Fascist, authoritarian attitude – even an attitude of contempt – towards the others, that showed itself in the way they ordered them about. There were these two distinct kinds of people, both of them representing reactions to the same situation of social change. You can react by weakly following or by leading, or trying to lead, in a highly authoritarian fashion. In both ways you get your security.

KULAMITRA: And those leaders are the dominant ones that people sometimes call individuals.

SANGHARAKSHITA: Yes, right. Dominant group members are often called individuals.

KULARATNA: But then the true individuals who arise and teach in a time of disorder will lead the way towards a new order.

SANGHARAKSHITA: Hopefully lead the way towards an entirely new social order.

KULARATNA: Which eventually, presumably, will break down in decay again.

SANGHARAKSHITA: Yes, the whole thing is cyclical, and therefore can never be done once and for all as regards society at large but needs to be done again and again and again. This brings us to something that will come in later: the Buddhas of the past, present, and future – and the Dharmas and the Sanghas too. Anyway, let's go on.

The Buddha is also *lokavidū*. *Loka* is 'world'. In Buddhism, especially in the Theravāda, there's this distinction or contrast between *loka* and *lokuttara*, the mundane and the transcendental. *Loka* is 'world' in the full sense, i.e. all conditioned existence, and *vidū* is one who knows in the sense of one who understands, who penetrates into. So the Buddha is 'the one who knows the world', the one who knows conditioned existence through and through, who *comprehends* conditioned existence. You can look at this in two ways. First of all, the Buddha is the one who knows the world in the purely spiritual or transcendent sense that he sees through conditioned existence: sees that it is conditioned, that it arises in dependence on conditions, on causes, even, that it is contingent, that it can't give permanent satisfaction, that it is impermanent and doesn't possess any permanent reality of its own. Secondly, the Buddha is a knower of the world in the sense that he knows the minds of people, understands the conditions under which they live, understands society. We certainly see in the Pāli texts that the Buddha knew what was going on. He is quite well informed about things, even acquainted with the political situation – certainly acquainted with the social setup, particularly the caste system.

KULARATNA: That's really interesting, because there's sometimes an idea that the spiritual person leaves the world behind.

SANGHARAKSHITA: Yes, the Hindu will have this idea. He will be a bit shocked if he sees, for instance, a monk reading a newspaper. Now clearly, in a sense, a monk ought not to occupy himself too much with newspapers. *You* can be a newspaper addict, but you can't lay it down as a hard and fast rule that a monk, i.e. a completely spiritual person, should never read a newspaper because that's worldly, and he should have nothing to do with anything worldly. This is the reasoning, but it's a false reasoning. Assuming that he is a spiritual person, and that his motive is spiritual, if he is working in the world he may need to know what is going on. He may need, therefore, to read newspapers. It's too easy to say, 'Worldly people read newspapers. Spiritual people don't. If you're a spiritual person you mustn't read a newspaper.' Or, 'He's reading a newspaper, he can't be a spiritual person.' That's too simplistic, too absolutist. Whether it is by reading the newspaper or in any other way, you need to know the world, because it's in the world that you are operating.

Incidentally, one could mention here, and maybe quarrel with, the expression 'giving up the world'. This is something you hear in India, and in the West too: that the monk 'gives up the world', as though he could find some vantage point entirely outside it and have nothing to do with it. That is not the case at all. He's 'in' the world as much as anybody else, but in a different way; or at least he tries to be in it in a different way. Again you see this attempt to shunt off the spiritual person, to make him socially irrelevant. In a sense, yes, he is *not* in the world. Or rather, he's not *of* the world, but he is *in* it. Orthodox Hinduism tries to make anything like Buddhism – or even some of its own spiritual traditions – socially irrelevant, and this is one of the ways in which it does this: by saying that the holy man, the spiritual man, has nothing to do with worldly things. It's true that he doesn't in a worldly way, but this sort of philosophy shouldn't be used to try to neutralize his influence on the existing society. In the Middle Ages, for instance, a monk might come to a king and expostulate with him that he ought to be more just and more compassionate to his subjects. What would the king usually say? 'Get back to your monastery. Get on with your prayers. *That's* your job – not to tell me how to govern the country.' It's only too easy for someone who's a bit revolutionary to be neutralized in this way. In the West, the revolutionary is neutralized by being incorporated into the establishment, which happens pretty quickly once he becomes successful. You see it time and time again. Look at the Beatles, for instance. In India they do it more by making you socially irrelevant, by putting you on a pedestal so high that you have no influence. They say things like 'Oh, you are so pure you couldn't possibly understand how bad and wicked we are! It's useless to give us advice we're incapable of following. In your pure compassion just pray for us and leave us to our well-deserved misery.'

KULANANDA: Please!

SANGHARAKSHITA: So the Buddha is a knower of the world both spiritually and in a more mundane sense. And then he is *anuttaro purisadammasārathi. Sārathi* is 'charioteer'. *Ratha* is 'chariot', *sa* is 'with', so it means 'the man who goes with the chariot, i.e. the charioteer. The Buddha is the charioteer – the leader, or guide, shower of the way – for *purisa*, 'men', who are *damma*, 'to be tamed' or 'to be controlled', that is to say, who are ready to be controlled, who want to be controlled.

KULARATNA: When you say men who want to be controlled, do you mean men who want to control themselves?

SANGHARAKSHITA: Yes, men who want to be shown how to control themselves. This raises the whole question of the meaning of control. *Damma* could be translated as 'restraint', in which case the Buddha is the charioteer – the leader or guide – for men who wish to restrain themselves. The suggestion is that the energies are going in the wrong direction and need to be redirected. In the *Dhammapada* the Buddha says that just as irrigators lead water, and fletchers fashion arrows and carpenters wood, so wise men control (*damayanti*) themselves.[190] It is the same word, *damma*, that is used here. The conception is more one of a natural force or natural energy which needs to be properly directed than of one that needs to be repressed or dammed up. You could even render *purisadammasārathi* as 'the guide for those who wish to direct their energies properly'.

KULANANDA: To become integrated.

SANGHARAKSHITA: To become integrated. Then there's the epithet *anuttaro. Anuttaro* means the highest or best or supreme; literally the unsurpassed. The Buddha is the highest or best or supreme guide for those who wish to restrain themselves or to direct their energies in the right way. Sometimes *anuttaro* is taken as a separate epithet, not as an adjective of *purisadammasārathi*, in which case it means simply: 'The Blessed One is the highest, or the unsurpassed', i.e. the highest kind of being: the fully Enlightened, liberated individual.

The fact that in Buddhism there is this idea of control or restraint – or at least redirection – of energies raises a question of considerable importance. People usually think of control or restraint so much in terms of repression that they're against the idea of any control or restraint at all. It is quite important to understand this matter properly.

KULANANDA: Perhaps one should think in terms of harmonization of energies.

SANGHARAKSHITA: That might be to gloss over the difficulty a bit. Maybe it's a question of recognizing that sometimes there are within yourself impulses that you just have to check. You have to realize that you can't always give vent to your feelings or impulses. If you get very angry and want to lash out at somebody, you have to check that. That's not to say that you need to repress the feeling of anger in the technical psychoanalytical sense – it's not to say that you should refuse to acknowledge that the feeling is there – but you may have to check or control the expression. Partly as a result of a polarized and misunderstood Freudianism people sometimes speak and think as though you just have to 'let everything hang out' – including lash out – in the full and literal sense, and that clearly is not desirable.

KULARATNA: I suppose the reason for that is that we've been so blocked and repressed that sometimes actually expressing it all is the first step towards redirecting energies.

SANGHARAKSHITA: Even so, you have to be aware of other people and consider them. Why should they have to pay the price for your self-expression – your self-development, even – if they don't want to? 'Control' has come to be rather a dirty word in some circles. In other circles control is regarded with too much favour. It's as though people are split, some wanting control in a higher, authoritarian, rigid, repressive way, and others not recognizing the need for any kind of control at all, even objective self-control. At least one needs to deflect one's energies from one object onto another.

Continuing, the Buddha is *satthā devamanussānaṃ*. *Satthā* is 'teacher', even 'guru'; *devamanussānaṃ* is 'of gods and men'. So the Buddha – the Blessed One – is described as the 'teacher of gods and men'. Now how is one to take that? Clearly it matters what is meant by god, or *deva*. *Devas* appear in Buddhist texts repeatedly, don't they? A *devatā* appears at the beginning of the *Maṅgala Sutta*. So what is a *deva*, or *devatā*?

KULAMITRA: A being that inhabits a world that is correlative of a more positive state of consciousness.

SANGHARAKSHITA: But what is that world essentially? Is it mundane or transcendental? Conditioned or unconditioned?

KULAMITRA: It's conditioned.

SANGHARAKSHITA: What therefore could one say about the *deva*?

KULAMITRA: A *deva* is a being of refined conditioning.

SANGHARAKSHITA: A being of refined conditioning. Is a being of refined conditioning necessarily at the same time an Enlightened being? No. So does a being of refined conditioning – or a *deva* – need the teaching or not?

ALL: He needs it.

SANGHARAKSHITA: Yes, he needs it.

KULANANDA: Could you say he's closer to Enlightenment than human beings are?

SANGHARAKSHITA: In a sense closer. In a sense further away. He's closer in the sense that his conditioning is more refined, but he's further away in the sense that his conditioning is *very* refined. Or, he is nearer because what separates him from Enlightenment is more refined, but further because such refined conditioning is more difficult to break through. That's the mythological explanation of the Buddha being 'the teacher of gods and men'. According to Buddhist tradition, conditioned existence

– the sphere of sentient existence – extends further than the world of modern science. (*Devas* don't appear in accounts of anthropology!) And the Buddha, the Enlightened One, is the guide or the shower of the way for all forms of sentient conditioned existence, whether lower or higher, grosser or more refined. Since the *devas*, the gods of popular mythology, are regarded as coming in the latter category, it follows that they are in need of teaching. One could say that this is one of the ways in which Buddhism asserted its superiority over the popular cults – by making the objects of those cults, the *devas*, into humble disciples of the Buddha. One could also look at it more psychologically, even in Jungian terms. Looking at it in this way – in a non-mythological, psychological, 'archetypal' sort of way – what is a *deva*?

KULANANDA: One could see it as representing the higher aspect of one's own being.

SANGHARAKSHITA: Yes, the higher aspect of one's own conditioned being. So if one looked at it in that way then in what sense would the Buddha be the teacher of gods and men?

KULANANDA: He would be taking you beyond even that.

SANGHARAKSHITA: He would certainly be doing that, but also more than that. One could say that the *deva* of mythology is seen as being 'out there', but in this more Jungian sense the *deva* is regarded as being 'in here'. Thus the Buddha is the teacher of gods and men in that he also enables one to see that divinities which one formerly projected are aspects of one's own – possibly higher – consciousness and in that way enables one to withdraw the projections. He enables you not to see the *deva* 'out there' but to experience him 'in here', and in this way to become more integrated.

Finally comes *buddho*, i.e. the Buddha, which we have already discussed. The complete formula runs: 'Such indeed is he, the Blessed One, the Worthy One, the Fully and Perfectly Enlightened One, the One Endowed with Knowledge and Practice, the Happily Attained One, the Knower of the World, the Unsurpassed Charioteer of Men to be Tamed, the Teacher of Gods and Men, the Enlightened One.' *Bhagavā ti*: 'Such indeed is the Blessed One'. The formula comes as it were full circle and ends, as it began, with *bhagavā*, 'the Blessed One'. Or we could take *satthā devamanussānaṃ* as the last of the epithets, in which case the reading is *buddho bhagavā ti*: 'Such indeed is the Buddha, the Blessed One'.

Then *Buddhaṃ jīvitapariyantaṃ saraṇaṃ gacchāmi*: 'To the end of (my) life I go to the Buddha for Refuge'. Why do you think the Going for Refuge follows on that recital of the epithets of the Buddha? It's because in order to go for Refuge you must know what you're Going for Refuge to – at least to some extent. It's the Buddha in the sense described here, in these epithets – not a being who created the world or anything of that sort – to whom one is Going for Refuge. And why 'to the end of (my) life'?

KULADEVA: It's not something you do just once. It's more dynamic.

SANGHARAKSHITA: In a sense it's something that you do just once, or once and for all, but again not, because it's something that you do continuously, as well as continually.

KULANANDA: Is Going for Refuge adopting a standard?

SANGHARAKSHITA: That applies more, maybe, to the Going for Refuge to the Dharma. But if you see Going for Refuge in terms of commitment, a commitment which is not for life is hardly a commitment at all. If you really commit yourself there's a quality of absoluteness about it. Since you can't actually see beyond this life, practically speaking in Going for Refuge you commit yourself for life. If, for instance, you really do now believe something to be true, you intend that you should believe it for life. It may so happen that you will change your mind later on and see things differently, but when *now* you see something as true you see it so totally that, so far as you are concerned, you see it as true for good, for the rest of your life. Commitment, being of the same total and absolute nature, cannot but be for life – or beyond it, if you can see beyond. The formula therefore says, 'To the Buddha I go for Refuge to the end of (my) life.' Not just for today or tomorrow.

KULAMITRA: So even if you do change your mind it doesn't change the fact that when you went for Refuge you saw it in that way.

SANGHARAKSHITA: Yes, it's like when you get married. You say, according to the Church of England service, 'Till death us do part', and that is genuinely your intention at the time, i.e. to stay married to that person until death. For one reason or another it may not work out like that, but ideally that is the intention.

Now there follow two stanzas. The opening salutation, the recital of the epithets of the Buddha, and the formula of going for lifelong Refuge are in prose, but the following lines are in verse.

*Ye ca Buddhā atītā ca*
*Ye ca Buddhā anāgatā*
*Paccuppannā ca ye Buddhā*
*Ahaṃ vandāmi sabbadā.*

This means the Buddhas of the past or of the time that has 'gone by' (*atīta*), the Buddhas of the future or of the time that has 'not come' (*anāgatā*), and the Buddhas of the present, or that time that has (just now) 'arisen' (*paccuppannā*) – that is to say, the Buddhas of the present *kalpa* or world period. In the verse you say, 'I (*ahaṃ*) ever (*sabbadā*) salute (*vandāmi*) the Buddhas of the past, the present, and the future.' This brings us to the question of cycles, to the point that a Buddha's work is never done once and for all. A Buddha arises: an individual arises, a true individual, a perfect individual. He gathers around him a number of other individuals, they create a spiritual community, a sangha, and this eventually has an influence on the whole of society. Under favourable conditions the whole of society may become virtually a sangha. But then the process of corruption sets in. Success leads to degeneration. The quality of people joining deteriorates, so your spiritual community becomes less a community of individuals. To the extent that they're not individuals the community becomes more of a group. Group pulls start operating, and then the whole society sinks. Eventually it ends up just like another group, and again, within that group, another individual has to arise, and that is the next Buddha. Thus the process goes on. Buddhism sees the final victory in this way: final victory for the individual, yes, but not final victory for society.

KULANANDA: That's how it treads the path between absolutism and nihilism. Because you can be very nihilistic and say, look, it's just going to collapse, just going to fall away, why should we bother? Or you can say we're going to save mankind for ever.

SANGHARAKSHITA: Though not mankind as a collective entity, because mankind is continually being renewed or replenished. But you can go on 'saving' individuals indefinitely, can 'save' more and more individuals.

KULARATNA: Each time a few might get out.

SANGHARAKSHITA: Yes. 'Group' or 'society' is only a collective term. Suppose there's a teacher teaching the fourth form in a school. He might say, 'What's the use of my work? The fourth form is always the fourth form! It never comes to anything.' But that's not the point. Individuals from the fourth form go up to the fifth form, that's the point, though the fourth form, in a sense, is always with you, always there. However brilliant the students of this year are, however well they go sailing up into the fifth form, at the beginning of next year there's another crop of fourth formers. You might think that your time was being wasted, because the fourth form is always there; but the fourth form in that sense is only an abstraction, not an actually existing entity. In the same way the work of the bodhisattva is never done, because fresh unenlightened individuals are always being produced. Yet at the same time there's optimism because more and more of those unenlightened individuals are becoming Enlightened individuals. Thus there is always the need for another Buddha, once the previous spiritual community has become a group and all knowledge of the path to true individuality has been lost. Another individual has to find it out all over again, and again communicate it to other people.

KULAMITRA: But even during the period of influence of one Buddha there are fluctuations, with the spiritual community becoming stronger and then weaker and again stronger and so on.

SANGHARAKSHITA: Oh yes, and you find this happening in different areas. If you study the history of Buddhist China, you will see that Buddhism rose and fell there many times. Now it's fallen. It may rise again. Some great teacher may arise in China. Historical Buddhism has not yet reached the end of the road by any means, though at present it's very much in retreat. It's been virtually wiped out in Mongolia, in Tibet, and in large areas of China. Now it's suffered great setbacks in Vietnam, in Cambodia, and in Laos. This is all within my lifetime, maybe within your lifetime. Even since the FWBO was founded Buddhism has suffered setbacks.

KULARATNA: Is there still Buddhism in Vietnam?

SANGHARAKSHITA: It's very difficult to say, but the fact is that there's a Communist regime now in control that is completely anti-religious. You can't wipe Buddhism out overnight, of course. I've got many friends in Vietnam, mostly Vietnamese monks. I don't know what's happened to them. I don't know what happened to the Van Hanh Buddhist University that some of them started, the rector of which, also a Vietnamese Buddhist monk, was a very good old friend of mine. At this university they had 2,000 students, many of them monks. I've no news at all what happened to them. I had a standing invitation there. When it started they wanted me to join it. But I know nothing of what's going on there now.[191] This is the way it goes. Buddhism tells us to expect nothing else: this is the world. It goes up, it comes down. Expect no kingdom of heaven on earth. Even Buddhism in its organizational or institutional form will not last for ever. But there's a constant possibility of renewal.

KULANANDA: The principle is eternal?

SANGHARAKSHITA: Buddhism wouldn't even say that. There are two permanent possibilities: to go up, or to go down. To be reactive, or to be creative. The individual – or person who *could* be an individual – has to choose each time.

As for the second of the two stanzas, it's really quite simple. 'For me there is no other Refuge (*n'atthi me saraṇaṃ aññaṃ*). The Buddha is for me the supreme Refuge (*Buddho me saraṇaṃ varaṃ*). By the power of this truth (*etena saccavajjena*) may the victorious-auspicious be mine (*hotu me jayamaṅgalaṃ*)! The only thing that really needs comment here is *etena saccavajjena*: 'by the power of this truth' or 'by the power of these words of mine'. It is a common Indian belief that the utterance of truth has a certain power or force, and can even bring about results in the objective world. This would be regarded nowadays as being completely unscientific, if taken literally, but what it suggests is that the utterance of truth –

something which you say with your whole being, which is true and which you utterly believe – is a really powerful thing, When you really do speak the truth in the full sense there's a certain weight, a certain power, behind your words. Traditionally in India it is the belief that that power is an objective, almost physical power which can bring about events or changes in the course of nature, which can work miracles, as it were – though perhaps they're just a symbolical way of emphasizing and underlining the psychological power which attaches to the utterance of truth. So, 'by the power of this truth, may the victorious-auspicious be mine.'

### Salutation to the Dharma

The *Dhamma vandana*, or 'Salutation to the Dharma', begins with *svākkhāto bhagavatā Dhammo*. It is important to understand that the word *dhamma* or *dharma* has a number of different meanings. For instance, *dhamma* can mean 'quality or attribute'; it can mean 'idea', in the sense of an object of the mind; it can mean 'law', the course or natural order of things; and it can mean 'cause'. *Dhamma* can also mean the ultimate truth or reality of things, and the teaching that reflects that reality. Here it's the last two meanings that are relevant: the *Dhamma* that we salute in the *vandana* is the experience in words, as a teaching, of the ultimate reality of things. When we speak of the Buddha-Dharma, i.e. the Buddha's Dharma, it means the expression by the Buddha, in words, of his realization of the ultimate truth or ultimate reality of things, his experience of the universal spiritual law. Thus *Dhamma* has this double meaning. There's *Dhamma* as the Buddha's actual teaching, there's *Dhamma* as truth or reality, and then there's both meanings together, that is to say there's *Dhamma* as the Buddha's teaching in the sense of his expression or communication of the ultimate reality of things. It is this which is meant here.

*Svākkhāto bhagavatā Dhammo* is 'the Dharma spoken by the Blessed One'. According to some commentators the Dharma is said to be spoken by the Blessed One in the sense that it is specifically the Dharma of the Blessed One, that is to say, of the Buddha: it is not any other person's Dharma, any other teacher's teaching. It is the Dharma which has issued from the spiritual realization of the Buddha, a perfectly Enlightened One. It is not something that has been fabricated intellectually or put together in an eclectic manner from various sources, and therefore it belongs to the Buddha. It has not been revealed or discovered in its fullness by anybody else before him, at least not in the present world period. It is the Dharma that belongs specifically to the Buddha and to nobody else: *bhagavatā Dhammo*. *Svākkhāto* means well spoken, well expressed, or even well communicated. This is quite important: that the Dharma is not only the Dharma of the Buddha, but that it is well communicated, that the Buddha has put it across properly. (Sometimes *svākkhāto* is translated 'well expounded', but this is a bit too formal.) The Buddha has fully communicated whatever it was necessary for the disciple to know. He has communicated it in various ways, sometimes by means of rational analysis of human experience, sometimes by means of moral exhortation, sometimes with the help of parables, or myths, or stories. So it has been fully and completely and adequately communicated or expressed: the Dharma is *svākkhāto*. Usually this is translated as 'well taught', but really it is 'well expressed' or 'well spoken', the literal sense of the word. Recently I've translated it as 'well communicated', which I think better conveys the essence of the meaning. So, 'Well communicated is the Dharma by the Blessed One'.

Then, the Dharma well communicated by the Blessed One is *sandiṭṭhiko*. This is usually translated as 'with immediate fruit', but it really means '(immediately) visible', that is to say, you see the results at once – as you do, for instance, when you practise the *mettā bhāvanā*. You don't have to wait until you die to experience them: you experience them immediately, in the form of a change in your own emotional state. There is no question of your having to depend on faith, in the sense of blind belief. You practise in accordance with the teaching, and you experience results in accordance with your practice. Thus you see for yourself that the Dharma works. There's no need for blind belief. The Dharma is *sandiṭṭhiko*: its results are '(immediately) visible'. But suppose somebody says to you, 'Ah, but we don't get immediate results! Sometimes we meditate for weeks and months on end, but nothing happens.' What do you say then?

KULARATNA: That's just what I was thinking, actually.

SANGHARAKSHITA: So what would you say?

KULANANDA: You can't get any immediate results, in a way; but at the same time I'm not sure how you *cannot* get immediate results, because you're coming in touch with whatever it is that's blocking you.

SANGHARAKSHITA: Right.

KULAMITRA: Perhaps they're just not the results that you are expecting.

SANGHARAKSHITA: Yes, and perhaps sometimes you even block off a result because you expect some other kind of result. When people meditate, they usually think success, 'a good meditation', means that they should feel really immersed, really blissful, and get carried away and float off. Well, in a sense it does mean that, but even though you may not get that kind of result immediately you will get *some* result immediately, even if it's simply coming up against your own blockages. Something is happening; something is being stirred up. But I think that if you were a normal, healthy, relatively integrated person, the first time that you sat and meditated you would get some tangible results, and therefore you would know that it worked. Blockages or hindrances, problems or difficulties arise subsequently, when you start getting more deeply stirred up as the meditation begins to take effect. In the old days, at least, quite a few people used to find that their first meditation was their best. When people are not anticipating anything – when they don't know what is going to happen – their minds are completely open. But if they do well the first time they meditate, then the next time, instead of really meditating, really concentrating, they start looking for, or trying to engineer, that particular experience, and to that extent they're not really concentrating, not really meditating. It can be that you have the 'same' experience again and again and again, but if you really go after it because you're attached to it, or because you'd like to have it for egoistic reasons, the chances are that you won't have it, won't gain it, won't experience it.

KULARATNA: So what's the remedy for that?

SANGHARAKSHITA: The remedy is to approach each sitting, or each session, with a completely new mind. Don't think in terms of doing something 'again'. Just think in terms of doing it – doing it 'just this once'. Because even though you sit and meditate every day, every day is different. You yourself are a different person when you sit. The weather is different, the atmosphere is different, the day ahead is going to be different, you're in a different kind of mental state, a different kind of mood, and so on. How can you have exactly the same meditation? It may be in the same general line of development, but it won't be a duplicate of yesterday's meditation, however good.

KULANANDA: It would be quite an exciting approach to sit down and say, 'What's going to happen today?'

SANGHARAKSHITA: That's right. But in a way that should be one's approach to everything: to life, or to other people. Otherwise you think that you know, you anticipate, you act in accordance with your anticipations, and in that way you get onto a definite track – the same old tramlines, as it were. Of course very often it happens that people do behave in the same way (broadly speaking) again and again, so that in your relationship with them you get into the habit of constantly repeating the same old pattern. You can't help that when dealing with people who are essentially reactive, and when dealing with yourself to the extent that you are reactive, but you have to resist it all the time. You resist it partly by being open all the time to things being new, or a little different, or even quite different. You resist it by realizing that you're not in fact doing the same thing over again, however much the same it may appear to be. When you meet your father, for instance, he *may* be the same dreary old father, and he *may* be expressing the same sentiments that you've heard a hundred times before, but you should not *anticipate* that. It may be that this time he'll be a bit different. But he's less likely to be different if you anticipate his *not* being different. It's the same in every situation. If you say to somebody, 'I know what you're going to say; I've heard it a hundred times before', then even if the situation isn't like that, you'll make it so, you'll make it boring and repetitive. One should always try to see what is happening now. How is the person now? What is the situation now? What is my experience now? Forget about yesterday. Forget about tomorrow. What is it like now? As a general rule, the more reactive a person, the more predictable they are, but the more creative the person is, the less predictable they are. Once a creative person has done something, even though it was totally unexpected, in retrospect you can see that it is in character. Take the example of creative writing. If somebody brings out a new book of poems or a new novel, you could not have anticipated that that is what he would bring out – assuming him to be a really creative person – but once he's brought it out, you can see its connection with all his previous work.

KULANANDA: Because a creative person is a continuous entity.

SANGHARAKSHITA: Yes, but you yourself, to the extent that you are not a creative person, or at least not as creative a person as he is, could not have anticipated or predicted it from his previous work, however well you knew it. Even if you knew Ibsen up to his thirty-sixth year, who could have predicted that he'd write *Brand*?[192] Apparently Shakespeare wrote things in a very odd sequence indeed. According to something I was reading recently, after *The Tempest* he wrote, or collaborated in the writing of, *The Two Noble Kinsmen*, which doesn't seem to follow on at all. As a general rule, one can say that the more reactive a person is, the more predictable he is. The less reactive, and the more creative, the less predictable. But even the reactive person doesn't react in exactly the same way every time. One ought to be open to the possibility of that slight difference too. If you anticipate, you are yourself being reactive, because you are going on the past, and the essence of reactivity is that it's completely determined by the past, whereas the creative is not ruled by the past, but opens up an entirely new perspective, an entirely new vista. So that's the Dharma as *sandiṭṭhiko*.

Then *akāliko*. The Dharma is *akāliko*, literally 'timeless': free from time, out of time. So what does this mean? It means that in principle it is never out of date. Sometimes the Dharma is called *sanātana* (Sanskrit) or *sanantana* (Pāli), which means 'eternal'. In the *Dhammapada* there is the verse:

> *Na hi verena verāni*
> *Sammant'īdha kudācanaṃ*
> *Averena ca sammanti –*
> *Esa dhammo sanantano.*[193]

This means: 'Here (in this world) hatred never ceases by hatred. It ceases only by non-hatred. This is the *sanantana Dhamma*, the eternal law' – the eternal truth, the permanently valid (psychological and ethical) principle. Its validity is not affected by time. Whether it's a thousand years ago, or now, or in a thousand years' time, as long as there are human beings, or sentient beings, with human natures as we know them, it will always be true that hatred never ceases by hatred but only by its opposite, which is non-hatred or *mettā*. This is an eternal law, not a law that changes from time to time. In the same way, the law of conditionality is an eternal law. The Dharma is a law in this sense. It's a truth which remains true irrespective of particular circumstances. It's as valid now as it was in the Buddha's time. There are certain things that have got mixed up with the Dharma historically, which were valid and useful then, but are not now: that's a different matter. But the basic, fundamental principles remain eternally true and eternally valid.

Then *ehipassiko*. *Ehi* means 'come' and *passa* means 'see'. The Dharma is of the nature of an invitation to come and see. In other words, it is not something to be taken on trust in the sense of blind belief, but something that you have to come and see for yourself. *Ehipassiko* is the adjectival form of the word. The Dharma is the *ehipassiko* Dharma: the 'come-(and)-see' Dharma. This goes down very well with the new Buddhists in India. They're very much opposed to what they call blind belief, though they tend to equate the Buddhist attitude with pure rationalism, which is rather unfortunate. But certainly Buddhism has this emphasis of coming and seeing for yourself. Talking about it in Helsinki recently I said that it's like when you've got to know somebody and they're maybe a bit interested in the FWBO, though they've never actually been along to a centre. They ask you, 'Well, what's it like? What do you do? What's the atmosphere like? What sort of people are present?' Perhaps you say, 'Well, I can't really tell you. You'll just have to come and see for yourself.' Sometimes people want to know all about it while remaining as far away from it as they possibly can. They don't want to come and see! They just want to stay away and hear, then write a book about it, telling the world what it's really like. Therefore it's the *ehipassiko* Dharma, the Dharma which says, 'Come and see for yourself. Don't take anything on trust, even from the Buddha.'

KULARATNA: This is what you've translated as 'of the nature of a personal invitation'.

SANGHARAKSHITA: That's right. It's a bit of a paraphrase. It's much more direct and idiomatic in Pāli. *Ehi! Passa!* In the Buddha's day the first ordinations of 'monks' – as we call them now, unfortunately – were when the Buddha said, '*Ehi, bhikkhu!*' or 'Come, monk!' That made him a monk. The first 'ordinations' were conducted in that way by the Buddha. There was no apparatus of ordination in the more ceremonial sense, as there is now. Somebody came along to the Buddha, heard what he had to say, and was impressed by that. The Buddha saw that he was ready to lead the spiritual life, so he said, '*Ehi, bhikkhu!* Come, monk!' By addressing him as 'monk' he actually made him one! It's a form of *saccavajja* or '(the power of) truthfulness'. He saw that he *was* a monk so he called him one, and that made him a monk. There was no formal Going for Refuge and taking the precepts at the very beginning of Buddhism, even for what are now called *bhikkhus*. There was just what's called the *ehi bhikkhave upasampadā*, the ordination by the Buddha's utterance of the words 'Come, *bhikkhus*!' The usual translation into English, 'Come, O monks!', is a bit stilted. In the original it's much more forcibly put: *Ehi, bhikkhu!* 'Come, monk!' Just that, and you're ordained. You're in the sangha then.

The next epithet of the Dharma is *opanayiko*. *Upaneti* is 'to lead to', 'to conduct', or 'to carry along', so *opanayiko* means leading forward, or leading onward, or – as it's sometimes translated – progressive. The Dharma is of such a nature that it leads you on or leads you forward step by step and stage by stage. You could even say that it is evolutionary, developmental. It is a path of regular steps – eventually, at least.

In Helsinki we talked quite a bit about regular steps, and I made the point that in the FWBO everything, to begin with at least, is 'irregular', and you only gradually get onto the path of regular steps – the path of regular steps meaning that you perfect an earlier stage before starting to develop a later stage. So many people start in the middle, as it were, but by practice and experience they learn that they can't perfect the middle stage while an earlier stage remains imperfect, so they go back a bit and develop that earlier stage more and then come forward again: from the path of irregular steps they get onto the path of regular steps.[194] In Helsinki the question arose originally with respect to ordination. I mentioned that someone in England had said on the first anniversary of his ordination that only on that day did he feel that he was ready for ordination. One of the Finnish Order members said that she felt the same. The rest were a bit surprised, or a bit puzzled, by this. So I said that it was an example of the path of irregular steps leading to the path of regular steps. In a sense, though only in a sense, you are ordained when you are not ready for ordination. But after being ordained, and maybe only after being ordained, you become ready for ordination: you pass from the path of irregular steps to the path of regular steps. In that sense therefore, I said, everybody is ordained irregularly, and everything in the FWBO is irregular – that being the nature of the situation now. People know mentally far more than they are ready to practise. Maybe they're trying to practise some advanced form of Zen meditation before they've really learned to concentrate, or maybe they're trying to get into the Tantra or something like that. So, all right, you can't stop them from doing that. But if they are really into it, and if they're sincere, after a while they realize that they're only getting so far: something is getting in the way. So they have to come back and make their foundation firmer and then they can go forward more successfully. In this way from the path of irregular steps you go forward to the path of regular steps. Hardly anybody goes onto the path of regular steps straight away, because people know too much intellectually. They think they've left all the elementary stuff behind because they're 'on' those more advanced steps, but they're on them just mentally: they've read about them, they know about them.

It's only very simple people, who have not read about Buddhism and don't know anything about it just mentally, who can tread the path of regular steps. In the old days, you didn't get hold of books on Buddhism and read them and in that way become interested. You saw some *bhikkhus* living as *bhikkhus* – saw a group of the Buddha's followers living in accordance with his teachings – and you were attracted by that and wanted to join them. So you went along to the monastery and presented yourself. You weren't given a book to read: you were just given work to do. You had to sweep the monastery compound, or work in the kitchen. You might be given a simple meditation. When you'd done those things really well, you'd be given the next thing to do. The teacher would give you only what you were willing and able to practise at that particular time. When you'd done it, he'd give you something else to do, something else to practise. In that way you'd go through the path of regular steps. But that's no longer possible, because you can read all about the goal, and all about what it's like when you get there, before you've even taken the first step! These days everybody, at least in the West, with very few exceptions, is necessarily on the path of irregular steps. Everything is irregular. In a way we're doing everything wrong. That's the way it has to be. But if you really are making an effort, from the path of irregular steps you get onto the path of regular steps, and then you make more solid progress.

Some schools carry this to an extreme, almost deliberately. You start off by being Enlightened, or thinking that you're Enlightened, and you gradually have to catch up with yourself. Some people, for instance, might start trying to meditate without giving up parties or getting a bit drunk at the weekend. Fair enough. In the old days you would be told: stop going to parties, give up alcohol, observe the precepts strictly, then you can start meditating. You can't tell people that now so, all right, you let them start meditating before they've even thought of observing the precepts, and maybe they get a bit into it. But sooner or later they find they can't get any further. They'd like to get more deeply into it, but they can't. So they think, 'What's holding me back?' Maybe they ask you and you say, 'Well, it's the rest of your life which is pulling in the other direction. You have to start sorting things out a bit. Lead a quieter life. Don't go to so many parties. Don't get drunk. Just take a little drink every now and then.' If they follow this advice, they will find their meditations getting better, and in this way they will get a bit more onto the path of regular steps. That's how it works.

The Dharma is progressive. It's constantly leading forward. If it isn't leading you forward it isn't the Dharma – at least not for you. It's not working for you in the right way, maybe because you're taking it in the wrong way, or maybe because you haven't got into that aspect of the Dharma which is suited to your needs, suited to your temperament. It should be leading you forward all the time. Every year, or every few months, there should be some discernible progress. Maybe you can't see it yourself – after all, you see yourself every day, every minute – but it should be perceptible to those who see you from time to time.

KULARATNA: If you're not changing, then it's not the Dharma you're practising.

SANGHARAKSHITA: Changing is not enough. It's got to be a change for the better. Switching from beer to whisky, or from blondes to brunettes, would be a change, but it wouldn't exactly be a change for the better in the spiritual sense.

So one of the essential characteristics of the Dharma is that it is progressive. It's of such a nature that if you practise it, it cannot but lead you forward to higher and ever higher levels of being and consciousness.

KULARATNA: Well, that's what it is, really. It's what moves you forward.

SANGHARAKSHITA: It's like a stream into which you get and which carries you forward if you allow it to. A little word of warning in this connection. The new Buddhists in India, and Hindu intellectuals sympathetic to Buddhism, like to think of it as progressive in the modern, secular sense, in the sense of material improvement. Clearly one must distinguish that kind of progress from spiritual progress.

KULARATNA: That's just change.

SANGHARAKSHITA: That's just change. It may be a necessary change. We should make it clear that we're not against material improvement as such. But we certainly don't confuse that with the onward progressive movement of the Dharma itself in the spiritual life of the individual.

Than *paccataṃ veditabbo viññūhī ti. Paccataṃ* means 'personally'; *veditabbo*, 'to be known'; and *viññūhī*, 'by those who are wise', by those who understand. The Dharma is of such a nature that it should be known and understood personally by the wise. That is to say, it is to be understood from one's own actual experience, not from the testimony of another. As regards the Dharma, another's experience is no substitute for your own. The Dharma is essentially something which you must experience for yourself – if you are wise. It's something that only the wise can experience. If it isn't experienced personally, if it's just hearsay, it isn't really the Dharma so far as you are concerned.

KULARATNA: Something I've noticed is that earlier on, when I came along to the FWBO, and had *kalyāṇa mitras* and so on, I'd take quite a few things on trust which fairly recently I've been thinking out for myself and usually agreeing with what I was told or had picked up. It's almost as though sometimes you have to take things on trust until you find out for yourself.[195]

SANGHARAKSHITA: You do, but you take them on trust provisionally, and subject to your own future investigation. You don't take them on trust absolutely, as if that ends the matter. It's not that you've been told, you believe, and that's all there is to it. There are, of course, the three levels of wisdom (*prajñā*), which are quite important – the *suta-mayā-paññā*, the *cintā-mayā-paññā*, and the *bhāvanā-mayā-paññā*. (These are the Pāli terms.) The *suta-mayā-paññā* means the wisdom or understanding you get just by hearing. Here hearing means learning. You read a book, say, about Buddhism, and you understand the Buddha's teaching from that exposition. This is the wisdom that comes from learning, and it is quite valid. It is what you have to do first. You have to be open; you have to hear what the Dharma has to say. Then comes the second stage, the *cintā-mayā-paññā*. *Cintā* means thought or reflection. You turn what you have learned about the Dharma over in your mind and understand it for yourself, as it were intellectually. The *suta-mayā-paññā* is understanding what has actually been said, whereas the *cintā-mayā-paññā* is more like understanding the why and the wherefore of what has been said. This first is a sort of formal understanding, the second is more substantial. One consists in understanding the meaning of what has been said, in the sense that it is clear, intelligible, and internally consistent, whereas the other consists in understanding, through the exercise of one's own intellectual powers, the meaning of that meaning, i.e. the fundamental principles involved and their implications. Then the *bhāvanā-mayā-paññā* is when you practise and meditate and actually experience for yourself the truth of what you have heard about, and understood and reflected upon intellectually. All these stages have to be gone through by the disciple. First you hear, then you reflect, then you meditate and experience for yourself. So when you hear, you take on trust that what has been stated is correct. But then you try to understand it for yourself, try to experience it for yourself, and then you know, yes, it is so. What I heard, what I understood, was correct. You don't start with an initial scepticism; you start with provisional acceptance. But then you examine it for yourself, and reflect on it, and try to make it an experience for yourself, especially through meditation.

So these are the attributes of the Dharma: that it is well-communicated; that it is the special Dharma, as it were, of the Blessed One, i.e. the Buddha; that its fruits – of one kind and another – are immediately visible; that it is timeless, i.e. eternally and universally valid; that it invites one to come and see for oneself; that it is progressive, leading one on to higher and ever higher stages or levels of experience; and that it is to be personally experienced by the wise, each one for himself. The complete formula for the Dharma therefore runs: 'Well communicated is the Dharma of the Blessed One – the immediately visible, the timeless, the inviting, the progressive, (the Dharma) to be personally experienced by the wise.' It is in that Dharma that, as long as life lasts, you go for Refuge. The two stanzas that follow are the same as in the Buddha *vandana*, with Dharma taking the place of Buddha: 'the Dharma of the past, the Dharma of the future, and the Dharma of the present, I ever salute. For me there is no other Refuge. The Dharma is for me the supreme Refuge. By the power of this truth, may the victorious-auspicious be mine!'

### Salutation to the Sangha

The Sangha *vandana* or 'Salutation to the Sangha' begins with *supaṭipanno bhagavato sāvakasaṅgho*, and here it is the characteristics of the Sangha that are described. Sangha of course means, as we would say, 'spiritual community'. This is another of those words which has a general, popular meaning in modern Indian languages, and about which you have to be very careful when speaking on Buddhism in India. In India generally *sangh* means an association, a society, a group. The word has no specifically spiritual connotations.

Here in the Sangha *vandana* the Sangha is characterized as the *sāvakasaṅgho*. One can look at this in two different ways. If one looks at it in terms of the fully developed Buddhist doctrine then it's the community of *śrāvakas*, in the sense of followers of the Hīnayāna, as distinct from bodhisattvas. But that later doctrinal distinction does not really come in here, so one can virtually ignore it and try to see the word *sāvakasaṅgho* in terms of the more primitive teaching. Looked at in this way, it's the community of the Buddha's disciples in the widest sense. The word *sāvaka*, or *śrāvaka* in Sanskrit, is usually translated as 'disciple', but the literal meaning is 'hearer': the *sāvaka* is one who hears. This is quite significant, because in hearing you're completely passive. You just receive: you don't have to do anything. In the case of sight you have at least to look, to turn your head, direct your gaze. But when it's a question of hearing the sound waves impinge on the drum of the ear and that's that. You're completely passive, completely receptive. So the *sāvaka* is not just the disciple. He's the hearer: he's the one who receives, the one who takes in through the ear. That was quite literally the case in those early days, because that was the way of learning in a world in which there were no books. *Sāvaka* can therefore suggest the spiritual community of those who are completely receptive to the Buddha's teaching, who open themselves to it, offer no resistance to being penetrated by it. The use of this word *sāvaka*, or disciple as we would say, does suggest the importance of receptivity in the spiritual life. But you've got to be receptive to the positive, not just to everything indiscriminately, not to negative influences. In this case that sort of consideration doesn't apply, because the *sāvakasaṅgha* is the *bhagavato sāvakasaṅgho*, i.e. the spiritual community of those who are disciples of – who are open to, receptive to – the Buddha and his teaching.

They are described as being *supaṭipanno*; this is the first of the attributes of the Sangha, the hearers of the Buddha's teaching. *Paṭipanno* means 'going' or 'proceeding' and *su* means 'good', 'well', 'happily', so the Buddha's disciples are the community of those who proceed well and happily – who proceed positively, perhaps we could say. 'Positively proceeding is the community of the Buddha's disciples' or 'the community of the disciples of the Blessed One'. You notice the use of the word *bhagavato* here, the more devotional term for the Buddha, which is more in keeping with the word *sāvaka*. *Bhagavan* as it were corresponds to the word *sāvaka*: the *sāvakas* are receptive to him because he is the Blessed One, and because they regard him in that way they are his disciples. Thus they are well, or happily, or positively proceeding. This is one of the characteristics of the spiritual community. So what does this suggest? It suggests that the Sangha is something active, that it's a community of people engaged in practice, in actually treading a path, following a certain method of development. And they're doing that well, happily, properly, positively. That's the first characteristic of the Sangha.

Then *ujupaṭipanno bhagavato sāvakasaṅgho*. Similarly, that community of the disciples of the Buddha is *ujupaṭipanno* or 'straightly proceeding'. (*Uju* means 'straight' in the quite ordinary, colloquial sense.) The disciples proceed straight. What do you think that means?

KULARATNA: Directly.

SANGHARAKSHITA: Directly, by the shortest route. They don't go straying off into the bypaths. The *Tao Te Ching* says, 'The great way is broad and plain for all to see, but the people love the bypaths,'.[196] In other words, they get interested – over-interested, let's say – in astrology, or in things like flying saucers. Things like that have a certain connection with the spiritual life, perhaps, but they are rather peripheral from the spiritual point of view, so that if you give the greater part of your time and energy to one or another of them, you're definitely straying off onto a bypath. You've left the main road, as it were, the great way. You're no longer proceeding straight. To be 'straightly proceeding' is very important, but it can be misunderstood. Keeping on the main road doesn't mean toeing the line all the time and doing what you're supposed to do. It means keeping on the broad straight path of your own actual development. It doesn't mean being a good boy, being a good Buddhist – being a good Order member – in the narrow sense. It means occupying yourself consistently with what conduces to your overall development as a human being. It means at each turn of the road asking yourself, 'Which step is a way forward for me? What action should I take in order that I may grow in this situation?' The community of the Buddha's disciples are those who are following a straight path in this sense, in other words, who are primarily if not solely occupied with their individual spiritual development.

*Ñāyapaṭipanno bhagavato sāvakasaṅgho*. *Ñāya* means 'method' or 'system', and *ñāyapaṭipanno* is therefore usually translated as 'proceeding according to method', or 'methodically proceeding'. Sometimes it's translated as 'proceeding by rule', but it's not really that: *ñāya* is definitely 'method' rather than 'rule'. Do you know what is meant by method? What does proceeding according to method, or methodically proceeding, convey to you?

KULARATNA: It suggests regular steps.

SANGHARAKSHITA: Regular steps, or proceeding systematically. For instance, people who haven't done much in the way of meditation think that meditation just means sitting down and musing. But there is a method, a systematic technique, almost, of getting concentrated, e.g. counting the breaths or doing the *mettā bhāvanā* practice in a certain sequence of stages. All that pertains to method. There's a definite way of going about the spiritual life: it's a practical thing. There are certain definite things to be done in a certain order. It doesn't just happen. It's this aspect which is covered by the word *ñāya*. You go about leading the spiritual life methodically, systematically, in a practical way, not just in a vague, general, dreamy way, hoping for the best. For instance, if you are greedy as regards food you know that you've got to tackle that weakness systematically. You've got to adopt a certain definite method. Maybe you've got to take a vow that you won't eat between meals, or maybe you've got to give up certain things that you're particularly fond of. This is tackling that particular difficulty systematically, in a methodical fashion – not just hoping that the greed will go away some time. So 'methodically proceeding is the community of the Buddha's disciples'. They're not satisfied with a general feeling of going along. They're taking concrete, positive steps in a methodical, practical way to ensure that they actually do develop – just as they do in the case of meditation. When they meditate, they don't just meditate: they do the mindfulness of breathing, or a visualization practice, or the recollection of the six elements. There's no such thing as just meditating – not unless you're very advanced and can just sit down and go straight into a higher state of consciousness. So one goes about the spiritual life methodically.

And then, *sāmīcipaṭipanno bhagavato sāvakasaṅgho*. The community of the Buddha's disciples is proceeding together, proceeding harmoniously: *sāmīci*. Usually *sāmīci* is rendered 'properly', but as it comes from a word meaning 'connected, in one', it is best rendered 'harmoniously'. It is very important that the Sangha should proceed harmoniously. Why do you think this is?

KULARATNA: Well, if the people who are putting all these things into practice aren't getting on with each other, you can say there's something seriously wrong.

SANGHARAKSHITA: And what do you think that could be? They're all doing the same meditations, sharing the same philosophy, living in more or less the same way, but they're not proceeding harmoniously. Why is it? What's getting in the way? What *could* get in the way?

KULANANDA: Negative emotions.

SANGHARAKSHITA: But let's assume, in this instance, that they're all doing the *mettā bhāvanā*, and they don't have negative emotions – at least not while they're actually meditating. But still they don't really get on. What is it, usually, that comes in the way, apparently?

KULARATNA: Competition.

SANGHARAKSHITA: Yes, competition comes in the way.

KULANANDA: Personalities.

SANGHARAKSHITA: Personalities too. Personalities seem to be the biggest factor. People are very different as personalities: their temperaments are very different. You don't get on, and don't really proceed harmoniously, when the common element which is provided by your common practice and common way of life is not powerful enough to resolve, or to transcend, the personal differences of temperament.

KULANANDA: So if the members of a community, for example, aren't getting on with each other, what they should do is put more and more effort into their own practice.

SANGHARAKSHITA: Actually, yes. They should put more effort into both their own individual practice and their practice together. That must be the common basis. It's one of the characteristics of the community of the Buddha's disciples that they get on together, that they proceed harmoniously. It's not *playing*, except to the extent that play in a positive sense is also included in the path, but they're travelling on the path harmoniously and together.

It's very easy to operate just on the level of personality and to be very much influenced by personal likes and dislikes, even in very trivial ways. You might not like people with ginger hair, or the way someone eats might annoy you, or the way they talk. I've known such things happen. There is no objective reason for such reactions, but they nevertheless do occur. Sometimes it may happen that you just don't like the way people are. You can't fault them as regards actual behaviour, perhaps, but you just don't like that type of person. Maybe they remind you, even if very distantly, of your father, or of some hated brother, or of someone you knew at school who was very nasty and mean to you. Sometimes these sorts of likes and dislikes can influence you really powerfully, and almost determine your life, or at least certain very important aspects of it.

In a spiritual community, especially as it gets bigger, you're going to have all sorts of people, of so many different kinds of temperament. It should be possible for them to proceed harmoniously together. If they experience any difficulty, they just have to strengthen that common element which is provided by their common practice or practices.

KULARATNA: I think sometimes you get difficult situations in a community because the common commitment is enough to stop people from just giving up and going off, but still not quite enough for them to get over the differences between them.

SANGHARAKSHITA: Then there's the whole question of communication within the spiritual community. There may not be actual temperamental difficulties, but there may not be very free and open communication. Some members of the spiritual community may be a little blocked, and since that prevents the free flow of communication, they may be jogging along together pretty well but there won't be that positive and dynamic togetherness. That seems to be aroused when people work on something very concrete together. I've certainly seen this happening at Aryatara, which formerly was a pleasant but rather sluggish sort of place. It's really dynamic now, especially since Nagabodhi went there and more especially since the St Michaels Road project got going. This project seems to have galvanized and unified all their energies.[197]

So these are the characteristics of the spiritual community – among others. They are the ones that were more relevant, perhaps, in the Buddha's day. Not that they're not relevant now, but there are other characteristics of the spiritual community that I'm sure we could think of in addition to these. But to begin with, at least, it is positively proceeding, straightforwardly or directly proceeding, methodically or systematically proceeding, and unitedly and harmoniously proceeding. That's quite a lot to get on with for the time being.

*Yadidaṃ cattāri purisayugāni*
*aṭṭha purisapuggalā*
*esa bhagavato sāvakasaṅgho*

These words describe not just the general characteristics of the spiritual community, but the kind of people of whom the spiritual community in the highest sense – that is to say the Āryasaṅgha – consists. It consists of *cattāri purisayugāni*, these four pairs of *purisas*, that is to say, of the *aṭṭha purisapuggalā*, or the eight persons who are individuals, or the eight individuals who are persons: the translation can be varied. You've got two terms here. You've got *purisa*, which literally means 'male', and *puggala*, which means something more like person. So although the terms don't really correspond in the literal sense, let's translate *purisa* by 'person' and *puggalla* by 'individual'. Edward Conze, it is true, translates *puggalla* by 'person', but let's do it the other way round. We shall then get: 'These fours pairs of persons, that is to say, those eight persons who are individuals – it is they who are the spiritual community of the Buddha's disciples.' So who are those 'persons who are individuals' who make up the Āryasaṅgha, the community of the Buddha's disciples in the highest sense?

KULARATNA: You've got the Stream Entrant and the one who has realized the fruit of Stream Entry, the once-returner and the one who has realized the fruit of once-returning, the non-returner and the one who has realized the fruit of non-returning, and the *arhant* and the one who has realized the fruit of arhantship.

SANGHARAKSHITA: As I mentioned before, this was a later classification. The earliest teaching seems to have spoken simply in terms of one who was 'going upstream' (*uddhaṃsota*). But here in the Sangha *vandana* you've got a fourfold classification of the members of the Āryasaṅgha worked out on the basis of the number of fetters broken and the number of births, or rebirths, remaining. Among these four (or eight) persons the crucial one is the Steam Entrant, and therefore it's on Stream Entry that I personally put all the stress – because that is more accessible, more immediate, and more practical. So first of all there's the Stream Entrant. Technically speaking, the Stream Entrant is one who has broken the first three out of the ten fetters. You know what they are, don't you?

KULANANDA: Personality view, dependence on rites and ceremonies as ends in themselves....

SANGHARAKSHITA: And the third one is *vicikicchā*, which is doubt and indecision. One needs to rephrase these terms, even to reinterpret them. I do it in this way. *Sakkāya-diṭṭhi* is 'self-view'. It is the view that I am what I am, a fixed unchanging entity. It is the view that I cannot change. If you have this sort of view, well, how *can* you change? In order to change you have to accept the possibility of change. In other words, you have to accept the fact that your self, as you know your self at present, is not the ultimate, irreducible, unchangeable you. If you regard what you are now as a fixed datum, something that cannot be changed, no progress is possible. This attitude can be rationalized in various philosophical forms, as it was in the Buddha's day. But with or without such rationalization, most people do basically feel themselves to be what and who they are, and they can't imagine themselves, really, as being very different. It is this, basically, which is *sakkāya-diṭṭhi*, 'personality view' or 'self view'. It's the view that I am what I am and nothing's going to change me. In the past I've given various examples of this. A man says, 'Well, look, I've got a bad temper. Too bad: that's the way I am. I was born that way. There's nothing I can do about it: you'll just have to get on with it. If you want to be friends with me you'll have to accept the fact that I've got a bad temper. That's the way God made me: I can't change.' This is *sakkāya-diṭṭhi*. If you have this view, no progress is possible, no individual development is possible. This is the first fetter. If you really accept the possibility of radical change in you as a person, or as an individual, then you break the first fetter, and having broken it, you are open to further change, further development. This openness is absolutely essential. If you're not willing to change, if you're not willing to grow, what spiritual life can there be? We could therefore paraphrase *sakkāya-diṭṭhi* as 'unwillingness to grow', and the breaking of this particular fetter as 'willingness to grow'.

KULANANDA: *Sakkāya-diṭṭhi* is not just the lack of a belief of an intellectual sort.

SANGHARAKSHITA: Oh no! It's not just that you don't accept a particular philosophy. Not at all. As a Buddhist you won't, of course, accept certain philosophies which are rationalizations, basically, of this kind of attitude of resistance to growth, but you may intellectually accept the alternative philosophy – even intellectually accept Buddhist philosophy, the teaching of no self – but still in practice remain completely bound by this first fetter and make no effort whatever to change or grow or develop. You find Buddhists in the East saying, 'I'm a Buddhist already. There's nothing I have to do about it. I was born one. That's the way I am. I don't need to practise Buddhism: I was *born* a Buddhist.'

KULARATNA: It's failing to take responsibility for yourself, isn't it?

SANGHARAKSHITA: Yes. In a passage which I've quoted in a lecture Artaud says, in effect, that one should not accept oneself as the person one was born as.[198] That's just given to you on a plate; you shouldn't accept that as *you*. That's just the raw material, which you proceed to develop and fashion, not exactly in your own way, but in the best way for you. You don't accept yourself ready-made from your parents, or from your general social and cultural conditioning.

KULANANDA: What a dreadful life that would be!

SANGHARAKSHITA: That's most people's life. They accept themselves ready-made: they don't remake themselves. Yeats says:

> Myself must I remake
> Like that William Blake
> Who beat upon the wall
> Till Truth obeyed his call.[199]

Thus the first fetter represents resistance to change, reluctance to grow. There's no real spiritual life – no real entering the Stream – until you can break that. You don't start developing until you accept the possibility, even the necessity, of change in you; which means *not* accepting your present personality, your present conditioning, your present way of doing things, your present way of living, as ultimate. On the contrary, it's complete openness to change.

The second fetter is *sīlabbata-parāmāsa*: dependence on moral rules and religious observances as ends in themselves. It doesn't mean not using them at all, not making use of them. It means being stuck in them and thinking that if you go through the right motions that's enough. It's external, mechanical observance. The *sīla* and the *vata*, the moral rules and the religious observances, are all meant to help one to grow and develop, but it's possible to *not* use them in that way. Instead of making use of them you just go through the motions, especially if going through those sorts of motions is socially respectable or acceptable. You go through the motions, but inwardly you remain unchanged. This is what *sīlabbata-parāmāsa* really is. Sometimes I've translated it as 'the fetter of conventional religiosity'. It hides from you, and hides from others, the fact that you are not changing and have no intention of changing – but you go through the motions of changing. You go to church, which is supposed to indicate that you are spiritually reborn, according to Christianity. It's the same in some Buddhist countries; it's respectable to go to the vihara and to feed the *bhikkhus*. Once I was talking with Prince Latthakin of Burma, with whom I stayed for six months in Kalimpong,[200] about the last days of the Burmese monarchy. When he was quite young Prince Latthakin had been married to the second daughter of King Thibaw, who was still living with him and whom I also knew, and he used to tell me quite a bit about the old days. As you can read in the history books, King Thibaw had the unpleasant habit of disposing of his relations, and the Burmese custom was that people were executed by being trampled to death by elephants. In the case of members of the royal family, they were put into red velvet bags – the red velvet was imported from Holland – and the elephants trampled on these bags. He disposed of nearly a hundred of his relations in this way, mostly half-brothers and half-sisters, children of the previous king. Apparently he was a very bloody-minded man. There was an absolute reign of terror in the palace, and in the end the British deposed him. Prince Latthakin told me all about this, but then he said, 'But, you know, King Thibaw was a very good Buddhist. He always fed the monks.' Prince Latthakin was no fool, but he said this quite seriously. All the time the massacres were going on King Thibaw would invite a hundred monks to the palace each day and give them alms. He was a very good Buddhist! Even that act of generosity was a little bit of goodness, you could say, a tiny scrap of *puṇya*, not counterbalancing, of course, but nevertheless distinct from, that enormous mass of *pāpa*. But basically it was an example of *sīlabbata-parāmāsa*. The king was going through the motions. He fed monks, endowed temples, gilded images – but look at the way he was really living! But he thought he was a good Buddhist, and other people thought so too.

KULARATNA: You get the same thing with art, don't you, that it becomes respectable and socially acceptable, whereas its call can be quite revolutionary.

SANGHARAKSHITA: So *sīlabbata-parāmāsa* is essentially going through the motions of religion, spiritual life, individual development, but without actually meaning it. I sometimes say that this particular fetter represents conventional religiosity.

Thirdly, there's *vicikicchā*, which is doubt and indecision. It's a sort of wavering, an inability to make up one's mind, even an unwillingness to make up one's mind, which means, really, a refusal to commit oneself. This ties up with the other two fetters, because if you really want to change – if you are not attached to your old self, and don't consider it ultimate and final – you're willing to commit yourself to the future, willing to commit yourself to developing as an individual. But if you don't want to do that you'll make all sorts of excuses, you'll go through the motions of trying to make up your mind, you'll shilly-shally, you'll wobble, you'll rationalize – and that's all included under *vicikicchā*. *Vicikicchā* means unwillingness to make up your mind. If you make up your mind, then you have to commit yourself. If you commit yourself, you have to change. If you want to change, you have to commit yourself. They're all interconnected. *Vicikicchā* is the vague, woolly attitude that refuses to think things through to a conclusion, because that might mean you have to make some changes. You're in a sense deliberately indecisive; you go intellectually woolly and refuse to think because thinking might mean that you clarify things in such a way that certain decisions or lines of action are indicated, and you want to avoid that.

KULANANDA: I sometimes actually feel that process happening.

SANGHARAKSHITA: You confuse the whole issue, so that you can avoid having to make up your mind and commit yourself, avoid having to adopt a certain line.

KULARATNA: Some people have got a real talent for it, haven't they?

SANGHARAKSHITA: Oh yes!

KULANANDA: Sometimes when that happens you've got a glimmering of what's going to be the result of coming to that conclusion, so you deliberately don't come to a conclusion, and then you're crippled by not doing whatever it is.

SANGHARAKSHITA: Sometimes I've said that these three fetters could be paraphrased as scientific psychology, conventional religion, and academic philosophy. In the case of academic philosophy you consider all conceivable philosophical options, but you never commit yourself to any of them. You weigh Plato against Aristotle, and Descartes against Spinoza, but you never even *think* of committing yourself to the practical implications of these philosophies. And what about the first fetter as the fetter of scientific psychology? Well, scientific psychology is purely descriptive. It just lists the mental contents and describes them as they are. There's no suggestion of any possibility of change. As for the second fetter as conventional religion, that's obvious, isn't it?

KULANANDA: Modern psychology or psychiatry is very often based on getting a person to be able to live with himself, accept himself as he is.

SANGHARAKSHITA: Yes, whereas in a sense that's the last thing he should do. There is a sense in which you should accept yourself as you are, to start off with, but that also includes, surely, accepting your capacity for change and development – not accepting the kind of person you are now as something fixed and final and unalterable. You don't have to learn to live with your bad temper; you can get rid of your bad temper, or develop a good temper. If you've got some physical defect that cannot be remedied, you have to learn to live with that, because it cannot be changed. If you are born short, you just have to accept the fact. If you weren't born beautiful, too bad. You just have to make up for it by developing a pleasant character. But if it's a bad habit or mental attitude, you ought not to be encouraged to live with that because it can be changed.

These are the first three fetters. If you are willing to change, willing to grow, willing to develop; if you don't ever just go through the motions of developing, don't adopt any particular method of developing and treat it as an end in itself, without reference to its being a method of development; and if at the same time you're ready actually to commit yourself – then you enter the Stream. Then, in other words, a permanent, irreversible change starts taking place. And then, further on, or further up the Stream, you break, or first weaken, other fetters. It has been pointed out that the first three fetters are, as it were, intellectual. They're something to be worked out intellectually, something to be understood. But fetters four and five go deeper: they're more emotional. It's not that the first three fetters are simply matters of theoretical understanding. That they certainly are not. But they're more accessible intellectually. But with fetters four and five you come up against emotional, even unconscious, factors. Let's look at the full list in the *Survey*.

> The *sakṛdāgāmin*, or once-returner, succeeds in weakening, though not in actually breaking, the fourth and fifth [not second and third] fetters of sensual desire (*kāma-rāga*) and ill will (*vyāpāda*).[201]

I've translated *kāma-rāga* here as 'sexual desire',[202] though that's probably a bit narrow, and *vyāpāda* as 'ill will'. They're both very, very strong. Not just strong emotionally – it's even more basic than that. They're more like tendencies of the whole being.

In order really to understand what they're like, one has to go back to the whole distinction – or even division or cleavage – between subject and object. All our experience is influenced by, modified by, even vitiated by the fact that it takes place within the framework of the subject–object distinction. There's a basic, fundamental schism between subject and object and therefore a sort of tension between them. You as subject are either strongly drawn towards the object or strongly repelled by it or from it. The fact that there is this schism between subject and object – the fact that everything is looked at in this way, or distorted in this way – is ignorance, *avidyā*. Then on the basis of that ignorance there takes place the development of craving, of *tanhā* or *kāma-rāga*, which basically is the impulsion of the subject towards the object, or its repulsion by it. Not only that. Ill will, or *vyāpāda*, arises when your movement towards the object, your impulsion towards the object, your powerful attraction towards the object, your longing to unite with the object, which actually is not possible within the subject–object framework, is frustrated or impeded by some third factor. Then your craving turns into ill will directed towards the impeding factor.

*Kāma-rāga* is desire or craving in general, but it is said to be sexual craving, or sexual desire, in particular. You could say this is because the sexual object represents the object in a special sort of way, because when there is a sexual object present your impulsion or propulsion towards it is strongly marked. Actually, this is what happens all the time with objects in general, not only with specifically sexual ones, but in the case of the specifically sexual object the tendency is intensified, so that it becomes more obvious, more evident. It's the same in principle with regard to something to eat, or something to look at. The object of sexual desire is a sort of 'object par excellence' and sexual craving, therefore, is in a way craving par excellence, or craving in a very representative capacity. Do you get the idea? And suppose you are confronted by a very desirable and attractive sexual object, and are on your way to unite with that, and some third party intervenes, well, what is your reaction? It's *vyāpāda* pure and simple. It might be your best friend cutting you out, but at least momentarily you'll feel quite murderous, perhaps, depending on the strength or intensity of your desire. And all of this takes place within an overall framework of *avidyā*.

As long as you consider yourself as a separate individual or ego there is ignorance, and there must therefore be this kind of craving – this impulsion or propulsion towards the object – with the continual possibility of frustration and, therefore, of ill will, aversion, and resentment. It's not so difficult to understand that one can and must change, and really accept that. It's not so difficult to realize that it's no use just going through the motions of change. It's not so difficult to give up shilly-shallying and commit oneself. But to start dismantling that overall framework of ignorance, that overall framework of subject–object, and therefore to weaken that kind of craving and that kind of aversion, is much more difficult. But this is what one does in the case of the fourth and fifth fetters. You start working on your craving, which is not just ordinary desire but the basic impulsion of the subject towards the object, the subject as it were trying to complete itself, not by transcending the subject–object distinction but by hugging the object towards itself, which can only be done for a certain length of time or to a certain extent. It's here that the sexual paradigm is again very useful. Why are you attracted to the sex-object? In the case of the woman – often the sex object for a man – there's something out there that you want because you feel that it will make you complete. If you start developing that woman within yourself, start developing your own femininity so that you don't project it onto the sex-object and try to unite with it there, then you'll be free, or relatively free, from that strong craving for that particular object.

In the same way, when you try to overcome, or resolve, the subject–object distinction, when you try to get above that, there's no longer any question of your moving towards the object and trying to incorporate the object in yourself, which you can't actually do anyway. All you can do is get beside it and sort of squeeze it to yourself, and after a while it's taken away, or goes away. You've lost it, so you have to do the same thing all over again. You find that very much with sex, taking that as a paradigm again. The satisfaction only lasts for a while, then you have to start all over again, because you haven't done what you wanted to do, basically, which was to unite. That's not possible. The only way you can really unite is by developing that projected element or that projected aspect within yourself. It's the same within the general framework of the subject–object relationship. You have eventually to rise above the distinction of subject and object, which is done initially by developing a more refined individuality – a less coarse ego, as it were – with a finer movement towards a finer object, not a gross, clumsy, heavy, clutching movement towards a gross, clumsy, heavy object. Do you see what I mean? You have instead a soft, delicate, diaphanous, tender subject, very gently moving out to a relatively refined, subtle, graceful object. In that way the grossness and heaviness of the subject–object distinction is refined. It's not literally getting rid of it or rising above it – one mustn't take this expression literally. It's refining it, making it more diaphanous, more transparent, more subtle, more delicate.

KULAMITRA: Is that what you're doing in visualization practice?

SANGHARAKSHITA: Yes, but it's a very basic thing, to refine that raw energy which is moving towards its object *all the time*. Therefore it's said that the once-returner only weakens the fourth and fifth fetters. If you just succeed in weakening the fourth and fifth fetters, then you become a once-returner. And then, of course, if you break them completely, you become a non-returner. You are not reborn in the lower worlds at all, but gain Enlightenment directly from one or another of the Pure Abodes.

KULANANDA: You never experience those states of consciousness again.

SANGHARAKSHITA: You never experience those states of consciousness or those corresponding objective situations again: that is to say, the *kāmaloka* or world of sensuous desire, the *rūpaloka* or world of form, or even the *arūpaloka* or formless world. According to doctrinal tradition you're reborn on a higher, rather special level, at the summit of the world of form, which is neither mundane nor perfectly transcendental, the Pure Abodes, and gain Enlightenment from there.

KULAMITRA: What's the difference between these stages of entering the path and experiencing the fruit of the path, in the case of the Stream Entrant, once-returner, and so on?

SANGHARAKSHITA: 'Path' is the volitional aspect, when one actually does the things that pertain to Stream Entry, and 'fruit' is when, by virtue of your having engaged in those particular skilful volitions, you actually are a Stream Entrant and enjoy the mental states pertaining to Stream Entry. It corresponds to the distinction between *karma* and *vipāka* in the twelve ordinary *nidānas*. As you know, there's a cause process of the present life, an effect process of the present life, and so on.[203] *Magga* or 'path' corresponds to cause process, and *phala* or fruit corresponds to effect process.

KULAMITRA: So the first one is while certain things are happening.

SANGHARAKSHITA: You're in the process of becoming: you're exerting yourself in the appropriate way. In the case of the fruit of the result, you experience the appropriate consequence of that exertion and are as it were in enjoyment of it.

KULANANDA: It occurs to me how important communication is with regard to the fourth and fifth fetters, because within the context of communication you're working within a tension, you're not necessarily caught up in either pole, so things are more diaphanous.

SANGHARAKSHITA: One does find that. In real communication it's as though a solid subject and a solid object are no longer there. It's more like a relative polarization. The polarization is not absolute, as it usually is in ordinary contact with people.

KULANANDA: So to the extent that we really communicate, to that extent we are once-returners: but that doesn't seem ... I mean one can sometimes communicate and sometimes not communicate. So I think to draw these hard and fast distinctions can be misleading.

SANGHARAKSHITA: This links up with the Vajrayāna, in which there are what some writers like to call sexo-yogic practices. These arouse everybody's interest and curiosity at once, but the Vajrayāna is not really like that. It simply takes the sexual situation as a sort of paradigm, to begin with at least, because in that situation there is this very definite polarization in the grossest and almost crudest sense. There's a polarization between male and female, and the consequent powerful attraction and repulsion between them, and, therefore, the possibility for both craving and aversion. The Vajrayāna tries to refine this from a sexual congress to an actual communication. If I were to put it diagrammatically – this has only just occurred to me – it could be done like that. Has anyone got a pencil and paper? One could say that what usually happens between people is something more like this.

*fig. 1*

There's a subject, and there's an object – though each of course is both subject for itself and object for the other – and there's just this infinitesimal point of contact in the middle: otherwise there's a complete polarization. Then you could say it becomes a bit more like a peanut.

*fig. 2*

You could even substitute a dotted line for the hard line bounding the subject and the object. This represents the subject–object polarity existing more within a framework of unity, almost. And then you have something more like this.

*fig. 3*

And then you could say you have something more like that,

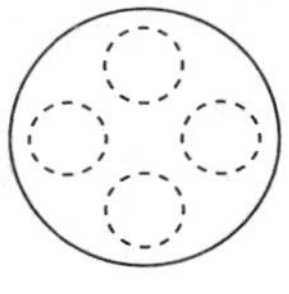

*fig. 4*

or even something more like that.

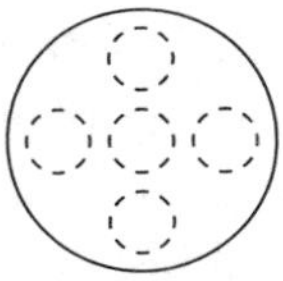

*fig. 5*

One of the aims of the Vajrayāna is depolarization, but you have to start with a polarization before you can depolarize. That's why the Tantra sometimes starts with sex – taking that as a paradigm for that extreme situation of polarization between subject and object. You will notice that some of the *sādhanas* are concerned with the resolution of the tension between subject and object, especially the Mañjughoṣa *stuti* and the Mahākaruṇika *sādhanas*.[204] If you do these practices, you do actually get an experience of a state in which subject and object are not as fully polarized as usual, and you get that experience also in communication with people – when it becomes real communication. There is polarization without that tension.

KULAMITRA: Which is why it's so much more difficult to experience real communication between a man and a woman.

SANGHARAKSHITA: Because the polarization is so powerful. On the other hand there has to be a little bit of polarization in communication, otherwise it's too weak, too tepid. When you like someone in a vague, acquaintance-like sort of way, you never communicate, of course. There has to be a modicum of tension: not so much that communication is sharply polarized and you set up the figure-of-eight situation, but on the other hand not so little that the situation is slack and tepid and there's nothing to work with.

KULAMITRA: That tepidness is just a sort of non-individuality, isn't it?

SANGHARAKSHITA: Well, it's non-relating. You've got to relate before you can communicate.

So you can see that the transition from breaking the first three fetters to breaking, or even weakening, the fourth and fifth is quite an important one, and something that most people involved with the spiritual life don't even begin to touch upon. It's not very often that even those who succeed in breaking the first three fetters can get on to breaking the fourth and fifth, or even weakening them, which would make them a once-returner. Finally, the *arhant* breaks all the remaining five fetters. We won't go into those in detail because they're a bit irrelevant at the moment. We'll just look at them. They're *rūparāga*, or desire for rebirth in the higher world of form, or on the archetypal plane; *arūparāga*, or desire for existence in the formless world, the world of formless consciousness, one could say; *māna* or conceit, which is the idea of oneself as equal, superior, or inferior to anybody else (here there's no comparison at all, because there's virtually no polarization); *uddhacca* or restlessness, in the sense of just the tiniest possible movement of the most rarefied subject towards the most rarefied object; and, of course, *avijjā* or ignorance, by breaking which one breaks the fetter of the subject–object structure completely.

KULANANDA: In a way, we don't have to worry about those things so much.

SANGHARAKSHITA: No. Once you enter the Stream, there's a natural momentum that carries you forward.

KULARATNA: So it's the first three we've really got to work on.

SANGHARAKSHITA: It's the first three – and also the beginnings of the fourth and fifth. The Vajrayāna seems to tackle those quite effectively.

KULAMITRA: The first three, you could say, are a recognition of the non-fixed nature of the ego, and later on you realize that even that isn't quite right – in fact you progressively realize that even a non-fixed idea of an ego is too fixed.

SANGHARAKSHITA: Yes, that's right. So the spiritual community, the community of the Buddha's disciples, consists of these four pairs of persons, these eight persons who are individuals: the Stream Entrant, the once-returner, the non-returner, and the *arhant*, all subdivided to 'path' and 'fruit'. The Stream Entrant, it is said, will be reborn on earth not more than seven times, the once-returner only once, and the non-returner not at all (he'll be reborn in the Pure Abodes and will gain Nirvāṇa directly from there). And the *arhant* is liberated here and now, in this life itself, and has no further rebirths remaining. Perhaps one shouldn't take this question of number of rebirths too literally, but you can see the general sense of it: that the objective repercussions of one's conditioned mental states become, as it were, less and less gross, more and more subtle.

KULANANDA: There's been a feeling in the Movement that even something like Stream Entry is beyond us.

SANGHARAKSHITA: One shouldn't really feel that. As I pointed out on the Order convention, so long as you aren't a Stream Entrant you can fall right back and right away. It's only after Stream Entry that you become irreversible from Enlightenment: that is, you cannot fall back. You may not make much progress, but you cannot fall back onto the wheel, as it were. If you haven't entered the Stream, you could give up the path completely, give up all your efforts to evolve, forget all about Buddhism, forget all about the Order. You could just drop out and be what you were before, if not worse. So Stream Entry is very, very important, and this is what it consists in: the breaking of those three fetters, i.e. in the actual realization (1) that one isn't, ultimately, what one is now, and that one *can* change, and is willing to change; (2) that there's no use just going through the motions of development: you have really to develop; and (3) that you have to commit yourself to that process of change and development without wavering and without rationalizing, and give your whole being and all your energy to that. In the Buddha's day people became Stream Entrants, it seems, at the same moment, virtually, that they went for Refuge. In a way, in the highest sense, Going for Refuge and Stream Entry are the same thing: but in the case of most people the Going for Refuge is a separate thing from the Stream Entry: it precedes it and, in a way, is a sort of anticipation of it.

KULANANDA: It can be like a purely intellectual formula.

SANGHARAKSHITA: You could say that Going for Refuge is like going through the motions of Stream Entry; but going through them in a positive, healthy way that prepares you for the real thing.

KULAMITRA: It is in a way seeing these three things, but at a lesser level – at a more mental level only, with less power.

SANGHARAKSHITA: Yes, with less power.

KULANANDA: Perhaps it's weakening those things ...

KULARATNA: Do you think it possible to become dependent on meditation in a 'dependence on rites and ceremonies' sort of way?

SANGHARAKSHITA: There are two things here. One is going through the motions of meditation, that is to say, it just becomes a habit that you go into the shrine-room, chant a bit, sit there quietly, but actually you're not meditating, in the sense that you're not generating positive, higher states of consciousness: you're just sitting there in a quiet, relaxed, dreamy sort of way. That would be one way of falling victim to meditation as *sīlabbata-parāmāsa*. The other way would be actually experiencing higher states of consciousness but becoming attached to them and not wanting anything to do with the world or other people, just wanting to remain in those higher states of consciousness, so that they become an end in themselves.

KULARATNA: That's hedonism.

SANGHARAKSHITA: Yes, it's the higher hedonism.

KULANANDA: But it's okay at the moment ...

SANGHARAKSHITA: Right. For those immersed in the lower hedonism, the higher hedonism represents a considerable advance. It's progress, in a way. Also, you mustn't exclude that hedonic element – even that lower hedonistic element – in the sense of regarding pleasure, or pleasurable sensation, as somehow evil or undesirable. We've got so much in the way of our guilt-ridden Christian heritage to contend with that we have to be a bit cautious here. Pleasure is all right. Pleasurable sensation is all right, lower or higher. The danger arises when it becomes the basis for strong craving or strong attachment. Higher meditative experiences are intensely pleasurable, and it's right that they should be so, but the pleasurableness mustn't prevent one from going on to even higher experiences. What usually happens is that we see the object and move towards it; but the essence of the aesthetic attitude is that you just contemplate it, and enjoy it, and appreciate it for its own sake without moving towards it. As Schopenhauer pointed out, in aesthetic appreciation and enjoyment there's a suspension of craving, or a suspension of desire, and that provides the analogy between the aesthetic and the spiritual.[205] In the case of the spiritual approach, it's not that you close your eyes to the beauty of the object, but you don't want to possess it, you're content just to enjoy it contemplatively.

KULANANDA: In a way you can't have an ethical relationship with someone unless you're in communication with them.

SANGHARAKSHITA: Yes, you can't have an ethical relationship with someone unless your attitude towards them is a responsible one. Otherwise it's merely exploitative.

KULANANDA: And your attitude must be other-regarding: you are aware of them.

SANGHARAKSHITA: Before leaving the four pairs of persons, the eight persons who are individuals, maybe we should point out that one can use the word individual in three distinct senses. First of all there is what I call the statistical individual, one who is an individual in the sense that he's got a separate body, but is really mentally part of the group, the crowd, the herd. Next there is somebody who is an individual psychologically. He does think for himself, he has a measure of self-awareness, and he isn't one of the group; but he isn't a Stream Entrant. An individual in the highest sense is one who is a Stream Entrant or more. That is the true individual, and that is what the *puggala* represents. The individualist is simply a stronger member of the herd – a statistical individual who happens to have more strength or more cunning than other members of the same group.

Then follow more epithets of the community of the Buddha's disciples. *Āhuneyyo* means worthy of offerings, worthy of worship, or worthy of respect. If you yourself are not an individual, if you yourself are not a member of the spiritual community, your natural attitude towards those who are should be one of respect. *Pāhuṇeyyo* means worthy of hospitality, deserving to be a guest. When members of the spiritual community arrive you should open your doors to them, in the sense that you should be open to them both materially and spiritually. *Dakkhiṇeyyo* means that the members of the spiritual community are deserving of gifts and donations: you should give to them, help them, support them, in any way that you can. This should be your natural response. Finally, *añjalikaraṇīyo*. This means worthy of being revered with folded and uplifted hands. In other words, you should have towards members of the spiritual community not just ordinary social respect, but even a positive – almost religious – devotion.

KULANANDA: It's a sort of natural aristocracy.

SANGHARAKSHITA: Yes, but it's not a question of anybody saying, '*I* am an individual and *you* are not, and you ought to respect me!' It's more a question of people keeping open the channels of communication. If the channels of communication are open, then it will be naturally felt that one person has got more to give, whereas the other is more on the receiving end, relatively speaking. The situation may change from time to time. In a certain situation, one person may be the receiver, the other the giver, and in another situation the roles may be reversed. It's a question of being open to what the situation actually is. An individual doesn't regard his individuality as a position which he has established, and which he has to assert in relation to others. If he does that he's not an individual: he's simply an individualist, a dominant or dominating member of the group. We find this sometimes in connection with the question of seniority within the Order. Certainly people who are more senior, more experienced, should be respected by other members of the Order, but your seniority is not something on which you can take your stand, and from which you can assert yourself in such terms as 'I am a senior Order member, and therefore you ought to do what I say' or 'I am the one to lead!' It doesn't follow. If you are inclined to adopt that attitude, you may be senior technically, but you're not senior in terms of real maturity.

KULARATNA: That's seeing the Order as a sort of group.

SANGHARAKSHITA: Yes, indeed.

KULANANDA: It can be very difficult for more senior Order members to stand receptive to more junior Order members when the occasion arises.

SANGHARAKSHITA: It's going to get increasingly difficult. Those of you who are junior now may be having quite a happy time challenging the senior ones, but wait until *you* become senior, and you're challenged by an even more virile generation of even younger Order members! Let's wait and see! You may have quite a tough time in the future. On the other hand, if you've really kept up to scratch it will be fun being challenged by the younger ones; you'll thoroughly enjoy their spirit and their efforts to challenge you, but you'll know that you can deal with it. You know it's just like a play, so you will quite enjoy it. You will like to see them doing that sort of thing because it's part of the way they grow. As between any two people – certainly within the context of the spiritual community – there can be no question of anybody claiming to be superior. This is a very important point. I emphasize the 'claiming' here. The chances are that one of the two will be superior, but there's absolutely no need to make any point of it at all, much less still to insist upon it. If both are open, then it will become evident who is relatively more the giver and who is relatively more the receiver. That will be felt and experienced by those concerned. Nobody needs to seek to establish that as a formal position: that's totally unnecessary and anti-spiritual, and it's totally out of place within the spiritual community.

KULANANDA: You could say, couldn't you, that if someone asks for your respect they don't deserve it.

SANGHARAKSHITA: Yes, right. One begins, if one begins from any position at all, from a position of complete equality. That is the position from which you start, because before you are really open with one another – before you have any real communication – how do you know who is superior and who is inferior, if in fact those are terms to be used at all? You just don't know. So you assume that the other person is as good as you are, you assume that you are as good as the other person, until such time as, having opened up to real communication, it begins to be apparent to both of you that in fact there are certain inequalities, or perhaps even overall inequalities, and then you adjust to each other accordingly, in a quite natural, spontaneous manner. You should be open to the possibility of even the youngest and newest Order member having something to teach you, or give you, or show you, even if he may not overall be more mature than you. It may be that there's an overall superiority to you on his part: you have to be open to that possibility as well. In short, you start off thinking he's just as good as you and you're just as good as him, you start communicating, and you see where it leads, see what the actual situation is.

If people start off with a rigid dogmatic assumption of equality, then they are not able to communicate. If they assume that they are necessarily as good as anybody else, however much they 'communicate' they will never discover any superiority in anybody else. If they've got that dogmatic view of equality, they will never discover your superiority – if in fact you are superior – and there will be no communication, because they will be trying to communicate on false terms. In other words, if you are superior to them and they are insisting on being 'equal', no real communication will be possible, because they are blocking you off. They are not willing to receive from you, which would be the natural thing if you are superior to them, or more experienced, more mature, than they are. If they are so hung up on this dogma of everybody being the same, that will effectively block the channels of communication. If they really believe that there's nothing they could possibly learn from you, well then, they won't, they won't learn anything. But if within the spiritual community there's any attempt to assert a position of superiority or seniority, then that immediately turns the situation from a spiritual community to an ordinary group. You're seeking to exercise power instead of emanating *mettā*.

KULAMITRA: How does one go about restoring the balance if that happens?

SANGHARAKSHITA: The first thing is that you actually see what is happening. You realize it, you recognize it. You don't do it yourself, or if you are doing it, you stop; and you point out to others where necessary that this is what they are doing. Point it out with good will. If they really are committed and sincere, and if they are doing it, and you point it out to them, they will see it. It's a very important point, a very important distinction.

KULANANDA: They won't be able to work with others within the spiritual community if they exercise power instead of *mettā*.

SANGHARAKSHITA: That's true. By the way, I'm using the word power here in a different sense from that in which Chintamani uses it in his articles, and in which I sometimes use it. That's a bit confusing, but there are these different usages.

KULANANDA: Power in the group sense is seeking to dominate. If they have any real power, it's obvious.

SANGHARAKSHITA: But one could say that in dealing with the people who are not individuals, the use of power cannot be ruled out. If you as an individual are not to be overwhelmed by the members of the group, you may have to use it in self-defence, to protect yourself.

KULANANDA: You could even use it for their own good.

SANGHARAKSHITA: Yes, though here one is on rather dangerous ground. Perhaps we shouldn't even say that in public! Otherwise you become like Plato's guardians, or like Big Brother, knowing what is good for other people, which is quite a dangerous situation – though sometimes it may occur.[206] That situation cannot be ruled out altogether.

KULANANDA: But it must be real, and not just a rationalization.

SANGHARAKSHITA: It mustn't just be a rationalization of your own desire to dominate.

Anyway, these also are characteristics of the spiritual community: that they are to be respected, received hospitably, made offerings to, and even revered, by those who are not members of the spiritual community. But this recognition of the spiritual community should be natural and spontaneous. It can't be insisted upon.

Finally, the spiritual community is also *anuttaraṃ puññakkhettaṃ lokassā ti*: the supreme, or unexcelled, field of merit for the world. This needs a bit of explanation. If you plant a seed in a field, what happens? It germinates: you get something from it later on. In the same way, according to tradition, if you make an offering, if you give something to someone who is spiritually worthy, from that offering merit accrues to you which helps you to have a good rebirth. It is also believed that the more meritorious, the more holy, the person to whom you make the offering, the greater the amount of *puṇya* (Pāli *puñña*) that will redound to you. Since the spiritual community, the Sangha in the sense of the Āryasaṅgha, contains all these highly developed individuals – the Stream Entrants and so on – it is the best field of merit, the best field in which to sow the seed of your offering in order to reap fruit in the form of merit. One could look at this sociologically, because this doctrine secures to the monks (in the technical sense) their support from the laity. The laity believe that by supporting them, by making offerings to them, they are benefiting themselves. That has a sociological, even a spiritual, value, but it can be looked at in another way too. For instance, it can be looked at rather as in my aphorism: 'One should not waste time helping the weak. Nowadays it is the strong who need help.' If you help someone who is strong, that's better than helping someone who is weak, because the strong person will do more with that help. Looked at in that way, it would seem that making offerings to those who are less meritorious or less holy is not a good investment for those who are not members of the spiritual community. It does tend to be a bit like this in some Theravādin countries. The ordinary laity lead a quite unspiritual life, and they don't take Buddhism very seriously, but they make lots of offerings to the monks, who are taking Buddhism at least a bit more seriously than they are. They believe that they're earning merit in that way, and that that will secure them a good rebirth and blessings in future lives. This isn't a very good way of practising the Dharma, though there's some value in it. It's better to look at the spiritual community as a source of inspiration for your own spiritual life and practice, and as being the people who are really able to use your cooperation and to help you just by being what they are, than to regard them as a good area of investment for your offerings.

These, then, are the qualities or attributes of the Sangha. The complete formula for the Sangha *vandana* therefore runs:

> Happily proceeding is the fellowship of the Hearers of the Richly Endowed One, uprightly proceeding,... methodically proceeding,... correctly proceeding,... namely, these four pairs of Individuals, these eight Persons.
>
> This fellowship of Hearers of the Richly Endowed One is worthy of worship, worthy of hospitality, worthy of offerings, worthy of salutation with folded hands, an incomparable source of goodness to the world.

It is to that Sangha, to that spiritual community, that one goes for Refuge as long as one's life lasts. Then follows the verse:

> To all the Fellowships that were,
> To all the Fellowships to be,
> To all the Fellowships that are,
> My worship flows unceasingly.
> No refuge but the Fellowship,
> Refuge supreme, is there for me.
> Oh by the virtue of this truth,
> May grace abound, and victory!

That, then, is the *Tiratana Vandanā*, the 'Salutation to the Three Jewels'. There's probably much more that could be said on it, but I think we've dealt with it fairly adequately, at least for the time being.

# THE THREEFOLD REFUGE

A seminar on *The Threefold Refuge*
held at Padmaloka in May 1978

Present: Sangharakshita, Anandajyoti, Dhammarati, Dharmananda, Kulananda, Kularatna, Lalitavajra, Lokamitra, Mahamati, Ratnajyoti (later named Maharatnajyoti), Ratnavira, Sagaramati, Sthiramati, Vairocana, Ray Daguerre, Martin Redman (later ordained as Vidyaratna), Phil Shann (later ordained as Indrabodhi), Graham Steven (later ordained as Harshaprabha).

# INTRODUCTION

SANGHARAKSHITA: In the course of these ten days we shall be studying three different texts. The first is this little booklet on *The Threefold Refuge* by Nyanaponika Thera, the second is the Sevenfold Puja, and the third is the chapter on 'Milarepa and the Novices' as translated in *Buddhist Texts Through the Ages*, edited by Dr Conze.[207] You will notice that there's a certain pattern – a sort of system – here. In dealing with the subject of the threefold Refuge, that is to say, refuge in the Buddha, Dharma, and Sangha, we shall be going into what is virtually the Theravāda or Hīnayāna; in covering the Sevenfold Puja, and trying to understand it in some depth, we shall be dealing with the Mahāyāna; and when we come on to 'Milarepa and the Novices' then, of course, it will be a matter of the Vajrayāna. In the course of ten days we shall in a sense be covering, of course not completely, all three *yānas*, i.e. the three main stages of the historical development of Buddhism.

*The Threefold Refuge* is divided into two chapters. The first contains Buddhaghosa's exposition of a passage in the *Majjhima Nikāya* dealing with the Refuges which comes at the end of the *Bhayabherava Sutta*. The *Majjhima Nikāya* or collection of middle-length sayings of the Buddha is part of the Theravāda Pāli canon, and Buddhaghosa is the great Theravāda commentator who has written or compiled commentaries on the Pāli canonical texts as well as the monumental *Visuddhimagga* or 'Path of Purity'. Nyanaponika's second chapter consists of his thoughts and comments on Buddhaghosa's exposition, and this falls into two sections: the first offering some general reflections on Going for Refuge and the second offering his reflections on Buddhaghosa's commentary on the *sutta* passage. It will be better for us to go through the booklet not in that order but starting off with the first half of Nyanaponika Thera's thoughts and comments, beginning on page 9, then back to Buddhaghosa's exposition, and then go forward again with the remainder of Nyanaponika Thera's thoughts and comments from page 17 onwards. If we plunge straight into Buddhaghosa's exposition, which is a bit technical, before going through the meaning of the Threefold Refuge in general we may get lost.

I

# GOING FOR REFUGE

## What Makes One A Buddhist

> In all Buddhist lands the followers of the Enlightened One profess their allegiance to him and his liberating doctrine by the ancient, simple and yet so touching formula of 'taking refuge', or, more literal and more expressive, by *going for refuge* to the Triple Gem. (p. 9)[208]

The important point that emerges here is that what makes one a Buddhist is the Going for Refuge. In other words, the Going for Refuge is a uniting factor. To the extent that you are a Buddhist at all you go for Refuge. Notice that Nyanaponika Thera insists on the fact that it is a *going* for Refuge. The significance of that we shall see in greater detail later on. As you probably know, the usual rendering is 'taking refuge', but as Nyanaponika says, 'Going for Refuge' is more literal and also more expressive. It's more literal because that is exactly what the Pāli says. *Gacchāmi* is 'I go', not 'I take'. And it's more expressive because it gives better expression to what actually happens. Going for Refuge is an action on your part of, as it were, going from one place to another, one state to another. It doesn't consist in your *taking* something. When you go it suggests a change taking place in you, but taking suggests only that you've added something to yourself. You've increased your property, as it were. 'Going for Refuge' is therefore always to be preferred to 'taking refuge'.

> The going for refuge, as this figurative expression itself suggests, is or should be a conscious act, and not the mere profession of a theoretical belief, still less the habitual rite of traditional piety. The protecting refuge *exists*, but we have to go to it by our own effort. It will not come to us by itself, while we stay put. The Buddha, as he repeatedly declared, is only the teacher, 'pointing out the Way'.[209] Therefore, the going for refuge, expressive of Buddhist faith (*saddhā*), is, in the first place, a conscious act of *will* and determination, directed towards the goal of liberation. Hereby the conception of faith as a mere passive waiting for 'saving grace' is rejected. (p. 9)

The Going for Refuge should be a conscious act. That is the main point that emerges here. Notice that Nyanaponika says 'not the mere profession of a theoretical belief, still less the habitual rite of traditional piety'. This is, of course, what it has become for most people in most Buddhist countries. How could it be a mere profession of theoretical belief? And how does that differ from the habitual rite of traditional piety? Is there, in fact, a distinction between these two?

SAGARAMATI: A theoretical belief can be accepting it rationally, whereas in the case of the habitual rite of traditional piety you just don't think about it.

SANGHARAKSHITA: You just do it because everybody else does it. You could say that the first is what happens in the case of the degenerate *dhammānusārin* or 'doctrine-follower' and the second is what happens in the case of the degenerate *saddhānusārin* or 'faith-follower', these two representing the predominantly intellectual and the predominantly emotional and devotional type of character.[210] If you're predominantly an intellectual type the Going for Refuge tends to mean for you simply the acceptance of certain ideas. If you're predominantly of the emotional and devotional type the Going for Refuge tends to be simply the reciting of something because everybody else recites it and this gives you a positive feeling of togetherness. It's the first that we tend to find in many Western Buddhist circles and the second in Buddhist countries in the East. In the West, until quite recently, if people said that they were Buddhist it tended to mean that they believed in or accepted certain Buddhist doctrines on intellectual or rational grounds. Not that they necessarily lived in accordance with those doctrines, but that was their Going for Refuge – the acceptance of those doctrines or the profession of that particular theoretical belief. In the East, as we know, it's a question of the 'habitual rite of traditional piety'. You're taken along to the temple when you're quite small. You join in the recitations. You don't even know what they mean to begin with. You grow up like that and maybe in the whole course of your life you never really come to understand the meaning of what you're saying. You just repeat the formula, admittedly with some sort of piety or some sort of feeling, but it doesn't get much beyond being the act of a group. It is not an expression of individual commitment to the Three Jewels.

'The protecting refuge exists, but we have to go to it by our own effort. It will not come to us by itself, while we stay put.' Do you think this is strictly true? Didn't the Buddha go to people, without being invited? Wasn't that a case of the refuge coming to them?

DHAMMARATI: It's more the opportunity.

SANGHARAKSHITA: The opportunity, yes. You could say that the Jewel comes to you, but the Refuge doesn't come to you.

LOKAMITRA: You have to go for Refuge.

SANGHARAKSHITA: You have to go for Refuge. The Refuge may come to you, but not as Refuge, if you see what I mean? As Jewel it may come to you, but not as Refuge. The Buddha can be right there in front of you, but unless you go for Refuge that isn't of much use to you, is it? There are many instances in the Pāli canon of the Buddha going to people, even speaking to people, teaching people, but nothing happens. They didn't go for Refuge. For them, he wasn't a refuge, because they hadn't gone for refuge in him.[211]

So, 'The Buddha, as he repeatedly declared, is only the teacher "pointing out the Way".' Do you think this is strictly true, or do you think there's more to it than that?

MAHAMATI: He also inspires us.

SANGHARAKSHITA: Yes. I think the Theravāda tends rather to leave out this element of inspiration. Nyanaponika reflects, to a great extent, a somewhat liberal Theravādin point of view, but still a quite Theravādin point of view. The Mahāyāna Buddhist would emphasize the element of inspiration. The fact that it's the Buddha pointing out the Way makes a tremendous difference, and the Theravāda tends to overlook that. In fact you could go so far as to say that if the Buddha doesn't point it out, it isn't the Way, or that to the extent that the Buddha points it out it is the Way and to the extent that he doesn't it isn't. Those of you who lead classes or give talks will know from your own experience that to the extent that you speak from your own experience, what you say is convincing, and communicates, and is the Dharma for the people there. If you're just producing it from a book it isn't so convincing. It doesn't really communicate. It doesn't feel like a Way for them.

'Therefore,' he concludes, 'the going for refuge, expressive of Buddhist faith (*saddhā*), is, in the first place, a conscious act of will and determination, directed towards the goal of liberation.' So clearly, in order to go for refuge according to this interpretation, one should have some idea of what liberation is all about. What form do you think that idea takes initially? Can one really conceive of it in the ultimate sense? What do you want liberation *from*, at least to begin with?

VAIROCANA: You want liberation from suffering, of course.

SANGHARAKSHITA: You want liberation from suffering. But how refined to begin with is your conception of suffering?

VAIROCANA: It's your initial insight.

SANGHARAKSHITA: That suggests that it isn't just a matter of will and determination. It's also a matter of insight. Nyanaponika makes the point later on that there's not only will and determination but also understanding and faith. You can't really separate these. In a sense, yes, will and determination come first – but will and determination directed towards what? Liberation. Liberation from what? Suffering. How can you understand anything about liberation from suffering? Only through insight. So it seems that there must be some insight first. But what do we mean by insight in this connection? Is it a transcendental insight or does it fall short of being that?

LOKAMITRA: If it was transcendental you'd be taking the supramundane as your …

SANGHARAKSHITA: Yes. So what is it, then, if it isn't a transcendental insight?

VAIROCANA: Just spiritual.

SANGHARAKSHITA: Probably intelligent is the right word. It's not just rational. It has an emotional side, because it results in action, in will and determination. Perhaps the best word for that kind of insight is just intelligence. You have an intelligent understanding of the fact of suffering which is not merely theoretical and rational and …

DHAMMARATI: (interrupting) I didn't say rational.

SANGHARAKSHITA: No, but this is the distinction that is made, between the rational and the emotional, I was saying that the rational plus the emotional equals what we call the intelligent, which is an insight, yes, but a mundane insight, not insight in the transcendental sense. This suggests that before you can go for refuge, even in the mundane sense, there must be some degree of integration in you of your reason and your emotion, in the form of what we call intelligence. So 'Hereby the conception of faith as a mere passive waiting for "saving grace" is rejected.' Do you think that the emotional nature of faith has received sufficient emphasis in this passage?

VAIROCANA: He's just harming the Christian idea of faith.

SANGHARAKSHITA: Yes, in the last sentence he's clearly rejecting that.

VAIROCANA: He doesn't say much about joyousness of faith. He doesn't seem to be emphasizing a spiritual experience or anything.

SAGARAMATI: But joy would be included under will. He speaks of 'a conscious act of *will*' and in will I imagine he would include all the *saṃskāras*, which would include the emotional side of things.

SANGHARAKSHITA: Yes, if one wanted to look at it technically joy could be regarded as included in will. But even so, is that made sufficiently explicit, or emphasized? Really it isn't, is it? So why do you think that is?

VAIROCANA: Does it go back to the Hīnayāna point of view again?

SANGHARAKSHITA: In a way it does, but one must say that in the Theravādin countries there *is* faith in an emotional sense. If you read books about the Theravāda you might get the impression that it's very dry and unemotional and purely rational, but if you actually meet Theravādins – especially lay people – you get the impression of a tremendous faith in the emotional sense. So why do you think it is not insisted on at all here?

RAY: He seems to be aiming more towards our rational than towards our emotional side.

SANGHARAKSHITA: Yes.

SAGARAMATI: Because faith in that more emotional sense can be taken for granted.

SANGHARAKSHITA: No, I don't think it's that. I think the key is perhaps to be found in that last sentence, 'Hereby the conception of faith as a mere passive waiting for "saving grace" is rejected.' He's throwing away the baby with the bathwater, I think. He's so concerned that people should not think of Buddhist faith in the Christian sense of just blind belief or a purely passive attitude that he's almost forgotten that faith – I was going to say *even* Buddhist faith, but perhaps I should say most of all Buddhist faith – is an emotional state. It's not just a tepid 'confidence', which is the way some modern Theravādin writers are very fond of translating *saddhā*, playing down the emotionality of the state. If anything, the emotionality of it should be played up, but dissociated from all the things that we tend to associate faith with in the West, such as blind belief, fanaticism, and authoritarianism.

SAGARAMATI: Is Nyanaponika European?

SANGHARAKSHITA: Yes, he's a rather intellectual European Buddhist, a Theravādin. He's writing mainly, I imagine, for Western Buddhists, or prospective Western Buddhists, so he's playing down the whole emotional, devotional side of Buddhism. I think that is a mistake. It's bound up with the belief that many Eastern Buddhists have, especially Theravādins, that Western intellectuals are the most favourable soil for the planting of the seed of the Dharma and that the Dharma should therefore be presented in exclusively intellectual terms. I think this is a complete misunderstanding. Because he wants to appeal to Westerners he does seem to play down, or at least not emphasize, the emotional nature of faith, but this doesn't conform with practice and experience in the Theravādin countries, where *saddhā* is definitely a very emotional thing, and quite rightly so. It is because of this sort of presentation of the Dharma that we get in Buddhist circles in the West so much of what he himself calls 'the mere profession of a theoretical belief', so much of the Going for Refuge in that sense – and why Buddhism doesn't become a matter of actual practice and changing one's life, but remains just an intellectual study. It's because this emotional element is not sufficiently present. You only change when your emotions are involved. You may be able to see the need for change clearly enough, but you only actually start to change when the emotions come in. So it isn't correct to say that the Buddha is only the teacher, pointing out the Way; he's also the inspirer.

MAHAMATI: Playing down the emotions also seems to be playing down being receptive.

SANGHARAKSHITA: This is true. It's true that Buddhist faith is not 'a mere passive waiting for "saving grace".' It does include an element of receptivity. With the rightful rejection of passivity there is also, if one isn't very careful, an implied rejection of receptivity too. Even within the context of the Theravāda the disciple is called the *sāvaka*, 'the one who hears', which implies receptivity – not passivity but receptivity. What do you think is the difference between passivity and receptivity? How could one formulate that?

VAIROCANA: Passivity doesn't seem to be very active. With receptivity you're actively taking in, whereas passivity seems to suggest that you're just sort of sitting back.

SANGHARAKSHITA: But what is this 'actively taking in'? Isn't it a bit of a contradiction in terms? Can't you be receptive and just take in? Is that not possible?

VAIROCANA: It doesn't have to be an emotional response to what you're taking in. You have to be sort of active. You have to be in communication, I suppose, with what you're taking in.

KULARATNA: Receptivity is directed towards something whereas passivity isn't.

SANGHARAKSHITA: Passivity isn't. Passivity has no aim and object, as it were. But when you're being receptive, you first of all see what you're going to be receptive to and you *want* to open yourself to that because it is good to be open to that. You could say that you have to make yourself receptive, that is, make yourself active. To be receptive isn't easy. It requires a lot of hard work, because one's normal state is either to be active or to be passive, but not to be receptive. So you're going to have to work hard on yourself to make yourself open to something of a higher, more ideal nature. Only then can you be receptive. At the moment of being receptive, well, you are receptive: you're neither active nor passive. But to make yourself receptive, to get yourself into that sort of mental state, requires a great deal of hard work, because you need to remove all sorts of blockages that you may have and open the channels of communication, free yourself from reactivity, so that as soon as whatever it is starts flowing into you, you don't start reacting against it and shutting it out, but allow yourself to remain open and receptive. That isn't easy. When you're passive you tend to allow yourself, out of laziness or indifference or sloth or torpor, to be played upon by whatever happens to come along, but receptivity is a far, far higher state. So reject passivity by all means, but not receptivity. You see the difference? You could say that passivity is a dull, almost sleepy state, whereas receptivity is not only open, but very bright, very alert. It's very aware also, because you see what it is that you're being receptive to. You see the value of being receptive. In fact, it's very difficult to distinguish between seeing the value of something and being receptive to that. If you're not really receptive to it, you can't see what it is, and if you can't see what it is, you can hardly be said to be receptive to it,

RATNAJYOTI: So you couldn't really have a 'mere theoretical belief' – or could you?

SANGHARAKSHITA: It depends how you define belief. You can't really have a theoretical Going for Refuge, any more than you can have a merely traditional Going for Refuge. They only appear to be such. Somebody may say, 'I'm a Buddhist. I go for Refuge because I accept the *anattā* doctrine', but if that seems to have no repercussions at all in his life and experience he is not a Buddhist, he has not gone for Refuge. He hasn't really accepted the *anattā* doctrine. As the *anattā* doctrine is a spiritual teaching, there cannot really be a purely theoretical acceptance of it, I would say. If you accept it only theoretically you're only thinking that you are accepting it. Your theoretical acceptance is theoretical. If you fail to act upon something which, when understood, is automatically to be acted upon, then you have not understood it. You could say that the truths in Buddhism are of such a nature that to understand them is to act upon them, and not to act upon them is not to understand them. If somebody doesn't act upon something it shows that he hasn't understood it. There may be a theoretical comprehension of the concepts through which that teaching is expressed, but that's quite different from an understanding of the teaching itself. If you understand, you understand via your intelligence, which is not only reason but also emotion, so that you don't only understand, you act upon your understanding, because you *feel*.

There's no such thing as a Going for Refuge in the sense of 'a mere profession of a theoretical belief', any more than there is the familiar Going or Refuge which is simply 'the habitual rite of traditional piety'. In both cases one deceives oneself if one thinks that one is Going for Refuge. You may understand the concepts in which the Buddha's teaching is expressed very well, but if you don't act upon them you've not gone for Refuge, and that theoretical understanding itself doesn't constitute a Going for Refuge. On the other hand, you may repeat the Refuges and Precepts, along with lots of other people, with a tremendous amount of emotion, but if you don't really understand what it's all about and if it is simply a group emotion which you are experiencing, if Buddhism is for you simply a cultural matter, then you haven't gone for Refuge.

It seems to me that these are the two extremes: on the one hand thinking that you've gone for Refuge because you have understood, or think you have understood, the Buddha's teaching considered just theoretically, as a 'philosophy'; and on the other hand thinking that you've gone for Refuge when really you've only been born and brought up in a Buddhist country and have repeated the appropriate formula from an early age. You're more likely to find the first extreme in the West among people who read books about Buddhism and belong to Buddhist societies, while the second you'll be more likely to find in the Eastern Buddhist countries, among people who have been brought up as Buddhists, or 'born as Buddhists', as they will tell you, though of course that's a contradiction in terms. How can you be born as a Buddhist? Do you go for Refuge as you come out of your mother's womb? You don't know anything about it! As we shall see later on, the mundane refuge is broken at the time of death, according to orthodox or, let us say, Theravādin teaching, which is also accepted by the Mahāyāna. When you are born, you are born without a refuge, even a mundane refuge. You may be born with a transcendental refuge carried over with you from a previous life, in which case you'll be born presumably being mindful and self-possessed. But you aren't born as a Buddhist simply because you are born in a Buddhist family. In that case you have to go for Refuge, later on in life, as a result of your own intelligence, your own understanding, your own feeling for the Refuges.

The only way in which you can go for Refuge is to have a definite will, a definite determination, directed towards a higher state of freedom of which you have some inkling, into which you have some insight, not in the transcendental sense, but in the sense of an understanding and upon which you *act*. That is what Going for Refuge really means or really implies.

There's one aspect of the Going for Refuge and faith which is *entirely* overlooked here but which is very, very important. Can you think what that might be? It was indirectly touched upon by somebody a little earlier. It's connected with the Buddha as inspiration as well as just teacher.

STHIRAMATI: The contact with the sangha.

SANGHARAKSHITA: There's contact with the sangha, yes. But it's not specifically that.

STHIRAMATI: With your own guru.

SANGHARAKSHITA: With your own guru, yes. Well, taking it in more appropriate emotional terms.

SAGARAMATI: There's probably the fact that it's joy.

SANGHARAKSHITA: There's joy, yes. That is what we have referred to before. But put it even more strongly than that. There's another word than joy: a more refined word – a more aesthetic word, let's say.

VAIROCANA: Rapture.

SANGHARAKSHITA: Rapture. Or delight. But what is it that you delight *in*? If the subjective side is delight, what is the objective side?

GRAHAM: The Three Jewels.

SANGHARAKSHITA: Yes, but under what aspect?

KULARATNA: Receptivity.

SANGHARAKSHITA: No, that's subjective. What is the objective correlate, as it were, of your delight? What is it that fills you with delight?

GRAHAM: Beauty.

SANGHARAKSHITA: Beauty, of course! But does this passage say anything about beauty? It isn't only a question of Going for Refuge because you see a need for liberation, because you want to be liberated. There's another whole aspect. One can take delight in the beauty of the spiritual, as it were, or, one might even say, in the spiritual beauty of the Buddha, and this rouses one's feelings of delight and joy and rapture which may impel one to go for Refuge. This aspect seems to be entirely overlooked here, though it does figure quite prominently in the Buddhist life of people in Eastern Buddhist countries, including Theravādin Buddhists.

ANANDAJYOTI: There's the story of Ānanda. Doesn't he see the beauty of the Buddha and that caused him to go for Refuge?

SANGHARAKSHITA: That's right. In the *Śūraṅgama Sūtra* the Buddha asks Ānanda what prompted him to become his disciple, and Ānanda replies, in effect, that he was attracted and fascinated by the spiritual beauty of the Buddha.[212]

What Nyanaponika says about the Going for Refuge, though correct as far as it goes, tends to overlook this aspect, so that, generally speaking, there is a devaluation of the whole of the emotional side of the spiritual life. He is very conscious that he's addressing a predominantly Western, or Western-educated, audience and wants to avoid the imputation of anything like Christian faith or blind belief. In any case, being a Theravādin, he is predisposed to play down the part of faith. Theoretically, many *bhikkhus* do this. They may have quite a bit of faith and devotion themselves, but for one reason or another they will play it down ('Buddhism is for the intellectual', 'Buddhism is for the highly educated', etc.) and rather depreciate the genuine faith of ordinary people. There's a feeling among quite a few Theravādin *bhikkhus* that emotion or devotion is somehow rather second rate and that a devoted Buddhist is a sort of second-class Buddhist. The well-read, intellectual Buddhist is the *real* Buddhist. Some Theravādin *bhikkhus* believe quite strongly that it's the Western intellectual who is the most favourable field for the propagation of the Dharma, although from what I've seen personally of Western intellectuals, I'd say that that isn't so at all, even when they do have an interest in Buddhism.

LOKAMITRA: I went to a vihara in London recently and met the head monk, a Sinhalese who's been in England for twenty-five years, and asked him how he saw the future of Buddhism in the West. He said he saw it as never being a large movement because it was something only for intellectuals, and so I said, 'Well, surely it hasn't got much chance then.' He said, 'Oh well, others will be attracted to it for peace of mind and so they'll meditate and so on.' That is, they were the second line.

SANGHARAKSHITA: It's also got something to do with the fact that in Ceylon Buddhism as a purely spiritual tradition died out quite a few centuries ago (it has been revived a little in more recent times) and *bhikkhus* became the intelligentsia. They became the learned class, the cultured class, and they attached great importance to purely intellectual attainments and tended to think of Buddhism and the religious life exclusively in that way. One could almost say, if one wanted to be a little unkind, that such *bhikkhus* can hardly give what they haven't got themselves, so they tend to look to their opposite number in the West, which is usually the academic, rather than to the man in the street, as it were, who has got a relatively integrated head and heart and who might be *really* able to go for Refuge. They can't speak his language. They can speak, usually, only the language of the intellectual, the academic. This means that their presentation of Buddhism in the West is quite severely slanted. It's as though they don't want very much to do with ordinary people in the West. They hardly know what to say to them. This is a very, very severe limitation.

MAHAMATI: Is this emphasis on the intellectual more historical, or does it derive from the original Theravādin scriptures?

SANGHARAKSHITA: It derives from the scriptures to some extent, because the scriptures include the Abhidhamma. The Abhidhamma certainly discusses the emotions, but it does so in a theoretical way, and the way in which the Abhidhamma is studied, nowadays at least, is more or less just academic. It is not studied as a living thing. I think one must say that for many centuries the Theravāda has had a tradition of intellectualism, as regards the *bhikkhus*.

This brings us to quite an interesting point. In the Theravādin countries you find the lay people very often have tremendous faith and devotion, or at least they're emotionally involved in Buddhism, but very often they don't know much about it. The monks know quite a lot about it. They're the experts in it. They've studied the texts. They very often know Pāli, or even Sanskrit. They're very cultured, witty, intelligent people. But they're not all that emotionally involved in Buddhism, except as the institution to which they belong. There's a sort of split, I've found, between the very intellectual *bhikkhus* and the very devoted lay people, and intellect and emotion tend not to come together, though sometimes you get a lay Buddhist who is very devoted and who has also studied the Dharma, and occasionally you get a *bhikkhu* who is not only well versed in the scriptures but has some devotion. So you've got a split in the Theravāda community, and one often wishes one could bring these two things together much more. The *bhikkhu*, especially in Ceylon, has become very much the professional, almost the Buddhist academic, and in modern times the *bhikkhus* have tended to take up teaching positions in colleges and universities, while the lay people have great faith and devotion but not much understanding of the teaching. There's this sort of split, and the *bhikkhus* tend to rather devalue faith and devotion. They're almost ashamed of it, apologising for its external manifestations in the form of pujas and chanting. 'These are just for the lay people, just for the devoted people. We don't bother about such things. We study the scriptures. We're the real Buddhists.' They confuse wisdom with purely theoretical understanding.

VAIROCANA: It's strange that they know so much about Buddhism, but yet they don't realize that!

SANGHARAKSHITA: This is true, but it holds good of everybody in some measure. If we ask ourselves how much we understand of Buddhism, as I suggested in one of my lectures on Zen, the answer is that we probably understand quite a lot.[213] We know about the four noble truths and the Noble Eightfold Path, about karma and rebirth, Nirvāṇa, and dependent origination. We know about *śūnyatā*, bodhisattvas, and the Pure Land. What a lot we know! But how much are we able to practise? This is a universal phenomenon. It seems to be connected with the stage of human evolution in which we are at present. Our head races so far ahead of our heart! At least, head and heart don't go in the same direction. The heart has its own little preoccupations – not exactly parallel with those of the head.

What we must be quite clear about is that Buddhism, essentially, is an integrated teaching. Nyanaponika himself makes the point later on, at least theoretically, that there must be deep emotional involvement.

Theoretical understanding alone doesn't make one a Buddhist. You can know a lot about Buddhist philosophy from an academic point of view, and yet be miles away from being a Buddhist in the sense of Going for Refuge. We have to be very careful when we encounter books about Buddhism which are written purely from this intellectual – or rather, not to misuse the good word intellectual, from this academic point of view.

### Faith-Followers and Doctrine-Followers

> In the Commentary, translated above, there is the remarkable statement that the expression 'going for refuge' is meant to convey, in addition, the idea of 'knowing' and 'understanding'. This points to the second aspect of going for refuge, namely as a conscious act of *understanding*. Hereby unthinking credulity and blind faith based on external authority are rejected. (p. 10)

SANGHARAKSHITA: As we saw in connection with the previous paragraph, since your Going for Refuge is an act of will and determination directed towards the goal of liberation, you have to have at least some idea of what liberation is all about, some idea of what you're going to be liberated from. The element of understanding therefore necessarily arises and, as Nyanaponika points out, in the commentary he has translated – which we'll be going into later – it is said that the expression 'going for refuge' is meant to convey, in addition, the idea of 'knowing' and 'understanding'. This is a very important point.

This points to the second aspect of Going for Refuge, that is to say, to the fact that it is not only a conscious act of will and determination but also 'a conscious act of *understanding*'. All the same, it comes back to the old point that 'Hereby unthinking credulity and blind faith based on external authority are rejected.' That's quite true. So they are. But one needs to bear in mind that devotion in the sense of higher emotional experience, or rapture – or delight, even – in the Buddha, are certainly not rejected. So the 'Going for Refuge' is an act, a conscious act of will and determination, and it also involves understanding.

> The commentator emphasizes this aspect by describing the going for refuge as a state of mind, not relying on others (*aparapaccaya*).

On many occasions the Master warned his disciples not to accept his teachings out of mere trust in him, but only after personal experience, practice, and reflection. Here it may suffice to remind us of the famous Sermon to the Kālāmas:

'Do not go by hearsay, nor by tradition, nor by people's tales, nor by the authority of Scriptures. Do not go by reasoning, nor by logic and methodical investigations, nor by approval of speculative views, nor moved by reverence, or by the thought: "The Recluse is my teacher!"'[214] (p. 10)

SANGHARAKSHITA: There's a seeming ambiguity in the first sentence. If you go for Refuge you begin by Going for Refuge to the Buddha, so aren't you relying on the Buddha? In what sense does the Going for Refuge involve not relying on others? What is reliance?

RATNAJYOTI: Does he mean that it's an individual decision, a choice you make yourself?

SANGHARAKSHITA: Yes.

VAIROCANA: You've got to make way for yourself, because you're relying on others for your constant inspiration and guidance.

SANGHARAKSHITA: Yes. If 'not relying on others' is emphasized too much – and it seems to be a little here – the whole aspect of *kalyāṇa mitratā*, spiritual friendship, is ignored. It is quite true that you don't rely on others to make your decisions for you, but especially in the early days of your spiritual life you rely on others for inspiration, encouragement, instruction, and so on. You could say that you don't rely upon others insofar as the act of Going for Refuge itself is concerned, but you do very much rely upon others to help you to get to the point where you're able to go for Refuge and to continue Going for Refuge. So long as your Going for Refuge is only mundane, you may be unfaithful to it at any time, and in order to maintain its existence you need the constant spiritual support of other members of the spiritual community to remind you, inspire you, exhort you, and criticize you if necessary. You're not relying in the sense that you are not expecting others to do for you what you can only do for yourself, but you're certainly relying on them to give you that help which you need and which you yourself cannot provide.

SAGARAMATI: The others in this case would be the group. You're 'not relying' for any enjoyment or pleasure or anything like that.

SANGHARAKSHITA: Just as in one's anxiety to reject the group one should be careful not to reject the spiritual community, so in one's anxiety to emphasize that the Going for Refuge is an individual, personal act, one must not reject or seem to reject the *kalyāṇa mitratā* – and it does seem that this passage tends a bit in that direction. If somebody like Nyanaponika doesn't actually say that in not relying upon others you should be careful that you don't reject the whole idea of *kalyāṇa mitratā* – and the passage certainly doesn't say that – it would seem that he doesn't even think of that possibility.

MAHAMATI: Maybe he's being a bit individualistic and rationalistic.

SANGHARAKSHITA: It does seem rather like that. 'On many occasions the Master warned his disciples not to accept his teachings out of mere trust in him, but only after personal experience, practice and reflection.' This would seem to hold good of the *dhammānusārin* but not of the *saddhānusārin*. Traditionally Buddhism, including the Theravāda, divides disciples into three classes. There is the *dhammānusārin* or 'doctrine-follower', the *saddhānusārin* or 'faith-follower', and the *kāyasakkhin* or 'body-witness'. I go into this distinction in my book *The Three Jewels*.[215] The *dhammānusārin* is the person whose approach to the spiritual life is predominantly intellectual. That's not to say he's an intellectual in the modern sense. He does practise the Dharma, he is a genuine follower, but his point of contact is doctrinal, or intellectual. He understands the Dharma first, then practises it – but he does actually practise, even though his understanding is introductory to his practice. He tends to rely more upon himself. He tends not to be so closely connected with a guru or to be inspired so much by him. He gets his inspiration from the Dharma via its 'philosophy' as he understands that. In the case of the *saddhānusārin* or faith-follower, the point of contact is more emotional or devotional. He's not all that much interested in the philosophy of Buddhism, but attaches great importance to contact with the teacher, the guru, and tends to accept and put into practice whatever the teacher tells him. The *dhammānusārin* and the *saddhānusārin* are both real followers, and both are equally valid types of disciple according to the traditional Theravāda teaching. The *kāyasakkhin* or body-witness is more difficult to understand. 'Body' here means something like 'individual personality', so the *kāyasakkhin* is the one who is simply the witness or observer of the sum total, the 'body', of his own bodily and mental states. He's more like the yogi, who experiences higher and higher states of consciousness, and who, from those higher states of consciousness, doesn't exactly look down upon the lower ones with which he clearly identified himself but sees them as his body 'out there'. In other words, he progressively dissociates himself from his grosser personality. These are the three main types of disciple.

It would seem that when Nyanaponika says, 'On many occasions the Master warned his disciples not to accept his teachings out of mere trust in him, but only after personal experience, practice and reflection', this applies to the *dhammānusārin*. The *saddhānusārin* – to say nothing of the *kāyasakkhin*, who studies his own experience – trusts the Buddha to begin with, and he practises on that basis. He might be inspired by the Buddha's very appearance. He doesn't feel any need for 'personal experience, practice and reflection' before accepting the teachings. He believes them from the beginning and puts what he believes into practice at once. The majority of Buddhists in Buddhist countries are of this type – I mean those who actually follow the Dharma, not those who simply conform for cultural or ethnic reasons – but this sentence doesn't seem to recognize their existence.

'Here it may suffice to remind us of the famous Sermon to the Kālāmas: "Do not go by hearsay, nor by tradition, nor by people's tales, nor by the authority of Scriptures".' This is often quoted, but not so often quoted is what follows in the text: 'Do not go by reasoning, nor by logic and methodical investigations.' Usually when the *Kālāma Sutta* is quoted in the West, people quote only the first part, in other words they think that the *Sutta* is saying, 'Think it all out for yourself. Just follow your own reason, your own ideas.' But then the *Sutta* goes on to say, 'Do not go by reasoning.' So why should you not go by reasoning?

KULANANDA: The lower mind tends to take it over.

SANGHARAKSHITA: Yes. Reasoning is only too often rationalization. In any case you can only reason from premises, and how are you to know that your premises are correct? What gives you your premises? So, 'Do not go by reasoning, nor by logic and methodical investigations.' If you were to methodically investigate Buddhism, studying all the books on Buddhism and what all the different schools have said, and in that way try to build up a correct picture of Buddhism, that would be a methodical investigation, but it wouldn't get you very far. 'Nor by approval of speculative views.' Sometimes you hear an idea and you think, 'Oh, I like that!' You're naturally drawn to it, and accept it. But you shouldn't do that. 'Nor moved by reverence.' This is reverence not in the sense of faith but in the sense of respect. You shouldn't accept a view out of respect for anybody. Here the idea of the group comes in. You could say that most people in Buddhist countries accept the Buddha's teachings out of respect in this sort of way. 'Or by the thought: "The Recluse is my teacher!"' Why should you not accept the teachings on this basis, thinking that the *samaṇa* – this could mean the Buddha, or it could mean any *bhikkhu* – is your teacher? If you accept out of *saddhā*, that's all right; but if you accept *thinking* that the Recluse – the *bhikkhu*, or the Buddha even – is your teacher, then this is not really accepting. But what sort of conception of the relation between teacher and disciple does that suggest, if you accept out of respect?

VAIROCANA: It's the reverence thing.

SANGHARAKSHITA: Yes: in the wrong way, of course.

VAIROCANA: It wouldn't make you a faith-follower, would it?

SANGHARAKSHITA: No, it wouldn't.

GRAHAM: It would be a passive faith.

SANGHARAKSHITA: It would be passive, for one thing. But what more than that would such a relation suggest?

ANANDAJYOTI: It's like a rather blind hero worship projection.

LOKAMITRA: It would be a passive faith. It's just an academic teacher.

SAGARAMATI: This is the acceptance of the conventional set-up of the society we live in.

SANGHARAKSHITA: Yes, it's that. Here you follow a particular teaching as you might follow a particular football team. It becomes a sort of group thing. You've got your group set-up: the head of the group is the teacher, and since you want the group of which you're a part to continue, you accept whatever the teacher says, to maintain your group in existence. Just as you might say, 'My country right or wrong', in the same way you say, 'My teacher right or wrong'. If you've got that sort of attitude towards the teacher, it means that the teacher has become the head of a group. Accepting what the teacher says in order to maintain the identity and solidarity of the group is quite a different thing from accepting, as a *saddhānusārin*, what the teacher says out of genuine individual faith and devotion towards him. So if you're not to go by hearsay, if you're not to go by tradition or by people's tales, nor even to go by reasoning, by logic and methodical investigations, what are you to go by?

A VOICE: Faith.

SANGHARAKSHITA: Yes, faith. You can certainly go by faith in the Buddhist sense.

SAGARAMATI: There must be something in the experience that makes it such that there's no doubt.

RATNAJYOTI: An objective. I mean, you practise for a period and objectively you would either see the value of that or not.

SANGHARAKSHITA: But it would seem, in the case of the *saddhānusārin*, the Going for Refuge antedates anything of that sort.

DHAMMARATI: Some experience of vision.

SANGHARAKSHITA: Yes. There's what one might describe – in a way in contradictory terms – as a sort of mundane vision, which is what intelligence is. It can be predominantly intellectual in colouring as in the case of the *dhammānusārin* or predominantly emotional in colouring as in the case of the *saddhānusārin*, but there is an element of what one can only describe as vision and therefore an immediate response, whether intellectually or emotionally mediated.

It would seem that the whole trend of Nyanaponika's explanation – reflecting, as it does, Theravādin attitudes – is to confuse the intelligent with the purely rational and the devotional with blind faith, and therefore instead of encouraging the intelligent, it encourages the merely intellectual or theoretical, and instead of rejecting only blind faith it also rejects the genuinely emotional and devotional. That would seem to be quite wrong. I'm sure this is not his conscious intention, but his whole language and approach seems to point in that direction.

KULARATNA: Perhaps he finds it difficult to distinguish between blind faith and genuine devotional thoughts.

SANGHARAKSHITA: But how is it that one finds that difficult?

SAGARAMATI: You can't feel it.

SANGHARAKSHITA: It would seem that in the case of the ordinary person there is a sort of oscillation between purely theoretical understanding and blind faith, whereas in the case of the more developed person there is a more progressive integration between the genuinely intellectual and the genuinely emotional. It's rather like in the Middle Ages when you get the scholastic philosophers who are intellectual to the point of scepticism and the masses who are faithful to the point of fanaticism – and the one manipulating the other. The *Kālāma Sutta* is very often quoted only in part, but it's important to remember that it does also reject reasoning and logic. If you quote only the first half, the suggestion is that you have to work things out by means of your own unaided thinking. There is, or there was – I'm a bit out of touch now – quite a lot of this sort of individualistic approach and attitude among Western Buddhists, or perhaps I should say among English Buddhists: 'You've got to study it yourself, think it all out yourself, not rely on anybody else, not have any contact with anybody else.' This was very much the attitude of a lot of people with whom I came into contact during my first few years back in England. There was no conception of *kalyāṇa mitratā* at all. Your Buddhism boiled down to reading about Buddhism yourself in your spare time. Perhaps you'd go to a weekly class, a weekly lecture, but no more than that, and of course you had a full-time job which might or might not accord with the principles of right livelihood.

> It is a threefold knowledge that is, or should be, implied in the act of going for refuge. It is a knowledge answering the following questions: Is this world of ours really such a place of danger and misery that there is a need for taking refuge? Does such a refuge actually exist? And what is its nature? (p. 10)

This is quite clear. Let's go straight on to the next paragraph. This gives a further explanation.

> There are many who do not see any need for a refuge. Being well pleased with themselves and with the petty, momentary happiness of their life, they are fully convinced that 'all is well with the world'. They do not wish, or are not able, to look beyond their narrow horizon. For them neither the Buddha nor any other great religious teacher has yet appeared. But the majority of men know very well, by their own bitter experience, the hard and cruel face of the world which is only temporarily hidden by a friendly mask. There are some others who, sufficiently aware of a fellow being's actual existence, add to that personal experience by observation of other lives. And there is a still smaller number of people who are able to reflect wisely on both experience and observation. Particularly to those latter ones 'whose eyes are less covered by dust', life will appear as a vast ocean of suffering, of unfathomable depth, on the surface of which beings swim about for a little while, or navigate in their fragile nutshells of which they are very proud. True, there are spells of calm on the waters when it is pleasant to float upon a smooth sea, or to prove and to enjoy the strength of one's body by a long swim. But those with open eyes and minds are not deceived by these short moments of respite: they know the overpowering fierceness of a storm-swept sea, they know the dangerous currents and whirlpools in it, and the demons and monsters of the deep. They know that, even under the most

> favourable conditions, the feeble strength of man will soon be exhausted by the impact of life's elemental forces. The vicissitudes of life give no chance of maintaining permanently, during the unlimited sequence of transformations, even the lowest degree of happiness, even the lowest standard of moral worth. There is nothing to gain by traversing ever anew the infinite expanse of life's ocean, in any of its regions. There is only the same senseless repetition of the ups and downs, of ebb and tide. Faced by the ever-present perils of life and by its essential monotony, there will be only the one cry for refuge in a heart and mind that has truly grasped its situation within the world. A refuge is the one great need of all life and 'going to it' the one sane act demanded by that situation. (pp. 10–11)

SANGHARAKSHITA: This is very well expressed, isn't it? It's quite eloquent. Do you think it's true?

VAIROCANA: (Doubtfully) Yes.

SANGHARAKSHITA: Yes, it's true, but do you think it's the whole truth?

MAHAMATI: It's very pessimistic.

VAIROCANA: No, it's not all that pessimistic.

DHAMMARATI: It's the same perspective as the earlier stuff, that's all.

SANGHARAKSHITA: Yes, it is. In other words, it seems to take into consideration only the approach of the *dhammānusārin*. If we distinguish between the conditioned and the Unconditioned, *saṃsāra* and Nirvāṇa, it suggests that you can be repelled by *saṃsāra* and that, if you have a little understanding, a little insight, you *are* repelled by *saṃsāra*, but it doesn't seem at all aware that you can be attracted by Nirvāṇa, or attracted by the Unconditioned, especially as embodied by the Buddha, or by members of the spiritual community who are more spiritually developed than you are. It therefore suggests that the Going for Refuge is motivated *only* by disillusionment with the *saṃsāra*. That is certainly an important aspect, and it may be decisive for a lot of people, but there are other people who hardly think about *saṃsāra* but who are attracted by the intrinsic value and beauty of the spiritual life itself, you could say of Nirvāṇa itself, of the Buddha himself. This passage doesn't take them into consideration at all. They are more like the *saddhānusārins*. They're fascinated by the beauty of the Unconditioned and they just want to go towards that. That is their motivation for Going for Refuge. Do you see the difference? Why do you think there is this one-sided emphasis in Nyanaponika, perhaps in the Theravāda tradition itself?

DHAMMARATI: Because they never pay any attention to the life of the Buddha, but just go on studying the teaching.

SANGHARAKSHITA: Yes. They don't take into account the life of the Buddha.

VAIROCANA: There's a formulation of the four noble truths which is a bit like this. They mention sickness and the cause of sickness, but nothing is said about the positive state of health.

SANGHARAKSHITA: As I've pointed out in the *Survey*, the teaching of conditioned co-production or dependent origination is the basic Buddhist teaching, but the Theravāda seems to have lost sight of the positive half of that process. Certainly they're fully aware that 'in dependence upon ignorance there arise the *saṃskāras*, in dependence upon the *saṃskāras* arises *vijñāna*, in dependence upon *vijñāna* arises the psycho-physical organism' and so on up to 'in dependence upon becoming there arise birth, old age, disease, and death'. But they've lost sight of 'in dependence upon suffering there arises faith, in dependence upon faith arises joy, in dependence upon joy arises delight' – though it is there in the Pāli scriptures. There is this one-sidedness in the relatively modern Theravāda tradition.[216]

But there's something even more important than that. I think that they've lost sight of something which we do find in the Mahāyāna. It's there in a way in the Theravāda, though very hidden and obscure, but it's certainly brought out much more strongly and clearly in the Mahāyāna. This is the teaching that each individual human being has an affinity for the truth, or an affinity for Enlightenment, or even – to use more poetic language which mustn't be pressed too literally – has the seed of Enlightenment in himself or herself. Because you've got this seed in you, you will be attracted by the Buddha, who represents the seed in its full growth and efflorescence. It's because you've got that possibility of Enlightenment in you that you're drawn and attracted to Enlightenment when you see it represented or embodied before you. But the Theravāda doesn't bring out this point. In the technical language of the Mahāyāna, this seed of Enlightenment is called the *Tathāgata-dhātu*.

The one-sided emphasis in Nyanaponika harks back to the Theravādins forgetting, or not taking into consideration, the positive aspect of conditioned co-production. We suggest growth and progression along a more and more positive series, but they can see spiritual life only in terms of rejection and therefore the Going for Refuge only in terms of disillusionment with *saṃsāra*, not of attraction to Nirvāṇa.

MAHAMATI: Is there a correlation between the doctrine-follower who is disillusioned with *saṃsāra* and the faith-follower who is attracted to Nirvāṇa and the hate and the greed types?

SANGHARAKSHITA: It could be. It could be that the *dhammānusārin* is more of a hate type, usually, and the *saddhānusārin* more of a greed type, usually, though I'm sure you could also find at least a few *dhammānusārins* who were greed types. It's as though one type arrives at the Unconditioned almost by accident, by a process of rejection of the conditioned, while the other arrives at the rejection of the conditioned almost by accident, by way of an attraction to the Unconditioned. You could say that the first kind of person approaches the Unconditioned backwards. They're standing facing the conditioned, and they're rejecting it, they're going further away from it, but they're looking at it all the time. They're walking backwards, and before long they bump into the Unconditioned. They turn and recognize it, though they haven't been thinking in terms of the Unconditioned, they've been thinking in terms of getting away from the conditioned. As for the other type, they're attracted by the Unconditioned from the very beginning. They might be right down in the mire, but they're looking towards the Unconditioned. So they're moving towards the Unconditioned and then, when they've got quite near to it, they turn around and think, 'Good heavens, where's the conditioned gone?' and see that it's a long, long way behind. This seems to be the basis of the difference.

On the whole, it must be said, the Hīnayāna represents more the first sort of approach – whether it is really the *dhammānusārin*'s approach or not – and the Mahāyāna very much the second.

RATNAVIRA: Do you think there are a lot of people in this country at the moment, especially young people, who are stuck in the first sort of situation, who are fairly disillusioned with the conditioned but who haven't exactly bumped into the Unconditioned? There's certainly a lot of very cynical people around.

SANGHARAKSHITA: Well, not only have they not bumped into it, they haven't even seen it in the distance! This is quite a sad state to be in. You're disillusioned with the conditioned but you've no idea, even, of the Unconditioned. You just drift around quite aimlessly, or you devote yourself to something or other in a quite cynical, exploitive way, just whiling away the time until you die, 'You have to do *something*', people say, especially if they've got a lot of energy. They don't really believe in anything, but they've got all this energy, so they just play some sort of game for the time being: whether it's football or philosophy.

You could say that in a way the Mahāyāna has more faith in human beings, in the individual, than does the Theravāda. It has the faith that there is in every human being a kind of spark, to use a poetic expression which wouldn't stand up very well to a rigorous Abhidharma-type analysis, and that on account of that spark of Enlightenment or whatever, the individual is drawn, at first not very consciously, towards something higher, something better, even towards whatever is highest and best. The Mahāyāna has the faith that this spark is at work within the individual all the time, amidst all sorts of mistakes and wanderings. The Theravāda tends to think more in terms of an almost rational seeing-through of the imperfections of the conditioned, on account of which you just give up the conditioned. I don't know whether psychologically this is a very good approach – not that the psychological is necessarily the decisive factor. Do you think it would have much effect on people who come along to classes at the Buddhist centre if you were to try simply to disillusion them with the conditioned rather than to inspire them by holding up a positive spiritual ideal? Which do you think works better?

DHAMMARATI: I think the effect of your disillusioning them would be that they were put off Buddhism and wouldn't come back a second time.

SANGHARAKSHITA: What Nyanaponika says in this rather eloquent paragraph is absolutely true, but the danger is that if you try to put this sort of approach over to people you merely make them cynical unless you can also hold up some very positive ideal – or better still *show* them a much more positive way of life. If you say, 'What's the use of running around playing games and jumping about? In fifty years' time you will be decrepit, dragging yourself around. As for women, they may be blooming and beautiful now, but think what they'll be like in forty years time: withered old crones!' If you systematically go through the whole of life in this way, you might convince people of the imperfections of the conditioned and make them rather cynical, but you're not very likely to inspire them to follow the spiritual path. People need to be inspired rather than disillusioned; this is what it comes down to. Nyanaponika seems to work more on disillusioning people, but for Buddhism to succeed in the West, we need to be able to inspire people with a positive ideal, so that they get away from the conditioned by natural stages, as it were.

STHIRAMATI: It's like the path is the inspiration as well. The inspiration is the other half of it. You're not really showing them a path by talking exclusively in terms of disillusionment.

SANGHARAKSHITA: No, you're not.

LOKAMITRA: I feel that there is something rather sick about this sort of approach, which I think is the approach behind the so-called *vipassanā* teaching, though that teaching seems to have got a bit more positive recently. Maybe I'm not the one to say this, but it seemed to me that it quite perverted the Buddha's teaching.

SANGHARAKSHITA: If you do adopt this 'disillusioned' approach, what is it that you've got to be careful of?

GRAHAM: Nihilism.

SANGHARAKSHITA: Nihilism, yes. You're confusing disillusionment with simple disgruntlement. Sometimes you get people adopting this sort of attitude, not because they've really seen through conditioned existence but because they're dissatisfied and disgruntled and they've got a grudge against life, as it were, and want to run it down. It's not because they've seen in a spiritual sense at all. According to the Buddha's teaching, if you really see what human beings are like, then you'll see even the most attractive woman as a walking skeleton. But if you've been unsuccessful in your particular courtship and you start saying, 'Oh well, women are just bags of bones,' that isn't the result of your insight: it's just a result of your disappointment. You can adopt this disgruntled sort of attitude with regard to life as a whole. You haven't really seen through it; you're just disappointed because you haven't been able to get out of it what you wanted, and that is quite a different thing. I think that behind this so-called *vipassanā* as currently taught there's a lot of disgruntlement, not actual disillusionment.

LOKAMITRA: What I felt was that people's growth was being stunted and inhibited: that was the major effect.

KULARATNA: Disillusionment is quite a positive thing. You're losing illusion, and showing your real emotions.

SANGHARAKSHITA: But disgruntlement isn't positive at all: it's an expression of resentment. You could even say that this sort of approach on the part of the followers of the pseudo-*vipassanā* is in fact an approach of refined resentment, which explains why they play down the element of devotion and why they're not very happy about things like pujas – because how can you really get into those if you're in a state of resentment and disgruntlement? For those you need positive emotion. You need inspiration.

RAY: I'm wondering if this is partly due to historical reasons. Today perhaps people need a very positive approach – there are so many potentially threatening things going on – whereas in the Buddha's time …

SANGHARAKSHITA: Yes. In the Buddha's time I'm sure people were emotionally very healthy, so that if one adopted this approach of disillusioning people, they took it in a very healthy way, because they weren't disgruntled, so this sort of approach could be very inspiring to them. But it wouldn't be inspiring to most people in the West nowadays, I think, even if it were put across genuinely, and still less if it was put across in a purely academic or cynical way.

LOKAMITRA: Another thing. The teachings as we've got them in the Pāli canon are just one aspect of the whole situation. You'd see all the Buddha's disciples around. You'd see them communicating.

SANGHARAKSHITA: You'd see them very happy and joyful. As the *Dhammapada* says, 'Happily we live!'[217]

LOKAMITRA: And then the teaching would be the final 'lift up', as it were.

SANGHARAKSHITA: So it's not that what Nyanaponika says here isn't true. It's absolutely true, but the emphasis on this sort of approach is only one possible emphasis. There is the other approach that one must also bear in mind, the one represented by the more *saddhānusārin* approach. Disillusionment can very easily be confused with disgruntlement, and then, instead of disillusioning people you just make them disgruntled. I think we can sum up the points we have been making by saying that it's both more effective and intrinsically better to try to draw people into the spiritual life rather than to drive them into it.

SAGARAMATI: That means you must have something attractive.

SANGHARAKSHITA: Right. It needs to be something genuinely attractive. It mustn't be just a little gimmick: it must be the real thing that they're shown as really attractive.

> But, granting its necessity, does a refuge from the world's ills actually exist? The Buddhist affirms it and proves by that affirmation to be anything but a pessimist. The refuge to which he turns his steps is the triad of the Buddha, his Doctrine, and the Fraternity of holy disciples. Being what is most precious and most pure, it has been called 'The Triple Gem'. But the fact that it provides the final refuge, and not only a temporary shelter, cannot

otherwise be proved than through the actual attainment of that refuge by those who are going to it. (p. 12)

SANGHARAKSHITA: Here one is continuing the *dhammānusārin* approach. You've seen the unsatisfactoriness of the conditioned and you're looking for an alternative to that, a refuge from that. In the case of the *saddhānusārin* you see the refuge first, before the unsatisfactoriness: you see it to begin with, maybe by accident. In the case of the *saddhānusārin* it may be that, rightly or wrongly, you're quite happy in the world, you're having quite a good time, you're quite enjoying yourself, but then in some strange way you come into contact with Buddhism and you think, 'Well, this is even better!' You're not *looking* for a refuge because you don't feel the need for one, but you encounter the refuge nonetheless – perhaps as a result of good karma committed in the past, we don't know – and when you encounter it you're naturally, almost instinctively, drawn to it. In the case of some people it seems to happen like this. They haven't been thoroughly disillusioned, or been driven to desperation by all the painful, traumatic experiences of life. They have had a quite happy, healthy, wholesome, carefree existence, and would have been quite happy going on with it, but it so happens that they encounter Buddhism and feel, 'Here is something even better!' Or perhaps it seems to be the next step for them to take, the next stage in more or less the direction they were going in already.

So the explanation here holds good only for the person who has been disillusioned, who sees the need for a refuge and has started looking for one. In the case of the person with the more devotional, more emotional, more aesthetic approach, he may have found his refuge, paradoxically, even before he felt the need of any refuge. It's like when you're young and you start reading. To begin with you read anything you can lay your hands on – if you're a reader at all, that is – any grubby comic, or cheap novel, or dictionary. But one day, by sheer chance, you happen to read some Shakespeare or Milton, and you think, 'Well, this is ten times, a hundred times, better', and then you go on reading that sort of thing and give up reading your grubby comics. But it's not that you get so fed up with the comics that you start thinking, 'Where can I find a refuge from this sort of stuff? Where can I find a better kind of literature?' It doesn't usually happen like that, does it? Just by accident you stumble upon something better.

All at once you see, you feel, how much better it is. You were quite happy with your comics, so long as you didn't encounter Shakespeare; but having encountered Shakespeare you find he has the same human interest, but so much better! The same imagination, but so much greater! From then on you're sold on Shakespeare, and you give up the comics. For many people Going for Refuge is much the same. Going to parties was all right. Having a good time, earning money, making a living – it was all fine. But when you come into contact with the Dharma you think, 'Well, how much better!' It's not that you're violently disillusioned and then go in search of the Dharma. I think this is the experience of many people. Some people are disillusioned. They have a really painful life. They're looking for some kind of refuge, some sort of way out, some sort of cure, even. But I think that such people are likely to be quite a small minority among the kind of people who come along to us in the West, so we've got to attract, draw, and fascinate people, not point out to them the miseries of *saṃsāra*. They'll see those for themselves – maybe not see them as miseries but see them as not especially attractive.

LOKAMITRA: You have to have both, don't you? You can't have someone who is disillusioned Going for Refuge without having a positive attraction towards…

SANGHARAKSHITA: Although what Nyanaponika says almost implies that you can. I think you can't. Otherwise, as I said, you're like the man who's walking backwards away from *saṃsāra*. If you're just walking backwards you might go in the wrong direction, whereas if you fix your eye on a goal in the distance and move towards it you're moving away but at the same time you're also moving towards.

LOKAMITRA: I would have thought that disillusionment is quite common among people who come along to FWBO centres.

SANGHARAKSHITA: I would call it disgruntlement. My impression is that there isn't much genuine disillusionment around. People would like to have plenty of money if they could get it, but most of them haven't been able to. That's much more like disgruntlement than disillusionment.

MAHAMATI: Some people who go to centres could easily get side-tracked because they think there's pleasure in the spiritual life, and may go after that – and maybe there isn't complete disillusionment.

SANGHARAKSHITA: I think that if you are really progressing spiritually, then when you look at mundane things you will be disillusioned. You will see right through them. But if you're thinking of your spiritual life in more positive terms and travelling towards an attractive goal, you won't be thinking all that much about the mundane anyway. When you do happen to think about it or look towards it, yes, you will see through it: that will be the disillusionment. But your spiritual life won't consist in a constant preoccupation with the mundane even by way of seeing through it.

RATNAVIRA: So you're not actually engaging with the conditioned very much at all. Your attraction to it just falls away, very much as a sort of side track.

SANGHARAKSHITA: The danger is, and there *is* a danger, that your preoccupation with the Unconditioned is purely theoretical. But this is where the emotional or devotional element has to come in. There must be that genuine devotion to the Unconditioned, otherwise you'll just be disgruntled as regards the mundane and have a purely theoretical preoccupation with the Transcendental which is the sort of situation that you find some people in. That is their Buddhism. I think this is the position of some of these '*vipassanā*' people: disgruntled with the mundane and preoccupying themselves in a purely theoretical way with the Transcendental.

ANANDAJYOTI: If they only see one side of the insight, they don't see the beauty side. They only see that conditioned things are insubstantial, instead of trying to develop also insight to the Unconditioned.

SANGHARAKSHITA: I think I'd go so far as to say that it's very doubtful whether one can really see through the conditioned without some glimpse of the Unconditioned.

LOKAMITRA: But they seem to leave that out entirely.

SANGHARAKSHITA: To look after itself, as it were. But as a method of approach that simply doesn't work.

LOKAMITRA: So if the doctrine-follower approach was followed through properly, it would include this more positive approach.

SANGHARAKSHITA: Oh yes. I've been using the expression 'doctrine-follower' rather loosely. You could say, if you liked, that the doctrine-follower is attracted more by intellectual beauty, whereas the faith-follower is attracted more by sensuous beauty. The mathematicians tell us that there's a very ethereal beauty in mathematical equations which absolutely fascinates them.

### How The Three Jewels Become The Three Refuges

> The Triple Gem has objective existence as an impersonal idea or ideal as long as it is known and cherished, in so far it is doubtlessly a still persisting and active source of energy for the world. But it is transformed from an impersonal idea to a personal refuge only to the extent of its being realized in one's own mind and manifested in one's own life. Therefore the existence of the Triple Gem in its characteristic nature as a refuge cannot be proved to others than those who find this refuge in themselves by their own efforts. (p. 12)

SANGHARAKSHITA: Is this clear? 'The Triple Gem has objective existence', that is to say, there is a Buddha, a Dharma, and a Sangha 'out there', 'as an impersonal idea or ideal as long as it is known and cherished'. It isn't quite clear, actually, is it? The Buddha surely exists even if he isn't known and cherished, and so does the Dharma, and the Sangha, but not as a refuge. But the text doesn't clearly say that. Yes, the Three Jewels exist objectively, but they become refuges only as a result of your personal attitude towards them. They're not refuges in themselves. They're jewels in themselves, you could say, but not refuges in themselves. The Three Jewels become the Three Refuges only when you make them such by Going for Refuge. When you go for Refuge to the Three Jewels, the Three Jewels become the Three Refuges for you. He rightly goes on to say, 'But it is transformed from an impersonal idea to a personal refuge only to the extent of its being realized in one's own mind and manifested in one's own life.' This is perfectly true.

'Therefore the existence of the Triple Gem in its characteristic nature as a refuge cannot be proved to others than those who find this refuge in themselves by their own efforts.' This is quite important. You can talk about the Three Jewels to others who haven't gone for Refuge, and they can understand what you mean, but you can hardly talk about the Three Refuges. *That* they must know from their own experience. You can talk only in a very provisional way about Going for Refuge or, to use the term that we often use, about commitment, but you can't fully explain to people what commitment is. It's something they have to experience for themselves. You can explain the framework within which the commitment takes place, but you can't communicate very much about the commitment itself. This is why one finds, I think, that so many books 'about' Buddhism have an air of unreality. The facts are all there, the dates are all there, and there are explanations of the teachings, but you feel, 'This is not the Buddhism that I'm in touch with. This is not the Buddhism that I'm trying to practise.' Why? There's no feeling of Refuge pervading the whole thing. The author has not gone for Refuge, and that makes a tremendous difference. The facts are there, but the most important fact of all is not. All the information is there, but there is no understanding. You recognize everything – it's the same four noble truths, the same conditioned co-production, the same four *dhyānas*, the same doctrine of *śūnyatā* – but it seems completely unreal. It doesn't seem to be what you're concerned with in the least. It doesn't seem to be Buddhism. You recognize it but it's like a complete stranger. There's no commitment.

There is this expression, 'In so far it is doubtlessly a still persisting and active source of energy for the world', and Nyanaponika here comes a bit closer to the idea of inspiration, but he doesn't quite make it. Yes, the Buddha, Dharma, and Sangha are sources of spiritual energy and inspiration for the world, but this needs to be insisted upon much more. It's when one starts responding to that, even without being disillusioned with mundane existence, that one starts Going for Refuge – in the case of some people at least. One goes for Refuge because one feels so drawn by that energy, so inspired by it.

Reflecting on what we have considered so far, it seems that if you try to approach the spiritual life simply by way of disillusionment, you lose sight of what the spiritual life essentially is, or at least lose sight of something that was brought out much more clearly in the case of the approach through faith and devotion: the spiritual life as essentially a process of growth. In the case of the Theravāda that has been lost sight of mainly because of their truncated conception of conditioned co-production, which leaves out what I call the positive *nidānas*: in dependence upon suffering arises faith, in dependence upon faith arises joy, and so on. There are various versions of this process in the Pāli canon – the seven *bojjhaṅgas* are a version of it – but the series of the positive *nidānas* and the progressive, spiral principle which this series exemplifies tends to be lost sight of. One thinks of the spiritual life only in terms of a process of cessation, or in terms of the series of negative *nidānas*, not in terms of the progressive uprising of the series of positive *nidānas*, so one loses sight of the Buddhist conception of the spiritual life as a process of growth and development.

You may remember that at the very beginning of his career the Buddha saw living beings as like a bed of lotus flowers in different stages of development, and this really strikes the keynote.[218] But what is it – to pursue the analogy further – that makes the flower grow? What does it grow towards?

A VOICE: The sun.

SANGHARAKSHITA: The sun. So you are not to imagine the flower as trying to get away from the soil. The flower doesn't think, 'I want to get as far away as possible from this nasty soil, and all this manure and muck that has been put about my roots.' The flower is simply trying to get nearer and nearer to the sun, and in the process it does in fact leave the soil further and further behind. It's as though the Theravādins see the growth of the spiritual path almost exclusively in terms of the plant getting away from the soil in which it grows, or even trying to uproot itself. They do not see it in terms of the plant trying to grow towards the sun. The sun is lost sight of altogether, and that seems to be the great weakness of that particular approach.

VAIROCANA: Does this mean that a person who is walking backwards must sooner or later have to turn round and walk forwards?

SANGHARAKSHITA: I expressed that by saying that sooner or later you bump into the Unconditioned, as it were. So, yes, you might have to turn round if you are genuinely disillusioned and genuinely walking backwards away from the conditioned, because – to continue the analogy – you might not go in the right direction. You might be walking away backwards but bump into some other aspect of the conditioned. Instead of going straight up from the earth like that [raises hand], you might curve round [hand describes curve] and bump into some other less obvious aspect of the conditioned, because after all the conditioned is all the time exerting its gravitational pull.

> The refuge becomes and grows by the process of going to it. (p. 12)

That's very well put. It grows by your own process of committing yourself personally to the Three Jewels. To the extent that you commit yourself to the Three Jewels, to that extent the Three Jewels become, for you, the Three Refuges.

> By effort, earnestness and self-control
> Let the wise man make for himself an island
> Which no flood can overwhelm.[219]

> The refuge exists for us only in so far as something within ourselves responds and corresponds to it. Therefore the Sixth Zen Patriarch said: 'Let each one of us take refuge to the Three Gems within our mind!'[220] (p. 12)

The *Dhammapada* quotation illustrates this little aphorism, as one might call it, that 'The refuge becomes and grows by the process of going to it.' 'By effort, earnestness, and self-control' – and we had better add mindfulness – 'Let the wise man make for himself an island which no flood can overwhelm.' You make the Three Jewels into a refuge – into an island – by your own effort. Also, 'The refuge exists for us only in so far as something within ourselves responds and corresponds to it.' He's getting a little closer to the Mahāyāna position, though very cautiously, and he quotes the Sixth Zen Patriarch as saying, 'Let each one of us take refuge to the Three Gems within our mind!' How literally can we take that? Are the Three Refuges really in our own minds? Are they purely subjective? In which mind are they, anyway? Don't take it for gospel just because the Sixth Zen Patriarch is supposed to have said it. After all, we've been a bit critical as regards the whole Theravāda, so don't let's be credulous as regards Zen. 'Let each one of us take refuge to the Three Gems within our mind!' Surely the Three Gems are outside our minds? Surely that's the whole purpose of them – to be something outside ourselves, something that we go out towards. Or is there an ambiguity here?

KULANANDA: We take Refuge to the extent that they are within our minds.

SANGHARAKSHITA: Well, you could say that the Going for Refuge is within our mind – not in the sense, though, that it's purely mental and not emotional as well – but surely the Refuges themselves remain outside our minds. We're Going for Refuge to the Buddha – is the Buddha inside our own mind? If so, which mind? Do we see him?

RAY: Is it to our higher self, as it were, to what we are potentially?

SANGHARAKSHITA: You could put it that way. As I said earlier on, the Mahāyāna view is that the seed of Enlightenment is within us. Therefore the seeds of the Buddha, Dharma, and Sangha are within us. So your Going for Refuge could be explained as your watering and nourishing of those seeds within yourself so that gradually they grow into the fully developed Buddha, Dharma, and Sangha. But to the extent that you identify yourself with your ordinary mind, to that extent the Three Jewels in their full developed form are outside you, not inside you. So far as your present experience is concerned, they're in your own mind only in a very germinal fashion. You could say that they are within you on some deeper level – that deeper level also being your own mind in some deeper sense – but you have to be very careful not to use that sort of expression in a slick, sophisticated way as if to suggest that they're all there in one's own mind already and that one therefore does not have to do anything about it by way of spiritual practice – which is the way some people in the West take these Zen sayings. 'Let each one of us take refuge to the Three Gems within our mind' really means, one could say, let each of us develop within ourselves, from a seed form into a fully developed form, those potentialities which are the Three Jewels. Going for Refuge means developing our potentialities for Enlightenment.

This passage stresses the subjective side more than what had been said previously did. It's true that you could not go for Refuge unless you had some affinity for the Refuge, which again brings us back to the Mahāyāna point of view. Unless you are a potential Buddha you cannot be an actual Buddha. Only a potential Buddha can go for Refuge to the Buddha – that is, to the actual Buddha. And this is why Nyanaponika himself says, 'the refuge exists for us only in so far as something within ourselves responds and corresponds to it.' This is very true.

LOKAMITRA: Could you say that the Jewels would be the external aspect and the Refuges the internal aspect, referring to what you said earlier about the Three Jewels?

SANGHARAKSHITA: Yes. The Refuge, you could say, is entirely within yourself because the Three Jewels become the Refuge for you on account of your particular attitude towards them. The aspect of Refuge is the subjective aspect, and so, by the act of your Going for Refuge, you make the Three Jewels, jewels for you – that is to say, you make yourself into the Three Jewels.

KULANANDA: So you could say that we don't really go for Refuge, but rather that we begin to go for Refuge.

SANGHARAKSHITA: We begin to go for Refuge, yes. This brings up the point that the Going for Refuge is not something that you do once and for all, but a continuing process and, in the case of the mundane Going for Refuge, a process that can come to a halt at any moment, if you aren't careful. So let's not take the Sixth Zen Patriarch's statement too much as a matter of course. The Three Gems are not within our own minds as yet except in a very potential form, but they come to be more and more within our own minds, or we ourselves become more and more transformed into the Three Gems, by virtue of our Going for Refuge to them as perceived outside ourselves, or as though outside ourselves.

> With regard to the first refuge, in the Buddha, the Master himself said, shortly after his Enlightenment:

> 'Like me the conquerors will be
> Who have attained to the defilements' end.'[221] (p. 13)

'Conquerors' here translates Jinas, which is a synonym for Buddhas. So 'These Buddhas who have attained to the end of all defilements' – that is, all *kleśas*, all negative emotional states, all impurities – 'will *be* like me.' This suggests that by the process of Going for Refuge to the Buddha you gradually transform yourself into a Buddha: the aim of your Going for Refuge is that you yourself should become like a Buddha, or be a Buddha. The process of Going for Refuge is a means by which you transform your own potential Buddhahood into actual Buddhahood – though, as I've said before (I think in the seminar on the *Sūtra of Huineng*), we have to be really careful how we use this language of potentiality, saying that we are potentially Buddhas and so on.[222] Yes, in principle we are Buddhas – very much in the abstract – but we shouldn't allow that fact to distract us from the task of actualizing that in practice – and certainly one might say that some Mahāyāna Buddhists have allowed themselves to be distracted in that way.

> Concerning the second refuge, in the Dhamma, the Buddha said shortly before his decease:
>
> 'Be ye islands unto yourselves, be ye a refuge unto yourselves! Take no other refuge! The Dhamma be your island, the Dhamma be your refuge; take no other refuge!'[223]
>
> In the commentarial literature it is said (in reference to another passage, but applicable to the one just quoted):
>
> 'The Dhamma is called "self" (*attā*), because, in the case of a wise one, the Dhamma is not different from himself and because it pertains to his personal existence.' (p. 13)

The explanation is necessary because there seems to be a contradiction. The Buddha is represented as saying, 'Be ye islands unto yourselves, be ye a refuge unto yourselves!' But also, 'Let the Dhamma be your island, let the Dhamma be your Refuge!' That seems contradictory, doesn't it? – that you should take Refuge in yourself and also take Refuge in the Dharma. The commentary resolves the contradiction in this way: 'The Dhamma is called 'self' (*attā*), because, in the case of a wise one, the Dhamma is not different from himself and because it pertains to his personal existence.' In other words, in the case of a wise person – one who truly understands, who has insight – what was objective has become subjective, and what was the Dharma 'out there' has become the Dharma 'in here'. The Dharma has been realized, and to that extent he has become one with the Dharma. In Going for Refuge to the Dharma he goes for Refuge to himself; or, to the extent that he has realized the Dharma, when he goes for Refuge to himself, to that extent he goes for Refuge to the Dharma. This is why when you become a Buddha – when you become Enlightened – you don't go for Refuge to anyone or anything outside yourself, because you yourself are the Refuge: you are at one with the Refuge. The one who goes for Refuge and the one who *is* the Refuge coincide.

So when the Buddha says 'go for Refuge to the Dhamma, go for Refuge to yourself', he is suggesting that Going for Refuge to the Dharma is effective, or is truly a Refuge, only to the extent that it is a personal experience. Your *really* Going for Refuge to the Dharma is a Going for Refuge to yourself. So long as you are Going for Refuge to the Dharma and not Going for Refuge to yourself, you are not Going for Refuge to the Dharma. But when you're Going for Refuge to yourself, to the extent that you have realized the Dharma, to that extent you are Going for Refuge to the Dharma.

So you go for Refuge to the Dharma and also to yourself. Then the objective side is there, and the subjective side is there too. The Dharma is not simply an idea existing within your own mind in the sense of your own limited consciousness. It is an objective reality, a transcendental reality existing 'out there', so you have to go for Refuge to that. That's the objective side. But the act of Going for Refuge also consists in your actually experiencing the Dharma, in the Dharma becoming part of you, in you yourself becoming transmuted into the Transcendental. This is the subjective aspect. Both aspects must be there, because in the ultimate analysis Dharma transcends the distinction between subject and object. There has to be an objective approach and a subjective approach, so that you get 'to' that which is neither subject nor object.

> The third refuge, the Sangha, being the community of holy disciples, is the great and inspiring model for emulation. The actual foundation of that refuge is the capacity inherent in all beings to become one of the Eight Noble Beings who form the Sangha of the refuge.

The Sangha, the object of the third refuge, is 'the community of holy disciples'. In the Hīnayāna or Theravāda context the community is explained as consisting of the two kinds of *arhant*, the two kinds of non-returner, the two kinds of once-returner, and the two kinds of Stream Entrant. In the Mahāyāna it includes the bodhisattvas too, but essentially the Sangha in this sense of the Āryasaṅgha is the community of all those with at least some personal experience of the transcendental path. They are the sources of true inspiration and guidance. Once again he refers to the fact that 'the actual foundation of that refuge,' i.e. the Refuge of the Sangha, 'is the capacity inherent in all beings to become one of the Eight Noble Beings who form the Sangha of the refuge', i.e. to become either *arhant* or non-returner and so on. In the case of the Mahāyāna, of course, they attach importance only to the capacity or potentiality to become a fully Enlightened, perfect Buddha. Arhantship and so on are regarded as lower ideals. You're able to go for Refuge to the Buddha only because you are able to become a Buddha yourself. You're able to go for Refuge to the Dharma only because you're capable of being transformed into the Dharma. In the same way you're able to go for Refuge to the Sangha only because it is possible for you too to be a member of the Sangha.

He rightly says that the Sangha in the sense of the Āryasaṅgha 'is the great and inspiring model for emulation', but I'm afraid that in the Theravāda this ideal of spiritual fellowship remains rather a dead letter. The Āryasaṅgha is pretty remote for most Theravādin Buddhists, because some of them – if not all of them, in Ceylon, say – believe that the age of the *arhants* is past, so that you have only non-*āryas* and there's no real source of inspiration around any more. But the Mahāyānists don't see it like that at all. Even on a lower level, the modern Theravāda perhaps doesn't appreciate sufficiently what the Buddha himself said about the indispensability of *kalyāṇa mitratā* for individual spiritual development. In the Theravāda they tend to think much more in terms of a monastic order, which they do not believe is an Āryasaṅgha, and an almost blindly obedient laity. But the truth is that there is always spiritual fellowship among those who are trying to follow the spiritual path and to grow and develop. In the Theravāda, the idea of that sort of spiritual fellowship isn't very strong. There may be a great deal of warmth and kindliness and so on, but it seems to pertain much more to the group than to the spiritual community.

The Mahāyāna text *The Jewel Ornament of Liberation* points out that though the Buddha is a *kalyāṇa mitra*, in fact *the kalyāṇa mitra*, and though the great bodhisattvas are *kalyāṇa mitras*, so far as ordinary human beings are concerned the best *kalyāṇa mitra* is just another ordinary human being who helps you at the right time with a few words of friendly advice.[224] This is what *kalyāṇa mitratā* means for most people. Forget about Buddhas and bodhisattvas and *arhants* and so on; you probably wouldn't recognize them if you met them. What you need is contact with someone who can help you onto the next stage of your development. It's *kalyāṇa mitratā* in this basic, elementary sense that is of practical importance. Clearly the spiritual community in this sense will be important for you and relevant to you only if you are actually trying to develop, otherwise you'll be quite content to keep a purely imaginary Āryasaṅgha around as a remote object of worship, without its implying or involving any direct personal contact. When the modern Theravādin thinks of the Āryasaṅgha, he doesn't think of anyone with whom he's in actual contact – he thinks of Sāriputta, Moggallāna, Ānanda, and the Buddha's other disciples, who lived 2,500 years ago. No doubt their example can be quite inspiring, but if you yourself want to develop you need something more than that, you need actual, almost physical contact with people who are more advanced than you are and who can inspire you and give you some guidance; this is what *kalyāṇa mitratā* means for you. But this isn't stressed very much in the modern Theravāda.

LOKAMITRA: Very often they don't think so much of the community, but of the isolated individuals who have attained to that state of arhantship, so in a way it's not really the Sangha they are Going for Refuge to but…

SANGHARAKSHITA: A collection of isolated individuals.

LOKAMITRA: Exactly.

SANGHARAKSHITA: So it's not the community, it's not the communication that takes place on that level. Even if, in countries like Thailand or Burma, one does hear of someone who is believed to be an *arhant*, he's usually reported to be living in the depths of some forest all by himself and hardly anybody has ever seen him. There's not a whole community living together and being in contact with other people. What seems to be missing in the case of the Theravāda conception of the Āryasaṅgha – as in the case of the whole Theravāda conception of growth – is a series of intermediate links so that each person is in contact with the next link, the next stage upon the spiritual path – and that's all that you need for the time being.

LOKAMITRA: It's a totally open situation. It will take you as far as you need to go: to Buddhahood.

## Changing the Terms of the Problem

> We turn now to the third subject of the knowledge implied in taking refuge, i.e. to the ultimate nature of the threefold refuge.
>
> We have seen that the refuge becomes attainable and even perceptible only by way of the living roots, by the actual foundations it has within the average mind. Like the lotus it arises within the waters of worldly existence; there it develops and from there it takes its nourishment. But what is still immersed in the ocean of worldliness and suffering cannot be the ultimate refuge, the place of safety and bliss. It must not only assuage, but finally transcend the world of danger, fear and ill, like the lotus that rises above the surface of the water and remains unsullied by it. Therefore the consummate refuge meant in the traditional formula is of supramundane nature, *lokuttara*, i.e. world-transcending. (pp. 13–14)

SANGHARAKSHITA: This is quite an important point. What is really being said is that the Refuge cannot be just remedial. It cannot be something which simply makes conditions in the *saṃsāra* a bit better, or just bearable. It must be something that enables you to transcend them altogether. The approach here is still that of disillusionment, but from that point of view what he says is quite valid. A Refuge is not something that provides you with an amelioration of existing conditions. A Refuge is something which in a way changes the terms of the problem. To put it into contemporary language, one could say that some kind of adjustment therapy can't be a Refuge. It's not enough that you should be helped to happily adjust to the *saṃsāra*, however successfully. You should be enabled to go beyond it altogether. Again, the approach is that of disillusionment.

GRAHAM: Sometimes I wonder if that's the case with Transcendental Meditation. They do try to make you live with the present situation.

SANGHARAKSHITA: Yes, it's a bit misleading that they call a particular technique of meditation 'transcendental', though in their own practice their experience of meditation itself may well be so, for all we know, but they certainly do seem to encourage people to adjust to the existing state of affairs rather than to transform it. I believe they're practising Transcendental Meditation in the Pentagon!

The point that Nyanaponika is making is that if one is disillusioned with conditioned existence – if one wants to *escape* from conditioned existence – one can do that only by having recourse to a Refuge which is not itself part of the conditioned, not itself mundane, in other words which is transcendental. This is a very important point. It is the whole difference between the psychological, however refined, and what we'd call the spiritual in the stricter sense, i.e. the transcendental. It's not enough to adjust to the world and get by. You have to go beyond it into another dimension altogether, which would result in a radical change in your whole way of life.

> Consequently, the first refuge is not the recluse Gotama, but the Buddha as the personification of world-transcending Enlightenment (*bodhi*). In the *Vīmaṃsaka Sutta* it is said of the Noble Disciple: 'He believes in the Enlightenment of the Exalted One.'[225]

SANGHARAKSHITA: All right, let's think about that. 'The first refuge is not the recluse Gotama' (*samaṇa* Gotama, the historical person, that is to say) 'but the Buddha as the personification of world-transcending

Enlightenment (*bodhi*).' The implication is that you can distinguish between the two, but do you think you can? When you go for Refuge, is it that you go for Refuge not to the *samaṇa* Gotama but to the Buddha? Is that a valid distinction? There are texts where the disciple says, 'I go for Refuge to *Gotama* Buddha',[226] but leaving that aside for the moment, is it correct to distinguish between Going for Refuge to the *samaṇa* Gotama and Going for Refuge to the Buddha as Buddha? Do you in fact know the Buddha apart from Gotama the Buddha or others who, historically speaking, have gained Enlightenment? How do you know that there is such a thing as Buddhahood? Have you reasoned yourself into it, or do you know of its existence through historical personages who have been, or who are, Enlightened? What does it mean to say that the first Refuge is not the recluse Gotama, but the Buddha? Can you really separate the two? When Gotama became Enlightened, was there a sort of split, so that you could say that on this side it's Gotama and on that side it's the Buddha, and I go for Refuge to that side but not this side, to the Buddha but not to Gotama?

SAGARAMATI: It depends on how you see Gotama, doesn't it?

SANGHARAKSHITA: In what way?

SAGARAMATI: Well, take the time when he made the mistake of teaching those monks to meditate on death and they committed suicide.[227] It's not that aspect that you go for Refuge to. You don't go for Refuge to his ordinary mind or the way he treats you.

SANGHARAKSHITA: But what you go for Refuge to is surely still Gotama. Surely Buddhahood is not something grafted onto the Gotama bit, as it were, without any essential connection with it. In other words, if the recluse Gotama and the Buddha could really be separated it would not be meaningful to speak of anybody gaining Enlightenment, or of Gotama gaining Enlightenment. I think that here Nyanaponika, like other Theravāda writers, is being over cautious and trying to dissociate himself a bit too sharply from historicity. You do go for Refuge to Gotama the Buddha, according to some texts, but you don't go for Refuge to the accidents of his historicity: perhaps one could put it that way. The Buddha is an Enlightened human being. You don't go for

Refuge to the Enlightenment only. You go for Refuge to the Enlightened humanity, because the Enlightenment has been realized by a concrete, living, individual human being, and that's what you want to be, not some abstract Enlightenment but an Enlightened human being. And when you are Enlightened, that's what you'll be – an Enlightened human being. So even if 'the first refuge is not the recluse Gotama' it must at least be a human being. Besides, 'Buddha' means an Enlightened human being, so there doesn't seem to be much basis to the distinction between the recluse Gotama and the Buddha. The distinction seems to be rather unreal. Saying 'Consequently, the first refuge is not the recluse Gotama, but the Buddha' is really saying 'Consequently the first refuge is not the human being called Gotama who happens to be a *samaṇa*, but an Enlightened human being.' The only sense one can make of Nyanaponika's statement is that one should not attach too much importance to the historical accidents of the Buddha's career – to the fact that he was a *samaṇa* (in another kind of situation, he might just as well have been a non-*samaṇa*), or that he was an Indian, or that he lived 2,500 years ago. What you must attach importance to is the fact that he was a human being, because the Buddha is an Enlightened human being, and this is what you want to be.[228]

VAIROCANA: In Tibet, don't they put up a poster of Padmasambhava rather than the Buddha? As long as you've got somebody that has attained Enlightenment then that's okay, because it doesn't make any difference if it's Gotama or anyone else.

SANGHARAKSHITA: It doesn't matter which human being it is, so long as it is a human being. This is not what Nyanaponika says, and as a Theravādin he might not be too happy with Padmasambhava. But the Refuge has to be specific. It can't be abstract and general.

SAGARAMATI: But isn't it possible to go for Refuge to, say, somebody like Mañjughoṣa? I wouldn't see Mañjughoṣa as an Enlightened human being – I certainly wouldn't look at it like that.

SANGHARAKSHITA: Well, even a bodhisattva, one might say, is a human being.

LOKAMITRA: An Enlightened state of being, could you say that?

SAGARAMATI: But that would be in you.

SANGHARAKSHITA: Your personal objective, presumably, is to be an Enlightened human being. So if what is potential in you is actual in the object of Refuge, your object of Refuge, inasmuch as you want to be an Enlightened human being, must be an Enlightened human being. Otherwise it cannot be an object of Refuge for you. The Refuge represents what you want to become and what you are able to become.

SAGARAMATI: I always see it as something existing completely outside any sphere of being, whether human or otherwise.

SANGHARAKSHITA: This is true, but then, again, there is the question of the distinction between the conditioned and the Unconditioned. If in fact *śūnyatā* is *rūpa* and *rūpa* is *śūnyatā*, when you attain *śūnyatā* you still have *rūpa*. That *rūpa* may be that of a human being, or of a *deva*, or of a bodhisattva, but there will be a *rūpa*. It's not that you attain a one-sided, as it were abstract, *śūnyatā*. So if you wish to be an Enlightened *human* being, then you can go for Refuge only to an Enlightened human being, but if you just want to be an Enlightened *being*, then you may go for Refuge to an Enlightened human being, or a Enlightened bodhisattva, or an Enlightened god, if there is such a thing in Buddhism. So perhaps one should amend the phrase 'human being' and just say 'being', Enlightened being.

The point is that Enlightenment must by definition be embodied in some form of sentient existence, and as we ourselves are human beings at present we therefore think of our object of Refuge as an Enlightened human being. But if we are aware that there are other possibilities of existence – even post-Enlightenment existence – other than human, then we can express that realization by saying that the object of our Going for Refuge is an Enlightened being – not necessarily even an Enlightened human being.

LOKAMITRA: How would this fit in – that you attain Enlightenment at the point of death, in the *bardo* state?

SANGHARAKSHITA: It depends on your view of the *bardo* state. You could say that in the *bardo* state you're in a sort of heavenly state. If you were to attain Enlightenment in that state then you'd be an Enlightened god, in a subtle form of existence. You'd be a sort of *gandharva* – a sort of Enlightened god like the beings in Sukhāvatī, who are 'Enlightened gods' or gods on the way to Enlightenment.

LOKAMITRA: So you're always in a state of being.

SANGHARAKSHITA: Yes, as far as I can see, whether Enlightened or unenlightened, you're always in a state of being. This is quite an important point, but one which is not brought up explicitly, so far as I know, by any writer on Buddhism. It's been overlooked entirely – but it should not be overlooked, since otherwise there is one-sidedness.

SAGARAMATI: But that doesn't fit in. I mean you've got karma and *karma-vipāka*, but karma is equated with consciousness and that determines the being and the being is seen as the result of action, so it's identified with *vipāka*. When you're Enlightened you're not creating any *vipākas*, therefore there is no being.

SANGHARAKSHITA: That depends on the definition of being. According to the Mahāyāna the state of Enlightenment is a state of non-duality in which you no longer distinguish between conditioned and unconditioned, but if one wants to express that state of non-duality one can only express it in the language of duality. As an Enlightened being you are both conditioned and unconditioned, though at the same time neither conditioned nor unconditioned. To the extent that you are unconditioned you are Enlightened. To the extent that you are conditioned you are a being. In this sense there is being. At this level there is no question of time, therefore no question of conditionality – therefore no question of karma and no question of *vipāka*. So at this level the Enlightenment is not karma in the ordinary sense, nor is the being a *vipāka* in the ordinary sense. As I said, one is always a being, either in the *vipāka* sense or let us say in the '*sattva*' sense – i.e. as irreversible bodhisattva.

SAGARAMATI: But there is never any absolute Being.

SANGHARAKSHITA: There is never any absolute, abstract Being. One is always *a* being. The object of one's Refuge is therefore always a being, but an Enlightened being, whether human or non-human.

KULARATNA: What about the story of somebody who gained Enlightenment just as he died and Māra, seeking to find him, found no trace?[229]

SANGHARAKSHITA: He found no *vipāka*. Māra could not see the '*sattva*'. He could only see what was conditioned, not what was unconditioned, so he found no *vipāka*. The idea that upon bodily death the Buddha ceases to exist is specifically rejected. *Vipāka* ceases, anything mundane ceases, but cessation does not express the whole truth of the situation. On the other hand, it's not a question of anything unchanging continuing to exist in time, because that would involve a sort of abstraction. Thus one is always a being, either an Enlightened being or an unenlightened being.

Anyway, that's a bit metaphysical. Perhaps we'd better get back to the question of Gotama. If you're attracted to 'Gotama the Buddha' as an exotic, specifically Indian figure – or if you regard him as the ninth incarnation of the Hindu god Vishnu – then you are not attracted to him as Gotama the *Buddha*; you do not go for Refuge to the Buddha.

> The Dhamma of the second refuge is not the faint, fragmentary, or even distorted picture of the Doctrine as mirrored in the mind of an unliberated worldling (*puthujjana*). (p. 14)

It's very good to bear this in mind. As you know, Buddhism distinguishes between *āryas*, those with insight in the transcendental sense, and those without it, who were called *puthujjanas* or worldlings or ordinary people. The Dharma represents, in its ultimate nature, something transcendental, absolute, ultimately real. So in the mind of the worldling, who has not got any insight at all, really – any *transcendental* insight – there can only be a faint, fragmentary, and even distorted picture of that Dharma or Doctrine. (Maybe to call it 'Doctrine' here isn't very satisfactory.) First of all, your unenlightened mind – your mind which doesn't even have a spark of insight – sees the Dharma faintly. However well you may have studied it, however much you've read about it, you have only a very, very faint glimmer of the Dharma in your mind. Then, your picture of the Dharma is fragmentary: great chunks of it are missing. There are vast areas of which you know nothing whatever, not even theoretically. Finally, it's not only faint and fragmentary but distorted in accordance with your own particular emotional and mental condition. It's very good to bear this in mind: that so long as one has not developed any transcendental insight, one's understanding of the Dharma will at best be faint, fragmentary, and distorted – and that applies to all books about Buddhism written by unenlightened people. However good they may seem to be – however clear, however intellectual, however well-informed – they're faint, fragmentary, and distorted. So long as one is a *puthujjana*, at best one just has a glimpse of the Dharma. One can't possibly claim to have understood it.

> It is the supramundane Eightfold Path and its consummation in Nibbāna. (p. 14)

That's what the Dharma really is! But we mustn't understand it too scholastically. What is meant by 'the supramundane Eightfold Path and its consummation in Nibbāna'? It doesn't mean that there's a step one, and a step two, and a step three, and then finally there's the goal at the end of step eight. It means having a vision of a great stream of transcendental experiences and attainments flowing in the direction of what we can only call the Absolute. Not that we see the Absolute. We just see the stream disappearing over the horizon and posit the Absolute over the horizon. This is what seeing the Dharma really means: having a vivid, direct vision of the whole process of the Higher Evolution. This process is typified in the Supramundane Eightfold Path. In its broadest sense, the process of the Higher Evolution comprises both the mundane and the Supramundane Eightfold Path. The latter constitutes the Path of the Higher Evolution par excellence.

> The commentator underlines the supramundane nature of the second refuge by saying that the Dhamma as an object of learning (*pariyatti-dhamma*) is only in so far included in the refuge as it arises in the Holy Disciple together with the fruition of stream-entry etc., i.e. only in so far as it is a formulation of that consummate knowledge acquired on the four stages of sanctity. (p. 14)

'The Dhamma as an object of learning' is included in the Refuge, not in the sense of book-learning, but in the sense that it consists of what one learns from one's own transcendental experience. Perhaps I should say a word or two about the mundane and the supramundane Eightfold Path. It's not usually understood that the Eightfold Path as we usually encounter it in books, beginning with *samyak-dṛṣṭi*, is in fact the transcendental Eightfold Path. Step one doesn't really come first in most people's experience of the spiritual life. The *samyak-dṛṣṭi* of the supramundane or transcendental Eightfold Path is Perfect Vision, in the sense of an insight into the Transcendental, and the remaining seven steps represent the transformation of one's whole life in accordance with that transcendental vision. But there is also the subdivision of the path into *śīla*, *samādhi*, and *prajñā*. These stages are progressive. You start off with *śīla* or ethics, then you practise *samādhi* or meditation; as a result of practising meditation you develop insight, and that gives you *prajñā*. When the Eightfold Path is enumerated in the usual way the order is, in effect, changed. *Prajñā* (represented by *samyak-dṛṣṭi* together with *samyak-saṅkalpa*) comes first, *śīla* (represented by right speech, action, and livelihood) comes next, while *samādhi* (represented by effort, mindfulness, and concentration) comes last. Do you see this? When you subdivide the mundane Eightfold Path in accordance with the threefold division of *śīla*, *samādhi*, and *prajñā*, that means starting with right speech, action, and livelihood, proceeding to right effort, mindfulness, and concentration, and finishing with right intention and understanding.

People usually treat the transcendental path as though it were the mundane path, which makes nonsense of them both. Perfect Vision is not the first step of the mundane path, but the first step of the *transcendental* path. In terms of the threefold vision the first step of the mundane path is *śīla*, in other words right speech, right action, and right means of livelihood. When it is said that the Eightfold Path is a progressive path, i.e. progressing from *śīla* through *samādhi* to *prajñā*, this refers to the mundane path. Not understanding the distinction between the mundane path and the transcendental path, people try to practise the transcendental path as though it were the mundane path, which makes nonsense of their practice. Perfect Vision is degraded to mere intellectual understanding of the teaching. Do you see what I'm getting at? We really need a chart to illustrate this! Most Theravādins have forgotten, in practice, the distinction between the mundane Eightfold Path and the transcendental Eightfold Path. When they give a lecture on the Eightfold Path, therefore, they quite rightly start off with *samyak-dṛṣṭi* or Perfect Vision, but not understanding that this is Perfect Vision in the sense of insight into the Transcendental, and mistaking the Transcendental for the mundane and the mundane for the Transcendental, they will tell one that Perfect Vision or 'right view' as they call it, means a rational understanding of the Dharma and that this rational understanding is the basis on which you are to proceed. First you understand rationally, and then, in accordance with your rational understanding, you follow all the other steps. They don't explain that in following the transcendental Eightfold Path you first of all have a spiritual vision – a transcendental vision – and then transform your life in accordance with that vision. All modern Theravādin expositions of the Eightfold Path in effect explain the eight 'steps' – to call them that – in the order in which they occur in the transcendental path, but they explain them as though they were the mundane path, which as I said makes nonsense of the whole thing.

MAHAMATI: Is that to say that the supramundane Eightfold Path wasn't intended for beginners?

SANGHARAKSHITA: Yes. The transcendental Eightfold Path, which is the Eightfold Path usually cited, is not intended for beginners, though that isn't realized. In a complete path you have mundane *śīla*, leading to mundane *samādhi*, leading to transcendental wisdom. Or, enumerating the stages at greater length, you first of all have *prajñā* in the sense of a rational understanding of the Dharma. (That comes first, you have a path of regular steps.) On the basis of that *prajñā* in the sense of a rational understanding of the Dharma you practise mundane ethics. On the basis of your practice of mundane ethics you practise mundane *samādhi*. As a result of practising mundane *samādhi*, you develop *prajñā* in the transcendental sense. As a result of practising *prajñā* in the transcendental sense you're enabled to practise *śīla* in the transcendental sense. By practising *śīla* in the transcendental sense you come to practise *samādhi* in the transcendental sense. If you explain it in the usual way, taking the steps of the Eightfold Path as arranged in the transcendental path but giving them a mundane explanation, it appears that the beginning of the supramundane Eightfold Path is a rational understanding and that it culminates in ordinary mundane concentration. This makes nonsense of the whole scheme, and devalues it considerably.

LOKAMITRA: So if one doesn't take that approach, one has to make it clear that this path operates on two levels.

SANGHARAKSHITA: The transcendental Eightfold Path begins with spiritual insight, transcendental insight; but that is led up to by mundane meditation, which is led up to by mundane ethics, which is led up to by rational understanding.

LOKAMITRA: So it is okay to present the mundane Eightfold Path as long as we...

SANGHARAKSHITA: If you want to present the mundane Eightfold Path, you have to start with rational understanding, from there proceeding to the practice of ethics on the basis of that rational understanding, and from there proceeding to the practice of mundane meditation on the basis of that mundane morality. By practising mundane meditation you have the spiritual i.e. transcendental experience, which is the first step of the transcendental Eightfold Path – which is the Eightfold Path usually enumerated, though people don't realize it.

Thus, even an apparently simple thing like the Eightfold Path isn't properly understood. Most exponents of the Eightfold Path nowadays start off with Perfect Vision – with right view, or right understanding, as they usually put it – but they don't give the proper explanation of it. It just becomes something purely rational. In other words, because the first 'step' has been wrongly explained the whole of the transcendental path is explained in mundane terms. This is what happens. You don't have a transcendental path left at all.

SAGARAMATI: I believe that somewhere in the *Majjhima Nikāya* the Buddha makes this distinction quite clear, and he puts the two of them side by side.[230]

SANGHARAKSHITA: Yes, but like other things this has been entirely forgotten by modern Theravādins, at least in their popular expositions. The transcendental path – in terms of the three stages – reads: wisdom, morality, meditation. The mundane path reads – in those terms – morality, meditation, and wisdom.

KULARATNA: But it does start off with a rational understanding.

SANGHARAKSHITA: Not in this threefold enumeration. Usually you get mundane *śīla*, mundane *samādhi*, transcendental *prajñā*. This is the mundane path, culminating in the transcendental. If you apply these terms to the transcendental Eightfold Path then you will get transcendental wisdom, transcendental morality, transcendental meditation. Here all three are transcendental, because the transcendental insight transforms first your conduct and then your whole emotional attitude. It's quite important to understand this, since otherwise you devalue the whole path, which is exactly what most modern Theravādins do. You're exhorted by such Theravādins to have a rational understanding of the Dharma, and then on the basis of that to practise conventional ethics, and then to concentrate the mind, and that's your following of the Eightfold Path, whereas the *real* explanation would be for you to achieve by means of your prior practice – by means of your following the preliminary path of rational understanding, mundane ethics, and mundane concentration – a transcendental insight which gives you a direct contact with ultimate reality and, as a result of that, to transform all your external activities, and your whole emotional attitude – which is a very different thing and much closer, you could say, to the Mahāyāna.

One can't help noticing, going through these paragraphs of the text, that the Theravāda seems to have limited everything, and given very demeaning interpretations of the Dharma.

> The Sangha of the third refuge is not the all-inclusive congregation of monks, having all the weaknesses of its single members and sharing in the shortcomings attaching to any human institution. It is rather the fraternity of holy disciples, not necessarily monks, who are united by the invisible tie of common attainment to the four stages of sanctity. In other words, it is likewise of supramundane nature. It is the assurance of possible progress to the world-transcending heights of a mind made holy and pure. (pp. 14–15)

This is very true. It's the common spiritual attainment – the common *transcendental* attainment – that makes the Sangha in the highest sense, and members of this sangha are not necessarily monks. This is a point made in the Pāli texts themselves, but for the ordinary lay person in the Theravādin Buddhist countries of South-East Asia the 'sangha' means the monks. They wouldn't think of including a non-monk in that category. Even if you think of the Āryasaṅgha historically, it's Sāriputta, Moggallāna, Ānanda; you don't get any lay *arahant*'s name mentioned or thought of. There *are* lay *arhants* according to tradition, but I'm sure that no Theravādin Buddhist could tell you the names of any of them. I'm not so sure that I can remember any of the names myself, though I know these things are there in the scriptures.[231] So this is again a very important point: that the Sangha, in the spiritual sense, is not to be identified with any ecclesiastical body. It may well be that those living as monks are much more likely to be *āryas*, are much more likely to be on the transcendental path; but not necessarily so. Thus the spiritual community, in the highest sense is a purely *spiritual* community, not exactly regardless of the way in which they live, but regardless of what one can only describe, in the light of history, as their formal ecclesiastical position. The sangha in the fullest sense is all those who are on the path, both mundane and transcendental, but the 'Sangha', in the highest sense, is the community, past, present, and future, of those on the transcendental path, regardless of whether they are technically monks or laymen, nuns, or laywomen.

In the case of the WBO and the FWBO, we stress the Going for Refuge, in the deepest sense, as the uniting factor – as what pulls everybody together and creates a sangha, creates a spiritual community, creates an order. Whether you're living in a community or whether you're living alone in the forest doesn't make any fundamental difference.

> By this threefold knowledge, about the need, existence, and nature of the refuge, the going to that refuge becomes a conscious act of *understanding*. (p. 15)

So much for understanding. Let's go on now to the emotional element, which, perhaps significantly, doesn't get quite so much attention.

## The Emotional Basis

> This knowledge and understanding forms the firm basis of the third, the *emotional*, aspect of taking refuge, having, as it were, three facets: confidence, devotion and love. The knowledge of the existence of a refuge provides the basis for a firm and justified confidence, for the calmness of inner assurance and the strength of conviction. The knowledge of the need for a refuge instils unswerving devotion to it; and the understanding of its sublime nature fills the heart with love towards the highest that can be conceived. Confidence is the firmness in faith; devotion is the patient endurance in loyal service and effort; and love adds the element of ardour, warmth, and joy. In the sense of these three constituents, the going for refuge is also a conscious act of wise *faith*. (p. 15)

SANGHARAKSHITA: Earlier we saw that the emotional can itself be the basis, the starting point. This statement of Nyanaponika's is true from the standpoint of the *dhammānusārin*, or doctrine-follower, but for the *saddhānusārin* or faith-follower it would be the emotional element, the faith, which came first. Emotion would be the basis. Do you see how this works out in detail? In this last paragraph of the text, knowledge and understanding leads to faith. How would faith lead to knowledge and understanding?

MAHAMATI: Through one's commitment to the spiritual life one would learn....

SAGARAMATI: You must take an interest in what you are doing.

SANGHARAKSHITA: Exactly: you take an interest in it! Suppose you went to an art gallery, and were at once fascinated by a particular painting. You would ask yourself, 'Who is it by? What is it about? What is it that attracts me to it?' In this way your emotional interest would lead to a search for understanding. It's just the same in the case of faith. You may never have even thought of taking any interest in religion, never studied comparative religion, never thought about life very much, but almost by accident you come into contact with something of Buddhism, or with the life of the Buddha, and without knowing anything about it you're at once attracted. Then you start asking yourself, 'Well, what is it that I've become attracted to?' and you discover that it's Buddhism – and then you discover what Buddhism is. You learn about conditioned co-production, about the teaching of the Void and so on. In this way faith leads to understanding in the case of the faith-follower. This attraction is not, of course, a superficial attraction to the exotic, but a deep and heartfelt response to the spiritual essence of Buddhism unmediated by conceptual symbols.

What Nyanaponika says here about knowledge and understanding forming the firm basis of the third, the emotional aspect of taking Refuge, is very true, but it is more true for the doctrine-follower than for the faith-follower. The faith-follower, it seems, follows an opposite procedure.

'...And the understanding of its sublime nature fills the heart with love towards the highest that can be conceived.' Do you think that this is quite correct? There's probably an ambiguity in the word 'understanding'. Do you have to understand the sublime nature exactly before you can feel any love? Maybe the doctrine-follower does, but the faith-follower certainly doesn't. Perhaps there's too hard and fast a distinction here between understanding and love. It's as though the assumption is that love is completely blind – that love towards the Highest is almost exclusively a product of the understanding, and that love itself needs to be supplemented. But it is doubtful whether, in this sort of spiritual context, love does exclude understanding in that sort of way. One might even doubt whether understanding really does exclude love.

'Confidence is the firmness in faith.' What do you think that means? What is confidence?

DHARMANANDA: It's knowing that you can rely on something.

SANGHARAKSHITA: But how does that sort of feeling develop? Does it not come only with time, with repeated experience, as in the case of one's dealings with people? You can only be sure that you can rely on somebody after knowing them for quite a time, or after having been in various situations with them. Sometimes, if you are quite experienced, and have had quite a few dealings with people, you can know in advance that somebody is going to be unreliable, but you can't be absolutely certain that any given person is going to be really reliable in any given situation. That comes only when you've known them for some time.

So in what way would confidence, in that sense, be 'firmness in faith' – faith in the Three Jewels or Three Refuges? How would that apply?

SAGARAMATI: It would only come about through your practising over a period of time.

SANGHARAKSHITA: You'd learn that your faith was justified: that the Three Jewels or Three Refuges hadn't let you down. In that way your faith would acquire firmness, and that firmness is what Nyanaponika calls confidence. So confidence represents a sort of consolidation of faith over a long period of time, when you know from your own experience that you're not going to be let down, that you can rely on the Three Refuges, that they are, in fact, a Refuge, that the Refuge 'works'.

Probably this is easiest to see in the case of the Sangha Refuge – not quite in the sense of the Āryasaṅgha, but more in the sense of *kalyāṇa mitratā*. You find over a period of time that it *does* work, that you *do* gain energy, that you *do* gain inspiration from *kalyāṇa mitratā*. Thus your faith in the Sangha becomes confidence in the Sangha. You know, for instance, that if you are feeling depressed, and you go along and meet a few Sangha members, you are going to be uplifted, you are going to be inspired again. You *know* that. So you don't have simply faith, you have confidence, based on previous experiences.

RAY: I saw an implication here, of confidence being not only towards something outside yourself but becoming confidence in yourself also.

SANGHARAKSHITA: Well, it's confidence in oneself to the extent that one has oneself become identified with, or transformed into, the Refuge. If you become your own good friend, then you can have confidence in yourself as a good friend of yourself. You can have confidence in yourself in the ordinary sense if you know from experience that you can rely on yourself in certain situations. Suppose someone asks you to be retreat organizer. If you have done it twenty times before, you will have confidence that you can do it. It's not a question of faith; you know you can do it in the light of your previous experience. But if you've never done it before, you may have faith that you can do it, but you won't have confidence that you can do it unless it's a blind confidence. But having done it on the basis of your faith that you could do it, and having realized that you could do it because you have done it, that faith becomes consolidated as confidence in yourself, based on your knowledge and experience of yourself in a particular situation.

This consolidation of faith into confidence is quite an important thing and it requires time. The length of time required presumably depends upon the intensity of your practice and experience, or even on accidental factors like the nature of the situations in which you find yourself. If you repeatedly find yourself in crucial situations, then your faith will have an opportunity of consolidating itself into confidence pretty rapidly. You may, for instance, be a young Order member suddenly left in charge of a centre. After a few months your faith in yourself will have developed into confidence, because you will have had to do all sorts of things connected with the activities of that centre and will know that you are able to do them.

So what do you think would be the general effect of having consolidated one's faith in the Buddha, faith in the Dharma, faith in the Sangha, and faith in oneself into confidence over a period of time?

LOKAMITRA: Deepening of commitment.

DHARMANANDA: A growing strength, which you could transmit to others.

SANGHARAKSHITA: Yes. But something more general than that. Perhaps it's expressed to some extent by this word 'firmness' in the text.

LOKAMITRA: Lack of conflict?

SANGHARAKSHITA: Well, that's implied by commitment, isn't it? Surely you'd become very solid, unshakeable, unflappable. You wouldn't get upset, you wouldn't get excited, you wouldn't worry. You'd be quite calm, quite steady, quite sure. These are the sort of characteristics that you would develop. You'd become Acala- or Akṣobhya-like,[232] and it would inspire confidence in those around you that even when other people lost their heads, you didn't lose yours. Even when other people lost their faith, you didn't lose yours. When other people started doubting, you didn't. When other people became anxious, you remained calm and confident. That sort of confidence can only come over a period of time. Other factors being equal, the older you grow the more confident you should become in this sense. Assuming that you start off with faith in the Three Refuges and faith in yourself, as the years go by you should become more and more confident. Things that really bother the young Mitra, or even the young Order member, shouldn't bother you any more. You just take them in your stride; you don't even think about them. You just go sailing on. Lack of money, no buildings, nowhere to live – you don't bother. You know it's going to be all right. You have that confidence, because you've done it all before so many times, and you've come out in the end quite successfully, so you think, 'Why worry?

What about 'Devotion is the patient endurance in loyal service and effort'? This is the second aspect of faith. First of all there came confidence, which is firmness in faith, and now there comes devotion, which is defined as 'the patient endurance in loyal service and effort.' Do you think that definition is quite right? It's all right as far as it goes, but do you feel that anything is missing?

KULANANDA: It's love that's missing.

SANGHARAKSHITA: Love is going to be mentioned separately, I think, whether rightly or wrongly. It seems to me that *joy* is missing. 'Devotion is the patient endurance in loyal service and effort.' That may be how it is at the beginning. That may be what the word devotion literally means: that you devote yourself to something. But I would say that devotion in the Buddhist sense must involve an element of joy and spontaneity, sooner or later. Certainly this 'patient endurance in loyal service and effort' is necessary. That's the basis, and that's how it usually is for a very long time, because it isn't easy to be devoted. The joy and the spontaneity don't come all at once, very often. But sooner or later they must come, they should come. Nyanaponika does go on to say that 'love adds the element of ardour, warmth, and joy', because without that the 'patient endurance in loyal service and effort' can be a bit of a drag, even in the case of the most sincere people. If you were simply plodding along with endurance and effort you might become a bit resentful in the end, especially if you thought that others weren't equally devoted and the work was all being left to you. All the same, he does not emphasize joy, and spontaneity is not even mentioned.

### A Conscious Act of Will

> We may now define the going for refuge as *a conscious act of will directed towards liberation, based upon knowledge and inspired by faith;* or briefly: *a conscious act of determination, understanding, and devotion.* (p. 15)

SANGHARAKSHITA: Once again this definition, especially the first part of it, seems more applicable to the Going for Refuge of the *dhammānusārin*, the doctrine-follower. How could one word it so as to make it more applicable to the Going for Refuge of the *saddhānusārin*, the faith-follower?

KULARATNA: Something like a spontaneous emotional response to something higher?

SANGHARAKSHITA: A spontaneous emotional response to something higher resulting in active investigation into the nature of that object. Something like that. If one wanted to be a little strict, one might say that the definition of Going for Refuge given by Nyanaponika is so general that it leaves the Refuges out. 'A conscious act of will directed towards liberation…,' But is it just directed towards liberation? Where does the Buddha come in? The definition is too general, too abstract, one might say.

KULARATNA: Is it rather impersonal?

SANGHARAKSHITA: Yes, it is rather impersonal, which is all right from the point of view of understanding, but not from the point of view of emotion. Once again it is a definition of Going for Refuge in terms of the *dhammānusārin*'s approach, rather than in terms of the *saddhānusārin*'s approach. As for the brief definition, 'A conscious act of determination, understanding, and devotion', that's far too general. You can have all sorts of conscious acts of determination, understanding, and devotion that wouldn't be acts of Going for Refuge.

SAGARAMATI: It's all up to you. It's all to do with yourself. It's all things that are happening to you.

SANGHARAKSHITA: Yes, it *is* all up to you. It's *your* Going for Refuge. But it's also your emotional response, not just your understanding. The emotional response can be the starting point, with ramifications into understanding and will, just as understanding can be the starting point, with ramifications into will and emotion.

> These three aspects of taking refuge have their counterparts in the volitional, rational, and emotional sides of the human mind. Therefore, for a harmonious development of character, the cultivation of all three is required. (p. 15)

SANGHARAKSHITA: What does this really mean? What is it really saying about the Going for Refuge?

RATNAVIRA: That it has to involve your entire being.

SANGHARAKSHITA: It has to involve your entire being. In other words, it's a total thing. Man has these three different aspects, the volitional, the rational, and the emotional, and though one shouldn't differentiate them too rigidly, all three have to be developed. That doesn't mean that one develops them separately, as though they really are divisible. It means that your whole being, your whole personality, has to be fully developed. Then, when it comes to Going for Refuge, you have to go for Refuge with your whole being, not only volitionally but also emotionally and in terms of understanding. Perhaps the most important point is that if the Going for Refuge is a total thing – if you have to go for Refuge as a whole person – you have to be a whole person to begin with. If your emotions are tied up somewhere or other, if you have some big emotional hang-ups so that your emotions are not free, not at your own disposal, how can you go for Refuge with those emotions? They're hanging behind. So how can you go for Refuge totally? You can't. But Going for Refuge is by very definition a total thing. So in order to go for Refuge totally you have to be a total person, that is to say a whole person. In other words, you have to be happy, healthy, and human to begin with.

Clearly very few people are whole. There will always be some deficiency, as it were. To begin with, your Going for Refuge is usually either predominantly volitional, or predominantly in terms of understanding, or predominantly emotional. Probably you're luckiest if it's predominantly emotional, because the emotions provide the driving force.

MAHAMATI: What would it be if it was predominantly volitional? What does that mean?

SANGHARAKSHITA: Probably a predominantly volitional Going for Refuge would be a wilful, i.e. a will-full, effort. At the same time, although there is this threefold distinction of will, understanding, and emotion, I'm doubtful if one can really separate the volitional from the emotional, even to the extent that one can separate the aspect of understanding from the emotional. Perhaps one should speak simply in terms of the rational and the emotional. These are the two great aspects of personality.

SAGARAMATI: Isn't there a sort of power aspect, corresponding to the volitional?

SANGHARAKSHITA: Yes, the power aspect – the aspect of energy would correspond to the volitional; but then the emotional too is energy.

SAGARAMATI: Power or energy can be without those more refined and positive qualities associated with feeling, though, can't it?

SANGHARAKSHITA: Yes. Inasmuch as there are two great aspects of human personality one could say that one's Going for Refuge is either predominantly intellectual or predominantly emotional, but probably the predominantly emotional refuge is more truly a refuge in the sense that it is more complete. It is more complete because an emotional Going for Refuge in the true sense – I don't mean a sentimental Going for Refuge – would take along with it a larger part of yourself, inasmuch as we're much more bound up in our emotions than we are in our understanding or intellect. So a person who really *felt* like Going for Refuge would be in a much more promising position than one who merely *thought* it would be a good thing to do. Do you see the distinction? You might be quite convinced intellectually that Going for Refuge would be a very good thing to do but not actually move in that direction. But on the other hand you might feel emotionally that it was a very good thing to do and throw yourself into it, without understanding very much what you were throwing yourself into – you would discover that only gradually, later on. That would be a better thing for you to do, provided that you threw yourself in within the context of the spiritual community, and received instruction later on to clarify your predominantly emotional Going for Refuge so that it became illuminated with understanding.

LOKAMITRA: If you don't have contact with others in the form of a spiritual community, then it's more likely to be a rational Going for Refuge – would you say that?

SANGHARAKSHITA: Possibly it's more likely to be predominantly rational.

LOKAMITRA: Or the danger of a rational Going for Refuge is more there, in that spiritual fellowship brings out the positive emotional side. Certainly I've noticed this among people who don't have contact with...

SANGHARAKSHITA: If you have a predominantly emotional Going for Refuge, you're much more likely to appreciate and seek out spiritual fellowship within the spiritual community. But if you have a predominantly intellectual Going for Refuge then, even to the extent that it is a genuine Going for Refuge and not just a theoretical thing, you'd be much less likely to enjoy and seek out the spiritual fellowship of the spiritual community, so you'd probably tend to remain more or less where you were spiritually, because you'd be relatively isolated from others and therefore from the inspiration that spiritual fellowship can provide.

SAGARAMATI: It's very hard to judge what is driving somebody, isn't it? People might be driven emotionally to want to go for Refuge, or to join the sangha, but at the same time the object of their emotions can be such that it is nothing to do with getting involved with spiritual development.

SANGHARAKSHITA: But then it wouldn't be really a Going for Refuge, would it?

SAGARAMATI: It's quite difficult to discriminate.

SANGHARAKSHITA: I don't think so. Let me give a concrete example. Suppose someone happened to pick up a copy of *The Light of Asia*, which is a poetical version of the life of the Buddha up to the time of his Enlightenment.[233] They could be so moved and stirred by it that they felt like Going for Refuge. They might not even know that it was called 'Going for Refuge', but the attraction they felt towards the Buddha as depicted in those pages, or towards the ideal of Enlightenment as reflected in the life of the Buddha, would be so strong, and they would feel so definitely that this was the direction in which they wanted to go that it would be, in effect, a Going for Refuge. There is a possibility of that sort of thing happening. But that's quite different, and quite recognizably different, from the case of somebody who's had a not very happy home life, a not very happy marriage, a not very happy job situation, and who feels that he'd like to get away from it all and then hears that there's an organization called the FWBO that's got rather lovely little places in the country where it's quiet and peaceful, and feels he'd like to go there. That isn't an urge in the direction of Going for Refuge, but something quite different, and with experience one could spot this difference, presumably.

Also, one must recognize that people can be emotionally driven, as well as emotionally drawn – that is to say, emotionally driven *from* the *saṃsāra*. Their experience of life has been so bitter and painful that they experience a sort of emotional disillusionment which is not just disgruntlement. They really are looking for some completely radical alternative, and without knowing exactly what that alternative is, they're in a state of preparedness to commit themselves to it. They haven't seen through the mundane in a cool, detached, intellectual way; they've had such a bitter and painful experience of it that they genuinely don't want anything more to do with it. That is a form of Going for Refuge. But it is not easy to sort out the different forms a genuine Going for Refuge can take, or to disentangle the genuine from the not-so-genuine. They may even be mixed in one and the same person. There may be all sorts of elements confusing the issue. There may be a central thread in the form of a very genuine Going for Refuge, entangled with all sorts of other threads which are nothing to do with Going for Refuge. If one is thinking in terms of Going for Refuge, or even thinks of oneself as already having gone for Refuge, one has to ask oneself such questions as, 'What direction am I going in? Am I really Going for Refuge, and in what way? Do I really want to grow? Am I prepared to grow *up*, and to grow *out of* various things? Do I have a genuine urge to reach forward to some stage beyond?'

RATNAJYOTI: Nietzsche says something to the effect that one must know what one wants and that one wants it.[234] Is that the same?

SANGHARAKSHITA: If you simply know that you want it, that's more like the *saddhānusārin*, but if you know what you want, that's more like the *dhammānusārin* – though really you need to have both in the end. The danger with the more emotional approach, is that your urge to go for Refuge may be quite pure but you may get involved with a group or a movement that doesn't enable you to bring that incipient Going for Refuge to fulfilment. You may even confuse the object of Refuge. Having been inspired by your reading of *The Light of Asia* you might happen to drift into some beautiful old cathedral and think, 'Maybe I ought to become a monk. After all, it's not all that different, the Buddha's life and the life of a Christian monk.' Thus your Going for Refuge, though genuine to start with, might be deflected and destroyed.[235] Do you see the sort of possibility I have in mind? Or you might read that the Buddha had meditated under a bodhi tree, and then see a poster: 'Transcendental Meditation' and think that that's the right direction. That would be a mistake – or at least you wouldn't get very far. It is therefore important not only to experience that you go for Refuge but also to know what you go for Refuge to. You must know that it really and truly is a Refuge. The predominantly intellectual person, the person of the more *dhammānusārin* approach, knows the *what* all right, but he might not find it so easy to experience the *that*, might not find it so easy to experience that he must go for Refuge. He might understand 'This is what I should go for Refuge to,' but at the same time he might not be experiencing so positively that 'I'm Going for Refuge'.

Because of the danger of confusing the object of Refuge it becomes more and more necessary for the more emotionally oriented person to find refuge with, or to have contact with, a genuine spiritual community. I was almost going to say that if you establish contact with a genuine spiritual community you can almost forget about the Dharma. In such a case it's not that you're not in contact with the Dharma. You *are* in contact with it, as it is embodied in the spiritual community. That is what makes it a spiritual community. So you can forget about the Dharma in a conceptual, intellectual sense if you are in contact with the spiritual community, because the spiritual community is based on the Dharma, is the embodiment of the Dharma, so that through the spiritual community you're in contact with the Dharma in a *living* way.

RATNAVIRA: That happens quite often. Thinking of my own experience, I used to do quite a lot of reading of books on Buddhism and so on. It's all just a sort of general line.

SANGHARAKSHITA: I remember an amusing experience of mine in a centre somewhere. A group of us were discussing the Dharma, and it was becoming really interesting and several people seemed to be getting quite a lot out of it. Then somebody said, 'We'd better stop now, because according to the programme we've got to listen to one of Bhante's taped lectures!'

MAHAMATI: I noticed that in one of the Buddhist publications in the States, put out by Trungpa Rimpoche's group, nearly all the writers had a PhD in Buddhist Studies.

SANGHARAKSHITA: There's nothing wrong in having a PhD in Buddhist studies, but one suspects that in at least some cases that's all they've got. If you've got that in addition to genuine Buddhist qualifications, that's fine: it's an extra piece of equipment.

If ever you are in the painful position of having to choose between the Dharma and the Sangha, choose the Sangha every time – provided it really is the Sangha, not just a Buddhist group. If it really is the Sangha, really is the spiritual community, you've got the Dharma there too, because the spiritual community embodies the Dharma in terms of love. You need not read, you need not study: just be in contact with the spiritual community – not just in social contact, but in real, living, spiritual contact, with meditation and Dharma discussion, living and working together as fellow members of the spiritual community. That itself *is* practising the Dharma! You can remain in isolation and have a whole library of books on Buddhism, as some people do, but never come in contact with another Buddhist, never mind the spiritual community, and even pride yourself on the fact. In that case you aren't getting very far. An isolated Buddhist is a contradiction in terms. If you are unavoidably isolated, that is not your fault; but if within a few miles there are other Buddhists, or at least other people calling themselves Buddhists, and you make no attempt to establish contact with them, then it's very doubtful whether you really are a Buddhist in the sense of one who has gone for Refuge, because where is your Sangha Refuge? Strictly speaking, it is the Āryasaṅgha that is the object of Refuge; but so far as most ordinary Buddhists are concerned, for all practical purposes the Sangha Refuge is the other Buddhists with whom one is in personal contact.

> Will, understanding and faith support each other in their common task; will, transformed into purposive action, frees faith from the barrenness and dangers of emotional self-indulgence; it prevents intellectual understanding from stopping short at mere theoretical appreciation. Will harnesses the energies of both emotion and intellect to actual application. Understanding gives direction and method to will; it provides a check to the exuberance of faith and gives to it its true contents. Faith keeps will from slackening, and is the vitalizing and purposive factor in intellectual understanding. (pp. 15–16)

SANGHARAKSHITA: This paragraph explains how well understanding and faith cooperate. 'Will, transformed into purposive action, frees faith from the barrenness and dangers of emotional self-indulgence.' How might that be? In what way does faith become barren, or emotionally self-indulgent? Do we see actual instances of this? Or is emotional self-indulgence in respect of faith an unreal danger for most Western Buddhists? What is emotional self-indulgence in this context? Do we come up against this?

KULANANDA: Yes.

SANGHARAKSHITA: In what way? What form does it take? How do we recognize it?

KULANANDA: Well, going into particular states of being for their own sake, like listening to music just for the particular emotional experience in itself, becoming attached to that.

SANGHARAKSHITA: But this is emotional self-indulgence in connection with faith.

MAHAMATI: I would say this wouldn't be faith.

SANGHARAKSHITA: Perhaps there are two possibilities. First of all there's the possibility that you have genuine faith, but that it becomes an object of emotional self-indulgence. Take the parallel example of compassion. Suppose you read in the newspaper about some terrible disaster in which a lot of people have suffered. You feel quite sorry for them. You feel, maybe, just a little touch of compassion. But then what happens? Your 'self-conscious' mind (in the not very positive sense of the term) says, as it were, 'Look, I'm being compassionate! How compassionate I am!' And you start enjoying the feeling of being compassionate, quite detached from your feeling for the people who are suffering. In this way the so-called compassion, though genuine to begin with, becomes a sort of emotional self-indulgence. Similarly, you might be in the shrine-room chanting and experiencing genuine faith and devotion, but then you become a bit self-conscious and think, 'Oh look how devoted I am!' You start enjoying your own feeling of devotion, which means it becomes directed towards you, not the Buddha. This is emotional self-indulgence. The faith and devotion are genuine to begin with but then self-consciousness, even ego-consciousness, creeps in and spoils that genuine devotion. With any kind of skilful action or skilful mental state, this sort of self-consciousness can creep in and appropriate the positive, skilful experience for itself in a self-indulgent way, and when that happens of course it ceases to be skilful and becomes unskilful.

VAIROCANA: In some cases you can have such a strong sense of ego that it can lead to fanaticism.

SANGHARAKSHITA: Indeed, yes. But there's also the possibility that you can start off not with faith and devotion, but with an attitude of emotional self-indulgence. There can be some chanting going on in the shrine-room and you are there, but you've no feeling of devotion: you just want to enjoy the experience of the chanting and appropriate it for yourself, so that you can feel good, almost in a therapeutic way. This would be an example of emotional self-indulgence without genuine faith and devotion coming first.

KULARATNA: It seems to be a psychological rather than an ethical state.

SANGHARAKSHITA: Yes. You want to experience the state not because it is skilful but because it is pleasant. Skilful mental states are pleasant, but if you want to experience them because they're pleasant, even though the skilfulness includes the pleasant, it becomes emotional self-indulgence.

KULANANDA: Is there any way of avoiding this appropriation?

SANGHARAKSHITA: Oh dear! It's quite difficult, because self-consciousness goes on developing more refined forms. Suppose you start off being full of faith and devotion. After a while you start becoming aware that you are experiencing faith and devotion and then you start appropriating it to yourself and becoming emotionally self-indulgent. Then a further awareness supervenes: 'Oh, this is what I am doing! This is not very skilful,' so that again there's a somewhat more genuine faith and devotion, and for the time being you are purged of that self-indulgent element. But then, after a while, a little voice within you says, 'Oh look, wasn't I clever!' This is what happens. One has to keep a constant check on oneself and constantly eliminate the wrong kind of self-consciousness.

SAGARAMATI: I think this happens during the practice of *mettā*. You forget about yourself, you get a good feeling going, and then you realize, 'Oh, my meditation's going well!'

LOKAMITRA: In a way our skilful states are at the mercy of our unskilful states of mind.

SANGHARAKSHITA: The only remedy is to be aware – and to put oneself into the faith and devotion so powerfully and so totally that the possibility of that sort of self-consciousness or somewhat alienated awareness arising is greatly reduced. That's why it's very good to be really busy, because then you've no time to think about how busy you are. Suppose the puja was quite elaborate and that instead of just sitting there chanting you had to do various things at various times: light certain candles or offer certain flowers. You'd be so busy doing all those things that you'd have no time to think of yourself as doing them. In this way the whole process would remain more skilful and therefore more genuinely devotional. That's perhaps one of the reasons why one has elaborate pujas in some forms of Buddhism.

Sometimes it's good to allow yourself to be carried away, but you can be carried away mindfully, as when you're playing music. Maybe you're playing a very difficult piece. You're carried away, but at the same time you're fully aware. Yet although you're fully aware you've no time to think of yourself as being carried away, because then you'd spoil the music. You can think of yourself as being carried away when you're listening, but not when you're playing, I imagine, unless your mind becomes very subtle indeed.

So, 'Will, transformed into purposive action, frees faith from the barrenness and dangers of emotional self-indulgence; it prevents intellectual understanding from stopping short at mere theoretical appreciation.' This is only too true. 'Will harnesses the energies of both, emotion and intellect, to actual application. Understanding gives direction and method to will; it provides a check to the exuberance of faith and gives to it its true contents.' Is exuberance of faith something that we usually experience in the Western Buddhist context? No. The flower of our faith is not very exuberant in its growth. It's usually a poor, sickly little plant that requires constant tending, 'Faith keeps will from slackening, and is the vitalizing and purposive factor in intellectual understanding: ' It's pretty clear that all these three cooperate, isn't it?

DHAMMARATI: In *Sayings, Poems, Reflections* you said something along the lines that the will is a myth.[236] We either did something or didn't do something. There is no such thing as the will.

SANGHARAKSHITA: I wasn't referring to will in the sense of the sum total of psychic energy available to the conscious subject, which is the sense in which the term is used by Nyanaponika, but to will in the sense in which the term is used in discussions about free will, i.e. about whether the will is free or bound. Will as abstracted from the concrete, psychic situation of doing or not doing, and made the subject of such discussions, is a myth. In that saying I was concerned to deny not the psychic reality of the act of volition as such but the existence of a 'will' separate and distinct from that reality.

## A Total Commitment

> The presence of these three aspects is the distinguishing feature of true Buddhist faith (*saddhā*). In the conception of faith, as found in all other world religions, only the emotional aspect is stressed (assurance, devotion, and love). The two other aspects, will and understanding, are absent, or in an undeveloped state, being impeded by the dictates of the creed. The element of self-responsible will is supplanted by the postulate of obedience, by authoritarian guidance, and by submission to the will of a God. Understanding is replaced by dogmatic belief, demanding or implying a sacrifice of intellect. (p. 16)

SANGHARAKSHITA: So, 'The presence of these three aspects,' that is to say, will, understanding, and faith, 'is the distinguishing feature of true Buddhist faith.' What is one to make of that statement? Of course you could turn it around the other way and say that it is the presence of those three aspects which is the distinguishing feature of true Buddhist faith. If understanding is part of the definition of faith, is not faith part of the definition of understanding? But do Theravādin writers ever make faith part of the definition of understanding? No, they don't. It's as though there's a tendency or inclination to rationalize faith but not to devotionalize understanding. So rather than saying that it's the presence of these three aspects that is the distinguishing feature of the true Buddhist faith, it might be better to say that for Buddhism Going for Refuge is a matter of total commitment. Speaking in terms of the presence of will, understanding, and faith being the distinguishing feature of true Buddhist faith seems to be a rather roundabout way of saying that. If you say that the definition of faith includes understanding, surely you must also say that the definition of understanding includes faith.

I've mentioned in the *Survey* that in certain contexts – I was thinking of the Jōdo Shinshū Buddhist context – it would be possible to understand faith as the emotional counterpart of wisdom.[237] Faith in the sense that the Jōdo Shinshū Buddhists use the term is, in fact, wisdom, expressed in emotional terms. But what about 'the conception of faith as found in all other world religions'? Do you think it a fair criticism that in these religions 'only the emotional aspect is stressed'? 'The two aspects, will and understanding, are absent, or in an undeveloped state, being impeded by the dictates of the creed.' Do you think that this is a fair point?

VAIROCANA: It seems to be true of Christianity, which encourages a blind faith without any real understanding.

GRAHAM: I would have thought it was true of Islam too.

SANGHARAKSHITA: Perhaps the explanation of that will involve seeing how 'The element of self-responsible will is supplanted by the postulate of obedience, by authoritarian guidance, and by submission to the will of a God. Understanding is replaced by dogmatic belief, demanding or implying a sacrifice of intellect.' Perhaps the impression of authority and obedience is central in the case of Christianity and Islam.

SAGARAMATI: With regard to their attitude towards the other religions?

SANGHARAKSHITA: Yes, and with regard to the fact that their understanding of faith virtually excludes understanding and will in the Buddhist sense.

SAGARAMATI: Is that like the guy who burned all the books in the Library at Alexandria and said that everything that's worth knowing is in the Koran, so you can burn everybody else's knowledge.

SANGHARAKSHITA: He is supposed to have said, 'Either what is in these books is in the Koran, or it is not. If it is in the Koran, we don't need these books. If what is in them is not in the Koran, then we need them even less.' So they were burned.[238] So how does this concept of authority arise? People don't realize how strong it is in the religious sphere – in Christianity, in Islam, and in fact in all the theistic religions – and therefore how strong is the idea of obedience, and also the idea of guilt. Where does it come from, this conception of authority? What *is* authority?

VAIROCANA: They just create an absolute authority out of air, on behalf of God.

SANGHARAKSHITA: But what *is* that? What *is* authority? What do we mean by authority?

DHAMMARATI: It's an idea that somebody's got a better understanding of a situation than you can possibly have, so they lay down the way it is and insist that you conform to it.

SANGHARAKSHITA: I'm thinking of something even more basic than that.

SAGARAMATI: Isn't it that they've got power?

SANGHARAKSHITA: They've got power! This is what authority is, essentially: greater power. So if it's a question of greater power, then what is it, really?

KULARATNA: You're afraid of them.

SANGHARAKSHITA: No, I'm not thinking in that sort of way.

GRAHAM: Group conditioning.

SANGHARAKSHITA: It's something to do with the group. It's not anything spiritual – it's an absolutely basic point, that within the spiritual context the question of power cannot arise. This is the basic point of difference between Buddhism and the theistic religions: the fact that according to these religions God is more powerful than you. He has made the world. He has made you. He has created everything. He is almighty. There may be in the cosmos a power which is greater than you; Buddhism would not deny that, but it would deny that it is anything spiritual, anything unconditioned. The Unconditioned has no power. The Unconditioned is not a power, whereas God is conceived of as a power. In other words, God, in a sense, is Nature. He is the God of Nature: the greater power.

You, conceived of as a biological organism, are small and frail, so the rest of Nature seems infinitely more powerful than you. A hurricane can sweep you away, a flood can drown you, fire can burn you, a thunderbolt can strike you dead; but that is just power – a greater power than you. But the question of power doesn't come into the spiritual context – into spiritual life, spiritual experience, spiritual community. There, power is completely irrelevant.

KULANANDA: It's a more subtle form of power ... and spiritual hierarchy.

SANGHARAKSHITA: No, I wouldn't say that. I think it would be very dangerous to say that. In the spiritual hierarchy there's no power at all, not even a more spiritual kind of power – defining power in the way we have. I think it would be much safer, and much truer, to say that in the spiritual hierarchy there's no question of power. There's no question of those higher in the hierarchy having power over those lower in the hierarchy.

KULANANDA: Doesn't vision bring power?

SANGHARAKSHITA: Not in this sense. Here one is obviously using the word power in the sense of that extra weight that the group has in relation to the individual. Here I mean by individual simply the member of the group.

KULANANDA: Power is a potential force.

SANGHARAKSHITA: A potential force. In Christianity, in Islam, God is conceived of as more powerful than you, and therefore capable of crushing you, so all that you can do is submit. The greatest sin is disobedience. This is illustrated by the myth of the Garden of Eden. Even if, as a Christian, you accept that it is only a myth, only a symbol – accept that that particular episode didn't historically take place – you still believe in the truth it contains, which is that it is a sin to disobey God. The modern Christian may not believe there was a woman called Eve who ate an apple and then gave it to her husband to eat, against the command of God, but they still believe that sin consists in disobedience to the commands of God as expressed in the Decalogue, through the words of Christ in the New Testament, and so on. Sin is disobedience; disobedience is sin. If you have to obey someone more powerful than you, and do what he says because he says it and the ultimate sanction is with him, the ultimate sanction being that he can send you to hell for disobedience, how can you speak in terms of freedom? What happens to your will? In the theistic religions your will is crippled. Moreover, if you are having to obey someone whom perhaps you don't want to obey, you could feel only resentment. This is what somebody once said about Cardinal Newman: 'He believed in God, but he didn't like him.'[239] That is the situation of many Christians. They believe in God, but they don't like him, because he is always telling them what to do. But suppose you know what God wants you to do, suppose you know what the commandments of God are, or think you know, because the priests or the Bible have told you, but suppose you don't want to obey those commandments and in fact don't obey them. Suppose you even go against them. What would be your feeling? It would be one of guilt. Further, suppose you think that you can't hide anything from God because he is all-knowing and he will get you in the end because he is all-powerful. What would be your state of mind then?

A VOICE: Fear.

SANGHARAKSHITA: Fear. Even terror, even despair. In this way you become emotionally crippled. So what has been said is very true. We may have painted a rather lurid picture of Christianity. On the highest and most refined theological level God may not be simply power. But that is how it works out for the ordinary believer, even today, whether Catholic or Protestant. 'The element of self-responsible will is supplanted by the postulate of obedience, by authoritarian guidance, and by submission to the will of a God. Understanding is replaced by dogmatic belief, demanding or implying a sacrifice of intellect.' For instance, you might be told that God wants you to do a certain thing, that it is God's commandment. You might start thinking that this wasn't reasonable, and say, 'Surely God, if he is good and just, could not want me to do this.' But then the priest says, 'Ah, that's doubt! That's the voice of the devil, tempting you. That's unregenerate reason.' So you have to suppress the voice of your own reason, because you're told it's the voice of the devil. Thus your understanding is stunted, your will is crippled, and your emotions are perverted, because God is power.

If you're not careful, when you come into Buddhism you may easily think of the Buddha in this sort of way. Do you see what I mean? The Buddha has no power to punish you at all: it's very important to remember that. If you disobey the Buddha – assuming the Buddha to issue 'commands', or at least to tell you what he thinks you ought to do – the Buddha has no power to punish you whatever. The Buddhist attitude is that the Buddha points out what it would be good for you to do in your own interest. It's up to you to see or feel that for yourself and act upon it. There are no threats.

We must recognize, though, that in some Buddhist scriptures it does *seem* that there are threats. For instance, the Buddha may say, 'If you perform unskilful actions, you will suffer.' If you're not careful this can be given the kind of emphasis that makes it sound like a threat, especially when some scriptures go on to describe the sufferings of the different hells.[240] Even though the hells are not permanent, if you're not careful you can tend to present the prospect of suffering in them as a sort of threat, which means invoking power. Since power pertains to the group, you can take it as a maxim that if in this so-called spiritual or pseudo-spiritual context anybody starts threatening painful consequences, then one is concerned not with a spiritual community, but with the interests of a group. To the extent that people are members of a group, to the extent that they are not individuals, they'll only be susceptible to the dictates of power. It's only an individual who can respond to a purely spiritual appeal, as we may call it.

LOKAMITRA: By that, do you mean that when reading the scriptures which talk of sufferings in the hells and so on, to the extent that one is not a true individual one can quite easily take these things the wrong way and won't see the purely spiritual appeal, as it were?

SANGHARAKSHITA: No, I wasn't saying that. If there is just the statement, 'If you perform unskilful actions, you will suffer', that is a sensible, calm statement addressed to the individual, and therefore it could be described as a spiritual teaching, a teaching of the Buddha. But if someone starts elaborating on it and saying that if you do this or don't do that, then you will go to hell and burn there for millions of years, and they give descriptions of all the torments of hell, one cannot help suspecting that they are trying to coerce you. And if they're trying to coerce you they're not functioning spiritually. They're not functioning as an individual, but in the interests of the group – because maybe it is in the interests of the group that you should act or not act in a particular way, and the group wants to reinforce that with supernatural, pseudo-spiritual sanctions. Thus, the person who threatens you and invokes power in that way, even though he uses religious language, is in fact functioning as the spokesman of the group, not as the mouthpiece of the spiritual community, not as an individual. How can you tell whether someone is using power, or whether they are just appealing to you, spiritually, as an individual?

SAGARAMATI: There'd be some *mettā*.

SANGHARAKSHITA: There'd be some *mettā*. Also, they won't try to make you feel guilty. If you feel that someone is trying to make you feel guilty, and if in fact they *are* trying to make you feel guilty, even with regard to something which is actually unskilful, they're using power when they should be using *mettā*. It may be, of course, that you yourself feel guilty, when someone speaks to you with *mettā* about your unskilful behaviour, because of your own previous group and authority conditioning. That's another possibility. But if you detect that somebody else, though using the language of religion, the language of Buddhism, is trying to coerce you and pressure you and frighten you and make you feel guilty, then he's functioning as the spokesman of the group. Do you see this? It's a very delicate matter. If one individual speaks to another as an individual he can only speak with *mettā*. He can't invoke power in the sense of the greater weightage that the group has in relation to the statistical individual.

A great deal of what passes for religion in the world, including a great deal of Christianity and of all the theistic religions, has nothing to do with spiritual life. It's a matter of group politics. You get examples of this during wartime, when the Archbishop of Canterbury comes forth and blesses the troops, telling them to fight for King and Country because that is the will of God. Clearly, supernatural sanctions are being applied to the interests of the group. It has nothing to do with the genuine spiritual teaching of Christianity – assuming that there is such a thing. He's just invoking a supernatural sanction in the interests of a particular political group. It's not that on their own level the interests of the group should not be defended, but there's no need to invoke pseudo-spiritual sanctions.

MAHAMATI: Do you think that the language of theism is not necessary to (inaudible) ...

SANGHARAKSHITA: It seems so, because, you know, God is the ruler of the world. He's a great natural force. This is why the Manichees and the Cathars and the rest distinguish between the God of this world, the God of the Old Testament, and the spiritual God, as it were, who had nothing to do with the creation of the world. According to them the world was created by a sort of demon who was the God worshipped by the Christians and the Jews. What the Manichees said, in a way, was quite right. If you worship the one who creates the world, you're worshipping a sort of demon, from a spiritual point of view.

MAHAMATI: You're worshipping *saṃsāra*.

SANGHARAKSHITA: Yes, you're worshipping *saṃsāra*. You're worshipping the deification of *saṃsāra*. You're worshipping a natural force. The spiritual is on a quite different level. The Manichees make a very important distinction between the God of the Old Testament and the God of the New Testament: the God of the Old Testament being a God of power, in our terminology, the God of the New Testament being a God of love in the true sense. This is why in the Middle Ages there were the Albigenses and other similar groups.[241] They altogether rejected the Catholic Church, or *the* Church as it was then, because it had become a political power structure, and was not a spiritual community, not a true Church. The minute you start invoking power in the interests of so-called religion it ceases to be religion. You can't persecute people, you can't be intolerant, you can't try to force people to follow your own religious path, as the Christians have repeatedly done. You can't try to frighten people into being good. You can only encourage, you can only clarify, you can only inspire – you can't function in any other way, spiritually speaking. Not only can you not coerce, you can't bribe either; you're just appealing to people's greed then.

SAGARAMATI: What about us, the FWBO, in relation to the positive group? You can say that the negative group is all around, and even what is left of the positive group; but the positive group uses means in order to go against that pressure of the negative group, so that you could actually be fighting a negative group which to you would be inconsistent with establishing a positive group.

SANGHARAKSHITA: Well, you might consider yourself justified in doing that, but you'd have to assure yourself that in defending the positive group in that way, you really were able to preserve the positive group and that in the process of fighting for the positive group, the positive group itself did not become a negative group. It would be a matter of the individual decision and the individual person. It wouldn't be possible to lay down any hard and fast rule beyond what I've already said.

I remember reading something about the Crusades, and about one of the late emperors of Byzantium, the Eastern Roman Empire. Christian historians have blamed him very bitterly for being so diplomatic, even perfidious. He kept playing all sorts of diplomatic games, making promises and breaking them, but as more than one modern historian has pointed out, his whole purpose was to avoid war. The Christians of the Latin Church criticized him for not going out and fighting a straight battle, with lots of slaughter, and for breaking his word, but he considered breaking his word, and saying one thing to this party and another to that, to be preferable to warfare and the loss of human life. He managed to stave off war for a number of years, and he thought that a better and a more civilized thing to do, but the Latin Christians didn't.[242] This whole question of authority is very important. I've only just touched upon it this morning, but it is very important to realize, in broad general terms, that there's no place for authority in the spiritual life or in the spiritual movement. This makes things much more difficult in some ways, because you can rely only upon persuasion, upon genuinely convincing people of the rightness of a certain line of action. You can't threaten them, or coerce them, or bribe them, or do anything of that sort, which means there has to be lots of discussion, even lots of argument.

> Against such a one-sided emphasis on emotional faith, Buddhism
> moves from the very beginning of its spiritual training towards
> wholeness and completeness, i.e. towards a harmonious

> development of mental faculties. Therefore the act of going for refuge in its true sense is accomplished only if there is connected with it at least a minimal degree of purposeful will and genuine understanding. Only in that case, faith (*saddhā*) will have the quality of a 'seed' attributed to it by the Buddha, i.e. of a seed productive of further growth. The element of will in that seed of faith will grow until maturing into the irrepressible desire for liberation (*muñcitu-kamyatā-ñāṇa*) which is one of the advanced stages of Insight (*vipassanā*; see *Visuddhimagga*).[243] The element of initial understanding in true faith will grow into penetrative wisdom that will finally transform the assurance of faith into the inner certitude conferred by realization. (pp. 16–17)

SANGHARAKSHITA: There's a particular doctrinal formula which makes clear the emphasis of Buddhism on wholeness, or the fact that it 'moves from the very beginning of its spiritual training towards wholeness and completeness'. What doctrinal formula do you think that is? Can you remember that? It makes it *very* clear.

SAGARAMATI: The five spiritual faculties.

SANGHARAKSHITA: Yes, the five spiritual faculties of faith, wisdom, energy, meditation, all bound together by awareness or mindfulness. The Buddha does say in the Pāli canon that faith is the seed (*saddhā bīja*),[244] but Nyanaponika adds that although this is true – you can't deny the words of the Buddha – it's the seed only if it's connected with 'at least a minimal degree of purposeful will and genuine understanding'. The text, of course, doesn't say that. The text simply says faith is the seed. The point is that all one's faculties – all the different aspects of one's personality – have to be involved. That the Going or Refuge is a total commitment has been sufficiently stressed. It's probably better to say just that it must be total, and involve all of you, rather than try to work out the different proportions of the different so-called separate faculties.

> Taking refuge by way of thoughtless recital of the formula is a degradation of that venerable ancient practice. It deprives it of its true significance and of its efficacy. 'Going for refuge' should be the expression of a genuine inner urge, in the same way as, in

> ordinary life, one may be urged by the awareness of a great danger to seek without delay the refuge of a place of safety. (p. 17)

SANGHARAKSHITA: The illustration is from the more intellectually oriented approach. In that opening sentence Nyanaponika is referring in a cautious way to the practice in Theravādin countries of reciting the Refuges and Precepts, on all possible occasions but in a very mechanical way – and that certainly doesn't make one a Buddhist. Recited in this way it becomes a sort of slogan of the Buddhist cultural group, which certainly is a degradation; the word is not too strong. Such 'thoughtless recital... deprives it of its true significance'. This is what I call the cultural Going for Refuge, which is an expression of cultural, ethnic identity, as you get it in Ceylon, Burma, and so on.

> When taking refuge, one should always keep in mind the implications of this act, as outlined above. This will be, at the same time, a beneficial training in right mindfulness. One should always ask oneself how the presently undertaken act of going for refuge could be translated into terms of will and understanding. Seeing that the house of our life is ablaze, it will not do merely to worship the safety and freedom that beckons outside, without making an actual move to reach it. The first step in that direction of safety and freedom is taking refuge in the right way, i.e. as a conscious act of determination, understanding, and devotion.

SANGHARAKSHITA: I don't know why it is – despite what we looked at earlier – but the author seems to be really afraid of too much emotion. He is much more afraid of that than of too much understanding. Actually, so far as most Western Buddhists are concerned, it is the paucity of emotion and devotion that they should be afraid of, or aware of, rather than any deficiency of understanding. It's almost as though he's got it the wrong way round. Maybe it's because he's living and working in Ceylon, where he is surrounded by lots of apparently very devoted people, people who are very emotionally involved with Buddhism, and who are reciting the Refuges and Precepts day and night without understanding them, and he feels a need to stress the understanding aspect. But that certainly doesn't apply to the West – not as regards genuine faith and devotion, anyway.

## 2
# BUDDHAGHOSA'S EXPOSITION

### A Stream of Tendency Making for Righteousness

Having dealt with Nyanaponika's introductory thoughts and comments on the Refuges in general we'll go back now to Buddhaghosa's exposition of a passage in the *Majjhima Nikāya* dealing with the Refuges, as translated by Nyanaponika. First comes an introductory paragraph by the translator.

> After listening to the Buddha's discourse called 'Fear and Dread', the Brahman Jānussonī becomes a lay follower of the Buddha, by taking the Threefold Refuge. The words used by him differ slightly from the usual formula in so far as in the latter the words 'the Lord Gotama' are replaced by 'the Buddha'. (p. 1)

We find this sort of thing happening quite often at the end of a discourse by the Buddha. The person to whom the discourse is addressed is so impressed that they spontaneously go for Refuge on the spot. In some cases the Buddha has said very little; but that little is enough.

Buddhaghosa's comment, here slightly abridged, runs as follows:

> 'I go for refuge to the Lord Gotama' (*bhavantaṃ Gotamaṃ saraṇaṃ gacchāmi*). This means: The Lord Gotama is my refuge

> and my guiding ideal. I am going for refuge to the Lord Gotama. I resort to him, follow and honour him, in the sense of his being the Destroyer of Affliction and the Provider of Weal. Or: I know and understand him to be of such a nature. (p. 1)

You notice that here the commentator paraphrases by saying, 'I am going for refuge to the Lord Gotama.' Gotama is mentioned, not the Buddha. You remember the discussion earlier about Going for Refuge to the Buddha, not to Gotama, but as I mentioned, in many cases one does go for Refuge to Gotama, to the historical Buddha, not just to the abstract ideal of Buddhahood. So in these words the commentator brings out more fully the significance of the Going for Refuge. 'I go for refuge to the Lord Gotama (*bhavantaṃ Gotamaṃ saraṇaṃ gacchāmi*). This means: The Lord Gotama is my refuge and my guiding ideal.' What 'guiding ideal' means we shall see later on.

I don't think I am anticipating, but there are one or two points to be clarified here. 'I resort to him, follow and honour him, in the sense of his being the Destroyer of Affliction and the Provider of Weal.' Why do you think that last clause is added?

KULARATNA: Isn't that what we talked about before, that you're not Going for Refuge to him because he's a prince of the Sākya clan?

SANGHARAKSHITA: Exactly. The point is made in several places in the commentarial literature that if you were yourself a member of the Śākya clan, you might 'go for Refuge' to the Buddha thinking that he was a distinguished member of your clan and that it was right and proper that you should honour him as such in this way. But that would not be Going for Refuge to Gotama *the Buddha*. Or you might go for Refuge to him because many other people – distinguished people – went for Refuge to him and you thought you might as well join in. For this reason it is said that you go for Refuge 'in the sense of his being the Destroyer of Affliction', which is the negative side, as it were, 'and the Provider of Weal', which is the positive side. So is there any shade of difference between the meaning of these expressions? 'I resort to him, follow and honour him.' What would you think is meant by 'I resort to him'? What does having resort to someone usually mean?

SAGARAMATI: That you'd go to him for help.

SANGHARAKSHITA: You'd go to him for help. This is the one to whom you naturally turn for advice, help, guidance, inspiration. And then, 'follow him'. This is clear enough, isn't it? Whatever advice you receive, whatever teaching you receive, you put it into practice. But why do you think 'honouring' is mentioned separately from 'resorting' and 'following'? Perhaps this expresses the more devotional side of the spiritual life, the more 'giving' side. You're not just making use of the Buddha, as it were, for your own admittedly positive purposes. You have a genuine regard and admiration for him for his own sake. 'Or: I know and understand him to be of such a nature.' This is explained in the next paragraph, so let us go into that.

> This last explanation is based upon the fact that, in the Pāli language, the verbal roots denoting 'going' (*gati*) may also have the meaning of 'knowing' (*buddhi*). Therefore the words 'I go for refuge to the Buddha' may also be taken to express the idea: 'I know and understand him to be the refuge.'

SANGHARAKSHITA: This is obviously quite important – that one knows and understands the Buddha to be the Refuge as well as actually Going for Refuge to the Buddha. Yet again it represents an extra emphasis on the whole intellectual side of the process, even though reinforced by the appeal to the meaning of the word 'going' in Pāli.

SAGARAMATI: He always wants to qualify faith by bringing in understanding, but he doesn't qualify understanding by faith.

KULARATNA: This is Buddhaghosa, isn't it?

SANGHARAKSHITA: Yes, this is Buddhaghosa, but as translated and explained by Nyanaponika, who is perhaps even more in the intellectualist tradition than Buddhaghosa himself. This reminds me of an instance in which the Mahāyāna, on its own level, does exactly the opposite. You could say that if the Theravāda is constantly qualifying the devotional by the intellectual, the Mahāyāna very often qualifies the intellectual by the devotional – or even more than that. There is a passage in the *Perfection of Wisdom in Eight Thousand Lines* which discusses the question of how a bodhisattva may know that he is irreversible from Supreme Perfect Enlightenment, or, in other words, what the signs of irreversibility are. One of the signs is that if he is asked a question about the Unconditioned, or about Nirvāṇa, or about Wisdom, an irreversible bodhisattva will always bring compassion into his reply.[245] This is a sign that he is irreversible because it shows the beginnings, at least, of a complete unification of wisdom and compassion, so that he can no longer speak exclusively in terms of either the one or the other. He can no longer speak in this way because he has to some extent transcended the duality between *saṃsāra* and Nirvāṇa, conditioned and Unconditioned, wisdom and compassion. Therefore he has to bring compassion into his reply, even if it was not brought into the question. This illustrates very well the overall tendency of the Mahāyāna. In Nyanaponika's text we see devotion constantly being qualified by understanding, but in the Mahāyāna we see understanding even on the highest level, that of wisdom, being constantly supplemented not just by emotion but by compassion. In the case of the Mahāyāna you have wisdom already present. Wisdom is implied by the sort of question that is supposed to be put to the bodhisattva, which is why in answering it he cannot but bring in compassion. There is nothing else left to bring in. He is not in any way qualifying or trying to reduce wisdom, or to make it anything less than it is. He is just bringing in an extra dimension; he is concerned with ultimate truth. But one does feel that in *The Threefold Refuge* an attempt is being made to cut devotion down to size, as it were. One feels that the author doesn't want it to get out of hand. He wants not simply to supplement it with understanding but almost to reduce it, limit it.

> 'I go for refuge to the Dhamma.' The word *dhamma*, i.e. the Doctrine or the Law, is derived from the verb *dhāreti*, to keep or to bear. In accordance with that derivation, the Dhamma may be regarded as refuge, because it keeps, upholds and supports the beings by way of preventing their fall into the states of woe[246] by way of enabling a life according to instruction (as given by the Dhamma), by way of attainment of the Path, and by realization of the extinction (of suffering). Accordingly, the Dhamma (meant in the formula of refuge) is the (supramundane) Noble Path as well as Nibbāna. Besides, it is the attainment of the noble fruitions

(of the stream-enterer, the once-returner, the non-returner, and the saint), and also the Dhamma of Learning (laid down in the Scriptures; *pariyatti-dhamma*). (p. 2)

SANGHARAKSHITA: This is very important. It makes clear what the Dharma is in the primary sense by means of a reference to the etymology of the word *dhamma*, which is derived from the verb *dhāreti*, meaning 'to keep' or 'to bear' or 'to uphold'. Sometimes I give the analogy of the law of gravitation. Suppose you jump into the air and you come down. What is it that makes that possible?

GRAHAM: Gravity.

SANGHARAKSHITA: The law of gravity. If the earth did not exert a gravitational pull on you, in the absence of gravity you wouldn't ever come down again: you'd just go up and up indefinitely. So it's the law of gravity that makes that jump possible. In the same way, it is the Dharma that makes possible your skilful activities. Do you see that? There is, as it were, a law in accordance with which your skilful activities are followed by happiness, your unskilful activities by suffering. The law on the basis of which we are able to go from a lower to a higher state, from a less skilful to a more skilful state, from a less conscious to a more conscious state, is what we call the Dharma. This is what the Dharma actually is: the force in the universe that supports your individual moral and spiritual effort. We have to be careful here, though. The Dharma isn't a natural law. It is supramundane. It is transcendental. It isn't 'in the world' in the literal sense. We see no trace of it in nature. We see it only in human life, in human experience. Nature reveals only part – or God in the Manichaean sense reveals only part. Nature reveals only a cyclical order, not a spiral order. It's only when you come to the level of the individual consciousness that the spiral order begins to emerge. This is what the Dharma essentially is.

There's a very interesting definition by Matthew Arnold which purports to be a definition of God but which is much more suitable as a definition of Dharma: 'a stream of tendency making for righteousness'.[247] It doesn't sound much like God, does it? It doesn't sound very much like Christianity. It sounds more like Buddhism, except that in Buddhism it would be more than righteousness; it would be 'a stream of tendency making for Enlightenment'. Again, we mustn't always speak in terms of a law, just as in the case of the law of gravity, you mustn't imagine that there is a law governing objects from the outside. It's not exactly that it is just a manner of speaking; it's a bit more than that, but just as we mustn't imagine the law of gravity existing apart from material objects, in the same way we mustn't set the Dharma up as a sort of agency or force or power outside the individual, outside skilful, mundane, and transcendental actions and events.

So the Dharma is essentially whatever it is that assists us to move from lower to higher levels of being and consciousness. It is that which makes possible, or underlies, the whole process of the Higher Evolution. You could even say that the process of the Higher Evolution itself is Dharma. We are following the Dharma when we come into contact with that process of the Higher Evolution, when we become one with it, so that it is functioning as it were through us and we become part of that process. This is what the Dharma essentially is, and what following the Dharma essentially is, too.

Doctrines, specific teachings, are just applications or exemplifications of that law of the Higher Evolution. This is why it says at the end of the paragraph, 'Besides, it is the attainment of the noble fruitions (of the stream-enterer)' etc. That is to say, the Dharma is the transcendental path as actually experienced by living human individuals, 'and also the Dhamma of Learning (laid down in the Scriptures, *pariyatti-dhamma*)'. This latter is very secondary. So first of all, the Dharma is the law of the process of the Higher Evolution, secondly, it is that law as experienced, in varying degrees, by individuals; and thirdly, it is that law as reflected in actual, specific teachings contained in the scriptures. Living in accordance with the Dharma means living in accordance with the process of the Higher Evolution.

SAGARAMATI: Couldn't you say that there is something like that law of the Dharma at work in the lower evolution? Because there is development from lower forms of life to higher forms of life.

SANGHARAKSHITA: Yes, you could say that, but then that leads you into very deep waters metaphysically speaking, and into the question of immanence. What does one mean by immanence, for instance? It's probably safer to say that the crest, as it were – the positive crest – of the lower evolutionary process provides the basis for the arising of the process of the Higher Evolution. When you begin to speak in terms of the Higher Evolution being immanent in the process of the lower evolution, then you get into quite deep waters metaphysically. You could probably speak in that way with proper qualification, but you could also be misunderstood. The Yogācāra school does try to speak in this sort of way, especially in *The Awakening of Faith*. There it speaks of a mutual 'perfuming' of the conditioned and the Unconditioned.[248] That is metaphysics, and whether it's strictly necessary to speak in that way is a question. The Theravāda would certainly not consider it necessary to speak in that sort of way. But the human mind can't help wondering about it, especially the philosophic mind. Because the question does arise: are the two, the conditioned and the Unconditioned, different in an ultimate sense? Is there never any contact between them? If there is never any contact between them – if there never has been any contact between them – then how is it possible for the one to act as the basis or support for the arising of the other? Is it not possible that from the beginningless beginning there has been some infinitesimally faint reflection of the Unconditioned in the conditioned which provides the seed (to mix one's metaphors) for the development not only of the Unconditioned in the midst of the conditioned but even for the development of the Unconditioned itself? One can't help wondering in that sort of way. In other words, is the Transcendental – or the Dharma in the sense of the Transcendental Dharma – the support even of the conditioned, even of the process of the lower evolution, not simply of the Higher Evolution? I don't think these questions can be answered very easily, but they do arise, and for some people at least they need some sort of solution.

MAHAMATI: I think in your article on the bodhisattvas you said that one could say there were two ultimate realities.[249]

SANGHARAKSHITA: Yes, it is the standpoint of the Theravāda, or of the Hīnayāna generally, that there are two ultimate realities. But there is a very important proviso. Two ultimate realities mean an ultimate dualism. But to an experience such as ours, which is dualistic, that is to say, constituted in terms of subject and object, ultimate reality cannot present itself other than dualistically. So long as we are operating with our dualistic consciousness we cannot perceive anything other than duality. From that standpoint, which is the standpoint of the Theravāda, of the Hīnayāna in general, or even of practical Buddhism generally, dualism is ultimate. For the dualistic mind, dualism is ultimate.

MAHAMATI: I was surprised, because I thought Buddhism could say very little if there weren't two ultimate realities, not one ultimate.

SANGHARAKSHITA: Well, the Theravāda doesn't admit a metaphysical position. The Theravāda operates with these two categories of the conditioned and the Unconditioned. It thinks of the spiritual life as a process of transition from the conditioned to the Unconditioned, but it doesn't go into the metaphysical question as to whether the conditioned and the Unconditioned are two aspects of one higher reality. It doesn't consider it necessary to do that, because the standpoint of the Theravāda, and this seems to have been the Buddha's own standpoint, was strictly practical. So methodologically, if not metaphysically, the conditioned and the Unconditioned are your two ultimate categories. They're ultimate methodologically for the Theravāda, but the question of whether they are metaphysically ultimate is left open, because the Theravāda leaves metaphysical questions open when they have no practical implications. The Mahāyāna, rather more boldly – some might say recklessly – took the matter up and resolved the conditioned and the Unconditioned into a third category, *śūnyatā*, which was higher than either and included both. But what is it that posits *śūnyatā*? This is also a very important question. If it is only the dualistic subject, or a subject which is part of a duality of subject and object, positing *śūnyatā*, then *śūnyatā* itself becomes dualistic. So probably, in a way, the Theravāda position is the safer one, because to venture into Mahāyāna metaphysics you need to be not only spiritually aware but also intellectually very sophisticated.

For all practical purposes Buddhism is dualistic. We ourselves are subjects experiencing objects: the framework of our experience is dualistic. We cannot but think dualistically, cannot but experience dualistically, and even when we think of the non-dual, that which is neither subject nor object, we make it an object, and we, as subject, are thinking of it. We are self-excluded from it. By making it an object we falsify it, because how can the subject think or experience as subject that which is neither subject nor object? It's impossible. It's self-contradictory. If you were able to experience or think it you couldn't experience it or think it. Hence the paradoxes of the Mahāyāna, of the 'Perfection of Wisdom' teachings. How can the subject attain that which is neither subject nor object? Therefore the bodhisattva's attainment is a non-attainment, or there is both attainment and non-attainment.

Anyway, that's going rather far afield. For all practical purposes, Buddhism is dualistic. I must admit that in that article you mentioned I made this point in a sense deliberately to shock people, because they usually think that Buddhism is monistic, or non-dualistic. But one should be very careful about making statements like that. The Theravāda certainly, for practical purposes, methodologically, is dualistic. Buddhism, to the extent that it is a practical system, is dualistic, and you can even make out a case for metaphysical dualism, as regards Buddhism, just as easily as a case for metaphysical non-dualism. But *practically* speaking, whether it's the Theravāda, or the Mahāyāna, or Zen, or Tantra, the basis is dualistic. Sometimes Zen, as well as the Tantra, professes to have a non-dualistic basis, but if you look into it more closely you'll find that in fact it's not so.

SAGARAMATI: Regarding the idea of the spiral way, the path of the Higher Evolution, I've always thought of the spiral as arising out of the conditioned. It's another form of the conditioned. Is it in that sense more ...

SANGHARAKSHITA: It arises out of the conditioned in the sense that it arises in dependence on it; but you couldn't therefore really describe it as another form of the conditioned.

SAGARAMATI: You mean the spiral part of conditionality is actually under the influence of the Transcendental?

SANGHARAKSHITA: Yes, that is so. But there is, of course, the intermediate band where one feels the pull of both, and where the conflict is not yet resolved. You are on the spiral but you are on that section of the spiral which is at the same time part of the round. You can't work that out diagrammatically very well, but that is actually how it is. But there is that point of no return beyond which the spiral is not part of the round. So you've got (1) the round only, where you can only go round and round; (2) that intermediate band of experience which can be part of the round and also part of the spiral – it's a sort of transition from the round to the spiral proper; and (3) the spiral proper, from which regress is not possible. So where does the difficulty come in?

SAGARAMATI: Well, I've always seen it like on the one hand you've got the Transcendental and on the other you've got the conditioned. In the conditioned there are basically two types of conditionality. There's a lower type of conditionality and there's also the like of what you said, the Dharma as a process of growth but which is still *moral* in a sense.

SANGHARAKSHITA: This would be that part of the spiral which is also part of the mundane. But beyond that – beyond the point of irreversibility, beyond the point of Stream Entry – there is a section of the spiral which is not part of the mundane, not part of the world, something that doesn't have a place in the mundane at all.

SAGARAMATI: That's the Unconditioned, isn't it?

SANGHARAKSHITA: Perhaps the difficulty arises out of a conflict of modes of expression, that is to say, a conflict between speaking of processes and speaking of things. We speak of the spiral path, and that is a process. But we also speak of 'the Unconditioned', as though it was a thing. This is not altogether satisfactory. Perhaps we should not speak of the Unconditioned as though it was a thing at all, but only of that furthest point of the spiral process beyond which you cannot see. Not that there's a static thing called the Unconditioned at the end of the spiral process. Perhaps you can speak of the conditioned as a thing, though in the light of modern physics perhaps you shouldn't do even that, but you certainly cannot think of the Unconditioned as a thing. You should think of it only as that hypothetical furthest point of the process of the spiral path.

So there's the Dharma as that stream of tendency making for Enlightenment, which is not any part of the mundane – except for that intermediate band, as I've called it; there's that stream of tendency as reflected in, or actually experienced by, those who have made themselves one with it in its higher, purely transcendental reaches, and then there's that same stream as reflected in specific spiritual teachings contained in the scriptures. This is what the Dharma essentially is. I think it's quite important to think of it in this sort of way.

LOKAMITRA: You said that the law wasn't a natural law but a transcendental law?

SANGHARAKSHITA: In other words, it's not a law which you can discover or detect at work in the natural world anywhere other than in human experience.

LOKAMITRA: But isn't it just the same process of conditionality? Isn't it natural law when looked at in a cyclical way, and the transcendental law, the spiral or creative conditionality, when looked at in a spiral way?

SANGHARAKSHITA: Again it's a question of terminology. If you speak in terms of a single process of conditionality you transcend the dichotomy of conditioned and unconditioned, mundane and transcendental, because if you use the term conditionality in that sense it's used as an all-inclusive term that includes both the so-called conditioned and the so-called Unconditioned. In that way it equates with *śūnyatā*, which is neither mundane nor transcendental, because it transcends that duality. This is a point which has not been developed at all by the Theravāda. I've developed it in a paper that I wrote in 1949 and which I'm thinking of putting together with other papers, published and unpublished, for a little volume.[250] But the *pratītya-samutpāda* or *paṭicca-samuppāda* (i.e. conditioned co-production) mentioned in this paper is an all-inclusive formula. It includes both the mundane and the Transcendental. So the term conditionality – though again, as I've said, this involves a conflict of terminology – includes both conditionality and non-conditionality, i.e. both cyclical conditionality and spiral conditionality. Perhaps one should invent some other term for that total process. Maybe *śūnyatā* would do. It is that process which makes possible both modes of what we've called conditionality, the cyclical *and* the spiral. But the spiral type of conditionality is transcendental, the cyclical is mundane. So the *pratītya-samutpāda*, as an all-inclusive law, cannot be described either as exclusively mundane or exclusively transcendental.

KULARATNA: Can you define what you mean by transcendental in this context?

SANGHARAKSHITA: That's quite difficult. The Pāli and Sanskrit word is *lokuttara*: that which is 'beyond the world'; that which is not subject to the cyclical process; that which grows from good to better, from better to best, irreversibly. In terms of process, the transcendental is that which is irreversibly cumulative. It is that which is not subject to old age, disease, and death, that which is not subject to suffering or impermanence, in the sense of the cyclical process, and that which is ultimately real.

SAGARAMATI: But in that definition the transcendental path starts with *śraddhā*.

SANGHARAKSHITA: No, it doesn't. The positive series of *nidānas* or links starts with *śraddhā*, and the transcendental series starts with *yathābhūta-jñānadarśana* or knowledge and vision of things as they are.

SAGARAMATI: But there is a spiral from *śraddhā* to...

SANGHARAKSHITA: Yes, but that section of the spiral is not only part of the spiral process but also part of the round, the cyclical process, because there can be recession from it.

SAGARAMATI: It's like the two can be mixed then?

SANGHARAKSHITA: The two are identical. Something does not cease to be positive because in dependence upon that positive, a negative can arise. But that is the mundane positive. In dependence upon the transcendental positive, a negative cannot arise. Only a further positive, a higher positive, can arise.

SAGARAMATI: So if in dependence upon *śraddhā* or faith there arises joy, that's the transcendental order?

SANGHARAKSHITA: No. It is simply the *spiral* order. It would be confusing to call it the transcendental order.

SAGARAMATI: But that's going from a positive to a greater positive, isn't it?

SANGHARAKSHITA: That's true, but it's simply spiral. The spiral process has got these two sections: mundane spiral and transcendental spiral. But to call the whole thing transcendental would cause confusion.

KULARATNA: Is not the mundane spiral transcendental?

SANGHARAKSHITA: No, because the transcendental section of the spiral is *irreversibly* cumulative. The mundane part is only reversibly cumulative. It *can* be undone.

KULARATNA: So that's the key thing: when we pass the point of no return, that's when it's transcendental.

SANGHARAKSHITA: You can't fall then, in terms of the path. That's when it becomes transcendental.

SAGARAMATI: In the lower spiral, the mundane spiral, there's a possibility of heading towards the Transcendental. There's also a possibility of falling back.

SANGHARAKSHITA: That's right, yes. It's as though the line of the spiral and the line of the round cross each other. That positive experience occupies the nexus between the two. It can take a turning onto the round, it can take a turning onto the spiral. It's at the point of intersection between the two. For instance, I spoke of emotional self-indulgence. You may have a positive feeling of faith and devotion, but if your self-consciousness intervenes and appropriates it for itself that sets up a movement away from the spiral to the round, whereas if your self-consciousness hadn't intervened, and if instead your faith and devotion had given rise to joy and delight, that would have been a movement up the spiral – not the transcendental but the mundane spiral, but still the spiral nonetheless.

SAGARAMATI: It's as if at each turn on the spiral there's a round.

SANGHARAKSHITA: Yes, indeed there is, until you get to that point of no return. That is why, if you find yourself in a highly positive state, you should be very aware, because you can become self-forgetful, lose your awareness, and sink very easily into a negative state, or at least into an unskilful state. You get carried away. It's a question of energy, too. When I was in Kalimpong some of my young Nepalese friends used to get into trouble with women. Nepalese Hindu society doesn't offer many opportunities for that sort of activity, so it used to be interesting to see what the pattern was when it did happen. It was nearly always after, or in the course of, some religious festival. They'd be really enjoying the festival, maybe feeling devotional and listening to devotional music, but then they would become a bit unmindful. There would be lots of people around, it would be late at night.... That's when one must watch oneself, and not allow oneself to be carried away, when one's spiritual life is going well, when one feels in a positive mood, because it's easier to be carried away then. So you swing from the spiral, that is to say from that part of the spiral which is also part of the round, onto that part of the round which is just part of the round. You're not safe, as it were, until you get up to that point of no return.

**Part and Parcel of The Sangha**

> 'I go for refuge to the Sangha.' The Sangha is (here) the community of (holy) monks which is united by the communion of right view and virtue (*diṭṭhi-sīla saṅghātena saṃhato'ti saṅgho*). (p. 2)

SANGHARAKSHITA: This is rather interesting. It is not only Buddhaghosa who says this. In the Pāli canonical texts too the Sangha is sometimes defined as 'the community of (holy) monks', that is, monks who are *āryas*. But that is surely a mistake. 'The Sangha is (here) the community of (holy) monks which is united by the communion of right view and virtue.' No, it certainly isn't that, because it's the Āryasaṅgha, and those who are not monks, those who are *upāsakas*, can by virtue of their higher spiritual attainments be members of the Āryasaṅgha. This is the Theravāda teaching as well. So this statement of Buddhaghosa's is not quite correct. It's a slip. But anyway, it's interesting that the members of the sangha are said to be 'united by the communion of right view and virtue'. What seems to be missing?

A VOICE: Devotion.

SAGARAMATI: *Samādhi.*

SANGHARAKSHITA: Yes, once again the emotional factor seems to be missing. You could say that *samādhi* represented that, inasmuch as *samādhi* includes intense happiness, joy, bliss, delight, peace, and so on.

> That is to say: the Sangha (meant in the formula of refuge) is the group of the eight noble beings (*ariya-puggala*; those in possession of (1) the path of stream-entry, (2) the fruition thereof, etc).' (p. 2)

SANGHARAKSHITA: This is of course from the Theravāda or Hīnayāna point of view. The Mahāyāna would also include the great bodhisattvas in the Āryasaṅgha, but putting it very broadly beyond the distinction of Hīnayāna and Mahāyāna, the Āryasaṅgha is all those who have become one as it were with the spiral subsequent to that point of no return. It consists of those who are at one with that stream of tendency making for Enlightenment to such an extent that they can no longer fall back from it into the round.

LOKAMITRA: If you had a transcendental vision, Bhante, you're on the path of Stream Entry. But surely at the same time you'd be experiencing the fruits of Stream Entry because you'd had that vision.

SANGHARAKSHITA: Not according to the Theravāda teaching. It's analogous to what happens in the case of karma and *vipāka*. There is an action, a willed action, and then, subsequent to that, there is an experience which is the result of that willed action. For instance, you perform a skilful action and you experience happiness; you perform an unskilful action, you experience pain. Subsequently, on the transcendental path, you make an effort, you break certain fetters: that is the experience of the path. Then, as a result of your breaking those fetters, as a result of your experiencing the path, there comes to you an experience of enhanced freedom, enhanced expansion. This is the fruit.

LOKAMITRA: So the path is a process of breaking those fetters.

SANGHARAKSHITA: In the Theravāda the path is spoken of in terms of the breaking of the fetters.

LOKAMITRA: So it could in fact be before the fetters are broken. It's a question of terms which I'm not quite sure of. If you see the fetters being broken at an exact point then it's hard to see the difference between path and fruit, whereas if you see the path as the process of breaking the fetters, which starts as you're aspiring to be an individual, and ends after you've actually broken ...

SANGHARAKSHITA: There doesn't seem to be any difficulty at all. Take the case of a prisoner who is literally bound. Someone provides him with a file – that corresponds to the preparatory practices prior to the attainment of the transcendental path. But the prisoner also actually breaks the fetters: that corresponds to the experience of the transcendental path as distinct from the fruit. As the prisoner steps out of the fetters a free man he experiences great joy, happiness, and expansion: that corresponds to the experience of the fruit. This is the nature of the distinction. So with regard to the Stream Entrant, and with regard to the once-returner, the non-returner, the *arhant*, there is this distinction between path and fruit: the path being the more volitional side, or what you actually do, and the fruit representing the experience that comes to you, almost like a *vipāka*, as a result of what you have done.

KULARATNA: But they're not necessarily to be seen as temporary, one thing after the other...

SANGHARAKSHITA: Well, the latter comes after the former. The experience of the fruit comes after the experience of the path. Where's the difficulty? There isn't really any difficulty at all. If there seems to be a difficulty it's maybe because the word 'path' is used here in a technical sense and you're thinking of the path in general all the time. Experience of fruition is also part of the path in a more general sense.

SAGARAMATI: The fact is that people are confused, saying that there are these eight persons, and it seems a really strange sort of way to split them up.[251]

SANGHARAKSHITA: In the *Tiratana Vandanā* or 'Salutation to the Three Jewels' the term is *aṭṭha purisapuggalā*. Here the *puggalā* seems to refer to the four i.e. the Stream Entrant etc. and the *purisa* to the eight i.e. to the Stream Entrant etc. as divided according to *magga* and *phala*, though the question of what interval elapses between the experience of *magga* and the experience of *phala* can be raised. One gets the impression that even if it is not instantaneous, the transition from the one to the other is very rapid, so that it is rather a refinement of analysis to speak of eight distinct persons rather than simply of four.

LOKAMITRA: It seems almost ridiculous to do so, unless the fruits, i.e. the experience of *phala*, come some time afterwards.

SANGHARAKSHITA: I don't remember any definite statement to this effect in the Pāli canonical literature but it seems that the fruit is experienced almost immediately after the path. According to Nyanatiloka, *phala*: literally 'fruit, fruition', i.e. result, path-result, 'denotes those moments of supermundane consciousness which immediately after the moment of path-consciousness are flashing forth, and which, till the attainment of the next higher path, may during the practice of Insight (*vipassanā*) still recur for innumerable times.'[252]

KULARATNA: So time on the path is almost a momentary thing.

SANGHARAKSHITA: Yes, but the Theravāda, for some reason or other – I'm not quite clear why – considers it important to make this distinction between *magga* and *phala*. It's always brought in when the *arhant* and the other Holy Persons are discussed.

SAGARAMATI: There's another person prior to the Stream Entrant as well, isn't there?

SANGHARAKSHITA: There's the *gotrabhū*, but that's a further refinement or analysis brought in by the Sarvāstivādins. In the Theravāda the *gotrabhū* is one who experiences what Nyanatiloka terms 'the lightning-like transitional stage between the state of a worldling and that of a *sotāpanna*'.[253] In the Sarvāstivāda, however, *gotra* means something like 'spiritual lineage' and *gotrabhū* is more like 'determination of spiritual vocation' when, from the Hīnayāna point of view, one definitely sets oneself in the direction of individual liberation alone or in the direction of Supreme Perfect Enlightenment as a Buddha, in other words on either the *arhant* path or the bodhisattva path. I think this is a false alternative.

There is a definite psychological basis for the distinction between *magga* and *phala*, as I explained by way of the example of the man in prison. When you're struggling with your fetters, or even at the moment of breaking them, it's as though you are bound and free at the same time. But when you experience the state of being completely free, the fetters no longer being there, that's quite a different experience. It's that experience which the Theravāda refers to as *phala*. It's simply the *experience* of *magga*.

SAGARAMATI: It isn't like even the Buddha's own experience of Enlightenment. There was that time he spent in the woods, I think you mentioned one or two examples, where he's got accustomed ...

SANGHARAKSHITA: That was the path of bodhisattvahood, not the path of the *arhant*, with reference to which this distinction between *magga* and *phala* is made. This would be the technical reply, but really the matter is more abstruse than that and requires further elucidation.

SAGARAMATI: When the compassion arose that was the bodhisattva path?

SANGHARAKSHITA: Traditionally speaking the Buddha, having aimed at full Enlightenment from the beginning, i.e. from the time of his life as the ascetic Sumedha, was following the bodhisattva path, so distinctions that pertain to the *arhant* path are not relevant in his case. That is what the Theravādins would say. Whether that is a completely adequate reply is another matter.

SAGARAMATI: I was thinking of a distinction between his attainment of Enlightenment and the fact that he had to get used to the idea of his Enlightenment: that was the *fruit* of his Enlightenment experience.

SANGHARAKSHITA: You could say that in the same way that *magga* and *phala* are analogous to karma and *vipāka*, wisdom and compassion are analogous to them. First you experience wisdom, which is seeing through the conditioned, and then, as it were, you reach the state of freely functioning with that wisdom, and that is compassion. You could say that there was an analogy there. That would be going beyond the Theravāda explanations, but you could certainly say that. You could say that wisdom, or insight, corresponded to becoming free; compassion corresponded to what you did with your state of freedom.

> In order to gain proficiency with regard to this subject of 'refuge', one should be acquainted with the following method of exposition, dealing with (1) the word *saraṇa*; (2) the going for refuge (*saraṇāgamana*); (3) who is going for refuge?; (4) the divisions; (5) the results; (6) the defilements; (7) the breach. (p. 2)

SANGHARAKSHITA: I think we'll have to leave these points until tomorrow because it's already one o'clock. Before we close, are there any general points arising out of what we've done so far this morning?

MAHAMATI: Can you just say a few words about Buddhaghosa?

SANGHARAKSHITA: Buddhaghosa was Indian by birth. Not much is known about him. He seems to have lived in the fifth century and is supposed to have been a brahmin of Bihar who, on being converted to Buddhism, became a monk and went to Ceylon, where he studied the Sinhalese commentaries on the Pāli canonical texts and translated them into Pāli. He also wrote that encyclopaedic exposition of Theravādin Buddhism called the *Visuddhimagga*, or 'Path of Purification' of which we have two English translations, and is the great scholastic authority of the Theravāda right down to the present day; there has been nobody else like him. On account of his literary work he is highly esteemed. In Theravādin countries they esteem first the Pāli Tipiṭaka, then the *Milindapañha*, the 'Questions of King Milinda', a non-canonical work, and then the writings of Buddhaghosa. These three are considered the most authoritative, and in that order. There is a life of Buddhaghosa in Pāli called *Buddhaghosuppatti*, which has been translated into English.[254] Buddhaghosa is the greatest exponent of the Theravāda, corresponding to Vasubandhu for the Sarvāstivādins. He isn't very philosophical, though he is very interesting. There are a number of commentaries which go under his name but which modern scholars think are not actually by him. But some of the most important commentaries are certainly his.

I couldn't help thinking that Buddhaghosa's definition of the Dharma was extraordinarily broad in the true sense, and contrasts very strongly with the way that the modern Theravādins look at the Dharma. They look at it in a very narrow, literal-minded sort of way. He also makes it clear that 'Dharma' has very little to do with 'religion' as that term is usually understood in the West.

> (1) As to the meaning of the word *saraṇa*, the commentator relates it, not in the sense of a linguistic derivation, but for the purposes of exposition, to the verb *sarati*, 'to crush', having the same meaning as *hiṃsati*, 'to kill'. The refuge is explained in that way, because, for those who are taking that refuge, it kills and destroys danger and fear, suffering and the defilements leading to evil destiny. The refuge is a name of the Triple Gem. (pp. 2–3)

SANGHARAKSHITA: So the commentator does not give 'a linguistic derivation' (what we would describe as a scientific etymology), but what we would regard as a fanciful etymology based purely upon verbal resemblance. Buddhist commentators very often do this. I think I once said, probably in the *Survey*, that it's bad etymology in the scientific sense but that it often makes good sense from a Buddhist point of view.[255] So here 'the commentator', that is to say Buddhaghosa 'for the purpose of exposition', for the purpose of making what he considers the real meaning of the word 'refuge' clear, derives it from the verb *sarati*, 'to crush' in the sense of *hiṃsati* or 'to kill', that is to say, to crush, destroy, wipe out, kill, eliminate. So, 'The refuge is explained in that way' – that is to say, as a crushing or a destroying or a killing, 'because, for those who are taking that refuge,' for those who go to that refuge, 'it kills and destroys danger and fear, suffering and the defilements leading to evil destiny.'

What is meant by evil destiny? These are the *duggatis*: rebirth as an animal, as a hungry ghost, or as a being in hell – or rather, in a state of purgatory. This explanation of the meaning of the word 'refuge', connecting it with *sarati*, 'to crush', clearly reflects what we described earlier as the approach of the doctrine-follower, rather than that of the faith-follower. But it certainly is an aspect of refuge that 'it kills and destroys danger and fear, suffering and the defilements leading to evil destiny'.

Another explanation: The Buddha destroys fear in beings by promoting their happiness and by removing harm from them. The Dhamma does it by making the beings cross the wilderness of existence and by giving them solace. The Sangha does it by (enabling devotees) to obtain rich results even from small religious acts (like homage, offerings, etc). (p. 3)

SANGHARAKSHITA: The Triple Gem collectively destroys danger and fear, suffering and the defilements, but each individual Refuge, Buddhaghosa is saying, does it in a specific way. Do you notice anything in particular about that last item – how the Sangha does it? What does it assume?

LOKAMITRA: A split between the monks and the lay devotees.

SANGHARAKSHITA: Yes. Even though the Sangha has been defined as the Āryasaṅgha, clearly for practical purposes it is identified with the *bhikkhu* sangha in a quite conventional sense. Clearly the devotees here are the lay devotees, and clearly they are not expected to practise the Dharma seriously themselves, but simply to make offerings to the *bhikkhus*, to do them homage and derive at least some benefit from that. What this really means is that on account of the 'split' between the sangha, between the order of monks, and the laity, the Sangha is ceasing to be a refuge, or is a refuge to a very limited extent indeed.

There is the conception, which one finds very strongly in Theravādin Buddhism, in the Hīnayāna generally, and even in the Mahāyāna to some extent, of the Sangha – theoretically the Āryasaṅgha, but in practice the *bhikkhu* sangha – as a *puṇyakṣetra* or 'field of merits', the idea being that any offering made to them bears especially abundant fruit. Thus it is that in Theravādin countries you find that it's one of the functions of the sangha to provide the lay devotees, the *upāsakas* in that debased sense of the term, with opportunities of making merit. The idea behind this is that the ordinary lay Buddhist does not take the Dharma very seriously – is perhaps not in a position to take it very seriously – but he does need some merit to ensure happiness for himself in this life and in future lives. So how is he to obtain that merit? He can't gain it by meditation, because he doesn't meditate. Perhaps he can't gain it even by observing the moral precepts: perhaps he's breaking them all the time. So what can he do? He can make offerings to the monks and pay them outward respect. In this way he can earn merit, and that merit will help him obtain a better rebirth. It will remove danger and fear (in terms of the present explanation), at least to the extent of helping him avoid painful rebirths later on. Here you can see a great decline from the ideal of sangha. The sangha is no longer something to which you belong, to however humble an extent, or of which you are a member, however imperfect. The sangha is not something which is inspiring you, as a member, to follow the path. The sangha, in this sense, is simply a body of people who are, at least theoretically, following the path themselves, and who give opportunities to you, since you are not able really to follow the Path, to make a bit of merit by making offerings to them. This is really a decline, a degeneration.

The ordinary lay person in Theravādin countries – even though he may call himself an *upāsaka*, which means virtually nothing more than a 'born Buddhist' – does not regard himself as a member of the sangha. In practice the sangha is identified exclusively with the *bhikkhu* sangha, and the lay person regards it as his function to support the sangha in that sense. He does not consider himself to be a member of it. He's just a 'born Buddhist', just a lay devotee, just an *upāsaka* in the devalued sense of the term. Thus the average layman in Theravādin countries, however good and pious he may be, does not have a sense of belonging to the spiritual community and as being committed. In other words, he doesn't take the Going for Refuge seriously. He recites it, sure enough, but it's simply a cultural act. It shows that he's a 'Buddhist' in the purely cultural sense, not that he's committed to the spiritual path and wishes to evolve.

This conception of the sangha as the field of merits (and it surely *is* a field of merits) and of the lay devotee as simply making merit by making offerings to the *bhikkhu* sangha came in very early. After all, the full-time followers were monks, and they needed to be supported. That's all right. But unfortunately it became the sole duty of the Buddhist living at home to support the monks rather than to practise the Dharma seriously himself. So 'the Sangha does it,' that is to say, destroys fear in beings, 'by (enabling devotees) to obtain rich results even from small religious acts.' It's a good investment! I don't know how happy Nyanaponika himself really is with this approach, but he's paraphrasing or expounding what the commentator says. But you see how easy it is. Instead of following the path yourself, you support somebody else who is following it. It's certainly good to support those who are following the path to a greater extent than you can yourself, but you must be careful that supporting someone following the path does not become a substitute for following it yourself – and this is definitely what happens in the Theravādin countries. It's almost as though they employ the *bhikkhus* to keep up the Dharma so that they themselves need not bother about it too much. This is one of the reasons why they are very strict with their *bhikkhus*: because the *bhikkhus* have to practise the Dharma not only for themselves but, in a sense, for the laity too. If a *bhikkhu* commits some misdemeanour, other *bhikkhus* will not be hard on him, but the lay people will be very hard on him, because they feel that their faith is being undermined and their source of merit depleted.

In some of the Theravādin countries – I certainly noticed this with the Sinhalese – it's as though the lay people practise Buddhism vicariously through the *bhikkhus*, and this isn't a very healthy state of affairs. Even admitting that some people may practise the path in a more advanced way and that, if they have no material resources of their own, they may need to be helped by those who have such resources, the people with resources should still practise the Dharma themselves in ways other than just helping others who are practising if they wish to be considered Buddhists. That's certainly our approach in the FWBO. If you call yourself a Buddhist it means that you go for Refuge. If you go for Refuge you really practise, earnestly and sincerely, whatever your socio-religious position may be. Whether you're living at home or whether you've literally gone forth, you must still practise. It's not enough merely to support those who are practising, and if that's all you do, you can't really believe in what they're doing. So why do you support them? It can't be for purely spiritual reasons. You support them because it's part of your national culture, perhaps, or because it's a respectable thing to do. It gives you the reputation of being a pious person, and thereby you have a certain amount of weight, a certain amount of influence.

So if you are a Buddhist, if you yourself really and truly go for Refuge, you cannot regard the sangha as something outside of yourself which it is merely your duty to support. You are part and parcel of the sangha in however humble a capacity, and as such you are supposed to be practising the Dharma and following the path yourself by your own efforts. To say of the sangha, as Buddhaghosa does, that it destroys danger and fear by enabling devotees to obtain rich results even by small religious acts like homage, offerings, etc., is to take away the main function of the sangha, which is to act as a source of spiritual inspiration and guidance for all its members, even the humblest – perhaps most of all for the humblest. To think of it in our own terms, there might well be people who supported the Western Buddhist Order and the FWBO quite generously, but if they confined themselves simply to doing that we wouldn't regard them as Buddhists – not if they were not actually practising the Dharma themselves. To the extent that it is *dāna* or giving, supporting is a practice, but by itself it is not enough, because they could be supporting us for reasons that were entirely non-spiritual. Such a person couldn't be regarded as a Buddhist because they would not have truly gone for Refuge, even though they might join in the recitation of the Refuge formula in the course of a puja if they happened to come along to one.

This explanation of the meaning of *saraṇa* is very one-sided, isn't it? It stresses revulsion from the conditioned rather than attraction to the Unconditioned. But perhaps we said enough about that already.

## A Very Positive State of Mind

> (2) The going for (or taking) refuge is a state of mind in which defilements are destroyed owing to the faith in, and veneration for, the Triple Gem; a state of mind which, without relying on others (*apara-paccayo*), proceeds by way of taking the Triple Gem as its guiding ideal (*parāyaṇa*). (p. 3)

SANGHARAKSHITA: This is quite a bit more positive. It suggests that one has the Triple Gem – the Buddha, the Dharma, and Sangha – in view, as it were, and that one has faith in and veneration in the Three Jewels. Quite a bit more could have been said about this. It's not just a question of faith: it's also a question of joy, delight, and so many other positive states – possibly all the different positive states. In the positive mental events listed in the Abhidharma, faith is the first one to be enumerated, and even if it's not the most important of the positive mental events it certainly occupies the leading position among them. If one's mind is filled with faith, devotion, joy, love, and delight as one is engaged in contemplating the attractiveness of the Triple Gem, there's no room for the defilements. This is a very important point.

There'll be a little bit about this 'guiding ideal' (*parāyaṇa* is also translated as 'the way to the beyond') later on. The suggestion here is that when you go for Refuge you regard the object of refuge, especially the Buddha, as an ideal – an ideal being something which you can take as the norm of your own conduct, something which shows you what you can become. So this is a somewhat more positive approach. You are drawn to the Triple Gem. You have faith in it, you feel love towards it, you take delight in it, and because your mind is filled with all those mental events there's no room for any of the defilements. But it must be emphasized that you don't just have faith in, or take delight in, the Triple Gem in a merely aesthetic way. It's not purely contemplative. You also take the Triple Gem as your 'guiding ideal'. You think, 'This is what *I* would like to be like. This is what I would like to *become*. This is what I'm *going* to become.' Thus it's 'a state of mind which, without relying on others (*apara-paccayo*), proceeds by way of taking the Triple Gem as its guiding ideal (*parāyaṇa*)', i.e. as something to be personally attained.

ANANDAJYOTI: What exactly is meant by 'without relying on others'? On other people?

SANGHARAKSHITA: We talked a bit about this on the first day. You're not completely without reliance, because you are relying on the Triple Gem itself; but you are Going for Refuge to it as a result of your own personal decision. You're not Going for Refuge, or going through the motions of Going for Refuge, simply because others are Going for Refuge. It's an individual act on your part. You're not Going for Refuge as a member of a group.

Returning to the main subject, it's a very positive state of mind indeed that is envisaged here, a state of mind so wrapped up in the Three Jewels, so full of positive, skilful mental states that there is no room for any defilements at all. This suggests that if you've really and truly gone for Refuge you never have any mental defilements. They're all destroyed. And when they're permanently destroyed, that's the transcendental Going for Refuge. You could also put it the other way round and say that when you have any unskilful mental states then, at that moment, and to the extent that you have the unskilful mental states, you're not Going for Refuge, and therefore to that extent you're not a Buddhist.

Do you see the point? In this way you can see how your Going for Refuge fluctuates. Sometimes it's stronger and brighter. At other times it's rather dim and weak and faint. There might even be times when it's in abeyance altogether, as far as one can see – if one has sufficient mindfulness even to look and see.

LOKAMITRA: There's something important which comes from that, which is that when one is in an unskilful state, faith goes, and if there's no faith then one ceases to see the spiritual community as a spiritual community and sees it only as another group. One then tends to react to it, and to one's spiritual friends, in this sort of way. One closes the gates, as it were, locks oneself out.

SANGHARAKSHITA: Yes, or one regards this spiritual community, the sangha, just as the field of merits in an almost cynical way. I have met Sinhalese lay people who didn't really believe in Buddhism but who still supported the *bhikkhus* because it was the done thing. They cheerfully and cynically supported them, or gave them things, in a spirit of almost worldly friendship. They liked them, they got on well with them, but they didn't take them very seriously. Their attitude was that the *bhikkhus* were good chaps, they knew Pāli, some of them were good writers, so okay, we'll give them some food, make them a few presents. They were quite happy to do this for the *bhikkhus*, but you could hardly call it the giving of *dāna* in the ordinary sense. They had no faith. Perhaps what was said earlier on has another implication: that to the extent that you're in a negative mental state you're not Going for Refuge. To the extent that you're depressed, gloomy, resentful, or disgruntled you're not Going for Refuge. One mustn't exaggerate, because if and when you are in that sort of negative emotional state you can still cling on to the Refuge by force of overall conviction, but it certainly isn't a very real thing for you when you're in that sort of state.

> (3) Who is going for refuge? It is a being endowed with a state of mind as described above. (p. 3)

This is very short and simple, isn't it? It defines who is a Buddhist. A Buddhist is one who is in a state of mind in which defilements are destroyed owing to faith in and veneration for the Triple Gem. So if your defilements are not destroyed by your faith in and veneration for the Triple Gem, you're not a Buddhist. This is very clear and very uncompromising. To the extent that you're overcome by greed, craving, hatred, ignorance, and delusion, and all their derivatives, to that extent you are not Going for Refuge – *cannot* go for Refuge – and to that extent you're not a Buddhist. One could therefore say that you're a Buddhist when you have the Triple Gem clearly in mind, when you have faith in it, take delight in it, and so on, and when on account of your faith and delight in it, your defilements are at least suspended, held in abeyance, if not actually destroyed. (They can be destroyed only by way of insight.) You can also be said to be a Buddhist if – in addition to all that – you regard the Triple Gem as your guiding ideal, that is to say, if you regard it not as something to be admired and worshipped from a distance but as something to be personally experienced and eventually to be realized by you as a result of your following the spiritual path. Someone endowed with this state of mind is a being who is Going for Refuge. In other words, first you're conscious of the Triple Gem. Then, being conscious of the Triple Gem, your mind is full of skilful mental states. Thirdly, because your mind is full of skilful mental states there's no room for unskilful mental states. And fourthly, you make the Triple Gem your guiding ideal: you resolve to tread the path and realize the Triple Gem for yourself, to *become* the Triple Gem. If you do these four things, then you're one who is Going for Refuge.

> (4) The going for refuge has two main divisions: it may be mundane or supramundane. (p. 3)

This is *lokiya* and *lokuttara* in Pāli, sometimes translated as worldly and transcendental, or mundane and transcendental. So let's see what these divisions are.

> The supramundane refuge is taken by those who have a (true) vision of the Noble Truth (*diṭṭha-sacca*; i.e. by the eight noble beings). In the path-moment (of stream-entry, where any trace of the fetter of doubt has been removed), the supramundane refuge succeeds in exterminating any blemish that may still attach to the going for refuge. It has Nibbāna as its object, and in its function it comprises the entire Triple Gem (in that object of Nibbāna).

> The mundane refuge is taken by worldlings (*puthujjanas*; i.e. all those, monks or laymen, who are still outside of the four stages of sanctity). It succeeds in effecting a temporary repression of the blemishes attaching to their going for refuge. Its objects are the noble qualities of the Buddha, Dhamma, and Sangha. It consists in the acquisition of faith (*saddhā*) in these three objects. It is this faith in the Triple Gem that is referred to when, among the ten meritorious acts (*puññakiriyavatthu*), the 'straightening of views' (*diṭṭhujjukamma*) is defined as Right Understanding rooted in faith (*saddhāmūlika sammā-diṭṭhi*). (pp. 3–4)

So 'The supramundane refuge is taken by those who have a (true) vision of the Noble Truth (*diṭṭha-sacca*; i.e. by the eight noble beings).' In other words, supramundane or transcendental refuge is taken by those with at least some transcendental insight, some Perfect Vision. Here it says 'of the Noble Truth', presumably meaning the four noble truths. By 'the path-moment' is meant the moment when one attains to the transcendental path by means of that transcendental vision. Not only the fetter of doubt is removed at that moment, of course, but all three of the lower fetters. 'The supramundane refuge succeeds in exterminating any blemish that may still attach to the going for refuge', that is to say, which may still attach to the mundane Going for Refuge. It exterminates blemishes in the form of unskilful mental states. 'It has Nibbāna as its object, and in its function it comprises the entire Triple Gem (in that object of Nibbāna).' In other words, the supramundane refuge has the Unconditioned as its object – not the object of thought but the object of actual experience by transcendental insight, at least to some extent – and in that Unconditioned, as experienced, is comprised, virtually, the Buddha, the Dharma, and the Sangha. The Buddha is in his essence unconditioned on account of his complete realization of Nirvāṇa. The Dharma is in its essence unconditioned because it is the sequence of unconditioned or transcendental states culminating in Nirvāṇa. And the Sangha, of course, is unconditioned because it consists essentially of those who have realized and experienced those transcendental states and stages culminating in Nirvāṇa. When one has the Unconditioned as one's object and goes for Refuge to that, experiences that, then one is Going for Refuge to the entire Triple Gem. Thus, transcendental Going for Refuge occurs when one has, through transcendental insight, a personal experience of the Transcendental, of the Unconditioned, and that proceeds by way of the breaking of the first three fetters – the fetter of self view, the fetter of doubt, and the fetter of dependence on moral rules and religious observances.

KULANANDA: Can those fetters be broken to an extent and then come back again?

SANGHARAKSHITA: No, they are broken once and for all. They can be weakened, and you can get a kind of insight, but this is something intermediate between mundane intellectual understanding and insight in the full sense. In the case of the Stream Entrant they are finally broken. They don't come back again. Thereafter one has – I won't say no self-view, but no self-view up to a certain level. There are still subtler forms of self-view, otherwise you would be fully Enlightened, but certainly the grosser forms of self-view are broken, as well as the grosser forms of doubt and the grosser forms of dependence on moral rules and religious observances.

SAGARAMATI: So there can be subtler forms of unskilful states.

SANGHARAKSHITA: In a sense one could say that. It's a matter of terminology.

SAGARAMATI: It's just the grosser unskilful states that are described,

SANGHARAKSHITA: Yes. One could say that essentially the object of the transcendental Going for Refuge is the Unconditioned itself, Reality itself. When you go for Refuge to that, or rather, when, from the Hīnayāna point of view, your experience of that is at least that of the Stream Entrant, then your Going for Refuge is a transcendental Going for Refuge, because the Buddha, Dharma, and Sangha are pre-eminently comprised in the Unconditioned, in the Transcendental. This is going a bit off the track, but you could say that if somebody had an experience of the Transcendental to the extent of breaking those first three fetters without ever having heard of Buddhism, then they would be Going for Transcendental Refuge to the Buddha, Dharma, and Sangha even though in a conventional sense they were not Buddhist. They wouldn't know what they were doing in those traditional Buddhist terms, but that would in fact be what they were doing. Whether that sort of instance does occur, presumably we wouldn't know.

'The mundane refuge is taken by worldlings (*puthujjanas*, i.e. all those, monks or laymen, who are still outside of the four stages of sanctity).' This means those people who are not any of the Four Noble or Holy Persons. 'It succeeds in effecting a temporary repression of the blemishes attaching to their going for refuge'. In other words a temporary repression of the defilements, particularly those which directly affect the genuineness of the mundane going for Refuge. 'Its objects are the noble qualities of the Buddha, Dhamma, and Sangha. It consists in the acquisition of faith (*saddhā*) in these three objects.'

So the essential difference between the Going for Refuge in the transcendental sense and in the mundane sense is basically a difference between the experience of the Unconditioned and faith in the noble qualities of the Buddha, Dharma, and Sangha.

RATNAVIRA: In a sense you could say that until you've actually had the experience of the Transcendental you don't really know what you're Going for Refuge to.

SANGHARAKSHITA: No, you know only its attributes. The objects of the mundane Going for Refuge are the noble qualities of the Buddha, Dharma, and Sangha. You certainly see the qualities, the external manifestations. You might for instance understand through the scriptures the Buddha's kindness, gentleness, compassion and so on, and feel great faith in the qualities of the Buddha, Dharma, and Sangha, but what the Three Jewels really were in truth, in their depth, in their essence, you wouldn't know. You could only know that by direct spiritual, that is to say transcendental, experience, and then of course you would be Going for Refuge in the transcendental sense. You can have faith in the noble qualities of the Buddha, Dharma, and Sangha just as in ordinary life you can admire somebody without actually knowing or understanding them, or as you can admire or appreciate, to some extent at least, a great work of art without really being able to enter into the mind of the person who produced it. In the case of the transcendental Going for Refuge the defilements are permanently destroyed, whereas in the case of the mundane Going for Refuge the faith and devotion that you feel for the Triple Gem are strong enough to hold the defilements in temporary suspense, but not strong enough to destroy them altogether. That can be done only by an actual experience of the Transcendental, of the Unconditioned.

This also points to the fact that so long as your Going for Refuge is only mundane you're much more dependent on a positive environment. If your Going for Refuge is transcendental, if you're a Buddhist in the highest sense, you can't *not* go for Refuge. You *can't* fall back. In a sense, it doesn't matter where you are, whether you're working in a factory or in a beautiful calm, quiet retreat centre. Your Going for Refuge can't be shaken. But if your Going for Refuge is mundane it can be shaken very badly – indeed it can lapse, it can fall into abeyance. And what does it depend upon for its existence? It depends upon faith. So if your Going for Refuge is only mundane, and if that mundane Going for Refuge depends upon the presence of faith, what sort of environment do you need above all?

A VOICE: The spiritual community.

SANGHARAKSHITA: Well, above all you need an environment that sustains your faith, which means a spiritual community. If you're living most of the time in an environment that does not sustain your faith (which doesn't mean keeping up your belief, but creating a positive, joyful, happy atmosphere 'around' the Three Jewels), then your Going for Refuge may wither away altogether. So long as your Going for Refuge is mundane you can't afford to stray away from the spiritual community very far or for very long. If you're separated from the spiritual community for too long, you're in danger of sustaining your Going for Refuge almost by force of will, without actually feeling it.

SAGARAMATI: Surely you could get that through your meditation practice, if it was such that when you went into it you tended to get into that feeling, and that would support you.

SANGHARAKSHITA: It would, provided you were able to keep up your meditation. But if you were living outside the spiritual community, in some other kind of group, it might be very difficult for you to keep up your meditation. Meditation sometimes goes wrong, even when external conditions are all right. What is going to sustain you then, at least for a few days? It can only be some outside factor, and by definition that isn't present in your environment if you are living in a kind of group other than a spiritual community. It still comes back to the spiritual community, in the long run at least, because if your meditation goes wrong, the spiritual community can give you the positive support that will help you to get back into the meditation.

So long as you cannot depend upon yourself completely for the continuation of the positive mental state of faith in the noble qualities of the Three Jewels, you need some inspiration from outside yourself. In other words, you need people who are themselves in a positive mental state in this sense, and who can encourage and help you to get back into that, or to stay in that – and that means the spiritual community. As long as your Going for Refuge is not transcendental, you can't even rely on your meditation.

Let us suppose, for the sake of argument, that all the members of the spiritual community also go for Refuge in the mundane sense. The chances are that there would be some at least who would be in a positive state of mind. It would be highly unlikely that the whole mundane spiritual community would lapse simultaneously, which means that it would become merely a Buddhist group. The reasonable chances are that you would always find some people around who were genuinely Going for Refuge, even though it was the mundane Going for Refuge, and who, therefore, would inspire and encourage you when your own Going for Refuge had lapsed, emotionally speaking, for the time being.

LOKAMITRA: If all the members of the spiritual community are Going for Refuge in the mundane sense, is it possible for those members to develop?

SANGHARAKSHITA: Well, if they were all Going for Refuge only in the mundane sense then clearly some of them at least would have to start Going for Refuge in the transcendental sense. How is that possible? It can only be by means of contact with others who themselves go for Refuge in the transcendental sense. This is excluding the possibility of someone like a *pratyekabuddha* achieving that transcendental Going for Refuge by means of his own individual meditation, or even his own individual study, without any external support. That is possible, but I think it would be very rare for someone to win through to the Transcendental Path without any kind of personal contact with anybody else who had won through to it. I don't want to exclude the possibility altogether, but it's quite unlikely. To rise to that transcendental level you need contact with someone who is already to some extent on that level. One therefore has to hope that within the spiritual community there are at least some who have gone for Refuge in the transcendental sense. They will sustain everybody else, because their Refuge will never fail, whatever happens.

LOKAMITRA: If there aren't those people, could you call it a spiritual community?

SANGHARAKSHITA: It depends how you use the word 'spiritual'. We use it in an ambiguous manner in the FWBO. Used in one way it is contrasted with the transcendental community, but used in another it isn't. As contrasted with the transcendental community it is a spiritual community but not a transcendental community. If you do not contrast it in this way then there is an ambiguity. In this case there might be a spiritual community in the sense of a group of people, who were normally in an emotionally positive state, but it wouldn't be a spiritual community in the sense of an Āryasaṅgha, a Sangha containing at least some *āryas* or Noble or Holy Persons. I would say that a spiritual community in the full sense would have to contain at least some who had gone for Refuge in the transcendental sense.

LOKAMITRA: In order to make that higher development possible for the other members.

SANGHARAKSHITA: In order to make it possible for more and more people, yes, though I don't exclude the possibility of some of them winning through to the Transcendental as a result of the sheer momentum of their meditation practice and their study of the Dharma, or their spiritual practice in other ways.

'It consists in the acquisition of faith (*saddhā*) in these three objects' – that is to say, the Buddha, Dharma, and Sangha. 'It is this faith in the Triple Gem that is referred to when, among the ten meritorious acts (*puññakiriyavatthu*), the 'straightening of views' (*diṭṭhujjukamma*) is defined as Right Understanding rooted in faith (*saddhāmūlika sammā-*

*diṭṭhi*).' There's no reference given for this particular list of the ten meritorious acts. It's different from the ten *kusaladhammas*.[256]

### The Surrender of Self

> This mundane refuge is of four kinds: (a) the surrender of self (*atta-sanniyyātana*); (b) acceptance (of the Triple Gem) as one's guiding ideal (*tapparāyaṇatā*); (c) acceptance of discipleship (*sissabhāvū-pāgamana*); (d) homage by prostration (*paṇipāta*).[257]
>
> (a) The surrender of self[258] is expressed as follows:
>
> 'From today onward I surrender myself to the Buddha… to the Dhamma… to the Sangha.'
>
> *Ajja ādiṃ katvā ahaṃ attānaṃ Buddhassa niyyādemī Dhammassa Sanghassā'ti.*
>
> This is the giving over of one's self to the Triple Gem. It may also be done in this way:
>
> 'To the Exalted One I am giving my self, to the Dhamma I am giving my self, to the Sangha I am giving my self – I am giving my life! Given is my self, given is my life! Until my life ends, I am taking refuge in the Buddha! The Buddha is my refuge, my shelter and my protection.'
>
> *Bhagavato attānaṃ pariccajāmi, Dhammassa Sanghassa attānaṃ pariccajāmi, jīvitañca pariccajāmi. Pariccatto yeva me attā, pariccattaṃ yeva me jīvitaṃ. Jīvita pariyantikaṃ Buddhaṃ saraṇaṃ gacchāmi. Buddho me saraṇaṃ leṇaṃ tānan'ti.* (p. 4)

SANGHARAKSHITA: What does this 'surrender of self' remind one of? What does it convey? How would one describe it in a word? What it represents is what we usually call a total commitment. One could say that it's Going for Refuge in the sense of surrender of self, total commitment, that constitutes the *upāsaka* ordination. Normally one experiences a mundane Going for Refuge at the time of the *upāsaka* ordination – I don't think many people, at that moment, would experience a transcendental Going for Refuge – but it is nonetheless a total commitment on that mundane level.

MAHAMATI: I was talking to somebody who had just become a Muslim. He said that when you become a Muslim you give up your will, and that he imagined that probably that is what it is like when you become a Buddhist.

SANGHARAKSHITA: But what is meant by giving up one's will?

SAGARAMATI: Giving up your selfishness.

KULANANDA: The words mean surrendering to a higher authority.

SANGHARAKSHITA: Yes. This is what we were talking about earlier. You could say that there are two kinds of giving up one's will. One is submitting one's will to a greater and higher will, a will which from the Buddhist point of view is still mundane, and the other is giving up one's will because one sees the futility of it all, because one sees right through the delusion of that self to which, or to whom, that will pertains. Do you see the difference? It's quite true that even when you submit your will in what we would regard as the negative sense of the term to a bigger or more powerful one, you experience a sort of liberation, a sort of freedom, but it's a freedom from responsibility, which is not a very positive thing. Sometimes it's a great burden to have to think, and be responsible, and take your own decisions. It's a great burden to be an individual, and sometimes when the demands made upon you as an individual are quite extreme, it's a relief to surrender your individuality. But that kind of surrender would be regarded as a backward step in Buddhism. It would be a backward step just to hand over responsibility to the boss, the chief, the leader, or God, and we would tend to think that the Muslim, surrendering his will to God, would be doing just that. This is quite an interesting point. You make over your will to some higher authority and experience what is really an infantile freedom from responsibility.

SAGARAMATI: That's probably tied up with the idea of the will of God. Something happens, and he saves you from further harm. It's an attitude of 'It's nothing to do with me.'

SANGHARAKSHITA: That does result in a feeling of liberation, or of freedom from responsibility, but it is more like the freedom of the child who leaves everything to his parents. There is a difference between that and the surrendering of oneself, the giving up of oneself, in the sense of a dedication of oneself to a higher ideal – an ideal which *you* must grow up into, which *you* must reach, which *you* must realize. In the case of the ideal you realize it only by a complete transformation, which means giving up yourself as you are now for the sake of yourself as you can and will be. If one were to use the language of surrender, one could say that when you surrender to the Buddha you are not submitting your will to the Buddha's will in the same way that the theist is submitting his will to the will of God. So what are you doing? If the Buddha is not the big boss overruling your small will with his big will, what is he?

GRAHAM: You're accepting the path.

SANGHARAKSHITA: You're accepting the path, which means accepting the gradual unfoldment of the process of your own development. You're accepting the possibility of development – the necessity of development, in a sense – for yourself.

LOKAMITRA: Is self-surrender the best term for this?

SANGHARAKSHITA: I think it's a fair translation of the Pāli term *saraṇa*, but whether it's the sort of expression that we should use in English I don't know. It does rather suggest handing yourself over and becoming a sort of slave, submitting your will to that of another, which is not the Buddhist view at all. The new, ex-Untouchable Indian Buddhists don't like the term 'surrender' because for them it's all part of a common pattern – that you surrender to God and at the same time to the higher caste people. They see it as one and the same thing; and it's true, it is the same. It's not easy for those brought up in an authoritarian, theistic tradition to understand this Buddhistic 'surrendering' of yourself, which is not a surrendering to some other will simply more powerful than your own. Buddhist surrender is more like receptivity to a higher influence, so that you yourself may be transmuted into that influence. In the case of the theistic religions it's a question of the lower degree of power submitting itself to the higher degree of power, but in the case of Buddhism it's a question of the lower level of spiritual experience opening itself to the higher level of spiritual experience, so that it may itself rise to that, and experience that.

LOKAMITRA: Rajneesh has said something like, 'You submit yourself and I'll do the rest.'

SANGHARAKSHITA: There's a great deal of difference between submitting yourself and being receptive. If he means by 'submit yourself' just 'Be receptive to whatever I have to offer', that's fair enough. But if he sees himself as the head, the boss, of a group or a movement, and if others have simply to submit to his judgement and allow themselves to be used by him, this is completely anti-spiritual. Perhaps he's not very clear himself about the difference between submission and surrender. The other extreme is, of course, that the individual, while retaining his freedom and not submitting to any other higher power, does not open himself, does not become receptive to higher spiritual influences, but just goes his own way, on his own level. That is just individualism. True surrender is not submitting to a higher power, but opening yourself up to a higher spiritual influence. It's easy to confuse these two things, and which one Rajneesh is calling for is perhaps ambiguous. But there is no doubt which Buddhism calls for. By all means open yourself to higher spiritual influence. This is what surrender really means. This is what commitment really means. But it's not a question of submitting yourself to a more powerful will within the framework of what is simply the group.

(b) The acceptance of the guiding ideal.

'From today onward the Buddha is my Guiding Ideal, the Dhamma, and the Sangha. Thus may you know me!'

*Ajja ādiṃ katvā ahaṃ Buddhaparāyano Dhammaparāyano Sanghaparāyano. Iti maṃ dhāretha.*

It is illustrated by the following verse spoken by Āḷavaka:

'From village to village, from town to town I'll wend my way, lauding the Enlightened One and the perfection of His Law.'[259]

Thus the acceptance of the guiding ideal by Āḷavaka and others has to be understood as equalling their going for refuge. (p. 5)

SANGHARAKSHITA: How does the acceptance differ from the surrender of self? *Is* there a difference?

DHAMMARATI: In the case of the latter maybe you're actually recognizing the ideal and its qualities.

RATNAJYOTI: The surrender is like the dedication, the acceptance of practice.

SANGHARAKSHITA: There is a footnote by Nyanaponika on the meaning of this term 'guiding ideal':

*Pārāyaṇa* is, in ordinary usage, a synonym of *saraṇa*, having the meaning of resort, support, etc. Here when denoting a particularly distinguished way of taking refuge, it is probably intended to be taken in a strict sense, as often used in religious literature, Pāli as well as Sanskrit: the going to the highest, the way to the beyond, the chief or best aim; the essence. We have therefore ventured upon the above free rendering by 'guiding ideal'.

SANGHARAKSHITA: Does this seem a particularly distinguished way of taking Refuge? Not really! There is a chapter in the *Sutta-Nipāta*, the *Pārāyana Vagga*, translated by Hare as the chapter of 'The Way to the Beyond', which is the literal translation of *pārāyana*. So one might speak of 'the acceptance of the way to the beyond', and yes, one might consider that tantamount to the Going for Refuge, but in what way is this little incident of Āḷavaka an illustration of that acceptance of the way to the beyond? There doesn't seem to be much connection. If you accept the Buddha, Dharma, and Sangha as your way to the beyond – your way to transcendence, to the Unconditioned – then yes, surely that is tantamount to Going for Refuge. But it doesn't seem that Āḷavaka was really doing that. He was simply going from place to place praising the Buddha, Dharma, and Sangha. Does that, in itself, really amount to an acceptance of the guiding ideal? One would have thought not. It may well be that he *was* practising, *was* Going for Refuge, but does it amount to accepting the guiding ideal? It does not seem specific or clear enough to amount to an acceptance of the Buddha, Dharma, and Sangha as the guiding ideal or *pārāyana*. After all, in India today there are plenty of Hindus who will go from place to place, and stand up on platforms praising the Buddha, Dharma, and Sangha, but they certainly don't go for Refuge. They remain good Hindus, or good brahmins, or good observers of the caste system. So praising is not enough. Certainly, to say that the Buddha is one's way to the beyond, one's way to the Transcendental – likewise the Dharma, likewise the Sangha – is tantamount to Going for Refuge, but we can't say that this passage from the *Sutta-Nipāta* illustrates that mode of Going for Refuge. If the praise was completely sincere perhaps it would, but that isn't explicitly stated, so I don't think this is a very good illustration of acceptance of the guiding ideal. Perhaps Buddhaghosa was hard pressed to find an illustration. This sometimes happens. This acceptance of the guiding ideal is mentioned in tradition, but where is an actual example of it to be found? For want of anything more suitable, he cites this passage from the scriptures.

(c) The acceptance of discipleship:

'From today onward I am the Disciple of the Buddha, the Dhamma, and the Sangha. Thus may you know me!'

*Ajja ādiṃ katvā ahaṃ Buddhassa antevāsiko Dhammassa Saṅghassa. Iti maṃ dhāretha.*

This is illustrated by the following passage expressing Kassapa's acceptance of discipleship that has to be understood as equalling his going for refuge:

'Fain would I see the Master! The Exalted One, him would I wish to see! Fain would I see the Blessed One! The Exalted One, him would I wish to see! Fain would I see the Enlightened One! The Exalted One, him I would wish to see!

'Then I prostrated myself before the Exalted One and addressed him thus: The Exalted One, O Lord, is my Master, and I am his disciple!'(pp. 5–6)

SANGHARAKSHITA: One thing that emerges from these different passages, and from this discussion of the different forms of mundane refuge, is that the Going for Refuge is not invariably expressed in the words, 'I go for Refuge'. For instance, in the acceptance of the guiding ideal one says, 'The Buddha is my guiding ideal.' One doesn't say, 'To the Buddha I go for Refuge', though this is what it means. In the same way, when one says, 'From today onward I am the Disciple of the Buddha', in effect one is saying, 'I go for Refuge to the Buddha.' This suggests that one must beware of identifying the Going for Refuge with any particular set of words, or any specific procedure. One may go for Refuge without actually saying those words. It's what happens within you – your own experience, your own intention – that counts. Normally, when one goes for Refuge, one says, 'To the Buddha for Refuge I go', etc., but certainly in the early days of Buddhism, during the Buddha's own lifetime, it wasn't quite so cut and dried as that. One disciple might say, 'I go for Refuge to the Buddha', but another might say, 'The Buddha is my teacher.' Another might say, 'The Buddha is my *pārāyana*, my guiding ideal.' But it all meant the same thing. One mustn't insist too strongly on the importance of a particular set of words, a particular formula. It might be that the tradition is nowadays that you always say, 'To the Buddha for Refuge I go', but we shouldn't think that the Going for Refuge is necessarily or invariably associated with that particular set of words. You could genuinely, spiritually, go for Refuge without using that formula. It has been more or less agreed among Buddhists down through the ages that it is the Going for Refuge formula rather than any other which will be used, but there are alternative formulations in at least some of the early Pāli texts.[260] Just as it's possible to *not* go for Refuge even while reciting the formula of the Refuges, in the same way, even though you do not actually recite the formula of the Refuges you may, in fact, spiritually be Going for Refuge.

DHAMMARATI: Is Buddhaghosa saying, then, that those four kinds of mundane Refuge are just four different ways of expressing the same thing? Or are they distinct in themselves?

SANGHARAKSHITA: It isn't clear. He says, 'This mundane refuge is of four kinds.' The word 'kinds' is ambiguous. It seems to me as though what he really means is that there are four different forms of the mundane refuge. All of these four kinds of people – those who surrender themselves, those who accept the guiding ideal, those who accept discipleship, and those who pay homage by prostration – are in fact Going for Refuge, so it seems to be more a question of four different forms of mundane Going for Refuge associated with expressions or phrases other than that of the literal Going for Refuge.

LOKAMITRA: Nyanaponika takes it as a gradation, I think.

SANGHARAKSHITA: Yes, he does. We shall go into that later on. For the time being, so far as Buddhaghosa is concerned, it's just a question of four kinds of mundane Going for Refuge. Whether or not it's a gradation we'll see later on.

The word for 'disciple' here is *antevāsiko*, which literally means someone who 'lives in' with you and who, therefore, is closely associated with you. The more usual word for disciple is *sāvaka* or 'one who hears', but here the context is a specifically monastic one. A *bhikkhu*, when he becomes ordained into the *bhikkhu* sangha, normally has two teachers. One is called the *upajjhāya*, the other is called the *dhammācariya* or *ācariya*. In relation to the *upajjhāya* he is a *saddhivihārika*. In relation to the *ācariya* he is an *antevāsika*. Both terms imply or suggest actually living with the teacher, not just coming for lessons every now and then, or being a disciple in a general sense, but learning from the teacher by attending upon him, by close personal association. It's part of the traditional Indian conception of discipleship, both Hindu and Buddhist, that full discipleship involves living with the teacher and serving him, doing things for him, associating with him and learning from him by a process of association. It's discipleship in this sense that is meant, rather than discipleship in the sense of accepting the teacher's ideas, as it were from a distance. This 'living in' with the Buddha, and thereby with the Dharma and the Sangha, is what is meant by discipleship as the third kind of mundane refuge.

One might say that discipleship in this sense in our context would mean living in a residential spiritual community. You might even say that if you really wanted to live in a spiritual community, and to be part and parcel of it, that's tantamount to wanting to go for Refuge, because that is what the spiritual community – whether residential or non-residential – is doing. If you want to join the spiritual community, knowing and understanding what it really is like, it really means that you want to go for Refuge.

This emphasis on discipleship as personal association is suggested in the passage expressing Kassapa's acceptance of discipleship: 'Fain would I see the Master. The Exalted One, him would I wish to see!' This suggests personal association, personal contact.

SAGARAMATI: On the other page it says, 'Thus may you know me!' It's almost like saying, 'You won't know what I'm really like. This is what I am really interested in.'

SANGHARAKSHITA: *Iti maṃ dhāretha* literally means, 'Thus hear me,' i.e. 'Thus bear me in mind.' In other words it is a mutual acceptance, a mutual recognition. It is not that you simply regard yourself as somebody's disciple, but that *they* regard you as their disciple also. It's mutual. So, 'May you know me in this way.' It's not one-sided.

(b) Homage by prostration: [261]

'From today onward I shall give respectful greeting, devoted attendance, the *añjali*-salutation (by folding the palms and raising the hands) and homage only to those three; the Buddha, the Dhamma and the Sangha. Thus may you know me!'

*Ajja ādiṃ katvā ahaṃ abhivādana-paccuṭṭhāna-añjalikamma-sāmīcikammaṃ Buddhādīnaṃ yeva tiṇṇaṃ vatthūnaṃ karomi. Iti maṃ dhāretha.*

This way of going for refuge consists in showing deep humility towards the Buddha, the Dhamma, and the Sangha. (It is illustrated by the Brahmin Brahmāyu's homage after his being deeply stirred by a stanza spoken by the Buddha.)[262] (pp. 6–7)

SANGHARAKSHITA: 'From today onward I shall give respectful greeting.' That suggests that you're receptive and welcoming, as when someone comes round to your house to see you. You're glad to see them: that's your initial reaction. So you 'give respectful greeting to the Buddha, the Dhamma, and the Sangha'. 'Devoted attendance' suggests that you look after them, wait upon them, stay near them, associate with them. As for 'the *añjali*-salutation', this is made by placing the palms together and raising the hands. You give these three things 'and homage [as the fourth] only to those three: the Buddha, the Dhamma and the Sangha'. This suggests a certain exclusivity. 'Homage by prostration' means that you give respectful greeting to the Buddha, the Dharma, and the Sangha, you give them devoted attendance, you give them the *añjali*-salutation, the salutation of genuine, heartfelt respect, you give them homage, and you give these four things *only* to the Buddha, the Dharma, and the Sangha. You do not give them to other teachers or other teachings. You've committed yourself to the Buddha, the Dharma, and the Sangha. You're following that path. In the case of those living in the Buddha's day, you're not following any of the other teachers who were around at that time. You've definitely devoted yourself to the Buddha, the Dharma, and the Sangha. 'This way of going for refuge consists in showing deep humility towards the Buddha, the Dhamma, and the Sangha.' 'Humility' seems to be Nyanaponika's own word. It isn't really suggested by this passage, is it? Is humility quite the appropriate word?

GRAHAM: Friendliness.

SANGHARAKSHITA: It's more like respectful or reverential friendliness, though it isn't *just* friendliness. 'Humility' has, perhaps the wrong sort of Christian connotation. Humbling yourself suggests an attitude such as is adopted towards a superior power rather than an attitude of receptivity towards a spiritual influence.

But what about not giving respectful greeting to any teacher or teaching or community other than the Buddha, the Dharma, and the Sangha? Does that mean you shouldn't show any respect at all to other teachers or to other teachings? What is the distinction?

SAGARAMATI: You don't go for Refuge to them.

SANGHARAKSHITA: You don't go for Refuge to them, but it's not a question of actually Going for Refuge, even though 'homage by prostration' is one of the four kinds of mundane refuge. It's a question of showing respect in the more ordinary sense. So what should be one's attitude towards other teachers and teachings?

KULANANDA: Openness.

SANGHARAKSHITA: Openness? But if you've committed yourself to the Buddha, Dharma, and Sangha, what are you being open to?

DHARMANANDA: You'd be open to the sincerity, perhaps, of other teachings.

SANGHARAKSHITA: But how are you open to their sincerity? What does that really mean? Well, you recognize their sincerity, certainly. What is the kind of attitude which you find in the early Pāli texts with regard to other teachers, teachings, and so on? What is the minimum that is expected of the Buddhist?

VAIROCANA: To be tolerant of them.

SANGHARAKSHITA: To be tolerant of them, yes, to be polite when you meet them, to be courteous. Certainly this at least is expected. But do you think respect is a term that could be used in this connection?

MAHAMATI: Not if you think it's wrong-headed.

SAGARAMATI: You could respect their views, in a sense, for them. They're following a path, and you can respect the fact that they've got a right to follow that path.

SANGHARAKSHITA: But that is more like recognizing than respecting. You recognize their right to follow their own path, certainly. You recognize the right of every individual to follow the path that he sees as the best, or the right path. You may consider them wrong, and you may wish to discuss the matter with them and try to convince them, but you'll be courteous. You'll observe the decencies of discussion. You'll be tolerant. You won't try to make them change their minds or their views by force, or by unfair means of any kind. You will give them respect as human beings, even though not as teachers; but you won't respect their teachings if you think that they are mistaken. It is quite important to understand this, because it means following a middle way. On the one hand you don't say, 'What they teach is the same as what we teach, and just as good', but on the other hand you don't condemn them or wish to persecute them. Your attitude is not fanatical. You recognize their right to follow the path of their own choosing. Even if it differs from your path – even if you consider them entirely mistaken in their choice – you don't forget that they are human beings, and you are tolerant and courteous, and even friendly. This is the Buddhist attitude. Christians sometimes think that if you are of a different faith, it's their duty to be rude to you, but this is certainly not the Buddhist view. The Christians honestly feel that they are doing God a service in being rude to you. I know this, because I've had the experience of Christian missionaries being rude to me in India.

LOKAMITRA: I had a Christian come up to me in India. He said, 'How come you've forsaken the religion of your country?' He was really upset and used quite strong words.

SANGHARAKSHITA: Well, you should say, '*You've* forsaken the religion of *your* country!'

LOKAMITRA: I just wanted to get away from him as quickly as possible.

SANGHARAKSHITA: Yes: sometimes they are quite impossible people.

LOKAMITRA: But I couldn't help laughing at the situation.

SANGHARAKSHITA: Buddhism is as it were saying, 'However much you may differ, and however wrong you may consider other people to be, you must never forget that they also are human beings, and that, like you, they are trying to find some solution to the problems of existence' – though that does not mean that you should compromise or weaken your own views, your own commitment, in any way.

> Homage by prostration may be of four kinds: being paid towards (senior) relatives, out of fear, towards one's teacher, and towards those deserving highest veneration. Only the latter case – i.e. the prostration before those worthy of highest veneration – is to be regarded as 'going for refuge'; the three other cases do not count as such. Only if referring to the highest (in one's scale of values), refuge is taken or broken, respectively. (p. 7)

SANGHARAKSHITA: Homage by prostration has a wide application, not just a specifically Buddhist one. In India prostration, or bowing down before others, or touching their feet, is just a part of ordinary social life. You behave in this way to senior relatives: to mother, father, elder brother, elder sister, aunt, uncle, grandparents, and so on. It's just the social custom. This is not what is meant by homage by prostration in the Buddhist context, that is to say, as equivalent to Going for Refuge. Secondly, there's paying homage by prostration 'out of fear'. If you prostrate at someone's feet out of fear, if you humble yourself before some more powerful member of the group, this is not Going for Refuge in the Buddhist sense. For example, if you're sentenced to death by the king, and you throw yourself at his feet and beg for mercy, this is not Going for Refuge. Thirdly, there's homage by prostration 'towards one's teacher', which here seems to mean a secular teacher, because in India you prostrate yourself in front of your secular teachers as well as your spiritual teachers, or at least this was the old custom. And fourthly, there's homage and prostration 'towards those deserving highest veneration', and only that, the text says, is to be regarded as Going for Refuge.

KULANANDA: Would this refer to members of the Āryasaṅgha?

SANGHARAKSHITA: Well, it's interesting that Nyanaponika inserts in brackets, 'in one's scale of values'. I assume that this is his own interpolation, but what do you think it means? This is quite an interesting point.

KULANANDA: He seems to assume that the scale of values will be the scale of values of one who goes for Refuge. So it would be a Buddhist scale of values.

SANGHARAKSHITA: It's as though he's asking you to suppose that, on looking around, you find that you're in contact with all sorts of people, at all sorts of levels of development. Some may be Buddhists, some non-Buddhists. But if your homage by prostration spontaneously goes to the person or persons who, within the range of your experience, represent the highest, then that can be counted as a Going for Refuge, because you are heading in the right direction, as it were. Leaving aside karma, it's not your fault if within your particular context there are no fully Enlightened beings, or even any bodhisattvas or Stream Entrants. But if you naturally gravitate towards whoever is most highly developed, that may be counted as a Going for Refuge within the limited context that you are in. If it's your principle to pay homage by prostration to whoever is the highest within your range of experience, then clearly as soon as your range of experience is enlarged you will be Going for Refuge to something genuine, something truly spiritual, assuming that not to be present within your circle already. The principle of Going for Refuge is there, in the sense of a natural tendency to pay homage to whatever is spiritually the highest in your immediate environment.

What Buddhaghosa means by 'highest' is a little ambiguous. Presumably it means highest in the scale of spiritual attainments, but whether or not that scale is limited to those within the Āryasaṅgha is left unclear, or at least not directly stated.

> Therefore if a member of the Sakya or Koliya clan worships the Buddha, thinking: 'He is our relative', no refuge is taken in that case. (p. 7)

SANGHARAKSHITA: That is to say, no refuge is taken if he is worshipped simply as a relative. You might say this applies to many Indians who revere the Buddha just because he was born and brought up in India, or at least he taught there. It depends on where you draw the border, but at present the birthplace of the Buddha is definitely within the boundaries of Nepal, but Indians always say he was born in India, and was the greatest of the sons of India.

> Or, one may think: 'The recluse Gotama is honoured by kings and has great influence. If he is not worshipped, he might do me harm.'

> If, thinking thus, one worships out of fear, no refuge is taken in that case. (p.7)

SANGHARAKSHITA: This sort of motivation for paying homage by prostration just does not constitute a Refuge.

> Furthermore, a person remembers to have learned something from the Blessed One while he was a Bodhisatta, an aspirant to Buddhahood; or, after his attaining Buddhahood, one has received from the Master advice relating to worldly knowledge. If for these reasons, one regards the Buddha as one's teacher and worships him, no refuge is taken, in that case too. (p.7)

SANGHARAKSHITA: That's quite interesting, isn't it? If a person recollects teachings received from the Buddha before he became a Buddha, and worships him as his teacher in respect of those teachings, then he does not go for Refuge, because the Buddha might have taught mistaken things before his full Enlightenment. Similarly, if after his Enlightenment one has received from the Buddha advice relating to worldly knowledge, and if for this reason one regards the Buddha as one's teacher and worships him, no Refuge is taken. What do you think is meant by 'worldly knowledge', and what would the Buddha be doing giving advice relating to worldly knowledge?

SAGARAMATI: 'Worldly knowledge' means knowledge about family problems.

SANGHARAKSHITA: Family problems. Psychological problems. Unless the teaching is directly related to the spiritual path, and ultimately to the transcendental spiritual path, and unless one accepts the Buddha as the teacher of such teachings, then even if one worships him, one does not go for Refuge. By making these points, Buddhaghosa, and through him the whole Buddhist tradition, is making a very strong and clear distinction between what pertains to the group and what pertains to the spiritual community. One has to distinguish between what one does as an individual in the true sense and what one does merely as a member of a group. You may remember that in the case of the Maharishi lots of people followed him and practised Transcendental Meditation because the Beatles had done so. It's a little bit like that.

> But if one pays worship to the Buddha in the conviction 'This is the most venerable being in the world,' only by such a one is refuge taken. (p. 7)

SANGHARAKSHITA: This makes what is meant by 'in one's scale of values' a bit clearer. But how is one able to tell? Is one really able to judge that 'this is the most venerable being in the world'? One might have to admit that one might not be able to do so, but if one goes for Refuge to what one genuinely feels to be the highest and best within the range of one's experience and contacts, the highest and best which is accessible to one, practically speaking, then one is in principle Going for Refuge.

SAGARAMATI: Take the teaching of the orthodox Christian church, or of the Gnostics, say. If someone found that that was the highest and committed themselves to it, would that be good for them?

SANGHARAKSHITA: If you had made a thorough search in one's immediate environment and attached yourself to whatever was highest in that environment, as far as you could see, you would be going in the right direction. Even if it wasn't a Refuge in the full Buddhist sense, at least it would be going in the direction of Going for Refuge, because you would have been following the right principle already. Suppose, for instance, that you are looking for a river, or even for the ocean, but you happen to come across a stream instead. So far as you can see it's the best stream in the neighbourhood, the broadest, the freshest and clearest – so you follow it. If you follow it for long enough, with enough perseverance, you'll find that it joins a bigger stream, even a river. You follow that, and you find it linking up with a bigger river still. In that way you come to the main river, and through *that* you come to the ocean. But this is because throughout you've followed faithfully the guiding principle that you're looking for a bigger and bigger body of water. The principle of Going for Refuge is to allow oneself to be attracted towards the best and highest with which one is in personal contact, even if within the range of one's contacts Buddhism is not as yet included. If you follow that principle you are in principle Going for Refuge.

SAGARAMATI: I think that's where the contact between faith and understanding comes in.

SANGHARAKSHITA: I would call it incipient Refuge, if you want an expression for it. In my talk at the Order convention I spoke in terms of effective Refuge.[263] Effective Refuge, which as I think I made clear is the normal Going for Refuge in the Western Buddhist Order, constituting the *upāsaka* ordination, seems to correspond with the surrender of self, or with total commitment. But I would call what we're talking about now incipient Refuge.

> On the other hand, the going for refuge remains unbroken in the following situations. A male or female lay devotee who has taken refuge in the Triple Gem, worships a (senior) relative, thinking: 'He is my kinsman'. Even if that relative is a recluse of another faith, the refuge in the Triple Gem is unbroken; still less can it be said to be broken if it is not a recluse or a priest. (p. 7)

Because you're respecting that kinsman just as an elder kinsman, not as a spiritual teacher.

> When prostrating before a king, out of fear: 'If he who is honoured by the whole country is not worshipped, he will do me harm!' – in that case too the refuge is unbroken. If one has learned any science, art or craft even from a non-Buddhist, and one worships him in his capacity as one's teacher, in that case too the refuge remains unbroken. (p. 8)

This seems quite clear and straightforward, just a matter of common sense. In other words, it's the intention and inner understanding that counts, rather than the external action. When you pay homage by prostration to the Buddha, recognizing the Buddha as Buddha, that is equivalent to Going for Refuge, but if you pay homage by prostration to a senior kinsman simply as a senior kinsman, or to a secular teacher simply as a secular teacher, this is not a Going for Refuge to that person and therefore does not conflict with one's Going for Refuge to the Buddha.

SAGARAMATI: So you can stand up for the queen then.

SANGHARAKSHITA: If you're simply respecting the traditions or customs of the group to which you belong then your Refuge is not broken. Is there any further point arising out of that? What do you think of a situation in which your homage by prostration to someone in whom you do not take Refuge might be regarded by others as indicating that you have gone for Refuge to that person when in fact you have not? How should you behave then? Suppose you go to India. You're a Buddhist, you go for Refuge only to the Buddha. Suppose you enter a Hindu temple. The polite thing to do is to bow to the images, but suppose your Hindu friends took that as a sign that you accepted the Hindu gods in the same way as they did and went for Refuge to them, just as you do to the Buddha. Would it be more skilful not to bow before those Hindu images, even at the risk of displeasing your Hindu friends, rather than allowing them to wrongly think that Buddhists can or do go for Refuge to Hindu gods?

VAIROCANA: You'd be better not bowing down to them, I think. You'd be better displeasing people, rather than letting them mistake you as having gone for Refuge to Hindu gods.

SANGHARAKSHITA: Suppose they feel you've disrespected their gods?

VAIROCANA: That would just be too bad.

SANGHARAKSHITA: Perhaps you should make your position clear before you go along to the temple. You could say, 'I'm quite happy to accompany you, but so far as I am concerned it's just an interesting experience, an opportunity to see the art and the architecture. I won't be going as a worshipper. If you're ready to accept that, then I'm ready to accompany you.' It's the tradition, by the way, in Theravādin countries, that *bhikkhus* never salute images of gods. Even Hindu monks (sannyasins) do not do so, on the grounds that the Hindu gods are usually married and the sannyasin should not salute married persons. It's the custom that the sannyasin, on entering a temple dedicated to married gods, simply chants some verses of blessing. He does not salute the gods. So anybody in Buddhist yellow robes would not be expected, if the Hindu concerned knew his own religion, to salute Hindu gods, because almost all of them are married. There are pairs of divinities such as Brahma and Sarasvatī, Vishnu and Lakshmi, Shiva and Parvati, and so on. Being married, they are, in a sense, lay people, and the Indian tradition is that the celibate monk does not salute lay people. If you go to India in yellow robes, you're not expected to return the salutations of traditionally-minded Buddhists. They do not expect it, and would be shocked if you did. You might feel it rather impolite not to return their salutation, but they would feel it to be very much out of place if you, as a *bhikkhu* or even as an *anagārika*, wearing yellow robes, were to return their salutation. Theravādin Buddhists would be horrified if a *bhikkhu* returned their salutations.

KULANANDA: Wouldn't that be a good thing to do?

SANGHARAKSHITA: If you decided skilfully to break with custom and return a lay person's salutation, and were not just doing it out of ignorance. But then you'd have to take the consequences. If you offend people's group susceptibilities, which might be justified sometimes, you mustn't be surprised if they come back at you in a very unpleasant way. You must be prepared for that, and take it into consideration – not just be all hurt and disappointed when it happens. In Mahāyāna countries there is not the same sort of feeling about the *bhikkhu* not returning the salutations of the laity. Why do you think that is?

SAGARAMATI: Because of the bodhisattva ideal.

SANGHARAKSHITA: Yes. Monks and lay people all accept the bodhisattva ideal, so they regard themselves as all being essentially on the same path, and all equally possessing Buddha-nature. The monk, in a way, respects the lay person as much as the lay person respects the monk. It may be that the lay person is a little more respectful to the monk, but the monk will normally return the salutation of the lay person, within the Mahāyāna context. There's quite a bit to be said on both sides of the question, as it were. But unless one really knows what one is doing it is best, when one goes abroad to Buddhist countries, to follow the local Buddhist custom – unless it is something which is definitely unskilful, like the eating of meat on the part of the Sinhalese, Burmese, and Thai monks.

LOKAMITRA: What about non-Buddhist teachers you happen to be friendly with?

SANGHARAKSHITA: Well, you can certainly salute them, but just as senior, respectable people with some kind of position in society. Lay Buddhists understand that their *bhikkhus* have to relax a bit when dealing with people of this sort, though they certainly wouldn't be happy with the idea of *bhikkhus* prostrating themselves. At best, a little bow would be in order.

LOKAMITRA: That won't be taken by non-Buddhists as an act of homage?

SANGHARAKSHITA: No, not if it was just a little bow. If you did a full prostration, then yes, they would naturally think that you were accepting that person on his own terms, but if you just raised your joined hands in an *añjali* salutation they probably would not misunderstand. That's just part of general social courtesy. The teacher himself, if he had a little savoir-faire, would return it in the same way. He would recognize that you were not a disciple of his, and were not behaving as such, but merely being polite, so he would be polite too. Some non-Buddhist teachers are arrogant, and try to create an impression that you are their disciple by *not* being very polite, and by *not* returning your salutation; but you soon get to know them and behave accordingly. You don't salute *them*! If they want to play that sort of game, you're able to play it too. Or you show a bit of off-handedness in some other way. If you've been caught out, if you have saluted them politely but they have just given you a blessing as though you had come as a disciple, then you bear that in mind and later on say something to make clear what the situation actually is. They soon get to know.

### The Fruits of Going for Refuge

> Results: The fruit of the supramundane refuge, in the sense of being its karmic result (*vipāka-phala*), is the four fruitions of monkhood (*sāmañña-phala*) ... (p. 8)

One shouldn't take this 'four fruitions of monkhood' too literally. Lay people also, even according to the Pāli texts, can attain these fruitions, so they're not specifically or exclusively 'fruitions of monkhood'. The word *sāmañña* is not very well translated by 'monkhood', but we'll let that pass.

> ...viz, the fruition of stream-entry etc. The fruit in the sense of advantage or blessing (*ānisaṃsa-phala*) is the destruction of suffering; further, the blessings mentioned in the following scriptural passage: 'It is impossible, O monks, that a person endowed with insight (*diṭṭhi-saṃpanno*, i.e. stream-enterer, etc.) should regard any conditioned thing as permanent, enjoyable, or an ego; that he should take the life of his mother, his father, or a saint; that, with a thought of hate, he should shed the blood of the Blessed One: that he should cause a split in the community of monks; that he should choose another teacher. There is no possibility of that.'[264]
>
> But the fruit of the mundane refuge is only the attainment of favourable rebirth, and the attainment of property and enjoyment. (p. 8)

SANGHARAKSHITA: Is the distinction clear, or do you think the mundane refuge is being played down a little bit? Surely it is the mundane refuge which leads into, is the basis of, the transcendental refuge. In a non-technical sense is that not its greatest 'fruit'?

KULARATNA: It seems almost to be equating the supramundane refuge with monks and the mundane refuge with lay people.

SANGHARAKSHITA: The fruits of the supramundane refuge are the higher spiritual, even transcendental, attainments: destruction of suffering, and so on, and the fact that one becomes incapable of performing the more extremely unskilful actions. As for the fruits of the mundane refuge, yes, they include 'the attainment of favourable rebirth, and the attainment of property and enjoyment', but surely there is also the fact that it provides one with access to the higher spiritual life itself: the transcendental refuge, the spiritual community, and so on.

RAY: I see that 'attainment of property' is often mentioned in Pāli texts,...

SANGHARAKSHITA: That's because people are so fond of it!

RAY: Is it some sort of reward for practising the spiritual life?

SANGHARAKSHITA: Well yes, it is, in a way. The general Buddhist idea is that the performance of meritorious actions of a mundane nature improves your worldly status, whether in future lives by way of better or higher rebirth, or in this life by way of longevity, increase of happiness, increase of property, and so on. This is a very firmly held Buddhist belief.

VAIROCANA: Doesn't Christmas Humphreys say somewhere that people are reborn into middle-class families, with plenty of money, owing to their previous good lives and all the rest of it?[265] It seems quite a distortion of the word 'karma'.

SANGHARAKSHITA: If you perform skilful actions, certainly you will be reborn in a happy state, but if you're reborn in a happy state it is not necessarily because you performed skilful actions in the past. It can be due to what we can only describe as accident. It must be recognized that the law of karma is quite frequently applied in this 'Christmas Humphreys' sort of way, even in the East, but the ex-Untouchables of India are very strongly against this. They've been told for generations by the brahmins, 'You've been born as Untouchables. You were born in this miserable condition, at the very bottom of the social system, as a punishment for your bad deeds in previous lives. You must accept your punishment, otherwise there's no possibility of improvement for you.' Quite naturally, the ex-Untouchables bitterly resent this presentation of the law of karma, which has become a rationalization for social injustice. The Christian might say that it was the will of God, who created rich and poor – in the words of the hymn, 'The rich man in his castle, the poor man at his gate, he (i.e. God) made them high or lowly, And ordered their estate.'[266] In the same way the Hindus would say of brahmins and 'Untouchables' that karma made them high or lowly, and ordered their estate – the brahmins of course being the high ones. Because in his previous lives the brahmin performed good deeds, and was noble and pure, he is born as a brahmin in this life, and because the Untouchable was devoted to all sorts of criminal pursuits, never thought about religion, and was greedy and malicious, he is born as an Untouchable. This is what the Untouchables were taught. But this is clearly not the Buddhist view of the workings of karma.

LOKAMITRA: Surely the best rebirth is one that brings you in contact with the Dharma.

SANGHARAKSHITA: There is that point too, yes.

LOKAMITRA: That needn't necessarily mean being materially well off.

SANGHARAKSHITA: The question is: What really is a good result of karma?

VAIROCANA: It's odd that that's not mentioned here. All it's got is property and enjoyment and things. It seems rather strange that Buddhism should stress that point.

SANGHARAKSHITA: Well, this is very much the attitude you find, certainly in Theravādin countries: that the practice of the Dharma – to the extent that you *do* practise it, e.g. by the giving of *dāna* – is for the sake of worldly prosperity and enjoyment. You get this very strongly in India too. This is why I often say that the Indians are not a deeply spiritually-minded people, although they claim to be. What their spirituality usually amounts to is a firm belief that worldly benefits can be obtained by magical means, which is a very different thing. The average Indian wants progeny, property, money, enjoyment, and pleasure, but he deeply believes that these things can be obtained in some sort of magical way, especially with the help of the blessings of people who are spiritually developed and who have therefore got magical powers. Any Indian holy man will have thousands of disciples if he's at all well known. But what are they mostly after? They're after his blessings, as a result of which they hope to have more worldly things, more property, more worldly enjoyments of every kind. They do not come to him because they want to learn anything spiritual from him. They want his blessing: 'May I pass such-and-such an examination, may I get a better job, may I get promotion. Please give me your blessing.' This is their so-called religiosity in many, many cases. And this is why you often find that the very rich people – merchants – go to holy men. They go because they want a *big* blessing. They might build him a vihara, and they hope to get a very big blessing indeed for that! But then the merchant, having spent all that money on constructing the vihara, makes even vaster profits as a result of that really big blessing, or so he believes. So we mustn't be deceived by appearances of religiosity or spirituality.

Some Indian gurus make a sharp distinction between devotees and disciples. Your devotees are those who help and support you for the sake of a worldly blessing. They're not interested in spiritual life. Your disciples, who are fewer in number, are those who are with you for the sake of actually following your teaching and trying to attain to some spiritual development. All the more reputable Indian gurus understand this clearly. They function in both ways, and they don't confuse their disciples with their devotees. But some less scrupulous gurus, who are in the blessings business, as it were, refer to what are in fact their devotees as their disciples. Thus, someone might have two or three million 'disciples', but it doesn't mean that there are two or three million people who are following his spiritual teachings. What it means is that there are two or three million people who believe that he is sufficiently spiritually developed to have magical powers, so that if they can only please him, or win his favour in some way, then he will bless them, and they will become more prosperous, more powerful, enjoy life more, and so on. I'm afraid this sort of attitude is reflected here in Buddhaghosa, and Nyanaponika too. You find it in the Theravādin Buddhist countries to a great extent. The lay person – using the expression in the more conventional traditional sense – follows his religion for the sake of material benefits, not for the sake of his individual spiritual development, much less still that of others. Religion is a good investment.

The spread of science and technology in the East undermines this whole attitude, because people see that prosperity comes through technology, not magic. Technology is the enemy of magic. Psychologically, magic is probably better for you than technology, but technology probably works – in some ways at least – better than magic. Throughout the East – it has already happened in the West – people are switching from magic to technology, and religion, in the mass sense, is losing a lot of support, because people were into it not for the sake of spiritual development, but for material results. Those results, they now see, they can get from technology. Technology is a more powerful magic. They keep a bit of Hindu philosophy, or Buddhist philosophy, or whatever, for reasons of cultural patriotism, but really they believe in technology now, just as they believed in magic before. Technology works. It actually *gives* them material benefits. It works *better* than magic. So don't run away with the idea that Hindus are deeply religious. They'll tell you that, and they'll tell you how materialistic the West is, but they're no less materialistic themselves. If anything, they're more materialistic, I would say. But they believe in magic as a means to the fulfilment of their materialistic ambitions. Or at least this is what they have believed traditionally. It's beginning to weaken now.

GRAHAM: Do you think this belief in technology has been totally ingrained in Tibet now?

SANGHARAKSHITA: I should think it has been, at least with the younger generation that's grown up since the Chinese invasion in 1950. We really don't know much about what's going on there, but I think they are probably convinced that when it comes to building roads and hospitals, technology is better than magic. And if you see religion in terms of magic, when you see that technology is more powerful and more effective, you not only give up magic but you give up religion at the same time, because for you religion was just magic.

A VOICE: Was this materialistic attitude also prevalent in Tibet?

SANGHARAKSHITA: The Tibetans certainly were and are very materialistic, but I would say from my personal contact with Tibetans that despite that, they are on the whole much more deeply imbued with genuinely spiritual ideas than the Hindus. I was interested to notice that when Tibetans started coming down into India as refugees, they regarded the Hindus as very irreligious people. They felt that they didn't take their religion seriously, and that they weren't very generous. So I would say that despite the strong magical element in Tibetan Buddhism, the spiritual element was also very strongly present, and very accessible. There were many Tibetans following Buddhism as a spiritual path – probably not the majority, but certainly a substantial number. Certainly Buddhism as a spiritual path was to be found in Tibet – there's no doubt about that, despite the prevalence of what I've called magic. But for the majority of people, even in Tibet, Buddhism was magic. For the average villager it was magic. It was what the lama did to help make the crops grow, and what the lama did for you after your death, so that you got a better rebirth. But there were enough people in Tibet committed to Buddhism as a path of higher spiritual development for one to be able to say that Buddhism as a spiritual tradition was definitely well established in Tibet. One could hardly say that about the Buddhism of Ceylon.

MAHAMATI: Could it be that India didn't develop industrially in the same way as the West because their magic was better, because it was more attractive?

SANGHARAKSHITA: You could say that. And psychologically, as I said, probably magic is better for you than technology.

SAGARAMATI: It doesn't make a noise.

SANGHARAKSHITA: Or at least it makes a very pleasant noise.

VAIROCANA: Why would you say it was better for you psychologically?

SANGHARAKSHITA: That's quite a big question. For one thing it's less alienating. Magic is more in touch with nature. Technology tends to alienate you from nature. You could also say it feeds your greed because it's much more effective than magic. On the other hand, technology has brought definite material advantages to a large number of people who would almost certainly otherwise have lived in an extremely miserable manner, especially in the colder countries. In the warmer countries it doesn't matter so much if you don't have technology, because your requirements are fewer, and you can live more simply, but in the colder countries such as those of Europe, life for the average person before technology was very hard and squalid indeed, and it was only slightly tempered by magic. On the whole, taking a very long-term view, as far as the lives of the majority of people are concerned it's probably better that we have technology rather than magic, though technology has many unfortunate features. It's not so enjoyable as magic, unless you like fast cars and motor bikes, or record players, come to that.

Anyway, let's bring this discussion to a conclusion. It's really not enough to say that 'the fruit of the mundane refuge is only the attainment of favourable rebirth, and the attainment of property and enjoyment'. That seems a very sordid ideal indeed. The truth is that the mundane refuge leads straight on to the supramundane, the transcendental, refuge. That's its principal fruit, surely.

> Defilements: In three cases the mundane refuge is defiled and without great brightness and radiating influence: if connected with

> ignorance, doubt and wrong views. The supramundane refuge is free from any defilements. (p. 8)

Ignorance, doubt, and wrong views are all 'intellectual' defilements. It suggests that defilement, essentially, is the absence of transcendental vision, of Perfect Vision, of insight. All the negative emotions spring from that. And the supramundane refuge, the transcendental refuge, 'is free from any defilements'. It's not quite clear what is meant here. It could mean that only the supramundane refuge has great brightness and radiating influence, but one could also take it as meaning that even the mundane refuge possesses that great brightness and radiating influence when, at least temporarily, severed from ignorance, doubt, and wrong views. In that case the 'brightness' would be the brightness of mundane emotional positivity, not the brightness of transcendental vision. The text says, 'In three cases the mundane refuge is defiled', but probably 'in three ways' would be better.

RATNAJYOTI: You spoke of the absence of doubt and wrong views. Is that the same as Perfect Vision?

SANGHARAKSHITA: Yes, if they are permanently absent. Again, it is not clear in the case of the mundane refuge whether the absence of wrong views implies *samyak-dṛṣṭi* (or *sammā-diṭṭhi*) in the sense of right view or in the sense of Perfect Vision. Do you see what I mean? One could look at the passage as meaning that if one was possessed of right view, as distinct from Perfect Vision, even that right view would be sufficient to make your mundane refuge of great brightness and radiating influence. On the other hand it could be taken to mean that it's only when you've got Perfect Vision that the Going for Refuge has that great brightness and radiating influence – in other words, only when it's transcendental. The passage itself isn't at all clear. I would say it was a question of degree. Surely even your mundane Going for Refuge has some brightness and radiating influence, at least in the sense of emotional positivity. Faith is present, even if it's only mundane. But certainly, when the Refuges are the object of the transcendental Going for Refuge the brightness and radiating influence are greater and of course permanent, not just intermittent. This should have been made clearer. 'The supramundane refuge is free from any defilements.' Well, that's clear enough.

> A breach of the mundane refuge might be blameable or blameless. It is blameable when occurring as a going for refuge by self-surrender etc. to other religious masters: in that case the breach will have undesirable results. The breach is blameless at the time of death, as it will not cause any karmic result. The supramundane refuge is without breach. Even in another existence a holy disciple will not turn to another master. (pp. 8–9)

SANGHARAKSHITA: It's an interesting idea, that one's mundane refuge is severed at the time of death, but I wonder if it's necessarily so. What do you think is the reasoning behind this?

VAIROCANA: The mundane refuge is a conscious thing that you do if you're wanting to start out on the spiritual life. Perhaps if you're reborn you're not conscious of it.

SANGHARAKSHITA: You might not be conscious of it, but if you had genuinely gone for Refuge, even by way of a mundane refuge, in this life, surely you would be drawn to Buddhist surroundings in your next life?

SAGARAMATI: This suggests that the mundane refuge is purely part of your conditioning.

SANGHARAKSHITA: Yes, it does. But even if it's part of your conditioning, the effects of that conditioning can surely continue. Probably it would be more correct to say that there *may* be a breach at the time of death, because whether there actually is a breach or not will depend upon the sort of environment into which you are reborn as a result of your karma. You could be reborn into a Buddhist environment and pick up the threads of your old interests again, in which case there wouldn't be a breach – except insofar as even the mundane refuge has to be a conscious thing. Over the period of death, and during the early months of one's life in the new body, there'd be a breach, as it were, in the continuity of human consciousness. Whether that would amount to a real breach of the mundane refuge could be argued, perhaps.

LOKAMITRA: Then you get the case of being born a Buddhist but at the same time not yet on the transcendental path.

SANGHARAKSHITA: You can be born a Buddhist in the sense of Going for Refuge in the mundane sense. You can't be regarded as being born a Buddhist simply because you're born into a Buddhist family without yourself Going for Refuge even in the mundane sense, but you can, perhaps, be born Going for Refuge, in which case you would be a born Buddhist to that extent.

KULARATNA: Perhaps if you'd only taken mundane refuge you might be drawn to rebirth in a Buddhist environment but you'd have to go for Refuge again to put more seeds …

SANGHARAKSHITA: But you have to take that new decision to go for Refuge again every minute anyway. What constitutes the breach? What length of time is involved? In a sense one is breaching one's mundane refuge all the time. You breach it, then you remember it, then you renew it. Why should the breach that occurs at death be such a special instance?

LOKAMITRA: I don't like to make it sound like a time of reckoning, but there's a time when past weighty karmas and habitual karmas and so on will be able to resolve themselves – either skilful or unskilful ones – so that even though one has managed to get on a fairly positive and creative path now, there may be things that one has done even in past lives that could negate that and cause a breach of one's refuge.

SANGHARAKSHITA: Yes, that's true. This is why I say that it would be more correct to say that there *may* be a breach at the time of death than that there is *necessarily* a breach. There may be one, but it seems there may not be. Certainly there may be no greater breach at the time of death than one might have experienced many a time in the course of the present lifetime.

LOKAMITRA: But if one's mundane refuge has been sincere then one will ultimately reap the benefits of it.

SANGHARAKSHITA: It does seem so. For instance, take the case of sleep. When you are asleep, are you Going for Refuge or not? Death is analogous to sleep, just as the *bardo* state is analogous to dream. So are you Going for Refuge when you are asleep? In some cases you may be, because you may actually dream that you are Going for Refuge, dream that you are reciting the Refuges and Precepts. It is affecting you to that extent. On the other hand it may be completely wiped out during your sleep state, so far as one can tell. That means that your Refuge is in abeyance night after night, which means that it is in abeyance for a third of your life. So what's so special about death? Why should your mundane Going for Refuge not survive death if it can survive sleep? Or perhaps it doesn't survive sleep. Perhaps you ought to renew it every morning, as some Buddhists in fact do. You do in a sense renew it by at least reciting the Refuges and Precepts from time to time.

LOKAMITRA: But you have a dream state.

SANGHARAKSHITA: So it could be that during the bardo state you are Going for Refuge, even if it was only the mundane refuge. It could be so, if the mundane refuge was quite powerful. This is possible, I think.

LOKAMITRA: But presumably that current of Going for Refuge would continue.

SANGHARAKSHITA: Presumably that current would continue, in which case there would not be a breach of the Going for Refuge, even at the time of death.

DHAMMARATI: In the case of death do you quite have that radical new set of choices that you have when you wake up in the morning? You're still in your community. You've still got the Sangha to liberate you.

SANGHARAKSHITA: But then you might, after death, as the result of your previous good karma, 'wake up' in the midst of a Buddhist environment, in which case there could be that possibility of continuity of the Going for Refuge. But if you woke up in the midst of quite a different kind of environment maybe that possibility wouldn't be there, and the 'current' continuing from the previous existences would perhaps just die out, at least for the time being.

DHAMMARATI: Would it be fair to assume that the possibility wouldn't be there, that there would be a breach?

SANGHARAKSHITA: Perhaps Buddhaghosa is a bit too hard and fast. Perhaps we should simply say that when there is a breach of the Refuge at the time of death, that breach is blameless. But maybe one can't even say it's absolutely blameless, because you are responsible for the fact that your refuge is not strong enough to continue through and after the process of death. All that one can say is that at least you haven't deliberately curtailed it. Or can one even say that? In a sense you *have* curtailed it, because you have deliberately abstained from making those efforts which would have ensured its continuance. Perhaps the old scholastic, Buddhaghosa, is trying to be a bit too cut and dried in his treatment of the subject, as scholastics only too often are, and is not doing justice to the complexity of life and the complexity of experience: not on this occasion, anyway.

LOKAMITRA: But if you are on the transcendental path there's no doubt that you will get rid of all your unskilful karmas by that....

SANGHARAKSHITA: Ah, not all of them. To the extent that your Going for Refuge is a transcendental one, whether that of the Stream Entrant or any other noble being, to that extent defilements are destroyed.

LOKAMITRA: So it is not necessarily the case that one has this sort of continuity established once and for all?

SANGHARAKSHITA: I think it would be fair to say that it's not necessarily the case.

LOKAMITRA: So until that continuity is established once and for all, one has to really make that decision, I suppose, make that commitment.

SANGHARAKSHITA: Perhaps it's good that one at least recites even the formula of the Going for Refuge as often as possible. At least it acts as a reminder.

SAGARAMATI: Don't you think that if you had some negative weighty karma surely that would have come up the last time you died and breached your Going for Refuge?

SANGHARAKSHITA: Well, you might have committed some in this life itself, either prior to your Going for Refuge or in those intervals when it was in abeyance.

SAGARAMATI: But even if you've led an un-Buddhistic life – you know, you've been unskilful, though you haven't committed a murder or anything like that – you can pretty well suppose that your next life will be more or less a continuation of this. There won't be anything really unexpected that can be disruptive.

SANGHARAKSHITA: No, one would think not. One would expect not. It's unlikely that *vipākas* of weighty karmas would pop up from the remote past. This is a rather popular way of looking at things which is not justified by the teaching. It is assumed that you might have killed someone millions of lives ago, and that pops up in the next life. But weighty karmas are exhausted much more quickly than that, according to the Abhidharma.

SAGARAMATI: There's also the idea of faith. To the extent that you have faith, actually some of it does follow through from life to life.

SANGHARAKSHITA: Yes, and if your natural tendency is in the direction of that which is highest, then surely that would carry over. Even a mundane tendency of that sort would carry over. That tendency in the direction of the highest is in principle a Going for Refuge. So perhaps Buddhaghosa has been a bit too dismissive of the mundane Going for Refuge.

# 3
# NYANAPONIKA'S COMMENTARY

## An Individual Act

We've gone through the first part of Nyanaponika's thoughts and comments and we've studied Buddhaghosa's exposition of the passage in the *Majjhima Nikāya* where the brahmin Jānussonī goes for Refuge. We now come on to Nyanaponika's further thoughts and comments on that commentarial passage, and with that we're going to conclude our study of the Threefold Refuge.

> In the commentarial passage translated above, a precious document of ancient Buddhist practice is preserved, showing the thoughtful and discriminating way in which the devotees of old took refuge in the Triple Gem. Four different formulas are mentioned, given in what seems to be a descending order beginning from the highest form, the complete self-surrender, and ending with the lowest, the homage by prostration. (p. 17)

One must bear in mind that Nyanaponika is living in Ceylon. He is very aware of the fact that in Ceylon, and in other parts of the Buddhist world, the recitation of the Refuge formula has become very mechanical, just a matter of ritual observance, so he is stressing 'the thoughtful and discriminating way in which the devotees of old took refuge in the Triple Gem'. But I think the real point is not so much that the devotees of old took refuge in a thoughtful and discriminating way as that at the time of the Buddha there were various ways of Going for Refuge. Subsequently he doesn't succeed in showing that those different ways of Going for Refuge did in fact survive after the Buddha's time, when things became quite standardized.

LOKAMITRA: These different ways, how much did they correspond, as Nyanaponika makes out, to different levels of Going for Refuge, and if they do correspond to different levels?…

SANGHARAKSHITA: He's not quite sure about it. He says that the four different formulas of Going for Refuge are 'given in what seems to be a descending order'. We'll go into that a bit more later on, when he deals with each one individually.

> It is greatly to be regretted that the information we can derive from the commentarial passage in which these formulas are embedded is rather scanty. Many questions that come to our mind are left unanswered, as for instance: Have these four formulas been used instead of the traditional one, or in addition to it? By whom and on which occasions have the three lower kinds been used? Have they been administered to the devotees in a similar fashion as it is done today in the case of the traditional formula? (pp. 17–18)

SANGHARAKSHITA: It seems to me, as we go through this passage, that Nyanaponika is trying to feel his way towards something. What do you think that is?

SAGARAMATI: He's trying to feel his way back in time to what it would have been like if the Buddha had actually been present.

SANGHARAKSHITA: No, I wasn't thinking of that. It is something more general, in a way more basic, more essential.

DHAMMARATI: The change that has to come about in somebody who goes for Refuge.

SANGHARAKSHITA: Yes, but even more strongly than that.

SAGARAMATI: Just in what feeling Going for Refuge actually is.

SANGHARAKSHITA: Maybe that's putting it a bit too broadly. It seems to me that he's trying to feel his way back to the Going for Refuge as an individual act, an act that marks the beginning of your spiritual life. He uses the word 'initiation', which is certainly not used in modern Ceylon or modern Burma in this connection. In other words, he's very indirectly expressing dissatisfaction with the state of affairs in contemporary Ceylon, at least, where the Refuge formula has become simply something that you recite in a ritual way en masse on various occasions, just part of the collective proceedings. The *bhikkhu* who is officiating recites the Refuges and Precepts in Pāli, and you recite them after him in unison with everybody else. Perhaps we in the West don't always realize this. If you're born and brought up in a Buddhist country, you're born and brought up reciting the Refuges and Precepts, so there is no time, no definite point in your life, when you consciously and deliberately go for Refuge in a way that marks a turning point in your life. It doesn't function as a sort of initiation. It doesn't mark a new life. It's just a formula you've been reciting ever since you can remember. It doesn't mean anything special to you.

Nyanaponika has a sense, it seems, that this is all wrong. He knows quite well what the Going for Refuge meant in the Buddha's day, but he's also aware that in present-day Ceylon it has become for the vast majority of people just something that you recite with thousands of other people on the occasion of festivals and so on. It's lost its significance as an expression of the individual's conscious commitment to the Buddhist way of life, and he'd surely like to revive that significance. So this is what he's feeling his way towards. He's wondering, it seems to me, whether these other formulas, which are different from the Going for Refuge formula but have the same essential meaning, were in use not only in the time of the Buddha but also subsequently in Ceylon, and did in fact represent a greater awareness of the Going for Refuge as an individual act; and he wonders whether it might be possible to revive something like that in present-day Buddhist world. Perhaps he's thinking, 'The going for refuge formula, so far as the Buddhists of Ceylon are concerned, is so stale. They're so used to it. It doesn't have that sense of an individual commitment. Maybe we could try out some of these other formulas, which were perhaps in use in that way in ancient times, not just in the Buddha's day, and maybe that could lead to Buddhists in Ceylon, and in the East generally, taking the Going for Refuge, or what amounted to the Going for Refuge, more seriously as individuals than they do at present.'

In effect that would mean adopting the position of the FWBO, because this is exactly what we've done. We've made the Going for Refuge something quite special, which it was in the Buddha's day, but which it isn't in almost all Buddhist countries today. We've recognized it as being, as it was in the Buddha's day, the central and decisive act in the Buddhist life. The Going for Refuge represents your commitment of yourself as an individual to your own spiritual self-development, your commitment of yourself to the path of the Higher Evolution, and it's that which makes you a Buddhist. That is a sort of initiation, and it's interesting that he uses this word 'initiation' in this passage. He says, 'Does the plural form used in the Pāli sentence refer to an assembly of devotees that witnessed the act' – just as in the case of our own *upāsaka* ordinations – 'or, what seems to be more probable, was it merely a respectful way of addressing the spiritual teacher (guru) or the monk who may have administered that special formula of refuge, perhaps as a kind of initiation?' Do you see how he's feeling his way towards what is virtually our own position, though without coming very much out into the open, as it were, because after all he's living and working in Ceylon, and he has to be quite careful what he says? He seems to be suggesting – he doesn't make the point very clearly – that in ancient Ceylon also it might have been felt that the refuge formula had become of more or less purely ritual significance, being used simply en masse, and that maybe some *bhikkhus* had therefore made use of these other formulas for more individual purposes. He seems to be wondering about this possibility.

A VOICE: This was written prior to 1965.[267] Do you think there has been any change since?

SANGHARAKSHITA: I rather doubt it. 1965 is quite a few years ago, but there has certainly not been any evidence of any change in Ceylon in this respect.

'It is greatly to be regretted that the information we can derive from the commentarial passage in which these formulas are embedded, is rather scanty. Many questions that come to our mind are left unanswered, as for instance: Have these four formulas been used instead of the traditional one, or in addition to it?' It seems to me that this is rather begging the question. It seems to me that Buddhaghosa, who was after all a commentator.... But perhaps I had better say a bit more about Buddhaghosa before I go on. As I mentioned the other day, Buddhaghosa was the great Theravādin commentator on the Pāli Tipiṭaka, and had a very thorough knowledge of those texts. That comes out very clearly in all his writings. He knew them backwards and forwards and inside out. He cited a vast number of passages, and within his limits was a very acute commentator. So of course he knew quite well that the standard Going for Refuge formula was, well, the standard one. In his day, presumably, as nowadays, that was the formula that was always used: 'To the Buddha for Refuge I go, to the Dhamma for Refuge I go, to the Sangha for Refuge I go.' Nonetheless, in going through the scriptures he finds there are passages in which people who were impressed by the Buddha's teaching, and were clearly committing themselves to that teaching, gave expression to that commitment not in the standard formula but in some other formula. Instead of saying 'I go for Refuge to the Buddha', they said 'I surrender myself to the Buddha.' So Buddhaghosa has to account for this. He has to tidy things up. Quite rightly he came to the conclusion that these were simply different ways of Going for Refuge and that the people using those alternative formulas – which were not, of course, formulas for them, but their own spontaneous utterances – had in fact gone for Refuge. So, in his usual systematic, scholastic way he coins terms for these alternative ways of Going for Refuge – or maybe previous commentators no longer known to us had coined those terms already. He therefore speaks of the four different kinds of mundane refuge, in order to account for those scriptural passages, and to make it clear that when, having met the Buddha and listened to his teachings, those people gave expression to their feelings in the particular way that they did, they were in effect Going for Refuge, even though they didn't express themselves in what afterwards became the standard Going for Refuge formula.

I don't think it's likely that these alternative formulas, as we may call them, were ever in actual use in Ceylon as Nyanaponika seems to think they might have been. What he is trying to do is to find a precedent. He knows quite well that if there is to be any more individual Going for Refuge in modern Ceylon – if the Going for Refuge is to be taken more as an initiation – you've got to find some precedent for that in the Pāli literature and the Theravāda tradition, and this is what he is desperately searching for. It's all got to be justified by tradition. So he's thinking that maybe these alternative formulas were used in ancient times, perhaps even in ancient Ceylon. (He doesn't actually refer to Ceylon, but this is clearly how he is thinking.) Maybe even at that time the standard Going for Refuge formula, the '*Buddhaṃ saraṇaṃ gacchāmi*', had got a bit rusty, so when someone wanted to make an individual commitment, teachers in those ancient times might have administered these other formulas as a sort of special initiation. Maybe he's thinking, 'If they did it, then perhaps we could do it too. It would only be continuing an ancient Theravādin, Sinhalese custom. It wouldn't be an innovation. It wouldn't be dragging in the wretched Mahāyāna or actually changing anything.'

It's a deep conviction of the Theravādin Buddhist that in the Theravāda tradition nothing has been changed, and nothing ever *can* be changed, though that's wrong on historical grounds. Of course many things were changed, but they won't admit that, just as the Roman Catholics won't believe that there has been any real change within the Catholic Church. They believe that they had a pope and bishops right from the beginning, though historical research shows that they came much later. Likewise, in Ceylon they believe that Buddhism as they have it has existed unchanged right from the time of the Buddha, so that it's not possible to introduce anything new. If you want to introduce something which is relatively new you therefore have to find a precedent in their own tradition. This is what Nyanaponika is trying to do, it seems to me. He realizes that for there to be any real, living Buddhism there must be an individual commitment. He knows that perfectly well. Since the Going for Refuge formula as used in Ceylon nowadays does not represent that individual commitment he is searching around for another formula, but he's got to search around for it in the Pāli literature, in the Theravādin tradition, preferably in Ceylon, and he thinks he might have found it here in the commentarial passage he has translated. He is therefore wondering whether these expressions, tantamount to Going for Refuge, found in the Pāli scriptures, on the part of people who come in contact with the Buddha and his teaching, could subsequently have been used as alternative formulas, as it were, for more serious-minded people who took their Buddhism as an individual commitment. He's feeling his way towards something like our own position, but he's not nearly bold enough about it.

DHAMMARATI: Why does he suggest that the other three were lower kinds of Going for Refuge? He seems to devalue them, suggesting that Buddhaghosa devalues them in comparison with the first form.

SANGHARAKSHITA: He seems to take the surrender of self as the highest, and the other three, i.e. acceptance of the guiding ideal, acceptance of discipleship, and homage by prostration, as lower. There isn't any tradition of what these really mean, other than the scanty information he gives, but as he looks at them, and tries to make sense of them, it seems to him that they represent a descending order of importance.

So, Nyanaponika asks, 'Have these four formulas been used instead of the traditional one, or in addition to it?' Clearly these alternative forms of words were used by people, as recorded in the scriptures, but whether those words were used as additional formulas we just don't know. I think it's unlikely. 'By whom and on which occasions have the three lower kinds been used? Have they been administered to the devotees in a similar fashion as is done today in the case of the traditional formula?' That is to say, in the case of the '*Buddhaṃ saraṇaṃ gacchāmi*' formula. There's no evidence of that, and I think it's quite doubtful.

> Those three lower kinds, namely, have in common the last sentence, being a call to witness: 'Thus may you know me!' (*Iti maṃ dhāretha*). (p. 18)

Here he's feeling his way towards the idea of a small spiritual community that is the witness to a particular individual's Going for Refuge as a personal commitment to the spiritual path. Here again he's feeling his way towards something like our own position.

> Does the plural form used in the Pāli sentence refer to an assembly of devotees who witnessed the act or, what seems to be more

> probable, was it merely a respectful way of addressing the spiritual teacher (guru) or the monk who may have administered that special formula of refuge, perhaps as a kind of initiation? (pp. 17–18)

In the Indian languages, to address someone in the singular is less polite than to address them in the plural. We had this in English originally. 'You' is plural, not singular, and 'you' was a more polite form of address than 'thou'. Eventually 'you' became the polite way of addressing everybody, so the distinction was obliterated. When the distinction was still used, the Quakers would not distinguish between people as being high or low and therefore would not say 'thou' to some and 'you' to others. They said 'thou' and 'thee' to everybody, to emphasize that they were no respecters of persons. For the same reason, they refused to take off their hats in the presence of the nobility, or royalty, or magistrates. They insisted on behaving in the same way towards everybody. Now, of course, everybody says 'you' to everybody, but some old-fashioned Quakers still say 'thee' and 'thou'. There's something of that sort here. One says, for instance 'you' rather than 'thou' to 'the spiritual teacher (guru) or the monk who may have administered that special formula of Refuge, perhaps as a kind of initiation.' Nyanaponika makes this point because he knows very well that the customary way of reciting the Refuges and Precepts in Ceylon isn't anything like an initiation, but he's wondering whether that ever did exist – presumably, in Ceylon.

> In any case, the concluding 'call to witness' gives to those utterances a strong emphasis and the solemnity of a vow distinguishing it from the general formula of refuge. The commencing words too: 'From today onward…' are stressing that character of a definite and personal dedication, as distinguished from an impersonal ritual. They mark the day of the first utterance as initiating a new period in the life of the devotee. Both the beginning and the end of these three modes of refuge are an echo of the earliest formulas of conversion, reported in the Suttas: 'I take refuge in the Lord Gotama, the doctrine and the community of monks! May the Lord Gotama know of me as an upāsaka! From today, as long as life lasts, I have taken refuge! (… *upāsakaṃ maṃ bhavaṃ Gotama dhāretu, ajjatagge pāṇupetaṃ saraṇaṃ gataṃ*.') (p. 18)

Nyanaponika is clearly struggling with the degenerate situation in Ceylon, where the repetition of the Going for Refuge formula has become what he calls an impersonal ritual. He'd like to get back to something more like what the Going for Refuge must have been in the Buddha's day, but he seems to feel that the Going for Refuge formula itself has been so misused for so long that one would need some other formula as an expression of one's more individual commitment. He's wondering whether these alternative formulas that occur in the scriptures, and which he thinks might have been used in that sort of more individual way later on, could be used.

SAGARAMATI: Who would use them? *Upāsakas* or monks?

SANGHARAKSHITA: I assume that *upāsakas* would, because the *bhikkhus* have their ordination ceremony. To spell it out more clearly, make it more explicit, what he has in mind is this. He's apparently thinking: Let people in Ceylon, in Burma, in Thailand, go on reciting '*Buddhaṃ saraṇaṃ gacchāmi, Dhammaṃ saraṇaṃ gacchāmi, Saṅghaṃ saraṇaṃ gacchāmi,*' on these big festive occasions. Let them recite it all together in their hundreds and thousands without bothering very much about what it means. But in the case of the lay Buddhist, the *upāsaka*, who wants to start taking Buddhism seriously, let there be a sort of initiation for him, and let one of these other formulas be used for that. He seems to be thinking that that particular person who has been born a Buddhist, and who has hitherto not taken Buddhism seriously, but who now wishes to take it seriously, could repeat one of these other formulas in front of a *bhikkhu*. They could repeat this formula thinkingly, whereas in the past they have unthinkingly repeated the Going for Refuge formula. Suppose the surrender of self formula was used. The person who wanted to become a real *upāsaka*, a real Buddhist, as distinct from a born Buddhist, would come in front of the *bhikkhu*, the *bhikkhu* would recite '*Ajja ādiṃ katvā ahaṃ attānaṃ Buddhassa niyyādemī Dhammassa Sanghassā'ti*', he would then recite it after him, and that would be a real initiation into Buddhism. This is exactly what we've done with the Going for Refuge and the ten precepts. When we start operating in India the ex-Untouchable Buddhists, who have become Buddhist en masse, will continue reciting the Three Refuges and the *five* precepts – we won't interfere with that – but anyone who wants to become an *upāsaka* in our sense will recite the Three Refuges and the *ten* precepts. In other words, it will be something different, something special, representing an individual commitment on their part as distinct from the mass adoption of Buddhism associated with the Three Refuges and the five precepts.

LOKAMITRA: Here you're making a distinction, though, again according to precepts, which is a distinction between *upāsakas* and *bhikkhus* in the old way. Do you see what I mean?

SANGHARAKSHITA: Yes. I am not really making a distinction in respect of observing of precepts, because in many cases the five precepts are just a formula to those who are reciting them, not anything that they take seriously. It's a flag that they wave.

LOKAMITRA: But there is the danger that one would be taken to be a Buddhist in our sense not because one goes for Refuge but because one takes the ten precepts as opposed to the five precepts.

SANGHARAKSHITA: It might be, but we'll have to make that clear, because you can't alter that situation. You can't stop people reciting the five precepts! What are you going to do?

LOKAMITRA: Then of course there would be the individual ceremony.

SANGHARAKSHITA: Yes. It's the individual Going for Refuge that counts. Recently I summarized the situation in a sort of aphorism which I haven't yet committed to writing but which I'll tell you now. It goes, 'Buddhism is not a service industry.' So what does that mean? What is a service industry?

A VOICE: Something which supports the whole.

ANANDAJYOTI: It's advisory, in a sense.

SAGARAMATI: It just maintains.

SANGHARAKSHITA: Yes, a service industry is an industry that maintains. Can you give an example?

SAGARAMATI: Well, the television repair industry keeps everybody's television working.

LOKAMITRA: The railways. Transport. Catering.

SANGHARAKSHITA: Catering, yes. These are all service industries. So what do I mean by saying that Buddhism is not a service industry?

LOKAMITRA: It's not something that maintains the status quo.

SANGHARAKSHITA: It's not something that maintains the status quo. Maintains it in what particular way?

SAGARAMATI: A sort of psychological way.

SANGHARAKSHITA: By 'blessing' it and 'consecrating' it. When I say that Buddhism is not a service industry I mean that our main task is not simply to perform ceremonies that bless ordinary worldly activities. This implies that ultimately religion as usually understood is more or less a service industry. You have a class of professionals who carry on the service industry and a class of customers. The former are called the priests and the latter are called the laity. We don't want that. We don't want a situation in which we've got a core of full-timers who are running a religious service industry, with swarms of customers who make vigorous and continuous demands for ceremonies of various kinds which you fulfil. But this is what it could be like. Among the ex-Untouchables one is always being asked to perform ceremonies of some kind or other. Such ceremonies have a certain place, but one must be very careful that there is not created a division between the ordinary Buddhists who stay at home and who recite the Refuges and Precepts without taking them too seriously, and the full-timers, whether they are monks or *anagārikas* or whatever, who are allegedly concerned with Buddhism but who are in fact simply operating that service industry, so that that is the only distinction between them. In India, this is the great danger. We're not so much in that kind of danger in the West, but certainly we are over there.

VAIROCANA: It has happened here. There have been funeral services conducted by the Order.

SANGHARAKSHITA: I'm not saying that funeral services shouldn't be conducted, but we should be very careful how we get into things of this kind. We shouldn't become just an agency for blessing the activities of secular life and helping people to feel good about them and to preserve the status quo. This is certainly what has happened in America in Buddhist circles. You should see some of the Buddhist magazines and journals we get from them! It's absolutely terrible, absolutely pathetic.

LOKAMITRA: That's among the Japanese and Chinese, isn't it?

SANGHARAKSHITA: Some of the Caucasians too. Some of the Buddhist magazines and papers we get are exactly like local parish magazines, just reports of parish pump activities, photographs of weddings and funerals and giving of certificates, and Buddhist Sunday School outings and Boy Scout troops. There is the danger that Tibetan Buddhism will eventually go this way in the States, because they do not stress the Going Forth; they do not stress giving up anything. Anyway, maybe that's quite a different story, but one can see the beginnings of it already.

VAIROCANA: It happened in Edinburgh. A couple came along who wanted us to marry them, but we didn't do it. We gave them the address of Samye Ling.

A VOICE: Their situation was different because they were going to Greece and it seems that in Greece a marriage is not recognized unless it has been conducted by a religious ceremony of some kind. So they wanted a Buddhist ...

SANGHARAKSHITA: I'm not saying that there should be a hard and fast rule that we should never perform these ceremonies. It's largely a question of proportion. If most of your time is taken up in this way then clearly you are becoming just a service industry. If you have the odd funeral, or even the odd blessing of a marriage, well, never mind. It may be necessary to do that sort of thing occasionally, but it shouldn't be one's principal occupation. Each case can be considered on its individual merits, and there might be occasions when we decide to do as people wish. But certainly we shouldn't become, as religions tend to become, what I call a service industry, as even Buddhism sometimes is in the East, quite wrongly. Our function is not to service people's secular needs in this sort of way.

This 'calling to witness' is very interesting. What makes it interesting is the fact that the 'initiation' in terms of which Nyanaponika is thinking, or what we would call the public ordination, takes place in the midst of an assembly of devotees – within a circle of already committed people, as we would say.

KULANANDA: It shifts the emphasis from the internal to something external as well.

SANGHARAKSHITA: So what do you think is the significance of this? Why should it be external as well as internal, objective as well as subjective?

VAIROCANA: It's a case of standing up and being seen as a Buddhist, instead of saying to *yourself* 'I'm a Buddhist' but not telling anyone. You can conceivably do that, but in this case you stand up in front of everyone and say 'Yes, I am a Buddhist.' That's the importance. You *could* go back on your word later on, but ...

SANGHARAKSHITA: Clearly it must start in your own mind, but if it stops there it isn't fully real.

KULANANDA: It needs to move into the realm of activity.

SANGHARAKSHITA: Into the realm of what is sometimes termed 'the public reality' – and you do exist in the public reality. If you only go for Refuge in your own mind it isn't really complete, because you also exist as a person among other persons. If you don't make it clear to them that you've gone for Refuge, in a sense you haven't fully gone for Refuge.

But there's another way in which we can look at it, a more philosophical way. We have touched upon this before. It refers to the relation between subject and object. I've often mentioned that our own experience takes place within the framework of the subject–object duality. According to Buddhism that subject–object duality is not absolutely, not ultimately real. In the state of Nirvāṇa, of *śūnyatā*, of *prajñā*, there is no distinction between subject and object. This is basic Buddhist thought. So that which is, or which purports to be, either exclusively subject or exclusively object is to that extent removed from the ultimately real. In other words, if you have subject and object together you're closer to ultimate reality than you are if you have only subject or only object separately. Do you see this? It's true that even when you have subject and object together, you're still far removed from ultimate reality, but when you have just one of them by itself you're even further removed. So long as you are functioning within the framework of subject and object, if you want to get as near, within that framework, to ultimate reality as you can, then you must operate in terms of both subject and object. Therefore, if you want your Going for Refuge, your mundane Going for Refuge, to be as near to ultimate reality, in a manner of speaking, as you can make it, then it must be a subjective and an objective process. It must be something which you do for yourself alone, which you experience for yourself and by yourself, and it must also be something which takes place within the public, objective reality. The private ordination represents the first. It's your Going for Refuge *by yourself*. It's your own individual act. But you're not an individual existing in a vacuum, you're an individual existing in an objective world as another object, another person, for other people – specifically, as a committed person for other committed people. So your Going for Refuge is, I won't say incomplete, but not as near to ultimate reality as it might be until you've proclaimed it in front of other people, especially other similarly committed people. This is why we have both the individual Going for Refuge and the private ordination *and* the Going for Refuge as witnessed by other committed individuals, in other words the public ordination.

KULARATNA: This sort of thing can apply to anything that we do, if you try to make a balance between subjective and objective aspects.

SANGHARAKSHITA: (Break in recording) Usually we do quite naturally. When we don't there's a definite reason why we don't which is perhaps not a very healthy or spiritual reason. This is why the whole conception of religion as an essentially private affair is completely wrong.

SAGARAMATI: Somebody said that your religion is what you do when you're on your own.

SANGHARAKSHITA: 'Religion is what you do with your solitude.' I think it was Whitehead who said this.[268] It's half the truth, but only half. There's also what you do when you're with other people. Religion is that too.

MAHAMATI: Does this tie in with the principle of *yin* and *yang*?

SANGHARAKSHITA: I would say that was a different kind of distinction. It is not that *yin* is subject and *yang* is object, or vice versa.

KULARATNA: It might tie in with individualism and altruism.

SANGHARAKSHITA: Yes, it might tie in with something like that.

SAGARAMATI: I must admit that I always find that it's out of balance. There's an objective world, but the objective world can't change me. It's only my own subjective volition that can change me. So there is an imbalance.

SANGHARAKSHITA: You have to start with the individual commitment, though some, of course, would say not. Some would say that you could start off without any real feeling of individual commitment, but you might be convinced, on purely intellectual grounds, that you ought to be committed, so you go through the external motions as, say, when you participate in the puja in the hope that eventually you'll start feeling some devotion. It can work that way round. But even that begins with your as it were 'individual' conviction that participating in the puja could sooner or later 'work' for you if you participated in it, even without your experiencing any feeling for it.

RATNAJYOTI: Is that view quite valid?

SANGHARAKSHITA: Which view?

RATNAJYOTI: The second one you gave, the objective one.

SANGHARAKSHITA: When you say quite valid, you mean does it actually work?

RATNAJYOTI: Yes.

SANGHARAKSHITA: It seems that quite a number of people have found that it does work, yes.

RATNAJYOTI: It can affect consciousness.

SAGARAMATI: It's equally true to say that you as a subject can't grow without external support. You can't do it on your own, as it were.

SANGHARAKSHITA: You can't do it on your own because you can't even *be* on your own in order to *do* it on your own to start with. Is anybody ever absolutely on his or her own? It's very, very doubtful indeed.

SAGARAMATI: Even just thinking about somebody is not being on your own.

SANGHARAKSHITA: Yes. Even if you're not thinking about them they may be thinking about you. That could affect you. There are other forms of life, even if there are no human beings around. Even if you went into the forest you'd be in contact at least with plant life. That is alive to some extent, even sentient – some would say even conscious to some extent. So you are not alone.

KULANANDA: You are part of the web of consciousness.

SANGHARAKSHITA: Yes. It's a question of degree. It has been said that if you try to eliminate the subjective element as much as is practicable you end up with science, if you try to eliminate the objective element you end up with the arts, especially music, and if you try to hold a balance between the subjective and the objective elements, that is religion. You can see those possibilities, whether you label them in that particular way or not, i.e. you can have an objectivity almost completely devoid of subjectivity, and a subjectivity almost completely devoid of objectivity, and you can also have a position where you try to hold a balance between them. Whether the holding of that balance is to be identified as religion or not, when one holds the balance in that way, inasmuch as you have a balance between the subjective and the objective, you are nearer to ultimate reality, which is, in a manner of speaking, both subjective and objective, and neither subjective nor objective.

This whole question of 'calling to witness' is therefore quite interesting, and Nyanaponika also seems to find it so. We don't, in our public ordination, have anything like a calling of the assembly to witness. In a way it isn't necessary, because there they actually are witnessing and participating. But they do let fly their threefold shout of '*sādhu*', which gives expression to their recognition – which means acceptance, in this case – of what has happened.[269] You get that echo coming back from the universe around you or from the spiritual community around you, the echo of your own commitment, your own Going for Refuge.

## Starting Afresh

> The commentator explains the three lower modes of refuge merely by reference to scriptural passages which do not enlighten us very much. From this fact we may conclude that in Buddhaghosa's time and environment those modes of refuge were no longer a living practice, but only a reminiscence for which explanation had to be sought in literature. Otherwise the commentator would certainly have dealt with them in greater detail and probably illustrated them by some stories which he is usually so fond of relating. The fourth and highest mode of refuge has obviously been more familiar at that time and was probably still in use by those undergoing strenuous meditative practice, as evinced by a passage in the *Visuddhimagga* which we shall quote later. (pp. 18–19)

SANGHARAKSHITA: Nyanaponika is suggesting here that these alternative procedures had been practised once upon a time but that by Buddhaghosa's time they had died out. Buddhaghosa had to find some basis in Pāli literature for those procedures, so he selected the episodes which he quotes and regarded them as illustrations of those particular modes of Going for Refuge, which they might not in fact have been. Perhaps he just fitted them in rather arbitrarily. There seems to be a little confusion as to which is the first and which is the fourth mode of mundane Going for Refuge. The three lower ones must be the last three, with the surrender of self being the first and highest mode. But he speaks here of the *fourth* and highest mode. Maybe that is reckoning backwards. He enumerates them first of all in descending order, but since here he refers to the fourth and highest presumably he is now reckoning in ascending order of importance. 'The fourth and highest mode of refuge has obviously been more familiar at that time and was probably still in use by those undergoing strenuous meditative practice, as evinced by a passage in the *Visuddhimagga* which we shall quote later'. Let's see what that is when we come to it.

> But despite the lack of authentic information, the following facts become sufficiently clear from the formulas themselves. The ancient devotees who coined and used them have been obviously very sensitive as to the deep significance of that act of going for refuge, perceiving it as a most momentous step, decisive for life. By making a fourfold distinction demanding a definite and personal choice, they made provision for saving the performance of that act from becoming a soulless habit. The ancient devotees knew well the implication of that apparently simple act and have been aware of the sacred responsibilities resulting from it. They knew that taking refuge is actually consummated only by a complete self-surrender to the Triple Gem, without any reservations. In the lesser modes of the act, there is still something of the presumed self that is kept back; it is a going for refuge with reservations. Nevertheless these lesser modes too are definite steps towards the highest, and should be consciously cultivated. As in any harmonious mental development, here too the higher level will not exclude the lower one but absorb it into its wider compass. In trying to obtain a clearer picture of those four modes, we shall therefore start not from the highest, but from the lowest level. (p. 19)

As Nyanaponika says, from the fact that there are these terms which Buddhaghosa is trying to explain it is clear that at some stage or other, whether in Ceylon or perhaps before that in India, there were people who were very much concerned with the significance of the Going for Refuge as an individual act. But the mere fact that even by Buddhaghosa's time very little was known about these things, and the general scantiness of the information available, shows that the significance of Going for Refuge as an individual act must have died out quite early in Ceylon. In some Buddhist countries even the *bhikkhu* ordination wasn't so much an individual act. Thousands of *bhikkhus* would be ordained at the same time, sometimes just for a short period. Even that came to have a more or less ceremonial significance.

Clearly Nyanaponika is trying to revive the significance of the Going for Refuge – whether in terms of the traditional formula, or some other formula – as a much more individual act, and a much more spiritually significant act, than it is at present, say, in Ceylon. I rather think he has an uphill task.

LOKAMITRA: With regard to this 'fourfold distinction demanding a definite and personal choice', do you think he's trying to say that there's still a place for those who aren't really Going for Refuge?

SANGHARAKSHITA: Well, it amounts to what I said about the ex-Untouchables and their recitation of the five precepts. You can't stop them doing it. In the case of people in Ceylon, they may have been misusing the Going for Refuge formula, but what are you going to do about it? They'd be up in arms if you tried to stop them reciting it. So you've got to find some alternative. In Nyanaponika's case the alternative has to be well within the Pāli tradition, otherwise no one in Ceylon, or in the Theravāda world generally, is going to accept it. This is why he is trying to bring out the significance of the material he finds in this one commentarial passage. He can give us just one passage, out of all the thousands of pages of commentaries, on such an important matter.

LOKAMITRA: It seems a bit wrong, in a way, that an ill that has happened in Buddhism, i.e. this distinction in the Going for Refuge: that the Going for Refuge is only taken sincerely if you're a monk, is …

SANGHARAKSHITA: Even in the case of the monk, in the Theravādin countries it's obscured, because they don't really think in terms of the monk Going for Refuge. He's just being ordained; he's becoming a monk; he's joining the service industry. Sometimes it really means not much more than that.

KULARATNA: There isn't really a ceremony for proper Going for Refuge at all.

SANGHARAKSHITA: No, actually there isn't, strange as it may seem. In the Theravādin Buddhist countries there is no such ceremony. It must be said that the Mahāyānists – the Tibetans, and the Chinese Buddhists – take the Going for Refuge much more seriously and have a proper Going for Refuge ceremony. The Tibetans take the Going for Refuge so seriously that they have even got different kinds of Going for Refuge and taking of precepts. They will not always take all the precepts. Some will take the Going for Refuge with only one precept, others with two, or with three. They take it as seriously as that because they say that if they take it in that formal way they absolutely must observe it. They would rather take only those precepts that they are actually going to observe. You might, of course, say that if you really and truly go for Refuge that should surely carry you through at least a few precepts because the precepts represent the practical application of the Going for Refuge. Nonetheless, the Tibetans are very strict and very serious about this. But you could say that in the Theravādin countries, normally at least, there is no individual Going for Refuge, which is a terrible omission.

KULARATNA: Or at least there might be for individual people, but there's no ceremony in the shrine-room.

SAGARAMATI: In Theravādin countries, there is only the public ceremony?

SANGHARAKSHITA: Yes, though there are exceptions. For instance, if you want to take the eight precepts, it's not that you cannot recite them individually; you can do so, either by yourself or taking them from a *bhikkhu*. But even when you recite the Three Refuges and the eight precepts by yourself in front of a *bhikkhu*, it's probably your umpteenth time of reciting them, and just part of the general merit-making that is considered appropriate to the lay Buddhist. It's not that you ever come in a very special way and recite the Refuges and Precepts as it were for the first time, and consciously pledge yourself to Buddhism. In other words, there is no equivalent of the Christian ceremony of confirmation.

In all countries where a certain religion has become established this question of conscious individual commitment arises. In the early days of Christianity, when you wanted to become a Christian you were baptized. Baptism is what makes you a Christian. But nowadays in nearly all Christian countries, and in nearly all Christian churches, you are baptized when you are a baby. You can't understand the significance of it at that time, but you are still genuinely baptized: you are a genuine Christian. But there is a difficulty inasmuch as you have not committed yourself personally, and most churches solve this with the help of the rite of confirmation. When you are 12 or 13, or even 15 or 16, there is a sort of individual ceremony. Even though that too has become a formality for many people, it is a bit more individual than baptism as an infant. The confirmation service was developed so that when you've reached the years of discretion, you have an opportunity to commit yourself consciously to the Christian faith.

But in the Theravādin countries, there isn't anything like that. No one ever says, 'Well, here you all are, reciting the Refuges and Precepts ever since you could speak, without understanding the significance of what you were doing. Now let's have a special occasion when you take them consciously and deliberately, if you wish to do so, and commit yourself to the Buddhist path.' Nyanaponika clearly feels the absence of that kind of ceremony, and maybe there are serious-minded Theravādin Buddhists who would like something of that sort, but there's no provision for it. You can go in front of a monk and take the Three Refuges and eight precepts, but they're usually just taken for one or two days. It isn't a lifelong commitment to the Three Jewels, just a bit of extra merit-making.

This raises the whole question of how difficult it is to reform a religion, to use that term, once it has become corrupt. It's very difficult indeed, even when it's clearly shown that people have strayed away from the original teaching. People are so attached to what is customary and traditional: they don't want to change, and if you try to impose or bring about a change, it usually results in some sort of schism. The Roman Catholic Church wouldn't be reformed, so the Protestants broke away. That was the Reformation. One of the recent kings of Thailand tried, when he was a *bhikkhu*, before becoming king, to reform the Thai sangha, but he only succeeded in creating another *nikāya*, the Dhammayuttika Nikāya.[270] The old Mahā Nikāya remained unreformed. So it isn't easy to reform an established religion.

In the West, we've got a much better opportunity. We start afresh. There's no need for reform here, because there isn't any old Buddhism except for tiny pockets of Sinhalese and Thai nationals and just a very few English people. This is one of the things I thought very clearly quite early on, when I was at the Hampstead Buddhist Vihara – that we don't want to introduce the old corrupt way of doing things. I remember the particular incident which really made me think about such things, after coming back to this country in 1964. What happened was that I grew my hair just a little bit. While I was in India, of course, I shaved my head, but after I had been at the Hampstead Buddhist Vihara for a while I let my hair grow a bit. It wasn't beyond the regulation length, but some people who regarded themselves as Theravādin Buddhists – English people – got very upset about this, and I thought, 'It's already started here. It's time to check it before it gets any worse, before it goes any further.' The problem was this attachment to these very minute things. Strictly speaking I wasn't in the wrong, not even technically, but they thought I was. I knew the rule about the two-fingers'-breadth of hair, but they didn't.[271] They were under the impression that a *bhikkhu* should be clean-shaven on his scalp, though that is not actually the rule. I thought, 'Buddhism has only been here in England for a few years, but already they've got these rigid narrow-minded, blind, blinkered, ignorant attitudes, just as in Ceylon and other places. This must be stopped before it goes any further.' You can't altogether blame the English Theravādins; they've been wrongly taught.

After that I let my hair grow longer than ever. It was still very short, but enough to upset some people quite a lot – even people who called themselves Mahāyānists and were always reading books about Zen, which seemed really extraordinary. So I thought, 'Well, here's a chance to do things in the right way', and this is why, when the FWBO was started, I was quite clear in my own mind that we were going to do things in the right way right from the beginning. Whatever other people might think, however much they might disagree or disapprove, we were going to do things in the right way, without any compromise.

Sometimes at Sukhavati and other FWBO places *bhikkhus* have turned up, or at least people in yellow robes, with no real knowledge of Buddhism, no real commitment to it, but they've expected to be treated almost like *arhants*, because that's the tradition in Ceylon, but we just don't do that. We won't do it because it is so wrong, so against the real Buddhist tradition. So we don't have such an uphill task here in doing things in the right way – the real way, the Buddha's way even, we might say – as Nyanaponika seems to have in Ceylon. I don't think he'll be able to do much at all, though he sees the situation so clearly.

But we can do quite a lot here. We can get off on the right foot right from the beginning.

> Homage is the mental attitude, and the bodily and verbal expression, of reverence, resulting from the recognition and appreciation of something higher than oneself. It breaks through the first and hardest shell of pride and self-contented ignorance that knows of nothing better than one's own petty self. When encountering something higher, animals and undeveloped men – 'primitive', or 'civilized' – will mostly react by distrust, fear, flight, attack, resentment, hostility, persecution, etc., because they can view that higher form of life only as something different, alien, and therefore suspect. It is the sign of a truly developed human mind that it meets the higher with due respect, with admiration, and the wish to emulate. Recognition and appreciation of something higher is therefore the preliminary condition of spiritual growth, and true respect, resulting from it, forms the basis of moral education too. Kungfutse [i.e. Confucius] names respect (*li*) as the first of qualities of 'human-heartedness' (*jen*). (p. 20)

What Nyanaponika has to say here about homage in general is very true, very correct. We find that very often when people encounter something higher, they do 'mostly react by distrust, fear, flight, attack, resentment, hostility, persecution, etc., because they can view that higher form of life only as something different, alien, and therefore suspect'. One can indeed say that 'it is the sign of a truly developed human mind that it meets the higher with due respect, with admiration, and the wish to emulate'. That really does sum it up. 'Recognition and appreciation of something higher is therefore the preliminary condition of spiritual growth…'

Nyanaponika defines homage as 'the mental attitude, and the bodily and verbal expression, of reverence, resulting from the recognition and appreciation of something higher than oneself'. You notice it must be objective as well as subjective, i.e. bodily and verbal as well as mental. 'It breaks through the first and hardest shell of pride and self-contented ignorance that knows of nothing better than one's own petty self.' Do you think this is people's normal attitude, that there's nothing better than their own self?

KULANANDA: No.

SANGHARAKSHITA: One has to distinguish, don't forget, between 'better' and 'more powerful'. You can feel what sometimes is called healthy respect for someone who's stronger than you, but that is to be distinguished from reverence for someone who is better than you.

KULANANDA: I think it's quite right when people actually really do feel this, experience this.

SANGHARAKSHITA: That somebody else is really better than they are. It is, in a way, a very un- or anti-democratic attitude, isn't it? Democracy is usually understood to mean, or to imply, that everybody is as good as everybody else. Democracy certainly does mean equality before the law, but equality before the law does not mean absolute human equality. Do you see the difference? Everybody is equal before the law, but that does not mean that everybody is equal without qualification.

KULANANDA: Aren't those people professing a kind of false equanimity, under this guise of democracy, pretending they're seeing the good in everyone?

SANGHARAKSHITA: Yes. Or at least pretending they're seeing the good intentions in everyone.

DHAMMARATI: Do you think this is more an adult attitude and maybe found less with younger people? The young people who are coming to the Glasgow centre are so obviously emulating some of the Order members.

SANGHARAKSHITA: I think in a way there is a natural tendency in the very young generally, in children even, to trust, to look up to, and admire, and it isn't always simply the greater strength or the greater power of the adult that is looked up to, but almost in a way something better. But that natural tendency very often gets corrupted later on by pseudo-egalitarian ideas. Perhaps one could say that among adults in the West the attitude of genuine reverence is very rare. Perhaps children, or young people generally, are more open in this particular way.

ANANDAJYOTI: It's as though in the case of the adult one is prepared to accept a bit of quantitative difference but not a qualitative difference.

KULARATNA: I suppose it comes from a reaction against an oppressive social and class system.

SANGHARAKSHITA: That too. If you have had the experience, as many people must have had in the past, of being looked down upon, or ill-treated and exploited, by someone who as a human being was clearly inferior to you and your friends, but who happened to have a higher social position, you will surely feel very bitter about it.

LOKAMITRA: I would have thought it was almost inevitably a phenomenon of *saṃsāra*, this sort of behaviour.

SANGHARAKSHITA: I was reading the other day (I think it was in the *Life of Swinburne*) a letter written by a lord, I think it was, criticizing somebody and saying he was lacking in proper respect for rank and opulence. Yes, for rank and opulence! As recently as the end of the nineteenth century, it was the belief of people with rank and opulence that these things should be respected, that the wealthier, more powerful members of society deserve the respect of the lower orders. Clearly among the lower orders, or at least some of them, there must have been feelings of bitterness and resentment, and this perhaps led to a disinclination to look up to anybody in any way. There was an assertion of a contrary attitude, everybody being equal, or being the same. Maybe it's time we got back to a middle way. People are all human, and certainly there should be equality before the law, but everybody is not equal in the respect of the development of human attributes – not equal in respect of awareness, and so on. If one encounters someone who is more highly developed than oneself one should be glad of that, because it demonstrates that there is a higher possibility of development open to human beings, including you. It's good news for you that there's someone more highly developed than you. It would be a very pitiable state of affairs if no one was ever more highly developed than you were. But this is an attitude that a lot of people have nowadays: that no one is essentially any better than they are.

LOKAMITRA: If they recognize that, it implies that they have to do something themselves.

SANGHARAKSHITA: Also, if you recognize someone as more highly developed than you and at the same time recognize yourself as less developed than him, you feel inferior, because you think in terms of the group, which means that you are made to feel weaker in relation to his greater strength. You don't feel simply less developed in relation to his overall development. You feel lower in every way, in comparison with him, he being as it were in the higher position. You look at it in terms of dominance, especially if you are a man perhaps, not in terms of degree of spiritual evolution, so you feel almost as though you're being put down, relegated to a lower position, an *inferior* position, and you resent that. If you resent someone for being more highly developed than you are, you're not really seeing them as more highly developed, because if you really and truly could do that, you'd respect and revere them. You're simply seeing them as different, quantitatively different, more powerful. In other words, you're seeing them in group terms.

Until you start revering people you're not out of the group situation – in other words, you are not being an individual. To the extent that you are an individual, you can recognize someone as being more of an individual than you, and therefore to be revered by you. But to the extent that you're just a member of the group, all that you can recognize is superior strength and force. This is why sometimes people who are qualitatively superior are only recognized as being in some way superior when they start succeeding in a worldly way. That's the only way in which the average person can, perhaps, 'recognize' them. For instance, people may not be able to recognize somebody as a great artist, but as soon as he starts making a lot of money out of his art he is recognized as a rich man and respected on that account. You think, 'There must be something in his art; after all, look at all the money he's made out of it.'

There's an experience of my own in this connection, when I was in India, which I've pondered upon quite a lot. I used to go around giving lectures, but I must say that I wasn't taken very seriously by quite a lot of other *bhikkhus*. They thought, 'Yes, what Sangharakshita is doing is all right. It keeps him happy, and of course there's no objection to his preaching the Dharma if he likes.' But they didn't take me very seriously or think very highly of me. But when I bought a property in Kalimpong their attitude changed markedly. They took me seriously after that, because they saw I had the capacity to have mustered sufficient support to be able to buy a building. When I went down to Calcutta and Sarnath after purchasing the Triyana Vardhana Vihara, as it was then, I found that their attitude towards me had changed. They were much more friendly, and they took me much more seriously. It was almost as though they felt I was really one of them now. So long as I merely meditated, and merely preached the Dharma, I wasn't taken very seriously, but as soon as I became the owner of some ecclesiastical property I was taken quite seriously, and that really caused me to reflect. There are a number of incidents in my career like this, which have given me cause for reflection – like the incident of growing my hair. It's these little things that one can really learn a lot from.

VAIROCANA: Even as regards the Glasgow Buddhist Centre getting a place of its own, people take it much more seriously now that we own our own property.

SANGHARAKSHITA: But you're the same people, with the same sincerity, the same knowledge of the Dharma. Maybe you're a little more experienced since the early days, but essentially you're the same people, doing the same things. But one finds people will respect you, even if you are a spiritual person, not on account of anything spiritual but on account of material things.

VAIROCANA: They come in and see tape recorders and things like that, and are impressed by how well organized we are, and this sort of thing.

LOKAMITRA: Do you think faith as an aspiration to grow can be suppressed or repressed? The question comes from my experience of coming into contact with people and feeling they want to categorize me, but they can't quite do it, and they're not very comfortable because – it seems to me – they won't admit to that possibility in themselves, or that wider possibility.

SANGHARAKSHITA: But what's the connection? How does that come in?

LOKAMITRA: Well, there's this respect, which people don't have; but it seems to me it's something which is possibly in a lot of people, but it's held down, it's repressed.

SANGHARAKSHITA: If you start recognizing something higher in other people and respecting that, it makes a sort of demand on you, and perhaps people are not prepared to meet that demand.

LOKAMITRA: But I feel it's very definitely there, in quite a few people.

SANGHARAKSHITA: Some people do the opposite of suppressing or repressing faith. You find this in India, and in Buddhist countries. They put you on an exaggeratedly high pedestal, so as to give themselves an excuse for not making any effort at all. 'That's all right for you', they say. 'You are so clever, so learned, so devoted. We poor people cannot be expected to be like that.' This is not real respect. It's just a ploy.

SAGARAMATI: But in the case of what Lokamitra's talking about, emotions seem to get tangled up. If a feeling of respect that had been repressed in you is coming up, there are so many other associations coming up with it, some of them to do with the group, so you experience them at the same time and feel confused.

SANGHARAKSHITA: It's really that you're not able to distinguish between what pertains to the group and what pertains to the individual. You're not able to appreciate the difference between a more powerful member of the group and someone who is more truly evolved – more truly an individual – than yourself. Since you think of the person who is more highly developed than you as though he was simply a more powerful member of the group, you feel those emotions towards him, or have those attitudes which would be appropriate towards a more powerful member of the group. For instance, you may feel threatened. But how could someone more spiritually developed than you possibly be a source of threat? It's ridiculous, absurd. If you fear God, it means that you're not regarding God as a spiritual figure, only as a more powerful member of the group, *the* most powerful member of the group, the most powerful being in the universe – so, by definition, not a spiritual being. It's right that you should fear him, if he exists. What other attitude could you have towards him? The confusion consists in not being able to make the distinction between the more powerful member of the group and the individual who is more developed as a human being, or even more spiritually developed, than you are. Hence you feel towards that more developed individual emotions which are appropriate only in relation to that more powerful member of the group. Instead of revering them you hate them, or you feel resentful towards them. Sometimes, of course, in the case of ecclesiastical figures, you have got, instead of a truly more developed human being, just a more powerful member of your particular pseudo-religious group. A bishop or archbishop may sometimes be a more spiritually developed person, but very often he's just someone with more authority within the ecclesiastical group to which you belong.

This whole question of homage is really very important. You become capable of rendering genuine homage only when you start becoming an individual, and start being able to recognize individuality – greater individuality than your own – in other people. If you 'knock' people who are spiritually more developed than you, or if you can't recognize or appreciate their higher spiritual development, it means that you're still functioning within the limits of the group. On the other hand, you mustn't allow yourself to be bullied into recognizing someone as more spiritually developed who is simply the most powerful member of a particular group, even a religious group. You get this with some of the Tibetan lamas, in the sort of publicity that their disciples put out. It's all intended to impress you. For instance, the followers of the Karmapa emphasize that he's the *Fourteenth* Karmapa. So what? There's a one-hundred-and-first Archbishop of Canterbury and a two-hundred-and-something Pope. That you're the hundredth or the two-hundredth or the fourteenth of your line: what difference does that make? It's just trying to consolidate tradition and authority behind you, to make you the representative of something big and powerful. This is not the way to go about it. To the extent that you are more spiritually developed, you are more of an individual. That is the fundamental principle. What does it matter if you're the fourteenth this or the umpteenth that? It doesn't really matter at all. But if you try to impress the potential audience by citing this fact, you're basically trying to impress them with authority.

### The Sheer Fact Of The Buddha's Existence

> Therefore in man's relation to the Highest, i.e. the Triple Gem, true homage comes first. As a way of taking refuge, homage is the spontaneous expression of the deep emotion felt when becoming

aware of the existence and the significance of the supreme refuge. It is the emotional reaction in gratitude, veneration, and joy when feeling the full weight of the tremendous fact that there is actually a refuge from this universe of suffering. Therefore the commentator's illustration of this mode of taking refuge is not the habitual act of worship by confirmed devotees, but the highly emotional conversion of an aged brahmin who, deeply stirred, prostrates himself before the Exalted One, embracing and kissing his feet. (p. 20)

SANGHARAKSHITA: This sounds like a real Going for Refuge. Even though it's supposed to be the lowest form, it sounds like a real commitment. But of what kind? On whose part? What kind of person is Going for Refuge in this way?

DHAMMARATI: A faith-follower.

SANGHARAKSHITA: Yes, it's more like the faith-follower. Even though Nyanaponika does say that homage is 'the spontaneous expression of the deep emotion felt when becoming aware of the existence and the significance of the supreme refuge', is it necessarily a reaction to that particular fact?

SEVERAL VOICES: No.

SANGHARAKSHITA: No. What sort of fact *could* it be a reaction to?

KULANANDA: The Buddha's existence.

SANGHARAKSHITA: Yes. It could be simply the sheer fact of the Buddha's existence, as in the case of Ānanda in the *Śūraṅgama Sūtra*.[272] So in this context this kind of Going for Refuge, the Homage, seems to be not just homage in the ordinary sense but the act of Going for Refuge of the faith-follower. Perhaps one has to distinguish different degrees, or different levels. You could have, say, a recognition of the fact that there is something higher, maybe as embodied in the Buddha, but in a not very marked or strong way, and this could be homage in the ordinary sense. But the homage which amounts to Going for Refuge would seem to be the Going for Refuge on the part of the faith-follower, and that Going for Refuge would seem to be as total as the Going for Refuge by way of self-surrender. Taken in that sense, it seems to be not really the lowest. Why Nyanaponika seems to regard it as the lowest we shall no doubt see in a minute. What he says about the significance of homage in a general way is very true, but homage as Going for Refuge seems to go beyond homage in the general sense. It is a real Going for Refuge, on the part of a faith-follower rather than a doctrine-follower.

> Homage represents the emotional side of taking refuge, being its aspect as a conscious act of faith. Through its single-heartedness and humility, the act of doing homage by body, speech and mind prepares the disciple emotionally for complete self-surrender. It is an indispensable step to it, but, being deficient with regard to understanding and determination, it requires the supplementation by the following two stages. (pp. 20–1)

SANGHARAKSHITA: Again, it's this question of qualifying. But is it reasonable to say this? Do you think there is a valid distinction between homage as here defined and complete self-surrender?

KULANANDA: Not necessarily.

SANGHARAKSHITA: Not necessarily. Because if you are emotionally committed, well, you are totally committed. If you go for Refuge emotionally, surely you just go for Refuge completely. Does 'understanding' make all that difference?

SAGARAMATI: He seems to see the emotional side as almost passive, despite the description.

SANGHARAKSHITA: Yes, right.

RATNAVIRA: What is complete self-surrender? Isn't it a sort of emotional response?

SANGHARAKSHITA: Surely your emotional response, by virtue of the fact that it is an emotional response, will have sufficient inherent momentum to carry you on and through, and to cause you to practise. It's not just a self-indulgent thing. So homage isn't really just the emotional side of taking Refuge. It is in its own right a full and genuine form of Going for Refuge on the part of a more emotionally-oriented person. Is it even deficient with regard to determination? It should not be deficient on account of its emotionality, surely?

DHAMMARATI: Do you think that subdivision actually exists, or is it just a classification for convenience?

SANGHARAKSHITA: What do you mean?

DHAMMARATI: Well, could you have homage as a separate thing? It seems that a person who pays homage sees the qualities to which he's paying homage. There's an understanding implied, and because it's emotional there's also an impulse towards it. It seems almost as though they've taken a single event and classified it into its components according to convenience.

SAGARAMATI: There must be some understanding in the case of homage. If you see something's higher than something else, there is the understanding that this is higher than that. So there is a pattern.

SANGHARAKSHITA: The feeling isn't just feeling. In a sense, emotion isn't just emotion.

KULANANDA: He keeps talking about 'blind emotion'. Is there really such a thing?

SAGARAMATI: There is on a group level, but not on this level.

ANANDAJYOTI: It means that emotion has an object.

KULARATNA: If you really feel there is something higher then you understand that, and if you really understand it ...

SANGHARAKSHITA: ...You may not be able to conceptualize it. Maybe he's confusing understanding with an ability to conceptualize, or a readiness to conceptualize, an ability to put things into words in a smooth and easy way. There is a tendency in Sinhalese Buddhism generally to depreciate 'mere faith' and attach much more importance and value to the understanding of things in terms of the established tradition and being able to quote the right text and all that sort of thing. I've found that Sinhalese monks, and even monks of other traditions, sometimes have a rather patronizing attitude towards the 'good devotees' who don't have the philosophy of Buddhism at their fingertips, as it were, who are just very devoted Buddhists who simply meditate and are charitable, and observe the precepts, and who don't even know Pāli, don't know the scriptures.

> While homage is still a distant and one-sided relationship to the supreme, the devotee still being in the outer court of the sanctuary, *the acceptance of discipleship* is a direct approach to it. Through the process of learning, a mutual relationship is established, or we may even say, a gradual and partial identification of teacher, teaching, and pupil takes place. Here the mind of the disciple goes for refuge to supreme wisdom, and becomes gradually permeated by it. (p. 21)

He begins by saying, 'While homage is still a distant and one-sided relationship to the supreme, the devotee still being in the outer court of the sanctuary', but from the actual description of the 'aged brahmin who, deeply stirred, prostrates himself before the Exalted One, embracing and kissing his feet', it doesn't seem to be very distant. It might be one-sided, though it's even doubtful whether it's really one-sided, but it's certainly not distant. It doesn't sound as though he's really talking about actual homage at all. '*The acceptance of discipleship* is a direct approach to it.' Here perhaps, his attempts to regard these different kinds of refuge as representing a sort of graded system, in the case of these two at least, breaks down. Admittedly he put it forward a bit hypothetically, at the beginning. 'Acceptance of discipleship' is indicated by the formula: 'From today onward I am the Disciple of the Buddha, the Dhamma, and the Sangha. Thus may you know me!' and illustrated by the passage expressing Kassapa's acceptance of discipleship.

'Through the process of learning, a mutual relationship is established, or we may even say, a gradual and partial identification of teacher, teaching, and pupil takes place.' Here, as I mentioned earlier, discipleship involves an actual living together with the teacher, not a periodic visit to him or simply attendance at a class. 'Here the mind of the disciple goes for refuge to supreme wisdom, and becomes gradually permeated by it.' Even here it's as though Nyanaponika is trying almost to intellectualize the whole process. Here's the disciple, actually living with his teacher, learning from him, so that a mutual relationship is established, but nonetheless he says, 'Here the mind of the disciple goes for refuge to supreme wisdom.' He doesn't want even to say, 'to the Buddha, to the Enlightened personality'. He wants to make it a bit abstract and impersonal. It's true that the disciple does go for refuge to supreme wisdom, but the fact that that is brought in seems to indicate a certain bias towards the intellectual side of things.

STHIRAMATI: That process that he mentions there seems to be an emotional one, rather than an intellectual one.

SANGHARAKSHITA: Perhaps he's got an emotional prejudice in favour of the intellect!

> Through respect and humility acquired by true homage, the disciple has earned for himself the right of entry into the sanctuary of wisdom. Only if approached in that attitude of respect and humility, the guru, the spiritual teacher of the East, will impart his knowledge, as these qualities are the first indication that the disciple is ready to receive. (p. 21)

'Through respect and humility acquired by true homage, the disciple has earned for himself the right of entry into the sanctuary of wisdom.' What do you think about that sentence?

KULANANDA: It's almost like a chore.

SANGHARAKSHITA: What do you think about this word 'earn'? Earn! That doesn't seem quite the right word for this growing intimacy and enjoyment of the Dharma. He earns 'for himself the right of entry into the sanctuary of wisdom.' The language – one doesn't want to exaggerate this – is more the language of the group than the language of the spiritual community. It's almost like passing an examination which gives you the right to sit the higher examination. 'Only if approached in that attitude of respect and humility, the guru, the spiritual teacher of the East, will impart his knowledge, as these qualities are the first indication that the disciple is ready to receive.' There's a slight flavour of the group approach here. It's as though the teacher is a somewhat more powerful person whom you've got to approach in a very respectful way. I don't want to insist upon the language of this passage too much, but the flavour that one gets from it is not really a spiritual flavour.

ANANDAJYOTI: It's almost one of romanticism and mystery in some respects. You get this 'sanctuary'.

SANGHARAKSHITA: The pseudo-emotional along with the intellectual! 'The sanctuary of wisdom.' It's as though he thinks he ought to be feeling something and therefore uses expressions of this sort, but they give the game away. It's as though he imagines the guru saying to himself, 'Has this chap got humility? Has he got respect? Otherwise I'm not going to impart my knowledge to him.' It doesn't seem as though it's really quite like that. It must be something genuinely felt. It can't be put on or assumed. Note 'the spiritual teacher of the East'. It seems that by writing about it in this way, perhaps by writing about it at all, he's made it seem a much more artificial process than it actually is. Certainly learning, in the true sense, does happen in the East, even in Ceylon, but not really in this sort of way.

> If refuge is taken in the sense of discipleship, life becomes a constant act of learning, i.e. of adapting the mind to the standards set by the Buddha, the Dhamma, and the Sangha. It is the character of the wise that he is always willing and anxious to learn. (p. 21)

Again there's this slight flavour of the group, I'm afraid, though what he says is technically correct. 'Adapting the mind to the standards set by the Buddha, the Dhamma, and the Sangha.' That choice of words is unfortunate, because when people talk of setting up standards, and living up to standards – well, you know the sort of people who talk in this sort of way. Perhaps we shouldn't criticize him too much, though, because he is, after all, German by birth, and so perhaps is not quite aware of the connotations these expressions may have for native English speakers. 'It is the character of the wise that he is always willing and anxious to learn.' Well, this sounds like the typical good boy at school, doesn't it? It just needs to be better put: to be felt more. Maybe one should speak more in terms of openness and receptivity, rather than of the wise being 'willing and anxious to learn.'

> The acceptance of discipleship represents the rational side of taking refuge which is here a conscious act of understanding. It supplies the full and satisfying reasons for the act of homage, and adds, in that way, to the strength and loyalty of devotion. (p. 21)

SANGHARAKSHITA: I think learning in the ordinary sense is being confused with learning in the spiritual sense. It's in a way unfortunate that the word 'teacher' has got this double meaning: one who imparts information and one who inspires spiritually. These are in fact two quite different things, and in Ceylon the teacher has become simply the imparter of information about Buddhism, the imparter of information about Pāli grammar, the contents of the Pāli texts, the Vinaya rules, and so on. (I've gone into this a little bit in my review of Walpola Rahula's book *The Heritage of the Bhikkhu*.)[273]

KULANANDA: In a way it expresses his own rationalization. 'Full and satisfying reasons' come after the emotional response to justify it.

SANGHARAKSHITA: As though one's devotional Going for Refuge requires a sort of justification.

SAGARAMATI: I think the word 'rational' often gets confused with 'being conscious'.

SANGHARAKSHITA: Yes. It's almost as though you make up your mind to become a disciple of the Buddha and then go along to some teacher, just as you might come to a rational decision to take up the study of, say, carpentry or beekeeping and then go along to evening classes. That's the sort of ring it has. It's just not good enough.

> But man is not always devotee or learner. There remains much in life that cannot be mastered easily by faith and understanding

> alone. It requires a strong will and determination, as well as the skill of long experience, to change the course of the manifold habitual activities of life into the direction of the refuge. This task of making the refuge gradually the centre of one's life is performed by the third mode of taking refuge. (pp. 21–2)

He's trying to treat these three lower modes of Going for Refuge in a systematic way, one being devotional, the next being rational, and the third being volitional, but it doesn't really work out very well. But what he says is true. 'It requires a strong will and determination, as well as the skill of long experience, to change the course of the manifold habitual activities of life into the direction of the refuge.' It's true that this has to be done, but I don't think that these three different kinds of Going for Refuge, i.e. homage by prostration, acceptance of discipleship, and acceptance of the guiding ideal, can be distributed among the three faculties of emotion, reason, and will quite so neatly as he thinks – though his general point that in the act of Going for Refuge emotion, reason, and will are all involved is of course perfectly valid.

> In accepting the Triple Gem as his guiding ideal the disciple pledges himself to subordinate gradually all the essential activities of his life to the ideals embodied in the Triple Gem. He vows to give all his strength to the task of impressing this sacred threefold seal upon his personal life and upon his environment too, as far as he is able to overcome its resistance. The threefold refuge in its aspect as the guiding ideal, or as the determining factor of life, calls for complete dedication in the sphere of external activities. (p. 22)

This is all true, though whether it does actually represent the specific meaning of Going for Refuge in the sense of accepting the Triple Gem as guiding ideal is a bit doubtful, as he himself goes on to recognize.

> This, at least, is what we tentatively suggest as the meaning or this third variety of taking refuge, called in Pāli *tapparāyaṇatā*. In putting forward this suggestion, we followed the trend of our previous thoughts about the three constituents of Buddhist faith, and we took up, in addition, the hint given in the illustrative

> passage quoted by the commentary in this connection. The canonical text to which that quotation belongs tells of two deities who, after their conversion, vow to go through the world as 'divine missionaries' of the Dhamma. This example given by the commentary may be taken as representative of the general task of establishing the sovereignty of the Triple Gem in one's own and in others' hearts. (p. 22)

His general approach is, in a way, quite understandable. He distinguishes emotion, reason, and will, rightly saying that in the Going for Refuge all three must be involved. Then he's got the three different forms of Going for Refuge: one, representing the first step, he tries to classify as emotional; one, representing the second step, as rational; and one, representing the third step, as volitional. Presumably we'll have them all together in the fourth step, that is to say, the Going for Refuge by way of self-surrender. Thus the general way of looking at things is quite intelligible. But whether the different kinds of Going for Refuge can be pigeon-holed in that way is a bit doubtful.

> But this dedication to the service of the Triple Gem is still not the highest form of taking refuge to which the disciple should aspire. Still there exists in the disciple's mind a difference between the noble objective and the person working for it. The delusive ego has been retained: it rejoices at the success of the work, and grieves when it fails. In a subtle way, the work, instead of the Triple Gem, becomes the refuge. If identification of self and work is not complete the ego, as it were, hides in the work, and evades the call for full surrender to the true refuge. Progress beyond this step is possible only if the service of the guiding ideal is done in a highly detached way, without looking for any reward. (pp. 22–3)

This seems quite an important point, a point that we did talk about earlier: 'Still there exists in the disciple's mind a difference between the noble objective and the person working for it.' In other words, there exists what I've called self-consciousness, in the more negative sense. 'The delusive ego has been retained: it rejoices at the success of the work, and grieves when it fails.' It's saying, 'Here I am meditating. Look how well I'm meditating!' Or it gets upset, thinking, 'I'm not meditating very well.' It gets upset not so much because objectively it isn't meditating very well, but because *it* hasn't succeeded, *it* hasn't gained what it wanted to gain. 'In a subtle way, the work, instead of the Triple Gem, becomes the refuge. If identification of self and work is not complete the ego, as it were, hides in the work, and evades the call for full surrender to the true refuge.' In other words, if you're really and truly into something, and are doing it completely, then there's no energy left over to go into your self-consciousness about what you're doing, so that the ego can appropriate what you're doing, and be proud of it, or pleased with it, or sorry on account of it, and so on. You must be completely identified with what you are doing. The distinction between subject and object must disappear. It usually disappears whilst in states of non-awareness, but here it must disappear whilst awareness is retained – but not that 'separate, self-conscious' awareness which is more like alienated awareness. You must be completely into what you're doing, completely aware of it, but not aware of it as something outside yourself. You're not standing apart from what you're doing and looking at it from the outside, but being aware of it in the very act of doing it, if you see what I mean? Otherwise, as he very rightly says, if there's this 'delusive ego' as he terms it, outside, appropriating what you're doing, then you're not truly into what you're doing. This is quite well put, and quite correct.

So in effect you remain your own refuge. You're not really Going for Refuge to the Buddha, Dharma, and Sangha. As Nyanaponika says, 'In a subtle way, the work, instead of the Triple Gem, becomes the refuge.' In other words, the work becomes an end in itself. But at the same time it's not really an end in itself. It's for you! It's not for the sake of attaining Enlightenment. But 'if identification of self and work is not complete' – i.e. if you are not completely identified with what you are doing in an aware way, so that there's no self-consciousness standing separately from that and evaluating it – then what happens is that 'the ego, as it were, hides in the work, and evades the call for full surrender to the true refuge. Progress beyond this step is possible only if the service of the guiding ideal is done in a highly detached way, without looking for any reward.' I don't think this quite follows. He seems to have at the back of his mind somewhere the *Bhagavad Gītā* teaching. He'd probably be horrified at the suggestion, but that's what it seems to me he has in mind: detachment from the fruits of one's work in the

*Bhagavad Gītā* sense. But really the remedy is to put oneself completely into what one is doing.

The general point is that it's very rarely that we are so much into something that we lose our self-consciousness. There's nearly always a bit of ourselves, what I'm calling self-consciousness in this slightly negative sense, which is not involved, standing apart, and even appropriating. This is connected with *vicikitsā*, doubt. There's a little bit of yourself standing apart from what you're doing, not participating. That is really what doubt is: a reservation. You might be doing the puja so beautifully, so well, and with such devotion, but at the same time there's a little bit of yourself that is not into it and which is standing and either just watching, or even being a bit sceptical or even ridiculing a little bit – and that means that *vicikitsā* is present. When that *vicikitsā* is there, then, in Nyanaponika's language, 'still there exists in the disciple's mind a difference between the noble objective and the person working for it'. It's very rarely that people are so into what they're doing – whether it's meditation, or study, or even communicating with others – that there's no self-consciousness, very rarely that they're entirely identified with what they're doing, and in a way lost in it, but without losing their awareness. In such cases there's only the self-consciousness that is lost, not consciousness itself. We do sometimes experience this complete losing of ourselves, but generally at the same time we lose our awareness, and that's the great difficulty. Either we're not into things, or we're into them but we lose our awareness. We're either self-conscious in the wrong sort of way, or we're not conscious at all.

Maybe a good example of being completely into what you're doing – to use that expression – and completely identified with it, with no self-consciousness, no standing apart from it and evaluating it, is the example of the expert musician. He's quite aware of what he's doing, he's quite aware of the music, and of himself playing, but they're all blended, they're all fused together. There's no part of himself uninvolved and standing apart, no part of himself simply evaluating or even observing and appropriating. This may sometimes happen, but not with the really good musician, when he's playing at his best. He's completely absorbed in the music, completely identified with it. It's the same with meditation, or puja, or human communication. Sometimes you can be into a particular situation to such a small extent that only part of you is engaged in what you're doing, and the greater part of you is just – well, in extreme cases – alienated.

GRAHAM: Does that draw energy away from situations?

SANGHARAKSHITA: Oh yes, of course it does. So you may begin to feel that situation very difficult.

KULARATNA: Sometimes it's quite difficult to find the balance, though, of not losing your awareness and at the same time maintaining the flow of energy. You have to hold a bit of yourself back because you know from experience that you're prone to lose your awareness.

SANGHARAKSHITA: In the course of retreats we can see people, or even the whole retreat, go from one extreme to the other. We used to see this in the very early days of the FWBO. When people came on retreats they used to arrive a bit alienated, and without much energy, but as the retreat progressed they would start feeling a bit more relaxed and happy. They would become much more lively and communicative, but then you'd see the unawareness creeping in. They'd start becoming silly and rushing around. On one retreat, I remember, two or three women were running up and down the corridor shrieking, which wasn't very mindful. So then we had to impose – and 'impose' is probably the word – silence. This would make everybody more mindful. They wouldn't go back to their previous state of stiffness or blockage but they would be a bit less lively than before. In this way we would try to achieve a balance. If the silence went on too long they'd get a bit blocked, and you had to allow them to relax a little, all the time trying to get them into a middle position in which they had their energy freely flowing, and were happy and spontaneous, but in which they were also mindful and aware. This balance was very difficult to achieve. Sometimes you didn't achieve it for more than half an hour at a time. People were always going either this way or that.

So depending on whether people are more blocked or more exuberant, the corrective treatment is to be applied. If you are leading a retreat and you find on arrival that nearly everyone is emotionally blocked, that they are finding it difficult to communicate, and that nobody is talking to anyone else, you'd be ill-advised to start the retreat with a day of silence. You would need to encourage people to talk to one another. You would need to have communication exercises. On the other hand, if on your arrival you find everybody talking excitedly, and even rushing around and shrieking, you will need to encourage more mindfulness. You might need to have a day of silence almost immediately, to calm them down, or contain them. Anyway, this is a little by the way.

One gets the general impression that Nyanaponika is in some ways very good in his approach. He really is trying to find out the meaning of the Threefold Refuge, but it's as though he is hampered by the Theravāda tradition, or what it has become, and hampered by his situation in Ceylon.

### Self-Surrender and Spiritual Community

> This detached attitude towards work will be one of the many fruits of complete self-surrender to the Triple Gem. This last and highest form of refuge taken by the worldling is without reservations. If true understanding has told us before that nothing can be gained in saṃsāra (which is the objective aspect of self), then, consequently, nothing can be lost by the surrender of self (which is the subjective aspect of saṃsāra). Though this surrender of self is only the surrender of a delusion, it is a very hard sacrifice as all of us know. But if ever we wish to be free of the bonds of saṃsāra, this self-surrender has to be done at one time or another, and therefore it may as well be done today as tomorrow.
>
> The highest prize is won only by the highest stake, by the sacrifice of that illusive self that has assumed so much power that it requires the highest effort to break it. In taking refuge by way of self-surrender the disciple, in his modest way, will follow the example of the Exalted One who, in his last great struggle before Enlightenment, addressed his inner opponent, personified as Māra, with the following words: 'It's Muñja grass I wear! Shame be on life! Fain in the battle I would die, than to live further as a vanquished one!'[274] The Muñja grass was the crest of those ancient Indian warriors who entered battle with the vow 'to do or to die'. It should be the symbol of the spiritual warrior too. If any reservations, regrets, or reluctances are retained there will be merely a half-hearted attempt, instead of a single-minded effort which alone can bring victory.

If the grave step of taking refuge by self-surrender has once been taken, a feeling of lightness, unconcernedness, and fearlessness will enter the heart of the disciple. A self that has been renounced cannot and need not have any fear for a life that has been surrendered and that is kept now only on trust for the definite purpose of being used for the highest realization. Therefore in the early days of the Dhamma, those of determined mind who entered the 'field of spiritual action' (*kammaṭṭhāna*), i.e. who took up a subject of meditation to be cultivated up to sainthood, they used to start their work by taking the vow of self-surrender, as advised in the following passage of the *Visuddhimagga*:

'Having approached his noble friend (i.e. the meditation master) the meditator should first surrender himself to the Buddha, the Exalted One, or to his teacher, and then, possessed of a strong desire and a high resolve, he should ask for the subject of meditation. His surrender of self to the Buddha should be as follows: 'This personal existence of mind, I offer to thee, O Exalted One!' (*Imāhaṃ Bhagavā attabhāvaṃ tumhākaṃ pariccajāmi*). Because one who, without such a surrender of self, lives in lonely places will be unable to stand firm against fearful objects that approach him. He might return to the village, and, associated with lay folk, might take up a search that is wrongful and come to distress. But to one who has surrendered his self, no fear arises even when approached by fearful objects. Only gladness will arise in him when he reflects: 'Hast thou not, O wise man, on that earlier day surrendered thyself to the Buddha?'[275] (pp. 23–5)

SANGHARAKSHITA: A quite interesting point arises here. As Nyanaponika has mentioned earlier, this passage in the *Visuddhimagga* became a bit like a sort of initiation. But on what occasion did this happen? What is the context?

KULANANDA: The context of meditation.

SANGHARAKSHITA: The context of meditation. And that suggests that meditation was not something that people normally did. It even suggests that meditation was not something that monks normally did, because the meditator here is the monk, is he not? The *Visuddhimagga*, as quoted by Nyanaponika, says, 'He might return to the village, and, associated with lay folk, might take up a search that is wrongful and come to distress.' It's as though in the days of Buddhaghosa the practice of meditation had died out to such an extent that taking it up was a very special thing, and became almost equivalent to taking Buddhism seriously, and truly Going for Refuge. Actually, one could say that that is true at the present time in, say, Ceylon. The serious Buddhist is the Buddhist who meditates. Most Buddhists, even most *bhikkhus*, do not meditate, ever. The sign of the serious Buddhist in the East is that he meditates – especially in the Theravādin countries. It is therefore quite significant, even appropriate, that when one takes up the practice of meditation there is an initiation ceremony of this kind, because you're beginning to take the Dharma seriously, beginning really to practise the Dharma.

The psychology of it is also very interesting. By tradition you go off and meditate in the forest, in lonely places. Living and meditating in such places you might experience fear, which would get in the way of your meditation. But on account of what are you feeling fear? On account of self. You are afraid for your life – afraid you may die, or be killed. So what is the best way of getting rid of that feeling of fear? By surrendering yourself. So before you go away to meditate in these lonely, possibly fearsome places, you take that particular form of Going for Refuge, you surrender yourself – because then there's nothing for you to worry about. After all, you've given up your self. Why worry?

Thus it is quite reasonable and logical that the would-be meditator should take refuge by way of self-surrender. It is almost as though, inasmuch as when you become a meditator you become a serious practising Buddhist, you get a sort of initiation in the form of this 'alternative' Going for Refuge. This is about the only trace of an actual practice – an individual Going for Refuge, or something of that sort – that Nyanaponika can find in the whole of the Pāli literature. It also suggests how exceptional the life of meditation had become. Then, as now, apparently, the serious Buddhist, the one who really went for Refuge, was the one who meditated. This is, in fact, what you find in Ceylon, Burma, and Thailand today. The serious Buddhist is the meditating Buddhist. If you find a Buddhist meditating it means he is really trying to practise Buddhism seriously. He has made an individual commitment to it, which the majority of 'born Buddhists' do not. And they don't meditate. It's as though meditation is the key, or the sign, that someone in the East is serious about Buddhism. You find this among the Indian Buddhist ex-Untouchables too. Not many of them meditate, but those who do are the ones who take the Going for Refuge seriously.

LOKAMITRA: I met none in India. I met one or two Sinhalese monks, out of quite a few, who meditated.

SANGHARAKSHITA: When Anagarika Dharmapala wanted to take up the practice of meditation he could not find a single *bhikkhu* in the whole of Ceylon to instruct him. In the end he had to learn from a lay Burmese Buddhist. What do you think of that? The nearest he got to meditation in Ceylon was when he discovered a manuscript about meditation in an old monastery and was told by the possessor that he had never practised it himself, but that his teacher had practised it and gone mad.[276] Whatever practice goes on there now has been introduced subsequently to that during this century, from Burma mainly.

A VOICE: Does the practice of meditation remain an unbroken tradition in Burma?

SANGHARAKSHITA: That's very doubtful. It depends on the form of meditation. A very popular form of practice is what is called '*vipassanā* meditation', which is not quite the classical *vipassanā* of the Buddhist tradition generally, but a method that was supposed to have been discovered by a *bhikkhu*, U Narada, living in Burma at the beginning of the twentieth century. But it seems that this method was his own discovery, or his own invention. It was not that he was continuing any existing tradition.

> 'And again, in surrendering himself to his teacher, he should say, "This personal existence of mine, reverend sir, I offer to thee!" Because, without such a surrender of self, he will be unruly, stubborn, unwilling to accept advice; he will go about at his own will without asking the teacher's leave. And the teacher will favour him neither with material nor with spiritual help and will not instruct him in difficult books.' (p. 25)

That's the worst thing of all. He 'will not instruct him in difficult books'! There is an ultimate sanction.

> 'Not receiving this twofold favour, he will become unvirtuous, or return to lay life.' (p. 25)

Again, clearly it is a monk who meditates. This surrendering himself to the teacher is almost a Tantric touch, isn't it? It's interesting that one finds this happening in Ceylon of all places.

> This way of taking refuge by self-surrender is, of course, still far from the complete abolishing of egotism and self-delusion, but it is a powerful means to that end. It may mark the transition from the worldly or mundane refuge to which it still belongs, to the supramundane refuge at which it aims. (p. 25)

On the whole I can't help agreeing with Nyanaponika as regards the importance of self-surrender as an aspect of Going for Refuge, or even as Going for Refuge itself. It seems to me that this corresponds to what I've called effective Going for Refuge. It is a total commitment, to the extent that that is possible on the mundane level, and therefore, as Nyanaponika says, 'It may mark the transition from the worldly or mundane refuge to which it still belongs, to the supramundane refuge at which it aims.' Ideally, at least, the *upāsaka* ordination, or Going for Refuge within the context of the Western Buddhist Order, means this sort of Going for Refuge. But there's some difference. Let's go on and see that.

> The formulae of self-surrender, as given in our commentarial text, differ even in their external form from the three lesser modes of refuge in so far as they lack that concluding 'call to witness' characteristic of the other modes. From that we may conclude that this gravest of all vows was to be taken in the secrecy of one's heart, as befits the sacredness of that resolve. Here the presence of a witness as a kind of moral support for keeping the vow should no more be required; such a requirement would only prove that it is premature to take this step. Any publicity to it would only detract from this supreme dignity of the vow, and would render its

> observance more difficult by making the disciple too self-conscious or even proud. Needless to say that a deliberate parading of the vow would defeat its very purpose by reinstating the self that was to be surrendered. (p. 25)

SANGHARAKSHITA: So what do you think of this? Do you agree with what he says here?

KULARATNA: There's no conception of spiritual community.

SANGHARAKSHITA: There's no conception of spiritual community. After all, he's got to find an explanation of why that calling to witness is not found in the case of this particular formula, which he regards as the highest of the four. 'From that we may conclude that this gravest of all vows was to be taken in the secrecy of one's heart, as it befits the sacredness of that resolve.' What do you think of that? Does secrecy befit sacredness?

LOKAMITRA: No, not at all.

SANGHARAKSHITA: Not necessarily, no. One might well ask why the *bhikkhu* ordination is a public event. There is no private monastic ordination at all, if you leave aside the *pabbajjā* or 'Going Forth' *sāmaṇera* or novice ordination – not as practised nowadays. It's entirely a public event. 'Here the presence of a witness as a kind of moral support for keeping the vow should no more be required.' Well, why not? He himself admits that the Going for Refuge by way of self-surrender is mundane. It's only the transcendental Going for Refuge which can stand on its own feet. Surely moral support is still needed – in fact more than moral support. Spiritual support is needed: hence the spiritual community.

KULANANDA: There would be no need for a vow if there was no need for support.

SANGHARAKSHITA: Exactly. So, 'Here the presence of a witness as a kind of moral support for keeping the vow should no more be required.' That's more than you can expect of a vow which is merely mundane, a Going for Refuge which is merely mundane. It requires all the support it can get, however sincere it may be, because it is liable to be broken at any time, if you're not careful. 'Such a requirement would only prove that it is premature to take this step.' That seems very strange indeed, because in that case it would always be premature to take a mundane Going for Refuge, because it could be broken. 'Any publicity to it would only detract from this supreme dignity of the vow, and would render its observance more difficult by making the disciple too self-conscious or even proud.' This seems very tendentious. Having a Going for Refuge in the presence of the spiritual community – can this really be described as publicity? This seems to be special pleading. Maybe he has in mind the way things are done in Ceylon and other Theravādin Buddhist countries. For instance, at a *bhikkhu* ordination, if some rich man becomes a *bhikkhu* for a week, there's tremendous publicity. 'Oh, look at Mr So-and-so! He's so rich and powerful, but he's becoming a *bhikkhu* for a whole week! He's giving up this enjoyment, and giving up that!' Perhaps he's got in mind something of that sort. That would surely detract from the dignity of any vow '... and would render its observance more difficult by making the disciple too self-conscious or even proud.' That's a criticism that would apply to the three lower ways of Going for Refuge even more strongly, because since they are 'lower' surely the person's Going for Refuge in those ways will be even more liable to self-consciousness or pride. So I'm afraid his arguments aren't very sound. 'Needless to say that a deliberate parading of the vow...' But is it necessarily a parading, that you go for Refuge in the presence of the spiritual community? When you become a *bhikkhu* are you parading the fact, just because all the other *bhikkhus* are assembled there? '...would defeat its very purpose by reinstating the self that was to be surrendered.' I'm afraid that self can reinstate self at any moment whatever you do. Even if you didn't parade it, and had no publicity, and did it all by yourself in the secrecy of your own heart, the self would reinstate itself there. 'Look at me,' it would say. 'So meek, so humble. No publicity. I'm surrendering myself all by myself, with only the Buddha knowing.' The self can reinstate itself so easily whenever one is engaged in any mundane activity. In other words, this is a typical piece of well-meant scholasticism. He's just trying to make sense of and give some explanation for the fact that there is no calling to witness in the case of this form of Going for Refuge. But I'm afraid that in trying to explain in that way he's committed many other mistakes.

> The longer formula of self-surrender, enlarging upon the short sentence in the *Visuddhimagga*, has been rendered here into a Western language for the first time; and also its Pāli original seems to have evoked little attention in our day. If we reproduce that formula here, we do it in the hope that it will be received with the reverence due to that precious document of ancient devotion, hallowed by the efforts and achievements of those who may have practised in accordance with it. We add the earnest request not to make use of it lightly for the purpose of ordinary devotion, and not to take the vow rashly on the spur of a moment's enthusiasm. This solemn pledge should be taken only after having tested one's strength and perseverance for a long time, by minor observances and renunciations. We should beware of making those highest things of the spirit cheap and common by approaching them in too facile a way; by talking too glibly about them, or by taking them into our hands, dropping them again when interest fades, or our feeble fingers get tired. Therefore, if we are not sure of our strength, we should not take upon us the severe demands of self-surrender, but take our refuge by way of those lesser modes. For these will likewise prove to be powerful helpers to high spiritual achievements. (p. 26)

What he says about 'the severe demands of self-surrender' are exactly what we say about the *upāsaka* ordination itself.

> In making an actual and intelligent use of that fourfold devotional Road of the Ancients, we shall preserve the most popular religious practice in the Buddhist world, the going for refuge, from becoming stale and ineffective. We shall be able to turn it into a strong, life-giving current of devotion that will carry us one day to the Isle of Final Peace, to Nibbāna, where the refugee and refuge are merged into one.

Clearly his whole objective in writing this pamphlet and drawing attention to this ancient commentarial passage is a very worthy one. He really does feel that the Going for Refuge has been devalued, and he would like to see it valued more in accordance with its true worth. But he is, as we've also seen, rather severely limited by the tradition to which he belongs and the cultural context in which he finds himself, that is to say, the cultural context in Ceylon. We'll probably be going into this a bit in the lecture this evening, but if we could say, for instance, that the Going for Refuge by way of self-surrender corresponds to Going for Refuge as we understand it in the Friends of the Western Buddhist Order, that is to say in terms of *upāsaka* ordination, could we draw any parallel with these other ways of Going for Refuge? Where do we put them, from our point of view?

LOKAMITRA: I was just thinking that they're not so much different levels but they all go to make up what Going for Refuge should really mean.

SANGHARAKSHITA: More like different aspects.

LOKAMITRA: Yes. Certainly there should be the homage, acceptance of the guiding ideal, and so on.

SAGARAMATI: Probably rather than each one being a different grade, there are different grades in each one.

SANGHARAKSHITA: Whereas if you grade them on his basis, that is to say, the emotional, the rational, and the volitional, you're assuming that reason is superior to emotion and volition superior to reason, which doesn't seem very sound psychology actually. After all, there is emotion and emotion, i.e. emotion is of varying degrees of positivity and refinement. Anyway, I have attempted a gradation in the tape-recorded lecture we shall be hearing this evening.[277]

What is the overall feeling you get from this subject of the Threefold Refuge and the author's treatment of it? It's certainly a very important subject, in a sense *the* most important subject.

LOKAMITRA: He's certainly trying to do something about, or comment on, something which he sees wrong in the Buddhist world, but he's too tied in by …

SANGHARAKSHITA: Too limited by that world itself to be able to do very much.

LOKAMITRA: His revolt is a bit too feeble.

KULARATNA: Not so much feeble but rather one man alone trying to do this thing.

SANGHARAKSHITA: Yes, indeed. This is, in a way, what is surprising – that there's an entire absence of any feeling of spiritual community, as though there's no awareness that it even exists, or that it's even a possibility. There's the odd reference to the order of monks and the lay devotees, but there's no sense at all of the spiritual community. That really is amazing in view of what the Buddha has said, in the Pāli canon itself, on this subject. Where is *kalyāṇa mitratā* or spiritual friendship, which the Buddha, according to the Pāli texts, declares as the whole of the holy life – not even half of it?[278]

It did occur to me a few minutes ago that it will be very interesting to see how the Friends of the Western Buddhist Order gets on among the Indian ex-Untouchables,[279] because that will be a sort of halfway house to the Buddhist countries themselves. The next step would be establishing FWBO centres in Ceylon, or Burma, or Thailand, or Japan.

LOKAMITRA: Certainly from our work in India it would appear that we'd become quite quickly known in these other countries, probably much more quickly than in England.

SANGHARAKSHITA: Oh yes. This is very definitely so.

SAGARAMATI: This emphasis on the understanding aspect, as when we talk of it as emerging from the group, sounds as though the first indication these people had of a sort of growth is that intellectual growth away from the group. It's almost still at that level. It's the first spark of individuality that's coming up.

SANGHARAKSHITA: It doesn't go all that far.

SAGARAMATI: Is there a relationship between the rational mind and self-consciousness? Because that's the spark …

SANGHARAKSHITA: I think I've talked about this on previous occasions.

In a way reason represents a degree of alienation, but the alienation seems to have been an inevitable stage, almost, in the development of the individual, provided it doesn't go beyond certain limits.

SAGARAMATI: So reason could almost be equated with the first spark of self-consciousness, which is bound to be slightly alienated.

SANGHARAKSHITA: Yes. You see this in the history of Greek religion and philosophy. As reason emerges and people start thinking for themselves, reason is rather 'brittle'. You can't help feeling it's rather adolescent, rather immature: even Socrates' reasoning. It's clearly not very much in touch, sometimes, with deeper emotional factors. In emancipating yourself from the group you have also got to tear yourself away from a lot that is positive in yourself, emotionally speaking, because your emotions are tied up with the group. To emancipate yourself from the group to some extent means to alienate yourself from your own emotions.

SAGARAMATI: So a faith-follower is somebody who would tend to take himself out of the group rather than his rational mind.

SANGHARAKSHITA: Possibly – or the faith-follower is one who takes his emotions with him out of the group, whereas the doctrine-follower is one who, for one reason or another, leaves his emotions behind him in the group, and they have to catch up gradually.

# NOTES AND REFERENCES

Notes appended with (S) are by Sangharakshita, those appended with (N) are by Nyanaponika, and those appended with (D) are by Dharmachari Dhivan.

DHAMMAPADA

1 See *The Eternal Legacy*, *Complete Works*, vol. 14, p. 52.
2 Ibid., p. 53.
3 Guhyaloka, or the 'secret realm', is a valley in the Sierra Aitana mountains of southern Spain, where four-month long – and some shorter – ordination retreats for men have been held annually since 1987. At the top of the valley is the retreat centre; a house for the resident community is at the bottom, while midway between the two is a bungalow where Sangharakshita stayed when he visited the valley.
4 In Buddhist mythology, Māra is the ruler of the realm of sense desire (*kāmaloka*) as Brahmā is the ruler of the realm of archetypal form (*rūpaloka*). He is the Evil One (*pāpimā*), representing as he does the forces that obstruct the attainment of Enlightenment. (S)
5 'Here' (*idha*) refers to this world and 'there' (*pecca*) to the next world. (S)
6 A. P. Buddhadatta Maha Thera (*Dhammapadaṃ*: *An Anthology of the Sayings of the Buddha*, Colombo, n.d., p. 6) comments:

This is the only place in the Pāli where this word [*sahitaṃ*] occurs to indicate 'literature'. It is doubtful whether this was used here to mean the same thing. Another possibility here is to take this as two words *sa* and *hitaṃ* instead of one. If we take it as two words we have to translate it as: 'Though much he speaks about beneficial things'. (S)

7 The Immortal or Deathless (*amata*) is a synonym for Nirvāṇa. (S)

8 Like Cupid, Māra is thought of as carrying a bow and arrows, and his arrows are 'flower-tipped', the flowers being the pleasures of sense. (S)

9 *Kusa*-grass was used in Vedic rituals, hence 'sacred'. (S)

10 The Factors of Enlightenment (*bodhi-aṅgas* or *bojjhaṅgas*) are mindfulness (*sati*), investigation of mental states (*dhamma-vicaya*), energy (*viriya*), rapture (*pīti*), tranquillity (*passaddhi*), concentration (*samādhi*), and equanimity (*upekkhā*). (S)

11 According to tradition, these two verses were spoken by the Buddha immediately after his attainment of Enlightenment. (S)

12 The 'path of the sun' (*ādiccapatha*) is the sky. (S)

13 The gods of Brilliant Light (*ābhassara-devas*) in Buddhist mythology are a class of gods occupying in the celestial hierarchy a place immediately above the various Brahmās. Their subjective or 'psychological' counterpart is the second *dhyāna* or 'absorption'. (S)

14 'One whose stream goes upward' (*uddhaṃsoto*) is one the current of whose being is directed towards Nirvāṇa. (S)

15 Atula was a layman who blamed various *bhikkhus* in the ways mentioned by the Buddha. (S)

16 'Jambunada gold' is gold from the river of that name. (S)

17 The 'mother' is craving (*taṇhā*); the 'father' self-conceit (*māna*); the 'two warrior kings' are the two wrong views of eternalism and annihilationism; the 'kingdom' comprises the twelve bases (*āyatanas*), i.e., the six sense organs, including the mind, and their respective objects; while the 'revenue collector' (*sānucara*) is the passionate delight that arises in dependence on the twelve bases. Here *brāhmaṇa* is synonymous with *arhant*. (S)

18 The 'two learned kings' are the two wrong views of eternalism and annihilationism; the tiger is doubt (*vicikicchā*), which also happens to be the fifth hindrance (*nīvaraṇa*). (S)

19 Here the Sangha is the Āryasaṅgha, consisting of those of the Buddha's disciples, past, present, and future, who are Stream Entrants, once-returners, non-returners, and *arhants*. To these the Mahāyāna would add the great bodhisattvas. (S)

20 Manu is the Primeval Progenitor of Vedic tradition, and a 'son of Manu' is therefore a human being (cf. the expression 'children of Adam'). (S)

21 A 'yellow-neck' (*kāsāvakaṇṭha*) is a wearer of the yellow robe of the almsman (*bhikkhu*). (S)

22 The 'thirty-six streams (of craving)' are the three kinds of craving (*taṇhā*) – for sense pleasures, for existence, and for non-existence – multiplied by the six internal plus the six external bases (*āyatanas*). (S)

23 These are the words with which, according to the *Ariyapariyesanā Sutta* (*Majjhima Nikāya* 26), the Buddha responded when asked by a naked ascetic, shortly after his Enlightenment, who was his teacher. (S)

24 The five that are to be 'cut away' are the fetters (*saṃyojanas*) of self-view, doubt, dependence on moral rules and religious observances, lust, and ill will. These five bind one to the realm of sense-desire. The five that are to be 'abandoned' are the fetters of desire for existence in the realm of archetypal form, desire for existence in the formless realm, conceit, restlessness, and ignorance. These bind one to the realm of archetypal form and the realm of formlessness. The five that are to be 'cultivated' are the five spiritual faculties (*indriyas*) of faith, wisdom, concentration, energy, and mindfulness. (S)

25 The 'stream' (*sota*) is the process of repeated birth, death, and rebirth. (S)

26 In this verse there is a play upon words which I have tried to reproduce. (S)

27 Human bonds (*mānusaka-yogas*) are the desire for continued existence, or rebirth, in the human realm; 'celestial bonds' (*dibba-yogas*) are the desire for rebirth in the realm of the gods. (S)

28 In Buddhist mythology 'celestial musicians' (*gandharvas*) are a class of gods inhabiting the realm of the Four Great Kings. They are so called because they live on scent (*gandha*). (S)

### AUSPICIOUS SIGNS (*MAṄGALA SUTTA*)

29 The *Mahāmaṅgala Sutta* is the fifth *sutta* of the *Khuddaka-pāṭha*, a collection of nine short passages which seems to have been put together as a sort of primer for novice monks and nuns; its verses are still widely known and chanted in the Buddhist world today. The *Khuddaka-pāṭha* is the first collection to appear in the *Khuddaka Nikāya* of the Pāli canon. The text also appears as the fourth *sutta* of the 'Minor Chapter', the second chapter of the *Sutta-Nipāta*.

### JEWELS (*RATANA SUTTA*)

30 The *Ratana Sutta* is the sixth *sutta* of the *Khuddaka-pāṭha*, and also appears as the first *sutta* of the 'Minor Chapter',

the second chapter of the *Sutta-Nipāta*.

OUTSIDE THE WALLS (*TIROKUḌḌA SUTTA*)

31 The *Tirokuḍḍa Sutta* is the seventh *sutta* of the *Khuddaka-pāṭha*.

THE BURIED TREASURE (*NIDHIKAṆḌA SUTTA*)

32 The *Nidhikaṇḍha Sutta* is the eighth *sutta* of the *Khuddaka-pāṭha*.

LOVING KINDNESS (*KARAṆĪYA METTĀ SUTTA*)

33 The *Karaṇīya Mettā Sutta* is the ninth *sutta* of the *Khuddaka-pāṭha*, and also appears as the eighth *sutta* of the 'Chapter of the Snake', the first chapter of the *Sutta-Nipāta*.

LIVING WITH AWARENESS

34 *Satipaṭṭhāna* is actually *sati* + *upaṭṭhāna*, where *upaṭṭhāna* means 'establishing' or 'making present'. See for example Bhikkhu Anālayo, *Satipaṭṭhāna*, Windhorse Publications, Cambridge 2003, p. 29. (D)

35 *Sampajañña* is not 'usually translated as mindfulness of purpose'; it means 'clear comprehension' or 'clear knowing', and the idea of 'mindfulness of purpose' comes from the commentary's gloss on *sampajañña* which includes the idea of directing clear knowing to one's purpose. See Bhikkhu Anālayo, *Satipaṭṭhāna*, Windhorse Publications, Cambridge 2003 p. 143. (D)

36 This is a phrase from Robert Burns' poem 'To a Louse'.

37 Vinaya Piṭaka ii.193 (*Cullavagga* 7.3); see I. B. Horner (trans.), *The Book of the Discipline*, part 5, Pali Text Society, London 1975, p. 271.

38 For the ordeals Milarepa had to undergo, see Lobsang P. Lhalungpa (trans.), *The Life of Milarepa*, Book Faith India, Kathmandu 1997, pp. 47–70.

39 *Aṅgulimāla Sutta* (*Majjhima Nikāya* 86); see Bhikkhu Ñāṇamoli and Bhikkhu Bodhi (trans.), *The Middle Length Discourses of the Buddha*, Wisdom Publications, Boston 1995, pp. 710–17; or I. B. Horner (trans.), *The Collection of the Middle Length Sayings*, vol. ii, Pali Text Society, Oxford 1994, pp. 284–92.

40 *Larger Sukhāvatīvyūha Sūtra*, chapter 8, in, for example, E. B. Cowell et al. (eds.), *Buddhist Mahāyāna Texts*, Dover Publications, New York 1969, part 2, p. 28.

41 Bhikkhu Bodhi, *The Connected Discourses of the Buddha*, Wisdom Publications, Boston 2000, p. 1516. See also *Saṃyutta Nikāya* v.316–9 (54.8) (ibid. pp. 1770–3). At *Visuddhimagga* 269, Buddhaghosa says that the

mindfulness of breathing is 'foremost among the various meditation subjects of all Buddhas'. See Bhikkhu Ñāṇamoli (trans.), *The Path of Purification*, Buddhist Publication Society, Kandy 1991, p. 263; or Pe Maung Tin (trans.), *The Path of Purity*, Pali Text Society, London 1975, pp. 308–9.

42 *Satipaṭṭhāna Sutta*, *Majjhima Nikāya* 10 (i.57). See Bhikkhu Ñāṇamoli and Bhikkhu Bodhi (trans.), *The Middle Length Discourses of the Buddha*, Wisdom Publications, Boston 1995, pp. 145–6; or I. B. Horner (trans.), *The Collection of the Middle Length Sayings*, vol. i, Pali Text Society, London 1976, pp. 71–2.

43 For the story of Ajātasattu's visit to see the Buddha, see the *Sāmaññaphala Sutta*, *Dīgha Nikāya* 2 (i.47–86); M. Walshe (trans.), *The Long Discourses of the Buddha*, Wisdom Publications, Boston 1995, pp. 91–109; or T. W. Rhys Davids (trans.), *Dialogues of the Buddha*, part 1, Pali Text Society, London 1973, pp. 65–94.

44 Buddhaghosa, *Visuddhimagga* 268–9. See Bhikkhu Ñāṇamoli, *The Path of Purification*, Buddhist Publication Society, Kandy 1991, p. 262; or Pe Maung Tin (trans.), *The Path of Purity*, Pali Text Society, London 1975, p. 308. See also Buddhaghosa's commentary on the *Satipaṭṭhāna Sutta*, published as Bhikkhu Soma (trans.), *The Way of Mindfulness*, Vajirārāma, Colombo 1949, pp. 43–4.

45 The phrase *sabbakāya* means 'the whole body', and the idea that it means 'the whole body of breath' is the commentarial interpretation. See Bhikkhu Anālayo, *Mindfulness of Breathing*, Windhorse Publications, Cambridge 2019, pp. 37–40, 182. (D)

46 Buddhaghosa, *Visuddhimagga* 281–2; see Bhikkhu Ñāṇamoli, *The Path of Purification*, Buddhist Publication Society, Kandy 1991, p. 274; or Pe Maung Tin (trans.), *The Path of Purity*, Pali Text Society, London 1975, p. 323.

47 What Sangharakshita calls *samāpatti* here are actually *nimitta*. (See Nyanatiloka, *Dictionary of Buddhism*, Buddhist Publication Society, Kandy 1980, p. 126.) *Samāpatti* is a word meaning 'attainment' in relation to meditation. (D)

48 For weighty karma, see the *Abhidhammattha Saṅgaha*, published as Narada Maha Thera (trans.), *A Manual of Abhidhamma*, Buddhist Missionary Society, Kuala Lumpur 1987, pp. 294–5. See also *Who is the Buddha?*, *Complete Works*, vol. 3, p. 107.

49 The three 'marks of conditioned existence' (*lakṣaṇas*, Pāli *lakkhaṇas*) are enumerated and discussed in many places

in the Pāli canon, for example, *Saṃyutta Nikāya* 22 (iii.20–4). See Bhikkhu Bodhi (trans.), *The Connected Discourses of the Buddha*, Wisdom Publications, Boston 2000, pp. 867–71; or F. L. Woodward (trans.), *Book of the Kindred Sayings*, part 3, Pali Text Society, London 1975, pp. 19–23. See also *Udāna* 3.10. The *locus classicus* is *Dhammapada* 277–9. Sangharakshita discusses the *lakṣaṇas* in *The Three Jewels*, *Complete Works*, vol. 2, pp. 80ff.

50 W. B. Yeats, 'The Witch', from his 1916 collection *Responsibilities and Other Poems*.

51 This is a phrase from T. S. Eliot's poem 'Whispers of Immortality', first published in 1918.

52 This was 'Subhā of Jīvaka's Mango-grove', *Therīgāthā*, canto 14; see C. A. F. Rhys Davids (trans.), *Poems of the Early Buddhist Nuns*, Pali Text Society, London 1997, pp. 126–33. Subhā's sight was restored to her in the end.

53 The four *viparyāsas* (Pāli *vipallāsa*), the 'mental perversities' or 'topsy-turvy views', are listed in the *Vipallāsa Sutta*, *Aṅguttara Nikāya* ii.52. See Bhikkhu Bodhi (trans.), *The Numerical Discourses of the Buddha*, Wisdom Publications, Boston 2012, pp. 437–8; or F. L. Woodward (trans.), *The Book of the Gradual Sayings*, vol. ii, Pali Text Society, Oxford 1995, pp. 60–1. See also *The Three Jewels*, *Complete Works*, vol. 2, chapter 11, pp. 80ff.

54 *Udāna* 3.2. See, for example, J. D. Ireland (trans.), *The Udāna and the Itivuttaka*, Buddhist Publication Society, Kandy 1997, pp. 35–9.

55 See Buddhaghosa, *Visuddhimagga* 258–9 and 345–7 in Bhikkhu Ñāṇamoli (trans.), *The Path of Purification*, Buddhist Publication Society, Kandy 1991, p. 252 and pp. 340–3; or Pe Maung Tin (trans.), *The Path of Purity*, Pali Text Society, London 1975, pp. 295–7 and pp. 400–1.

56 Lama Anagarika Govinda, 'Look Deeper!', *Stepping-Stones*, vol. 1, no. 4, October 1950, pp. 78–9.

57 See *Visuddhimagga* 347ff. Bhikkhu Ñāṇamoli (trans.), *The Path of Purification*, Buddhist Publication Society, Kandy 1991, pp. 343ff; or Pe Maung Tin (trans.), *The Path of Purity*, Pali Text Society, London 1975, pp. 402ff.

58 See, for example, Nyanatiloka Mahathera, *Guide Through the Abhidhamma-Piṭaka*, Associated Newspapers of Ceylon, Colombo 1938, pp. 13–14, where *rūpa* is translated 'corporeality'.

59 H. V. Guenther, *Philosophy and Psychology in the Abhidhamma*, Shambhala, Berkeley and London 1976, p. 146.

60 *Visuddhimagga* 366 states that the four great elements are like the great creatures of a magician who 'turns water that is not crystal into crystal, and turns a clod that is not gold into gold....' Bhikkhu Ñāṇamoli (trans.), *The Path of Purification*, Buddhist Publication Society, Kandy 1991, p. 361; or Pe Maung Tin (trans.), *The Path of Purity*, Pali Text Society, London 1975, p. 423.

61 The most famous Perfection of Wisdom verse expressive of the ephemeral nature of things is found in section 32 of the *Diamond Sūtra*, here translated by Edward Conze:

> As stars, a fault of vision, as a lamp,
> A mock show, dew drops, or a bubble,
> A dream, a lightning flash, or cloud,
> So should one view what is conditioned.

62 *King Lear*, Act v, Scene iii.

63
> Now I a fourfold vision see
> And a fourfold vision is given to me
> Tis fourfold in my supreme delight
> And threefold in soft Beulahs night
> And twofold Always. May God us keep
> From Single vision & Newtons sleep.

William Blake, letter to Thomas Butt, 22 November 1802, quoted in Geoffrey Keynes (ed.), *The Letters of William Blake* (1956). In Blake's thinking 'Single vision & Newton's sleep' equates to a kind of single-minded materialism, whereas the 'fourfold vision' combines reason and imagination, sense and emotion.

64 *Paradise Lost*, book 6, lines 509–20.

65 See *Visuddhimagga* 178–196. Bhikkhu Ñāṇamoli (trans.), *The Path of Purification*, Buddhist Publication Society, Kandy 1991, pp. 173–90; or Pe Maung Tin (trans.), *The Path of Purity*, Pali Text Society, London 1975, pp. 205–25.

66 *Hamlet*, Act v, Scene i.

67 See *In the Sign of the Golden Wheel*, *Complete Works*, vol. 22, p. 82.

68 *Dhammadāyāda Sutta*, *Majjhima Nikāya* i.12; see Bhikkhu Ñāṇamoli and Bhikkhu Bodhi (trans.), *The Middle Length Discourses of the Buddha*, Wisdom Publications, Boston 1995, p. 97; or I. B. Horner (trans.), *The Collection of the Middle Length Sayings*, vol. i, Pali Text Society, London 1976, pp. 16–17.

69 See T. W. Rhys Davids and W. Stede, *Pāli–English Dictionary*, Pali Text Society, Oxford 1992, p. 370.

70 This simile is found in various places including the *Mahā-assapura Sutta*, *Majjhima Nikāya* 39 (i.276–7); see

Bhikkhu Ñāṇamoli and Bhikkhu Bodhi (trans.), *The Middle Length Discourses of the Buddha*, Wisdom Publications, Boston 1995, pp. 368; or I. B. Horner (trans.), *The Collection of the Middle Length Sayings*, vol. i, Pali Text Society, London 1976, p. 331. See also the *Mahāsakuludāyi Sutta*, *Majjhima Nikāya* 77 (ii.15–16), Bhikkhu Ñāṇamoli and Bhikkhu Bodhi, as above, p. 641; or I. B. Horner (trans.), *The Collection of the Middle Length Sayings*, vol. ii, Pali Text Society, Oxford 1994, pp. 216.

71 *Mahāparinibbāna Sutta*, *Dīgha Nikāya* 16 (ii.99). See M. Walshe (trans.), *The Long Discourses of the Buddha*, Wisdom Publications, Boston 1995, p. 244; or T. W. Rhys Davids (trans.), *Dialogues of the Buddha*, part 2, Pali Text Society, London 1971, p. 106.

72 This is a reference to Charles Baudelaire's prose poem 'The Eyes of the Poor' ('Les Yeux des Pauvres'), published posthumously in 1869 in the collection *Le Spleen de Paris*.

73 Buddhaghosa's commentary on the *Satipaṭṭhāna Sutta* has been published in English as Soma Thera (trans.), *The Way of Mindfulness: The Satipaṭṭhāna Sutta and Its Commentary*, Vajirārāma, Colombo 1949. Sangharakshita's comment doesn't seem to refer to a specific passage in Buddhaghosa's commentary, but the commentary includes a section on energy (pp. 141–3) and discussion of *ātāpī*, or ardent: 'Ardour is a name for energy' (p. 34), and the whole text gives an impression of the effort required, describing the Kuru people as 'earnest in the application of the Arousing of Mindfulness to their daily life' (p. 19) and the *bhikkhu* as 'a person who earnestly endeavours to accomplish the practice of the teaching' (p. 31), and even commends a monk who sustains his mindfulness while being eaten by a tiger from the feet upwards' (p. 24).

74 The methods of overcoming the hindrances, including 'cultivating the opposite', are described at *Visuddhimagga* 5; see Bhikkhu Ñāṇamoli (trans.), *The Path of Purification*, Buddhist Publication Society, Kandy 1991, p. 9; or Pe Maung Tin (trans.), *The Path of Purity*, Pali Text Society, London 1975, pp. 6–7. See also the *Vitakkasaṇṭhāna Sutta*, *Majjhima Nikāya* 20 (i.119–22); I. B. Horner (trans.), *The Collection of the Middle Length Sayings*, vol. i, Pali Text Society, London 1976, pp. 152–6; or Bhikkhu Ñāṇamoli and Bhikkhu Bodhi (trans.), *The Middle Length Discourses of the Buddha*, Wisdom Publications, Boston 1995, pp. 211–14.

75 The Duc de Sully, who represented the French king at the court of James I,

wrote 'The English take their pleasures sadly, after the manner of their country' in his memoirs of 1638.

76 Henry David Thoreau, *Walden* (first published in 1854), chapter 2, section 19.

77 For example, this is the last line of all the stories of Māra's encounters with *bhikkhunīs* in the *Bhikkhunisaṃyutta* of the *Saṃyutta Nikāya*. See Bhikkhu Bodhi (trans.), *The Connected Discourses of the Buddha*, Wisdom Publications, Boston 2000, pp. 221–30; or C. A. F. Rhys Davids (trans.), *The Book of the Kindred Sayings*, part 1, Pali Text Society, London 1979, pp. 160–70.

78 Samuel Butler, *Hudibras*, canto 3, lines 547–8. Butler was a Royalist and an Anglican, and wrote *Hudibras*, a long satirical poem, between 1660 and 1680, to poke fun at those on the opposing side: the Cromwellians and the Presbyterian Church, who had ruled Britain after the Civil War but were vanquished with the restoration of the monarchy in 1660.

79 This is the last line of D. H. Lawrence's poem 'Thought', which begins 'Thought, I love thought.'

80 *Udāna* 1.10, in F. Woodward (trans.), *Verses of Uplift*, Pali Text Society, London 1935, p. 10.

81 The Abhidhamma's list of ten fetters appears in a text called the *Dhammasaṅgaṇī* (1113–4). They are: (1) sensual lust (Pali *kāma-rāga*), (2) anger (*paṭigha*), (3) conceit (*māna*), (4) views (*diṭṭhi*), (5) doubt (*vicikicchā*), (6) attachment to rites and rituals as ends in themselves (*sīlabbata-parāmāsa*), (7) lust for existence (*bhava-rāga*), (8) jealousy (*issā*), (9) greed (*macchariya*), and (10) ignorance (*avijjā*). See, for example, C. A. F. Rhys Davids (trans.), *A Buddhist Manual of Psychological Ethics*, Pali Text Society, London 1974, p. 274.

82 See, for example, *Saṃyutta Nikāya* v.61 (45.179); Bhikkhu Bodhi, *The Connected Discourses of the Buddha*, Wisdom Publications 2000, p. 1565.

83 T. S. Eliot, 'Burnt Norton', part 1, in *Four Quartets*.

84 *Mahāparinibbāna Sutta*, *Dīgha Nikāya* 16 (ii.156). See M. Walshe (trans.), *The Long Discourses of the Buddha*, Wisdom Publications, Boston 1995, p. 270; or T. W. Rhys Davids (trans.), *Dialogues of the Buddha*, part 2, Pali Text Society, London 1971, p. 173.

85 See *Visuddhimagga* 143. Bhikkhu Ñāṇamoli (trans.), *The Path of Purification*, Buddhist Publication Society, Kandy 1991, p. 141; or Pe Maung Tin (trans.), *The Path of Purity*, Pali Text Society, London 1975, p. 166.

86 See, for example, *Vatthūpama Sutta*, *Majjhima Nikāya* 7 (i.37): Bhikkhu Ñāṇamoli and

Bhikkhu Bodhi (trans.), *The Middle Length Discourses of the Buddha*, Wisdom Publications, Boston 1995, p. 119; or I. B. Horner (trans.), *The Collection of the Middle Length Sayings*, vol. i, Pali Text Society, London 1976, p. 47.

87 The Buddha is represented as telling a simple account of his realization under the rose-apple tree in the *Mahāsaccaka Sutta*, *Majjhima Nikāya* 36 (i.246). See Bhikkhu Ñāṇamoli and Bhikkhu Bodhi (trans.), ibid., p. 340; or I. B. Horner (trans.), ibid., p. 301.

88 The *Mahāsatipaṭṭhāna Sutta* (*Dīgha Nikāya* 22) is substantially the same as the *Satipaṭṭhāna Sutta* which has been the subject of our study, but it has one important difference: it goes into the four noble truths in great detail. In the printed text six pages are dedicated to them, whereas the *Satipaṭṭhāna Sutta* covers them in one paragraph.

89

> I should dispel the suffering of others because it is suffering like my own suffering. I should help others too because of their nature as beings, which is like my own being.

*Bodhicaryāvatāra* 8.94 in Kate Crosby and Andrew Skilton (trans.), *The Bodhicaryāvatāra*, Windhorse Publications, Birmingham 2002, p. 128.

90 D. T. Suzuki, *Studies in the Laṅkāvatāra Sūtra*, Routledge and Kegan Paul, London 1930, p. 324.

LIVING WITH KINDNESS

91 P. B. Shelley (1792–1822), from his essay 'A Defence of Poetry' written in 1821 and first published in *Essays, Letters from Abroad, Translations and Fragments*, in 1840.

92 For more on the distinction between feeling and emotion see, for example, *Know Your Mind*, in *Complete Works*, vol. 17, pp. 503–4.

93

> How sharper than a
> serpent's tooth it is
> To have a thankless child!

*King Lear*, Act I. Scene iv.

94 *Itivuttaka* 1.3.7 in F. L. Woodward (trans.), *The Minor Anthologies of the Pali Canon*, part 2, Pali Text Society, London 1987, p. 130.

95 John Macmurray, *Reason and Emotion*, Faber and Faber, London 1947, p. 19.

96 Ibid., chapter 2.

97 See, for example, C. A. F. Rhys Davids, *Buddhism: A Study of the Buddhist Norm*, Williams & Norgate, London n.d.

98 See note 79, above.

99

> Energy is the only life and is from the Body and Reason is the bound or outward circumference of Energy.

William Blake, *The Marriage of Heaven and Hell, plate 4.*

100 The seminar participants were using Saddhatissa's

translation of the (*Karaṇīya*) *Mettā Sutta* as published in the *Buddhist Quarterly*, the journal of the British Mahabodhi Society, in the 1950s. The wording was slightly different from that in his translation of the complete *Sutta-Nipāta* published by Curzon Press, London, in 1985. The seminar participants also had available to them the translation by Robert Chalmers, which is occasionally referred to below.

101 Saddhatissa translates this word as 'welfare' in the 1985 edition.

102 For more on Dr Dinshaw Mehta, his life and friendship with Sangharakshita, especially during the 1950s, see 'The Monk and the Prophet' in *Complete Works*, vol. 21, pp. 599–619.

103 This is perhaps a kind of paraphrase of *Saṃyutta Nikāya* ii.25 (12.20), which describes the causal relationships of the twelve *nidānas*, stating:

> Whether, brethren, there be an arising of Tathāgatas, or whether there be no such arising, in each this nature of things just stands, this causal orderliness, this relatedness of this to that.

C. A. F. Rhys Davids (trans.), *The Book of the Kindred Sayings*, part 2, Pali Text Society, Oxford 1997, p. 21. Also Bhikkhu Bodhi (trans.), *Connected Discourses of the Buddha*, Wisdom Publications, Boston 2000, pp. 550–1.

104 Vinaya Piṭaka i.23 (*Mahāvagga* 1.14). See I. B. Horner (trans.), *The Book of the Discipline*, part 4, Pali Text Society, Oxford 1996, pp. 31–2.

105 The distinction between the path of regular steps and the path of irregular steps is a very ancient one. It goes back to sixth-century China, to the great Chinese teacher Zhiyi, who was the virtual founder of one of the greatest of all Buddhist schools, the Tiantai school. For an explanation, see Sangharakshita, 'The Path of Regular Steps and the Path of Irregular Steps', in *The Taste of Freedom*, Windhorse Publications, Birmingham 1997, p. 28 (*Complete Works*, vol. 11).

106 This was the teaching given to Bāhiya at *Udāna* 1.10. For Sangharakshita's commentary, see *Complete Works*, vol. 10, pp. 458–65.

107 The *mettā bhāvanā* is described by Buddhaghosa at *Visuddhimagga* 295–7; see Pe Maung Tin trans.), *The Path of Purity*, Pali Text Society, London 1975; or Bhikkhu Ñāṇamoli (trans.), *The Path of Purification*, Buddhist Publication Society, Kandy 1991, pp. 288–99, especially sections 11–12 on p. 290.

108 Spinoza, *Ethics III*, Proposition 30 (note).

109 This is maxim 99 in *Réflexions ou Maximes Morales*, published in 1665 by the French moralist Duc François de la Rochefoucauld.

110 *Bodhicaryāvatāra* 6.24 in Śāntideva, *The Bodhicaryāvatāra*, Kate Crosby and Andrew Skilton (trans.), Windhorse Publications, Birmingham 2002, p. 70.

111 *Measure for Measure*, Act II, Scene ii.

112 See *Visuddhimagga* 307. Bhikkhu Ñāṇamoli (trans.), *The Path of Purification*, Buddhist Publication Society, Kandy 1991, pp. 299–300; or Pe Maung Tin (trans.), *The Path of Purity*, Pali Text Society, London 1975, p. 353.

LIVING BEAUTIFULLY

113 For an account of what Sangharakshita means by the love mode and the power mode, see *The Ten Pillars of Buddhism, Complete Works*, vol. 2, pp. 361–3.

114 We have been unable to trace this. It could perhaps be an interpretation of a passage in the *Aṅguttara Nikāya* which lists four kinds of people: those who gain Nibbāna with effort in this life, those who gain Nibbāna without effort in this life, those who gain Nibbāna with effort upon death, and those who gain Nibbāna without effort upon death. See *Aṅguttara Nikāya* ii.155; Bhikkhu Bodhi (trans.), *The Numerical Discourses of the Buddha*, Wisdom Publications, Boston 2012, pp. 533–5; or F. L. Woodward (trans.), *The Book of the Gradual Sayings*, vol. ii, Pali Text Society, Oxford 1995, pp. 160–2.

115 *Dhammapada* 200 in Max Müller's translation (*Sacred Books of the East*, vol. 10: *The Dhammapada and Sutta Nipāta*, Clarendon Press, Oxford 1881).

116 *Udumbarika-Sīhanāda Sutta*, *Dīgha Nikāya* 25 (iii.55); see M. Walshe (trans.), *The Long Discourses of the Buddha*, Wisdom Publications, Boston 1995, p. 393; or T. W. and C. A. F. Rhys Davids (trans.), *Dialogues of the Buddha*, part 3, Pali Text Society, London 1971, p. 50.

117 'Epitaph for a Man Falling from a Horse', by William Camden (1551–1623). The saying may have become well known through Samuel Johnson. See J. Boswell, *The Life of Samuel Johnson* LLD, John Sharpe, London 1830, p. 543.

118 In February 1983 UK unemployment stood at a record high of 3,224,715.

119 See note 71 above.

120 *Tālapuṭa Sutta*, *Saṃyutta Nikāya* iv.306–8. See F. L. Woodward (trans.), *The Book of the Kindred Sayings*, part 4, Pali Text Society,

London 1980, pp. 214–16; or Bhikkhu Bodhi (trans.), *The Connected Discourses of the Buddha*, Wisdom Publications, Boston 2000, pp. 1333–4.

121 *Aṅguttara Nikāya* i.261, in Bhikkhu Bodhi (trans.), *The Numerical Discourses of the Buddha*, Wisdom Publications, Boston 2012, p. 342; or F. L. Woodward (trans.), *The Book of the Gradual Sayings*, vol. i, Pali Text Society, Oxford 2000, p. 239. Bhikkhu Bodhi's translation is: 'To laugh excessively, showing one's teeth, is childishness.'

122 Oscar Wilde's *The Picture of Dorian Gray* was first published in 1890.

123 This is the late fifteenth-century English morality play, *Everyman* (more correctly, *The Summoning of Everyman*). Sangharakshita read the play in his teens, and saw Leslie French's ballet *Everyman* based on the morality play, which premiered in London in 1943. 'So deeply was I impressed that when I tried to write an appreciation of *Everyman* I found my feelings too strong for expression.' *The Rainbow Road from Tooting Broadway to Kalimpong*, *Complete Works*, vol. 20, p. 86.

AUSPICIOUS SIGNS (*MAṄGALA SUTTA*)

124 E. M. Hare, *Woven Cadences of Early Buddhists*, Oxford University Press, London (reprinted) 1947. p. 40.

125 F. W. Woodward, *Some Sayings of the Buddha*, Oxford University Press, London 1973, p. 39.

126 See, for example, the *Sigālaka Sutta*, (also known as the *Sigālovāda Sutta*), in which the Buddha comes across a young man called Sigālaka standing in the river worshipping the six directions and explains that true worship of the six directions consists of carrying out one's duties in regard to six kinds of relationship. See *Dīgha Nikāya* 31 (iii.180–93); M. Walshe (trans.), *The Long Discourses of the Buddha*, Wisdom Publications, Boston 1995, pp. 461–9; or T. W. and C. A. F. Rhys Davids (trans.), *Dialogues of the Buddha*, part 3, Pali Text Society, London 1971, pp. 173–84.

127 The quotations are from E. M. Hare (trans), *Mahāmaṅgala Sutta, Sutta-Nipāta* 2.4, in *Woven Cadences of Early Buddhists*, Geoffrey Cumberledge, London 1945.

128 Trevor Ling, *The Buddha*, Temple Smith, London 1973, chapter 3, 'The Physical, Economic and Social Environment', pp. 37–49.

129 The story of the conversion of Anāthapiṇḍika and his donation of the Jetavana or Jeta Grove in Sāvatthī is told at Vinaya Piṭaka ii.154–9 (*Cullavagga* 6.4). See I. B.

Horner (trans.), *The Book of the Discipline*, part 5, Pali Text Society, London 1975, pp. 216–23.

130 The story of Visākhā's purchase of the East Park for the Buddha's use is told in the *Dhammapada Commentary* (*Dhammapada Aṭṭhakathā* i.413). See E. W. Burlingame (trans.), *Buddhist Legends, Translated from the Original Pali Text of the Dhammapada Commentary*, part 1, Pali Text Society, London 1969, pp. 79–80.

131 'The Buddha's Daily Habits', from the *Sumaṅgala-Vilāsinī*, Buddhaghosa's commentary on the *Dīgha Nikāya*, quoted in Henry Clarke Warren, *Buddhism in Translation*, Cambridge, Mass. 1906, pp. 91–5.

132 Her name was Rose Samdup. See *Facing Mount Kanchenjunga*, *Complete Works*, vol. 21, p. 241.

133 *Dhammapada*, chapter 5. See pp. 15–17 above.

134 This expression, which refers to 'blocked energy', was very much in vogue in the FWBO at the time this seminar was given. The release of blocked energies can be achieved particularly through meditation; see various references in *Complete Works*, vol. 5.

135 Sukhavati, meaning 'full of bliss', was the name given to the community at the London Buddhist Centre, which was constructed from a derelict fire station over the preceding three years. It was a huge, red-brick Victorian civic building and in it a team of men lived and meditated together, worked on the renovation, studied Dharma, and practised puja. To begin with, there was neither heating nor electricity and the work demanded great energy and commitment. The construction project provided valuable experience in building and fundraising for those involved, as well as in 'team-based right livelihood' and community living. The success of Sukhavati was in a way only half the story, as it quickly became a single-sex project limited to men. It would take the creation of Taraloka Retreat Centre five years later to provide a similarly pivotal situation for the women's wing of the Triratna Buddhist Community. For more on Sukhavati, see Vajragupta, *The Triratna Story*, Windhorse Publications, Cambridge 2010, chapter 2. Sangharakshita lived in a flat attached to Sukhavati from 1979 to 1985.

136 For example, the Sevenfold Puja used within the Triratna Buddhist Community is based on verses from Śāntideva's *Bodhicaryāvatāra*, chapters 2 and 3, evidence of the seventh-century Indian Buddhist master's deep devotion, while the ninth chapter of the same work expresses a deeply

philosophical understanding of the Perfection of Wisdom.

137 John St John's *Travels in Inner Space: One Man's Exploration of Encounter Groups, Meditation, and Altered States of Consciousness* was published by Littlehampton Book Services in 1977.

138 F. W. Woodward, *Some Sayings of the Buddha*, Oxford University Press, London 1973, p. 39.

139 The quotation from Samuel Taylor Coleridge (from his *Table-Talk*, 15 May 1833) begins:

> 'There is now no reverence for any thing; and the reason is, that men possess conceptions only, and all their knowledge is conceptual only.' For Sangharakshita's talk, see *Complete Works*, vol. 11.

140 Pundarika was the original Triratna Buddhist centre in North London, founded in 1972.

141 Padmasambhava was the historical-mythical bringer of Buddhism to Tibet, and his life story, *The Life and Liberation of Padmasambhava*, describes his meditations in the cremation grounds, and in 'The Cremation Ground and the Celestial Maidens' (chapter 5 of *Creative Symbols of Tantric Buddhism*, *Complete Works*, vol. 13, pp. 231–2), Sangharakshita describes how the cremation ground symbolizes the 'crucial situation', the situation which confronts you with your fears and challenges you to overcome them.

142 The sequence of twelve positive *nidānas* or links, also sometimes called the spiral path, begins when in dependence upon unsatisfactoriness (*duḥkha*) arises not craving (*tṛṣṇā*) but faith (*śraddhā*). A detailed description of this process is to be found in (for example) chapter 7, 'The Spiral Path', in Sangharakshita, *What is the Dharma?* (*Complete Works*, vol. 3, pp. 258ff). The speaker is here referring to the fact that the first seven *nidānas* are 'mundane' in the sense that one can fall back from them. The aim is to reach the 'point of no return', which comes with the transition from the seventh to the eighth *nidāna*.

143 This is a reference to the spiral path, the sequence of progressive stages by which one may escape the wheel of life and make spiritual progress. At a certain point on the spiral comes the 'point of no return' – the point at which your spiritual momentum will carry you irrevocably towards Enlightenment. Lokamitra here is referring to the stages of the spiral path that come before that point of no return. See chapters 6 and 7, 'The Gravitational Pull and the Point of No Return' and 'The

Spiral Path', ibid., pp. 250–3 and pp. 258–79.

144 The 'gravitational pull' is a term often used by Sangharakshita to refer to the 'pull of the conditioned' – the way we tend to stay within or get drawn back into the orbit of conditioned existence until such time as spiritual momentum allows us to escape that gravitational field and instead move towards the Unconditioned. For more about this, see chapter 6, ibid., pp. 241–57).

145 *Sāmaññaphala Sutta*, *Dīgha Nikāya* 2 (i.51). See T. W. Rhys Davids (trans.) *Dialogues of the Buddha*, part 1, Pali Text Society, London 1973, p. 65; also M. Walshe (trans.), *The Long Discourses of the Buddha*, Wisdom Publications, Boston 1995, p. 93.

146 *FWBO Newsletter* no. 35, Summer 1977, pp. 6–10.

147 W. Somerset Maugham, *A Writer's Notebook*, Heinemann, London 1949, p. 22.

148 Muhammad Ali (1942–2016), 'The Greatest', was an American heavyweight boxer, and one of the most famous sportsmen of the twentieth century.

149 *Dhammapada* 62.

150 *Complete Works*, vol. 1, pp. 538–51.

151 The Yogācāra tradition lists eleven positive (*kuśala*) mental events. For the list and a commentary on it, see chapter 7, 'The Creative Mind at Work', in *Know Your Mind*, *Complete Works*, vol. 17, pp. 549–90.

152 See, for example, *Sukhamāla Sutta*, *Aṅguttara Nikāya* i.146, in Bhikkhu Bodhi (trans.), *The Numerical Discourses of the Buddha*, Wisdom Publications, Boston 2012, p. 241; or F. L. Woodward (trans.), *The Book of the Gradual Sayings*, vol. i, Pali Text Society, Oxford 2000, p. 129.

153 *Measure for Measure*, Act II, Scene ii.

154 See *Sukhamāla Sutta*, *Aṅguttara Nikāya* i.146, in Bhikkhu Bodhi (trans.), *The Numerical Discourses of the Buddha*, Wisdom Publications, Boston 2012, pp. 240–1; or F. L. Woodward (trans.), *The Book of the Gradual Sayings*, vol. i, Pali Text Society, Oxford 2000, p. 128.

155 'The worst sin towards our fellow creatures is not to hate them, but to be indifferent to them: that's the essence of inhumanity.' From Act II, Scene ii, of George Bernard Shaw's 1897 play *The Devil's Disciple*.

156 This is a paraphrase of D. H. Lawrence's statement in his essay 'Education of the People' in *Reflections on the Death of a Porcupine and other essays*, Cambridge University Press, Cambridge 1988, p. 140.

157 This was placed in the December 1975 issue of

*Shabda*, the Order newsletter. The whole seminar is available on www.freebuddhistaudio.com. Here is an excerpt from the relevant section:

> When I was at Hampstead in my very early days in England, people would say: 'Let's have an informal discussion, let's do it informally', as if to say that that was somehow better or at least they were more comfortable with that. If you sat up on chairs or maybe round a table with your notebook in front of you they didn't like that, but if you were all sprawled all over the place, someone with his legs up on the mantelpiece and so on, that was fine, that was informal. There was a sort of underlying assumption that when people are formal they are not being themselves, and when they are being informal in a very studious and calculated way they are being more themselves.

158 H. T. Francis and R. A. Neil (trans.), *The Jātaka*, vol. iii, Pali Text Society, London 1973, no. 313, *Khantivādi-Jātaka*, pp. 26–9.

159 Śāntideva, *Bodhicaryāvatāra* 6.43.

160 The saying is from *Proverbs* 15: 1.

161 Sangharakshita describes witnessing this during his stay at Ramana Maharshi's ashram in *The Rainbow Road from Tooting Broadway to Kalimpong*, *Complete Works*, vol. 20, pp. 342–3.

162 See *Precious Teachers*, *Complete Works*, vol. 22, p. 402.

163 Sangharakshita learned these communication exercises in the early sixties from Muriel Payne, an English educationalist working in India who had found that teachers, generally speaking, taught very badly, and came to the conclusion that this was because they were not able to communicate, either with their pupils or with one another. She therefore devised a series of communication exercises. Sangharakshita gathered a couple of dozen friends and arranged for Miss Payne to conduct a series of workshops, at which she taught these exercises, which Sangharakshita was convinced brought one to a level of communication way beyond that which normally exists between people. 'During those exercises I experienced communication as I had never done before, especially when I did the exercises with her.' Each person says, turn by turn, a banal phrase such as, 'Do birds fly?' In Sangharakshita's experience,

> Through a verbal exchange that does not have any objective meaning you experience the other person

as though there is, one might almost say, a merging of your two beings – it is very like that experience of the angels merging that Raphael describes in *Paradise Lost*.

(Condensed from a conversation with Mahamati and Subhuti in 2009.) Some years later, when leading FWBO retreats, Sangharakshita introduced these exercises and they proved very successful.

164 *Fantasia of the Unconscious* was published in 1922. See particularly chapter 8, 'Education and sex in man, woman and child'.

165 See 'Education of the People' in D. H. Lawrence, *Reflections on the Death of a Porcupine and other essays*, Cambridge University Press, Cambridge 1988, pp. 123–6.

166 The American actress Shirley Temple (1928–2014) began her film career at the age of 3, and her curly hair and precocious talent were much admired, hence the imitation Sangharakshita remembers. (He was a contemporary of hers.) She retired from acting at the age of 22, and in later life became a diplomat, becoming America's ambassador to Czechoslovakia.

167 Shwe Zan Aung and C. A. F. Rhys Davids (trans.), *Points of Controversy*, Pali Text Society, London 1915.

168 Subhūti is the Buddha's interlocutor in this Perfection of Wisdom text; see Edward Conze (trans.), *The Perfection of Wisdom in Eight Thousand Lines and its Verse Summary*, Four Seasons Foundation, San Francisco 1995.

169 See note 4 above.

SALUTATION TO THE THREE JEWELS (*TIRATANA VANDANĀ*)

170 The text of the *Tiratana Vandanā* is found in several places in the Pāli canon, notably in the *Mahāparinibbāna Sutta*, *Dīgha Nikāya* 16 (ii.93–4). This translation is by Sangharakshita.

171 Vinaya Piṭaka i.20–1 (*Mahāvagga* 1.11). See I. B. Horner (trans.), *The Book of the Discipline*, part 4, Pali Text Society, Oxford 1996, p. 28.

172 See note 142.

173 The reference here is to an exposition by the nun Dhammadinnā in the *Cūḷavedalla Sutta*, *Majjhima Nikāya* 44 (i.304); see Bhikkhu Ñāṇamoli and Bhikkhu Bodhi (trans.), *The Middle Length Discourses of the Buddha*, Wisdom Publications, Boston 1995, p. 402; or I. B. Horner (trans.), *The Collection of the Middle Length Sayings*, vol. i, Pali Text Society, London 1976, p. 367. Sangharakshita explains his interpretation

of the passage in *Who is the Buddha?*; see *Complete Works*, vol. 3, p. 68.

174 This may be 'The Buddha and the Bodhisattva: Eternity and Time', the last lecture in the Bodhisattva Ideal series: 'The Buddha represents the goal, and the goal is attained out of time' (*Complete Works*, vol. 4, p. 201) – although that suggests that Enlightenment takes place in an entirely different, timeless dimension, not simply 'spread out over a period of several weeks'.

175 The Buddha's vision of humanity as a bed of lotuses is described at *Saṃyutta Nikāya* i.138; see Bhikkhu Bodhi (trans.), *The Connected Discourses of the Buddha*, Wisdom Publications, Boston 2000, p. 233; or C. A. F. Rhys Davids (trans.), *The Book of the Kindred Sayings*, part 1, Pali Text Society, London 1979, p. 174; also Vinaya Piṭaka i.6; see I. B. Horner (trans.), *The Book of the Discipline*, part 4, Pali Text Society, Oxford 1996, p. 9.

176 In Pāli *vandana* means 'verse', and *vandanā* is the plural (as in *Tiratana Vandanā*), but for the convenience of readers unfamiliar with Pāli and Sanskrit the editors have indicated most plurals by appending the customary -s suffix.

177 A blind man with a stick is the usual symbolic depiction of ignorance (*avidyā*), which is the first link in the chain of twelve *nidānas* depicted around the edge of the Tibetan wheel of life.

178 This seminar studied the Mahāyāna text called the *Ratnaguṇa-saṃcayagāthā* or 'Verses on the Accumulation of Precious Qualities', and the seminar transcript appeared in edited form as *Wisdom Beyond Words*; for the passage on *vidyā* see *Complete Works*, vol. 14, pp. 516–24.

179 There is a lot to be said about the *pratyekabuddha*, or 'solitary Buddha'. A very good account is to be found in Reginald Ray, *Buddhist Saints in India*, Oxford University Press, Oxford and New York 1994, chapter 7.

180 Team-based right livelihood was further developed in the years following this seminar, notably a gift business which began life as a market stall in 1980 and developed its own chain of shops, Windhorse: Evolution. It raised a lot of money for Triratna projects and hundreds of people worked in its teams. It closed in 2015. Other right livelihood businesses have come and gone over the years, and there are several in operation at the time of writing (2022), though none on the scale of Windhorse: Evolution.

181 Sangharakshita seems to have changed his view about mixed communities. In a seminar in

January 1980 on chapter 13 of *The Jewel Ornament of Liberation* (p.194), he said:

> It seems quite difficult to set up mixed communities, because over the last few years I have even encouraged people to do this.... In fact I thought in the past that there should be, just so that the whole spectrum was complete, so that people could see that there were all these possibilities for different sorts of people. And I still believe that there should be the whole range of communities, from the strict single-sex community that does not allow members of the other sex even on the premises, right round to the family-cum-mixed-cum-school type community, with children. I think eventually we need to have the whole spectrum, so that people who come into the Friends can say, well, where do I fit? Where would I best like to go? Which would be best for me?

182 Padmaloka Retreat Centre, a former farm in the village of Surlingham, Norfolk, was purchased in 1976 to serve as a men's retreat centre. Sangharakshita lived there for some years.

183 Kularatna, Lokamitra, and Padmavajra went to Poona (now Pune), India, to support Buddhist activities in August 1978; for Lokamitra's account of their work there, see *Complete Works*, vol. 10, pp. xl–xli.

184 The reference is to Aldous Huxley's dystopian novel *Brave New World*, which was published in 1932.

185 The Axial Age, a term coined by the German philosopher Karl Jaspers (1883–1969), refers to the period (around 800–200 BCE) during which a number of significant figures emerged: Confucius and Laozi, the Buddha, Zarathustra, Greek poets and philosophers, and Old Testament prophets. Sangharakshita's talk appears in edited form in *What is the Sangha?*, *Complete Works*, vol. 3, pp. 424–8.

186 Herodotus (c.484–c.425 BCE) was a Greek writer who was called 'The Father of History'. His *Histories* were an enquiry into the origin of the Greco-Persian Wars. Herodotus was a great traveller, and his wanderings covered a large part of the Persian Empire: he went to Egypt, and he also visited Libya, Syria, and Babylonia. He journeyed up the Hellespont (now Dardanelles) to Byzantium, went to Thrace and Macedonia, and travelled northward to beyond the Danube and to Scythia eastward along the northern shores of the Black Sea.

187 In 1928 the American poet T. S. Eliot (1888–1965) announced that he had

'adopted the position' of an Anglo-Catholic (Anglo-Catholicism being a movement within the Church of England). The English writer G. K. Chesterton (1874–1936) became a Roman Catholic in 1922, and four years later, in an essay called 'Why I am a Catholic', wrote:

> The difficulty of explaining 'why I am a Catholic' is that there are ten thousand reasons all amounting to one reason: that Catholicism is true.

Hilaire Belloc (1870–1953), also an English writer, in fact grew up in a Catholic family, but moved away from Catholicism as a young man, returning to it after a spiritual experience which he described in his book *The Path to Rome*.

188 The Divine Light Mission (DLM) was founded in India in the 1930s. In 1966, following the death of its founder, the 8-year-old Prem Rawat was accepted as the movement's teacher. While still very young he travelled to America, and the DLM was established in many Western countries in the 1970s and attracted a large following. Its ashrams were closed down in 1983, and the organization's name was changed to Elan Vital, Prem Rawat seeking to shake off the Indian characteristics of the movement and make it more universal. Further name changes followed, and the movement still exists in some countries. Ananda Marga was founded in India in 1955. Its goal is 'self-realization and the welfare of all', and its practices include yoga, meditation, and vegetarianism.

189 In June 1973, the Divine Light Mission organized a 'Festival of Love' at Alexandra Palace in London, which drew thousands of people.

190 *Dhammapada* 80 and 145.

191 Van Hanh Buddhist University was founded in 1964 in what was then Saigon (now Ho Chi Minh City); Thich Nhat Hanh was one of the founders. After the fall of Saigon, many of the university staff were persecuted. Today (2022) a Zen temple stands in what was once part of the university campus and is the base for the Buddhist Research Institute of Vietnam.

192 Henrik Ibsen (1828–1906) was a Norwegian playwright whose realist drama explores the moral and psychological dilemmas of his time. *Brand* is a tragedy in verse written in 1855. At that time, after having been a theatre director for some years, Ibsen had left his wife and gone into self-imposed exile from Norway; *Brand*, which was his first successful play, is about an extremely uncompromising pastor.

193 *Dhammapada* 5.

194 The distinction [between the path of regular steps and the path of irregular steps] is a very ancient one. It goes back to sixth-century China, to the great Chinese teacher Zhiyi, who was the virtual founder of one of the greatest of all Buddhist schools, the Tiantai school.

Sangharakshita, 'The Path of Regular Steps and the Path of Irregular Steps', in *The Taste of Freedom*, Windhorse Publications, Birmingham 1997, p. 28 (*Complete Works*, vol. 11).

195 *Kalyāṇa mitra* means 'spiritual friend'. As an of expression of one's commitment to practising Buddhism in the context of the Triratna Buddhist Community (the FWBO as it used to be), one can become a 'Mitra', a friend. What this entailed has changed over time, and at the time of writing (2022) it involves making three declarations: (1) I consider myself to be a Buddhist; (2) I am trying to practise the five ethical precepts; and (3) the Triratna Buddhist Community is the context in which I want to deepen my practice. In the early days of the FWBO, in order to formally become a Mitra one had to ask two Order members to become one's *kalyāṇa mitras*, to offer friendship and support on one's spiritual path, and this is what is being referred to here. This condition changed, but the practice of two Order members making a commitment to spiritual friendship with a third person (usually a Mitra but sometimes an Order member) continues, and is marked by a simple ceremony.

196 *Tao Te Ching*, chapter 53.

197 Sarum House (later named Aryatara) was the first FWBO residential community, in Purley, south London. Nagabodhi is an Order member. The St Michaels Road project involved the development of various right livelihood businesses and what became the Croydon Buddhist Centre.

198 This was the lecture called 'The Axial Age and the Emergence of the New Man'. It appears in edited form in *What is the Sangha?*; see *Complete Works*, vol. 3, p. 471. The quotation from the French theatre director Antonin Artaud (1896–1948) begins:

> I hate and renounce as a coward every being who consents to having been created and does not wish to have recreated himself.

199 W. B. Yeats, 'An Acre of Grass', 1936.

200 Sangharakshita's six-month stay at the guest cottage of Prince K. M. Latthakin or 'Burma Raja' as he was known, is recounted in *Facing*

*Mount Kanchenjunga*, chapter 7, *Complete Works*, vol. 21, pp. 117–36.

201 *A Survey of Buddhism*, *Complete Works*, vol. 1, pp. 177–8.

202 Sic; this was changed to 'sensual desire' with the ninth edition of *A Survey of Buddhism*.

203 The *nidāna* chain is a way of explaining the process of life, death, and rebirth, its twelve links of conditioned co-production representing the application of the general Buddhist principle of conditionality to the process of rebirth. See, for example, 'Conditioned Co-production and the Twelve Links', in Sangharakshita, *A Survey of Buddhism*, *Complete Works*, vol. 1, pp. 105–113, or 'Entering the Stream' in *The Meaning of Conversion in Buddhism*, *Complete Works*, vol. 2, p. 255.

204 This is reference to two *sādhanas* or visualization practices: Mañjughoṣa, the bodhisattva of wisdom and Mahākaruṇika, a form of Avalokiteśvara, the bodhisattva of compassion.

205

> Let us transport ourselves to a very lonely region of boundless horizons, under a perfectly cloudless sky, trees and plants in the perfectly motionless air, no animals, no human beings, no moving masses of water, the profoundest silence. Such surroundings are, as it were, a summons to seriousness, to contemplation, with complete emancipation from all willing and its cravings; but it is just this that gives to such a scene of mere solitude and profound peace a touch of the sublime. For, since it affords no objects, either favourable or unfavourable, to the will that is always in need of strife and attainment, there is left only the state of pure contemplation, and whoever is incapable of this is abandoned with shameful ignominy to the emptiness of unoccupied will, to the torture and misery of boredom. To this extent it affords us a measure of our own intellectual worth, and for this generally the degree of our ability to endure solitude, or our love of it, is a good criterion. The surroundings just described, therefore, give us an instance of the sublime in a low degree, for in them with the state of pure knowing in its peace and all-sufficiency there is mingled, as a contrast, a recollection of the dependence and wretchedness of the will in need of constant activity. This is the species of the sublime for which the sight

of the boundless prairies of the interior of North America is renowned.

Arthur Schopenhauer, *The World as Will and Representation*, vol. 1, trans. E. F. J. Payne, Dover Publishing, New York 1958, pp. 203–4.

206 The guardians or philosopher kings of the ideal state of Plato's *Republic* are the only people who can claim actual knowledge. Big Brother is the omnipresent authority figure of George Orwell's dystopian novel *1984*.

THE THREEFOLD REFUGE

207 The seminar on the Sevenfold Puja (which also took place in 1978) appears in edited form in *Ritual and Devotion in Buddhism* (*Complete Works*, vol. 11), providing most of the material for chapters 5 and 6–12, as well as some of the material for chapters 3 and 4. The seminar on 'Milarepa and the Novices' appears in edited form as 'The Song of a Yogi's Joy', in *Complete Works*, vol. 18, pp. 39–54.

208 Page numbers refer to Nyanaponika Thera, *The Threefold Refuge*, Wheel Publication no. 76, Buddhist Publication Society, Kandy 1965. However, the quotations are taken from the 2006 online edition at accesstoinsight.org.

209 See, for example, *Dhammapada* 276 and the *Gaṇakamoggallāna Sutta*, *Majjhima Nikāya* 107 (iii.6). See Bhikkhu Ñāṇamoli and Bhikkhu Bodhi (trans.), *The Middle Length Discourses of the Buddha*, Wisdom Publications, Boston 1995, p. 878; or I. B. Horner (trans.), *The Collection of the Middle Length Sayings*, vol. iii, Pali Text Society, Oxford 1993, p. 56.

210 The *dhammānusārin* (doctrine-follower) and the *saddhānusārin* (faith-follower) are two of the group of seven *ariya-puggalas* (noble disciples) enumerated in the Pāli canon. See, for example, the *Cūḷagopālaka Sutta*:

> Just as that tender calf just born, being urged on by its mother's lowing, also breasted the stream of the Ganges and got safely across to the further shore, so too, those bhikkhus who are Dharma-followers and faith-followers – by breasting Māra's stream they too will get safely to the further shore.

*Majjhima Nikāya* 34 (i.226) in Bhikkhu Ñāṇamoli and Bhikkhu Bodhi (trans.), *The Middle Length Discourses of the Buddha*, Wisdom Publications, Boston 1995, p. 321; see also I. B. Horner (trans.), *The Collection of the Middle Length Sayings*, vol. i, Pali Text Society, London 1976, p. 279. Sangharakshita introduces the two terms at the beginning of his talk 'A Vision of Human Existence', published in *Buddhism for Today and Tomorrow*, Windhorse Publications, Birmingham 1996, pp. 24–5 (*Complete Works*, vol. 11).

211 For example, see the *Ariyapariyesanā Sutta*, *Majjhima Nikāya* 26 (i.171): Bhikkhu Ñāṇamoli and Bhikkhu Bodhi (trans.), ibid., pp. 263–4; or I. B. Horner (trans.), ibid., pp. 214–5. This text says that the first person to meet the Buddha after his Enlightenment was an ascetic called Upaka. Upaka was very impressed by the Buddha's appearance – he had just gained Enlightenment, and his face was bright and shining – so he asked, 'Are you an Enlightened One?' The Buddha replied, firmly and emphatically, that he was. Unfortunately, Upaka was unable to believe him. He just shook his head sceptically and remarked, 'May it be so, friend,' and went on his way.

212 See the *Śūraṅgama Sūtra* in Dwight Goddard, *A Buddhist Bible*, Beacon Press, Boston 1966, p. 112.

213 See *The Essence of Zen*, *Complete Works*, vol. 13, pp. 344–7.

214 *Kālāma Sutta*, *Aṅguttara Nikāya* i.190 (3.65). We have not identified this translation, but for other translations, see Bhikkhu Bodhi (trans.), *The Numerical Discourses of the Buddha*, Wisdom Publications, Boston 2012, pp. 281; or F. L. Woodward (trans.), *The Book of the Gradual Sayings*, vol. i, Pali Text Society, Oxford 2000, pp. 172–4.

215 *The Three Jewels*, *Complete Works*, vol. 2, pp. 141–5.

216 *A Survey of Buddhism*, *Complete Works*, vol. 1, pp. 120ff.

217 *Dhammapada* 197–200.

218 The Buddha's vision of humanity as a bed of lotuses is described at *Saṃyutta Nikāya* i.138; see Bhikkhu Bodhi (trans.), *The Connected Discourses of the Buddha*, Wisdom Publications, Boston 2000, p. 233; or C. A. F. Rhys Davids (trans.), *The Book of the Kindred Sayings*, part 1, Pali Text Society, London 1979, p. 174; also Vinaya Piṭaka i.6; see I. B. Horner (trans.), *The Book of the Discipline*, part 4, Pali Text Society, Oxford 1996, p. 9.

219 *Dhammapada* 25.

220 *The Sūtra of Huineng* (*Platform Sūtra*), chapter 6; see, for example, *The Diamond Sūtra and the Sūtra of Hui-neng*, trans. A. F. Price and Wong Mou-lam, Shambhala Publications, Boston 1990, p. 104.

221 *Ariyapariyesanā Sutta*, *Majjhima Nikāya* 26 (i.171). We have not identified this translation, but for other translations see Bhikkhu Ñāṇamoli and Bhikkhu Bodhi

(trans.), *The Middle Length Discourses of the Buddha*, Wisdom Publications, Boston 1995, p. 264; or I. B. Horner (trans.), *The Collection of the Middle Length Sayings*, vol. i, Pali Text Society, London 1976, p. 215.

222 The relevant passage of the transcript of the seminar on the *Sūtra of Huineng* (given in 1974 and available at www.freebuddhistaudio.com) is:

> Some … Mahāyāna *sūtras* also have the same sort of language, or what seems to be the same sort of language, if you don't look into it carefully, as when Huineng says 'Mind is Buddha', which is practically saying you are Buddha and it's something to be uncovered and realized, rather than something to be achieved and created. It seems to me … that to speak in terms of achieving and realizing and creating and bringing into existence, as in fact the historical Buddha did, so far as we know from the Pāli texts, is much closer to our actual experience. We therefore credit it as much more true, and it seems to cut through a lot of misunderstanding and misrepresentation to put things in this way. Otherwise, if you go around telling people that they are Buddha, they don't take that to mean in their ultimate metaphysical depths, but that they themselves, just as they are, with their ordinary selves and ego, are Buddha. You are just attaching a very beautiful label to their ego rather than enabling them to transcend their ego and realize it's illusory.

223 *Mahāparinibbāna Sutta*, *Dīgha Nikāya* 16 (ii.100). See M. Walshe (trans.), *The Long Discourses of the Buddha*, Wisdom Publications, Boston 1995, pp. 245; or T. W. and C. A. F. Rhys Davids (trans.), *Dialogues of the Buddha*, part 2, Pali Text Society, London 1971, p. 108.

224 See Gampopa, *The Jewel Ornament of Liberation*, trans. Herbert V. Guenther, Shambhala Publications, London 1986, p. 33.

225 *Vīmaṃsaka Sutta*, *Majjhima Nikāya* 47 (i.320). See Bhikkhu Ñāṇamoli and Bhikkhu Bodhi (trans.), *The Middle Length Discourses of the Buddha*, Wisdom Publications, Boston 1995, p. 417; or I. B. Horner (trans.), *Middle Length Sayings*, vol. i, Pali Text Society, London 1976, p. 382.

226 See, for example, the *Brahmāyu Sutta*, *Majjhima Nikāya* 91 (ii.145); Bhikkhu Ñāṇamoli and Bhikkhu Bodhi (trans.), ibid., p. 754; or I. B. Horner (trans.), ibid., pp. 330–1.

227 See *Ānāpānasaṃyutta*, *Saṃyutta Nikāya* v.320–2; Bhikkhu Bodhi (trans.), *Connected Discourses of the Buddha*, Wisdom Publications, Boston 2000, pp. 1773–4; or F. L. Woodward (trans.), *The Book of the Kindred Sayings*, part 5, Pali Text Society, London 1979, pp. 283–5.

228 In the passage under discussion Nyanaponika is perhaps concerned not to make the historicity of the Buddha seem as important for Buddhism as that of Christ is for Christianity. Nonetheless, what one goes for Refuge to is not some purely abstract notion of Buddhahood but the living ideal of Enlightenment as actually realized in human life. (S)

229 *Saṃyutta Nikāya* (iii.124) tells the story of Vakkali, after whose death the Buddha, seeing a swirl of black smoke in the distance, says this is Māra looking for Vakkali's consciousness, but he won't find it, because Vakkali has attained nibbāna. See Bhikkhu Bodhi (trans.), *The Connected Discourses of the Buddha*, Wisdom Publications, Boston 2000, p. 941; or F. L. Woodward (trans.), *The Book of the Kindred Sayings*, part 3, Pali Text Society, London 1975, p. 106.

230 *Majjhima Nikāya* iii.72. See Bhikkhu Ñāṇamoli and Bhikkhu Bodhi (trans.), *The Middle Length Discourses of the Buddha*, Wisdom Publications, Boston 2001, pp. 934–5; also I. B. Horner (trans.), *The Collection of the Middle Length Sayings*, vol. iii, Pali Text Society, Oxford 1993, pp. 114–5.

231 In the *Mahāvacchagotta Sutta* the Buddha attests that among his disciples were many *bhikkhus* and *bhikkhunīs*, men and women who had gone forth and attained arhantship, as well as lay disciples, both men and women, who were well advanced on the path to Enlightenment, though not fully Enlightened. See *Majjhima Nikāya* 73 (i.490); Bhikkhu Ñāṇamoli and Bhikkhu Bodhi (trans.), *The Middle Length Discourses of the Buddha*, Wisdom Publications, Boston 1995, p. 596; or I. B. Horner (trans.), *The Collection of the Middle Length Sayings*, vol. i, Pali Text Society, London 1976, p. 168.

232 Acala, the 'Immovable', is a wrathful deity or *dharmapāla* of the Vajrayāna tradition, and the dark-blue Buddha Akṣobhya, the 'Imperturbable', of the eastern quarter of the mandala of the five Buddhas.

233 *The Light of Asia: The Great Renunciation*, based on the *Lalitavistara Sūtra* and first published in London in 1879, was written by Sir Edwin Arnold (1832–1904), an English poet and journalist.

234 Do you want to walk along? Or walk ahead? Or walk by yourself? One must know what one wants and that one wants. Fourth question of conscience.

This is the 41st maxim of the 'Maxims and Missiles' which begin Friedrich Nietzsche's 1888 work *The Twilight of the Gods*.

235 Here it is, of course, at best what I have elsewhere called the 'effective' Going for Refuge that is meant. The 'real' Going for Refuge cannot be deflected or destroyed. (S)

236 There is no such thing as the will. What we think of as the will is simply our idea of ourselves as performing an action. To say that we *will* to do something is meaningless. We do it – or do not do it. The will is a myth.

This aphorism first appeared in *Sayings, Poems, Reflections* in 1976, then in *Peace is a Fire* in 1979. See *Complete Works*, vol. 26, p. 16.

237 *A Survey of Buddhism*, *Complete Works*, vol. 1, p. 347.

238 The claim is that when Sayyiduna 'Amr bin al-'As conquered Alexandria a Christian theologian called John Philoponus showed him the library so Sayyiduna 'Amr wrote to Sayyiduna 'Umar regarding it. It is alleged that the Caliph wrote back saying: 'If those books are in agreement with the Koran, we have no need of them; and if these are opposed to the Koran, destroy them.' So 'Amr allegedly distributed the books among Alexandria's baths for burning: something that took over six months due to the sheer volume of books.

239 Sangharakshita may be misremembering here. According to Sangharakshita in a seminar on Nagārjuna's *Ratnāvalī* (Precious Garland), p. 34, it was John Middleton Murry who wrote something like this about Cardinal Newman. In *Know Your Mind* Sangharakshita says, 'It has been said of Cardinal Newman, for example, that he *believed* in God but he didn't trust him.' See both *Living Wisely*, p. 336 and *Know Your Mind*, p. 552 (*Complete Works*, vol. 17).

240 For example, in the *Devadūta Sutta*, *Majjhima Nikāya* 130, the sufferings of hell are described in appalling detail, and the *sūtras* of the Mahāyāna tradition describe the sufferings of beings in the eight hot hells and the eight cold hells.

241 The Albigenses or Cathars were a heretical Christian sect who flourished in southern France during the twelfth and thirteenth centuries. Their beliefs showed the influence of Eastern doctrines including that of rebirth. Their practices,

which included vegetarianism and celibacy, aimed to sever all ties with the material world of the body, which they regarded as impure. They aimed instead to direct the soul towards a non-material state of purity and bliss in the Holy Spirit. The Catholic establishment, by this time long entrenched in the wealth and power attendant upon its temporal authority, acted swiftly and violently in what became known as the Albigensian Crusade. These measures led directly to the 'Holy Inquisition', whose shadow would extend across Catholic Europe in three subsequent centuries of religious persecution. For Sangharakshita's review of a book on the subject, Arthur Guirdham's *The Great Heresy*, see *Alternative Traditions*, in *Complete Works*, vol. 8, pp. 420–5.

242 This was Manuel II Palaeologus (1350–1425).

243 Buddhaghosa refers to the desire for liberation at *Visuddhimagga* 651; see Bhikkhu Ñāṇamoli (trans.), *The Path of Purification*, Buddhist Publication Society, Kandy 1991, p. 674; or Pe Maung Tin (trans.), *The Path of Purity*, Pali Text Society, London 1975, pp. 795–6.

244 *Kasibhāradvāja Sutta*, *Sutta-Nipāta* 1.4, verse 2.

245 Edward Conze (trans.), *The Perfection of Wisdom in Eight Thousand Lines and Its Verse Summary* (*Aṣṭasāhasrikā Prajñāpāramitā*), Four Seasons Foundation, San Francisco 1973, p. 206.

246 That is, rebirth as animal, a ghost, a titan, or a being in hell.

247 This is perhaps a conflation of two quotations from Matthew Arnold (the nineteenth-century writer): 'The Eternal not ourselves, that makes for righteousness' (*God and the Bible*, Smith, London 1906, pp. 6–7) and 'the stream of tendency by which all things fulfil the law of their being' (*Literature and Dogma*, Macmillan, New York 1908, p. 37).

248 Aśvaghoṣa (attrib.), *The Awakening of Faith*, trans. Yoshito S. Hakeda, Columbia University Press, New York 1967, pp. 56ff.

249 It isn't clear what article is being referred to here.

250 This is 'Philosophy and Religion in Original and Developed Buddhism'. The paper was eventually gathered with others, as mentioned here, many years later, in a 2014 publication called *Early Writings*, now to be found in *Complete Works*, vol. 7. For this paper, see pp. 190–206.

251 The transcription is somewhat conjectural here.

252 Nyanatiloka, *Buddhist Dictionary*, Buddhist Publication Society, Kandy 1988, p. 125.

253 Ibid., p. 52.

254 The *Buddhaghosuppatti*, an account of the life of Buddhaghosa, is thought to have been composed in fifteenth-century Burma by a monk named Mahāmaṅgala. Generally regarded by Western scholars as legend rather than history, it was translated by James Gray and published in 1892; it is still available from the Pali Text Society.

255 *A Survey of Buddhism*, *Complete Works*, vol. 1, pp. 23–4.

256 According to South Asia Buddhist teaching, merit may be achieved through: (1) giving (*dāna*); (2) observing moral precepts (*sīla*); (3) meditation (*bhāvanā*); (4) showing respect to superiors (*apacāyana*); (5) attending to the needs of superiors (*veyyāvacca*); (6) transferring merit (*pattidāna*); (7) rejoicing in the merits of others (*pattānumodanā*); (8) listening to the Dhamma (*dhammasavana*); (9) preaching the Dhamma (*dhammadesanā*); (10) having right beliefs (*diṭṭhijjukamma*). This list is non-canonical but widely taught in the Theravādin Buddhist world.

257 In the following passage the sequence of the text has been partly changed. (N)

258 'Performed, e.g. by those devoting themselves to a subject of meditation' (addition in *Paramatthajotikā*).

259 *Āḷavaka Sutta*, *Sutta-Nipāta* 1.10, verse 12.

260 The words of Kassapa that Buddhaghosa quotes in the passage translated by Ñāṇaponika are from *Saṃyutta Nikāya* 16:11. For an alternative translation, see Bhikkhu Bodhi (trans.), *Connected Discourses of the Buddha*, Wisdom Publications 1999, p. 678.

261 In the *Paramatthajotikā*, this mode of Refuge is called *tapponatta*, the proclivity, inclination, or devotion to it, i.e. to the Triple Gem. (N)

262 See the *Brahmāyu Sutta*, *Majjhima Nikāya* 91 (ii.145); Bhikkhu Ñāṇamoli and Bhikkhu Bodhi (trans.), *The Middle Length Discourses of the Buddha*, Wisdom Publications, Boston 1995, pp. 753–4; or I. B. Horner (trans.), *The Collection of the Middle Length Sayings*, vol. ii, Pali Text Society, Oxford 1994, pp. 330–1.

263 This was the talk 'Levels of Going for Refuge', delivered on the Order convention at Padmaloka in 1978; see *Complete Works*, vol. 12, pp. 301–16.

264 *Aṅguttara Nikāya* i.27–8. See F. L. Woodward (trans.), *The Book of the Gradual Sayings*, vol. i, Pali Text Society, Oxford 2000, pp. 25–6; or Bhikkhu Bodhi (trans.), *The Numerical Discourses of the Buddha*, Wisdom Publications, Somerville 2012, pp. 113–4.

265 Christmas Humphreys (1901–1983) was an English barrister, and later a judge, whose theosophical interests led him to Buddhism. He wrote many books, widely read at a time when there was little available in English on Buddhism. He considers karma and rebirth in many of his works, in particular in a little book, *Karma and Rebirth*, John Murray, London 1943, but although he discusses the topic of good karma leading to favourable rebirth, so far as we can discover, he doesn't refer to class or wealth in this way.

266 This is the third verse of the well-known hymn, 'All Things Bright and Beautiful', first published in 1848 in Cecil Frances Alexander's *Hymns for Little Children*. The verse was considered outdated as early as 1906, when Percy Dearmer, choosing to omit it from *The English Hymnal*, said that the words reflected the 'passivity and inertia at the heart of the British Establishment in the face of huge inequalities in Edwardian society'.

267 Actually, in 1948.

268 The reference is to Alfred North Whitehead (1861–1947), a prominent English mathematician and philosopher who co-authored the highly influential *Principia Mathematica* with Bertrand Russell. 'Religion is what the individual does with his own solitariness' is repeated several times in Whitehead's *Religion in the Making*, which originated in a series of four lectures delivered in King's Chapel, Boston, Massachusetts, during February 1926. See Alfred North Whitehead, *Religion in the Making*, Cambridge University Press, Cambridge 2011, pp. 6, 37, 48.

269 '*Sādhu*' is a Pāli word which, used as an exclamation, means 'It is well!' or 'Excellent!' The Buddha himself is described in the Pāli canon as commending it:

> But, Cunda, if you think he has got the right meaning and expressed it correctly, … you should say: 'Good!' and should applaud and congratulate him, saying: 'We are lucky, we are most fortunate to find in you, friend, a companion in the holy life who is so well versed in both the meaning and the expression!'

*Pāsādika Sutta*, *Dīgha Nikāya* 29 (iii.129): M. Walshe (trans.), *The Long Discourses of the Buddha*, Wisdom Publications, Boston 1995, p. 432. To this day '*Sādhu!*' is exclaimed, or even shouted, usually three times, within many Buddhist sanghas to express rejoicing or approval.

270 This was Mongkut (1804–1868), who in 1824 was ordained as a Buddhist monk, taking the name Vajirayan.

In 1835 he began a reform movement reinforcing the Vinaya, and this evolved into the Dhammayuttika Nikāya. In 1851, after twenty-seven years as a monk, he ascended the throne of Thailand. Outside Thailand he is best known as the king in the musical *The King and I*, which is based on the memoirs of a woman called Anna Leonowens, who lived at the king's court from 1862 to 1867.

271 Vinaya Piṭaka ii.107 (*Cullavagga* 5.2), see I. B. Horner (trans.), *The Book of the Discipline*, part 5, Pali Text Society, London 1975, p. 144.

272 See Dwight Goddard (ed.), *A Buddhist Bible*, Beacon Press, Boston 1970, p. 112.

273 This review was first published in the *FWBO Newsletter* no. 28, p. 22. It appears under the title 'Religio-Nationalism in Sri Lanka' in *Alternative Traditions*; see *Complete Works*, vol. 8, pp. 459–76.

274 *Sutta-Nipāta* 3.2, verse 16.

275 This is Nyanaponika's translation in *The Threefold Refuge*, Wheel Publication no. 76, Buddhist Publication Society, Kandy 1965 p. 20. For alternative translations, see Buddhaghosa, *Visuddhimagga* 115; Bhikkhu Ñāṇamoli, *The Path of Purification*, Buddhist Publication Society, Kandy 1991, p. 114–5; or Pe Maung Tin (trans.), *The Path of Purity*, Pali Text Society, London 1975, pp. 134–5.

276 See *Anagarika Dharmapala: A Biographical Sketch*, in *Complete Works*, vol. 8, p. 91.

277 This could perhaps have been the lecture on 'Levels of Going for Refuge' given earlier that year on the Order convention at Padmaloka; see note 263.

278 *Maggasaṃyutta*, *Saṃyutta Nikāya* v.2: see Bhikkhu Bodhi (trans.), *The Connected Discourses of the Buddha*, Wisdom Publications, Boston 2000, pp. 1524–5; also F. L. Woodward (trans.), *The Book of the Kindred Sayings*, part 5, Pali Text Society, London 1979, p. 2.

279 For an account of the work of the FWBO in India, (where it was called the TBMSG), see the introduction to *Complete Works*, vol. 10. The 'next step' hoped for here has not so far been taken.

# INDEX

*apramāda* (Pāli *appamāda*) *see* non-heedlessness
archetypal, beings 139, 224, 398, 436, 496; *see also* mythic figures
archetypal realm, *see rūpaloka*
*arhant* (Pāli *arahant*)
Buddha as 462–3, 470
ideal 241, 448, 585
path 644
*arhants* (Pāli *arahants*) 7, 58, 209, 240, 275, 289, 290, 465, 467, 518, 530, 531, 585–7, 599, 642, 745n
*Ariyapariyesanā Sutta* 48, 547, 582–3, 746n, 768n
Arnold, E. 609, 610, 770n
Arnold, M. 631, 772n
arrogance (*atimānī*) 275–6
artists 397, 404, 452–3, 488
arts 61, 83, 154, 157, 158, 217, 349, 522, 707, 717
and sciences 404–6
*arūpaloka* 208, 527, 530, 746n
*āryas* (Pāli *ariyas*) 11, 18, 31–2, 35, 38, 58, 449, 585, 593, 599, 640, 659
Āryasaṅgha 41, 538, 585–7, 599, 612, 640–1, 647, 659, 672–3, 745n
fourfold, classification of 518–19, 594, 598, 641–3, 654, 656
asceticism 440, 447
ascetics or asketics 5, 8, 11, 24, 29, 37–8, 45, 52, 62, 485, 768n; *see also samaṇas*
Aśoka 184
*āsravas* (Pāḷi *āsavas*) 34, 37–8, 57, 373; *see also* defilements
destruction of 230, 466, 653
*aśubha bhāvanā* 123–31
attachment 208–9, 231, 241, 248, 275, 313–14, 410, 533; *see also* craving
to rules and rituals (*sīlabbata-parāmāsa*) 203, 206, 207, 208, 355–6, 518, 520–2, 713, 746n, 752n
*Auspicious Signs* (seminar on *Maṅgala Sutta*) xx, 379–454
Aung, Shwe Zan 761n
authority 211, 266, 296, 424, 489, 617–18, 624, 661–3, 720, 772n; *see also* power mode
Avalokiteśvara 130, 196, 398
Mahākaruṇika *sādhana* 529, 766n
*avidyā* (Pāli *avijjā*) 36, 57, 471–2, 524–5, 530, 752n, 762n; *see also* ignorance
awakening, *see bodhi*
*The Awakening of Faith* 633, 772n
awareness 101, 113–14, 422; *see also* mindfulness
alienated 111, 114–18, 120, 136, 202, 205, 257, 428–30, 614, 730–2; *see also* alienation
non-dual 205; *see also* dualism
pure 201–3
Axial Age 488, 763n, 765n

Bāhiya 202, 754n
*bāla* 8, 12, 384–5; *see also* spiritually immature person
*bardo* 591–2, 688–9
Baudelaire, C. 164, 751n
'the beautiful' or moral beauty 22, 249, 291, 348–53
beauty xii, 21, 127–8, 156, 157, 258, 423, 533, 568, 576–7
deeper or higher 125, 130–1, 555–6
Belloc, H. 489, 764n
*Bhayabherava Sutta*, Buddhaghosa's exposition on Refuges in 543–4
*bhikkhunīs* 752n, 770n
*Bhikkhunisaṃyutta* 752n
*bhikkhus* 7, 445–6, 667, 713, 770n; *see also* monks
ordination 507, 667, 738, 739
Blake, W. xviii, 139, 205, 257, 435, 520, 750n, 753n
blessings xii, 680
*maṅgala* translated as 380, 393, 397, 404, 441, 453
as a 'service' 682–3, 702–3
bliss (*sukha*) 12, 39, 49, 70–1, 156, 219–21, 223–4, 226, 230, 258, 298, 449; *see also* tranquillity
*bodhi* 261, 464; *see also* Enlightenment
Bodhi, Bhikkhu 121, 747–8n, 749n, 755n
*bodhicarya* or *bodhisattvacarya* 416, 448, 472; *see also* bodhisattva path

consciousness (*cont.*)
states of, *see under* states
transformation of 81, 98, 107–8, 222–3, 226
consumerism 282–3, 433–4
contact, sensory 181, 205, 210
and craving 200–2, 286–8
contentment (*santuṭṭhi*) xx, 8, 31, 45, 50, 201, 275–8, 285, 288–90, 309–10, 345, 427–8, 433, 435–6
conversion 699, 721, 729, 756n, 766n
Conze, E. 518, 543, 750n, 761n, 772n
corpse meditation 140–4, 146
craving 46–8, 110, 126–7, 151, 155, 173, 231, 249–50, 266, 276, 286, 288, 317, 745n; *see also* attachment, desire; lust; poisons; *taṇhā*
and contact 200–2, 286–8
and contentment 427, 533, 766n
thirty-six streams of 46, 746n
creative process, path as, *see* path, spiral
creativity 96, 167, 174, 194, 196, 340–1, 469–71; *see also* mind, creative
cremation or charnel grounds 140–2, 394, 758n
crucial situation 394, 403, 603, 758n
*Cūḷagopālaka Sutta* 767n
*Cūḷavedalla Sutta* 466, 761n

*dāna* 28, 416, 435, 650, 652, 682, 773n; *see also* generosity
*darśana* (Pāli *dassana*) 33, 333, 441–2, 446, 448
death 9, 11, 14, 18, 23, 24, 25, 28, 35, 40, 42–3, 140–8, 375–7, 568, 687–90, 755n, 770n
*bardo* 591–2, 688–9
meditation on 140–4, 146, 589
Deathless 21, 54, 57, 63, 64, 745n
defilements 583, 650–3, 656, 657, 685–6; *see also āsravas*
delight 11, 12, 20, 29, 30, 42, 45, 47, 48, 49, 50, 120, 157–8, 220, 243, 310, 331, 345, 351, 568, 569, 639, 641, 650–1, 653, 745n; *see also* pleasure
and attachment 18–19, 40, 46
in beauty 555–6
in illusion (*papañca*) 37
in unskilful action 350–1
desire, *see also* craving
for continuing existence (*bhava-rāga*) 208, 209, 752n
for the Dharma (*dhammachanda*) 156
for rebirth 530, 746n
sensual (*kāmacchanda or kāma-rāga*) 125–6, 156, 168–72, 201, 203–4, 208, 524–5, 752n, 766n
world of, *see kāmaloka*
*Devadūta Sutta* 621, 771n
*devas*, *devatās* and *devīs* 58, 226, 382–3, 446, 495–6, 591; *see also* gods
devotion 327–8, 344, 391, 470, 551, 559, 576, 600, 604, 613–14, 626, 629–30, 727, 740, 757n; *see also* faith; reverence
devotional practice 98, 116, 118, 217, 237, 280, 767n; *see also* chanting; puja; worship
*Dhammadāyāda Sutta* 155, 750n
Dhammadinnā 466, 761n
*dhammakathā* or *dhammasākacchā* 443–6
*dhammānusārin*, *see* doctrine-follower
*Dhammapada* xiii–xvi, xxii, 1–2, 4–8, 59, 227, 261, 347, 360, 384–5, 414, 422, 436, 440, 493, 505, 573, 580, 749n, 755n, 757n, 759n, 764n, 767n, 768n
Sangharakshita and 5–7
seminar on chapter 9 xx, 347–77
translation of xiii–xvi, xxii, 6–56, 384
translations of xv–xvi, 7, 59, 347–8
*Dhammapada Aṭṭhakathā* 757n
*dhammas*, *see dharmas*
*dhamma-vicaya* 212, 215–16, 225, 745n
Dhardo Rimpoche 358
Dharma (Pāli Dhamma) 266, 501, 630–2, 636, 646, 654
books xi, xvii, 365, 617, 771n
and *dhamma-vicaya* 215
discussion of, *see dhammakathā*
doctrine, and method distinguished 129–30, 227
epithets of in *Tiratana Vandanā* 501–12
eye 206

as a 'force' 631–2
hearing of 403–4, 436–9, 511, 512–13, 773n
as law 7, 9, 62, 501, 505–6, 630–1, 637
learning by heart xiv, 5–6, 79, 179–80, 185, 279
negative and positive approaches 566–77
negative terms, use of 229–30, 338, 373–4; *see also* nihilism
as 'the Norm' 255, 437, 444, 753n
oral tradition of, *see* oral tradition
'original' teachings 161, 183–4, 188–9, 237, 240–1, 712
practice, *see also caraṇa*; *dharmacarya*; training
capacity for (*sakko*) 269–72, 283, 351, 426–7, 585, 720
as process of growth and development 95, 156, 229, 579, 632, 636, 662
progressive nature of 507–10; *see also* path, spiral
reflection on, *see* reflection
as refuge 583–4, 593–8, 630–1, 647
study xvi, 34, 97, 155, 177, 198, 256, 278, 279, 281–2, 284, 337, 373–4, 551, 563, 611, 658, 659, 757n
*dharmacarya* (Pāli *dhammacariyā*) 416, 448, 472
*dharmakāya* 397
Dharmapala, Anagarika 736, 775n
*dharmas* (Pāli *dhammas*), *see also* mental objects
mindfulness of 82, 168–78, 188, 422
no self in (*dharma nairātmya*) 184
reified 183–4, 186
*dhātus* 133; *see also* elements
eighteen 200
Dhivan Thomas Jones xxi, xxii, 744
*dhyāna* (Pāli *jhāna*) 108, 156–7, 163, 196, 203, 208, 239–40, 256, 336, 342, 405, 745n; *see also under samādhi*; states, of consciousness
Buddha and 222, 753n
and insight 108, 109, 222–3, 226
*Diamond Sūtra* (*Vajracchedikā Sūtra*) 135, 439, 750n
Dickens, C. xvii, 85–6, 87–8, 152, 194, 205, 274, 397–8
*Dīgha Nikāya* 103, 156, 210, 234, 362, 380, 405, 460, 583, 748n, 751n, 752n, 753n, 755n, 756n, 757n, 759n, 761n, 769n, 774n
disciples 442, 511, 562, 682–3
of the Buddha 128, 269, 278, 347, 462, 464–6, 470, 507, 512–13, 518, 556, 573, 770n
as *śrāvakas* 436, 512–13, 551
discipleship 667–8
acceptance of 660, 665–8, 698, 724–8
discipline 18, 25, 44, 61, 97, 98, 104, 173, 185, 393, 406
discretion (*nipako*) 288–9
disillusionment 570–1, 573–6, 578–80, 587–8, 609
distraction 108, 116–17, 119, 153, 232; *see also* hindrances
*diṭṭhis*, *see* views
doctrine-follower (*dhammānusārin*) 546, 561–2, 565, 567, 569–70, 574, 577, 600–1, 605, 610, 646, 743, 767–8n
doubt (*vicikitsā* (Pāli *vicikicchā*) 65, 105, 168, 170, 175–6, 203, 206, 207, 209, 265, 360, 519, 522–3, 653–4, 655, 686, 731, 745n, 746n, 752n
dreams xii, 135, 164, 194, 313, 329, 688–9, 750n
dualism 630, 633–5, 637; *see also* non-duality; subject-object duality; thinking, dualistic
*duḥkha* (Pāli *dukkha*) 58, 129–30, 262, 302, 448–51, 466, 758n; *see also* four noble truths; suffering

earth 132–3, 135, 138, 139
eating 97, 113, 118–19, 361, 515; *see also* food
ecology 283
effort 11, 115–16, 242, 243, 516, 527, 578, 580, 755n; *see also vīrya*
perfect (*sammā vāyāma*) 57, 170
efforts, four right 170
egolessness 338–9

ego or 'I'-sense 120, 210, 230, 329, 385, 387–8, 525, 680, 729–30, 769n; *see also* self-view
Eightfold Path or Way 30, 39, 57, 58, 79, 80, 99, 225, 232, 235, 250, 415, 594–8, 630
elements 132–7, 183, 750n
Eliot, T. S. 125, 210, 489, 749n, 752n, 763–4n
emotional
 development 402–3
 energy 149–50, 152–5, 208, 341, 399
 self-indulgence 612–14, 639
emotions
 and ethics 151, 157, 161–2
 and feelings distinguished 150–1, 252, 304–5, 312, 317–18, 753n
 higher, more refined or spiritual 155–7, 253, 256, 313
 and integration, *see under* integration
 and intellectual clarity 197–8, 250–1, 254–5, 318; *see also under* reason
 lack of 431; *see also* energy, blocked; indifference
 negative 303–8, 312, 316, 335–6, 338, 435, 438, 686; *see also* unskilful, or negative states
 positive 115–17, 152–5, 157, 236–7, 313, 326, 330, 338, 345, 686; *see also* faith; *mettā*
  and insight 208, 250–1, 327–8, 345, 549, 576, 625
emptiness, *see śūnyatā*
energies
 control or restraint of 493–4
 unification of 83, 106, 154, 341; *see also* integration
energy 152, 212, 395, 403, 578, 607, 625, 746n, 751n; *see also vīrya*
 blocked 115, 216, 218–19, 302, 387–8, 435, 494, 517, 732, 757n; *see also* feelings, alienated
 and boredom 428–9
 emotional 149, 152–5, 208, 341, 399
 of *mettā* 253–4
 and 'psychic heat' 446–7
 and reason 257–8, 753n
 release of 156, 218–19, 316, 757n
enjoyment 8, 20, 31, 117–18, 119, 169, 201, 269; *see also* pleasure
Enlightenment 58, 81, 93, 95–6, 138–9, 222, 226, 230, 334, 464–72, 592–3; *see also bodhi*; Buddhahood; Nirvāṇa
 *ānāpāna-sati* and 102
 in the *bardo* 591–2
 Buddha as embodiment of, *see under* ideal
 private, *see pratyekabuddhas*
 seven factors of (*bodhyaṅgas* (Pāli *bojjhaṅgas*) 19, 79, 169, 212–26, 234, 242, 579, 745n
 three kinds of 465
equality 536, 715–16, 774n
 wisdom of 121, 224
equanimity (*upekṣā* (Pāli *upekkhā*)) 165, 212, 223–5, 251, 257, 263, 265, 322, 326–7, 338, 396, 432–3, 745n; *see also* indifference
 cultivation of, *see upekṣā bhāvanā*
eternalism 745n
ethical ideal 348, 351, 353, 360; *see also* 'the beautiful'
ethics xiv, 98, 217, 271, 289–91, 294–5, 348, 596–7, 598; *see also* morality; precepts; *śīla*
 and feelings 151, 156–7, 161–2
 and meditation 114, 345, 509
 and *mettā* 268–96
 and positive *nidānas* 224
 and self-responsibility 289–91
 and shame 25, 36, 294, 417–18
*Everyman* 375, 756n
evil 43, 52, 65, 304, 347, 348–50, 353–4, 357, 359, 362, 366–8, 370–1, 373, *see also* unskilful
evil one, *see* Māra
evolution
 higher 19, 268, 351, 400–1, 594, 632–3, 635, 695
 lower 204, 632–3
existence, conditioned or mundane 57, 228, 491, 495–6; *see also saṃsāra*
 'pull of', *see* gravitational pull
 six realms of 92–3, 144, 211, 342, 772n
 three characteristics of, *see lakṣaṇas*
 and the Unconditioned 569–70, 576–7, 591–2, 633–7, 759n
'ex-Untouchables' 464, 484, 662, 681, 700, 702, 710, 736, 742; *see also* India, new Buddhists in

faculties
five spiritual (*indriyas*) 79, 625, 746n
imaginative, *see* imagination
faith 128, 129, 327, 563–4, 568, 570, 579, 638, 746n; *see also* confidence; devotion; *śraddhā*; trust
blind or dogmatic 359, 559, 563–5, 616–17, 620
and Going for Refuge 546–59, 579, 600–4, 607–16, 624–5, 650–4, 656–7, 659, 722–4
and positive *nidānas* 224, 230, 345, 466, 638–9, 758n
three aspects of 606–7, 616, 728
and understanding or wisdom 327–8, 559–77, 600–1, 607–8, 616–17, 625, 629–30, 723, 727–8
faith-follower (*saddhānusārin*) 546, 561–5, 568–9, 573–4, 577, 600–1, 605, 610, 721–2, 743, 767–8n
families 102, 120, 177, 247, 285, 305, 313, 407–14, 430, 473–85, 763n; *see also* parents
nuclear xx, 150, 197, 475, 478, 480
Triratna/WBO and xx, 414–15
father 14, 40, 45, 87–8, 324, 408–10, 412–14, 419–21, 430, 482–4, 504
'father' and 'mother', as metaphors 41, 745n
fear 13, 30, 32–3, 40, 144–5, 254, 272, 377, 620, 646–8, 672, 674, 676, 734, 735, 758n
and contraction 162–3, 388
feeling 179, 187, 307; *see also vedanā*
worldly and unworldly 149, 155–7
feelings
alienated or indifferent 429–32, 435; *see also* alienation; energy, blocked
and emotions distinguished 150–1, 252, 304–5, 312, 317–18, 753n
and ethics 151, 156–7, 161–2
and karma 150–1, 161, 304–5
mindfulness of 149–59, 234
fetters (*saṃyojanas*) 12, 33, 51, 199–200, 201, 203–10, 240, 337, 341, 355, 641–4, 746n
first three 206–8, 209, 241, 518–19, 523–4, 531–2, 654–5
five higher 530
fourth and fifth 524–8, 530, 531
ten 203, 206, 462, 752n
fire xv, 25, 132–3, 135, 139, 217, 451
food 10, 67, 154, 155, 231; *see also* eating
contemplation of loathsomeness of 129
fool, *see bāla*; spiritually immature person
forbearance (Pāli *khanti*) 439–41, 446; *see also* patience; tolerance
form 179; *see also rūpa*
four immeasurables, *see brahma vihāras*
four noble truths 58, 80, 169, 203, 227, 231–2, 234–5, 237, 249–50, 448–9, 568, 654, 753n
freedom (Pāli *vimutti*) 201, 275, 331, 341, 466; *see also* liberation
friendliness 253, 310–12, 396; *see also mettā*
friends 120–1, 192–3, 283; *see also* spiritual, friends
*mettā* towards 251–2, 293, 310–12, 332, 431
friendship 86, 91, 149–50, 154, 217, 271, 310–11, 356; *see also* spiritual, friendship
FWBO (Friends of the Western Buddhist Order) xi, xvi, xx, 507–8, 599, 649–50, 695, 713, 741, 742; *see also* Triratna Buddhist Order; Western Buddhist Order
in India 486–8, 700–2, 742, 763n, 775n
institutions and facilities 363, 365, 433; *see also* centres; communities; retreat centres; right livelihood businesses
new lifestyle or society xx, 473, 487
as positive group or tribe 421, 624

generosity 33, 98, 297, 326, 331, 349, 352, 435, 521, 534; *see also dāna*
genius 193–4
ghosts 68, 205
great, *see mahābhūtas*
hungry 646, 772n
goal 258, 260–1, 328, 334, 335, 343, 575, 762n
and path 81, 100, 241, 263, 328, 434
goal-setting 93–9, 205, 214, 762n

God 617–23, 631, 771n
gods 12, 15, 33, 57, 58, 61, 70, 73, 592, 677, 746n; *see also devas*; supernatural beings
and goddesses 137, 139
realm of 28, 58, 239, 342, 746n; *see also* heavens
Going for Refuge to the Three Jewels 486, 497–8, 500, 507, 545, 554, 605–6, 651–3, 673, 675–6, 693–4
breach of 687–90
centrality of xxi, 695, 728
ceremonies 710–12; *see also* ordination
commitment to, *see under* commitment
and emotions/faith, *see under* faith
'formula' 666, 693–700, 710; *see also* Refuges, and Precepts, recitation
fruits of 679–85
FWBO and 599, 695, 741
as an individual act xxi, 651, 692–711
as initiation 694–5, 697, 699–700, 704, 734–5
intellectual 607–8; *see also* doctrine-followers
levels of xxi, 693, 721–2, 773n
cultural 554, 626, 648
effective 610, 676, 771n
real 721–2, 771n
motivation or 'drive' for 608–10, 722–3
and ordination, *see under* ordination
and precepts, *see* precepts
in puja 426
significance of xxi, 545, 695, 709–10, 740–1
and Stream Entry 532, 675
and 'taking refuge' 545, 625–6, 629
three aspects of 605–7, 612, 615–16
*The Threefold Refuge* seminar on xx–xxi, 541–743
transcendental and mundane 651, 653–9, 679–87, 737–9; *see also under* refuge
and understanding, *see* understanding
going forth xi, 17, 42, 102, 241, 261, 407, 441, 649, 703, 738, 770n
the good 15, 25, 155, 261–3, 362–3, 387
and the beautiful, *see* the beautiful
Gotama 41–2, 588–90, 593, 627–8; *see also* Buddha
*gotrabhū* 643
gratitude (Pāli *kataññutā*) 234, 323, 433–5, 471, 721
gravitational pull 336, 399, 402, 470, 486, 580, 635–6, 758n, 759n
gravity, law of 631–2
greed 685, 752n; *see also* craving; poisons
type 569
group 98, 163, 285, 313, 489–90, 563–4, 618, 663, 672, 676, 717
and individual 290, 418–19, 484, 488–90, 498, 534, 537, 547, 619, 621–2, 624, 651, 719–20, 743
positive 417–18, 420, 624
and spiritual community, *see under* spiritual, community
Guenther, H. V. 134, 472, 749n, 769n
Guhyaloka xiv, 7–8, 744n
guilt 273, 331, 450, 618, 620–2

habits 97, 172–4, 353–7, 362, 504; *see also* volitions
Hakuin 393, 395, 403
happiness 117, 162, 221, 249, 250, 266, 297–8, 308, 309, 310, 360, 452, 453; *see also* joy
signs of coming 382–4
Hare, E. M. 380, 413, 425, 436, 437, 441, 447, 451, 664, 756n
harm 301–4, 367–72, 415
harmony 295, 418, 515–17
hate type 569
hatred 9, 14, 31, 41, 48, 50, 54, 160, 203, 303–6, 431, 505–6, 680; *see also* anger; ill will; poisons
heart 197; *see also* mind (*citta*)
*Heart Sūtra* 181
heavens 23, 28, 56, 70, 128, 139, 373; *see also* gods, realm of
hedonism 287, 533; *see also* pleasure
hell xviii, 93, 139, 342, 371, 373, 620–2, 646, 771n, 772n
hierarchy 714–20; *see also* scale of values
of aliveness 138
spiritual 619

insight (*cont.*)
beings with, *see āryas*
and emotions or faith 208, 250–1, 327–8, 345, 549, 576, 625
equanimity and 119, 223, 257
and fetters, *see* fetters
initial 548–9, 554
*lakṣaṇas* and, *see lakṣaṇas*
meditation and, *see under dhyāna*; *vipaśyanā*
*mettā* and 252, 256, 257, 258, 260, 322–3, 333, 335–41
and *puṇya* 98, 401–2
reflection and, *see* reflection
and *saṃprajanya* 97–8, 100, 214
with small 'i' or capital 'I' 256
stage of spiral path, *see* knowledge, and vision...
and twofold *nairātmya* 184, 186
views and 207, 333–4
inspiration 115–16, 118, 152, 154, 309, 442, 548, 562, 571–3, 578
from the Buddha 628–9
through Dharma 5, 561
through meditation 153, 156, 196
through Sangha 159, 539, 560, 585, 602, 608, 650, 658
insubstantiality xv, 25, 110–11, 120, 127, 277
integration 165, 217–20, 221, 223, 270, 288, 496, 549, 565; *see also* energies, unification of
around the ideal 88, 93–4, 100
and clear thinking 193, 198
*dhyāna* and 108, 163
and emotions 116–17, 257–8, 273, 316, 343
reason and 255, 257–8
and *saṃprajanya* 88, 93–4, 100
as 'solid human base' 399; *see also* human, qualities, importance of
as unifying the mind 171–2, 178, 203
as 'wholeness' 198, 257, 624–5
intention 96, 175, 252, 272, 331, 340, 666, 676; *see also* motivation
intoxication 36, 400, 422–4
irreversibility 241, 592, 630, 636, 638–9; *see also* Stream Entry
*Itivuttaka* 253, 753n
*Jātaka* stories 439, 445–6, 760n
jealousy (*issā*) 253, 317, 752n
*The Jewel Ornament of Liberation* 586, 763n, 769n
Jōdo Shinshū school 616–17
Johnson, S. 363–4, 755n
joy 50–1, 210, 217, 220, 230, 331, 343, 345, 466, 549–50, 568, 604–5, 650, 721; *see also* happiness
sympathetic, *see* sympathetic joy

*Kālāma Sutta* 560, 562, 565, 768n
*kalyāṇa* 348–9; *see also* the beautiful
*kalyāṇa mitras* 510, 586, 765n; *see also* spiritual, friends
*kalyāṇa mitratā*, *see* spiritual, friendship
*kāmaloka* 156, 200, 527, 744n, 746n
*Karaṇīya Mettā Sutta* xviii–xix, 236, 247–8, 258, 260, 338, 341, 747n, 754n
Sangharakshita's commentary, *see Living With Kindness*
Sangharakshita's translation xiii, 71–2
karma 89–94, 110, 182, 204, 214, 527, 592
as 'actions have consequences' 358–9
and feelings 150–1, 161, 304–5
law of 110, 319, 370, 373–5
distortion of 681
merit-producing 398
and rebirth 92–3, 306, 342, 373, 395–6, 401, 687–91, 774n
*vipāka* 90, 93, 165, 527, 592–3, 641–2, 644, 691
and the supramundane refuge 679–82, 685
'weighty' 92, 108, 688, 690–1, 748n
*karuṇā*, *see* compassion
*karuṇā bhāvanā* 256, 258, 326, 344, 396
Kashyap, J. xii, 6, 422
*Kasibhāradvāja Sutta* 625, 772n
Kassapa 665–6, 668, 773n
*khandas*, *see skandhas*
*Khuddaka Nikāya* 4, 746n
*Khuddaka-pāṭha* xiii, 258, 746n, 747n
knowledge 403–4, 469, 599–600, 674, 725–6, 758n; *see also* understanding

accumulation of (*jñānasambhāra*) 397
of the destruction of the *āsravas* 230, 466, 653
intuitive 138, 207
threefold 566, 599
*vidyā* (Pāli *vijjā*) as 471–3
and vision... (*yathābhūtajñānadarśana*) 122, 230, 638
*kṣānti* (Pāli *khanti*) *see* forbearance
Kṣitigarbha 342

*lakṣaṇas* (Pāli *lakkhaṇas*) xv, 39, 110, 191, 748–9n
Lama Govinda 130, 749n
language 3–4, 465, 557; *see also* speech
conditional and imperative 264–7, 621–3
of development 229
of metaphor and poetry 196–7, 569, 570
of potentiality 583, 769n; *see also* Buddhahood, seed/spark of
problem or inadequacy of 135, 229, 230, 328, 592
*Laṅkāvatāra Sūtra* 239, 753n
Laozi 514, 763n, 765n
*Larger Sukhāvatīvyūha Sūtra* 95, 747n
Latthakin, Prince 143–4, 521, 765n
laughter 371, 372–3, 756n
Lawrence, D. H. 198, 257, 432, 443, 752n, 759n, 761n
lay followers 98, 236, 241, 446, 475, 486, 550, 599, 627, 649, 677–80, 770n; *see also* householders; *upāsakas*
and monks, *see under* monks
liberation (Pāli *vimutti*) 19, 230, 546, 548, 625, 772n; *see also* freedom
library
at Alexandria 617, 771n
Sangharakshita's xi, xvii
life stories 91, 94, 165
lifestyle 97, 98, 154, 217, 599, 649; *see also carana*
and commitment 473, 486–8
'easily supported' (*subharo*) 277–8
homeless wanderers (*parivrājaka*) 278, 285
monastic 278–80
light 6, 25, 28, 51, 171, 239, 314–15, 325, 327
*The Light of Asia* 609, 610, 770n
Ling, T. 381, 756n
literalism 188, 209, 229, 230, 334
livelihood, *see also* right livelihood; work
'light' (*sallahukavutti*) 274, 284
perfect or peaceful 57, 407, 415
*Living With Awareness* xvi–xviii, 79–243
*Living With Kindness* xviii–xix, 245–345
Lokottaravāda 185
lotuses 468, 579, 587, 762n
love 252–3, 256, 308, 312, 314, 431, 600, 601; *see also* affection; *mettā*
mode, and power mode 351, 537–8, 622–3, 755n
mother's 71, 247, 321–4
loving-kindness, *see brahma vihāras*; *mettā*
luck 380, 382–3, 385–6, 397
lust 10, 31, 36, 48, 50, 53–4, 63, 72, 129, 160, 746n; *see also* craving

Macmurray, J. 254–5, 753n
magic 682–5
*Mahāassapura Sutta* 156, 750–1n
*mahābhūtas* ('great ghost') 133–5, 137, 750n
*mahāmaitrī* 257; *see also mettā*, and insight
*Mahāparinibbāna Sutta* 156, 210, 460, 583, 751n, 752n, 761n, 769n
*Mahāsaccaka Sutta* 753n
*Mahāsakuludāyi Sutta* 156, 751n
Mahāsāṃghika school 185
*Mahāsatipaṭṭhāna Sutta* 753n
*Mahāvacchagotta Sutta* 770n
*Mahāvastu* 185–6
Mahāyāna 183–7, 543
perspectives 110, 184, 186, 197, 468, 568–70, 580, 585, 592, 629–30, 634–5, 641, 711
*sūtras* 266, 334, 769n, 771n
*maitrī*, *see mettā*

*Majjhima Nikāya* 48, 93, 102, 155, 156, 161, 171, 222, 466, 583, 588, 597, 599, 627, 669, 746n, 747n, 748n, 750n, 751n, 752n, 753n, 761n, 767n, 768n, 769n, 770n, 771n, 773n
  Buddhaghosa's exposition on MN4, *see Bhayabherava Sutta*
Malory, T. 221–2
Māmakī 121
mandala, of five Buddhas 121, 139, 202, 770n
*maṅgala*, translations of the word 380
*Maṅgala* or *Mahāmaṅgala Sutta* xiii, 374, 746n, 756n
  Sangharakshita's translation 61–2
  seminar, *see Auspicious Signs*
Mañjughoṣa 398, 590
*Mañjughoṣa stuti sādhana* 529, 766n
*Manusmṛti* 412
Māra 10, 13–15, 20, 28, 39, 46–7, 178, 366–7, 402–3, 453, 593, 733, 744n, 745n, 752n, 767n, 770n
marriage 414–15, 476–7, 479–82, 484–5
Mascaro, J. 348
materialism 136, 401, 510, 683–4, 750n, 772n; *see also* merit, '-making'
meditation 83–4, 97, 113–14, 299, 337, 358–9, 361, 364, 514–15, 625, 734–6; *see also dhyāna*; *samādhi*
  advanced practices 344, 508
  on death/corpse 140–4, 146, 589
  deeper/higher states of, *see under* states
  dependence on as a 'rite' 532–3
  on the Dharma (*bhāvanā-mayā-paññā*) 511
  distraction in, *see* distraction; hindrances
  and ethics 114, 345, 509
  expecting results 502–4
  and four right efforts 170
  on foulness/impurity of body, *see under* body
  insight, *see under dhyāna*; *vipaśyanā*
  just sitting 201
  and karma 92
  *mettā*, *see mettā*; *mettā bhāvanā*
  mindfulness of breathing, *see under* mindfulness
  and pleasure, *see* pleasure
  poetry as 259
  posture 103, 171
  preparation for 104, 170
  and psychic 447–8
  *sādhana* or visualization practice 526, 529, 766n
  *samāpatti* and *nimitta* 108, 748n
  *śamatha* and *vipaśyanā*, *see under śamatha*
  six element practice 109–10, 136
  solitude and companionship 102–3
  and spiritual community 657–8, 757n
  'Transcendental' 588, 610, 674
  under difficult conditions 393–5, 403
  walking (*caṅkamana*) 190
Mehta, D. 264–5, 754n
memory 84–8, 304; *see also* recollection
mental (or mind-) objects (*dhammas*) 82, 83, 167–70, 179, 182, 187, 199, 212, 215, 224, 227, 233–4, 242, 342, 651, 759n
  classification of 161–2, 166, 169, 203, 417, 438
  investigation of, *see dhamma-vicaya*
  and mind, *see* mind, and mental events
  mindfulness of, *see under dharmas*
mental events, *see* mental objects
merit (*puṇya* (Pāli *puññā*)) 21, 26, 30, 36, 45, 48, 61, 68, 69–70, 350, 395–401, 521, 773n
  accumulation of (*puṇyasambhāra*) 397, 405
  'body of' (*puṇyakāya*) 397–8
  field of (*puṇyakṣetra*) 538–9, 647–9, 652
  loss of 366–7
  '-making'and worldly attainments/property 98, 539, 680–3, 685, 711–12
  -producing action (*-kamma*) 398
  rebirth and 538, 647–8
  rejoicing in 165, 224, 327, 773n
  transferring 773n
meritorious acts, ten (*-kiriyavatthu*) 654, 659–60, 773n
metaphors 41, 94, 124, 195, 197, 204, 330, 342, 422–3, 451, 633, 745n; *see also* analogies; similes; symbols

mothers xx, 14, 45, 409–11, 418–21, 431–2, 443, 480, 482–4
love of 71, 247, 321–4, 327, 331
motivation 158, 174, 221–2, 237, 270, 568, 674; *see also* intention
or 'drive' for Going for Refuge 608–10, 722–3
*muditā*, *see* sympathetic joy
*muditā bhāvanā* 326–7
Murry, J. M. 620, 771n
music xii, 87, 117, 118, 154, 157–8, 202–3, 615, 707, 731, 746n
mythic figures 95, 137, 496; *see also* archetypal beings; *devas*
mythology 139, 186, 495–6, 502, 619, 744n, 745n, 746n, 758n

*nairātmya*, twofold 184; *see also* *anātman*; *śūnyatā*
*nāma* 133, 187
*nāma-rūpa* 133, 200
Nanda 128
Narada Thera 348, 748n
Narada, U 736
nature 136–9, 157, 158, 201, 236, 257, 383, 618–19, 631, 685
*nidānas*, *see also* conditionality, cyclic and spiral; conditioned co-production
cyclic or negative 200, 228–9, 471–2, 527, 568, 579, 754n, 762n, 766n
positive or spiral 220, 224–5, 229, 399, 466, 568, 579, 638, 758n
*Nidhikaṇḍa Sutta* xiii, 69–70, 747n
Nietzsche, F. 610, 771n
nihilism or annihilationism 498, 571–2, 745n
Nirvāṇa (Pāli *nibbāna*) 57–8, 62, 79, 229–30, 239, 250, 343, 653–4, 755n; *see also* Enlightenment
as cessation or snuffing out 58, 226, 227, 229–31, 261, 338, 451, 579, 593; *see also* disillusionment
as Further Shore 18, 47, 51, 55, 58, 767n
and *saṃsāra*, *see under saṃsāra*
as a verb 373–4
Noble Ones, *see aryas*
non-duality 339, 592; *see also* dualism
non-heedlessness (*apramāda*) 45, 173
Non-Returners (*anāgāmins*) 58, 127, 239–40, 342, 467, 518, 526, 531, 585, 642, 745n
no-self, *see anātman*
Nyanaponika Thera xx, 543, 545, 551, 744; *see also The Threefold Refuge*
Nyanatiloka Mahathera 643, 748n, 749n, 772n

Once-Returners (*sakadāgāmins*) 58, 240, 467, 518, 524, 526–8, 530–1, 585, 642, 745n
oral tradition 3–4, 20, 179–80, 184, 234–6, 279, 403–4
ordination 412, 507
*bhikkhu* 507, 667, 738, 739
ceremony
private or individual 705, 711–12, 738
public 704, 705, 708, 711
and Going for Refuge 660, 661, 676, 695, 700, 704, 705, 708, 709–10, 737–41; *see also* commitment, and Going for Refuge
into WBO 421, 457, 486, 507–8, 660–1, 676, 695, 700–1, 737, 740–1
retreats 363, 744n
witnessing 695, 698–9, 704–5, 708, 738
other-regarding perspective 120, 172, 182, 223, 236–7, 281, 290, 297, 326; *see also* altruism; mindfulness, and other beings

Padmaloka Retreat Centre 347, 457, 477, 541, 763n, 773n, 775n
Padmasambhava 394, 590, 758n
paganism 139; *see also* animism
pain 39, 127, 156, 304, 368–9, 449; *see also duḥkha*; suffering
and pleasure 149–56, 223, 353
Pāli 3–4
Pāli canon 4, 103, 132, 136–7, 160–1, 180, 184–5, 234–5, 347, 696; *see also* individual *Nikāyas*
*paritrāṇa sūtras* xii, xiii
reciting, *see* recitation

pure lands 95, 240, 282, 342
Pure Land schools 240

Radhakrishnan, S. 347
Ramana Maharshi 442–3, 462, 760n
rapture (*prīti* (Pāli *pīti*)) 31, 156, 212, 217–21, 224–6, 230, 345, 559, 745n
*Ratana Sutta* xiii, 63–6, 746n
*Ratnaguṇa-saṃcayagāthā* seminar 472, 762n
Ratnasambhava 121, 224
reactivity, *see* mind, reactive
realities, two ultimate 633–4
reality, ultimate 266, 501, 705, 708
realms, *see* worlds
reason, or intellect 197, 255, 304, 349, 562–3, 743; *see also* understanding
  and emotions 208, 254–5, 257–8, 304, 307, 316–17, 338, 343, 549, 558, 565
    and volitions xxi, 606–7, 612, 615–16, 620–1, 624–5, 728–9, 741
  and energy 257–8, 753n
  and imagination, sense and emotion 750n
rebirth 42–3, 144, 211, 341–2, 646, 746n, 766n, 771–2n; *see also* wheel of life
  avoiding 92–3, 207, 214, 228, 240, 531
  desire for 530, 746n
  favourable 98, 478, 680–2, 684, 685, 687–8, 774n
  karma and, *see under* karma
  and merit, *see under* merit
  *mettā* and 335–6
  numbers of times of 531
receptivity 83, 85, 112, 164, 276, 331, 387, 427–8, 436–8, 513, 551–3, 663, 727
recitation
  of canonical texts xii, xiii, 5–6, 79, 125, 126, 180, 236, 436, 546, 746n; *see also* chanting
  of mantras 116
  of Refuges and Precepts, *see under* Refuges and Precepts
recollection 87, 91, 93, 99–100, 222; *see also* memory
reflection xiii, 90–1, 109–11, 122, 146–7, 176, 177, 190–8, 217, 228, 280, 316
  on anger 316, 440–1
  on the Dharma (*cintā-mayā-paññā*) 511, 560, 561
  on five *skandhas* 180–3
  and food 119
  on four noble truths 231–2
  and insight 226, 338–9
  on *nidānas* 228
  Sangharakshita and 190, 713, 718
  whilst walking (*caṅkamana*) 190–1
refuge 547, 573–4, 602, 645; *see also* *saraṇa*
  going for, *see* Going for Refuge
  as 'island for oneself' 12, 35, 580, 583–4
  mundane 554, 654, 656, 680, 685–9, 705, 737
    four kinds of 660–79, 692–8, 708–10, 728–9, 737–8, 740
    and supramundane or transcendental 651, 653–9, 679–80, 686, 737–9
  need for 566–7, 574, 600, 608–10
  'taking' *see under* Going for Refuge
  ultimate nature of 587–99
Refuges
  and Precepts 700–1, 711
    recitation, of xxi, 547, 554, 625–6, 650, 689, 690, 692, 694, 699–701, 710–11, 712; *see also* Going for Refuge... 'formula'
  seminar on Nyanaponika's commentary about Buddhaghosa's exposition 543–4, 627–91
  Three 577–81; *see also* Three Jewels
rejoicing in merits 165, 224, 327, 773n
relationships 272, 313, 354, 533, 756n; *see also* sexual, relationships
relativism 265, 291, 488–90
reliance 114, 207, 284, 291–2, 559–61, 650–1
remorse (Pāli *ottappa*) 11, 43, 417
resentment 253, 294, 303, 305, 572, 620; *see also* ill will
respect 21, 265, 292, 294, 389–90, 408, 534–6, 563, 670–1, 717–20, 773n; *see also* reverence

suffering 25, 202, 352–3, 368–70, 548–9, 566–7, 753n; *see also* *duḥkha*; four noble truths; pain
used as example of conditionality by Buddha 227–8, 233
suicide 363, 589
*sukha*, *see* bliss
*Sukhamāla Sutta* 422–3, 424, 759n
Sukhavati, community 388, 393, 433–4, 474, 477, 713, 757n
Sukhāvatī, pure land 240, 592
Sully, Duc de 172, 751–2n
*śūnyatā* (Pāli *suññatā*) 19, 58, 186–7, 339, 374, 448, 578, 634, 637, 704; *see also nairātmya*
and *rūpa* 591
supernatural beings 136–7; *see also* gods
supernormal powers (*iddhis*) 28, 58, 165
superstition 380, 382
*Śūraṅgama Sūtra* 556, 721, 768n
*A Survey of Buddhism* 524, 568, 616–17, 646, 766n, 768n, 771n, 773n
*Sūtra of Huineng* 580, 768n
seminar 438, 583, 769n
*Sutta-Nipāta* xix, 258, 347, 625, 664–5, 733, 746n, 747n, 754n, 756n, 772n, 773n, 775n
symbols 108, 187, 195, 197, 266, 327, 619; *see also* metaphors
sympathetic joy (*muditā*) 165, 223, 251, 256–7, 326–7, 396, 432–3
cultivation of, *see muditā bhāvanā*

*Tālapuṭa Sutta* 371, 755n
*taṇhā* 58, 745n; *see also* craving
Tantra 216, 635; *see also* Vajrayāna Buddhism
Tantric initiations 442
*Tao Te Ching* 514, 765n
Taraloka Retreat Centre 757n
*Tathāgata-dhātu* 569; *see also* Buddhahood, seed of
Tathāgata/s 37, 39, 63, 334, 754n; *see also* Buddha/s
teachers
other 669–70, 676, 678–9, 680, 687
spiritual 271, 412, 442, 561–2, 563, 672, 676, 695, 699, 725–7, 736
technology 683–5
temperament 509, 516–17; *see also* body-witness; doctrine-follower; faith-follower
Temple, S. 443, 761n
therapy 88, 271, 283, 588; *see also* psychology
Theravāda 4, 185, 543; *see also* Hīnayāna
perspectives of 183, 236, 491, 548, 550–1, 556, 568–9, 579, 585–7, 596, 598, 629, 635, 644, 697
*Therīgāthā* 126, 749n
Thibaw, King 521
thinking
associative 194–5
clear or directed 175–6, 190–3, 206, 307, 317
conceptual 135, 187
dualistic 121, 138, 207, 210, 230; *see also* dualism
and emotions 197–8
original 194
*The Threefold Refuge*
book by Nyanaponika Thera xx, 543–4, 767n
seminar xx–xxi, 541–743
Three Jewels xxi, 45, 328, 547, 573, 578; *see also* Refuges, Three
unconditioned nature of 654
'within our mind' 580–3, 587
Tibetan Buddhism 121, 130, 684, 703, 711, 758n; *see also* Tantra; Vajrayāna Buddhism
tiger 41, 745n, 751n
*Tiratana Vandanā* xiii, 457, 642, 761n
Sangharakshita's translation 73–4
seminar, *see Salutation to the Three Jewels*
text in Pāli and English 458–60
*Tirokuḍḍa Sutta* xiii, 67–8, 747n
tolerance 670–1; *see also* forbearance
training 80, 262–3, 299, 330; *see also* *caraṇa*; *dharmacarya*
tranquillity (*praśrabdhi* (Pāli *passaddhi*)) 19, 24, 31, 51, 107, 110, 212, 219–21, 224, 745n; *see also* bliss
the Transcendental (*lokuttara*) 449, 470, 491, 576, 584, 587–8,

631, 633, 635–8; *see also* the Unconditioned; *and under* Going for Refuge; path; vision
Triratna Buddhist Community xvi, 757n, 765n; *see also* FWBO
commitment to 701, 765n
Triratna Buddhist Order, *see also* Western Buddhist Order
neither monastic nor lay xx, 486–7
trust 91, 213, 272, 292, 310–11, 336, 510–11, 560–2, 771n; *see also* faith
truth 258, 376–7, 500–1, 567
provisional 187, 198, 334
truthfulness and lying 28, 272, 302, 507

*Udāna* xiv, 128, 202, 286, 347, 749n, 752n, 754n
*Udānavarga* xiv, 4, 59, 347
*Udumbarika-Sīhanāda Sutta* 362, 755n
the Unconditioned 567–70, 618, 630, 636, 654–7; *see also* Nirvāṇa; the Transcendental
and the conditioned 576–7, 591–2, 633–7, 759n
unconditioned being (*sattva*) 592–3
understanding 391, 404, 473, 553–4, 578, 596, 597, 599, 626; *see also* knowledge; reason
and faith or emotion 559–77, 600–1, 607–8, 616, 625, 629–30, 723–4
right, *see* view, right
theoretical 358, 524, 554, 558–9, 565
unemployment 365–6, 420, 755n
unsatisfactoriness 110, 574; *see also* *duḥkha*
unskilful (*akusala*), *see also* evil
actions 92–3, 216, 266, 290, 318, 350–1, 354, 367, 421, 641, 680
or negative, states 351, 367, 437, 639–40; *see also* emotions, negative
roots, three (*-mūlas*) 303; *see also* poisons
untouchability 175
Upaka 768n
*upāsakas* 486, 640, 647–9, 699–701; *see also* lay followers
ordination 660–1, 676, 695, 700–1, 737, 740–1
*upekṣā* (Pāli *upekkhā*) *see* equanimity
*upekṣā bhāvanā* 326
uprightness (*uju*) 71, 171, 247, 268, 271–3, 343, 345; *see also* straightforwardness

Vajrayāna Buddhism 202, 471, 528–9, 531, 543, 770n; *see also* Tantra; Tibetan Buddhism
*Vatthūpama Sutta* 752n
*vedanā* 57, 82, 150–2, 181; *see also* feelings; sensations
vegetarianism 133, 486, 764n, 772n
veneration 21, 426, 461, 672, 721; *see also* reverence
verse xii–xiv, xvi, xviii, 347, 382–3, 762n; *see also* poetry
*vidyā* (Pāli *vijjā*) 471–5, 762n; *see also* appreciation, aesthetic; wisdom
Vietnam 500, 764n
view, right (*samyak-dṛṣṭi* (Pāli *sammā diṭṭhi*)) 207, 258, 263, 333, 596–7, 654, 659–60, 686; *see also* vision, perfect
views (*dṛṣṭis* (Pāli *diṭṭhis*)) 57, 176–7, 184, 752n
and clear thinking 192–3
fixed 147, 304, 317
and insight 207, 333–4
mistaken or wrong (*micchā-*) 44, 46, 53, 122, 184, 248, 333–4, 686, 745n
and fetters 206
self- *see* self, view
tolerance of others' 670–1
topsy-turvy (*viparyāsas*) 127, 749n
*vijñāna* (Pāli *viññāna*) 57, 181–2, 568; *see also* consciousness
*Vīmaṃsaka Sutta* 588, 769n
Vinaya 185, 775n
*vinaya*, meaning of word 406
*Vinaya Piṭaka* 269, 381, 464–5, 468, 579, 713, 747n, 754n, 756n, 761n, 762n, 768n, 775n
*Vipallāsa Sutta* 127, 749n
*vipassanā*, 'pseudo-' 571–2, 576–7, 736

*vipaśyanā* (Pāli *vipassanā*), *see also* insight
practice 84, 109–12, 643
and *śamatha* 84, 109–11, 240, 337, 339, 421
*vīrya* (Pāli *viriya*) 216–17, 225–6, 745n; *see also* effort; energy
lack of, *see* passivity
Visākhā 381, 757n
vision (*dṛṣṭi* (Pāli *diṭṭhi*)), *see also* *darśana*
mundane 564–5; *see also* view, right
perfect or transcendental (*samyak-* (Pāli *sammā-*)) xxi, 57, 205–6, 449, 451, 594–7, 641, 653–4, 686
single xviii, 139, 750n
spiritual 127, 258, 465, 596
the wise and 293
*Visuddhimagga* 129, 133, 142, 171, 300, 322, 543, 625, 645, 708–9, 734–5, 740, 747n, 748n, 749n, 750n, 751n, 752n, 754n, 755n, 772n, 775n
*Vitakkasaṇṭhāna Sutta* 751n
volitions (*saṃskāras* (Pāli *saṅkhāras*)) xxi, 57, 150, 181–2, 187, 205, 298, 471–2, 550, 568, 616, *see* also, habits; will
reason and emotion, *see under* reason
skilful 90, 252, 527
vows 699, 734, 737–40
of Amitābha 240
bodhisattva 80, 82, 342

water 132, 133, 135, 139
welfare, of others 251–2, 291, 299, 320, 322; *see also* altruism
and self 27, 290, 309, 322–3, 340
Western Buddhist Order (WBO) 418, 419, 650, 676, 737, 741; *see also* Triratna Buddhist Order
ordinations into, *see under* ordination
wheel of life or rebirth 200, 226, 228–9, 233, 338; *see also nidānas*, cyclic
Whitehead, A. N. 706, 774n
Wilde, O. 374, 756n
wilfulness 222, 385, 607
will 548–50, 554, 559, 605–7, 612, 615–16, 625, 626, 771n; *see also* volition
giving up one's 661–3, 766n
wisdom 197, 255, 256, 314, 625, 746n; *see also prajñā*; *vidyā*
and compassion 470, 630, 644–5
of equality 121, 224
and faith 616–17, 625
mirror-like 202
three levels of 511
the wise, or 'those who know' 11, 29–30, 65, 291–4, 296, 330–1, 417–18, 583–4; *see also paṇḍita*
Woodward, F. L. xi–xiii, 749n, 752n, 753n, 755n, 758n *and passim*
work xix, 117–18, 177, 194, 217, 243, 271, 278–82, 284; *see also* livelihood; unemployment
identification of self and 729–31
manual 282, 404–5
and Sukhavati 434, 757n
world, 'giving up the' 491–2
worldlings (*puthujjanas*) 593–4, 643, 654, 656, 733
worldly winds or opposites (*lokadhammas*) 452–3
worlds or realms 138, 157, 239
as correlations of consciousness 495, 527, 745n
of desire, *see kāmaloka*
of form (archetypal) *see rūpaloka*
formless, *see arūpaloka*
god 28, 58, 239, 342, 746n; *see also* heavens
six mundane 92–3, 144, 211, 342, 772n; *see also* human realm
worship 61, 388–92, 425, 756n; *see also* devotional practice; puja
writing 87–8, 193, 354, 361, 364, 505

*yānas*, three 543
Yeats, W. B. 117, 520, 749n, 765n
Yogācāra tradition 417, 633, 759n

Zen 7, 103, 279, 450, 558, 580–2, 635, 768n
Zhiyi 754n

# A GUIDE TO THE COMPLETE WORKS OF SANGHARAKSHITA

Gathered together in these twenty-seven volumes are talks and stories, commentaries on the Buddhist scriptures, poems, memoirs, reviews, and other writings. The genres are many, and the subject matter covered is wide, but it all has – its whole purpose is to convey – that taste of freedom which the Buddha declared to be the hallmark of his Dharma. Another traditional description of the Buddha's Dharma is that it is *ehipassiko*, 'come and see'. Sangharakshita calls to us, his readers, to come and see how the Dharma can fundamentally change the way we see things, change the way we live for the better, and change the society we belong to, wherever in the world we live.

Sangharakshita's very first published piece, *The Unity of Buddhism* (found in volume 7 of this collection), appeared in 1944 when he was eighteen years old, and it introduced themes that continued to resound throughout his work: the basis of Buddhist ethics, the compassion of the bodhisattva, and the transcendental unity of Buddhism. Over the course of the following seven decades not only did numerous other works flow from his pen; he gave hundreds of talks (some now lost). In gathering all we could find of this vast output, we have sought to arrange it in a way that brings a sense of coherence, communicating something essential about Sangharakshita, his life and teaching. Recalling the three 'baskets' among which an early tradition divided the Buddha's teachings, we have divided Sangharakshita's creative output into six 'baskets' or groups: foundation texts; works originating in India; teachings originally given in the West; commentaries on the Buddhist scriptures; personal writings; and poetry, aphorisms, and works on the arts. The 27th volume, a concordance, brings together all the terms and themes of the whole collection. If you want to find a particular story or teaching, look at a traditional term from different points of view or in different contexts, or track down one of the thousands of canonical references to be found in these volumes, the concordance will be your guide.

### 1. FOUNDATION

What is the foundation of a Buddhist life? How do we understand and then follow the Buddha's path of Ethics, Meditation, and Wisdom? What is really meant by 'Going for Refuge to the Three Jewels', described by Sangharakshita as the essential act of a Buddhist life? And what is the Bodhisattva ideal, which he has called 'one of the sublimest ideals mankind has ever seen'? In the 'Foundation' group you will find teachings on all these themes. It includes the author's *magnum opus, A Survey of Buddhism*, a collection of teachings on *The Purpose and Practice of Buddhist Meditation*, and the anthology, *The Essential Sangharakshita*, an eminently helpful distillation of the entire corpus.

### 2. INDIA

From 1950 to 1964 Sangharakshita, based in Kalimpong in the eastern Himalayas, poured his energy into trying to revive Buddhism in the land of its birth and to revitalize and bring reform to the existing Asian Buddhist world. The articles and book reviews from this period are gathered in volumes 7 and 8, as well as his biographical sketch of the great Sinhalese Dharmaduta, Anagārika Dharmapala. In 1954 Sangharakshita took on the editing of the *Maha Bodhi*, a journal for which he wrote a monthly editorial, and which, under his editorship, published the work of many of the leading Buddhist writers of the time. It was also during these years in India that a vital connection was forged with Dr B. R. Ambedkar, renowned Indian statesman and leader of the Buddhist mass conversion of 1956. Sangharakshita became closely involved with the new Buddhists and, after Dr Ambedkar's untimely death, visited them regularly on extensive teaching tours.

From 1979, when an Indian wing of the Triratna Buddhist Community was founded (then known as TBMSG), Sangharakshita returned several times to undertake further teaching tours. The talks from these tours are collected in volumes 9 and 10 along with a unique work on Ambedkar and his life which draws out the significance of his conversion to Buddhism.

### 3. THE WEST

Sangharakshita founded the Triratna Buddhist Community (then called the Friends of the Western Buddhist Order) on 6 April 1967. On 7 April the following year he performed the first ordinations of men and women within the Triratna Buddhist Order (then the Western Buddhist Order). At that time Buddhism was not widely known in the West and for the following two decades or so he taught intensively, finding new ways to communicate the ancient truths of Buddhism, drawing on the whole Buddhist tradition to do so, as well as making connections with what was best in existing Western culture. Sometimes his sword flashed as he critiqued ideas and views inimical to the Dharma. It is these teachings and writings that are gathered together in this third group.

### 4. COMMENTARY

Throughout Sangharakshita's works are threaded references to the Buddhist canon of literature – Pāli, Mahāyāna, and Vajrayāna – from which he drew his inspiration. In the early days of the new movement he often taught by means of seminars in which, prompted by the questions of his students, he sought to pass on the inspiration and wisdom of the Buddhist tradition. Each seminar was based around a different text, the seminars were recorded and transcribed, and in due course many of the transcriptions were edited and turned into books, all carefully checked by Sangharakshita. The commentaries compiled in this way constitute the fourth group. In some ways this is the heart of the collection. Sangharakshita often told the story of how it was that, reading two *sūtras* at the age of sixteen or seventeen, he realized that he was a Buddhist, and he has never tired of showing others how they too could see and realize the value of the '*sūtra*-treasure'.

## 5. MEMOIRS

Who is Sangharakshita? What sort of life did he live? Whom did he meet? What did he feel? Why did he found a new Buddhist movement? In these volumes of memoirs and letters Sangharakshita shares with his readers much about himself and his life as he himself has experienced it, giving us a sense of its breadth and depth, humour and pathos.

## 6. POETRY, APHORISMS, AND THE ARTS

Sangharakshita describes reading *Paradise Lost* at the age of twelve as one of the greatest poetic experiences of his life. His realization of the value of the higher arts to spiritual development is one of his distinctive contributions to our understanding of what Buddhist life is, and he has expressed it in a number of essays and articles. Throughout his life he has written poetry which he says can be regarded as a kind of spiritual autobiography. It is here, perhaps, that we come closest to the heart of Sangharakshita. He has also written a few short stories and composed some startling aphorisms. Through book reviews he has engaged with the experiences, ideas, and opinions of modern writers. All these are collected in this sixth group.

In the preface to *A Survey of Buddhism* (volume 1 in this collection), Sangharakshita wrote of his approach to the Buddha's teachings:

> Why did the Buddha (or Nāgārjuna, or Buddhaghosa) teach this particular doctrine? What bearing does it have on the spiritual life? How does it help the individual Buddhist actually to follow the spiritual path?… I found myself asking such questions again and again, for only in this way, I found, could I make sense – spiritual sense – of Buddhism.

Although this collection contains so many words, they are all intent, directly or indirectly, on these same questions. And all these words are not in the end about their writer, but about his great subject, the Buddha and his teaching, and about you, the reader, for whose benefit they are solely intended. These pages are full of the reverence that Sangharakshita has always felt, which is expressed in an early poem, 'Taking Refuge in the Buddha', whose refrain is 'My place is at thy feet'. He has devoted his life to communicating the Buddha's Dharma in its depth and in its breadth, to men and women from all backgrounds and walks of life, from all countries, of all races, of all ages. These collected works are the fruit of that devotion.

We are very pleased to be able to include some previously unpublished work in this collection, but most of what appears in these volumes has been published before. We have made very few changes, though we have added extra notes where we thought they would be useful. We have had the pleasure of researching the notes in the Sangharakshita Library at 'Adhisthana', Triratna's centre in Herefordshire, UK, which houses his own collection of books. It has been of great value to be able to search among the very copies of the *suttas*, *sūtras* and commentaries that have provided the basis of his teachings over the last seventy years.

The publication of these volumes owes much to the work of transcribers, editors, indexers, designers, and publishers over many years – those who brought out the original editions of many of the works included here, and those who have contributed in all sorts of ways to this *Complete Works* project, including all those who contributed to funds given in celebration of Sangharakshita's ninetieth birthday in August 2015, and to a further outpouring of generosity after Sangharakshita's death in October 2018. All these donors have made the publication of this series possible, and we are very grateful. Many thanks to everyone who has helped; may the merit gained in our acting thus go to the alleviation of the suffering of all beings.

Vidyadevi and Kalyanaprabha
Editors

# THE COMPLETE WORKS OF SANGHARAKSHITA

I FOUNDATION



II INDIA

## WINDHORSE PUBLICATIONS

Windhorse Publications is a Buddhist charitable company based in the UK. We produce books of high quality that are accessible and relevant to all those interested in Buddhism, at whatever level of interest and commitment. We are the main publisher of Sangharakshita, the founder of the Triratna Buddhist Order and Community. Our books draw on the whole range of the Buddhist tradition, including translations of traditional texts, commentaries, books that make links with contemporary culture and ways of life, biographies of Buddhists, and works on meditation.

To subscribe to the *Complete Works of Sangharakshita*, please go to: windhorsepublications.com/sangharakshita-complete-works/

## THE TRIRATNA BUDDHIST COMMUNITY

Windhorse Publications is a part of the Triratna Buddhist Community, an international movement with centres in Europe, India, North and South America and Australasia. At these centres, members of the Triratna Buddhist Order offer classes in meditation and Buddhism. Activities of the Triratna Community also include retreat centres, residential spiritual communities, ethical Right Livelihood businesses, and the Karuna Trust, a UK fundraising charity that supports social welfare projects in the slums and villages of India.

Through these and other activities, Triratna is developing a unique approach to Buddhism, not simply as a philosophy and a set of techniques, but as a creatively directed way of life for all people living in the conditions of the modern world.

For more information please visit thebuddhistcentre.com

## SANGHARAKSHITA.ORG

You can find out more about Sangharakshita's life, teachings, and the Buddhist movement he founded on his official website: sangharakshita.org